THE
WORKHOUSE
ENCYCLOPEDIA

THE
WORKHOUSE
ENCYCLOPEDIA

PETER HIGGINBOTHAM

The
History
Press

First published 2012

The History Press
The Mill, Brimscombe Port
Stroud, Gloucestershire, GL5 2QG
www.thehistorypress.co.uk

British Library Cataloguing in Publication Data.
A catalogue record for this book is available from the British Library.

ISBN 978 0 7524 7012 2

Typesetting and origination by The History Press
Printed in India

CONTENTS

INTRODUCTION

My first encounter with the workhouse, many years ago now, was while researching my family history. The death certificate of my great-great-grandfather Timothy revealed that he had died in the infirmary of the Birmingham workhouse in 1890. I had only the vaguest idea what this institution might have been like, but decided that 'sometime' I would look further into the topic. Some time later, looking at a Victorian Ordnance Survey map, I discovered that the town where I lived once had a large workhouse. Eager to discover more, I visited the local library. Although they had a large collection of books on the history of the nearby abbey, parish church, almshouses, grammar school, railway line and so on, the workhouse – demolished in the early 1930s – was virtually unrecorded apart from a couple of small press cuttings about Christmas festivities in the 1880s.

As I gradually began to read about the subject I began to become fascinated by the history of the institution and all its facets. Who were the inmates? Why were they there? How did they spend their time? What did they eat? How did they get out? What really fuelled my interests, however, was the discovery that, all over the country, many workhouse buildings still survived. I could actually go and stand at the entrance to the building where my great-great-grandfather had spent his final days. At the same site, I could identify the block that had once been the workhouse boys' school, or the building where able-bodied men had lived and worked.

After researching my local workhouse, I started to track down and visit former workhouse sites in the local area, then in the rest of the county. The project eventually extended to the whole of the British Isles and Ireland, from Shetland to Cornwall, and from Galway to Essex. Over the past few years, a fair number of the buildings I visited have been demolished. Others have been refurbished, most often for residential use. A few have continued in what they have been doing for the past 175 years, in providing some form of medical or residential care. The latter group have proved the most interesting. In many cases, the buildings still bear all the marks of their history with structures such as the dining hall, tramps' block or mortuary still identifiable.

The workhouse, which had initially seemed a remote and long-gone institution, was also coming to life through people with direct first-hand contact with the institution. In one establishment I visited, now housing the elderly, it was mentioned – in rather hushed tones – that one of the elderly female residents had lived there continuously since the 1920s, originally having been admitted as a pregnant and single young woman. For whatever reason, she had never left. I've also been fortunate enough to interview a man who was taken on as a workhouse clerk in 1929, and another who was a child inmate of a workhouse and later its associated children's homes. Perhaps most affecting of all was my encounter with a man who, for more than half a century, had been carrying the deep psychological wounds of a 1930s childhood spent in a workhouse institution. His shocking memories were of endless days of toil in the institution's laundry, and of physical and other abuse. Now in his sixties, and embarked on a course of psychotherapy, he was finally just beginning to come to terms with the emotional scars that had afflicted his life.

Despite such graphic encounters, it also became clear to me that workhouses were not always the relentlessly grim and heartless places that they are often portrayed. Popular descriptions of the workhouse all too frequently start with that unquestioned assumption and then merely look for evidence to support it. Although cases of appalling cruelty or abuse occasionally surfaced, a great many workhouse staff showed great humanity and concern for their charges. The inmates, too, were not always passive and submissive victims of their situation – there are numerous instances of them 'playing the system' or subverting the authorities to make life more tolerable. Over the years, physical conditions inside workhouses generally improved and regulations relaxed, with increased concern being placed on the morale of the inmates. For some individuals, the existence of the workhouse was a lifeline for which they were grateful and infinitely preferable to what their situation would have been outside.

Despite the many improvements that undoubtedly were made, though, the abiding impression from talking to anyone who ever went near a workhouse, as an inmate at least, was the enormous shame and stigma attached to the institution.

The end of the workhouse era is sometimes dated to 1930, when responsibility for poor relief – now known as public assistance – was taken over by local councils. Many former workhouses continued in use, however, rebranded as Public Assistance Institutions though virtually unchanged in their operation. In 1948, many ex-workhouse sites were absorbed into the bright new world of Britain's National Health Service, a change which is often also taken to mark the 'real' end of the workhouse. How slow its death pangs really were is starkly illustrated by a description of the former Downham Market workhouse in Norfolk which, by the 1960s, had become an elderly care home:

> In 1966, a new Master and Matron arrived: Mr and Mrs Lee. They were dismayed and astonished to find the antiquated practices still in place. The numbers living at the renamed 'Howdale Home' were approximately 170. Space between the beds was small, a chair width apart. The beds were little more than wooden pallets and covered with straw mattresses. All inmates were to be up by a certain hour, dressed and down stairs promptly for breakfast. The men were expected to walk along Ryston Road and gather kindling to fuel the fires to heat the water boilers. The hot water was needed to wash the linen. There was no central heating. One day early in their employment the Porter approached the Master and asked 'could he have permission to sleep at his own home that night?' On checking the duty list Mr Lee noticed that the porter had finished his duty that afternoon and was not expected until on duty again the following afternoon. An astonished Mr Lee explained that on their off-duty time employees could do what they wished. Mrs Lee said she had a hard task to change staff attitudes to the inmates. She had also trouble reporting and raising concerns to the representatives on the 'Board of Trustees', some lived out of county and had never visited. However, she persisted and eventually the Local Authority recognised the need for improvement. She says the best memory she has, is the great bonfire of disgusting straw mattresses.[1]

I never cease to be amazed at the number of different avenues down which my interest in the workhouses has led me, whether the legal and administrative systems governing poor relief, the architecture and layout of the buildings, what life was like inside them and how it changed over the years, and how the institution was perceived by those on the outside – be they journalists, reformers, artists or poets. Many books have been written about the workhouse and the poor relief system of which it formed a part. This volume, as far as I am aware, is the first which aims to try and cover the many and hugely diverse aspects of the workhouse and poor relief systems in a single A to Z encyclopedia. Whether you want to know the postal address of the Rotherham Union workhouse; the rules for visiting a workhouse inmate; the songs that might be sung at a workhouse concert; the total national poor relief expenditure in 1888; whether any workhouse buildings are haunted, the qualifications for being a workhouse master; the names of some famous workhouse inmates; the map reference for the Skye poorhouse; the official recipe for gruel; the names of the presidents of the Poor Law Board; whether workhouse inmates were allowed to drink tea or send and receive letters; or whether there was ever such a thing as workhouse humour, then this is the book for you!

TIMELINE OF WORKHOUSE AND POOR LAW HISTORY

Note: references are to England and Wales unless otherwise indicated.

1349   The Black Death reaches England. Ordinance of Labourers prohibits relief to able-bodied beggars.

1388   Statute of Cambridge restricts movements of labourers and beggars.

1494   Vagabonds and Beggars Act threatens vagabonds with three days in the stocks on a diet of bread and water.

1536   Dissolution of the monasteries begins. Vagabonds Act requires parishes to collect alms for those who cannot work and the able-bodied poor be obliged to perform labour.

1547   Statute of Legal Settlement provides for the branding or enslavement of sturdy beggars. The impotent poor are to receive relief and have cottages erected for their use.

1572   Vagabonds Act introduces the poor rate for relieving 'aged, poor, impotent and decayed persons'.

1576   Act for Setting of the Poor on Work requires towns to set up stocks of materials for the poor to work on; every county is to set up a House of Correction for those refusing to work.

1579   Scotland's Act for Punishment of the Strong and Idle Beggars and Relief of the Poor and Impotent defines parish responsibilities.

1597   Poor Relief Act requires appointment of Overseers of the Poor in each parish to collect poor rate and administer poor relief. Hospitals for the Poor Act encourages founding of charitable hospitals and 'working houses'. Scotland's 1579 Act restated with Kirk Sessions now responsible for enforcement.

1601   Poor Relief Act restates principles of 1597 Poor Relief Act with minor amendments.

1623   Hospitals Act makes permanent 1597 Hospitals for the Poor Act.

1630   Commissioners of the Poor established by Charles I to improve implementation of poor laws.

1647   London's Corporation of the Poor established.

1662   Poor Relief ('Settlement') Act allows parishes to remove newcomers 'likely to become chargeable'.

1676   Philanthropist Thomas Firmin opens a workhouse at Little Britain, Smithfield

1696   Bristol Corporation of the Poor established by Local Act of Parliament. Quaker workhouse opens in Bristol.

1697   Relief of the Poor Act protects settlement certificate holders from removal and requires badging of paupers.

1698   Bristol Corporation opens its first workhouse.

1700   City of London Corporation opens workhouse on Bishopsgate Street.

1703   Opening of House of Industry in Dublin authorised.

1723   Knatchbull's Act (Workhouse Test Act) allows parishes to set up workhouses, contract out their management and restrict poor relief to those willing to enter.

1725   *An Account of Several Workhouses...* workhouse directory published.

1741   London's Foundling Hospital founded by Thomas Coram.

1743   Edinburgh's Charity Workhouse opens.

1762   Poor Act requires metropolitan parishes to maintain records of children admitted into workhouses.

1766   Hanway's Act requires London pauper children under six to be housed in the countryside.

1777   Parliamentary returns on poor relief record around 2,000 workhouses in use.

1782   Gilbert's Act allows parishes alone or in union to run workhouses for non-able-bodied paupers, managed by Boards of Guardians.

1797   Eden's *State of the Poor* published.

1798   Andrew Bell sets up first school in England using the monitorial system.

1800   The Act of Union unites Ireland with Great Britain.

1801   Joseph Lancaster opens a school with alternative version of the monitorial system.

1804   Abstract of national overseers' poor-relief returns published – 3,765 parishes using workhouses.

1810   Badging of the poor abolished.

1811   National Society created to open schools using Bell's system.

1814   British and Foreign School Society formed to run schools using Lancaster's system.

1818   Vestries Act allows ratepayers up to six votes at vestry meetings. National overseers' poor-relief returns reveal 4,094 parishes using workhouses.

1819   Select Vestries Act allows parishes to elect an executive committee, giving ratepayers more control over poor relief.

1824   Vagrancy Act replaces twenty-seven existing statutes and reduces penalties for vagrancy.

1831   Hobhouse's Act allows parish committees to be elected only by resident ratepayers.

1832   Royal Commission appointed to review poor law operation and administration. Allotment's Act authorises vestries to let small portions of land, with income used to buy winter fuel for the poor.

1834   Report of 1832 Royal Commission published in March. Poor Law Amendment Act receives Royal Assent on 14 August. Poor Law Commissioners take office on 23 August.

1835   Abingdon becomes first new Poor Law Union on 1 January.

1836   Report of the Royal Commission on the state of the poor in Ireland published. Poor Law Commissioner George Nicholls tours Ireland.

1837   Civil registration introduced in England and Wales on 1 July extends workhouse system to Ireland, locally administered by Poor Law Unions. Admission to workhouses open to any person 'in sudden or urgent' necessity.

1838   Poor Relief (Ireland) Act passed on 31 July.

1840   Vaccination Extension Act provides free vaccination of infants, administered by Poor Law Unions.

1842   Poor Law Amendment Act allows casuals to be given work before release. Outdoor Labour Test Order allows poor relief to able-bodied male paupers satisfying a Labour Test. End of competitive tendering for union medical officer appointments. Edwin Chadwick reports on link between health and sanitation.

1844   Poor Law Amendment Act allows unmarried pauper mothers to claim against putative fathers. Outdoor Relief Prohibitory Order prohibits outdoor relief to able-bodied apart from in exceptional circumstances. Hanway's Act repealed.

1845   Poor Law (Scotland) Act passed on 4 August. Andover workhouse scandal erupts. Great Famine begins in Ireland. Civil registration introduced in Ireland on 1 April but only for non-Catholic marriages.

1846   Poor Removal Act grants irremovability after five years' residence in a parish. Government begins contributing to salaries of teachers in pauper schools. Convention of Poor Law Medical Officers formed.

1847   Poor Law Board replaces Poor Law Commission. Bodkin's Act makes relief of newly irremovable paupers chargeable to common union funds. Married inmates both over sixty can request their own bedroom. Out relief introduced in Ireland.

1848   Buller Memorandum calls for reduction in casual numbers. Emigration scheme for workhouse orphans launched. Poor-rate funded Christmas dinners sanctioned for workhouse inmates. General Board of Health created.

1849   Rate in Aid Act passed to aid Irish unions worst hit by the famine.

1850   Creation of thirty-three new Poor Law Unions in Ireland completed.

1851   Poor Law Apprentices Act requires regular visits by relieving officers to under-sixteens apprenticed or placed in service from a workhouse.

1852   Outdoor Relief Regulation Order broadens conditions for allowing out relief.

1853   Poor Law Medical Reform Association formed. Vaccination of children becomes compulsory.

1854   Youthful Offenders Act establishes Reformatory Schools for juvenile offenders.

1855   Civil registration introduced in Scotland on 1 January.

1856   Convention of Poor Law Medical Officers and the Poor Law Medical Reform Association merge to form Poor Law Medical Reform Association.

1857   Industrial Schools Act provides for care of vagrant, destitute and disorderly children. National Association for the Promotion of Social Science formed.

1858   Workhouse Visiting Society founded by Louisa Twining.

1862   Poor Law (Certified Schools) Act allows unions to maintain pauper children at independently run homes.

1864   Houseless Poor Act requires metropolitan Boards of Guardians to provide casual wards. Full civil registration system begins in Ireland on 1 January. Expensive medicines used by union medical officers can now be charged to poor rate.

1865   Union Chargeability Act: parish contributions to union funds based on its rateable value rather than number of paupers; union becomes area of settlement; residency required for irremovability reduced to one year. *The Lancet* exposes terrible conditions in many London workhouse infirmaries.

1866   Industrial Schools Act requires children on remand to be kept in workhouses rather than prisons. Dr Edward Smith proposes improvements in workhouse food. Association of Metropolitan Workhouse Medical Officers formed by Joseph Rogers.

1867   Metropolitan Poor Act ('Gathorne Hardy's Act') creates Common Poor Fund to finance medical provision for London's sick poor; Local Act status abolished for London parishes; Metropolitan Asylums Board (MAB) set up to provide care for paupers with infectious diseases and mental impairment.

1868   Merger of the Association of Metropolitan Workhouse Medical Officers and the Poor Law Medical Reform Association to create Poor Law Medical Officers Association.

1869   Poor Law Amendment Act abolishes remaining Gilbert Unions. Goschen Minute launches drive to reduce out relief.

1870   Elementary Education Act introduces compulsory elementary education and local School Boards. North-Western Fever Hospital in Hampstead becomes England's first state hospital. Association of Poor Law Medical Officers of Ireland formed. Metropolitan Common Poor Fund extended to cover maintenance of adult workhouse inmates.

1871   Local Government Board replaces Poor Law Board. Pauper Inmates Discharge and Regulation Act provides powers to delay release of 'ins and outs' and casual paupers returning to same workhouse.

1872   In Ireland, poor relief administration passes from Poor Law Commissioners to Local Government Board.

1875   Public Health Act creates rural and urban sanitary authorities. First female guardian elected.

1876	Divided Parishes and Poor Law Amendment Act allows Local Government Board to reorganise or dissolve unions, and allows married inmates to live together if either partner is sick or disabled.
1879	Workhouse opened by Rhayader Union, the last in England and Wales agreeing to do so. Workhouse Infirmary Nursing Association founded by Louisa Twining.
1880	Brabazon Scheme launched to provide handicraft activities for non-able-bodied inmates.
1881	Association for Promoting the Return of Women as Poor Law Guardians formed.
1882	Casual Poor Act allows workhouses to detain casuals for two nights.
1883	Trial of weekly fish dinners for workhouse inmates. Expenditure on children's toys allowed from poor rates.
1885	Medical Relief Disqualification Removal Act preserves voting rights of non-paupers receiving poor-rate-funded medical care.
1891	Public Health (London) Act gives free access to MAB hospitals for all Londoners.
1892	Allowances of tobacco and snuff sanctioned for certain classes of inmate.
1894	Local Government Act extends guardians' term of office to three years and abolishes *ex officio* guardians, plural voting, and property qualification for voting. *British Medical Journal* launches campaign to improve workhouse medical facilities. Allowances of dry tea for female inmates. In Scotland, poor relief administration passes from Board of Supervision to new Local Government Board.
1897	Use of pauper inmates for workhouse nursing duties prohibited.
1900	Major revision of workhouse dietaries.
1901	*Manual of Workhouse Cookery* published.
1902	Education Act replaces School Boards by Local Education Authorities and raises school-leaving age to fourteen.
1904	Registrar General allows use of euphemistic addresses on workhouse birth certificates.
1905	Royal Commission on the Poor Law and the Unemployed appointed.
1906	Departmental Committee on Vagrancy recommends use of police to supervise vagrants, and establishment of labour colonies.
1908	Children's Act gives local authorities new powers to keep poor children out of the workhouse.
1909	Old Age Pension for over-seventies introduced on 1 January. The 1905 Royal Commission Majority and Minority Reports published.
1911	Unemployment Insurance and Health Insurance begin in a limited form.
1912	MAB takes over management of London's casual wards.
1913	Major revision of workhouse regulations: unions can devise their own pauper classifications; workhouses now referred to as 'poor law institutions' and paupers as 'poor persons'. A husband can no longer compel his wife to remain with him in workhouse. No children to reside in workhouses after 1915.
1919	Ministry of Health takes over responsibility for poor relief from Local Government Board in England and Wales; Scottish Board of Health does likewise in Scotland.
1921	Irish Free State created and abolishes workhouse system. Metropolitan Common Poor Fund now subsidises outdoor as well as indoor relief.
1925	Rating and Valuation Act abolishes overseers and poor rates. Oakum picking abolished in casual wards.
1926	General Strike. Board of Guardians (Default) Act enables Boards of Guardians to be replaced by government officials.
1929	In Scotland, Board of Health replaces Department of Health.
1930	Local Government Act transfers responsibility for 'public assistance' to local councils on 1 April. Departmental Committee on casual poor recommends better casual ward conditions and staffing.

1931   Stone-breaking abolished in casual wards.

1932   Children and Young Persons Act replaces Reformatory and Industrial Schools by Approved Schools.

1944   Education Act introduces primary and secondary schools; boys and girls schools merged at the primary level; school-leaving age raised to fifteen.

1945   Family Allowances Act.

1946   National Insurance Act. National Health Service Act.

1948   National Assistance Act. Settlement laws abolished. National Health Service begins on 5 July.

1967   Remaining parts of 1601 Poor Relief Act abolished.

A TO Z ENCYCLOPEDIA

ABLE-BODIED

(*See*: **Classification; Deserving and Undeserving Poor; Dietary Class; House of Correction; Labour Test; Work**)

ACCOUNT OF SEVERAL WORKHOUSES

An Account of Several Workhouses for Employing and Maintaining the Poor was first published by the Society for Promoting Christian Knowledge in 1725. The book espoused the use of workhouses and charity schools and detailed the setting up and management of more than forty local workhouses then in operation, especially noting the financial benefits that could result from their use. The book was strongly influenced by the activities of the workhouse entrepreneur, Matthew Marryott. The success of the publication led to a second enlarged edition in 1732.
(*See also*: **Marryott, Matthew; Society for Promoting Christian Knowledge (SPCK)**)

ADMISSION TO A WORKHOUSE

(*See*: **Entering a Workhouse**)

ADDRESSES

In 1904, the Registrar General advised local registration officers in England and Wales that where a child was born in a workhouse, there need be no longer any indication of this on the birth certificate. Instead, the place of birth could be recorded as a euphemistic street address. For example, births at Liverpool Workhouse were thereafter recorded as having taken place at 144A Brownlow Hill even though no such street address actually existed. Similarly, Nottingham workhouse used an address of 700 Hucknall Road for this purpose, while Pontefract workhouse delighted in the pseudonym of 1 Paradise Gardens. Some unions, particularly in smaller

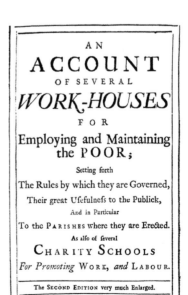

AN
ACCOUNT
OF SEVERAL
WORK-HOUSES
FOR
Employing and Maintaining
the POOR;
Setting forth
The Rules by which they are Governed,
Their great Usefulness to the Publick,
And in Particular
To the PARISHES where they are Erected.
As also of several
CHARITY SCHOOLS
For Promoting WORK, *and* LABOUR.

The SECOND EDITION very much Enlarged.

LONDON:
Printed by JOS. DOWNING, in *Bartholomew-Close*
near *West-Smithfield*, M.DCC.XXXII.

The cover of the 1732 edition of *An Account of Several Work-houses* – the first workhouse directory.

towns, invented a new name for their workhouse. The Trowbridge and Melksham workhouse thus became Semington Lodge, Melksham. Where a workhouse was located on a road such as Workhouse Lane, a renaming of the thoroughfare was sometimes carried out.

The same practice was adopted from around 1918 for the death certificates of those who died in a workhouse. It was not until 1921 that Scotland followed a similar course and recorded what were referred to as 'substitute' addresses for births and deaths taking place in a poorhouse.

The directory of poor law institutions in England and Wales (Appendix E) includes details of many of the euphemistic addresses adopted by workhouses.

AFTERCARE

The aftercare of young people leaving the workhouse to enter service or an apprenticeship became an increasing concern during the mid-nineteenth century. Following the 1851 Poor Law (Apprentices etc.) Act, union relieving officers were required to visit those under still under sixteen at least twice a year and ensure that they were being properly fed and not mistreated.

Following her appointment as the first female Poor Law Inspector in 1873, Jane Senior (often referred to as Mrs Nassau Senior) took a particular interest in matters concerning children, especially the education of girls. She also championed use of the cottage homes system. At her premature retirement due to ill-health in 1874, she outlined proposals for the creation of a national scheme for the aftercare ofo pauper girls leaving the workhouse, especially those aged of sixteen or more. Her ideas, taken up by Henrietta Barnett, led to the formation of the Metropolitan Association for Befriending Young Servants (MABYS). By the 1890s, the Association had more than 1,000 volunteers who visited girls at their workplaces, and helped them find accommodation and new employment, until they reached the age of twenty. MABYS and similar charitable organisations were helped by legislation in 1879 which allowed poor law authorities to contribute to their funds.

From 1882, the Local Government Board included a report from MABYS in its own annual report. During 1893, the Association had under its supervision 2,412 girls from Poor Law Schools and 955 from other institutions. Of the total, 1,700 were reported as 'satisfactory in their conduct and work', 740 as 'those against whom no serious faults have been alleged', 189 as 'accused of dishonesty, untruth, extreme violence of temper etc.', and thirty-two as 'having lost character or been in prison for theft etc.'[2]

After the First World War, MABYS was renamed the Mabys Association for the Care of Young Girls. It continued in existence until 1943 when its activities were taken over by the London County Council.

The Association for Befriending Boys was formed in 1898 and performed undertook similar activities to MABYS within the metropolitan area. Outside London, a similar role to MABYS was performed by the Girls' Friendly Society (GFS), established by the Church of England in 1875 and still in existence. The Society provided reports to Boards of Guardians on girls up to the age of twenty-one and also operated Homes of Rest and Lodges for girls who were unemployed. Unlike its London counterpart, the GFS limited its work to 'respectable' girls.

ALCOHOL

One of the most common rules applying to workhouse inmates was a general prohibition on alcoholic beverages, at least in the form of spirits, unless prescribed for medical purposes. Restrictions on other forms of alcohol, especially beer, varied at different periods in history.

The Parish Workhouse

At the Croydon workhouse, opened in 1727, the rules forbade any 'Distilled Liquors to come into the House' – a restriction perhaps aimed at the new habit of gin-drinking which was sweeping England at around this time.[3] At Hitchin workhouse, in 1724, it was reported that a lack of tobacco and gin was causing many inmates to 'get out as soon as they can'.[4] Brandy, too, appears to have been in a similar situation. Some of the parish poor at St Mary Whitechapel rejected the offer of the workhouse and 'chose to struggle with their Necessities, and to continue in a starving Condition, with the Liberty of haunting the Brandy-Shops, and such like Houses, rather than submit to live regularly in Plenty.'[5]

A century later, the 1832 Royal Commission investigating the operation of the poor laws, was told by the overseers for the London parish of St Sepulchre that intemperance was a major cause of pauperism: 'After relief has been received at our board, a great many of them proceed with the money to the palaces of gin shops, which abound in the neighbourhood.'[6]

Although the imbibing of spirits by workhouse inmates was usually prohibited, items such as wine, brandy and rum were often prescribed for medicinal purposes because of their supposed stimulant properties. The accounts for the Bristol workhouse in 1787 record the expenditure of £2 19s 7½d on 'wine, brandy, and ale for the sick'. At the Lincoln workhouse, in the winter of 1799–1800, colds and other ailments were so prevalent that the Clerk was instructed by the Board to purchase two gallons of rum 'for the use of the House'. Surprisingly, gin still occasionally features in workhouse expenditure – the 1833 accounts for the Abingdon parish workhouse include an entry for two pints of gin, although the precise use to which this was to be put is not revealed.[7]

Beer

One form of alcohol that was usually allowed to parish workhouse inmates was beer, something which at that time formed part of most people's everyday diet. Apart the attractions of its flavour, beer could provide a safe alternative in localities where the water supply was of dubious quality. Beer came in two main forms, strong ale and half-strength 'small' beer, the latter being a standard accompaniment for meals, often for children as well as adults.

Workhouse inmates sometimes had a fixed daily beer allowance such as the two pint quota imposed at the Whitechapel workhouse in 1725.[8] At other establishments it was available 'without limitation' as happened at the Barking workhouse and also at the Greycoat Hospital in Westminster, an institution purely for children.[9]

As well as being provided at meal-times, extra rations of beer were often given to those engaged in heavy labour such as agricultural work. At one time, female inmates working in the laundry at the Blything Incorporation's House of Industry at Bulcamp in Suffolk were each allowed a daily ration of eight pints.[10]

Many workhouses brewed their on beer on-site and their brewhouses contained all the paraphernalia associated with beer-making. In 1859, when the contents of the old Oxford Incorporation workhouse were sold off, the auctioneer's catalogue entry for the brewhouse listed the following items:

> Mash tub, underback, four brewing tubs, five coolers, five buckets, skip, tun bowl, tap tub, bushel, spout, malt mill, copper strainer, two pumps, brewing copper, three square coolers, with supports, spout, &c. Large working tub, two others, beer stands, three lanterns, &c., three casks, and strainer.

Alcohol in Union Workhouses

In post-1834 union workhouse, the consumption of alcohol – including beer – was generally prohibited except for sacramental purposes such as the taking of Holy Communion, or for medicinal use when ordered by the workhouse medical officer. A further exception was added in 1848, when it was allowed to be provided as a treat on Christmas Day.

As well as these general exceptions, some union workhouses revived the old practice of providing beer to able-bodied inmates engaged in certain types of heavy labour. In 1886 the Wirral Union was allowed by the Local Government Board to provide extra food and 'fermented liquor' to paupers employed in harvest work on land belonging to the guardians. In 1903, when an auditor surcharged a workhouse master for allowing beer to able-bodied inmates without such approval, the strange response came that if such an allowance were not made, 'some of the paupers would leave the workhouse.'[11]

The consumption of alcohol, like virtually every other activity that took place in the union workhouse, was carefully recorded and periodic returns made to the central authority. In 1893, the returns show an annual consumption per workhouse inmate in England and Wales of roughly half a pint of spirits, a quarter of a pint of wine and eighteen pints of beer.[12]

There were surprisingly large variations in the use of alcohol by different Boards of Guardians. In 1893, the Strand Union spent approximately 10s per head on alcohol for its inmates, while Wandsworth and Clapham's spent around 1d per head – less than 1 per cent of the Strand's expenditure. Some workhouses such as Greenwich used wine solely for sacramental purposes while others such as Woolwich issued wine and spirits for infirmary use. The Strand workhouse at Edmonton got through almost 10,000 gallons of beer during 1893, while Lambeth's two workhouses consumed only two pints between them.[13] There were also large regional differences in alcohol expenditure by workhouses. In the 1891 returns, the county of Rutland had the largest expenditure averaging 12s 10d per inmate, while the most abstemious county was Northumberland whose unions spent only 4d per head.

The 1880s and 1890s saw a large drop in alcohol consumption in workhouses. In part, this was due to the growth of the temperance movement in Britain. Pressure for a reduction in the use of alcohol or even its complete abolition came both from teetotal guardians and also from organisations such as the Workhouse Drink Reform League. As well as the consumption by inmates, the League criticised the imbibing of alcohol by workhouse staff and union officers, such as the barrel of beer consumed each week by the guardians at their weekly board meetings at the Wolverhampton workhouse. In 1884, the Local Government Board decreed that workhouse masters would be liable for the cost of any alcohol that was not supplied under medical instruction – a master at Islington subsequently faced a bill for over 200 gallons of porter consumed by his nursing staff.[14]

Attitudes were also gradually changing amongst doctors as to the medical efficacy of alcoholic beverages although this topic remained controversial until the beginning of the twentieth century. The London Temperance Hospital, which opened in 1873, prescribed almost no alcohol to its patients but achieved a very low mortality rate among it patients. The changing tide of medical opinion was also demonstrated by the British Medical Association: from 1880, tickets for its annual dinner did not include wine in the price.[15]

Reflecting the changes in attitude, alcohol consumption in workhouses in England and Wales almost halved between 1881 and 1893. Despite this downward trend, some doctors clearly remained convinced of the therapeutic effects of alcohol. In 1909 it was revealed that all seventeen inmates of the tiny Welwyn workhouse each received a daily pint of beer by order of the workhouse medical officer.[16]

(*See also*: **Christmas**; **Food**)

ALLOWANCE SYSTEMS

From the late eighteenth century until the passing of the Poor Law Amendment Act in 1834, various systems of 'allowance' – the subsidising of low wages from the poor rates – were adopted in many parishes.

One of the earliest allowance schemes was devised by Buckinghamshire magistrates in January 1795. For a working man and his wife, wages of less than 6s per week would be topped up to that amount from the poor rate. Couples with one or two small children would be guaranteed 7*s* with a further 1*s* for every additional child under the age of ten.[17] The Speenhamland System, formulated later in the same year, linked allowances to the current price of bread as well as the size of a recipient's family.

Critics of allowance systems believed they had a corrupting effect on able-bodied labourers, what an 1824 Select Committee on labourers' wages described as 'the degradation of the character of the labouring class'.[18] As the respondents to the 1832 Royal Commission from the parish of Hogsthorpe in Lincolnshire put it, such practices:

> brought numbers of the most hale labourers on the list of paupers, who previous to that would have shuddered at the thought of coming to a parish, but are now as contented to relief as they were before in a state of labouring independence.[19]

Wage subsidy schemes were also said to lower wages and so push more labourers into pauperism, with a resulting swelling of the poor rates bill. Not all ratepayers were necessarily unhappy with this situation. Even when the resulting rates bill was no different from what the cost of paying higher wages would have been, there could still be benefits from the allowance system for employers such as farmers: it allowed the outlay to be deferred until the next rate demand; higher rates might result in lower rents being charged for their property; and workers, especially those with several children, were often better off (and therefore happier in their work) with an allowance system.

Allowance systems were claimed by the 1832 Royal Commission to be prevalent in south England and spreading over the north, and were to be found both in rural areas and 'to a formidable degree' in towns. Eradicating this state of affairs was the main thrust of their report's proposals. However, it has been argued that their comments belie the report's own data and that 'the Speenhamland System as such had generally disappeared by 1832, even in the South.'[20] (*See also*: **Labour Rate System**; **Out relief**; **Roundsman System**; **Royal Commission – 1832**; **Speenhamland System**)

ALMSHOUSES

In England and Wales, almshouses were establishments providing free or subsidised accommodation for the elderly poor and funded by charitable endowment. They thus differed from poorhouses and workhouses, which were financed by the parish poor rates. Almshouses were often founded through a bequest from a wealthy person, with the residents required to be of good character and expected to offer regular prayers for their benefactor's soul. Almshouses were typically constructed as a row of small self-contained cottages, often placed near to the local parish church. More than 500 almshouses are still in operation in the United Kingdom.

In Scotland, the term almshouse was sometimes applied after 1845 to small parish-funded lodging houses for the poor.

In the nineteenth century USA, almshouses were similar to English workhouses and housing a mixture of the able-bodied poor, who were required to labour, and the 'impotent poor'. (*See also*: **Poorhouse; Scotland; Workhouse**)

ANDOVER WORKHOUSE SCANDAL

(*See*: **Scandals**)

APPRENTICESHIP

An apprenticeship was an extended period of training in a craft or trade, given to a child (most often a boy) by an established master in the trade.

The 1563 Statute of Labourers and Apprentices required that an apprenticeship of at least seven years should first be served by any person wishing to engage in any of the 'Arts, Occupations, Crafts or Mysteries' practiced in England at the time. Male apprentices had to be aged between ten and eighteen years, with the apprenticeship lasting until they reached at least the age of twenty-one. The operation of an apprenticeship was the subject of a legal agreement – an indenture – and usually involved the paying of a fee – the premium – to the master who would also provide the apprentice with board and lodging for the period of the apprenticeship.

Most apprentices were 'trade' apprentices, sponsored by their parents, and who would hope eventually to set up in trade themselves, perhaps as 'journeymen' (day labourers). However, the 1601 Poor Relief Act (and its 1597 predecessor) allowed parish overseers and churchwardens, with the consent of two Justices of the Peace, to apprentice out children under sixteen whose parents were considered unable 'to keep and maintain' them. Potential causes of such action could include the children being illegitimate, or the parents being dead or having abandoned them. The apprenticeship lasted in the case of boys until they were twenty-four, or for girls until they were twenty-one or, after 1601, were married.

The apprenticeship system allowed pauper children to be removed from ongoing support by the parish, and also provided them with a trade which reduced the likelihood of their needing poor relief in adult life. Under the Settlement Act of 1662, an apprentice took his, or her, settlement from his place of apprenticeship. It then became particularly attractive to try and place apprentices in a different parish which would then have responsibility should they later become a charge on the poor rate. Pauper apprentices did not usually learn highly skilled trades; instead, the boys would be taught 'husbandry' and the girls 'midwifery', effectively becoming labourers and household servants.

Some parishes prevailed upon their own ratepayers to take a pauper child for at least a year, or else face a £10 penalty. The allocation of such children could be based either on a rota system or take the form of a lottery. Such impositions were often extremely unpopular, with many householders preferring to pay the fine rather having to take in a child. Where a child was reluctantly received, the result might be it being overworked and poorly treated.

The more usual practice, however, was the payment of a premium, typically up to £10, to anyone willing to take a pauper child in for a set period, typically seven years, and train them in a trade. This was the route famously described by Charles Dickens in *Oliver Twist* when Oliver was offered, together with the sum of £5, as a 'porochial 'prentis'. The contract was conditional, as Dickens explained:

> 'upon liking' a phrase which means, in the case of a parish apprentice, that if the master find, upon a short trial, that he can get enough work out of a boy without putting too much food into him, he shall have him for a term of years, to do what he likes with.

In the late eighteenth and early nineteenth centuries, considerable use was made of orphaned workhouse children in the mills of the Midlands and northern England. Although some of these came from the areas surrounding the mills, many were provided by parishes in London and elsewhere in the south of England. The workforce at William and John Toplis & Co., a firm of worsted spinners and weavers at Cuckney, near Mansfield in Nottinghamshire, consisted almost entirely of parish apprentices. Some were local, while others came from London, Essex, Birmingham, Bristol and Hereford.[21]

The 1834 Poor Law Amendment Act left the apprenticeship system largely untouched, although its operation became the subject of much criticism. In the second annual report of the Poor Law Commissioners (PLC), James Phillips Kay – later better known as Sir James Kay-Shuttleworth – outlined the shortcomings of the apprenticeship system in Norfolk and Suffolk:

> The premiums offered with the children proved an irresistible temptation to needy persons to apply for an apprentice at the Hundred house, whether they wanted the services of the apprentice or not, or whether they could instruct him in any useful calling or not. Their sole object often was to secure the premium. Ten pounds or twenty pounds were wanted to pay a pressing demand. To avoid a warrant of distress for rent due, or for a bill for their stock in trade, some of these petty tradesmen eagerly sought the premium, and thus removed the imminent danger which threatened them. the future care of the apprentice, though a burden which they had often but slender means to encounter, had not such terrors as the present peril.
>
> The class of persons to whom the children were apprenticed were generally petty tradesmen of a low caste, who were usually unscrupulous in the neglect of their duties to the children. A parish apprentice is regarded as a defenceless child deserted by its natural protectors, and whose legal guardian, the parish, is only anxious to remove the burthen of its maintenance at the least possible cost, and with the least possible trouble.
>
> After a certain interval had been allowed to elapse, means were often taken to disgust the child with his occupation, and to render his situation so irksome as to make him abscond... many children have thus been driven to ruin.[22]

In 1842, the Royal Commission on Children's Employment in Mines and Manufactories discovered that workhouse boys in South Staffordshire, some as young as eight, were being sent on 'apprenticeships' of up to twelve years working in coal mines. In fact, the boys were usually employed as 'hurriers', conveying corves (large baskets) of coal from the coal face to the bottom of the pit-shaft from where it was raised to the surface. Their master was generally a 'butty' – a middleman between a mine owner and its workmen, who contracted to work the mine and raise coal or ore at so much per ton. The Commissioners heard with regard to South Staffordshire:

> That the number of Children and Young Persons working in the mines as apprentices is exceedingly numerous; that these apprentices are paupers or orphans, and are wholly in the power of the butties; that such is the demand for this class of children by the butties that there are scarcely any boys in the Union Workhouses of Walsall, Wolverhampton, Dudley, and Stourbridge; that these boys are sent on trial to the butties between the ages of eight and nine, and at nine are bound as apprentices for twelve years, that is, to the age of twenty-one tears complete; that, notwithstanding this long apprenticeship, there is nothing whatever in the coal-mines to learn beyond a little dexterity, readily acquired by short practice and that even in mines of Cornwall, where much skill and judgement is required, there are no apprentices, while in the coal mines of South Staffordshire the orphan whom necessity has driven into a workhouse is made to labour in the mines until the age of twenty-one, solely for the benefit of another.[23]

As a result of such revelations, unions in the coal-mining areas of South Staffordshire and the West Riding of Yorkshire were asked to provide detailed information on the children who had been apprenticed in the mining industry in recent years. Part of the 1841 return from the Dewsbury Union is shown below.[24] In each case, the master was a coal miner and no premium was paid.

Name of Child	Age Yrs–Mos	Apprenticeship Period	Name of Master	Residence
Joseph Gaunt	11-0	9 years	David Preston	Batley
Joseph Scott	10-0	11 years	James Robertshaw	Liversedge
John Howden	11-3	9 years, 9 months	John Fell	Batley
William Goodall	10-0	10 years	William Scaife	Thornhill
Shallam Lister	8-0	Went on trial and was returned in a few days	Valentine Wilkinson	Ditto
Joseph Booth	10-0	ditto	Richard Allatt	Denby
Thomas Townend	5-0	Went on trial and was returned in 16 days	William Bradshaw	Overton
Edward Robinson	9-0	Went on trial and is not yet bound apprentice	Jesse Speight	Flockton

Five-year-old Thomas Townend was a matter of some embarrassment for the Dewsbury Guardians as he was far too young to be bound as an apprentice. The guardians claimed that when he had been received from a township workhouse his age had been ascertained by informal enquiry and recorded as seven years. Once the error has been discovered, he had immediately been sent back from the mine. However, the Royal Commission were told that the boy had only been returned to the workhouse after his grandfather and friends had threatened to report the matter to the PLC.[25]

In their return, the Burton-upon-Trent guardians were at pains to point out the care they employed when placing children for apprenticeship: premiums in money were not allowed and the boys were instead provided with two full suits of clothes; any master applying for a boy was required to produce a certificate of character from the minister and officers of the parish in which he resides; a trial period of at least six weeks was required, at the end of which the boy was brought before the magistrates and strictly questioned as to his food, lodging, moral and religious instruction, and especially whether he had any objection to the apprenticeship being formalised.

The Royal Commission's report included evidence from workhouse apprentice, William Hollingsworth, revealing how he worked underground for up to sixteen hours a day:

I have no father or mother; my father was a shoemaker and has been dead five years, and my mother eleven; I lived with my sister at Crossfield six months after and rather better, and then went to the old workhouse; I was then apprenticed by the overseer of the parish of Halifax to Joseph Morton, the brickmaker, in the township of Southowram, where I remained two years. When he died. and I came here for a little while, Jonathan Oldfield, a collier, living at Bradshaw-lane, made application to the Board of Guardians for an apprentice; I was willing to work for him or anybody else, and went with him by consent of the Board on trial for a month; if I had remained with him I should have been bound until I was 21; I stayed with him five days; he gave me porridge for breakfast at half-past five, and then I went with his other two apprentices. with whom I slept, to the pit; each of us took a cake and a half for our dinners; we had no time to stop to eat it, but took it as we hurried; the first night I worked in the pit, which was

A boy with a harness and chain between his legs drags a heavy coal truck along a low underground passage in a mine at Halifax, Yorkshire. An official investigation in 1842 revealed that children as young as seven were being 'apprenticed' to work in mines, in some cases placed there by workhouses.

last Thursday, we remained until ten o'clock at night, and then all three came away together; the second night we stopped until nine, third night until half-past eight, and on the Monday until a quarter to eight; we had nothing during the whole of those days but the cake and half each, and nothing to drink; there was no water that we could get in the pit's bottom, and they would not allow us to go up to drink; I was very thirsty at times; my master never beat me, but he cursed enough at me because I was not sharp enough with the corves. I hurried without shoes one day, but was obliged to put them on again because the ground hurt my feet; the other apprentices told me that they worked until 10 and 11 o'clock at night regular. It was Mr. Joseph Stocks's Royd Pit that I worked in; I ran away from him Tuesday morning because he worked me so late; I was so tired when I got home to his house that I did not think I could stand it; after I left him I made application to come into the workhouse again.[26]

Girls, too, were occasionally sent to work down mines as the Commission found in reports from Halifax:

Patience Kershaw says:- I wear a belt and chain at the workings to get the corves [large baskets] out. The getters are naked, except their caps; they pull off all their clothes. I see them at work when I go up. They sometimes beat me, if I am not quick enough, with their hands; they strike me upon my back. The boys take liberties with me sometimes; they pull me about. I am the only girl in the pit. There are 20 boys and 15 men. All the men are naked. I would rather work in the mill than in the coal-pit.

Mary Barrett says:- I do not like working in pit, bit I am obliged to get a living. I work without stockings or shoes, or trousers; I wear nothing. but my shift.

Ruth Barrett, her sister, says:- I come down into pit in linings of old trousers, which I take off. I wear an old waistcoat and shift. I do not like working in pit; I would not do it if I could help it.[27]

Major legislative change eventually came in the 1844 Poor Law Amendment Act which transferred the responsibility for apprenticing paupers from parish overseers to Boards of Guardians and also abolished the compulsory taking of apprentices. The PLC subsequently issued an Order which required that a child being apprenticed must be at least nine years old and able to read and write its own name; the maximum period of apprenticeship was to be eight years; no premium was to be paid unless the child had some permanent infirmity; masters were

Burgh and Townfhip of }
  Kirkby in *Kendal.*   }

NOTICE IS HEREBY GIVEN,

That there are in

The WORK-HOUSE of the faid Town,

A Number of

BOYS AND GIRLS,

Ready to be put out as

PARISH APPRENTICES.

Thofe Perfons defirous of engaging any of them, may apply to CHARLES WAIDE'
Mafter of the faid Work-houfe.

N. B.   With the younger Part of them, a Premium will be given.

KENDAL: Printed by W. Pennington.

Copy of a handbill, thought to date from the 1820s, advertising the availability of boys and girls at the Kendal workhouse for being put out as parish apprentices.

given detailed duties with regard to the health, maintenance, clothing, and moral and religious instruction of their charges.[28] The PLC also expressed dislike of the 'servitude which is created by the apprenticeship of parish children'.[29] The Poor Law (Apprentices) Act of 1851[30] further improved the situation of workhouse apprentices, making their mistreatment an offence and requiring them to receive regular visits from their union's relieving officer.

Critics of the use of apprenticeship, such as Kay-Shuttleworth, proposed that pauper children should instead be provided with 'industrial training' within the poor law system, ideally in separate children's industrial schools, each serving a number of unions. Kay was particularly influenced by Mr Aubin's privately run school at Norwood which accommodated more than 1,000 residential pupils largely taken from metropolitan poor law unions. The work of the Central Society for Education and its 1838 publication *Industrial Schools for the Peasantry* also stimulated interest in this approach. Although only a small number of unions initially set up such establishments, there was a gradual decline in the use of apprenticeship for pauper children. It did not disappear entirely, however – between 1834 and 1863, the Norwich Incorporation apprenticed 130 boys into twenty trades, although 80 per cent of them went into shoe-making.[31]

(*See also*: **Children**; **Poor Laws**)

ARCHITECTURE

In the era of the Old Poor Law prior to 1834, many of the workhouses that were established were located in existing buildings that were adapted for the purpose. As the use of workhouses evolved, the construction of purpose-built premises become more common.

One of the earliest custom-built workhouses was at Newbury in Berkshire, where the town received a legacy to fund construction of the establishment which opened in 1627. The largely non-residential building occupied three sides of a quadrangle and included rooms for the various stages in the manufacture of woollen cloth. Sheffield Corporation's accounts from 1628 onwards record that they spent around £200 on the erection of a workhouse together with a stock of raw materials for providing employment. Little is known of the building other than it was timber-built and stood in its own orchard.

Incorporation Workhouses

The thirty or so towns, beginning with Bristol in 1696, that formed Incorporations under Local Acts invariably included a workhouse in their poor relief schemes. Some, such as Bristol, used existing premises, notably its impressive 'Mint' workhouse which was located in a former merchant's house. The majority, however, constructed new and often substantial buildings for the purpose. Hull's 'Charity Hall' workhouse, erected in 1698, had a three-storey U-shaped layout and comprised about forty-five rooms, wards, garrets, lobbies, school and dining-rooms, and workrooms. The Oxford Incorporation's workhouse, built in the 1770s, had a long two-storey main block with a boardroom and chapel at its centre. Males were housed to one side and females at the other, a division that was not then always the standard arrangement that it later became. As well as the usual dormitories, dining-rooms and kitchen, the Oxford workhouse contained a wool-carding room for the men and a spinning room for the women, a schoolhouse, bakehouse, brewhouse, salthouse, deadhouse, correction room, an apothecary's room, storerooms, workshops, and rooms for staff including work supervisors, gardener and

Right The remaining section of Newbury's 1627 workhouse, one of the oldest surviving workhouse buildings in England, now home to a local museum.

Below The Wangford Hundred Incorporation workhouse, built in 1766–67 at Shipmeadow in Suffolk. The building, like many other former workhouses, has now been converted to residential use.

housekeeper.[32] The master and matron's quarters were originally located in a corner of one of the side-wings, but were later moved to the centre to allow them a much better degree of supervision.

The rural Incorporations formed in East Anglia and elsewhere in the mid-eighteenth century often served thirty or forty parishes. The workhouses they erected, sometimes accommodating 400 or more, were typically of two or three storeys with a U- or H-shaped layout. The Wangford Hundred Incorporation's workhouse at Shipmeadow in Suffolk, opened in 1777, was an H-shaped red-brick structure, two storeys high with attics. The sides of the H were each 210ft long, with the central 'crossbar' of the H measuring 100ft. The building housed up to 350 inmates, including twenty-nine rooms for married couples, a dormitory for boys and single men, a dormitory for girls and single women, large work rooms, an infirmary with two wards for the elderly, a schoolroom, a guardians' committee room, a kitchen, a laundry, a granary, a linenhouse, various out-houses, two arcades 50ft by 20ft 'with Bogg Houses at the end of each', and quarters for the governor.[33]

Parish Workhouses

The eighteenth century saw an enormous growth in the provision of parish workhouses, especially with the passing of Knatchbull's Act in 1723. Many of these were simply adaptations of existing buildings, such as that opened in 1731 in rented premises at Eaton Socon in Bedfordshire. In 1736, the workhouse housed twenty-seven inmates – nine males and eighteen females – including six children. An inventory in the same year recorded that the workhouse had eleven rooms, six on the ground floor and five above, which were described as kitchen, buttery and little room adjoining, hall, parlour, brewhouse, great chamber, and four further chambers over the brewhouse. The 'little room next the buttery' contained thirteen 'jersey & linen wheels'. One of the upper chambers was a linen store, the others were used as bedrooms as was the parlour which contained six bedsteads. The twenty-seven inmates shared fifteen bedsteads and fourteen bolsters.[34]

The Poland Street workhouse of the parish of St James, Westminster, opened in around 1727. This 1809 view of a women's day-room by artist and caricaturist Thomas Rowlandson shows the inmates engaged in activities such as sewing and spinning.

The Thurgarton Incorporation workhouse at Upton, near Southwell, was opened in 1824. Its strict regime, compartmentalised layout and central hub, helped shape the union workhouses established following the 1834 Poor Law Amendment Act. The building has now been restored by the National Trust.

In towns such as Bury St Edmunds, Cambridge, Newark, Saffron Walden, Richmond (Yorkshire) and Whitehaven, the workhouse shared a site with a local gaol or 'House of Correction'. In 1776, a workhouse reformer visited Hinckley in Leicestershire where the same individual was both keeper at the gaol and also master of the adjoining workhouse 'in which the poor looked healthy, were cheerful, clean, and at work.'[35]

Where parish workhouses were erected for the purpose, the smaller ones generally resembled ordinary local houses. Others were rather more impressive structures – Maidstone's workhouse, erected in 1720, was described as 'a large and handsome Building of three Stories high, ninety one feet in Length, and twenty one in Depth, with a large Kitchin thrown behind'.[36] Some parish workhouses adopted, on a reduced scale, the layouts typical of the large Incorporation workhouses, such as the H-shaped plan of the St Paul Covent Garden workhouse erected on Cleveland Street, London, in 1778, or the U-shaped building at Bledlow in Buckinghamshire, dating from around 1800.

One of the largest parish workhouses in the country was that of St James, Westminster. In 1776, the building could house 650 inmates and was described as being constructed of brick, 146ft long, 40ft deep, 58ft high, and consisting of thirty-two apartments.[37]

The Early Nineteenth Century

The early nineteenth century saw architectural developments that were to become significant in workhouse design. One of these was the 'supervisory hub' – a central vantage point, usually part of the workhouse master's quarters, which provided views over all the inmates' exercise yards. The principle had already been implemented in prison buildings by architects such as William Blackburn. His design Ipswich County Gaol had four wings connected to an octagonal centre where the governor's quarters were located.[38]

An alternative supervisory arrangement, known as the panopticon, was put forward by the philosopher Jeremy Bentham. The panopticon was in the form of polygonal structure with a vantage point placed at its centre, giving a view into every part of the building. Although Bentham's grandiose scheme for a chain of 2,000-inmate panopticon-style workhouses was never implemented, the principle of central supervision was implemented in a number of workhouses such as those at Caistor (opened in 1800) and Ongar (1830).

Another development was increasingly strict separation of different classes of inmate, not just of male from female, but also of the aged and infirm from the able-bodied poor. This prin-

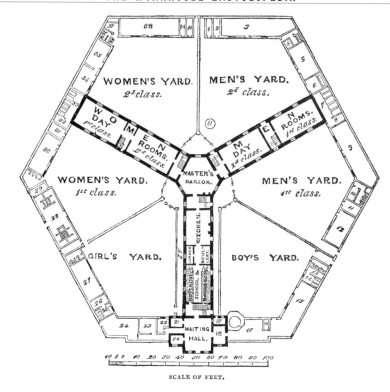

SCALE OF FEET.

The ground-floor layout of the model 'Y-plan' or hexagonal workhouse designed by Sampson Kempthorne and published by the Poor Law Commissioners in 1835. '1st Class' inmates were the elderly and infirm, while '2nd class' were the able-bodied.

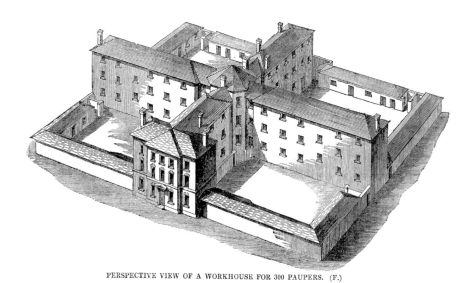

PERSPECTIVE VIEW OF A WORKHOUSE FOR 300 PAUPERS. (F.)

Sampson Kempthorne, Architect,

A 'bird's-eye view' of the Kempthorne's model 'square' workhouse plan, one of the most widely adopted designs for early union workhouses.

Sir Francis Head's model 'courtyard' plan placed workhouse buildings around a large quadrangle. The inmates' quarters, with rooms supposedly based on the size of a typical labourer's cottage, had no outward-facing windows.

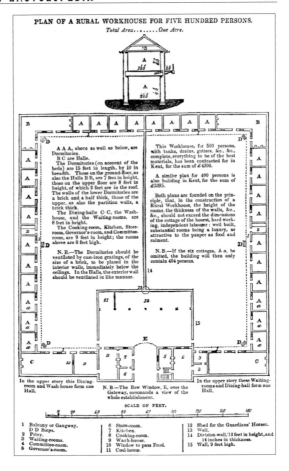

PLAN OF A RURAL WORKHOUSE FOR FIVE HUNDRED PERSONS.
Total Area........One Acre.

ciple was most clearly demonstrated in workhouses such as the one near Southwell in Nottinghamshire, erected in 1824 by the Thurgarton Hundred Incorporation. Male and female accommodation lay either side of the central hub and within each half the accommodation was strictly segregated between that for the 'guiltless' poor and the 'idle, immoral and improvident' able-bodied.

The Union Workhouse

Following the 1834 Poor Law Amendment Act, each new Poor Law Union was expected to provide a common union workhouse. Unions could either enlarge and adapt existing buildings, or erect a completely new purpose-built workhouse. By 1839, the Poor Law Commissioners (PLC) could report that over half of the then 583 Boards of Guardians in England and Wales had opted for the latter course.[39]

In 1835–36, the PLC published a number of model workhouse plans, most of which were by the young architect Sampson Kempthorne. Kempthorne's most influential design was the cruciform or 'square' layout. Its front entrance block contained a porter's room and waiting-room on the ground floor, with the guardians' boardroom above. To the rear were a children's school and dining room, connecting to the central hub where the workhouse master's quarters were located. Radiating from the hub were women's and men's wings, each divided into separate sections for the able-bodied and for the elderly and infirm. Day-rooms occupied the ground floor of each wing, and dormitories the upper floor. A fourth wing contained the workhouse kitchens, scullery, larder and stores. The spaces between the wings formed exercise yards which (sometimes further subdivided by walls) created separate areas for the different classes. The upper floors of the hub had windows in each direction giving a view over all the yards. The square perimeter of the buildings housed stores, workshops, laundry, mortuary etc. Unions erecting square-plan workhouses included Andover, Basingstoke, Devizes, Hastings and Newbury.

Kempthorne produced two other model designs. The first, the 'Y-plan', was based on similar principles to the square layout, but with three rather than four wings radiating from its hub; it was also known as the hexagonal design because of the shape formed by its perimeter. Unions building Y-plan workhouses included Abingdon, Bath, Chertsey, Frome, Grantham, Taunton and Warminster. Kempthorne's final design was the smaller and cheaper '200 pauper' plan published in 1836. This design was a truncated version of the cruciform layout but without a central hub. It was intended for use in more rural areas where pauper numbers were lower such as the Worcestershire unions of Martley, Pershore and Upton-upon-Severn. As well as producing model plans for the PLC, Kempthorne personally designed a number of individual buildings, notably the Abingdon workhouse, the first to be erected using the new model designs. Surviving examples of his work include the workhouses for the Andover, Crediton, Eton and Hastings Unions.

The other model design published by the PLC was the 'courtyard' plan devised by Assistant Poor Law Commissioner, Sir Francis Head. In this layout, the buildings lay around a large quadrangle. On three sides, the inmates' accommodation was arranged on two storeys and consisted of a large number of small dormitories, each around 15ft by 10ft, roughly based on the size of a typical poor labourer's cottage. Each dormitory could sleep eight inmates in four double beds. A single lavatory or privy was provided on each floor on each side of the workhouse. The inner courtyard was divided into male and female sides by a 12ft-high wall. The administrative offices, boardroom, master's quarters, kitchens, dining halls, store-rooms, washhouse etc. were placed at either side of the entrance archway on the fourth side of the quadrangle. Although Head's design proved to have a number of problems, it was taken up by around a dozen unions in Kent including Bridge, Dover, Faversham, Hoo, Maidstone and the Isle of Thanet, with Bridge being a good surviving example.

Workhouse Architects

The workhouse construction boom that took place in England and Wales between 1835 and 1838 provided a unique opportunity for young architects to make a name for themselves. It could also be lucrative, with an architect's fee usually being calculated as a percentage of the construction cost. At Beaminster, in 1837, the workhouse building contract was £4,500 with the architect's commission at 3½ per cent amounting to around £157. Workhouse designs were often open to competition, with the winner(s) receiving a fixed cash prize or a percentage fee if a design was subsequently executed.

Not surprisingly, Kempthorne had many competitors, perhaps most notably George Wilkinson, who later went on to design all of the union workhouses in Ireland. Wilkinson's first success was for the workhouse in his home town of Witney in Oxfordshire. The Witney guardians awarded him the contract after the initial appointee, Sampson Kempthorne, had committed the heresy of proposing a building made of brick for a town that was built almost entirely from Cotswold stone.[40] Wilkinson's designs can be seen in surviving buildings at Chipping Norton, Bridgend, Bromyard and Northleach, with many of his Irish workhouses still standing.

Some architects were active in a particular area of the country. In the east of England, for example, the majority of new workhouses were designed by William Donthorn (e.g. Aylsham,

The Bedminster Union workhouse, erected in 1837–38 at Flax Bourton in Somerset. The design, by George Gilbert Scott and William Bonython Moffatt, marked a trend away from radial layouts towards the use of parallel blocks.

Ely, Oakham), William T. Nash (e.g. Braintree, Buntingford, Royston) or William Thorold (e.g. Chelmsford, Rochford, Thetford). The partnership of John and William Atkinson was dominant in Yorkshire (e.g. Bedale, Guisborough, Howden).

The most prolific workhouse designers of this period were George Gilbert Scott and his partner William Bonython Moffatt. Scott, later knighted for his work on such prestigious projects as the Albert Memorial and the frontage of St Pancras Station, initially worked as an assistant to Sampson Kempthorne but soon set up on his own, taking on Moffatt as his assistant and then partner. Over the next ten years, the indefatigable Scott and Moffatt designed over forty workhouses across the breadth of England. They evolved their own distinctive layout which featured a long single-storey range at the front containing porter's lodge, boardroom, receiving wards and chapel. A central entrance archway led through to an inner courtyard either side of which were boys' and girls' yards. The main building, usually three storeys high, still retained a central hub containing the master's offices and quarters. To each side were male and female day-rooms and dining halls on the ground floor, with dormitories above. Behind were kitchens and scullery, workrooms, laundry, bakehouse etc. with a separate infirmary block at the rear. Examples of their work survive at Windsor, Williton in Somerset, and Witham in Essex.

Corridor-Plan Workhouses

Between about 1840 and 1870, new workhouse buildings moved away from the PLC's model radial plans. Influenced by Scott and Moffatt's designs, it became the norm to have a separate entrance block, linear main block, and hospital block all running parallel to one another. The main block generally had a central corridor along its length with rooms off to each side, unlike the earlier designs which were usually one room deep. The main block had the administrative functions at its centre, often surmounted by a tower, and with kitchens and dining hall to the rear, creating a building that was T-shaped.

Many of the new buildings of this type were in the north of England, which had initially held out against erecting new workhouses, and in London where many pre-1834 buildings had continued in use but had become too cramped. Around 150 corridor-plan workhouses were built in this period, with the later buildings often in the then fashionable Italianate style, with gables, pinnacles, projecting bays and Venetian windows. Unions erecting corridor-plan workhouses included Warrington (1849), City of London (1849), Bolton (1858), Preston (1865), and Rochdale (1873).

Pavilion Block Workhouses

From 1870 onwards, the trend in workhouse design was increasingly towards housing inmates of a particular category or condition in separate blocks or pavilions linked by covered walkways. Other facilities such as receiving wards, offices and stores, and dining hall and kitchens would occupy further blocks. This change coincided with widespread attempts to improve sanitary conditions and reduce the spread of disease which was thought to be largely airborne.

One of the earliest pavilion plan designs was used by the Chorlton Union for its new infirmary, built in 1864–66 and designed by Thomas Worthington. It comprised five well-spaced ward blocks, each accommodating ninety-six patients and linked by a covered way. It featured what became known as 'Nightingale wards' – long wards with pairs of opposing windows allowing a through draught. Beds, of which the optimum number was decreed to be thirty-two per ward, were placed along each wall either singly or in pairs between the windows. Sanitary facilities were placed in cross-ventilated towers attached to the outer ends of the wards. Worthington's design was commended by Florence Nightingale:

> Your hospital plan is a very good one: when completed it will be one of the best, if not the best, in the country... If you succeed in completing the buildings for anything like the money with due regard to the simple sanitary arrangements of so great a building, you will have

inaugurated a new era in building. And we shall hasten to imitate you; for you will have set up a model for the whole country.[41]

Probably the first entire workhouse built on a pavilion plan was at Madeley in Shropshire, erected in 1871–75. It comprised a central single-storey block containing dining hall and kitchen which was linked by covered ways to the two-storey accommodation blocks. Other separate blocks included an entrance block, infirmary, isolation block and workshops. By the end of the nineteenth century, virtually all new workhouses and workhouse infirmaries adopted a pavilion plan.

Infirmary Buildings

The improvement and expansion of workhouse medical facilities that took place from the 1870s onwards was visible in the large number of new infirmary buildings that were erected. This was most obvious in London where, following the 1867 Metropolitan Poor Act, the capital's poor law authorities were required to provide hospital accommodation on sites separate from the workhouse. In some cases the separate site was actually adjacent to the workhouse but had its own management. Among the large new infirmaries erected were those by St Pancras (1870), Lambeth (1877), Fulham (1878), Holborn (1879), St Marylebone (1881) and St Saviour's (1885). In a few cases, such as at Whitechapel and the City of London Union, a new workhouse was established with the old one being converted to infirmary use. Architects prominent at this period were Thomas Aldwinckle and Henry Saxon Snell, the latter also originating the cellular design for casual wards.

Outside London, although a few unions opened separate-site infirmaries such as Keighley (1871), Salford (1882), Croydon (1885), Halifax (1901), Southampton (1902), Leicester (1905) and Stockport (1905), most of the new buildings were at existing workhouse locations. Where completely new workhouses were opened such as those at Doncaster (1900), Hunslet (1903), Nottingham (1903) and Hammersmith (1905), the infirmary now occupied its own

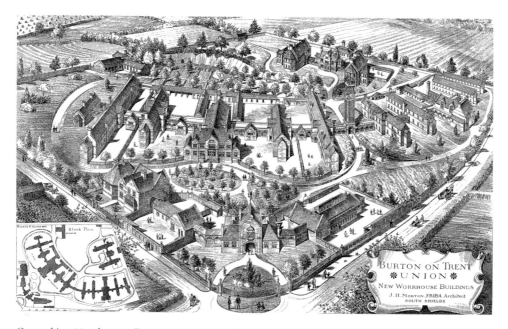

Opened in 1884, the new Burton-on-Trent workhouse was a typical pavilion-plan design. The separate blocks for each class of inmate, children's complex (right of picture) and central administrative block containing facilities such as the dining hall and kitchens, were linked by covered walkways.

Holborn's 1879 union infirmary on Archway Road, Highgate – one of the new separate-site infirmaries erected following the 1867 Metropolitan Poor Act. Henry Saxon Snell's design mixed pavilion-style blocks and, in the central portion, a novel arrangement of beds placed along internal partitions at right angles to the main walls.

large and distinct section of the site. In 1896, the parish of Willesden, formerly part of the Hendon Union, became a separate poor law authority. Interestingly, its first construction project, which began in 1900, was a parish infirmary. A workhouse was subsequently opened on the same site in 1908.

The Twentieth-Century Workhouse

By the start of twentieth century the construction and fitting out of new workhouses often reached an impressive standard. The new workhouse at Hunslet in West Yorkshire, opened in 1903, had two large steam-boilers to provide heating and hot water to all parts of the buildings, with the exhaust steam being condensed and recycled to reduce fuel costs. Electricity was generated on-site to provide power for 1,130 electric lamps placed throughout the buildings, and also to operate electric lifts in the infirmary pavilions, two fans in the kitchen block, the bake-house machinery, and the automatic boiler stokers. Nineteen telephones around the site were linked to a central switchboard at the porter's lodge.

Despite such advances, conditions in many of the older and smaller workhouses remained very basic. In 1930, the Great Ouseburn workhouse, also in West Yorkshire, was taken over by the West Riding County Council who found conditions to be primitive. Water was still being drawn from wells, heating was mostly by open fires, and electricity came from a paraffin engine. At the same date, the Saddleworth workhouse was still lit by gas, and was supplied with water from an adjoining private reservoir, although the water was not filtered in any way.
(*See also*: **Chapel**; **Electricity**; **Gas**; **Ireland**; Morrison (1999))

ART

The dramatic possibilities of the workhouse inspired a number of artists, with pathos often being a major element in such works. An early example was Charles West Cope's *Board Day Application for Bread* (1841) which was based on a visit to a meeting of the Staines Board of Guardians. It shows a young widow pleading for relief for her four children.

Above left An 1844 illustration from Frances Trollope's *Jessie Phillips* – Jessie undergoes a faint-inducing inquisition by the Board of Guardians.

Above right The 'Milk' of Poor Law 'Kindness' – an 1843 cartoon from the satirical magazine *Punch* following a report that in the Bethnal Green workhouse a five-week-old infant had been separated from its mother.

'Sunday music for the indigent poor: a concert given by the National Sunday league at the City Road workhouse.' An illustration from the *Graphic* magazine in 1901 – some of the audience (and band) appear less than attentive.

An ex-soldier, drawn as a mannequin and carrying his own broken-off leg, looks at a WD (War Department) signpost pointing to the workhouse. The illustration was a commentary on the lack of welfare provision for those returning disabled from the Boer War which ended in 1902.

The Warriors Return.

Illustrations for novels such as *Oliver Twist* and other works relating to the workhouse tended to be in a similar vein. Particularly notable are John Leech's drawings for Frances Trollope's 1843 novel *Jessie Phillips*, one of which also portrays the eponymous heroine fainting during an interview with the guardians.

The poor law was often a subject of attention for the satirical magazine *Punch* which was launched in 1841. Typical of its attacks was the cartoon captioned *The 'Milk' of Poor Law 'Kindness'* published in 1843 following a report that in Bethnal Green workhouse 'an infant, only five weeks old, had been separated from the mother, being occasionally brought to her for the breast.'

Sentimental images relating to the workhouse and other facets of poverty often featured in illustrated weekly magazines such as *The Graphic* which first appeared on 4 December 1869. Its inaugural issue carried an article on the Houseless Poor Act, a measure that obliged metropolitan unions to provide casual wards for 'destitute wayfarers, wanderers, and foundlings'. The accompanying picture, *Houseless and Hungry*, by Samuel Luke Fildes portrayed a line of homeless people applying for tickets to stay overnight in the workhouse. The engraving was seen by John Everett Millais who brought it to the attention of Charles Dickens. Dickens was so impressed he immediately commissioned Fildes to illustrate *The Mystery of Edwin Drood*. In 1874, Fildes later reworked *Houseless and Hungry* as an oil painting re-titled *Applicants for Admission to a Casual Ward*.

Another successful *Graphic* artist was Hubert von Herkomer whose credits included *Christmas in a Workhouse* in 1876 and *Old Age – A Study at the Westminster Union* in 1877. The latter formed the basis of von Herkomer's much admired 1878 oil painting *Eventide*. In the same year, James Charles West unveiled *Our Poor: A Bible Reading, Chelsea Workhouse*, an oil painting whose colourful sunlit scene of inmates contentedly reading and drinking tea made a striking contrast with the more usual murky depictions of workhouse interiors.

In 1901, maintaining its reputation for social realism, *The Graphic* published Clement Flower's illustration *Sunday Music for the Indigent Poor* which depicted the dining hall of the City Road workhouse where the National Sunday League were putting on a concert for the inmates.

ASSOCIATION FOR BEFRIENDING BOYS

(*See*: **Aftercare**)

ASSOCIATION OF METROPOLITAN WORKHOUSE MEDICAL OFFICERS

(*See*: **Medical Officers' Associations**)

ASSOCIATION OF POOR LAW UNIONS

Although many union guardians had been meeting at district and national conferences since the early 1870s, the formation of a body to represent their views did not take place until 1898. In that year, the national Association of Poor Law Unions was formally inaugurated, following the passing of the Poor Law Unions Association (Expenses) Act which allowed the costs of membership, within prescribed limits, to be charged to the poor rates. The Association became a lobbying group to represent the views of Boards of Guardians on all matters relating to the poor relief system.

(*See also*: **Poor Law Conferences**)

AUBIN'S SCHOOL

In 1825, Frederick Aubin became the proprietor of a privately run school on Westow Hill in Norwood, South London. The school, which had been founded in around 1819, housed and educated young pauper children sent from London parishes, under the terms of Hanway's Act of 1766.

An 1836 report noted that the average number of residents at the school was around 650, of which many were pale and weakly. Although the food provided was adequate (breakfasts and suppers of bread and butter with warm milk; dinners of roast or boiled beef or mutton with potatoes three times a week, pease-soup twice a week, suet or rice puddings once a week, bread and cheese once a week, and table-beer five times a week), the school was overcrowded and badly ventilated.[42] Two years later, it had expanded to house around 1,100 children aged under fifteen.

A particular interest in the school was taken by James Phillips Kay (later better known as Sir James Kay-Shuttleworth), Assistant Poor Law Commissioner and secretary to the Committee of Council on Education. Kay was a vocal campaigner for improvements in the provision of education and industrial training of pauper children. Kay held up Aubin's school as an example of what could be achieved in such an establishment, given the right direction. When Kay had first visited the school he noted that the children were 'chiefly orphans, deserted, illegitimate, or the offspring of persons undergoing punishment of crime, they are, in fact, children of the dregs of the pauper population of London, and have consequently been, for the most part, reared in scenes of misery, vice, and villainy.'[43] As to the school itself, Kay found little to commend it – the buildings were of a 'very defective character', the teaching was carried out using an approach known as the method of 'mutual instruction' otherwise known as the monitorial system, and the industrial training was limited to the sorting of bristles, and the making of hooks and eyes, with the girls also employed in making the beds and cleaning the rooms.

With Kay's encouragement, a number of changes were introduced at the school, including the employment of a chaplain and the introduction of the 'simultaneous' and 'synthetical' methods of teaching, with children under the constant attention of either a teacher or a candidate teacher. Children received alternate days of classroom education and industrial training which included tailoring, shoemaking, carpentry, blacksmithing, farm work and nautical instruction using a mast erected in the exercise ground. Singing and gymnastics were also instituted. The girls were employed in the household duties – scouring the floors, making the beds, cooking, waiting upon the teachers, washing, ironing, mangling, knitting and sewing. They were also employed in dairy work on the school's farm.

Despite Kay's favourable impression of the improvements at Mr Aubin's school, he still retained fundamental objections to the use of private contractors and continued to support the use of publicly run District Schools. Aubin's school continued in operation until 1849 when it was taken over by the newly formed Central London School District. Aubin was kept on as the school's superintendent, with his wife as matron, until his sudden death in November 1860.

(*See also*: **District and Separate Schools**, **Hanway's Act**, **Drouet's School**)

AUXILIARY HOME

An establishment. linked to a Certified Industrial School, for dealing with particularly difficult inmates or acting as a half-way house for those about to leave and enter employment.

From the 1920s, the term was also used in the Irish Free State for an institution, sometimes located in former workhouse premises, used to accommodate unmarried mothers and infants. (*See also*: **County Home**; **Industrial Schools – Certified**; **Ireland**)

BABY FARMS

(*See*: **Hanway's Act**)

BADGING THE POOR

The Poor Act of 1697 required that anyone receiving poor relief should wear a badge on their right shoulder. The badge, in red or blue cloth, was to consist of the letter 'P' together with the initial letter of the parish, for example 'AP' for Ampthill parish. The practice of badging was not new, however, and dated back to at least the previous century. In earlier times, its use might simply have been to identify paupers as being registered with the parish so that householders might be more amenable to giving them alms. By 1697, though, the wearing of such badges had acquired a stigma with its use acting as a deterrent against the claiming of parish relief. The use of badging was abolished in 1810. (*See also*: **Uniforms**, Hindle (2004))

BANDS

Many of the larger poor law children's establishments – especially district and separate schools, cottage homes sites, and training ships – ran a military-style boys' band. As well as teaching the boys musicianship, learning to play an instrument could lead to a future career in the forces as a military or naval bandsman. The bands often performed at fêtes or other local events with any income being used to buy new instruments or uniforms. In 1897, the band at Hackney's school at Brentwood had thirty-four boys in its 1st band and twenty-eight in the 2nd, with sixteen outside engagements carried out during the year.[44]

A rare example of a band being run at a workhouse occurred at Beaminster in Dorset where, between 1868 and his death in 1872, Thomas Beale held the post of schoolmaster. During this time he taught the boys to play the fife, and established the Union Fife and Drum Band which became popular with the townspeople. Occasionally, the workhouse children would process – in their workhouse uniforms – into Beaminster led by the band.[45]

BAPTISM

The baptism of infants residing in the workhouse, including those born there, was most commonly carried out at the church of the parish in which the workhouse stood. Baptisms in the workhouse were permitted 'only under circumstances which would justify the administrative of baptism in a private house' such as serious illness.[46] Where a chapel was erected at a workhouse, baptisms could be performed there subject to such a provision being included in the appointed clergyman's licence from the bishop of the diocese. (*See also*: **Religion**)

The boys' band, resplendent in their uniforms, at the Kensington & Chelsea District School for pauper children (later known as Beechholme) at Banstead in Surrey. The school's name can be seen on the bass drum.

BASTARDY

(*See*: **Illegitimacy**)

BASTILLE / BASTILE

One of the slang names for the workhouse, deriving from the penal institution of that name in Paris, perhaps reflecting the fortress-like nature of some early workhouse designs. G.R. Wythen Baxter's book *The Book of the Bastiles* was an early polemic against the post-1834 workhouse system.

(*See also*: **Book of Bastiles**; **Grubber**; **Spike**)

BATHS

(*See*: **Washing and Bathing**; **Turkish Baths**)

BEDS

In early workhouses, inmates sometimes took in their own bedding. In 1724, this was common practice at St Alban's workhouse[47] and a requirement at Hitchin.[48] It was, however, more usual for the workhouse management to furnish the sleeping accommodation.

Eden's survey in the 1790s found considerable variation in the beds that were provided. Bedsteads could be made from iron, as found at Preston workhouse, or have wooden bottoms as at Sunderland. The mattress and pillow could be stuffed with a variety of materials such as straw as at Norwich, chaff (grain husks and/or chopped straw) as at Ecclesfield in Yorkshire, or flock (tufts of wool) as used at Leeds and also at Leicester where the beds were said to be 'much infested with bugs'. A rather more comfortable time was had by the inmates of the workhouses at St Alkmund in Derby, Spilsby in Lincolnshire, and at Windsor where feather beds were provided. Bedding, such as that found at Chesterfield and Ecclesfield, could include a pair of sheets, a blanket and a rug or coverlet. Bed sheets were typically changed every three weeks.

An auction catalogue for the contents of the Oxford Incorporation workhouse catalogue in 1859 offered items from the former Old Ladies' Bedroom: five 3ft, three 4ft and one 2ft iron bedsteads, with each provided with a flock bed and bolster, a pair of blankets, a pair of linen sheets, and a rug. Items from the master's bedroom included a painted bedstead, flock mattress, feather bed, bolster and pillow, three blankets, two sheets and a coverlid.

The condition of workhouse beds sometimes left a lot to be desired. In 1865, *The Lancet* reported that beds at St Martin in the Fields were 'lumpy and comfortless' while at St Giles & St George, Bloomsbury:

> The iron bedsteads, as a rule, were short of six feet, and were not more than two feet five inches in width. In many cases the sacking was in rags, loose, and dirty, the beds of flock, with dirty ticks, in some cases extremely dirty, and the flock escaping on the sacking the blankets and sheets also were dirty and ragged. The sheets we were told were changed when required, and always once a fortnight – statements we could hardly credit when looking at the articles themselves.[49]

For the inmates of Irish workhouses, the standard provision was either a straw-filled mattress on a wooden sleeping platform, or – for the elderly, sick and infirm – there was the uncomfortable and narrow 'harrow' bed which comprised:

> Five parallel wooden bars supported at the foot on an iron crossbar and two iron legs, and at the head it rests on a continuous rail fixed on iron uprights about 6 inches from the wall, or, failing the rail, its place is taken by two legs; there is no bed head, the tick and pillows resting against the wall, and there are no sides. The bed is 2 feet 3 inches wide, stands about a foot from the ground, and on this is placed the straw tick.[50]

The worst sleeping arrangements, though, were undoubtedly those provided for tramps and other travellers accommodated overnight in the workhouse casual ward. In 1857, a party which included the Lord Mayor of London visited the West London Union's casual wards which for the men consisted of the floor of a twelve-stall stable while the women were found in an adjoining cattle-shed, huddled together on a rug on the bare ground, almost perished with cold, and without either fire or food.[51] In association wards, which were the norm for casuals up until the 1880s, beds could consist of a hammock-like canvas bed, a plank-bed with one end leant against a wall, a box or 'trough' bed containing a straw-filled canvas tick, a straw-filled pallet on the floor, or even just bare floorboards, with a rug for cover. The beds provided under the cellular system usually comprised a metal-framed bedstead with a wire mattress, for which two or three blankets were provided. Some workhouses offered the luxury of sheets, although these often concealed the very dirty state of other bedding. The sleeping quarters in casual wards were notorious for harbouring lice, fleas, or bugs which would make their appearance during the night. Gradually, things did improve, at least at some establishments. At the Wandsworth and Clapham workhouse in 1896, a visitor recorded that:

> The beds are as comfortable as one could wish to have. The bedding for old people those over 60 consists of a cocoanut fibre mattress, a flock bed, two sheets, two top blankets, one under blanket and counterpane, pillows and bolsters. Inmates under 60 years of age have the same bedding with the exception that the flock bed is missing.[52]

A cramped dormitory in the Coventry Union workhouse, which incorporated parts of the city's old Whitefriars monastery. Note the chamber-pot under each bed. (*Picture by kind permission of Coventry History Centre.*)

For much of the workhouse's history, for reasons of space or economy, bed-sharing was common amongst inmates. Although this was particularly the case with children, it could also apply to adults. At the Wisbech workhouse in 1724, children slept three to a bed while the elderly were two to a bed.[53] At Sevenoaks in 1841, sixty-two boys and two men occupied seventeen beds, fifteen of which were 6ft long by 4ft 6in wide, in each of which four boys slept; in the two others, which were about half the size, a man and a boy slept. There was a space of about 13in between each bed.[54] In 1844, a boys' dormitory at Southampton workhouse contained eleven double beds and one single bed in a space of 34ft by 14ft 6in. Two of the double beds had four occupants each, eight beds had three, and one had two, with the single bed used by one – thirty-five sleepers in all. In the same institution's venereal ward, double beds were shared by two patients exposing each 'by continued juxtaposition under the same covering, to the offensive and purulent discharges which are generated by the various forms of the complaint.'[55] The bed-sharing record, though, was probably held by Huddersfield workhouse where in 1848, up to ten children shared a bed.[56]

Another striking instance of bed-sharing was reported at Preston workhouse in 1866 by the inspector, Mr R.B. Cane:

> Many of the infirm people, men as well as women, are sleeping together two in a bed. The sick have not all of them a separate bed to lie upon. In the 'venereal ward' the patients affected with syphilis are sleeping together two in a bed. Two women, owing to a want of room, have lately been placed together in the same bed in the lying-in ward, both having just been confined.
>
> Four patients, two men and two boys, were lately sleeping together in the same bed in the 'itch ward.' Six men occupied two beds in this ward to-day, three in each bed. The man lying in the middle of the bed had his feet to the top of the bed, and his head came out at the bottom of it. The feet of the other two men were placed so as to be close to the head of the man who was lying between them.

Bed-sharing by adult male inmates, in operation at a number of workhouses in Lancashire until the 1860s, was deprecated by Cane as 'a most objectionable and indecent custom.'[57] Following his criticisms the practice appears to have been discontinued.
(*See also*: **Casual Ward**)

BEER

(*See*: **Alcohol**)

BENTHAM, JEREMY

Jeremy Bentham (1748–1832) was a legal reformer and utilitarian philosopher. He believed that people's behaviour was determined by the basic principle of seeking pleasure and avoiding pain, and that the value or utility of every action should be judged according to whether it tended to increase or reduce the happiness of the community as a whole.

Originally an advocate of a free-market approach in matters such as wages and interest rates, Bentham came to accept that there were certain areas where state intervention and central control were required, one of these being relief of the poor. His principle of greatest happiness demanded that everyone should be secure against starvation and the fear of it. However, this could only be achieved by instituting incentives to work and penalties for not working. Making it more attractive to work than to not work was the basis of the influential principle of 'less eligibility' which Bentham is usually credited with originating:

> If the condition of persons maintained without property by the labour of others were rendered more eligible, than that of persons maintained by their own labour then... individuals destitute of property would be continually withdrawing themselves from the class of persons maintained by their own labour, to the class of persons maintained by the labour of others.[58]

In 1796, Bentham published a grandiose scheme for 'Pauper Management'. This early example of privatisation proposed the formation of a National Charity Company that would construct a chain of 250 enormous workhouses, financed by a large number of small investors. Each workhouse would hold around 2,000 inmates who would be put to profitable work and fed on a spartan diet. Bentham's proposed workhouse design was based on the 'panopticon' principle where supervision of a polygonal building was carried out from a vantage point placed at its centre. The scheme was never implemented, however.

In his unfinished *Constitutional Code*, written during the 1820s, Bentham proposed a far-reaching centralised government based on thirteen powerful central ministries (Health, Education, Trade, Finance, Army, Navy etc.) including one for Indigence Relief.

Bentham's ideas undoubtedly influenced the conclusions reached by the 1832 Royal Commission on the Poor Laws. Several of the Commission's members were Benthamites, including the two largely responsible for its final report, Nassau Senior and Edwin Chadwick, the latter having worked for Bentham on the *Constitutional Code*. Another contributor, Walter Coulson, had also previously been Bentham's amanuensis. However, the administrative system that emerged from the 1834 Poor Law Amendment Act, with significant powers devolved to local Boards of Guardians, is not necessarily one that Bentham would have advocated. (*See also:* **Architecture**; **Chadwick, Edwin**; **Royal Commission – 1832**)

Part of Jeremy Bentham's scheme for a workhouse to hold 2,000 paupers. The five-storey circular building was to have a central observation point based on the 'panopticon' principle. Although used in the design of prisons such as Millbank, the panopticon layout as such was never adopted in workhouse buildings.

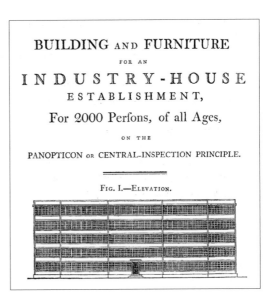

BUILDING AND FURNITURE

FOR AN

INDUSTRY-HOUSE

ESTABLISHMENT,

For 2000 Persons, of all Ages,

ON THE

PANOPTICON OR CENTRAL-INSPECTION PRINCIPLE.

FIG. I.—ELEVATION.

BILL OF FARE

(*See:* **Dietary**)

BIOGRAPHY

First-hand descriptions of workhouse experiences have been recorded in a variety of forms. Where the persons concerned have later achieved great success in some field, published biographies or autobiographies may include their accounts of workhouse life. The memories of less exalted individuals may be documented in local studies of individual workhouses, in the material collected by those researching their own family histories, or in evidence given to official bodies such as courts or parliamentary inquiries.

Perhaps the best-known workhouse resident was future film star Charlie Chaplin who in June 1896, at the age of seven, spent a few weeks in the Lambeth workhouse. He was then transferred to the 'Cuckoo Schools' at Hanwell where he stayed until January 1898. In his autobiography[59] Chaplin recounts the regular Friday morning punishment sessions in the gymnasium where all the boys lined up on three sides of a square. For minor offences, a boy was laid face down across a long desk, feet strapped, while his shirt was pulled out over his head. Captain Hindrum, a retired Navy man, then gave him from three to six hefty strokes with a 4ft cane. Recipients would cry appallingly or even faint and afterwards have to be carried away to recover. For more serious offences, a birch was used – after three strokes, a boy needed to be taken to the surgery for treatment.

Routine corporal punishment was also recalled by minister, mill owner and writer Charles Shaw whose book *When I was a Child* was published in 1903 under the pen name of 'An Old Potter'. In 1842, when Shaw was ten, his family spent some time in the Wolstanton and Burslem workhouse at Chell in Staffordshire. Shaw's account of the flogging of a boy who had run away was used by Arnold Bennet as the basis of a similar event in his novel *Clayhanger*.

Even more brutal events were chronicled by journalist Henry Morton Stanley, best known for tracking down missing explorer Dr David Livingstone. As a five-year-old orphan, Stanley – real name John Rowlands – entered the St Asaph workhouse in North Wales in 1847. Stanley's autobiography[60] recounts that the scourge of the workhouse was a one-handed schoolmaster called James Francis whose cruelty knew no bounds. Francis appeared to have been implicated in the death of a classmate of Stanley called Willie Roberts. On hearing of Willie's death, Stanley and several other boys sneaked into the workhouse mortuary and discovered his body covered in scores of weals. After a violent showdown with Francis in 1856, Stanley absconded over the workhouse wall and subsequently ran away to sea.

Politician Will Crooks had the rare distinction of being both a child inmate of the Poplar workhouse in London's East End then, in later life, becoming chairman of the Board of Guardians that ran the same establishment. Crooks' biography recorded his first return visit to the workhouse after becoming a guardian:

> We found the condition of things in the House almost revolting. The place was dirty. The stores were empty. The inmates had not sufficient clothes, and many were without boots to their feet. The food was so bad that the wash-tubs overflowed with what the poor people could not eat. It was almost heart-breaking to go round the place and hear the complaints and see the tears of the aged men and women.
>
> 'Poverty's no crime, but here it's treated like crime,' they used to say. Many of them defied the regulations on purpose to be charged before a magistrate, declaring that prison was better than the workhouse.[61]

There are a number of published accounts of life in poor law institutions by anonymous individuals. *Indoor Paupers*, which appeared in 1885 under the pen-name 'One of Them', purported to be a first-hand account by the inmate of an unnamed London workhouse. In contrast to the usual image of workhouse inmates being wholly oppressed and submissive, it described the various ways that inmates could subvert the regulations and exploit the system to their own advantage:

> There is malingering – a habit once only too well known in the British army. It consisted in self-mutilation by a skulker in order to secure an easy life in hospital, or, if need were, discharge. There are plenty of ex-malingerers in the workhouse; and these fellows never fail to instruct the youths round them in the secrets of their craft, and concerning the times and circumstances when they may be used with striking effects. They are used, too, and the results brought forward, first in the workhouse and then in the prison, to procure immunity from the more trying tasks and the more severe punishments.

In 1874, a Local Government Board report on the education of pauper children in the Metropolitan District included an account by 'W.H.R.' which was introduced as 'the autobiography of a pauper boy, showing his ascent from the condition of a street Arab to competence and respectability.' The author, whom research reveals to be William Hew Ross, provides a graphic account of life in the 1850s and 1860s at an unnamed union workhouse (clearly identifiable as Greenwich) and at the South Metropolitan District School at Sutton. At the workhouse, a black market operated in food:

> Every boy who was fortunate enough to have a halfpenny or a penny would directly after breakfast hang about the stairs leading to the bed-rooms to catch the old women who used to make the beds, and ask if they had an allowance of bread for sale. Many is the allowance (6 oz. bread) I have seen boys buy of the old women, and have also bought many myself. Boys also got into the habit of buying and selling their own rations. Thus, if Bob Jones coveted Joe Smith's top, he would offer Joe half his supper far it, At. the same time, perhaps, Bob had a mother in the house, who was certain to send by one of the bedroom women an allowance of bread for her boy Bob in the morning.[62]

At the age of four, William Golding entered the Stockbridge workhouse in Hampshire where his most vivid memory was the smell of carbolic soap and stale bread. He was later placed in the Southampton Union's children's homes where he spent the following ten years:

> We never had any names, we were all numbers. In the first house I was number 2, in the cottage home I was number 8, in the big house I was number 64. There was this particular boy, his name was Campbell. No-one knew his first name, no-one knew his parents. But he died at the age of eleven... I remember going to his funeral. There was only about two of use went. I remember going along the short distance from the infirmary to the graveyard. He was wheeled along on a basket-type bier, He was just buried in a pauper's grave – in an unmarked grave, and that was it.[63]

Personal recollections do not come just from the inmates of workhouses. The memoirs of workhouse medical officer Joseph Rogers, workhouse reformer Louisa Twining, workhouse chaplain Dennis Cousins, and Local Government Board Inspector Herbert Preston-Thomas all help to throw light on the institution. Preston-Thomas makes a revealing observation about the use of out relief in his area – Norfolk, Suffolk and Essex – at the end of the nineteenth century:

> In most Unions where pauperism was large I found that out relief was dispensed with the utmost freedom. Everybody seemed to have a keen sense of the disgrace of entering the workhouse, but none at all of receiving out relief. The former was regarded as an open shame,

the latter as a pecuniary arrangement not publicly known; and some Boards of Guardians favoured this view by not allowing the names of paupers to be published.[64]

Finally, a reminder that when it came to spirituality, it was not only the workhouse inmates who could learn from the chaplain. A former vicar of Bicester recalled:

> During my vicariate at Bicester I was also Chaplain to the Bicester Union House, and there I learned much from the spiritual experience of good and simple Christians who had drifted within its walls. I remember one particularly who had been a shepherd at Charlton-on-Otmoor. I simply sat at his feet to learn the Bible from him; he was literally soaked in it. I remember one day his telling me that he knew the Bible was true because he had tried himself the experiment of going before his sheep and calling them. What a simple and helpful way of establishing in one's faith the truthfulness of the Bible!
>
> Another man there came to me asking me to prepare him for Confirmation. 'But,' I said, 'you have often been at the Holy Communion: haven't you been confirmed?' He said, 'yes,' but he was a boy when he was confirmed and he did not think seriously about it and now he thought he would like to try it again![65]

A number of other personal recollections can be viewed, and in some cases heard, at the website www.workhouses.org.uk.

(*See also*: **Crooks, Will; Poetry; Rogers, Joseph; Twining, Louisa**)

BOARD OF GUARDIANS

(*See*: **Guardians; Jewish Board of Guardians**)

BOARD SCHOOL

Board Schools, which first appeared in 1872, were introduced by the 1870 Elementary Education Act. The schools were non-denominational and operated through a system which eventually included 2,500 School Boards, elected by local ratepayers. The Boards were innovative in that women were allowed to vote and stand for election. Boards had the power to levy a rate for setting up and running schools where existing voluntary provision was inadequate. In the latter part of the nineteenth century, many unions sent their workhouse children out to local Board Schools.
(*See also*: **Children; National Schools and British Schools; Workhouse Schools**)

BOARD OF GUARDIANS (DEFAULT) ACT

This Act,[66] which became law on 15 July 1926 in the wake of the General Strike, allowed the Minister of Health to suspend or 'supersede' any Board of Guardians that was deemed to have ceased (or was acting in a way that would make it unable) to discharge its functions. The union would then be administered by paid officials appointed by the Minister. The Act was immediately enforced in the West Ham Union which had become bankrupt, largely as a result of what were viewed by the government as excessive and improper out relief payments. Similar actions followed, both in distressed mining areas, at Chester-le-Street in Durham in August 1926, and at Bedwellty in Glamorganshire in February 1927.
(*See also*: **Guardians; Out relief**)

BOARD OF SUPERVISION

The central body overseeing the administration of poor relief in Scotland from 1845 until 1894. (*See also*: **Scotland**)

BOARDING OUT

Boarding out was the placing of parentless children with other families – what we now refer to as fostering. The practice was adopted by a few Poor Law Unions as early as the 1850s but it came into more general use in the 1870s. Children boarded out from workhouses had to be either orphaned or deserted, and aged between two and ten years old. The system was closely regulated and locally supervised by a union Boarding Out Committee. Foster parents, who were originally paid up to 4*s* per week, agreed to 'bring up the child as one of their own children, and provide it with proper food, lodging, and washing, and endeavour to train it in habits of truthfulness, obedience, personal cleanliness, and industry, as well as suitable domestic and outdoor work.'[67] From 1889, children could be boarded out beyond a union's boundaries – possibly some considerable distance away. By the end of the nineteenth century, around half the unions in England and Wales were using boarding out. Although occasional cases of ill-treatment or abuse emerged, these were far outweighed by stories of children filled with dread at the possibility of being taken away from their foster homes.

A different type of boarding out was sometimes adopted by unions which, for various reasons, could not provide all the workhouse accommodation required to house their indoor poor. This might be due to a temporary surge in numbers, for example during a period of high unemployment, or if a new workhouse was not yet ready for occupation, or because of building works at an existing workhouse site. In such situations, a union could pay for inmates to be accommodated in the workhouse of another union that was willing to offer spare places. Such arrangements were usually made between neighbouring unions but were sometimes more widely separated. For several years after its formation in 1896, the Willesden Union in Middlesex boarded out its paupers at the Risbridge Union workhouse in Suffolk and then at the Winslow Union workhouse in Buckinghamshire. After the First World War, a number of small rural workhouses closed and their former residents were boarded out elsewhere, as happened when the Bedale Union placed its inmates in the Beverley Union workhouse. (*See also*: **Children; Cottage Homes; Scattered Homes; Small Homes**)

BONE CRUSHING / BONE POUNDING

A labour task given to able-bodied male inmates which involved the pounding of old bones – usually by means of a heavy ramrod – into dust for use as fertiliser. In the 1845, there was a major scandal when it was discovered that malnourished inmates at Andover workhouse had been fighting over scraps of rotting meat left on some bones they were supposed to be crushing. The task was abolished soon afterwards. (*See also*: **Oakum Picking; Stone Breaking; Scandals; Work**)

BOOK OF BASTILES

In 1841, G.R. Wythen Baxter published *The Book of the Bastiles* – a compilation of newspaper reports, court proceedings, correspondence and other material that graphically illustrated some of the alleged horror stories relating to the New Poor Law. A typical item is given below:

An inquiry has taken place this week at Rochester, before the county magistrates, into several charges preferred against James Miles, the master of the Hoo Union-House, for cruelly beating several young pauper-children of both sexes. Elizabeth Danes stated that she was 13 years of age, and that the defendant, James Miles, had punished her three times while she was in the Union-House. The offence she had committed was leaving a little dirt in the corner of a room, and the defendant made her lie upon a table, and *took her clothes off*, and beat her with a birch-broom until blood came.[68]

(*See also*: **Opposition to the New Poor Law**)

BOY SCOUTS

The inception of the Boy Scouts movement in 1907 generated interest from boys in every walk of life. This included those in workhouses and their associated children's homes who, with the agreement of the Board of Guardians, might be able to join a local group. At the end of 1910, the Christchurch Union's cottage homes even formed their own troop – the 2nd Christchurch (Fairmile) – with the guardians making a grant of a penny per week to each boy joining. The Board also agreed to spend between 2 and 3s on each boy to buy his uniform and equipment.[69] When the Burton Latimer Boy Scouts troop started in about 1921, several boys from the Kettering Union's nearby cottage homes joined, with the guardians buying their uniforms. The following summer, four of the boys went to camp with the troop, the cost being raised by subscription from the guardians themselves not from union funds.[70]

A Scout troop, Cub pack and Girl Guide company were established at Queen Mary's Hospital in Margate, run by the Metropolitan Asylums Board for the treatment of children suffering from tuberculosis. Similar provision was also made at the Board's training colony at Darenth.

(*See also*: **Metropolitan Asylums Board**)

A troop of Boy Scouts from the Christchurch Union's cottage homes at their campsite.

A card advertising the holding of the Belper workhouse's annual sale of work produced by inmates under the Brabazon scheme.

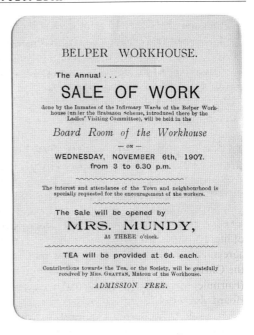

BELPER WORKHOUSE.

The Annual . . .

SALE OF WORK

done by the Inmates of the Infirmary Wards of the Belper Workhouse (under the Brabazon scheme, introduced there by the Ladies' Visiting Committee), will be held in the

Board Room of the Workhouse

— ON —

WEDNESDAY, NOVEMBER 6th, 1907.
from 3 to 6.30 p.m.

The interest and attendance of the Town and neighbourhood is specially requested for the encouragement of the workers.

The Sale will be opened by

MRS. MUNDY,

At THREE o'clock.

TEA will be provided at 6d. each.

Contributions towards the Tea, or the Society, will be gratefully received by MRS. GRATTAN, Matron of the Workhouse.

ADMISSION FREE.

BRABAZON SCHEME

The Brabazon Scheme was initiated in 1880 by Lady Brabazon who later became the Countess of Meath. It was intended to provide interesting and useful occupation such as knitting, embroidery or lace-making for non-able-bodied workhouse inmates who spent long hours confined to bed or in dayrooms. Training in the various crafts was provided by outside volunteers and the costs were initially borne by Lady Brabazon. The idea was slow to take off, with Kensington being the first to adopt it in 1883. However, it gradually spread, particularly when it was found that the goods produced were saleable which could make the scheme self-financing. By 1897, there were over 100 branches.

BRIDEWELL

(*See:* **House of Correction**)

BRITISH SCHOOLS

(*See:* **National and British Schools**)

BROADSIDE BALLADS

Sold in the streets for a penny or halfpenny between the sixteenth and early twentieth centuries, broadside ballads were popular songs of the day, often anonymous, and performed in taverns, homes or fairs. The words of the ballads, usually sung to a well-known tune, often commented on topical events including workhouse scandals or tragedies. Typical was *The Women Flogger's Lament of Marylebone Workhouse* published in 1856 after Richard Ryan, master of the St Marylebone workhouse, and two porters had been dismissed for beating young female inmates. Sung to the tune of 'Oh, Dear What Can the Matter Be', it begins:

Oh dear here's a shocking disaster,
My name it is Ryon (*sic*) a poor workhouse master,
I have now got discharged and my sentence is passed,. sirs.
Because I went flogging the girls.
The two flogging porters and me are crushed down. sirs,
One porter is green and the other is brown, sirs,
We would not have it happened for five hundred pounds, sirs,
Flogging the dear little girls.

Chorus
Oh where shall we wander, or where shall we roam, sirs,
As we walk through the streets folks won't let us alone, sirs,
Kicked out of the workhouse in Marylebone, sirs,
For flogging the sweet little girls.

Other titles relating to the workhouse or poor laws included: *The Poor Law Bastile*; *The Workhouse Door*; *Lines on the Death of a Most Cruel, Hard-hearted Overseer of the Poor*; *Joe Bradley, the Runaway Workhouse Boy*; and *A Night's Repose in Lambeth Workhouse* – inspired by James Greenwood's exposé of conditions in the Lambeth Casual Ward.

The Workhouse Boy, a parody of the popular song *The Mistletoe Bough*, was the macabre tale of a young workhouse inmate 'going to pot', which appeared in about 1836. The ballad is referred to in Dickens' *Bleak House* where shrill youthful voices taunt the Beadle with having boiled a boy and then chorus fragments of a popular song 'importing that the boy was made into soup for the workhouse'.

The Workhouse Boy
The towels were spread in the workhouse hall,
Our caps were hung up on the whitey brown wall;
We'd hoshuns of soup, and nothing to pay,
For keeping our Christmas holiday.
We'd a baron of beef, and pudden beside,
A beautiful one – it was Missus's pride
We feasted our eyes with the pudden and beef,
But as for our bellies, 'twas all make belief,
For the poor workhouse boy! Oh, the poor workhouse boy.

Rather more music hall than street ballad, *Standing at the Workhouse Gate* told the tear-jerking story of a widow and her children poised to ring the workhouse bell. At the last moment, however, 'the courage of her noble heart' gave her the resolve to try and survive outside.

'I'm tired,' cried one, 'of the soup I'm sick,
But stop here a minute – I'll play 'em a trick.
Bill Lovell,' says he, 'will you come and go,
Where the pudden is hid, I thinks I know.'
Away he ran and his pal began
The wash-house to search and the larder to scan.
And Bill Lovell cried, 'Now where do you hide?
I can't find the pudden nor you beside.'
Oh the poor workhouse boy! Oh, the poor workhouse boy.

He sought him next night, and he sought him next day,
He sought him in vain when a week passed way.
On the pantiles, the cellars, the coal-hole ('Why Not?')
Bill Lovell sought wildly but found him not.
A month flew by and his grief at last
Was just like a story of woe long past.
But Bill he still wept o'er his lonesome lot,
For his pal he felt certain had gone to pot.
Oh the poor workhouse boy! Oh, the poor workhouse boy.

The soup copper was cleaned out once a year,
The mops and the birch brooms were all brought near.
They put out the fire, they looked all around,
And what do you think in the copper was found?
A little boy's coat and a small-tooth comb
Showed very well that was a poor boy's tomb.
He'd lost his way and like poor Lovell too,
Had been for a month in a terrible stew.
Oh the poor workhouse boy! Oh, the poor workhouse boy.

(*See also*: **Entertainment**; **Poetry**; **Social Explorers**; Hepburn (2000); Symonds (2006))

BULLER MEMORANDUM

In August 1848, Poor Law Board president Charles Buller issued a set of recommendations relating to the treatment of the casual poor.[71] The so-called Buller memorandum was a response to the sharp increase in the numbers using casual wards that had taken place during the 1840s due to factors such as slumps in trade and the effects of the Irish famine. Buller urged unions to discriminate between the honest unemployed 'temporarily and unavoidably in distress' who were in search of work, and the 'habitual tramp or vagrant who simulates destitution'. It was suggested that the former category be issued with a certificate through which they might receive preferential admission or treatment at the workhouses along a particular route, while the latter might even be refused admission completely unless in immediate danger of starvation. In making this distinction, Buller suggested that local police officers be appointed as assistant relieving officers and take on the job of issuing casual ward admission tickets. In an overenthusiastic response to these proposals, some unions even went so far as to close their casual wards. The number of casuals relieved in England and Wales on 1 July 1849 was 5,662 – a drop of almost 60 per cent on the figure of 13,714 for the same date in 1848, just prior to the issuing of Buller's proposals.[72]
(*See also*: **Casual Poor**; **Casual Ward**)

BULLY'S ACRE

Originally a name used for the graveyard adjoining the Royal Hospital in Dublin, where no payment of burial fees was exacted. The term later became more widely used in Ireland as an informal term for a paupers' or famine graveyard, and is especially associated with workhouse burial grounds.
(*See also*: **Death**; **Ireland**)

BURIAL

(*See*: **Death**)

CAPTAIN SWING RIOTS

In the autumn of 1830, agricultural labourers across southern England began a series of protests against low wages, expensive food, and the growing mechanisation of farms. Threatening letters sent to land-owners and farmers were signed 'Swing' – the supposed although probably fictitious leader of the protests. Workhouses were also amongst the rioters' targets. On 22 November, a mob assailed the Selborne parish workhouse, turned out the occupants, burned or smashed the fittings and furniture, and pulled off the roof. The following day, an even larger mob, including the Selborne rioters, did the same to the workhouse at nearby Headley. The ringleaders were later transported to Australia.
(*See also*: **Rebecca Riots**)

CASUAL POOR

The 'casual', 'houseless' or 'non-settled' poor (usually known just as 'casuals') were those to whom a workhouse offered overnight temporary accommodation. Unlike ordinary workhouse inmates, casuals – typically vagrants, tramps, or those travelling in search of work – did not need to be settled in the union where they were applying for relief.

The poor law system introduced by the 1834 Poor Law Amendment Act originally made no provision for transient vagrants, with Boards of Guardians regarding vagrancy as a matter for the police rather than the poor law. However, several instances of tramps dying from exposure or starvation after being turned away from the workhouse door resulted in the Poor Law Commissioners having to compromise. In 1837, a new regulation was introduced which required food and a night's shelter to be given to *any* destitute person in case of 'sudden or urgent necessity'.[73] Workhouses gradually began to provide special accommodation for the casual poor – what became known as the casual ward – separate from the rest of the workhouse. From 1842, casuals were required to perform a task of labour before being released after their night's stay.

Rising Numbers

The casual poor grew to form a significant, albeit transient, part of the workhouse population. Increasing numbers in the early 1840s, particularly in London, led to a scheme for establishing six District Asylums for the capital's houseless poor, with similar establishments proposed for Birmingham, Bristol, Leeds, Liverpool and Manchester.[74] However, the plan never came to fruition and unions were left to make their own individual provision.

There were periodic attempts by the central authorities to keep the numbers of casual poor in check. In 1848, Poor Law Board president Charles Buller issued recommendations aimed at reducing the growing tide of casuals by deterring habitual tramps while still aiding those seeking work or in genuine distress. The 'Buller memorandum' achieved its aim with casual ward numbers being more than halved over the following decade.

By 1863, however, it had become apparent that many unions were evading their responsibilities towards the casual poor. Poor Law Board president Charles Villiers issued a circular reminding unions of their obligation to help the genuinely destitute. In London, the Metropolitan Houseless Poor Act of 1864 required each of the capital's poor law authorities to provide 'wards or other places of reception for destitute wayfarers and foundlings'. They were assisted in doing so by making the cost of casual relief chargeable to a common fund – this was initially provided by the Metropolitan Board of Works then, from 1867, by a new Common Poor Fund.

The subsequent resurgence of numbers applying for admission to the casual wards led in some areas to the introduction of way tickets to try and identify honest wayfarers. Way tickets, issued by the police or casual-ward superintendent, were for a specified duration along a particular route and endorsed at each workhouse visited. The ticket-holder was entitled to favourable treatment, such as being exempt from work tasks.

The numbers of casual poor continued to rise steadily. In 1905, the annual head-count on the night of 1 January recorded a total of 9,887 being relieved in England and Wales, more than six times the figure of 1,556 reported in 1855.[75, 76]

The 1904 Departmental Committee on Vagrancy

In 1904, in another attempt to put a halt to the growth in vagrancy, the Local Government Board instituted a Departmental Committee to inquire into the whole subject. The Committee's report, issued in 1906, laid the blame for the increase on 'the whims and wishes of the local administrators', i.e. Boards of Guardians, for their inconsistent and over-lenient treatment of habitual vagrants. The free refuges operated by charitable agencies were also viewed as encouraging vagrancy. The report included two main recommendations. First, that supervision of vagrants should be transferred from the poor law authorities to the police. Second, that labour colonies be established, perhaps by county and borough councils, where habitual vagrants could be detained for between six months and three years, with inmates being given a subsistence diet but able to earn small sums of money by their work. For *bona fide* work seekers, further use of the way ticket system was advocated. Other proposals included the licensing and control of charitably run free shelters, broadening the offence of 'sleeping out', and – recognising the efforts of campaigners such as Mary Higgs to improve the lot of homeless women – the receiving of female vagrants into the main workhouse rather than the casual ward. Despite the scale of the problem identified by the report, its proposals were almost entirely ignored and vagrant numbers remained high. On the night of 1 January 1910, a total of 10,392 inmates were housed in the country's casual wards.[77]

The persistence of the problem was, according to commentators such as Sidney and Beatrice Webb, the result of an ongoing failure to address the causes rather than the symptoms of vagrancy. There was also a tunnel-visioned focus on those vagrants who voluntarily applied for a night's lodging at a workhouse or other shelter.[78] These formed only a fraction of the national total of 30,000 estimated to exist by the 1904 Departmental Committee.

Some changes did take place in an effort to give greater consistency to the treatment of casuals. In 1912, control of almost all of London's casual wards passed to the Metropolitan Asylums Board. By 1914, the Board's efforts at rationalising the system had reduced the number of casual wards in the capital from twenty-eight to twelve. In 1913, the Local Government Board allowed Boards of Guardians elsewhere in the country to set up Joint Vagrancy Committees to coordinate provision for casuals in different areas.

The First World War and Beyond

The First World War saw a sharp decline in vagrant numbers and some casual wards were closed during the war years. During the post-war industrial depression, use of the casual wards again rose steadily, with a national total of 11,562 inmates being recorded on 1 January 1929. In the same year, the Ministry of Health instituted a Departmental Committee to examine, yet again, the situation of the casual poor.

The Committee's report noted the wide variation in treatment received by casuals at different workhouses, with some casual wards being regarded as 'infamous and intolerable'.[79] Its recommendations included improvements to the conditions in casual wards such as the sleeping accommodation, bathing facilities and the diet provided. The Committee criticised the widespread practice of releasing casuals after only one night's detention rather than the two demanded by the regulations. Those genuinely searching for work, it was argued, should be making use of employment exchanges rather than tramping the roads. Demanding work from casuals would deter those who had funds for alternative accommodation, although stone breaking was not viewed as a suitable occupation. The Committee strongly felt that the supervision of casual wards should be restricted to trained officers who could also identify those appearing to be sick or suffering from a mental disorder. The Committee encouraged the combination of local authorities which enabled the better provision of resources such as hostels or training centres for casuals who wished to improve their conditions. Recognition was also given to the efforts of voluntary agencies such as the Salvation Army, Church Army and Wayfarers' Benevolent Society in assisting former casuals better themselves.

Some of the Departmental Committee's proposals were implemented in the Public Assistance (Casual Poor) Order issued by the Ministry of Health in 1931 to the local authorities who were now responsible for administering public assistance following the abolition of the Boards of Guardians in 1930. The Order prescribed substantial improvements to casual ward conditions such as bathing arrangements and diet. Inmates holding a 'vacant ticket' as evidence of genuine unemployment from a labour exchange could leave on the morning after their arrival.

Who Were the Casual Poor?

The great majority of vagrants were men, with around 70 per cent being aged between thirty-five and sixty-five.[80] Women and children always formed a small fraction of the casual ward population and one that gradually declined. On the night of 1 January 1905, women formed just over 9 per cent of casual ward inmates, with children accounting for just under 2 per cent.

As to the characteristics of those using workhouse casual wards, views varied. The 1904 Departmental Committee distinguished four main sub-groups. First, working men travelling in genuine search of employment who, according to different opinions, formed between 1 and 20 per cent of the total. Second, 'work-shy' men willing to undertake short-term casual labour, but who objected to, or who were unfit for, permanent work. Third, habitual vagrants were those who claimed to be in search of work but who certainly had no desire to find it. Finally, persons who were old, infirm and often mentally ill who wandered from casual ward to casual ward.[81]

Another appraisal was made by former MP Frank Gray who made a number of undercover visits to casual wards in Oxfordshire in the late 1920s. The categories identified by Gray included: the 'real free, true, and genuine tramp', genuine workers seeking employment, labouring navvies, seafarers travelling between ports or between their home and a port, seasonal agricultural workers, professional beggars, habitual drunkards (a group which Gray considered to form the largest portion of all vagrants), habitual criminals, physical 'degenerates', mental 'degenerates', and youths – a group for which Gray had a particular concern.[82]

Evidence that vagrants included a significant proportion of those with mental problems was presented to the 1929 Departmental Committee. An informal examination of 592 casuals categorised more than a quarter as suffering from various mental problems such as feeble-mindedness, insanity, senility and psychoneurosis.[83]

(*See also*: **Buller Memorandum**; **Casual Ward**; **County Vagrancy Schemes**; **Labour Colony / Farm Colony**; **Oakum**; **Stone Breaking**; **Way Ticket System**)

CASUAL WARD

After 1837, when the poor law authorities became obliged to provide temporary overnight shelter for any destitute person, workhouses gradually set up special accommodation for this purpose. Initially, the casual poor were often housed in infectious wards as tramps and vagrants were widely regarded as potential carriers of diseases such as smallpox. Stables and outhouses were also pressed into service. Eventually, however, most workhouses erected a purpose-built casual ward, an institution which became popularly known by tramps and vagrants as the 'spike'.

In London and some other large towns, casual wards were sometimes erected on sites separate from the main workhouse. The usual arrangement, though, was for the casual ward to be placed at the edge of the main workhouse site, often with its own separate access gate. The wards were sometimes superintended by the workhouse porter, perhaps with his wife attending the female casuals. Some spikes were in the charge of a 'Tramp Major', usually a former tramp himself, and now informally employed by the workhouse.

Casual wards were intended to provide the most basic level of accommodation, inferior even to that in the main workhouse. One observer in 1840 reported that:

> In general they have brick floors and guardroom beds, with loose straw and rugs for the males and iron bedsteads with straw ties for the females. They are generally badly ventilated and unprovided with any means of producing warmth. All holes for ventilation in reach of the occupants are sure to be stuffed with rags and straws; so that the effluvia of these places is at best most disgustingly offensive.[84]

Entering a Casual Ward

The routine for those entering a casual ward began in late afternoon by joining the queue for admission – the number of beds was limited and late-comers might find themselves turned away. In fact, casual wards usually had two entrances, one for males and one for females – as in the main workhouse, segregation of the sexes was strictly observed.

A workhouse casual ward where inmates slept in hammocks slung between hooks on the wall and a metal rail. The poster (right) suggests that the location is in the vicinity of Reading in Berkshire.

At opening time, usually 5 or 6 o'clock in the evening, new arrivals would be admitted and searched, with any money, tobacco or alcohol confiscated. It was common practice for vagrants to hide such possessions in a nearby hedge or wall before entering the spike, although the items were often in danger of being removed by local children. Contraband such as cigarettes could also be smuggled in by various means. One ploy was to hide such items under the armpit, held there by sticking plaster. George Orwell's account of a visit to a spike in the 1920s revealed an unspoken rule that searches never went below the knee so that illicit goods could be hidden in the boots or stuffed into the bottoms of trouser legs.[85] Entrants were required to strip and bathe – in water that might already have been used by a number of others. They were then issued with a blanket and a workhouse nightshirt to wear, with their own clothes being dried and fumigated or disinfected. Each was given a supper, typically 8oz of bread and a pint of gruel (or 'skilly', as it was colloquially known), before being locked up for the night from 7p.m. until 6 or 7a.m. the next morning. Until the 1870s, the norm was for casual wards to have communal association dormitories where the inmates either slept in rows of low-slung hammocks or on the bare floor.

The following morning, a breakfast of bread and gruel would be served, usually at 6a.m. Following the Poor Law Amendment Act of 1842, casuals were required to perform a task of work for up to four hours before being released. The type of work demanded at each work-house was decided by the Board of Guardians. For male casuals, stone breaking and oakum picking were widely used. For females, labour tasks included oakum picking and domestic work such as scrubbing floors. In some unions, however, the work requirement was not enforced, with the guardians happy to be rid of casuals at the earliest opportunity.

Once vagrants had done their stint of work, or four hours had elapsed since breakfast, they were given a lump of bread and released to go on their way. However, even with an early start to the work, this meant that only half the day remained to tramp to another workhouse. The Casual Poor Act of 1882[86] made it a requirement for casuals to be detained for two nights, with the full day in between spent performing work. The casuals could then be released at 9a.m. in the morning after the second night, allowing more time to search for work or to travel to another workhouse. Those entering the casual ward on a Saturday evening were detained an extra day since no work was performed on Sunday. From 1871, return to the casual ward of the same union was not allowed within thirty days, the whole of metropolitan London count-ing as a single union for this purpose. Breaching this regulation would incur two extra nights' detention with work being performed on the days in between. To avoid this penalty, tramping circuits evolved linking a long progression of spikes before eventually returning to the first a month later. Nights at a spike might be interspersed with sleeping rough or in farm outhouses, especially in the summer months.

New Casual Ward Designs

In 1864, the Poor Law Board issued a circular containing advice regarding causal ward provi-sion.[87] Separate wards were to be provided for men and for women and children, each having a yard with a bathroom and water closet, and a work shed. It was also recommended that wards have raised sleeping platforms, divided down the middle by a gangway, and each side divided up by boards to give a sleeping space of at least 2ft 3in. A narrow shelf along each side of the room provided an area at the head of each compartment where clothes could be placed. Bedding was to consist of coarse 'straw or cocoa fibre in a loose tick', and a rug 'sufficient for warmth'. A temporary casual ward, designed by Henry Saxon Snell and clearly based on these recommendations, was erected at St Marylebone workhouse in 1867. Its walls were heavily decorated with 'improving' religious texts for the benefit of the establishment's occupants.

From around 1870, a new form of vagrants' accommodation began to be adopted, again developed by Henry Saxon Snell. It consisted of individual cells, very much like those in a prison, usually arranged along both sides of a corridor. Sleeping cells contained a simple bed, perhaps hinged so that it could be folded up against the wall when not in use. Work cells were

Above St Marylebone's new casual ward, with its coffin-like beds, opened in 1867. Scriptural texts printed in large red letters adorned the blue walls.

Right A cut-away illustration of a stone-breaking cell showing the metal grille through which the broken pieces of stone had to be passed.

usually fitted out for stone breaking, typically with a hinged metal grille which could be opened from the outside to allow unbroken lumps of stone to be deposited in the cell. The inmate then had to break up the stone into lumps small enough to pass back through the holes in the grille, or in a separate horizontal grid fitted beneath it. The broken stone could then be collected on the outside. There were variations in the design of stone-breaking cells – some had a bench on which the stone was broken, in others the work was done on the floor. Some designs had separate windows and grilles, while others used the grille itself as a glassless and very draughty window which, on being released from the outside, could also serve as a fire escape. Sometimes sleeping cells and work cells were separated, sometimes one led through to the other.

Views from the Inside

In 1890, William Booth, founder of the Salvation Army, published his book *In Darkest England and the Way Out* which included some accounts of conditions in London casual wards:

> J. C. knows Casual Wards pretty well. Has been in St. Giles, Whitechapel, St. George's, Paddington, Marylebone, Mile End. They vary a little in detail, but as a rule the doors open at 6; you walk in; they tell you what the work is, and that if you fail to do it, you will be liable to imprisonment. Then you bathe. Some places the water is dirty. Three persons as a rule wash in one water. At Whitechapel (been there three times) it has always been dirty; also at St. George's. I had no bath at Mile End; they were short of water. If you complain they take no notice. You then tie your clothes in a bundle, and they give you a nightshirt. At most places they serve supper to the men, who have to go to bed and eat it there. Some beds are in cells; some in large rooms. You get up at 6 a.m. and do the task. The amount of stone-breaking is too much; and the oakum-picking is also heavy. The food differs. At St. Giles, the gruel left over-night is boiled up for breakfast, and is consequently sour; the bread is puffy, full of holes, and don't weigh the regulation amount. Dinner is only 8 ounces of bread and 1 1/2 ounce of cheese, and its that's short, how can anybody do their work? They will give you water to drink if you ring the cell bell for it, that is, they will tell you to wait, and bring it in about half an hour. There are a good lot of 'moochers' go to Casual Wards, but there are large numbers of men who only want work.[88]

Many other accounts of life and conditions in the casual ward were provided by various 'social explorers' – usually well-heeled individuals who dressed themselves as vagrants in order to gain admission, and then published accounts of their experiences. One of the earliest and best-known undercover reports was James Greenwood's series of articles for the *Pall Mall Gazette* published in 1866. Typical of Greenwood's colourful prose was his description of the water 'disgustingly like weak mutton broth' in which tramps were expected, one after another, to take a bath.

Casual Ward Graffiti

An interesting sidelight on casual ward culture was provided by a collection of graffiti collected from various workhouses by Poor Law Inspector Andrew Doyle in 1865. Tramps often had colourful nicknames as shown by the following examples:

> The York Spinner, Dick Blazeanvy, Lancashire Crab, Dublin Smasher, and Bob Curly called for one night on their road for the tip at Birmingham.
> Saturday, 17th June, Bow Street, bound for Derbyshire, Amen–Wolverhampton Nipper and Belfast Jack was here 14th September 1865, bound for London.
> Notice to Long Cockney, or Cambridge, or any of the fraternity.–Harry the Mark was here from Carmarthen, and if anybody of the Yorkshire tramps wishes to find him he is to be found in South Wales for the next three months. –17th August 1865.
> Wild Scoty the celebrated king of the cadgers, is in Newgate in, London, going to be hanged by the neck till he is dead; this is a great fact.–Written by his mate.

Bow Street, Long Macclesfield, Welsh Ned, Sailor Jack, the Islington Kid, Wakefield Charley, and an Irish cabinet maker were located here 10th September 1865.

The graffiti often commented on the character of the relief afforded in different unions:

Beware of Ludlow–bare boards, no chuck.
Bishop's Castle Union Workhouse is a good place to be down in, but a damned bad lot of paupers about it.
This is a rum place for a fellow to come to for a night's lodging; you will never catch me here again.–Old Bob Bridley, Ok!

The workhouse of the Seisdon Union (at Trysull) appears to have a rather better reputation:

Dry bread in the morning, ditto at night,
Keep up your pecker and make it all right.
Certainly the meals are paltry and mean,
But the beds are nice and clean;
Men, don't tear the beds, sheets, or rugs,
For there are neither lice, fleas, or bugs
At this little clean union at Trysull.
But still at this place there is a drawback,
And now I will put you on the right track,
For I would as soon lodge here as in Piccadilly
If along with the bread they gave a drop of skilly,
At this little clean union at Trysull.
So I tell you again, treat this place with respect,
And instead of abusing, pray do it protect,
For to lodge here one night is certainly a treat,
At this little clean union at Trysull.
–Bow Street.

The End of the Casual Ward

By the 1920s, there was growing pressure for changes in the casual ward regime. Workhouses were increasingly reluctant to require casuals to perform punitive tasks such as stone breaking or oakum picking, preferring instead to give them useful jobs around the workhouse. Oakum, in any case, was no longer in demand by ship-builders. Supervising casuals all day on Sundays, when no work was required from them, often proved difficult.

Some changes came following a review in 1929 of the treatment of the casual poor by a Ministry of Health Departmental Committee. The Committee's report noted the wide variation in casual ward conditions. Criticisms included sleeping accommodation that was not fit for animals, poor or non-existent sanitary facilities, poor food – often served without cutlery, and a lack of work. Boards of Guardians appeared often to be apathetic to such conditions and reluctant to spend money on improving them. Interestingly, some of the worst run casual wards appeared to be the most popular – lax supervision, an absence of work and a lack of washing facilities all proving a positive attraction to some inmates.

Some of the Committee's recommendations were implemented in the Public Assistance (Casual Poor) Order issued in 1931, the year after responsibility for poor relief passed from Boards of Guardians to county and borough councils. Bathing arrangements now required the provision of clean warm water and unused towels. The casual ward dietary now omitted gruel and included a dinner of bread, cheese, meat, potatoes and some other vegetable. Stone breaking and oakum picking were no longer allowed as work tasks. Inmates holding a 'vacant ticket' – evidence of genuine unemployment from a labour exchange – could leave on the morning after their arrival.

There was a steady reduction in the numbers of casual wards operating during the 1930s, with 324 still in use in 1937.[89] The onset of the Second World War in 1939 was followed by a steep decline in those using casual wards and by 1944 all those still open had been shut until further notice. The 1948 National Assistance Act led to the establishment of 134 Wayfarers' Reception Centres, many of which were located in former workhouse casual wards and attached to what had often now become National Health Service hospitals. The numbers of Reception Centres was gradually reduced – by 1957, only sixty-five were in operation with just twenty attached to hospitals.[90] In a few cases, new purpose-built reception centres were erected such as that at Leeds opened in 1970 and demolished in 1998.

(*See also*: **Casual Poor**; **Metropolitan Asylums Board**; **Social Explorers**)

CATCH, GEORGE

George Catch, a former policeman, was a notoriously tyrannical workhouse master who held office at the Strand, Newington and Lambeth workhouses from around 1853 to 1870. His activities were documented by Joseph Rogers, the medical officer at the Strand, during Catch's tenure there. After finally being barred from ever again holding any workhouse post, Catch eventually threw himself in front of a Great Western train and was cut to pieces.

(*See also*: **Rogers, Joseph**; **Scandals**)

CERTIFIED SCHOOLS (POOR LAW)

The 1862 Poor Law (Certified Schools) Act[91] allowed Boards of Guardians to maintain pauper children at voluntary homes or residential schools that were inspected and certified for the purpose. The option applied to children who were orphaned or deserted or whose parents agreed to such a placement. The homes were mostly operated by charitable or religious bodies such as the Church of England or the Roman Catholic Church. A small number were also recognised as Certified Industrial Schools. Most certified poor law schools catered for a particular type of inmate such as Roman Catholic children, or those having a specific disability such as the blind, deaf or dumb, or with other physical or mental disabilities. Some were single-sex homes, while others took both boys and girls. On 1 January 1892, the number of certified poor law schools in operation in England and Wales was 171.[92]

(*See also*: **Children**; **Industrial Schools – Certified**; **Voluntary Homes**)

CHADWICK, EDWIN

Edwin Chadwick (1800–90) was born in Manchester but moved to London in around 1809 when his father became editor of the radical paper *The Statesman*. He later began training as a lawyer, supporting himself by writing articles for newspapers such as the *Morning Herald*. During the 1820s he became increasingly familiar with the social problems of the day and made the acquaintance of utilitarian thinkers such as John Stuart Mill and Thomas Southwood Smith. Chadwick's 1828 essay in the *Westminster Review* relating life expectancy to environmental conditions, and a subsequent piece on the organisation of the police force, brought him to the attention of Jeremy Bentham. In 1830, Chadwick was engaged to work on Bentham's *Constitutional Code* then, following the latter's death in 1832, gained a post as one of the twenty-six Assistant Commissioners for the newly inaugurated Royal Commission on the poor laws.

Chadwick was assigned to compile information on poor relief administration on London and Berkshire. His rapid accomplishment of the task, together with his Benthamite-leaning proposals for a new model of relief administration, led in 1833 to his becoming a full Commissioner.

Chadwick and fellow Benthamites Nassau Senior and Walter Coulson were responsible for writing the bulk of the Commission's final report published in the spring of 1834. Chadwick's main contribution was the section on 'remedial measures' whose central proposal was that relief to the able-bodied and their families should be only through a workhouse. Conditions in the workhouse were always to be 'less eligible' than those outside, a principle originally advanced by Bentham. Chadwick's role in formulating the report, subsequently enacted through the 1834 Poor Law Amendment Act, has led to his sometimes being described as the architect of the Victorian Poor Law.

As well as his poor law work, Chadwick spent part of 1833 involved in a separate Royal Commission examining working hours in textile mills. The Commission's report, written by Chadwick, resulted in the 1833 Factory Act. The Act banned the employment in factories of children under nine and limited the working hours of those under fourteen to eight hours a day with a one-hour dinner break. New officials – known as inspectors – were to ensure compliance with the law.

In 1834, to his huge disappointment, Chadwick was not appointed as one of the three new Poor Law Commissioners but was instead appointed as their secretary – a post thought more befitting to a man of his background.[93] George Nicholls was the only one of the trio with whom Chadwick formed any rapport but their alliance was disrupted by Nicholls' move to Dublin in 1838. Thereafter, Chadwick was increasingly sidelined from policy making, becoming even more bitter after not being promoted to succeed Thomas Frankland Lewis who resigned his Commissionership in 1839. Despite his unhappiness, Chadwick continued in the post of secretary until finally gaining his revenge at the inquiry into the Andover scandal in 1845. His revelations about lax procedures and an absence of formal meetings helped bring about the demise of the Poor Law Commissioners in 1847.

Throughout this whole period, however, Chadwick increasingly devoted his energies elsewhere, most notably to sanitary and public health matters. His influential 1842 report into

A bird's eye view of the 'Children's Home on the Moor' at Edgworth near Bolton, opened in 1872 by Methodist minister Thomas Bowman Stephenson. The home's 300 children included some placed there by poor law authorities under the 1862 Certified Schools Act.

the 'sanitary condition of the labouring population' demonstrated how health and lifespan were linked to the provision of good sanitation and clean water. In 1848, he became the first Commissioner of the new General Board of Health but retired in 1854 after his appointment was not renewed.

(*See also*: **Poor Law Commissioners**; **Royal Commission – 1832**; Finer (1952))

CHAPEL

Early union workhouse designs did not usually include a separate chapel, but with the dining hall serving as the venue for religious services. Separate chapel buildings became increasingly common, however. An early example was at Bath workhouse, where the foundation stone of a new chapel was laid at a ceremony on 10 February 1843, with the workhouse children singing a hymn. Remarkably, the building was erected almost single-handedly by a seventy-eight-year-old inmate, a former stone-mason named John Plass.

The addition of a chapel at a workhouse was often paid for by local charitable efforts or donations, such as the building funded in 1861 at Gainsborough by a Miss Anderson and containing a stained-glass window in memory of the union's former Clerk, Thomas Oldham.

From the 1850s, workhouse buildings often incorporated a dedicated separate chapel from the outset, such as the City of London workhouse on Bow Road erected in 1848–49, and at the Chorlton Union's new premises at Withington built in 1854–55. The plans for Oxford's new workhouse, erected in 1863–65, originally placed the chapel at the centre of the workhouse complex. However, it was finally erected separate from the main buildings, perhaps to allow it to have the conventional east-west orientation which the original design precluded.

(*See also*: **Religion**)

CHAPLAIN

(*See*: **Religion**)

In the chapel, as elsewhere in the workhouse, the sexes were segregated and the buildings often had separate entrances for men and women as seen here at the Tonbridge Union workhouse in Kent.

CHANNEL ISLANDS

Although independent of the legislation applying in Britain, several of the Channel Islands established poor-relief systems operating in a broadly similar manner.

In 1597, the Guernsey Synod introduced a parish-based poor relief system along similar lines to that introduced in England at around the same time. It was administered by lay officials called deacons, similar to the overseers in English parishes, who collected alms at Sunday church services and redistributed them to the needy poor. In the eighteenth century, several workhouses were built in Guernsey including, in 1741, the House of Charity in St Peter Port which later became Town Hospital. In 1751, following the pattern of Town Hospital, the parish of Castel set up a workhouse which later became known as Country Hospital. In the nineteenth century, Poor Law Boards in each parish administered poor relief through elected parish officials called the Procureurs of the Poor – comparable to the Boards of Guardians in England. In 1937, responsibility for poor relief passed from the parochial Poor Law Boards to the Public Assistance Authority.

The main establishment providing poor relief in Jersey was the Jersey General Hospital and its Poor Law Infirmary, originally founded in 1741. Until 1839 it was administered by a 'Comité des Pauvres' (Committee for the Poor). In the early 1900s, there was also a 'Maison des Pauvres' (poorhouse) at St Saviour's.

CHARITY ORGANISATION SOCIETY

The Society for Organising Charitable Relief and Repressing Mendicity, better known as the Charity Organisation Society (COS), was founded in London in 1869. Its membership included social reformer Octavia Hill and Charles Stewart Loch, who became its honorary secretary from 1875 until 1914. The Society's original aim was to organise the charitable relief efforts in each area so as to prevent overlap and competition between the large number of uncoordinated agencies that existed. The Society also believed that those in destitution could best be helped by a careful and scientific examination of their individual circumstances and, wherever possible, supported by private charity rather than poor relief. The poor should also be helped to become self-reliant by saving, through membership of friendly societies or sick clubs, or by support from their family, friends or neighbours. Only those unsuitable for being helped in this way should then be candidates for state-funded poor relief which would normally be by means of the workhouse.

The Society's philosophy complemented the crusade against out relief launched by the Poor Law Board's president George Goschen at the end of 1869, and subsequently pursued by the Local Government Board. Many members of the Society obtained election to their local Board of Guardians and were then successful in persuading the Board to reduce or virtually withdraw out relief as happened in more than a dozen unions including Stepney, Whitechapel, St George in the East, Paddington, Kennington, Manchester, Birmingham, Reading, Brixworth, Bradfield, Oxford, Ipswich and St Neots. The combined efforts of the poor law and the COS certainly had a marked effect on national out relief expenditure which fell from around £3.7 million in 1869 to just over £2.6 million in 1879, with the number of out relief recipients over the same period falling from 817,000 to 555,000. Less clear, however, is whether the drop in out relief claimants was due to their increasing thrift and self-sufficiency, or simply their turning to other agencies such as the Salvation Army or various church-run shelters.

The influence of the COS was in decline by the end of the nineteenth century, with many formerly strict unions now adopting a less rigid stance on out relief. Although the Society was well represented in the 1905 Royal Commission on the poor laws, it increasingly fell out of line with public opinion and continued to oppose 'indiscriminate' measures such as the old age pension introduced in 1909.

The COS was renamed the Family Welfare Association in 1946 and continues in operation today as the charity Family Action.

CHILDREN

Children always featured prominently in the poor relief system and how to deal with them was a major concern. A typical view, expressed as recently as 1903, was that:

> Pauperism is in the blood, and there is no more effectual means of checking its hereditary nature than by doing all that is in our power to bring up our pauper children in such a manner as to make them God-fearing, useful, and healthy members of society.[94]

Early workhouses were often targeted at children, especially those who were orphaned, abandoned, or otherwise lacking in parental care. As well as being protected and given a rudimentary education, children placed in a workhouse could be taught skills such as spinning or weaving. This would enable them to generate an income (and so pay for their keep in the workhouse) and, it was hoped, make them employable as adults and so not require poor relief.

Some workhouses were largely, or in some cases entirely, given over to children. The Bristol Corporation's first workhouse opened in 1698 took in 100 girls, with a second establishment the following year whose inmates included 100 boys. The City of London Corporation workhouse opened at Bishopsgate in 1700 housed up to 400 children who were taught to read and write, and worked at spinning and weaving.

In 1758, the parish of Lacock in Wiltshire opened what was in effect a workhouse for children. John and Mary Escott instructed the young inmates in spinning and carding wool and were paid a shilling a week for each child for which they also had to provide food and washing and the mending of clothes. In 1766, because of growing numbers, a pair of nearby houses were converted to a workhouse for the reception of 'Children who are too great a burthen to their parents, orphans and others by which means they may be brought up to labour and instructed in their Duty and be comfortably subsisted.'[95]

The majority of workhouse children, though, lived alongside adult paupers and in conditions, especially in London, that sometimes left much to be desired. In 1766, Hanway's Act required that children under the age of six in metropolitan workhouses be sent out into the countryside to live in privately run 'baby farms'.

The numbers of children resident in workhouses prior to 1834 are difficult to establish as they are not tabulated in sources such as the periodic national returns of poor relief (published in 1777, 1804 and 1818). In 1838, however, four years after the passing of the Poor Law Amendment Act, almost half of the workhouse population (42,767 out of 97,510) were children under sixteen.[96] Almost immediately, the central poor law authorities began to consider ways of removing the young from what was sometimes referred to as the taint of the workhouse. One of the most prominent advocates of this was James Kay-Shuttleworth who favoured the creation of District Schools serving a number of adjacent unions.

Over the next seventy-five years, a number of other methods were employed for dealing with pauper children. These included apprenticeship, emigration, boarding-out, cottage homes, scattered homes, small homes, training ships, and poor law certified schools – each described elsewhere in this volume. These various schemes took children out of the workhouse environment and provided them both with basic education and also, in most cases, some kind of 'industrial' training to equip them for employment in later life.

The official regulations relating to children living in a union workhouse were primarily concerned with their classification and accommodation, their diet, their education, and their discipline. Children under seven could live in the women's wards, with many workhouses operating some kind of nursery to provide care for the younger children while their mothers worked.

Inmates and staff of the Lambeth workhouse school at Norwood in Surrey. The building was erected in 1810 to house the parish's pauper children, as required by Hanway's Act, together with the elderly. After 1835, Lambeth continued to operate a poor law industrial school on the site.

Such nurseries were often little more than a bare room supervised by an elderly female inmate. From the age of seven, children resided in the boys' or girls' sections of the workhouse, with a daily 'interview' permitted if requested by either parent. In practice, meetings with parents were usually arranged to take place on Sunday afternoons. If children and parents were in different establishments, meetings might be much less frequent.

In the initial dietaries issued by the Poor Law Commissioners in 1835, children aged nine or above were allocated the same rations as adult females, while the younger ones were to be fed 'at discretion' – typically bread and milk for breakfast and supper, and an appropriately sized portion of the adult dinner. In 1856, separate children's dietaries were issued with versions for those aged from two to five and from five to nine. The breakfast and supper now included butter as standard, and the dinner menu provided four meat meals a week.

The education of workhouse children was required to include at least three hours a day of 'reading, writing, arithmetic, and the principles of the Christian religion, and such other instruction shall be imparted to them as may fit them for service, and train them to habits of usefulness, industry, and virtue.' Although the majority of union workhouses had their own schoolrooms, the increasing trend in the latter half of the nineteenth century was to send children out to local schools. Initially, this would probably have been to one of the many National or British Schools and then, from 1870, to one of the many Board Schools that were established. Workhouse children, being easily identifiable by their clothing, boots, or short haircuts, did not always have an easy time and were often stigmatised by their classmates.

As regards discipline, the rules regarding the punishment of workhouse children were extensive. The use of corporal punishment, or 'flogging', was restricted to boys who were under the age of fourteen, and could only be carried out by the schoolmaster or the workhouse master. Two hours had to have elapsed since the offence and the rod used had to have been approved by guardians. The refractory cell, used to confine those breaking workhouse rules, could not be employed for children under twelve either during the night or if it had no windows.

Life for workhouse children gradually improved over the years. By the 1880s, books, toys and games would often be provided, and occasional outings arranged to the seaside or countryside.

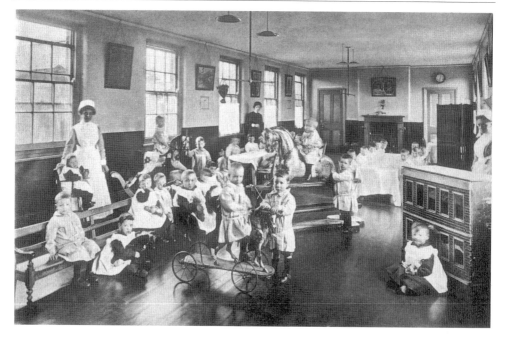

The nursery at the Ipswich Union's children's home in the early 1900s looks surprising well equipped with a horse on wheels, two rocking-horses and a doll's house. The lower portions of the windows appear to be rather dirty, or have been deliberately 'frosted' to prevent the children seeing out.

A party of children from the Aston Union's cottage homes at Erdington enjoy a trip in a charabanc on a seaside outing to Rhyl, North Wales, in about 1910.

For those living in the separate children's institutions set up by many unions, sporting activities such as football, cricket, swimming, gymnastics and athletics were provided. At the Holborn Union's school at Mitcham, a recreation room in the main block was used by boys and girls on alternate evenings. Entertainments provided for the children at the school included dancing, singing, magic lantern shows, Band of Hope (temperance) meetings, attendance at outside cricket and football matches, and occasional picnics and excursions.[97] Many children's establishments had a boys' wind band which might perform at local events such as fêtes.

Despite the growing provision of alternative forms of accommodation, in 1911 more than a third of the children receiving indoor relief were still being housed in workhouses or workhouse infirmaries.[98] In 1913, the Local Government Board decreed that no healthy child over the age of three should be living in a workhouse after 1915. Although the intervention of the First World War slowed progress in achieving this goal, at the start of 1922 just over 5 per cent of such children were in 'general' institutions, i.e. workhouses, although most of these were in special children's wards. At the same date, the overall total of 64,152 children in poor law institutions in England and Wales included 9,279 in scattered homes, 10,847 in cottage homes, 5,113 in District Schools, 6,181 in 'other' homes', and 749 on training ships. An additional 9,782 children were being boarded out, with around 17 per cent living outside their home union. A total of 9,485 children were housed in establishments not run by poor law authorities, of which 6,134 were in institutions – largely privately run – certified under the 1862 Poor Law (Certified Schools) Act.[99] By 1922, there were 217 schools certified for this purpose, most described as 'small orphanages'.[100]

(*See also:* **Apprenticeship**; **Bands**; **Boarding out**; **Certified Schools (Poor Law)**; **Cottage Homes**; **Discipline**; **District and Separate Schools**; **Emigration**; **Scattered Homes**; **Small Homes**; **Training Ships**; **Voluntary Homes**; **Workhouse Schools**)

CHRISTMAS

In the era of the parish workhouse, prior to 1834, Christmas Day – often together with the festivals of Easter and Whitsuntide – was the traditional occasion of a treat for most workhouse inmates. At the Bristol workhouse in the 1790s, the Christmas Day (and Whit Sunday) dinner included baked veal and plum pudding.[101] At the same date, Leeds workhouse inmates were given veal and bacon for dinner at Easter and Whitsuntide, roast beef at Christmas, and 1lb of spiced cake each at each of these festivals. At Carlisle on Christmas Day the workhouse inmates were allowed roast mutton, plum pudding, best cheese and ale. In 1828, inmates of the St Martin in the Fields workhouse received roast beef, plum pudding and one pint of porter each.[102]

However, in the new union workhouses set up following the 1834 Poor Law Amendment Act, things were rather different, at least to begin with. The Poor Law Commissioners (PLC) ordered that no extra food was to be allowed on Christmas Day or any other feast day. The workhouse rules also stated that 'no pauper shall be allowed to have or use any wine, beer, or spirituous or fermented liquors, unless by the direction in writing of the medical officer'.[103] Some unions apparently chose to waive the rules and celebrate Christmas in the traditional way. At Cerne Abbas, for example, the new workhouse's first Christmas dinner in 1837 included plum pudding and strong beer.[104] Most unions fell in line with the regulations, however. In 1846, when Christmas Day fell on a 'bread and cheese' day, a guardian at the Andover Union proposed switching the dinner for that day with that of the preceding 'meat' day. Even this modest suggestion was rejected.[105]

Irrespective of the question of festive fare, one indulgence was granted on Christmas Day. Along with Good Friday and each Sunday, it was a day when no labour, except the necessary household work and cooking, was performed by the workhouse inmates.

In 1840, the PLC conceded that extra treats could be provided, so long as they came from private sources and not from union funds.[106] Following the Queen's marriage to Prince Albert

A Christmas scene in the Whitechapel workhouse from the *Pictorial World* magazine in December 1874. Despite the festive mood, men and women were still strictly segregated.

in 1841, the Victorian celebration of Christmas took off in a big way, with the importing of German customs such as Christmas trees and the giving of presents. Dickens' *A Christmas Carol* also raised the profile of the event.

In 1847, the PLC entered into a protracted dispute with the Dudley Board of Guardians who – having always provided their inmates Christmas fare – had been surcharged by the union's auditor for repayment of the cost of the 1846 Christmas Dinner. Although the PLC upheld the surcharge, the workhouse rules were amended soon afterwards to allow special food to be served on Christmas Day.

By the middle of the century, Christmas Day (or more often Boxing Day, 26 December) had a became a regular occasion for the guardians to visit the workhouse and dispense food and largesse. The workhouse dining hall would be decorated and entertainments organised. The *Western Gazette*'s 1887 report on the Christmas festivities in Chard was typical:

> The inmates, thanks to the liberality of the Guardians and the kindness of Mr and Mrs Pallin, spent a very enjoyable time on Christmas Day and Boxing day. The pretty chapel was nicely decorated with holly and over the Communion-table was a cross of Christmas berries. On the walls were the words 'Emmanuel, God with us'. The inmates afterwards had cake and tea, which was much enjoyed. On Monday the usual festivities took place. The dining hall was elaborately decorated with evergreens, mottoes, gilded stars and Prince of Wales' plumes. ...The mottoes were of the usual; festive character but one, expressive of esteem, 'Long Life to Mr and Mrs Pallin' showed the feeling entertained by the inmates towards those put over them. Dinner was served at two p.m. and consisted of prime roast beef, potatoes, baked and boiled, and each adult had a pint of beer. One ounce of tobacco was given to each man, snuff to the old ladies, and oranges and sweets to the children. After tea, which comprised cake and bread and butter, a capital magic lantern display was given and was thoroughly enjoyed by young and old. Then followed some ancient ditties, sung by the old people, and those who liked tripped it merrily. Songs were sung by the Master,

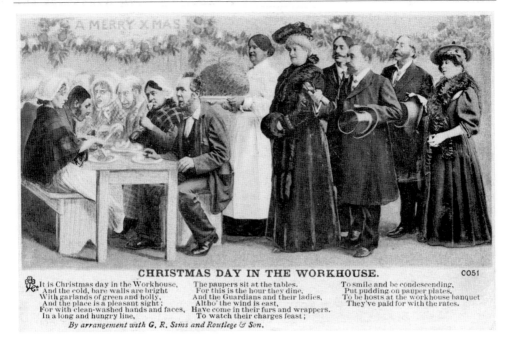

CHRISTMAS DAY IN THE WORKHOUSE.   C051

It is Christmas day in the Workhouse,   The paupers sit at the tables.   To smile and be condescending,
And the cold, bare walls are bright   For this is the hour they dine.   Put pudding on pauper plates,
With garlands of green and holly,   And the Guardians and their ladies, To be hosts at the workhouse banquet
And the place is a pleasant sight;   Altho' the wind is east,   They've paid for with the rates.
For with clean-washed hands and faces, Have come in their furs and wrappers.
In a long and hungry line,   To watch their charges feast;

By arrangement with G. R. Sims and Routlege & Son.

A postcard from the early 1900s illustrating a scene from the poem *In the Workhouse Christmas Day* – the guardians stand and look down upon the inmates eating their dinners.

> Porter and several friends, and a very enjoyable evening came to an end. Cheers were given for those who had strived to make them happy.

Such occasions were, however, seen by some as condescending and patronising. One of the best-known pieces of workhouse literature, the melodramatic ballad or monologue *In the Workhouse: Christmas Day*, was written from this standpoint. Its author, George R. Sims, was a campaigning journalist specialising in stories on poverty and poor housing published in the series entitled *How the Poor Live* and then in a column in the new *Sunday Referee*. His monologue, first published in 1877, told the story of an inmate whose wife had been refused out relief the previous Christmas and had starved to death rather than enter the workhouse and be separated from him. Here are the ballad's opening stanzas:

In the Workhouse: Christmas Day

It is Christmas Day in the workhouse,
And the cold, bare walls are bright
With garlands of green and holly,
And the place is a pleasant sight;
For with clean-washed hands and faces,
In a long and hungry line
The paupers sit at the table,
For this is the hour they dine.

And the guardians and their ladies,
Although the wind is east,
Have come in their furs and wrappers,
To watch their charges feast;

To smile and be condescending,
Put pudding on pauper plates.
To be hosts at the workhouse banquet
They've paid for with the rates.

Oh, the paupers are meek and lowly
With their 'Thank'ee kindly, mum's!'
So long as they fill their stomachs,
What matter it whence it comes!
But one of the old men mutters,
And pushes his plate aside:
'Great God!' he cries, 'but it chokes me!
For this is the day she died!'

Despite a number of flaws in its narrative (regulations allowed elderly couples to share a bedroom, and unions could always give short-term out relief in cases of 'sudden and urgent necessity'), Sims's ballad became immensely popular.

In the 1870s and 1880s, the temperance movement became influential in Britain and the Drink Reform League specifically campaigned for the banning of alcohol from workhouses. In 1884, the Local Government Board gave in and barred the supply of alcohol to workhouse inmates except under medical direction.

Fortunately, no such fate befell the traditional 'plum pudding' served up to workhouse inmates. The following recipe for a Christmas pudding for 300 persons comes from Pat Constable whose family includes several generations of workhouse master. The recipe was perfected by her parents Lionel and Annie Williams who ran several institutions including the former Bridport workhouse. They were, by then, fortunate enough to have the benefit of a food mixer to help prepare the mixture.

WORKHOUSE CHRISTMAS PUDDING FOR 300

Ingredients:
36 lbs Currants 42lbs Sultanas
9 lbs Dates
9lbs Mixed Peel
26 lbs Flour
16 lbs Breadcrumbs (prepared)
24 lbs Margarine
26 lbs Demerara Sugar
102 lbs Golden Syrup
102 lbs Marmalade
144 Eggs
2lbs 10oz Mixed Spice
13 lbs Carrots (prepared)

Method:
Cream fat and flour in Hobart mixer (to fairly thin consistency). Mix breadcrumbs with chopped dates and add to fat mixture Put shredded carrots and all dried fruit (washed) into separate bowl and mix thoroughly. Then gradually add the first mixture Add brown sugar, stirring all the time. Add marmalade. Add spice and stir well. Add eggs, which have already been well beaten. Finally add the hot melted syrup.

(*See also:* **Alcohol**; **Food**)

CHURCH

(*See*: **Religion**)

CLASSIFICATION

Upon entry into a workhouse, inmates were categorised according to a centrally specified system of classification which would determine certain aspects of their treatment whilst in residence, with different classes accommodated separately. In England and Wales from 1835, the classes defined were:

1. Aged or infirm men.
2. Able-bodied men, and youths above thirteen.
3. Youths and boys above seven years old and under thirteen.
4. Aged or infirm women.
5. Able-bodied women and girls above sixteen.
6. Girls above seven years old and under sixteen.
7. Children under seven years of age.

By 1842, the ages in classes 2, 3, 5 and 6 had been revised and were all set at the age of fifteen.

The term 'aged or infirm' had no legal definition but was generally applied to those aged sixty or over. Likewise, interpretation of the term 'able-bodied' was left to the discretion of each Board of Guardians, although was usually applied to those aged from fifteen to sixty who were in good health.[107]

A union could also further subdivide any of the seven main classes 'with reference to the moral character, or behaviour, or the previous habits of the inmates.' The most common use for this provision was to house women such as prostitutes and single mothers separately from other able-bodied women. The plans for the new workhouse at Greenwich in 1844, for example, show separate wards for 'bad women'. Men, too, could be subdivided in this way. In 1886, the

A 'male merit' ward at Birmingham workhouse in around 1910 where those judged to be of good character could enjoy more comfortable living conditions.

new Wandsworth and Clapham workhouse included separate areas for inmates of 'good' and 'bad' character on both the male and female sides. The City of London workhouse opened in 1849 included subdivisions for 'unruly' men and women. At Birmingham workhouse in the early 1900s, 'merit' wards provided more comfortable conditions for inmates judged to be sufficiently deserving.

Updated regulations in 1913 left it up to each Board of Guardians to adopt whatever system of classification they deemed appropriate based on 'considerations of age, character and behaviour'.[108]

(*See also*: **Segregation**; **Dietary Class**)

CLERK

The Clerk was a salaried officer appointed by each Poor Law Union's Board of Guardians who was responsible for the administrative aspects of the union's official business. The Clerk had to be at least twenty-one years of age and to provide a bond with two guarantors in case any financial irregularities arose.

The Clerk's main duties were:

- To take minutes at all the Board's meeting.
- To keep the union's accounts and minute books and to produce these for auditing.
- To conduct and file all the guardians' correspondence.
- To prepare all written contracts and agreements and to check that these were adhered to.
- To prepare all reports, answers, or returns required by the central authorities.
- To conduct the annual election of guardians.

As a compensation for all the additional work involved in organising the election of guardians, the Clerk received an extra payment plus a farthing per head of the population in parishes with a population of more than 500.

Since much of the workhouse's day-to-day book-keeping was carried out by the workhouse master, some unions appointed the same person as master and Clerk. This happened, for example, at Abingdon where in 1835 Richard Ellis took on the post of master at a salary of £150 per annum, and also that of Clerk at £75 per annum. However, the nature of the Clerk's work frequently benefited from legal training and a solicitor was often appointed to the post.

CLOTHING

Although clothing usually formed part of the relief provided in a parish workhouse, the practice of explicitly adopting a standard uniform seems to have been relatively rare prior to the appearance of 'reformed' workhouses such as those at Bingham and Southwell in Nottinghamshire in the 1820s. In these establishments, the wearing of a uniform formed part of the deterrent regime, along with a plain diet, a requirement for manual labour, and strict segregation of the sexes and of the infirm and able-bodied.

In the union workhouses established following the 1834 Poor Law Amendment Act, the wearing of a uniform was not explicitly demanded by the Poor Law Commissioners (PLC). The inmates' 'clothing' (the PLC never used the word 'uniform') was to be made out of 'such materials as the Board of Guardian may determine'[109] and 'need not be uniform either in colour or materials'.[110] In fact, a standard uniform was almost always adopted, but that was a local decision by each union. One exception was at the Saddleworth workhouse where in 1866 a Poor Law Inspector reported that 'the inmates are not clad in one uniform dress; the clothes of those who die in the workhouse are given out to be worn by those who survive'.[111]

The typical uniform worn by able-bodied female inmates – believed to be at the Leeds workhouse in the 1920s. The women's faces portray every emotion from grim resignation to cheery smiles. (*Picture by kind permission of Medical Illustration, the Leeds Teaching Hospitals NHS Trust.*)

The PLC proposed in 1835 that clothing should 'as far as may be possible, be made by the paupers in the workhouse'[112] no doubt imagining that this would both provide a useful work task and also be a cost saving. By 1840, however, 'possible' had become 'practicable', and by 1842 the suggestion had been dropped completely.[113] Although the making of uniforms and of shoes and boots did take place in some workhouses, many preferred simply to buy in such items.

Uniforms had several practical functions. Inmates' own clothes when they entered the workhouse might be dirty or in poor condition, and thus not suitable attire in which to work. The uniform provided a clean set of replacement clothing which would serve as a hard-wearing garb for labour and also stand up to washing in the workhouse laundry. Finally, the uniform provided a simple control mechanism over inmates' movements: leaving the workhouse in uniform without permission would constitute theft of union property and lead to an appearance before the magistrates and a possible sentence of prison with hard labour.

A longstanding practice at some workhouses was to mark out certain categories by a distinctive garment. At the Bristol Incorporation workhouse in 1834, prostitutes wore a yellow dress and single pregnant women wore a red dress.[114] At the Eton Union workhouse, according to a letter in the *Standard* on 3 January 1839, single mothers were made to wear 'a kind of felon's dress'. Later in 1839, the PLC issued a minute entitled 'Ignominious Dress for Unchaste Women in Workhouses' in which they deprecated such practices.[115] However, more subtle forms of such identification sometimes continued. At the Mitford and Launditch Union workhouse at Gressenhall in Norfolk, unmarried mothers were made to wear a 'jacket' of the same material used for other workhouse clothing. This practice, which resulted in their being referred to as 'jacket women', continued until 1866.

In 1837, the guardians of the Hereford Union advertised for the supply of inmates' clothing. For the men this consisted of jackets of strong 'Fernought' cloth, breeches or trousers, striped cotton shirts, cloth cap and shoes. For women and girls, there were strong 'grogram' gowns, calico shifts, petticoats of Linsey-Woolsey material, Gingham dresses, day caps, worsted stockings and woven slippers. ('Fernought' or 'Fearnought' was a stout woollen cloth, mainly used

A group of uniformed inmates at the Bosmere and Claydon Union workhouse at Barham in Suffolk in 1907. The well-dressed woman at the centre rear of the group may be a local volunteer involved in organising Brabazon work at the institution.

on ships as outside clothing for bad weather. Linsey-Woolsey was a fabric with a linen, or sometimes cotton, warp and a wool weft; its name came from the village of Linsey in Sussex. Grogram was a coarse fabric of silk, or of mohair and wool, or of a mixture of all these, often stiffened with gum.)

By the end of the nineteenth century, male inmates were usually kitted out in jacket, trousers and waistcoat. The most common headgear for men was the cloth cap although some unions, such as Doncaster and St Marylebone, later adopted the bowler-style 'billycock' hat. The uniform for able-bodied women was typically a simple blue-and-white-striped dress reaching to the calf, with a shift over. Elderly women generally wore a long gown, apron and shawl, with a bonnet or mop-cap.

Vera Underwood, daughter of the master and matron of Ongar workhouse in the early 1900s, later recalled:

> My mother made all the women's dresses, I think. They were blue and white striped cotton material, lined. Some wore white aprons and some did not. I think the ones who worked wore caps, and the dear grannies who did not work, bonnets. They had woollen material shawls to wear, and red flannel petticoats tied around the waist, thick black stockings and black shoes or boots. The men wore thick corduroy trousers, thick black jackets and black hats, grey flannel shirts, black thick socks and hobnailed boots.[116]

On finally quitting the workhouse, inmates had their own clothes returned to them. In 1839, the PLC ordered that long-time residents or children living there from an early age, or leaving to begin service or an apprenticeship, should be provided with a 'decent outfit of clothing'.[117]

In 1896, the Local Government Board reiterated its longstanding directive that inmates' clothing need not be uniform in colour or material. It also advised that when inmates were on temporary leave from the workhouse, their clothing should 'not be in any way distinctive or conspicuous in character'.[118] In the 1913 Poor Law Institutions Order, the advice given to unions was simply that workhouse inmates should be 'suitably clothed'.

(*See also*: **Badging the Poor**; **Laundry**; **Rules**)

COFFEE

Like tea, coffee became popular in England during the sixteenth century. However, it did not so quickly become a staple of working people's diets in the way that tea did. By the 1830s, coffee was being consumed in just a handful of workhouses, mostly in the north of England such as at Sheffield, Oldham, Bolton, Salford, Lancaster, Prescot and Sedbergh. Its provision was often as an 'indulgence' to the elderly or the sick, and sometimes also to women – an association it shared with tea.[119]

After 1834, coffee again rarely appeared on workhouse menus. An 1866 survey of the dietaries of sixty-five workhouses found that while fifty-two of them served tea to the elderly and infirm at breakfast, only three provided coffee.[120] Two years later, the Poor Law Board suggested that tea, coffee or cocoa should be allowed for the aged and infirm inmates at breakfast and supper, although tea or coffee should not be given to children except for supper on Sunday.[121]

Following the overhaul of workhouse diets in 1900, coffee was an item that could be offered to any inmate but its inclusion in the dietary was a decision for each Board of Guardians.
(*See also*: **Food**; **Tea**)

CONSOLIDATED GENERAL ORDER

A compilation and revision of all the General Orders issued to Poor Law Unions by the Poor Law Commissioners or their successors. It was first issued as part of the Commissioner's fourteenth annual report in 1847 and became the 'bible' of union and workhouse operation. It was periodically updated until 1913 when a major overhaul of the regulations relating to workhouses and associated establishments was issued as the Poor Law Institutions Order. The full text of the 1847 Consolidated General Order is included in Appendix P.
(*See also*: **Poor Law Commissioners**; **Poor Law Institutions Order**; **General Order**; **Special Order**)

CONSUMPTION

(*See:* **Tuberculosis (TB)**)

CONVENTION OF POOR LAW MEDICAL OFFICERS

(*See:* **Medical Officers' Associations**)

CORPORATION

(*See:* **Incorporation**)

COTTAGE HOMES

The cottage homes system grew out of European experiments in the institutional care of young people such as those at the Rauhe Haus in Germany in the 1830s and at the Mettray colony in France in the 1840s and 1850s. The Rauhe Haus developed the 'family principle' for the destitute children it housed. At Mettray, where 'family' groups of boys lived under the supervision of a house-parent, the approach proved successful in providing a remedial environment for the male juvenile offenders who were placed there.

The use of children's cottage homes in England was pioneered by charitable establishments such as the Home for Little Boys founded in 1865 at Farningham in Kent, the Princess Mary's Homes for Little Girls established in 1870 at Addlestone in Surrey, and the Barnardo's village home for girls at Barkingside in Essex opened in 1876. Adoption of the system for pauper children was proposed in an 1874 report to the Local Government Board by Mrs Jane Senior, the first female Poor Law Inspector. She criticised the large industrial or 'barrack' schools that had been set up by a number of unions as being unhealthy and also failing to give their inmates any individual attention. Cottage homes, housing children in household groups of 'no more than 20 to 30' in a rural environment, would instead be 'of a more home-like character' and provide a 'free and natural mode of life'.

In the mid-1870s, the unions of West Derby, West Ham and Bolton made tentative experiments with the cottage homes approach, although each used buildings erected on their existing workhouse sites. The West Derby and West Ham homes also housed fifty children – rather more than the maximum proposed by Mrs Senior. The first true poor law cottage home developments were established in South Wales by the unions at Swansea (1877), Neath (1878), and Bridgend and Cowbridge (1879), with schemes in England being opened by Birmingham (1879) and the Kensington and Chelsea School District (1880).

Cottage home schemes typically comprised a 'village' of small houses, often set around a green or along a street. In each house, a group of girls or boys of varying ages lived under the supervision of a house mother. Boys' homes sometimes had a married couple in charge with the husband also employed as an industrial trainer for the boys at the homes. The number of children in each house varied between schemes with fifteen to twenty gradually becoming the norm. As well as the houses and a school, larger cottage home sites could include training workshops, an infirmary, chapel, bakehouse, laundry, gymnasium, and even a swimming pool. Boys were taught practical trades such as shoemaking, tailoring, plumbing and joinery, while girls learned household skills such as sewing, cooking and cleaning to equip them for domestic service. A few occupations such as gardening were taught to both boys and girls. Cottage homes often also had a boys' military band which could provide a pathway into a career as a musician in the army or navy.

By the 1920s, around 115 unions operated premises which could be described as cottage homes although some consisted of just one or two houses located near to the workhouse. After the abolition of Boards of Guardians in 1930, many cottage homes sites were taken over by local councils and continued in operation, in some cases until the 1980s.

Girls dance around maypoles while the boys look on during the 1913 sports and inspection day at the Hackney Union's cottage homes at Ongar in Essex.

The boys' boot-making workshop at the Kensington & Chelsea School District cottage homes at Banstead in Surrey in about 1902. A rail hanging overhead is labelled 'Band Boots'.

Because of their location and domestic scale, cottage homes are some of the best surviving buildings from the workhouse era, most often now converted to residential use. Some of the most complete examples are those erected by the Leicester Union at Countesthorpe, the Newcastle Union at Ponteland, the Greenwich Union near Sidcup, and the Salford Union at Culcheth – the latter both still have swimming pools in operation.

As well as cottage homes for children, a few poor law authorities erected clusters of cottages for the elderly. The Bradford Union's 1903 development at Daisy Hill, for example, provided around twenty cottages placed either side of a central green, together with some communal facilities and staff accommodation.

(*See also*: **Mettray**; **Old People; Rauhe Haus**; **Scattered Homes**; **Small Homes**; Morrison (1998))

COUNTY HOME

After the creation of the Irish Free State in 1921, more than thirty former workhouses were converted for use as County Homes – somewhat analogous to the Public Assistance Institutions established in England and Wales after 1930. County Homes were primarily intended to house the aged and infirm poor and chronic invalids, although their inmates often included unmarried mothers and those with low-grade mental problems.

(*See also*: **Auxiliary Home**; **Ireland**; **Public Assistance Institution**)

COUNTY INSTITUTION

(*See*: **Public Assistance Institution**)

COUNTY VAGRANCY SCHEMES

(*See*: **Joint Vagrancy Committees**)

CREED REGISTER

A register of union workhouse inmates and their religious affiliation, often kept at the workhouse porter's lodge and available for inspection by local ministers of religion. Other information recorded in the register could include an inmate's admission and discharge dates, year of birth, trade, previous address, and nearest known relative.
(*See also*: **Records**; **Religion**)

CROOKS, WILL

William ('Will') Crooks was born in 1852, the third of seven children from a poor family in Poplar. At the age of eight, Will and four of his siblings spent three weeks in the Poplar workhouse and were then transferred for a period to the South Metropolitan District School at Sutton where, Crooks later recalled, 'every day spent in that school is burnt into my soul.'[122] The experience left a deep impression on Will, as did the sight of a bread riot in the winter of 1866 when a lorry delivering bread to the workhouse was stopped and its cargo looted by the starving unemployed.

As a worker at the East India Docks, he became involved in radical politics and was one of the leaders of the 1889 London Docks Strike. In March 1892, he successfully stood as a Progressive Party candidate in elections for the newly inaugurated London County Council.

Crooks petitioned the Local Government Board to lower the property qualification for election to the Board of Guardians from £40 to £5. As a result he was able to stand for election and subsequently became the first working-class member of the Poplar Board of Guardians. Crooks and his friend George Lansbury were the only two such men on a board of twenty-four members. On his first attempt at inspecting the Poplar workhouse, Crooks was refused admission but his resulting protests led to a new regulation giving any guardian the right to enter his union's workhouse at any reasonable hour. After becoming chairman of the guardians in 1897, he initiated a programme of reform in the running of the union and its workhouse including the abolition of uniforms and improving the quality of the food.

Crooks was a member of the Poplar Borough Council and, in 1901, became the first Labour Mayor of Poplar. He also helped to set up the National Committee on Old Age Pensions, believing that pensions were the only way to keep the elderly poor from entering the workhouse. In 1903, he successfully stood in a parliamentary by-election in Woolwich as the candidate for the Labour Representation Committee.

The generous out relief policies that became known as Poplarism brought Crooks before a

A portrait of Will Crooks who, as the title of his biography proclaimed, went from workhouse to Westminster.

Local Government Board inquiry in 1906 but, despite a number of criticisms being made of various aspects of the union's administration, he was largely exonerated.

Crooks lived all his life in Poplar and died on 5 June 1921.

(*See also*: **Lansbury, George**; **Poplarism**; Haw (1907))

DAILY ROUTINE

In 1835, the Poor Law Commissioners prescribed the following daily routine for able-bodied inmates:

	Rising	Breakfast	Start work	Dinner	Finish Work	Supper	Bedtime
25 March to 29 September	6a.m.	6.30 to 7a.m.	7a.m.	12 to 1p.m.	6p.m.	6p.m. to 7p.m.	8p.m.
29 September to 25 March	7a.m.	7.30 to a.m.	8a.m.	12 to 1p.m.	6p.m.	6p.m. to 7p.m.	8p.m.

The day began with the ringing of the rising bell which would continue to punctuate the rest of the day's proceedings. After rising from their beds, inmates would wash and dress themselves and tidy their beds. The master or matron then performed a roll-call in each section of the workhouse before all inmates who were able assembled in the dining hall. Communal prayers were read by the master before breakfast and after supper every day, and with grace being said before and after each meal. For the able-bodied, breakfast was followed by five hours of work, with the elderly and infirm retiring to their day-rooms – some individuals perhaps undertaking duties such as nursing or the supervision of children. The hour's break for dinner at midday was followed by a further five hours of work, followed by supper. The use of the time between 7p.m. and 8p.m. was unspecified and provided an informal recreation period. The timetable for the elderly, infirm or sick inmates was determined by each Board of Guardians.

On Sundays, together with Good Friday and Christmas Day, inmates were not required to labour, except in the necessary household work and cooking. Instead, inmates (unless declared Dissenters from the Established Church) were required to attend 'Divine Service' either in the workhouse – the dining hall often being used for this purpose – or, under supervision, at a local church or chapel. Sunday afternoons were often the time when meetings were arranged between parents and their children, or when concerts or lectures would be held.

As in most matters of workhouse operation, Boards of Guardians were able to modify the daily timetable to fit in with local requirements. At the Great Ouseburn workhouse in Yorkshire, for example, inmates had to go to bed at 6.30p.m. in winter as no candles were allowed.[123]

(*See also*: **Entertainment**; **Food**; **Religion**; **Work**)

The workhouse bell at Stourbridge in Worcestershire – its ringing punctuated the daily routine of the inmates.

DEATH

An example of the proceedings following the death of an inmate in a parish workhouse is provided in the rules of London's St Giles in the Fields workhouse in 1726:

> When any Person dies in the House, the Nurse attending that Ward shall immediately go for a Coffin and Shroud, and the dead Person shall be washed and laid in the Coffin; and then the Nurse, with, proper Assistance, shall forthwith bring the Corpse down to the Room appointed for that purpose.
>
> The Cloaths of Persons dying in the House shall (being first washed or cleaned) be brought into the Store-room; and such of them as are not much worn, shall be lodged there till wanted; but such as are very old, shall either be mended up, or cut to Pieces to mend others.[124]

If an inmate died in a union workhouse, the death was notified to any known next-of-kin who could, if they wished, organise a funeral themselves. If this did not happen, which was often the case because of the expense, the guardians arranged a pauper burial in a local cemetery or burial ground. This could either be in the parish where the workhouse stood or in the deceased's own parish if they or their relatives had expressed such a wish.

Most Irish workhouses had their own burial ground either at or near the workhouse site. This was not generally the case in England and Wales although examples can be found at the Blythburgh, Loddon & Clavering, Ellesmere, Bolton and Bury union workhouses. In London, the Cleveland Street workhouse of St Anne's Soho, later the Strand Union workhouse, had a burial ground at the rear of the premises which was in use until 1853. A few years later, excavations to lay the foundations of a new laundry block had to continue to a depth of 20ft before solid ground was reached beneath the skeletons unearthed by the digging.

Pauper burials were in unmarked graves, usually in an area of the cemetery reserved for this purpose, into which several coffins might be placed on the same occasion. The Poor Law Commissioners initially decreed that paupers should be buried as cheaply as possible, without even a bell being tolled at the funeral since this would incur extra expense. In response to public protests, the arrangements for funerals followed the 'less eligibility' principle – that a pauper funeral should be on a par with those of the lowest classes outside the workhouse.[125]

The Londonderry Union had a special coffin for transporting bodies to the burial ground. On its top was a hole where a warning flag was placed when the coffin was occupied.

A pauper funeral – the sight of which is supposed to have been the stimulus for the young Lord Shaftesbury's many philanthropic activities.

The coffins used in the burials were generally of the cheapest possible construction, either bought in or, in some large workhouses, made on-site in a carpenter's workshop. A layer of sawdust might serve as a lining, and a shroud was often absent, with the body buried naked or under a covering of paper or calico.[126]

In September 1883, *The Times* carried a report about the transport of pauper bodies to Colney Hatch Cemetery from Clerkenwell workhouse mortuary by an undertaker's sub-contractor. It had been alleged that a coach carrying five coffins, three of adults and two of children, had broken down on Exmouth Street with the coffins rolling into the road. It was also claimed that, for the sake of economy, bodies were kept in store until a batch of sufficient size was reached, resulting in offensive smells. The coffins were said to each be identified only by a name chalked on them and that during the journey the writing rubbed off. Although an investigation by a committee of guardians refuted the allegations, it was agreed that the union should acquire its own hearse, coach and horses for use at pauper funerals.

In 1867, a hearse costing £4 10s was acquired by Staffordshire's Leek workhouse. It was said to be of great pride to the workhouse master who justified the expense on the grounds that attendance at workhouse funerals had increased considerably.[127] Generally, though, few mourners were to be found at pauper funerals. At Bourne in 1901, the workhouse master reported that despite repeated invitations, workhouse inmates always declined to attend such events. This was perhaps a testimony to the old saying: 'rattle his bones, over the stones, he's only a pauper whom nobody owns.'

Under the terms of the 1832 Anatomy Act, bodies unclaimed for forty-eight hours could be sold or donated by workhouses and other institutions for use in medical research and training. The Act aimed to end the activities of 'resurrectionists' – most notoriously, Edinburgh's Burke and Hare – engaged in the lucrative trade of supplying corpses to medical schools. However, workhouses could not dispose of bodies in this way if the deceased or their relatives had formally registered their dissent. In reality, the often low levels of literacy amongst paupers, or a lack of foresight or awareness that such a fate might arise, meant that such objections were rare. Workhouses thus became a major source of bodies used for dissection in medical schools, either in return for money or the provision of medical facilities to the union. Although the 1844 Poor Law Amendment Act made it illegal for any officer connected with poor relief to profit personally from such activities, the practice continued, often secretively and sometimes illicitly. A scandal surfaced in 1858 when Alfred Feist, master of the St Mary Newington workhouse, was accused of illegally supplying pauper bodies to Guy's Hospital medical school. On the day of an inmate's funeral, any relatives present were allowed to view the body, but the coffin was then secretly switched. The fresh corpse was sent off for use at Guy's while the funeral proceeded with a coffin now containing the dissected remains of a different person that had been returned by the medical school.

(*See also*: **Mortuary**; Richardson (1987))

DESERVING AND UNDESERVING POOR

A problem which often preoccupied poor relief administrators was how to distinguish those who were deemed to be deserving of poor relief (the so-called 'impotent' poor, destitute through no fault of their own and powerless to remedy their situation) and those who were undeserving (because they were capable of supporting themselves but chose not to do so). The able-bodied who refused to work were easy to classify as 'undeserving'; those who were willing to work but unable to find employment were in a less clear-cut situation. The 1601 Poor Relief Act divided the poor into two groups. The first group – 'the lame, impotent, old, blind, and such other among them being poor' – were to be relieved through the provision of 'sums of money' and 'places of habitation'. For the second group, those able to work, a stock of flax, hemp, wool, thread, iron and other materials was to be provided, with imprisonment for those refusing to labour.

The 'workhouse test', enshrined in Knatchbull's Act of 1723, offered a self-selecting method to distinguish the deserving and undeserving, with those prepared to enter the workhouse automatically qualifying for relief. From 1782, in parishes adopting Gilbert's Act, the unemployed who were willing and able to work were to be housed and maintained from the poor rates until suitable work could be found for them. An avowed willingness to work rather than any actual performance of work thus made a person eligible for relief.

Allowance schemes such as the Speenhamland system which became popular in some areas at the end of the eighteenth century guaranteed minimum incomes to groups such as the poor, the sick and infirm, and to able-bodied labourers on low wages. During the early nineteenth century, it was increasingly argued that such schemes were giving rise to indiscriminate relief.

The 1834 Poor Law Amendment Act marked a return to the workhouse test with the intention that able-bodied paupers and their families would be offered only the workhouse. Some were still considered deserving of receiving out relief, however, such as cases of 'sudden and urgent necessity', to women newly widowed, and in cases of sickness, accident, or bodily or mental infirmity.

(*See also*: **Allowance Systems**; **Out relief**; **Poor Laws**; **Workhouse**)

DICKENS, CHARLES

(*See*: **Apprenticeship**; **Art**; **Broadside Ballads**; **Christmas**; **Documentary**; **Fiction**; **London**)

DIETARY

The scheme of meals served in an institution such as a workhouse, often with different foods or amounts being provided for different categories of inmate. The dietary in parish workhouses was sometimes referred to as its 'bill of fare'.

(*See also*: **Food**)

DIETARY CLASS

New inmates entering a union workhouse were assigned to a class (for example able-bodied male, infirm female etc.) which determined such matters as the section of the workhouse in which they were to reside. In addition, each inmate was assigned to a dietary class specifying the particular dietary they would receive. The classes mainly differed in the amounts rather than the types of food that they provided.

The classification of diets varied over the years. The one shown below was in use in the 1860s at the East Ashford Union workhouse:[128]

Class 1	Able-bodied men
Class 2	Old and Infirm Men
Classes 3 and 4a	Youths from 6 to 16 years
Class 4b	Boys from 2 to 6 years
Class 5	Able-bodied women
Class 6	Old and infirm women
Classes 7 and 8a	Girls from 6 to 16
Class 8b	Girls from 2 to 6 years
Class 9	Infants

Separate dietaries for the sick were introduced in the 1840s, with subdivisions of Low, Middle, and Full in which recipients were placed according to their medical condition. For women who had just give birth, a Lying-in dietary was also specified.

As part of the overhaul to workhouse diets in around 1900, three basic forms of diet were distinguished: the Plain diet (for healthy able-bodied adults), the Infirm diet (infirm but otherwise healthy adults), and the Children's diet (for those aged from three to fifteen). A new system of standard dietary classes was created based on these diets:[129]

Class 1.	Men not employed in work. [Plain diet.]
Class 1a.	Men employed in work. [As Class 1, but with a weekday lunch added.]
Class 2.	Men not employed in work. [Infirm diet.]

The women's dining hall at St Pancras workhouse in 1897. On the serving table at the rear stands some scales – any inmate could request that their portion be weighed out in front of witnesses if they suspected it was a short measure.

Class 2a.   Men employed in work. [As Class 1, but with a weekday lunch added.]
Class 2b.   Feeble men. [Special infirm diet with a daily lunch added.]
Class 3.   Women not employed in work. [Plain diet.]
Class 3a.   Women employed in work. [As Class 1, but with a weekday lunch added.]
Class 4.   Women not employed in work. [Infirm diet.]
Class 4a.   Women employed in work. [As Class 1, but with a weekday lunch added.]
Class 4b.   Feeble women. [Special infirm diet with an additional daily meal.]
Class 5.   Children aged from three to seven. [With a weekday lunch added.]
Class 6.   Children aged from eight to fifteen. [With a weekday lunch added.]

'Lunch' was a light mid-morning meal taken at around 10.30a.m.
(*See also*: **Classification**; **Food**)

DINING HALL

Most workhouses had a communal dining hall where the daily meals were eaten. In post-1834 union workhouses, segregation of the different classes of inmate was enforced in the dining hall as everywhere else in the building. Some workhouses placed partitions or screens down the middle of the dining hall, with separate entrances for men and women. Very large workhouses, such as that at St Pancras in London, even had separate dining halls for male and female inmates. By the end of the century, though, just having segregated seating and serving areas was generally considered sufficient.

In the 1830s, workhouse regulations demanded that during meals 'silence, order and decorum shall be maintained', though by 1842 the word 'silence' had been dropped.

Every workhouse dining hall was required to have a set of scales available. Any inmate who suspected that his allotted portion of food fell short of the regulation weight could demand to have it weighed in front of witnesses.

Generally being the largest room in the workhouse, the dining hall was also used for other communal activities and often served as the workhouse chapel. From the 1860s onwards, many workhouses began to host occasional entertainments for inmates such as musical concerts. These, too, would generally take place in the dining hall.
(*See also*: **Chapel**; **Entertainment**; **Food**)

DISCIPLINE

For those who broke workhouse rules, some form of punishment invariably followed. In the era of the parish workhouse, each institution operated according to its own rules. At Doncaster, in 1747, the workhouse regulations stipulated that the master and mistress 'are not to strike any of the grown up people but if they are disorderly are to put them into the dark hole till the visiting governor comes nor are they to strike any of the children but with a rod.'[130]

Inmates of Hackney workhouse in the 1750s could suffer a graded range of punishments. Anyone loitering or begging on the way to or from church on Sundays would lose their next meal. Anyone not turning up for a meal would lose their next dinner. Drunkenness, fighting or swearing at any time would be punishable by a spell in the stocks. Those refusing to work would be put on a bread and water diet or expelled from the house. In 1793, one particularly troublesome inmate was confined to the 'close room' for a week on a diet of bread and water.[131]

Another effective form of discipline was public humiliation. At Chichester, in 1756, the workhouse rules stipulated that anyone found guilty of lying would be:

A barred enclosure in Keighley's workhouse cellars may have been used as a 'refractory cell' for inmates who broke workhouse rules.

sett upon a stool during Dinner in the most public place in the Dining Room with a paper fixed on his or her breast whereon shall be wrote in capital letters *Infamous Lyar* and shall also loose that meal and for the second offence be put into the stock or wear the Pillory for two hours.[132]

Post-1834 union workhouses followed the rules set by the central authorities with two levels of misdemeanour defined. Lesser offences, such as swearing, gambling, insults, refusing to work or wash or keep silence, feigning sickness, or climbing over the workhouse wall, were termed Disorderly and punishable by a bread and potato diet for up to forty-eight hours.

An inmate who abused a member of the workhouse staff, repeatedly refused to obey the master or matron, hit another person, damaged property, was found drunk, carried out an indecent or obscene act, or disturbed a church service was deemed to be Refractory and punishable by up to twenty-four hours of solitary confinement, possibly plus a bread and potato diet. Workhouses usually had a refractory cell, often with no windows, used for this purpose.

Rather more unusual punishments are occasionally recorded. At the East Retford workhouse in April 1839, Selina Hill who had allowed another inmate to have 'very improper connections with her' was ordered to have her hair cut short, and not to be allowed to wear a cap for three months.[133] At the Strabane Union workhouse in Ulster, an inmate stealing money was given fourteen stripes with a rod and eight cold baths over four weeks, while 'throwing stones and annoying a lunatic' could be punished by twenty stripes, or twelve hours' confinement, loss of a meal, and a cold shower.[134]

Attempting to take alcohol into the workhouse, leaving whilst wearing the workhouse uniform, or other serious offences, could lead to an appearance before a magistrate. This path was occasionally taken by inmates of the casual ward if the facilities provided were less than they were prepared to countenance. Tearing up their workhouse clothing – colloquially known as a 'tear-up' – would generally result in a brief spell in a prison cell whose conditions (a single room, more food, and a stay of several nights) might well seem preferable.

Extensive rules governed the punishment of children. Corporal punishment was restricted to boys under the age of fourteen and two hours had to have elapsed since the offence. The refractory cell could not be employed for children under twelve either during the night or if it had no windows.

The workhouse system in Ireland after 1838 and the poorhouse system in Scotland after 1845 both broadly adopted the workhouse discipline rules used in England and Wales.

PRECAUTIONS AGAINST SMALL POX, FEVER, AND IN-
FECTIOUS AND CONTAGIOUS DISEASES GENERALLY.

Nelson's Patent Disinfecting Apparatus,

FOR THE USE OF

WORKHOUSES, HOSPITALS, LOCAL BOARDS, AND PUBLIC INSTITUTIONS.

J. NELSON & SONS have much pleasure in announcing that their PATENT DISIN-
FECTING APPARATUS continues to receive the most unqualified approbation of the
Officers of the numerous Institutions where it is in use; and they have received the
highest testimonials as to its efficacy in checking the spread of infectious and
contagious diseases, and in destroying vermin in clothes, bedding, &c. It is simple
and inexpensive in its operation, and can be readily managed by inexperienced
persons.

Prices and references on application to the Inventors and Patentees,

J. NELSON & SONS, Ironfounders, Hot Water and
Gas Engineers, 47, Briggate, Leeds.

An 1880 advertisement for a disinfecting apparatus manufactured by Nelson & Sons of Leeds. The base of the double-walled cabinet was heated with a row of gas jets and hot air rose between the inner and outer walls of the device, so heating its inner chamber.

DISINFECTION

All new inmates, whether entering the main workhouse or casual ward, gave up their own clothing which was then disinfected or fumigated to remove any vermin it might be harbouring. The process, colloquially known as 'stoving', was usually carried out in a cupboard or in a purpose-built disinfector. Purification of the contents could be achieved in various ways, such as by heating in dry air, heating in steam, or by fumigation with a sulphur candle. Whatever health benefits that resulted, heat treatment often left clothes the worse for wear:

> One man waxed eloquent with indignation. 'I was passing a workhouse when the chaps was coming out,' he said. 'I hadn't been in myself, but I seed one or two I knew and they had on good clothes the day before, they were all crumpled... and burnt in places. One man showed me his shoes; they had even put *them* in the oven, and the toes was turned up with the heat; he couldn't get them on his feet and had to walk barefoot.[135]

(*See also*: **Casual Ward**)

DISPENSARY

A secure location where medicines were stored and issued under the authority of a medical practitioner. The same premises might also be used for medical consultations. Nineteenth-century dispensaries, often charitably funded, were an important source of medical provision for the poor.

In 1851, Ireland's charitable dispensary system came under the control of the Irish poor law authorities, with the country then being divided up into dispensary districts each having its own dispensary and medical officer.

The Metropolitan Poor Act of 1867 provided for dispensaries to be set up by London's Poor Law Unions and parishes. By 1872, thirty-seven such establishments had come into operation across the capital, with six more under construction and seven others being contemplated.[136] Many were located adjoining a workhouse, workhouse infirmary or out relief office, while others were established in ordinary houses fitted out with a waiting room, consulting rooms and medicine store, with the dispenser also sometimes residing on the premises. Outside London, dispensaries were also established by unions such as Birmingham, Cardiff, Cheltenham, Gloucester, Kettering, Leeds, Liverpool, Manchester, Newport, Plymouth, Reading, Sheffield, Southampton and Wolverhampton.

(*See also*: Hodgkinson (1967); Cassell (1997))

DISTRICT RELIEF COMMITTEE

Where a union had one or more parishes whose entire area lay more than four miles from the Board of Guardians' regular meeting place, a District Relief Committee could be appointed from amongst the Guardians to deal with relief applications from those parishes.
(*See also*: **Relief Committee**)

DISTRICT AND SEPARATE SCHOOLS

One of the earliest proposals for housing pauper children in separate accommodation away from the union workhouse was for the establishment of District Schools, a scheme first outlined in 1838 by Dr James Kay (later better known as Sir James Kay-Shuttleworth) in 1838. Kay envisaged that each District School would serve a group of unions, perhaps with an existing workhouse in the area being converted for the purpose. Kay also commissioned model plans for new District School buildings from workhouse architect Sampson Kempthorne.

Kay argued that such establishments would allow children to receive a much better education, together with 'industrial training' – practical skills to equip them better for later life, such as manual trades for the boys and domestic training for the girls. Kay also believed that such schools would protect pauper children from what he saw as the 'polluting association' with the adult workhouse inmates. In such institutions, he claimed, poor law children:

> Would not be daily taught the daily lesson of dependence, of which the whole apparatus of a workhouse is the symbol... the district school would assume a character of hopefulness and enterprise better fitted to prepare the children for conflict with the perils and difficulties of a struggle for independence than anything which their present situation affords.[137]

The idea of separate establishments for workhouse children was not entirely new and Kay was particularly influenced by Mr Aubin's privately run school at Norwood which had over 1,000 residential pupils, largely taken from metropolitan poor law authorities. After the introduction of industrial training at the school, the banning of corporal punishment and improved conditions for teachers, great improvements had taken place in the children's performance and morale. As a result, the school became a much trumpeted showpiece of public education. Kay proposed a grandiose scheme for establishing 100 similar District Schools across England and Wales each accommodating around 500 children.

Another influential model was the Bridgnorth Union's school in the Shropshire village of Quatt. The school, which accommodated around eighty children, was set up in a large house on the estate owned by Bridgnorth Union guardian Mr Wolrych Whitmore. As well as receiving a basic classroom education, the boys cultivated the land and managed farm stock, while the girls did the housework.

Although the idea of industrial training was widely taken up, it was often on a small scale within existing workhouses and the provision of separate institutions for children was slow to happen. A few large industrial schools were established in the 1840s by single poor law authorities in the north of England such as the Manchester Union's Industrial School at Swinton, the Liverpool Vestry's Kirkdale Industrial School, and the Leeds Union's Moral and Industrial Training School. Separate schools were also eventually established at Brighton, Cardiff, Chesterfield, Cockermouth, Halstead, Hartismere, Merthyr Tydfil and Oxford.

Kay's proposals for the establishment of District Schools were incorporated into the 1844 Poor Law Amendment Act, allowing unions within a fifteen-mile radius (later extended to twenty miles) to form a School District for the purposes of setting up joint schools. The anticipated benefits of the larger District Schools included: economies of scale in teaching larger classes; the ability to provide industrial training in a wider range of subjects than a single

An aerial view of the Manchester Union's Industrial School at Swinton. In 1850, Charles Dickens' journal *Household Words* described it as 'a building which is generally mistaken for a wealthy nobleman's residence'.

The dining hall of the Central London District School at Hanwell where Charlie Chaplin was once an inmate. Now a community centre, much of the main building still survives.

The North Surrey District School at Upper Norwood, Surrey, in about 1905. Parts of the Crystal Palace are visible behind. The school, opened in 1850, housed up to 500 children from unions which included Croydon, Richmond, Kingston, Lewisham, Chelsea, Wandsworth and Clapham.

workhouse could offer; savings in the cost of staff, furniture, books etc., and the provision of better-quality staff who would be attracted to such establishments. Despite much encouragement by the central authorities, the scheme never took off, particularly outside London where only four School Districts were ever created: Reading & Wokingham (1849), Farnham & Hartley Wintney (1849), South East Shropshire (1849), and Walsall & West Bromwich (1869).

In the capital, three School Districts were formed in 1849 (Central London, South Metropolitan and North Surrey) which covered ten of the capital's thirty poor law authorities. However, a severe blow to the image of large pauper schools occurred in the same year when an outbreak of cholera at Mr Drouet's School, a privately run establishment at Tooting, resulted in the deaths of 180 of its 1,400 resident children. Despite ongoing efforts by the Poor Law Board, it was not until 1868 that three further School Districts (Forest Gate, West London and Finsbury) were created, although Finsbury was dissolved the following year. The Kensington & Chelsea School District was established in 1876 followed by Brentwood in 1877, the latter being dissolved in 1885. By the 1890s, London had five District Schools in operation covering fifteen unions, together with eleven individual separate schools at Bethnal Green, St George-in-the-East, Hackney, Holborn, Islington, Lambeth, St Marylebone, Mile End, St Pancras, Strand and Westminster. Two metropolitan parishes – Hampstead and Bloomsbury St Giles – had no schools of their own, with Hampstead sending its children to the Westminster Union's school at Tooting, and St Giles to the Strand Union's Millfield school at Edmonton.

District Schools, or 'Barrack' schools as they were often disparagingly known, became the subject of much criticism. Not only were they expensive to operate, but also proved to be a breeding ground for various infectious conditions such as ringworm and ophthalmia. In the last quarter of the nineteenth century, the development of alternative forms of children's accommodation such as cottage homes, scattered homes, and boarding out, were increasingly seen as being more flexible, economical, and better for the children who were placed there. A clear indication of the new direction came in 1880 when, after careful consideration of the various options, the Kensington & Chelsea School District opened its new cottage homes development at Banstead in Surrey which eventually housed more than 700 children.

(*See also*: **Boarding Out**; **Children**; **Cottage Homes**; **District and Separate Schools**; **Drouet's School; Ophthalmia; Ringworm; Scattered Homes**)

DISTRICT AND SEPARATE SCHOOLS IN IRELAND

Provision for the setting up of District Schools in Ireland was made in an Act of 1848 but, as in England and Wales, unions made very little use of the option. Only two were ever established, one in former town prison buildings at Trim in 1890 and serving the unions of Trim, Drogheda, Dunshaughlin, Navan and Kells, and the other in the former workhouse at Glin in 1893 serving the unions of Croom, Kilmallock, Limerick, Listowel, Newcastle and Rathkeale. The Glin workhouse had closed with the dissolution of the union in 1891.

Ireland's only separate poor law schools run by single authorities were those established by the North and South Dublin Unions. The North Dublin school, which became known as St Vincent's Home, was located at Cabra, at the north side of Dublin's Phoenix Park. The South Dublin Union's Pelletstown School stood just a few hundred yards away to the north-west. In March 1914, the two Dublin schools housed a total of 633 children, with those being maintained at the Trim and Glin schools numbering 337.[138]

DISTRICT MEDICAL OFFICER

To deal with the sick poor who were not resident in the workhouse, Poor Law Unions typically employed two or three District Medical Officers (DMOs), each of whom covered a portion of the union's area. Medical districts, usually based on groupings of parishes, had a maximum size of 15,000 acres in area or a maximum population of 15,000 persons.

DMOs were generally employed on an annual contract which, as well as attendance on the sick, usually required them to supply any necessary medicines. In 1835, the guardians' minutes of Abingdon Union recorded that James Hester was appointed at £110 per annum 'to include all cases of casual poor, accidents, surgery and midwifery, and to supply medicines, ointments, bandages and leeches.' From 1842, extra payments were made to DMOs for carrying out certain procedures or treatments as follows:

Compound fracture of the thigh	Five pounds
Compound fracture or dislocation of the leg	
Amputation of leg, foot or arm	
Strangulated hernia	
Simple fracture of thigh or leg	Three pounds
Amputation of a finger or toe	Two Pounds
Dislocation or fracture of the arm	One Pound

If the patient had several of these conditions on the same occasion, only one fee was payable. If they survived for less than thirty-six hours after treatment, only half the relevant fee was allowed. Extra fees could also be paid for attending a woman during or immediately after childbirth.

From 1857, unions could meet the cost of cod liver oil, quinine and other expensive medicines from the poor rates although not all chose do so, or would pay only for those used in the workhouse. The expectation that DMOs themselves should provide most if not all of the drugs they prescribed continued into the twentieth century. The effect of this policy was for some DMOs to prescribe cheap but ineffective or inappropriate remedies such as peppermint water or Epsom salts.[139]

(*See also*: **Medical Care**; **Medical Officers' Associations**; **Workhouse Medical Officer**)

DOCUMENTARY

Portraits of workhouse life come to us from a variety of sources including the works of novelists, poets and artists; the autobiographical accounts of inmates and staff; the reports resulting from official inspections and inquiries; and the newspaper stories relating to occasional workhouse scandals and other incidents.

Another source of published material is what might be called the documentary feature – usually in the form of a factual first-hand account of a visit to a particular institution, sometimes with commentary included. Such reports occasionally appeared in local newspapers and in weekly magazines such as *The Leisure Hour, The Sphinx, Sunday at Home, Household Words* and *All Year Round*, the latter two both edited by Charles Dickens.

A typical piece, written by Dickens himself, was 'A Walk in a Workhouse' which appeared in *Household Words* on 25 May 1850. The article featured an unnamed London workhouse belonging to the parish of 'St. So-and-so' and gained praise from Dickens:

> I saw many things to commend. It was very agreeable... to find the pauper children in this workhouse looking robust and well, and apparently the objects of very great care. In the infant school – a large, light, airy room at the top of the building – the little creatures, being at dinner, and eating their potatoes heartily, were not cowed by the presence of strange visitors, but stretched out their small hands to be shaken, with a very pleasant confidence. And it was comfortable to see two mangey pauper rocking-horses rampant in a corner. In the girls' school, where the dinner was also in progress, everything bore a cheerful and healthy aspect.

The 13 July issue of *Household Words* in the same year included 'A Day in a Pauper Palace' which described a visit to the Manchester Union's huge District School at Swinton. This was followed on 31 August by 'London Pauper Children', a report from the Central London District School in Norwood. Another piece from Dickens' own pen, 'Wapping Workhouse', appeared in *All Year Round* on 3 February 1860. A London District School also featured in a *Leisure Hour* article in 1866. Although unnamed, the establishment featured was probably the North Surrey District School at Anerley.

At the end of 1867, two articles bearing the ominous title 'A Workhouse Probe' were published in successive issues of *All Year Round*. Probably written by Joseph Charles Parkinson, both contained critical accounts of unnamed provincial workhouses which can be identified as Hursley in Hampshire and Leek in Staffordshire. The Hursley report noted the disgusting state of the water closets, and a cesspool under the windows of the lying-in and infectious wards which had remained unemptied for at least twelve years. The article on Leek drew attention to the treatment of vagrants at the workhouse who, in order to discourage them, were given no food or bedding.

In 1871, an account of a visit to the Chorlton Union workhouse appeared in *The Sphinx* magazine. Here is its description (with a literary allusion typical of such writing) of the dining facilities at the workhouse:

An immense kitchen, in which potato-hash had apparently been prepared by the cart-load in a series of huge boilers, first attracted our attention. Passing through this apartment we gained the dining-room. This place is fitted up with a series of fixed tables and seats arranged something like the pews in a chapel, the diners being seated side by side and back to back. The women do not sit with the men, but, like Dr. Johnson, at the publisher Cave's, partake of their food behind a screen, which screen runs up the centre of the room. The old people occupy the front seats, the middle-aged and young come next, and the children bring up the rear.[140]

An elderly inmate's first-hand account of life at the St Pancras workhouse was provided in an article by the Revd Frederick Hasting in an 1889 issue of *The Quiver*. The 'ladies' mentioned were presumably members of the Workhouse Visiting Society:

When you come out you have to ask the master for leave. You hand him your card, and he puts his initials on it. Directly some get out, they will go among their friends. They get asked to drink, and so eager are they, that they will almost 'bite the beer.' They know the public-houses where their friends go, and some find them out to get treated.

I have to pick oakum all the afternoon; I cannot do much. After tea we walk, or lounge, or go to the service. We have no prayers regular, only on Wednesday and once on Sunday. Sometimes ladies come on Sunday evening and sing, and bring tracts, and give us a little talk before the regular service. One lady has more and more people to listen to her each time she comes. I saw one man crying like a child – and not crocodile tears, sir. They don't know the good that a little human sympathy does to us poor cast-off hulks. We used to have an enter-tainment in St. Pancras, but we get none now. Sometimes we hear the music of the Salvation Army, and that is a pleasure to us for a time, as it passes; and even they don't know the cheer they give us poor fellows inside. When we are out some of the people look at us as if we were carrion. Some of the residents think our place lets down the value of their property.[141]

In 1888 and 1889, a sequence of documentary articles appeared in the *Sunday at Home* magazine under the collective heading 'Workhouse Life in Town and Country'. Places visited by the writer, a Mrs Brewer, included Liverpool, Manchester, Cirencester, Gloucester and Swindon, as well as several London workhouses.

Although published as part of a book rather than a magazine article, the German visitor J.K. Kohl's 1843 account of the North Dublin workhouse was very much in the documentary genre. Kohl did not conceal his disdain for the workhouse system, however:

A pauper, on entering the house, receives in exchange for his motley drapery, the gray uni-form of the house, with N.D.U.W.H. (North Dublin Union Workhouse) embroidered upon it in large letters. His liberty rags, together with hat, stockings, shoes, &c., are first carefully fumigated, and then, having been folded together, are marked with the name of their owner, and. deposited in the old clothes store. The pauper may at any time have his discharge, by simply intimating a wish to that effect to the governor, but to allow him to take with him the clothes worn in the workhouse would never do, or many would enter one day and go away again the next, merely for the sake of a new suit of apparel. Their old rags are therefore restored to them, and their ingenuity is again. taxed to discover the right entrance to their distorted sleeves. It must cost the poor a painful struggle when they waver between the servile N.D.U.W.H. costume, and the ragged *sans-culotte* drapery of freedom.[142]

As well as documentary reports for the general reader, some workhouse appraisals were aimed at a more specialised audience. Into this category come the detailed architectural descriptions of newly erected workhouse buildings that periodically appeared in trade journals such as *The Builder* and *Building News*. Reports of visits to workhouses also formed the heart of the campaigns for reform waged by the specialist medical journals, *The Lancet* and the *British Medical Journal* (BMJ).

For nine months, beginning in July 1865, *The Lancet* published accounts of visits by its 'commission' to London workhouses and their infirmaries which regularly exposed the poor standards of care, comfort and sanitation that existed in many institutions. At Bermondsey, for example:

> The wards for the infirm ... are excessively bad. Two of them especially, which are called 'Lazarus' and 'Aaron' respectively, are very dirty, and deficient in both light and air. The occupants were the most thoroughly 'pauperized' set we have seen in any of our visitations, herding together in a miserable manner in the midst of conditions which must render any medical treatment of their chronic diseases of little avail. Their water-closet and urinal (abutting on the deadhouse) stink so offensively as to poison the whole atmosphere of their airing-court.[143]

A similar approach was taken by the BMJ in 1894–95 in its campaign to improve conditions, especially nursing provision, in workhouse infirmaries which, particularly outside of London, often still left much to be desired. The journal published more than fifty reports by its investigators who travelled all over England and Wales, followed by a further twenty-eight in Ireland. Here is part of its report on the Totnes workhouse in Devon:

> The sanitary arrangements are of the old style: there is a closet for each block in the hospital, rinsed by the turning of a tap; that for the women is small and inconvenient; there is much more space on the men's side. The fixed bath on the women's side appeared to us to be most unsuitable for use by sick or old people; the raw edge of the metal, turned outwards at a right angle, is unprotected, and might be dangerous. The men's bath is movable. The water is pumped up, requiring the entire labour of one pauper. The water for the fixed bath is heated in a boiler in the hospital kitchen. In the infirmary there are movable baths; the closets are of the same style. and open immediately from the wards. We found no single closet sweet, and the urinal, also rinsed by tap, was in a foul condition. We came to the conclusion that the baths were not often used.[144]

DOMICILIARY RELIEF

An alternative name for out relief which was adopted by the Ministry of Health when they became responsible for overseeing poor relief administration in 1919.

(*See also*: **Out relief**)

DROUET'S SCHOOL

In 1825, Bartholomew Peter Drouet took over a privately run school at Surrey Hall, Lower Tooting, to the south-west of London. Drouet turned the school into an establishment for 'farming' pauper children from London parishes as required by Hanway's Act of 1766. Although Hanway's Act was repealed in 1844, Drouet's and similar establishments continued in operation for a further five years, taking pauper children up to the age of fourteen. The school had 723 children resident in 1846, with the number rising to just under 1,400 two years later.

Drouet's came to the attention of the Poor Law Commissioners in 1837 following allegations of cruelty at the school. Assistant Commissioner James Kay visited the establishment and discovered two boys chained to a log as a punishment. The boys had to sleep attached to the log and chain, an ordeal that could continue for up to a week. The boys' teacher, a former artillery captain, kept order in his classes through the use of a cane across the shoulders.[145]

In January 1849, the school became the centre of a scandal when a cholera epidemic broke out with the eventual death toll reaching 180. Criticisms of Drouet surfaced in a series of inquests initiated by Thomas Wakley, editor of the medical journal *The Lancet* and coroner for the county of Middlesex within whose jurisdiction some of the dead children came. The inquests recorded various verdicts to the effect that the victims had died of the effects of cholera, aggravated by inadequate food and warm clothing, overcrowding and poor ventilation. However, it was an inquest held at the Royal Free Hospital, where sick children belonging to the Holborn Union had been taken, that produced the most sensational outcome.

A succession of witnesses revealed that the children at Drouet's establishment were regularly underfed or given poor-quality food. One member of the Holborn Board of Guardians, Mr W. Winch, gave evidence about visits to the school during the previous year:

> The children were at dinner. They were all standing. I believe they never sit at meals. I cut up 100 potatoes, not one of which was fit to eat. These were served out to the boys. They were positively black and diseased...We asked the boys if they had any complaint of their food, and if they had, to hold up their hands. About thirty of forty held up their hands... Drouet became very violent, and... called the boys liars and scoundrels.[146]

Several of the school's children also gave testimony. Patrick Sheen said that he shared a bed with two other boys. He never had enough to eat but was frightened of being beaten if he said so. Boys from St Pancras who had run away had been birched and then dressed in girls' clothes for several days as punishment. Henry Hartshorn said that he earned a small amount of money shoemaking – a penny for each five pairs of slippers. Because he received so little food, he spent the money on sweets, apples and pears sold to the children by the school's nurses. He also paid a halfpenny for water because not enough was provided.

Other witnesses claimed that Drouet was slow in obtaining medical assistance which could have saved many of the victims' lives. It was noted that of the 155 children removed to the Royal Free Hospital, not one had died, unlike many of those who had stayed behind. Not a single case of cholera had occurred at Tooting outside the confines of the school.

The inquest jury found Drouet guilty of manslaughter and he then faced a criminal trial which began at the Central Criminal Court on 26 February 1849. The case was brought in the form of a specimen charge relating to the death of James Andrews and three other Holborn children. Despite the apparent weight of evidence showing Drouet's negligent treatment of the children

A view of Drouet's school for pauper children at Tooting where a major cholera epidemic broke out in 1849.

in his care, the defence successfully argued that there was no absolute proof that the child would have recovered if it had not been for Drouet's actions. On 16 April, following instruction from the judge, Mr Baron Platt, that there was no case to answer, the jury returned a 'not guilty' verdict.

The events at Tooting, and Drouet's subsequent trial, were the subject of four commentaries by Charles Dickens published anonymously in the weekly journal *The Examiner* between January and April 1849. Dickens was unstintingly critical of Drouet, the Boards of Guardians who used his school, the Recorder of the City of London, and the judge at Drouet's trial. He described the school as having been 'brutally conducted, vilely kept, preposterously inspected, dishonestly defended, a disgrace to a Christian community, and a stain upon a civilised land.'[147]

Following several months of illness, Drouet died in Margate at the end of July 1849.

(*See also*: **District and Separate Schools**; **Scandals**)

EARTH CLOSET

A chair-shaped device used as a toilet or latrine, invented in around 1860 by the Revd Henry Moules. Moules had discovered that a small amount of dry sifted earth scattered by each user into the closet's under-seat receptacle would quickly deodorise the deposited material. After re-drying, the mixture could be utilised a number of times before being employed as fertiliser. Although some use was made of earth closets, particularly in rural workhouses or in situations where no ready water supply existed, the water closet became the standard.

(*See also*: **Lavatory**; **Privy**; **Water Closet**)

EDEN, FREDERIC

(*See*: **State of the Poor**)

EDUCATION

(*See*: **Board School**; **Children**; **Teachers**; **National Schools and British Schools**; **Workhouse Schools**)

ELBERFELD SYSTEM

A scheme for administering poor relief originating in the German town of Elberfeld in 1853. Under the system, the town was divided into a number of poor law districts, with a number of *Pfleger* or almoners appointed in each district. The almoners, who were unpaid, had a role akin to that of the British system's relieving officer. Each was assigned a fixed number of poor relief cases to investigate, assess and monitor. The funding of any poor relief given came from the town council, which appointed a small committee to manage the system. Relief could be given to those not entirely without means, in order to prevent them becoming paupers. The system made no use of institutional relief such as the workhouse.

The Elberfeld system attracted much interest in Britain. In 1887, it was examined in detail by the Local Government Board but they concluded that it would 'almost certainly fail' and so the scheme was never implemented.[148]

ELECTRICITY

The use of electricity in poor law establishments for lighting and other purposes was something that developed in a rather haphazard way. One of the earliest electrical installations was at the hospital opened in 1871 by the Poplar and Stepney Sick Asylum District, where the facilities included 'a complete system of electric bells and telegraphic communication'.[149]

Towards the end of the nineteenth century, electric lighting and other equipment became a standard feature of new workhouses, workhouse infirmaries and the hospitals erected by the Metropolitan Asylums Board (MAB). Prior to the existence of any public supply, electricity was generated on-site by steam-powered dynamos, with large accumulator batteries being used to store power for use during the night. Dynamos could also be powered by gas, as happened at the MAB's Tooting Bec Asylum, or by a paraffin engine as employed at Yorkshire's Great Ouseburn workhouse.

At the MAB's Park Hospital, opened in 1897, the 'engine-room' electrical plant of three steam engines and dynamos provided power for lighting the hospital, telephones and electric fire alarms. In the same year, electric lighting was installed throughout King's Norton's new union infirmary, with arc lamps illuminating the grounds at night. The storage in the establishment's accumulator-house was sufficient for one night's supply.

The new workhouse and infirmary opened in 1903 at Hunslet, near Leeds, boasted a state-of-the-art electrical installation:

> The buildings are lighted throughout by electricity. There are two combined compound engines, each of about 41 E.H.P., and 4-pole dynamos in the electric light station next to the boiler house, as well as a set of storage cells for supplying the lights from about 10-30 in the evening to about 6 o'clock next morning, and also for supplying the electricity for other purposes during the day time. The engines will be run in the evening and in the early morning so as to make use of the cells as little as possible. On the switchboard, in addition to the usual instruments and appliances, a meter is provided for measuring the consumption of electricity in the building. The cells are charged by means of a booster so that the dynamos are always run at constant pressure. There are about 1130 lamps in the building of various candle powers.[150]

As well as in new buildings, electricity was installed in a number of existing workhouse premises. The Stoke-on-Trent workhouse had electric lighting by 1902. In 1912, electricity was installed at the Holywell workhouse in North Wales, replacing the old paraffin oil lamps. Other workhouses, however, such as Bridlington and Pontefract in Yorkshire, were still without electricity when the Boards of Guardians were abolished in 1930. Even the MAB's huge 'Imbeciles Asylum' at Leavesden had no electricity until 1931.
(*See also*: **Gas**)

EMIGRATION

The organised emigration of poor children dates back to a least 1619, when the London Common Council despatched 100 vagrant children to join the first permanent English settlement in North America, Jamestown in Virginia. Further parties followed in 1620 and in 1622 following the Indian Massacre of the settlers in Virginia. From the mid-1600s, the demand for labour in Britain's colonies led to the illegal emigration of hundreds of children through their 'spiriting', or kidnapping, a practice particularly associated with Scotland. This ended in 1757 after a number of Aberdeen businessmen and magistrates were exposed for their involvement in the trade.

In 1833, the Colonial Land and Emigration Commissioners (CLEC) were set up to manage a programme of free or assisted emigration to Britain's colonies such as Canada, Australia and

New Zealand. Workhouse inmates, or those in regular receipt of parish relief, were explicitly excluded from the CLEC schemes.

Provision for the emigration of the poor, paid for by an emigrant's home parish, was however included in the 1834 Poor Law Amendment Act. The Poor Law Commissioners (PLC) supervised this procedure and would, with a few exceptions (e.g. families of convicts or soldiers), usually sanction the emigration of any of its poor that a parish was prepared to fund. Responsibility for making the individual emigration arrangements, however, was in the hands of the Board of Guardians for the union of which the parish was a member.

In their first annual report, in 1835, the PLC noted the modest uptake of the Act's provision with a total of 320 persons having emigrated from eighty parishes, mostly to Canada. However, a year later things were looking rather different with 5,241 persons having been funded to move. Almost three quarters of the total were from Norfolk and Suffolk, with 250 emigrants from a single parish – Banham in Norfolk. In the following year, ending July 1837, the total fell to 1,112 – a figure which was rarely again to be exceeded. In 1842, just over 1,000 poor-rate-funded individuals emigrated, compared with more than 128,000 emigrating under the CLEC schemes. Nonetheless, in 1843, Member of Parliament Charles Buller claimed that Britain's emigration policy was one of 'shovelling out paupers to where they may die without shocking their betters with the sight or sound of their last agony.'[151]

By the mid-1840s, the destinations to which the PLC were prepared to support emigration were specified as 'some British colony, not lying between the tropics.'[152] In practice, the list of eligible destinations comprised: Canada, New Brunswick, Nova Scotia, the Cape of Good Hope, New South Wales, South Australia, West Australia, Van Dieman's Land (Tasmania), and New Zealand. Destinations to which emigration was prohibited by the PLC included India, the West Indies, Singapore, the Western Coast of Africa and the United States of America. Apart from a presumably patriotic disinclination to send British labourers to the USA, the PLC argued that they had much less influence over the treatment that emigrants might receive than would be the case in Empire countries.

The relative popularity of Canada and Australia as destinations for emigration went up and down. The Canadian cities of Quebec and Montreal offered a much shorter voyage than to Australia. However, emigration to Canada came to a halt in the winter months when the St Lawrence River was frozen. South Australia, which was proclaimed a colony in 1836, operated a free passage scheme until the spring of 1841. It was then suspended due to lack of funds until 1847, when various assisted emigration schemes were offered. Events such as the discovery of gold or diamond deposits could also boost each country's popularity.

In 1848, the CLEC began to open up its own scheme to paupers and a new drive was launched to encourage emigration to South Australia and New South Wales. It was proposed that orphans between the ages of fourteen and eighteen, who were of industrious habits and good character, free from all disease, and having been vaccinated against smallpox, should be considered for emigration. They would also be required to have a sufficient knowledge of reading, writing and arithmetic, and the principles of the Christian religion. Orphanhood was defined as having lost at least one parent. Female orphans were much preferred as candidates for emigration because males greatly outnumbered females in these colonies.

The orphan emigration scheme was taken up by Ireland's PLC at a time when the Great Famine was just beginning to subside. The Commissioners decided, however, to confine its use to females. In the first year of the operation, 2,219 girls emigrated from Irish workhouses with another 1,056 the following year. The overall level of poor law emigration from Ireland reached a high of 4,386 in 1851–52 with Quebec being the most popular destination – large parties arrived there from a number of west Ireland unions including Caherciveen (371), Clifden (340), Dingle (355), Ennistymon (376) and Kilrush (389).[153]

Despite its enthusiastic take-up in Ireland, the CLEC's Australian scheme was rather less used in England and Wales. However, the emigration of the poor from mainland Britain was given a boost in the late 1840s by two changes in the law. First, under the Poor Law Amendment Act of

1848, the financing of emigration could be charged to a common fund within each union, rather than having to be funded by the parish in which an emigrant was settled. Second, the 1850 Poor Law Amendment Act provided that a union could undertake the emigration of any 'poor orphan or deserted child under the age of sixteen years' that was in its care. The resulting increase in emigration peaked at a total of 3,271 in 1852 and then, as in Ireland, declined to a few hundred a year.

British Home Children

In the late 1860s, a number of British organisations and private individuals running homes for abandoned or orphaned children began to organise the emigration of parties of children to the colonies, with Canada being the most popular destination. Prominent amongst these individuals were Miss Annie Macpherson and Miss Maria Rye, both of whom organised the emigration and resettlement of several thousand children, many of whom came from workhouses. An added impetus was given to their emigration schemes in 1871 by a relaxation in the regulations and contracts that had formerly been required between Poor Law Unions and emigration agents.

Miss Rye's interest in emigration began in the early 1860s, helping educated young women emigrate to the British colonies, as a result of which she co-founded the Female Middle-Class Emigration Society. After several years of escorting parties of women and girls to Australia, New Zealand and Canada, she turned her attention to orphan and 'gutter' children, proposing their emigration to rural Canada and the western states of America. She took her first party of three children to Canada in June 1869, followed, in October 1869, by a group of seventy-five girls aged four to twelve, including fifty from Liverpool's Kirkdale Industrial School. Miss Rye established a Canadian base in a former court-house and gaol at Niagara-on-the-Lake. The home, which she named Our Western Home, was adapted to act as a holding home for 120 children. She also acquired a large house, known as Avenue House, at the south side of Peckham High Street in London where destitute girls were housed and educated. She obtained financial support for her work from a variety of sources including donations from readers of *The Times*, grants from the Canadian Government, and funding from the British poor law authorities.

In 1874, following adverse reports about the treatment received by some of the children and suggestions that Miss Rye was personally profiting from the public funds she had received, an inquiry was conducted by Local Government Board (LGB) Inspector Mr Andrew Doyle. Doyle visited Canada to interview around 400 children who had emigrated under Miss Rye's care and his report, published in 1875, expressed serious concerns relating to their welfare and aftercare. He found that young children tended to be adopted, and were generally well placed and treated with kindness and affection. Some older children were apprenticed or went into domestic service, but the majority were placed in farm service. Many who went into service suffered hardship, ill-treatment and deprivation. Many children had not been visited for several years and others had been lost track of altogether.[154]

Although Doyle's findings were vigorously disputed by Miss Rye, the emigration of pauper children was halted until 1883, mainly due to the lack of adequate ongoing superintendence of the children in their new homes. Despite this setback, Miss Rye continued her activities and over a twenty-five-year period placed around 5,000 girls in new homes in Canada. In 1895, she handed over her home and her work to the Church of England Waifs and Strays Society. Miss Macpherson's organisation, with homes in London, Ontario and Quebec, was taken over in 1920 by the Liverpool Sheltering Home, later merging with Dr Barnado's.

In April 1883, the LGB agreed new measures with the Canadian Department of Agriculture in Ottowa in relation to emigrant poor law children. During the rest of that year, the Board approved the emigration to Canada of a total of 133 pauper children. In the same year, approval was given for 296 other persons of whom ninety-five went to Canada, 105 to Australia, forty-two to the USA, twenty-eight to New Zealand, fifteen to Nova Scotia, five to New Brunswick, three to British Columbia, two to Cape Colony, and one to India.[155]

The rules governing the emigration and inspection of poor children emigrating to Canada were revised several times and in 1888, the Board published a guide for guardians in determining what would be a reasonable amount to pay to the persons entrusted with the children for the cost of taking them from Liverpool to homes in Canada. It noted that the charges made by the steamship companies for passages to Quebec and Halifax were £4 for adults and £2 for children under twelve. A 'kit' and bedding also had to be obtained by the emigrant at a cost of a few shillings. The railway fares from Quebec to places in Ontario, where most of the homes for the children were situated, ranged from £1 to £1 15s per adult, according to distance. Children between five and twelve years of age were conveyed at half fare.[156]

There was, however, still no compulsory ongoing monitoring of children in their new homes other than a single initial inspection. This changed in 1899 when the Canadian Ministry of the Interior agreed to arrange annual inspections, provided that they were paid for in advance by the child's union or parish.

(*See also*: **Migration**)

ENTERING A WORKHOUSE

Apart from a few special instances, entering a workhouse was a voluntary process. Most commonly, those seeking relief from a Poor Law Union would initially approach their local relieving officer or parish overseer. If the applicant was deemed not to qualify for out relief, an 'offer of the house' could be made – it was up to the individual if they accepted this. If they did so, they would be given a provisional order of admission which expired if not used within six days. Orders of admission could also be issued by the Board of Guardians, and workhouse masters could admit any person to the workhouse in the case of 'sudden or urgent necessity'.

The law viewed poor relief to any individual as also being given to his or her dependants. This meant that families were expected to enter the workhouse together – and also leave together, so that a man could not abandon his family to the care of the union. Variations to this principle did arise, however. In 1861, future politician Will Crooks, together with his younger siblings and disabled father, entered the Poplar workhouse, while his mother continued working and supporting the older children. From the 1870s, some unions made it a condition of out relief to able-bodied widows with several children that one or more of them be placed in the

The forbidding entrance to the union workhouse at Braintree in Essex. At the left are the porter's lodge and receiving wards, with the guardians' boardroom just visible at the right.

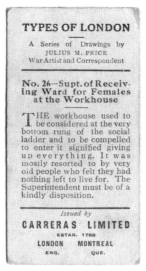

BLACK CAT
CIGARETTES

SUPT. OF RECEIVING WARD FOR
FEMALES AT THE WORKHOUSE

TYPES OF LONDON

A Series of Drawings by
JULIUS M. PRICE
War Artist and Correspondent

No. 26—Supt. of Receiv-
ing Ward for Females
at the Workhouse

THE workhouse used to
be considered at the very
bottom rung of the social
ladder and to be compelled
to enter it signified giving
up everything. It was
mostly resorted to by very
old people who felt they had
nothing left to live for. The
Superintendent must be of a
kindly disposition.

Issued by

CARRERAS LIMITED

ESTAB. 1788

LONDON   MONTREAL
ENG.   QUE.

Some large workhouses had staff dedicated to the processing of new arrivals. This cigarette card, dating from about 1919, shows the 'Superintendent of the Receiving Ward for Females' at a large London workhouse. As the text notes, she was expected to be of a 'kindly disposition'.

workhouse while the woman found employment. From the 1880s, a 'modified workhouse test' was sometimes implemented, making it possible for a man to reside in a workhouse while his family received out relief.

Entry into a workhouse could mean losing one's home if it was in rented accommodation since a landlord might not want to lose income by leaving the property empty for an indeterminate period. Furniture and other possessions were also at risk. Although the disposal of a destitute person's furniture was not demanded by poor relief regulations, it might well have already been sold to try and pay off debts, or be seized by a landlord in lieu of unpaid rent.

Formal admission to a workhouse was granted at the next meeting of the Board of Guardians. Until then, new arrivals were placed in a receiving or probationary ward, with males and females being housed separately. As well as the administrative formalities, new inmates would be required to bathe and then given workhouse uniforms, with their own clothes being disinfected and put into store. Children, but not adults, could be required to have their hair cut. Most importantly, no-one could be admitted to the main workhouse without first being examined by the medical officer in case they were harbouring any infectious condition that might be passed on to other inmates. Each new inmate would also be classified to determine their place of accommodation in the workhouse and their dietary provision.
(*See also*: **Classification**; **Clothing**; **Disinfection**; **Dietary Class**; **Leaving a Workhouse**; **Relieving Officer**)

ENTERTAINMENT

Although union workhouses were intended to be deterrent in character, life inside them was not always as unremittingly grim as it is often portrayed.

Perhaps not entertainment in its most obvious sense, the activities of the Workhouse Visiting Society from 1858 onwards no doubt brightened the lives of many workhouse residents. As well as providing visitors for those who would otherwise have none, members of the Society did readings of both religious and secular works, ran classes of instruction, taught handicrafts such as knitting, and encouraged workhouses to set up libraries.

For inmates who were bedridden or of restricted mobility the Brabazon Scheme, initiated in 1880, aimed to provide interesting and useful diversion through the learning of handicrafts such as knitting, embroidery or lace-making.

Name of Workhouse.	Inm'tes.	Men	Women.	Children.	Periodicals.	Newspapers.	Toys, &c.
ENGLAND.							
Ashton, near Manchester	776	330	284	162	None.	Odds and ends.	A few at Christmas.
Blackburn	96	53	23	20	None.	None.	Salvation Army *War Cry* and *Young Soldier*.
Bradford	500	300	200	...	Unsupplied.	Unsupplied.	
Bromley, Kent	299	185	114	31	The *Quiver* occcasionally.	None.	No toys or picture-books.
Bromsgrove	175	90	60	25	None.	Local.	From *Truth*.
Brentford Workhouse, Isleworth	460	241	165	54	Have papers, &c.	Have library of 2,000 books.	Fairly well.
Bury Union Workhouse.............	...	...	...	...	Too numerous to mention. There is a library.	Do.	Require some.
Cheltenham	404	157	141	106			
Christ's Church.......................	130	35	35	40	None.	Fluctuating.	None.
Coventry...............................	349	157	128	64	1, the *Quiver*.	3 weekly, 3 or 4 daily.	Yes, at Christmas.
Croydon	204	262	124	18	Well supplied.	Well supplied, except in the infirmary.	
Derby	514	196	162	156	Fairly well.	30 per week.	Fairly well.
Devonport	335	97	169	69	10 monthly.	None.	Not stated.
Dorchester	95	45	25	25	12 *Graphics* every fortnight.	Daily, one day old.	No toys mentioned.
Dunmow, Essex	171	96	37	43	Irregular.	2 weekly.	Well supplied.
Doddington, near Cambridge ...	137	60	33	44	*British Workman*.	Religious occasionally.	At Christmas.
Dudley.................................	642	271	239	122	6 monthly.	5 weekly.	A few at Christmas.
Eastville, Bristol	917	401	316	200	13 monthly.	20 weekly.	Not mentioned.
Epping Union	94	59	35	40	1 monthly.	2 daily.	A few.
Exeter—Union of St. Sodwell ...	319	154	101	14	Well supplied.	Well supplied, library 236 books.	Well supplied.
— Union of St. Thomas	172	76	51	45	None to depend on.	Very seldom.	Have toys, *require* picture-books.
Gateshead	526	147	167	212	None.	4 weekly.	A few from Uncle Toby at Christmas.
Great Yarmouth	500	200	200	100	Well supplied.	Well supplied, want books.	No toys.
Guiltcross Union, Kenninghall, Thetford	99	...	...	35	None.	None except a few old sometimes.	None.
Halifax.................................	458	251	156	51	Well supplied.	Well supplied.	Well supplied.
Hull—Union of Sculcoates	719	Not divided.		170	Sufficient.	Sufficient; indeed, very good.	Furnished by Guardians and friends.
— Union of Hull, Corporation of the Poor......................	591	Not divided.		100	Inadequate.	Inadequate.	Inadequate.
Hastings...............................	225	83	81	61	Fairly well supplied.	Inmates buy the daily papers.	Supplied.
Howden, Yorks	65	30	18	17	None.	Occasionally.	At Christmas.
Hampstead, West....................	262	128	114	20	No limit (?)	No limit (?)	Acceptable.
Hexham Union	Not mentioned.				Well supplied.	Well supplied.	Well supplied.
Huddersfield	Not given.			None.	5 monthly.	3 weekly, some 2 days old.	Papers given.
Kensington, St. Mary Abbots ...	810	300	480	30	Have a library.	Would be acceptable.	Children at Banstead.
Leeds Union	469	186	133	150	In plenty.	Plenty.	A few acceptable.
Leek Union	141	59	36	46	Irregular.	Irregular.	Well supplied.
Leicester...............................	634	...	...	...	Kyrie Society supplies.	Daily and weekly old papers.	
Lewisham	1050	250	250	50	Occasional bundles.	1 local.	Children drafted off to district school.
Liverpool, West Derby Union ...	2200	1000	1100	100	4 monthly.	None.	Very few.
London—Hackney	1090	560	480	50	Well stocked library.	Require more.	Require more.
— St. George's, Hanover-square	1532	1016	485	31	No regular supply.	8 daily, *Punch*, *Judy*, and *Fun* by lady visitors.	
Manchester—Union of North Brierley	260	170	70	20	12 *British Workman* and *Children's Temperance*.	None.	Fairly well off.

What an inmate might be reading in around 1890 at a time when workhouses relied on charitable donations of books, magazines and newspapers. Supplies varied enormously from 'none' at Blackburn to a library of over 2,000 books at nearby Bury.

An 1867 concert of comedy, music and song for the inmates of the Bethnal Green workhouse. The performers were the 'Delaware Minstrels' – an amateur company of Lombard Street bank clerks.

Right The programme for
a New Year's Day concert at
London's St Giles' workhouse
in 1904, inset with a newspaper
review of the event.

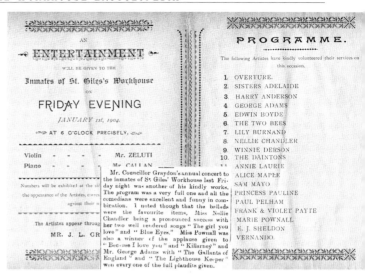

Below By the early 1900s, the
Sheffield Union workhouse
held an annual sports day.

Prior to the 1890s, supplies of books, magazines and newspapers for workhouse inmates came through donation from the public and other charitable sources. In 1864, the Haslingden guardians asked the Lancashire and Yorkshire Railway for permission to place collecting boxes at local railway stations, where travellers could place discarded books and periodicals. Eight years later, the guardians were apparently surprised to be told that one was full. One of the boxes was still in use at Bacup railway station in 1919. In 1891, the Local Government Board agreed that such supplies proved inadequate, and they could be supplemented from the poor rate. Guardians were encouraged to provide illustrated books and papers for the children and the sick, together with toys for the infants, and bats, balls and skipping ropes for the older children.[157]

As early as the 1860s, occasional concerts were being put on for inmates by visiting musical groups or bands such as that by the 'Delaware Minstrels' – a group of blacked-up bank Clerks – at the Bethnal Green workhouse in 1867. Home-made musical entertainments also frequently featured in the workhouse's Christmas or New Year celebrations, when inmates and staff would sing together, perhaps with some making solo contributions.

The period between supper and bedtime was, no doubt, a time when inmates entertained themselves. Any activity that might constitute gambling was strictly prohibited, with a ban on items such as dice and playing cards. In 1914, however, after Boards of Guardians had been given greater discretion in such matters, the inmates at Liverpool workhouse were permitted to play card games. Singing was undoubtedly popular, with workhouse inmates being among the sources used in the early 1900s by collectors of English folk songs such as Cecil Sharp, Ralph Vaughan Williams and George Gardiner. Gardiner collected more than 300 songs from inmates of workhouses including those at Bath, Portsmouth and Farnham in Surrey.[158]

According to the anonymous author of *Indoor Paupers* – a supposed first-hand account of workhouse life in the 1880s – informal concerts of songs, stories and recitations were regularly staged in the men's dormitory after 'lights out' on a Saturday night. On one occasion, the evening's offerings included a vivid account of a tiger-hunt in Upper India, a recitation of the poem *Lord Ullin's Daughter*, and songs such as *The Old Musqueteer, Tom Bowling, Meet Me by Moonlight Alone, Black-eyed Susan* and *The Red, White, and Blue*, with proceedings brought to an end by *Auld Lang Syne*.[159] While workhouse staff apparently turned a blind eye to such entertainments, it seems they could sometimes take place with official sanction. In 1867, an official report noted that at the workhouse of St Giles, Camberwell, parties of imbecile patients 'join the amusements of dancing and singing, which take place in the body of the house.'[160]

By the 1890s, outings to the countryside or to the sea, or to events such as tea parties, were regularly arranged for some workhouse inmates, particularly the elderly and the children. These were not always the sedate affairs that might be expected. From 1891, the residents of Camberwell's Gordon Road and Constance Road workhouses had an annual summer excursion to the seaside. For their 1896 day out to Bognor Regis, a special 650-seat train was chartered and at around 9a.m. the party set off. The group consisted mostly of elderly inmates aged sixty to ninety, together with a number of young children from the workhouse. They were also accompanied by a boys' band from the South Metropolitan District School. Dinner and tea were provided at the Bognor Town Hall after which the men were given tobacco, and the women and children sweets. However, many of the group had apparently obtained money from their friends and after being liberated from the workhouse had headed straight for the nearest public house before boarding the train. On arrival at Bognor, they had continued drinking and had then gone for their dinner at which beer was also served. After dinner, there were more visits to the local public houses. It was later reported that a number of cases had occurred of disorderly conduct and indecent behaviour on secluded parts of the beach.[161] The inmates of the Wandsworth and Clapham workhouse appear to have been rather more orderly. In May 1902, 430 of them visited the Grand Theatre and 420 the Shakespeare Theatre, with all except four behaving well.[162]

By the start of the twentieth century, workhouses could buy a piano or harmonium funded from the poor rates. In later years, more modern forms of entertainment gradually penetrated the institution. In 1925, the *Yorkshire Evening Post* reported that 'a wireless set with two loud-speakers has already been installed in the Beckett Street Workhouse, Leeds at a considerable cost, borne by the Board of Guardians, of £50.' Several patients in the infirmary also had their own crystal sets.[163] At Abingdon in Berkshire, some workhouse inmates even had a weekly trip to a local cinema.[164]

(*See also*: **Brabazon Scheme**; **Children**)

EPILEPSY

(*See*: **Mentally Ill**)

EX OFFICIO GUARDIANS

Ex officio is a Latin phrase meaning 'by virtue of one's office'. Justices of the Peace living within a Poor Law Union were automatically *ex officio* members of its Board of Guardians without needing to be elected. *Ex officio* guardians were abolished by the 1894 Local Government Act. (*See also*: **Guardians / Guardians of the Poor**)

EXAMINATIONS

The early 1900s saw the beginning of professional training and examination for some of those employed in poor relief administration. In 1903, the Metropolitan Relieving Officers' Association initiated a lecture course at the London School of Sociology and Social Work (LSSSW) – an institution set up by the Charity Organisation Society (COS). Initially for relieving officers, the training was later extended to union Clerks and workhouse officers, with the first examinations in 1906 recording a pass rate of more than 70 per cent. The scheme was then taken up by Liverpool University and elsewhere including the new London School of Economics which ran the course from 1912 following the collapse of the LSSSW.

The COS training scheme was acknowledged in the 1905 Royal Commission's Majority Report, with the suggestion that the system be continued and extended, eventually resulting in all poor law posts being filled by suitably qualified applicants. Although a Poor Law Examinations Board was subsequently formed, a requirement for the qualifications it awarded never became widespread amongst employers.

In Scotland, a Poor Law Examinations Board was established in 1909 by the Society of Inspectors of the Poor for Scotland to conduct examinations for the award of a Poor Law Diploma. (*See also*: **Charity Organisation Society; Poor Law Examination Board**)

EXMOUTH AND GOLIATH

From 1870–75, the Forest Gate School District operated a training ship called the *Goliath* moored on the Thames. It provided pauper boys from the District with instruction in all aspects of seamanship to help equip them for entry to the Royal or Merchant Navy. The scheme proved highly successful, but the ship was destroyed by fire on 22 December 1875 with the loss of twenty-three lives.

In 1877, a replacement vessel, the *Exmouth*, moored off Grays in Essex, took on the role but was managed by the Metropolitan Asylums Board and was available for use by all London's Poor Law authorities. In 1892, admission to the ship was extended to include up to fifty boys from parishes and unions outside the metropolitan area.

The *Exmouth* was an old wooden two-decked battleship, built in 1854, which had carried the flag of Admiral Seymour in the Baltic during the Crimean War. Boys were able to join the ship from the age of twelve. Their first task was to learn how to mend and patch their own clothes. They also had to learn how to wash their clothes, and keep their lockers and contents in good order. Each boy had his own hammock which was stowed during the day, leaving the decks clear of bedding. As well as learning the skills of sailing, rowing, sail and rope-making, gunnery, and signalling, the boys continued ordinary school work and other physical activities such as swimming and gymnastics. The ship had its own band and a separate bugle band.

In 1896, 137 pauper boys entered the Royal Navy from the *Exmouth*, compared with a total of 135 from all other training ships in the country combined. In 1899, of 372 boys discharged from the *Exmouth*, 149 entered the Royal Navy, 135 the mercantile marine, fifty-eight joined the army as musicians, and thirty returned to their respective parishes.

Uniformed boys performing dumb-bell drill aboard the Training Ship *Exmouth* in 1904.

In 1903, the ship's hull was found to be in an unsafe condition and was condemned. A replacement of similar appearance, but built of iron and steel, was commissioned from the Vickers company in Barrow-in-Furness. The new *Exmouth* was towed round the coast to Grays where she was inaugurated in August 1905.

The *Exmouth* had a companion vessel, a brigantine called the *Steadfast*, used for cruising and to provide the boys with practical training in seamanship. The original *Steadfast* was condemned in 1894 and replaced by a new vessel of the same name. Onshore at Grays, a playing field, swimming bath and infirmary were provided in an old manor house called Sherfield House.

In 1945, the *Exmouth* became *HMS Worcester* – part of the Thames Nautical Training College. She continued in service until the college's closure in 1968 and was broken up a few years later. (*See also*: **Metropolitan Asylums Board**; **Training Ships**)

FAMOUS NAMES WITH WORKHOUSE CONNECTIONS

A number of individuals who later became famous had workhouse connections. They included film actor/director Charlie Chaplain (inmate of Lambeth workhouse and Central London District School, 1896–98), author Catherine Cookson (laundry supervisor at South Shields, Tendring and Hasting workhouses, 1920s–30s), politician Will Crooks (inmate of Poplar workhouse and South Metropolitan District School, 1861), author Len Deighton (born in St Marylebone workhouse, 1929), 'Little Sweep' Valentine Gray (Alverstoke workhouse, early nineteenth century), TV presenter Gilbert Harding (born at Hereford workhouse where his parents were master and matron, 1907), 'Elephant Man' Joseph Merrick (inmate of Leicester workhouse 1880–84), journalist Henry Morton Stanley (inmate of St Asaph workhouse 1847–56), and alleged 'Jack the Ripper' victim Martha Tabram or Tabran (Whitechapel casual ward, 1881). In the USA, 'Calamity Jane' was admitted to the Gallatin County poorhouse in 1901, two years before her death at the age of fifty-two. (*See also*: **Biography**)

FARM COLONY

(*See*: **Labour Colony / Farm Colony**)

FARMING THE POOR

Farming the poor was the practice of contracting out parish poor relief administration to a third party, an early example of privatisation. Most often, the contractor engaged to run the parish workhouse was paid either an annual lump sum or a weekly or monthly rate for each inmate in residence. As well as their board and lodging, the contractor would provide the inmates with work and could keep most or all of any income generated. Contracts were usually open to competitive tendering, with the cheapest bid usually being the most successful. Farming the poor could be a financially lucrative occupation, with some contractors – most notably Matthew Marryott – being involved in the operation of multiple workhouses.

Sir Frederic Eden, in his 1797 survey of the poor in England, described the operation of farming at the Farnham workhouse:

> The contractor is allowed the use of the house and furniture, and the earnings of the Poor, and receives £1,000 a year for which he is bound to maintain the Poor of every description, but not bear the expense of removals, appeals, or other law contests. There are at present (Oct., 1795) 124 inmates, of whom 50 are old and infirm, and generally about the same in winter. There are a few out-pensioners, but the payments are very trifling, as it is more for the interest of the contractor to offer the Poor who apply for relief no alternative but the house. The infirm who can work are employed in picking wool, the children attend the carding machine, spin, etc., and are taught to read twice a day. Boys and girls, men and women sleep in different quarters of the house. The contractor says he keeps no account of expenses or earnings.

Farming the poor was widely adopted in London by parishes whose workhouses were full or which did not possess their own workhouse. In some cases, farming was used to deal with troublesome inmates. Some London contractors had large 'poor farms' housing 300 or more inmates drawn from as many as forty different parishes.[165] Following Hanway's Act of 1776, London's pauper children were required to reside at least three miles from the capital in accommodation that was mostly privately run.

After 1834, the use of contractor-run accommodation for paupers largely disappeared. One exception was the City of London Union whose reluctance to build a workhouse led it to continue using contractors until the late 1840s. Although Hanway's Act was abolished in 1844, some young children continued to be 'farmed' for a number of years.

The use of contractors resurfaced following the 1862 Poor Law (Certified Schools) Act which allowed pauper children to be housed in privately run accommodation certified as fit for the purpose. The boarding-out or fostering of children by Poor Law Unions, which became increasingly popular from the 1870s, was arguably yet just another variant of farming the poor. (*See also*: **Boarding Out**; **Certified Schools (Poor Law)**; **Hanway's Act**; **London**; **Marryott, Matthew**; **Workhouse Test**)

FARMS

(*See*: **Gardens and Farms**)

FEEBLE-MINDED

(*See*: **Mentally Ill**; **Metropolitan Asylums Board**)

FICTION

Like artists and poets, the writers of novels and short stories found the workhouse a valuable source of inspiration. The workhouse was invariably cast as a place of brutality, oppression and inhumanity, with factual accuracy never getting in the way of a good story.

The quintessential workhouse yarn was Charles Dickens' novel *Oliver Twist*. Oliver's immortal words, 'Please sir, I want some more', and the gruel he wanted seconds of, epitomise most people's image of the workhouse and its horrors. Here is the famous dining hall scene:

> The room in which the boys were fed, was a large stone hall, with a copper at one end: out of which the master, dressed in an apron for the purpose, and assisted by one or two women, ladled the gruel at mealtimes. Of this festive composition each boy had one porringer, and no more – except on occasions of great public rejoicing, when he had two ounces and a quarter of bread besides.
>
> The bowls never wanted washing. The boys polished them with their spoons till they shone again; and when they had performed this operation (which never took very long, the spoons being nearly as large as the bowls), they would sit staring at the copper, with such eager eyes, as if they could have devoured the very bricks of which it was composed; employing themselves, meanwhile, in sucking their fingers most assiduously, with the view of catching up any stray splashes of gruel that might have been cast thereon. Boys have generally excellent appetites. Oliver Twist and his companions suffered the tortures of slow starvation for three months: at last they got so voracious and wild with hunger, that one boy, who was tall for his age, and hadn't been used to that sort of thing (for his father had kept a small cook-shop), hinted darkly to his companions, that unless he had another basin of gruel per diem, he was afraid he might some night happen to eat the boy who slept next him, who happened to be a weakly youth of tender age. He had a wild, hungry eye; and they implicitly believed him. A council was held; lots were cast who should walk up to the master after supper that evening, and ask for more; and it fell to Oliver Twist.
>
> The evening arrived; the boys took their places. The master, in his cook's uniform, stationed himself at the copper; his pauper assistants ranged themselves behind him; the gruel was served out; and a long grace was said over the short commons. The gruel disappeared; the boys whispered each other, and winked at Oliver; while his next neighbours nudged him. Child as he was, he was desperate with hunger, and reckless with misery. He rose from the table; and advancing to the master, basin and spoon in hand, said: somewhat alarmed at his own temerity:
>
> 'Please, sir, I want some more.'
>
> The master was a fat, healthy man; but he turned very pale. He gazed in stupefied astonishment on the small rebel for some seconds, and then clung for support to the copper. The assistants were paralysed with wonder; the boys with fear.
>
> 'What!' said the master at length, in a faint voice.
>
> 'Please, sir,' replied Oliver, 'I want some more.'
>
> The master aimed a blow at Oliver's head with the ladle; pinioned him in his arm; and shrieked aloud for the beadle.
>
> The board were sitting in solemn conclave, when Mr. Bumble rushed into the room in great excitement, and addressing the gentleman in the high chair, said,
>
> 'Mr. Limbkins, I beg your pardon, sir! Oliver Twist has asked for more!'
>
> There was a general start. Horror was depicted on every countenance.

'For MORE!' said Mr. Limbkins. 'Compose yourself, Bumble, and answer me distinctly. Do I understand that he asked for more, after he had eaten the supper allotted by the dietary?'

'He did, sir,' replied Bumble.

'That boy will be hung,' said the gentleman in the white waistcoat. 'I know that boy will be hung.'

Dickens' story – subtitled *The Parish Boy's Progress* – first appeared in 1837 in the monthly magazine *Bentley's Miscellany*, although it had probably been evolving in Dickens' mind for several years. Its writing and publication came at a particularly significant point in poor law history, when – in the wake of the 1834 Poor Law Amendment Act – the old parish-run workhouses were being replaced by new, deterrent union institutions. Dickens' novel presents us with a rather muddled mixture of the two. The Beadle, for example, was a parish official or constable who had no role in the running of a union workhouse. We are told that Oliver's workhouse was some seventy miles from the capital, yet Oliver's experience of being 'farmed out' to the countryside was peculiar to London workhouses, Most significantly, Oliver, having reached the age of nine, would – under the new regime – have been entitled to the same 'dietary' as an adult woman which would have added at least a portion of bread to his meal of gruel. Interestingly, Dickens' later journalistic writings about the workhouse, for example *A Walk in a Workhouse* (1850), give a more positive view of workhouses than that presented in *Oliver Twist*.

Although many workhouses have been suggested as *the* one which inspired *Oliver Twist*, by far the strongest contender is the Cleveland Street workhouse in London's Fitzrovia district, erected in the 1770s for the parish of St Paul's, Covent Garden, and becoming the Strand Union workhouse in 1836. For two periods totalling five years, Dickens lived just a few doors away from the building.

Like *Oliver Twist*, Frances ('Fanny') Trollope's novel *Jessie Phillips: A Tale of the Present Day* was originally serialised, its instalments originally published between December 1842 and November 1843. It dealt with difficulties faced by the eponymous heroine after her seduction by the local squire's son. The novel railed against the effects of the so-called 'bastardy clause' in the 1834 Poor Law Amendment Act which effectively made illegitimate children the sole responsibility of their mothers. Women who were unable to support themselves and their offspring would have to enter the workhouse. As was typically the case, Jessie's accommodation in the workhouse placed her among those judged to be of a similar character to herself:

> The first unexpected misery which sufficed to shake her courage was the finding herself shut up with, and constantly surrounded by, some of the vilest and most thoroughly abandoned women that the lowest degradation of vice could produce. One of the nineteen parishes which formed the Deepbrook union was on the coast, and included in its population many of that wretched class of females which a seaport town is sure to produce. When sickness, accident, or age, drove any of these miserable creatures to such extremity of want as to leave them no resource but the parish, they were immediately consigned to the Union workhouse; and deeply would many of those whose vote and interest have aided the arrangement which makes this necessary, very deeply and profoundly, would they be shocked could they be made aware of the tremendous mischief which such Union produces.
>
> ... [One] may still find in every village of England honest, virtuous, hard-working females, who, in case their power of labour fails, have no resource but the workhouse against certain death by starvation, but who are as morally undeserving of having such association forced upon them as the noblest and most justly honoured matron in the land. IF THIS BE TRUE, let every Christian in the country ask himself if 'further amendment' be not wanted.[166]

In 1844, a further Poor Law Amendment Act did indeed restore the ability of a woman in Jessie's situation to apply for an affiliation order against the father of their child.

The workhouse scenes in Arnold Bennet's 1910 novel *Clayhanger*, set in the Staffordshire Potteries, were based on parts of the autobiography of 'An Old Potter', Charles Shaw, published seven years earlier. In 1842, at the age of ten, Shaw and his family had spent several weeks in Wolstanton & Burslem Union workhouse at Chell. Here is Bennet's version of events:

The Bastille was on the top of a hill about a couple of miles long, and the journey thither was much lengthened by the desire of the family to avoid the main road. They were all intensely ashamed; Darius was ashamed to tears, and did not know why; even his little sister wept and had to be carried, not because she was shoeless and had had nothing to eat, but because she was going to the Ba-ba-bastille; she had no notion what the place was. It proved to be the largest building that Darius had ever seen; and indeed it was the largest in the district; they stood against its steep sides like flies against a kennel. Then there was rattling of key-bunches, and the rasping voices of sour officials, who did not inquire if they would like a meal after their stroll. And they were put into a cellar and stripped and washed and dressed in other people's clothes, and then separated, amid tears. And Darius was pitched into a large crowd of other boys, all clothed like himself. He now understood the reason for shame; it was because he could have no distinctive clothes of his own, because he had somehow lost his identity All the boys had a sullen, furtive glance, and when they spoke it was in whispers.

In the low room where the boys were assembled there fell a silence, and Darius heard someone whisper that the celebrated boy who had run away and been caught would be flogged before supper. Down the long room ran a long table. Someone brought in three candles in tin candlesticks and set them near the end of this table. Then somebody else brought in a pickled birch-rod, dripping with the salt water from which it had been taken, and also a small square table. Then came some officials, and a clergyman, and then, surpassing the rest in majesty, the governor of the Bastille, a terrible man. The governor made a speech about the crime of running away from the Bastille, and when he had spoken for a fair time, the clergyman talked in the same sense; and then a captured tiger, dressed like a boy, with darting fierce eyes, was dragged in by two men, and laid face down on the square table, and four boys were commanded to step forward and hold tightly the four members of this tiger. And, his clothes having previously been removed as far as his waist, his breeches were next pulled down his legs. Then the rod was raised and it descended swishing, and blood began to flow; but far more startling than the blood were the shrill screams of the tiger; they were so loud and deafening that the spectators could safely converse under their shelter. The boys in charge of the victim had to cling hard and grind their teeth in the effort to keep him prone. As the blows succeeded each other, Darius became more and more ashamed. The physical spectacle did not sicken nor horrify him, for he was a man of wide experience; but he had never before seen flogging by lawful authority. Flogging in the workshop was different, a private if sanguinary affair between free human beings. This ritualistic and cold-blooded torture was infinitely more appalling in its humiliation. The screaming grew feebler, then ceased; then the blows ceased, and the unconscious infant (cured of being a tiger) was carried away leaving a trail of red drops along the floor.[167]

Other nineteenth-century novels featuring workhouses include: *Scenes from Clerical Life* (George Elliot, 1857) set in 'Shepperton' which was based on Chilvers Coton, the home of the Nuneaton Union workhouse; *Far from the Madding Crowd* (Thomas Hardy, 1874) in which 'Casterbridge Union' was based on the Dorchester workhouse; and *Captain Lobe* ('John Law' [Margaret Harkness], 1888) with scenes set in the Whitechapel workhouse.

Workhouse events in George Orwell's 1931 essay *The Spike* were later reused in his 1933 novel *Down and Out in Paris and London*. Although based on first-hand experience, Orwell does not identify the location of the workhouse described in *The Spike*. However, in *Down and Out...*, it is named as 'Lower Binfield' (a fictitious name also appearing in *Coming Up For Air*) and described as lying to the south of 'Cromley', a coalescence of 'Croydon' and 'Bromley'.

After the stay at the spike, some of the tramps were said to be heading for Croydon. The location of Orwell's spike is therefore perhaps Godstone.
(*See also*: **Art**; **Documentary**; **Poetry**; **Plays**)

FIRE

As in any large institution, fire was always a hazard in workhouse buildings and over the years a number of major outbreaks occurred.

Perhaps the worst ever workhouse fire broke out at 2a.m. on 24 February 1767 at Chester's Roodee workhouse, used for spinning cotton. The building, which then housed 200 children in addition to the adults, was totally destroyed. Seventy-seven died, including sixty children, twelve men and five women. A report in the *London Chronicle* recounted horrifying scenes of inmates running naked from the building, while others jumped from windows and the roof. A party of thirty men was employed to dig out the bones and dead bodies but without success – it was assumed that they had all burnt to ashes. Rather more fortunate were the inmates of London's St Saviour's workhouse, a large building entirely constructed of wood, which caught fire in August 1817. Although the building was completely destroyed, there were no fatalities.

One of the country's largest workhouses, Liverpool, suffered two major fires. The first, in 1796, destroyed one of its wings. In the second, on 7 September 1862, the church and one of the children's dormitories were destroyed, with twenty-one children and two nurses burnt to death.

In 1856, the South Metropolitan School District's school at Sutton was severely damaged by a fire discovered at 2a.m. in a blanket store. Fortunately, none of the 900 children in residence was harmed. On New Year's Day 1890, a disastrous fire broke out at the Forest Gate District School with two dormitories being destroyed and twenty-six boys dying from suffocation.

In 1886, the Chelmsford Union workhouse was almost completely destroyed by a fire and had to be largely rebuilt. In 1890, the female wing at the Newcastle-under-Lyme workhouse burnt down. The following year, a blaze at the South Molton workhouse in Devon was caused by an oil lamp being broken and resulted in the deaths of three inmates.

Major fires at two workhouses resulted in their permanent closure. The Westhampnett Union workhouse in Sussex was completely burnt out in 1899 although the external staircases on the four-storey building allowed all the inmates to escape. In 1922, the St Faith's Union workhouse near Norwich was gutted by a fire and never re-opened.

The wooden training ships, where some workhouse boys were placed, were particularly vulnerable to fire. Casualties included the *Goliath* in 1875 with the loss of twenty-three lives, the *Cumberland* in 1889, the *Wellesley* in 1914 and the *Warspite* in 1918.

FISH DAYS

Days of the week when the eating of meat was prohibited. In 1562, Elizabeth I added Wednesday to the existing fish days of Friday and Saturday; although portrayed as a religious devotion, its rather more practical purpose was to aid an ailing fishing industry and to conserve meat stocks. Defying the ban was punishable by a £3 fine or three months in prison.
(*See also*: **Flesh Days**)

FLESH DAYS

Days of the week, usually limited in number, when meat was served to workhouse inmates.
(*See also*: **Fish Days**)

Above The workhouse fire brigade at Stoke on Trent which had its own small fire station. The firemen were all workhouse officers with other full-time duties and were given regular training by members of the town's fire brigade.

Right Staff and inmates hold a fire drill at the St Faith's Union workhouse near Norwich, date unknown. The training paid off – there were no casualties when the building was gutted by fire in 1922.

FOOD

The food provided to inmates of the workhouse over the three centuries or so of its existence varied considerably and was determined by a number of factors. First, it reflected the usual diet of the particular time such as would be eaten in the home of a person of modest means. That, in turn, would be determined by the particular food preferences in different regions of the country, for example of wheat versus barley, or bread versus potatoes. The food served in a workhouse would also indicate the nature of the regime, with a deterrent institution offering a more restricted diet than would be provided at a more benign establishment. Generally, though, the staples of most workhouse diets were bread, soup or broth, cheese, various 'puddings', and with meat usually served two or three times a week.

Food in the Parish Workhouse
A typical workhouse 'bill of fare' in the 1720s was that adopted by the parishes of All Saints and St Andrew, Hertford:

	Breakfast	Dinner	Supper
Sunday	Bread and Cheese	Meat	Broth
Monday	Broth	Pease-Porridge	Bread and Cheese
Tuesday	Bread and Cheese	Hasty Pudding	Bread and Cheese
Wednesday	Bread and Cheese	Meat	Broth
Thursday	Broth	Frumety	Bread and Cheese
Friday	Bread and Cheese	Ox-Head	Broth
Saturday	Broth	Hasty Pudding	Bread and Cheese

Pease-porridge was a thick broth made from dried peas. Hasty pudding was a type of custard made by boiling up milk and flour or oatmeal. Frumety contained wheat grains with the husks removed and again boiled up with milk.

The term 'porridge' covered a rather wider range of dishes than it does today. At the Hunslet workhouse near Leeds in 1761, the weekly menu included milk porridge, water porridge and drink porridge. Although it is tempting to view these simply as regional variations on hasty pudding, perhaps with 'drink porridge' being equivalent to gruel, things are not that simple – the 1724 menu at Barking workhouse included milk porridge in addition to hasty pudding and oatmeal hasty pudding. Use of the term 'porridge' in its usual modern sense of oatmeal boiled in water seems to have begun during the nineteenth century.

Exactly when gruel – a thin oatmeal porridge – began its well-known association with the workhouse is unclear. *An Account of Several Workhouses*, first published in 1725, made no mention of the dish. One of the first references to gruel on a workhouse menu is in the 1742 bill of fare at St Margaret's, Westminster, where it was served at breakfast three times a week.[168]

Some parish workhouse diets were surprisingly ample in their provision. One of the most generous was that at Brighthelmstone (Brighton) workhouse which in 1834 provided three meals a day with no limits on quantity. Men received two pints of beer a day, children one pint, and women a pint of beer and a pint of tea. There were six meat dinners in the week and the inmates were served at table with the governor carving for the men and boys, and the matron for the women and girls. The complete diet is shown below:[169]

BREAKFAST:	Women: One pint of tea, with bread and butter. Men, boys and girls: Bread and gruel (of flour and oatmeal) excepting some old men, who are allowed a pint of tea, with bread and butter.
DINNER:	Monday: Pease soup, herbs, &c. with bread men and women a pint of table-beer; boys about half a pint. Tuesday: Beef and mutton puddings, with vegetables; the beer, &c., same as Monday. Wednesday: Boiled beef and mutton (sometimes pork with it), hard puddings, bread, vegetables, &c.; beer same as before. Thursday: Mutton and beef-suet puddings; beer same as before. Friday: Beef and mutton puddings, with vegetables; beer same as before. Saturday: Irish stew-meat, potatoes, herbs, &c.; beer same as before. Sunday: Boiled beef and mutton (sometimes pork with it), hard puddings, bread; vegetables, &c.; beer same as before.
SUPPER:	Women: One pint of tea, with bread and butter or cheese. Men and boys: Bread and butter or cheese; men, one pint of beer or tea each; boys, about half a pint. Girls and small children: Bread and butter; drink, milk and water.

The beer and tea served at Brighton were not the uncommon luxuries that might be imagined. Beer, in the form of weak 'small beer', was widely consumed, both as a pleasant beverage and also as an alternative to local water supplies which might be less than wholesome. Tea, introduced to Britain from China in the mid-1600s and originally very expensive, had by the nineteenth century become affordable by all and a staple item of many people's diets.

Food in the Union Workhouse

The union workhouses established after the 1834 Poor Law Amendment Act were intended to be deterrent in nature, with conditions outside always more attractive – even for the lowest-paid labourer. Workhouse food reflected this principle. In 1835, the Poor Law Commissioners issued six dietaries – weekly meal plans – with each union adopting one for use in its workhouse. The dietaries were plain and repetitive. They varied in their inclusion of foods such as potatoes, rice, porridge and suet-pudding, but all included a substantial proportion of bread and cheese. Cooked meat was generally served twice a week.

Dietary for able bodied Men and Women.

		Breakfast.		Dinner.					Supper.*		
		Bread.	Gruel.	Bread.	Cooked Meat.	Potatoes.	Soup.	Suet or rice Pudding.	Bread.	Cheese.	Gruel or Broth.
		oz.	Pints.	oz.	oz.	lb.	Pints.	oz.	oz.	oz.	Pints.
SUNDAY	Men	6	1½	4	5	½	–	–	6	–	1½
	Women	5	1½	3	5	½	–	–	5	–	1½
MONDAY	Men	6	1½	4	–	–	1½	–	6	1	–
	Women	5	1½	3	–	–	1½	–	5	1	–
TUESDAY	Men	6	1½	4	–	–	1½	–	6	–	1½
	Women	5	1½	3	–	–	1½	–	5	–	1½
WEDNESDAY	Men	6	1½	4	–	–	1½	–	6	1	–
	Women	5	1½	3	–	–	1½	–	5	1	–
THURSDAY	Men	6	1½	4	5	½	–	–	6	–	1½
	Women	5	1½	3	5	½	–	–	5	–	1½
FRIDAY	Men	6	1½	–	–	–	–	14	6	–	1½
	Women	5	1½	–	–	–	–	12	5	–	1½
SATURDAY	Men	6	1½	4	–	–	1½	–	6	1	–
	Women	5	1½	3	–	–	1½	–	5	1	–

OLD PEOPLE, of 60 years of age, and upwards may be allowed 1oz. of Tea, 5oz. of Butter, and 7oz. of Sugar per week, in lieu of Gruel for Breakfast, if deemed expedient to make this change.
CHILDREN, under 9 years of age, to be dieted at discretion, above 9 to be allowed the same quantities as Women.
SICK to be dieted as directed by the Medical Officer.
*SUPPER—The Gruel or Broth may be substituted for the Cheese, and vice versa.

H. BRADFORD, PRINTER, THAME.

The weekly menu for able-bodied inmates adopted by the Thame Union in Oxfordshire in 1836, based on the Poor Law Commissioners' suggested 'No. 1 Dietary'.

The quality of workhouse food was often poor. Charles Shaw, once an inmate of the Wolstanton and Burslem workhouse at Chell in Staffordshire, recalls his reaction to the 'skilly' (gruel) served there:

> I had heard of workhouse skilly but had never before seen it. I had had poor food before this, but never any so offensively poor as this. By what rare culinary-making nausea and bottomless fatuousness it could be made so sickening I never could make out. Simple meal and water, however small the amount of meal, honestly boiled, would be palatable. But this decoction of meal and water and mustiness and fustiness was most revolting to any healthy taste. It might have been boiled in old clothes, which had been worn upon sweating bodies for three-score years and ten. That workhouse skilly was the vilest compound I ever tasted, unutterably insipid, and it might never have been made in a country where either sugar or salt was known.[170]

The gruel served as the Poplar workhouse in the 1890s was even worse, as Will Crooks later recalled:

> The staple diet when I joined the Board was skilly. I have seen the old people, when this stuff was put before them, picking out black specks from the oatmeal. These were caused by rats, which had the undisturbed run of the oatmeal bin. No attempt was made to cleanse the oatmeal before it was prepared for the old people.[171]

Although some workhouses grew vegetables, raised pigs, or baked their own bread, food was mostly bought in from local suppliers with price rather than quality being the primary consideration. Workhouse food supplies were also an easy target for the widespread practice of adulteration. Milk could be watered down and flour or chalk then added to restore its bulk, bread could be made from an inferior grade of flour or have chalk or alum added, and oatmeal could be substituted by cheaper but less nutritious barley meal. Not only were paupers given second-rate food to begin with, but adulteration could reduce its quality even further. Following the 1872 Adulteration of Food, Drink and Drugs Act and the 1875 Sale of Food and Drugs Act, the inclusion of ingredients to add bulk or weight to a food product had to be declared to the customer and any adulteration injurious to health became punishable by a heavy fine.

Dietary Improvements

Unions were allowed to request changes to the dietary they used but for many years this was a lengthy administrative process. Some improvements in the dietary came about in the 1860s, largely as a result of the work of the Poor Law Board's medical officer, Dr Edward Smith. In 1866, Smith surveyed sixty-five workhouses in the north of England and found wide variations in the dietaries in use. Even where the same dishes were being served, they often varied widely in their preparation. The amount of oatmeal used in a pint of gruel, for example, ranged from a miserly ¾oz of oatmeal per pint at Easingwold to a glutinous 4oz at Scarborough.

As a result of his investigations, Smith proposed numerous improvements to the diets provided in workhouses and devised a set of new 'proper' dietaries with recommendations as to the composition and cooking of food, as well as such matters as its distribution and serving. He also made the radical proposal that a knife, fork and spoon should be supplied to each inmate. Applying his medical mind to the culinary art, his recommendations for cooks included a mine of practical advice such as:

- For making soup, meat should be cooked slowly from the outset to extract the juices; otherwise it should first be plunged into boiling water to seal the juices in.

- Potatoes should sometimes be boiled and sometimes roasted. Roasted potatoes lose more in weight than boiled, but the loss is of water so that a given weight of roast potatoes is more nutritious.
- Peas should be cooked until quite soft but not so much that they entirely break down.
- Milk should not be boiled but simply made hot.

Smith's dietary proposals were not imposed upon Boards of Guardians but provided for their information and advice. However, unions were now required to submit recipes to the central authority when requesting dietary changes.

In the last part of the nineteenth century, workhouse food slowly improved. This was partly brought about by a decline in the price of imported American grain in the 1870s which brought down the price of bread, allowing larger portions to be provided at the same cost. A number of other basic foodstuffs either held their price or became cheaper during this period, for example there was an increase in the availability of products such as cheap tinned meat from Australia. In 1883, more than 100 unions took part in a trial to provide inmates with once-a-week fish dinners. Although generally successful, both in broadening the diet and also in saving money, some unions gave up the experiment because of the difficulty they experienced in cooking fish in large quantities.

The 1900 Dietary Revolution

By the end of the nineteenth century, the Local Government Board acknowledged that the existing workhouse dietary system was unsatisfactory. The system of fixed portions, where each inmate received an exact amount of each particular item whether they wanted it or not, was leading to considerable wastage, especially of bread. The elderly and infirm inmates who made up an increasing proportion of the workhouse population often were literally unable to eat their way through the equivalent of a modern large loaf each day. Children, too, often had widely varying appetites. It was also becoming accepted that better food would be good for the health and morale of inmates.

In 1897, a committee was appointed to review dietary matters and concluded that the Board should frame, with medical advice, 'a sufficient number of diets to meet the varying tastes of different localities, and to limit the choice of the guardians to the dietaries so framed.' In 1900, the Workhouse Regulation (Dietaries and Accounts) Order transformed the framework of workhouse dietaries established in the 1830s. The Order designated three basic forms of diet – Plain (for healthy able-bodied adults), Infirm (for infirm but otherwise healthy adults), and Children's (for those aged from three to fifteen).

The weekly pattern of meals provided in each diet was selected by each union from a list of approved 'rations'. For each weekday breakfast or supper, the Plain diet offered eleven different combinations and amounts of bread, milk, cheese, porridge and gruel. On Sunday, a choice

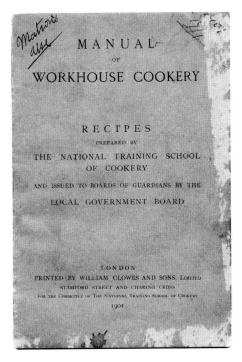

The 1901 *Manual of Workhouse Cookery*, compiled by the National Training School of Cookery, was intended to ensure that all the inmates' food was prepared in the same way at every workhouse.

of six breakfast/supper rations was available comprising bread plus either butter or margarine, and tea, coffee or cocoa. A typical Plain diet dinner was boiled beef served with bread, dumplings, and potatoes or vegetables. The Infirm diet could included such comforts as butter, margarine, jam, marmalade, treacle, plain cake, seed cake, tea, coffee or cocoa. The breakfast/supper rations available in the Children's diet broadly followed the Infirm diet but with the occasional inclusion of cold boiled bacon, an egg, or bread and dripping. The various dinner options included savoury mince, bread and potatoes or vegetables, followed by roley-poley pudding, rice or semolina. In the spring and summer months, the basic dietary could be supplemented by seasonal additions of stewed rhubarb, or other stewed fruit, onions, watercress and lettuce. With the exception of boiled or roast beef meals, no two dinners should be repeated in the same week.

Further new regulations required that sufficient water was to be supplied at dinner with a separate mug for each person, and that salt was to be provided at all meals for all classes. Pepper, vinegar and mustard, however, were to be provided at the guardians' discretion.

To reduce wastage, each inmate was now initially served only a proportion of their bread allowance but could ask for more to make up their full allowance if they so wished. Children's portions were no longer required to be weighed out; instead, each child was served 'according to appetite'. Unserved children's food could be re-used at a future meal on the same or the following day.

To assist unions in their adoption of the new system of dietaries, the Local Government Board commissioned a new thirty-two-page cookery book, *The Manual of Workhouse Cookery*, which was published in 1901. It contained recipes for all the dishes which were contained in the 1900 Order's schedule of rations. The distribution of the new cookery book to workhouse kitchens also aimed to ensure that all the dishes were prepared in a way that was simple, economical and standard.

(*See also*: **Alcohol**; **Dietary Class**; **Gardens and Farms**; **Tea**; Higginbotham (2008))

FOUL WARD

(*See*: **Venereal Disease**)

FUMIGATION

(*See*: **Disinfection**)

FUNERALS

(*See*: **Death**)

GAMBLING

After 1834, one of the activities most strictly forbidden in union workhouses was that of gambling, with items such as dice and playing cards explicitly barred. New workhouse regulations introduced in 1913 gave Boards of Guardians much greater discretion in such matters. The following year, after some discussion, the guardians at Liverpool decided that possession of playing cards would now be permitted.

(*See also*: **Entertainment**)

GARDENS AND FARMS

The cultivation of ground and the rearing of livestock was frequently a feature of workhouse operation. Garden produce could provide the workhouse with a cheap and ready source of food, while any surplus could be sold off and generate funds for the running of the house. Another benefit of a garden was that it offered a convenient and regular form of employment for the inmates of the workhouse. Finally, training pauper children in agricultural or horticultural work could equip them with skills that would make them employable in their later life, rather than being a drain on the poor rates.

Relatively little is known about early workhouse gardens. In 1724, the St Paul's parish workhouse in Bedford was noted as having 'a little Garden for Herbs, Onions, &c.' At the Solihull parish workhouse, opened in 1742, the male inmates kept pigs and grew turnips, cabbages, potatoes, peas and beans. In 1797, residents of the workhouse at Tiverton were 'regularly supplied with vegetables from a large garden adjoining'. At the same date, the Preston workhouse had 20 acres of the local common enclosed for its use 'for keeping cows, horses, and pigs; raising potatoes, &c.' Preston's workhouse inmates were employed in 'husbandry, gardening, and other occupations'. The overseers' accounts for the parish of Cogges in Oxfordshire in 1802–04 record payments for seeds and plants for the workhouse garden while at Abingdon the workhouse accounts for 1833 list the purchase of '1000 plants' at a cost of 3s.

The new union workhouses erected after the passing of the 1834 Poor Law Amendment Act were often located on large green-field sites where productive gardens could readily be established. In May 1849, the Abingdon workhouse master Richard Ellis – clearly a gardening enthusiast – reported to the Poor Law Commissioners on the matter of 'Profitable Employment of Paupers on Workhouse Land'. Ten acres of land at the rear of the workhouse had been turned over to growing vegetables – swedes, mangold wurzels, parsnips, carrots, potatoes, peas and barley. As well as supplying vegetables for the use of the inmates, the sum of £100 had also been credited to union funds. In the wake of the Irish famine, potatoes had been particularly successful, fetching an average price of 11s 3d per sack. Ellis also revealed that being allowed to work in the garden was seen as a perk for the well-behaved inmates and, in the case of elderly men, could benefit their health.[172]

During the 1840s, many workhouses introduced various forms of industrial training for the children in their care, with agricultural work being popular in rural areas. From 1846, the government's Committee of Council on Education (CCE) began inspecting workhouse schools and their reports indicate that much of the cultivation of workhouse gardens, fields and farms was being undertaken by the older boys. The CCE's returns of 'Farming Accounts' from different workhouses indicate the type and quantity of the produce being grown. The 1853 return for Wakefield recorded that 3 acres of land were being cultivated, with a further 2 'lying waste'. The wide range of crops being grown at Wakefield included cauliflower, cabbages, potatoes, turnips, swede, parsnips, leeks, onions, celery, radishes, lettuces, parsley and other herbs. Some of these were used in the workhouse while others were sold off.[173] In the same year, farming operations at the Wisbech workhouse made a profit for the year of over £80 and employed around forty boys in raising pigs and in growing vegetables such as potatoes, parsnips, peas, carrots, turnips, and onions.

Some workhouses kept cows which could provide milk and butter for the workhouse. The most popular livestock kept by workhouses, though, were pigs, which were fattened up with food waste from the workhouse kitchens and generally then sold off. Unlike vegetables, pigs were often not kept for the workhouse's own use since a whole pig included a large proportion of prime cuts which were not considered suitable fare for paupers. The bacon occasionally served up to workhouse inmates consisted of just the cheapest meat, which might be bought in from outside. Here, again, is, Richard Ellis, unravelling the economics of pig-rearing:

> By keeping, upon an average, twelve large pigs, which we purchase in a very poor condition, (spayed sows being preferred,) we can use all our spare offal from the garden, and this descrip-

The Holborn Union's workhouse farm at Mitcham in 1896. As well as the piggery, the site also had its own gasworks which supplied the workhouse.

tion of pigs will eat it, and get half fat upon it. We obtain a large quantity of manure from them, and, with a small purchase of stable dung, are enabled to manure the ground sufficiently. The liquid obtained from the washhouses, privies, &c., is all conveyed into close cesspools in the garden, from which it is pumped, and conveyed between the rows of the crops, particularly mangold wurtzel, by which means this plant attains a weight of from 20 to 25lbs. each, and sells at 20s. per ton. In winter the liquid manure is pumped up and distributed over such parts of the ground as are dug in, and the ground is trenched and prepared for spring crops. A gravel pit is kept always open for the employment of those who are not otherwise employed the gravel sold to surveyors and others produces more than sufficient to purchase manure and straw for the piggery.

Where the workhouse site had insufficient space for turning over to agricultural use, the guardians might be able to buy or rent additional land nearby. In 1856, the Tonbridge Union purchased an additional 12 acres for this purpose. In some cases, such as the Mitford and Launditch Union at Gressenhall, and the Holborn Union at Mitcham, a separate workhouse farm was established where inmates provided the bulk of the labour. The Mitcham farm was unusual in also having its own gas-works which supplied the workhouse. The largest of these agricultural enterprises was probably the Doe Royd dairy farm set up in around 1898 by the Sheffield Board of Guardians. Produce from the farm was used to supply the Sheffield workhouse and union infirmary. However, a veto by the land's owner, the Duke of Norfolk, meant that pauper labour was not used on the farm.

Flowers did not usually feature in workhouse gardens, at least the ones to which access was allowed by the inmates. An interesting exception was recorded, somewhat disparagingly, by the Poor Law Board in 1870 when they noted that an unnamed Lancashire workhouse, possibly Chorlton, had erected a greenhouse to supply the infirmary with blooms.[174] In 1895, the *British Medical Journal* (BMJ) visited a number of workhouses across the country. At Hatfield, the BMJ correspondent complained that:

> The airing courts are dreary prison-like yards, asphalted, the garden, with its wealth of flowers, being behind the house out of sight. We are at a loss for the reason why the sick poor are so carefully excluded from the use of the gardens; it would surely relieve the monotony of their lives to be allowed to walk among the flower beds.

Only very occasionally, the BMJ discovered, did English workhouses brighten their grounds with flowers. One of the rare instances was Truro, where the men's airing courts had grass and flowers. Irish workhouses, the journal reported, could be rather more generous in this matter. At the North Dublin workhouse, the master had turned a waste piece of ground into a pleasant garden for the elderly, with trees, shrubs, flowers, grass and comfortable benches. The South Dublin workhouse, too, housed its old women in small huts around three sides of a garden where there were seats, flowers and grass.

By the 1920s, however, some English workhouses were clearly gardening in a more domestic style. Workhouse plans of the period often feature kitchen gardens, glasshouses, cold-frames and garden shelters.

Workhouse garden restoration projects have been carried out at workhouse museums such as Southwell and Ripon. The Vestry House museum at Walthamstow also has a small garden containing plants known to have been grown by workhouse inmates in the eighteenth century.

GAS

At the start of the Victorian period, most domestic lighting was in the form of candles and oil lamps. This began to change from the 1830s onwards, when gas production and distribution companies were formed in many towns. In workhouses, as in other buildings, the use of gas – initially for lighting then later for cooking and electricity generation – became popular. In some workhouses, gas still provided the only form of lighting in 1930 when the Boards of Guardians were abolished.

One early adopter of gas lighting was the Abingdon Union workhouse in Berkshire, where in October 1835 the guardians agreed that 'the Workhouse be forthwith lighted with Gas'.[175]

Large institutions, especially those lying away from towns, sometimes manufactured their own gas. Such schemes were employed at the Central London District School at Hanwell, where gas was made in a detached gas house, and at the Mitcham workhouse, where operating the gas-works – located on the nearby union farm – also provided work for the inmates.

As today, escaping gas was a potential hazard. In December 1907, the workhouse at Knighton in Radnorshire was the scene of a gas explosion which destroyed part of the building. (*See also:* **Electricity**)

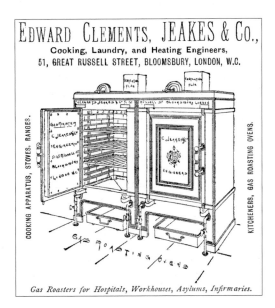

EDWARD CLEMENTS, JEAKES & Co.,
Cooking, Laundry, and Heating Engineers,
51, GREAT RUSSELL STREET, BLOOMSBURY, LONDON, W.C.

Gas Roasters for Hospitals, Workhouses, Asylums, Infirmaries.

An 1870 advertisement for a 'gas roaster' manufactured by Edward Clements, Jeakes & Co. and supplied to institutions such as workhouses, hospitals and asylums.

GENERAL ORDER

A directive from the Poor Law Commissioners applying to all Poor Law Unions and parishes and requiring parliamentary approval.
(*See also*: **Special Order**; **Poor Law Commissioners**)

GHOSTS

The misery, cruelty and death that are sometimes associated with workhouses have, perhaps not surprisingly, sometimes led to suggestions that some former workhouse buildings still harbour the ghosts of those who once lived there. Some, such as that at Stockport, have even been the subject of ghost-hunting TV programmes.

Typical ghostly happenings include strange noises or smells, the sounds of voices, and apparitions of former residents or staff. Such events may be reported either inside the workhouse itself or close nearby. At Tewkesbury, for example, residents of properties built on the site of the former workhouse graveyard have reported hearing the sounds of crying children.

Some of the best-known haunted workhouse sites are in Ireland. At the Londonderry Union, a particularly strict matron at the workhouse was said to have fretted herself to death after accidently starving three small boys to death in a punishment cupboard. As punishment for some misdemeanour, the children had been locked up for a few hours in the cupboard which was located in a remote part of the building. Just after placing them there, the matron received news that a relative was ill and went to visit them for a few days, taking the keys of the cupboard with her. On her return she rushed to the black hole, but the children had perished. It is said that the children are to be heard running up and down the top corridor, while the matron haunts the grounds, wringing her hands. Another child ghost is supposed to tug or push at visitors to the building. After the site became a hospital, night nurses often saw a female ghost. One nurse, who herself underwent an operation, awoke to find a woman dressed in white, placing an extra blanket on the bed, before disappearing through the wall of the room.

Also in Ireland, at the former Limavady workhouse, later used as a hospital, the sound of crying babies has been heard in the area around the former maternity ward. Sightings were also reported of a nurse in an old-fashioned cape with a red hood sitting on the bridge at the front of the hospital. Hospital nurses are said to have regularly heard at 3a.m. what sounded like a nurse with a wooden leg.

GILBERT UNION

A group of parishes jointly administering poor relief under the provisions of Gilbert's Act of 1782. A Gilbert Union could operate a common workhouse for the elderly, the sick and infirm, and orphan children. The able-bodied, however, were not to be admitted but instead found employment near their own homes. Management of a Gilbert Union was through a Board of Guardians whose members were elected by the ratepayers in each of the Union's member parishes. A visitor was also appointed by Justices to oversee operation of the Union.

Joining a Gilbert Union required a parish to obtain the agreement of two-thirds of its ratepayers and the consent of two Justices of the Peace. Membership of a Union was limited to parishes lying within ten miles of the Union's workhouse.

Around eighty Gilbert Unions were eventually formed, together with a few Gilbert Parishes who had individually adopted Gilbert's Act. The membership of many of the Unions fluctuated over the years as parishes joined or withdrew.

The 1834 Poor Law Amendment Act allowed existing Gilbert Unions to remain in operation. This came to be a matter of much regret for the central poor law authorities whose introduction of new Poor Law Unions in areas such as the West Riding of Yorkshire was severely hampered as a result. A few Gilbert Unions were subsequently persuaded to dissolve themselves, or were forced to do so through legal technicalities regarding their operation. All remaining Gilbert Unions were finally abolished in 1869 with their member parishes being distributed amongst adjacent Poor Law Unions.

A list of Gilbert Unions (and Gilbert Parishes, marked *) is included below:

Berkshire:	Wallingford
Cumberland:	Whitehaven
Derbyshire:	Brassington, Rosliston, Shardlow
Durham:	Darlington
Essex:	Ongar
Hampshire:	Aldershot & Bentley*, Alverstoke & Gosport, Farnborough, Headley, Winchester
Kent:	Archishop's Palace, Bearsted, Birchington, Eastry, Elham, Faversham, Harbledown, Martin, Petham, St Mary Cray & Orpington, River, Selling, Teynham & Linstead, Tudeley & Capel, Whitstable
Lancashire:	Caton
Leicestershire:	Appleby, Ashby-de-la-Zouch, Barrow-on-Soar, Glenn Magna, Lutterworth, Melton Mowbray, Ratby, Sapcote, Stathern, Stretton, Ullesthorpe
Lincolnshire:	Caistor, Claypole, Winterton
Norfolk:	Acle, Aldborough, Bawdeswell, Booton, Brinton & Melton Constable, Gimingham, Hackford, Oulton, Reepham-cum-Kerdiston, St Faith's, Taverham
Nottinghamshire:	Arnold & Basford, Thurgarton & Upton, Ruddington, Bingham
Staffordshire:	Alstonefield, Tutbury
Surrey:	Ash, Farnham*, Hambledon, Reigate
Sussex:	Arundel*, Easebourne, Eastbourne, East Preston, Glynde, Sutton, Thakeham, Westhampnett, Yapton
Warwickshire:	Bedworth, Exhall, Meriden, Rugby
Westmorland:	Eamont Bridge, Kirkby Lonsdale, Kirkby Stephen, Milnthorpe
Wiltshire:	Mere
Yorkshire:	Bainbridge, Barwick, Bolton-by-Bowland, Carlton, Giggleswick, Great Ouseburn, Lawkland, Leyburn, Lockington, Paghill or Paul, Great Preston, Saddleworth*

GILBERT'S ACT

(*See*: **Gilbert Union**; **Poor Laws**)

GIRLS' FRIENDLY SOCIETY

(*See*: **Aftercare**)

GOSCHEN MINUTE

The memorandum was issued in November 1869 by the president of the Poor Law Board, George Goschen, who was concerned at the rising expenditure on out relief in London.[176] Goschen expressed particular concern that the roles of the poor relief system and of charitable

Porridge (Sturrow.　Sican-Gwyn).

Ingredients.

4 ozs. Oatmeal
Water and Salt, a sufficiency } To make 1 pint.

Method.—Add the oatmeal gradually to the boiling water with the salt; stir till it is thick and smooth enough, and boil for twenty minutes, or until cooked.

Gruel.

Ingredients.

2 ozs. Oatmeal
½ oz. Treacle
Water and Salt, a sufficiency } To make 1 pint.

Allspice to be used occasionally.

Method.—As for porridge.

The difference between porridge and gruel is made clear by these official recipes from the 1901 *Manual of Workhouse Cookery.*

organisations should be clearly defined and coordinated so as to prevent inefficiency, duplication or abuse in the use of either's resources. The publication of Goschen's 'minute' marked the beginning of a period of the stricter administration of out relief which was to be given only to the totally destitute, with those in lesser need, such as those receiving inadequate wages, seeking assistance from charitable sources. Goschen's initiative came in the same year as the formation of the Charity Organisation Society which aimed to co-ordinate and support the activities of private charities and to encourage self-help amongst those receiving charity.
(*See also*: **Charity Organisation Society**)

GRUBBER

One of the slang names for the workhouse, along with Spike, Bastille etc. perhaps derived from 'grub' (a colloquial word for food) or from a term used to describe a person who works hard, especially in a dull, plodding way.
(*See also*: **Spike**)

GRUEL

A thin oatmeal porridge.
(*See also*: **Food**)

GUARDIANS / GUARDIANS OF THE POOR

A committee elected or appointed to administer poor relief in a particular area. The term dates back to at least 1696 when the City of Bristol Incorporation was formed for this purpose, with four guardians being elected from each of twelve wards in the city. Under Gilbert's Act of 1782, guardians were 'nominated' by a public meeting of ratepayers and then formally appointed by local magistrates.

After 1834, the local management committee for a Poor Law Union was its Board of Guardians. Guardians were elected at the start of April each year by the ratepayers in each member parish in the union, with candidates themselves being required to occupy property of a certain value. In addition, local magistrates could be *ex officio* guardians by virtue of their office, with the same powers and duties as those of elected guardians.

Boards of Guardians varied considerably in size. One of the smallest was at the Gravesend and Milton in Kent with a total of just eight guardians representing the union's two constituent parishes, while the Board at Great Boughton in Cheshire comprised 103 guardians from 101 parishes.

The Board met at a fixed time either weekly or fortnightly, usually in a boardroom at the workhouse. The quorum for business to be conducted was three. The usual order of business at each meeting was:

1. Minutes of last meeting
2. Business arising therefrom
3. Continuance of relief, and the applications of relief made since the last meeting.
4. New applications for relief
5. Reports upon the state of the workhouse, and all books and accounts
6. The treasurer's account
7. Any other business

The guardians were responsible for the financial management of the union and could be personally liable to repay the cost of any expenditure that was subsequently deemed by the authorities to have been inappropriate. In a few extreme cases of financial irregularity or mismanagement, such as the over-liberal payment of out relief, Boards were suspended by the central authorities with the union administration temporarily being carried out by centrally appointed officials. This fate befell thirty-eight overstretched unions in Ireland during the great famine in 1846–47 when 'vice-guardians' were installed, and again after the General Strike of 1926 when the Boards of Guardians at West Ham, Chester-le-Street and Bedwellty were 'superseded' under the provisions of the Board of Guardians (Default) Act.

The latter part of the nineteenth century saw the beginnings of a change in the composition of Boards. Although suitably qualified women had never been barred, it was not until

The Hull Board of Guardians with their chairman wearing his chain of office at the centre of the front row. Although this view dates from 1912, there is still a notable absence of women from the Board.

1875 in Kensington that the first female guardian, Martha Crauford Merington, was elected. By 1895, the number of female guardians in office had risen to 839.[177] A lowering of the rating qualification from £40 to £5 in 1892 was soon followed by the election of many working-class guardians, such as Will Crooks and George Lansbury at Poplar.

Prior to 1893, guardians had no automatic right of admission to their union's workhouse. In January of that year, the Local Government Board issued an order allowing guardians entry to their workhouse at any reasonable hour. Credit for this change was claimed by Crooks and Lansbury who had raised complaints after being denied access to the Poplar workhouse.

The Local Government Act of 1894 introduced further significant changes. Guardians were now elected for three years rather than one year.[178] *Ex officio* guardians were abolished although Boards could co-opt up to four suitably qualified additional members. Plural voting and rating qualifications were also done away with.

Boards of Guardians in England and Wales were abolished on 1 May 1930, when responsibility for poor relief, or public assistance as it then became known, was taken over by county and borough councils. Even then, guardians did not totally disappear – the new local authority body administering public assistance was often called the Guardians Committee.

(*See also*: **Jewish Board of Guardians**; **Poor Laws**; **Poor Law Unions**)

HANWAY'S ACT

Jonas Hanway's Act of 1766 required that all pauper children under six from metropolitan parishes were required to reside at least three miles from the capital until they attained the age of six. The nursing and maintenance of each child was to cost at least 2s 6d per week.

To satisfy these requirements, parishes sent their children to a variety of out-of-town establishments, sometimes known as 'infant poorhouses' or 'baby farms', many of which were privately run. In its reply to the 1832 Royal Commission, the parish of St Luke reported that its infant paupers were put out to nurse at Southgate where an average of fifty children were under the care of three nurses. Similarly, St James, Westminster, put its infant poor out to nurse at Wimbledon.

A view from Barnet Hill of a row of cottages (right) which formerly housed the 'infant workhouse' operated by the London parish of St Andrew's, Holborn.

Shoreditch had its own establishment at Baker Street in Enfield, with a resident master, matron and 'suitable assistants'. St George's, Southwark, had an infant poorhouse which stood opposite to Lewisham's workhouse, while that used by Islington was at Fords Green, Lower Edmonton. Other establishments were located at Hendon (used by St Clement Danes), Merton (St Mary Magdalen, Bermondsey), Heston (St Giles in the Fields & St George, Bloomsbury) and Barnet (St Andrew Holborn and St George the Martyr). One of the largest such institutions was Mr Aubin's school at Norwood which served a number of London's parishes.

Hanway's Act was repealed in 1844 although some of the existing children's establishments continued in operation for a number of years. The 1855 Post Office Directory recorded the St George's infant poorhouse as still housing 175 inmates.

(*See also*: **Aubin's School**; **Children**; **London**)

HAIR

Although children in a union workhouse could be compelled to have their hair cut, the same was not true for adults unless required for medical reasons. At large workhouses, a barber could be employed on a contract basis or even taken on as a full-time employee to cut the hair of inmates who desired it. At Abingdon workhouse in 1836, John Abel was appointed as workhouse barber and required 'to attend at the Workhouse, and cut the Children's hair at least once a month, to shave the male paupers once a week, and attend at all times when required by the Master for shaving and hair-cutting, and to receive for his services nine guineas per year.[179]

HEADQUARTERS HOME

(*See*: **Scattered Homes**)

HEATING

The most common form of heating in workhouse rooms was an open fire, burning wood or coal. In many cases, particularly in smaller rural workhouses, this was still the only form of heating in use when the Boards of Guardians were abolished in 1930. Apart from directly warming a room, open fires could also be used to heat water via a back boiler which was then circulated through pipes around the room or building.

Central heating systems, with pipes or radiators linked to a central boiler, were often fitted in larger workhouses and in new buildings such as the City of London workhouse on Bow Road, erected in 1848–49. By the end of the nineteenth century, new workhouse buildings frequently had large engine houses where steam was produced to heat the buildings, heat hot water, pump water from wells, and power electric dynamos. At the new Hunslet Union workhouse, opened in 1903:

> The heating and hot water supply is on the low pressure principle, steam being supplied to heat water in generators, two of which are placed under each block, one for heating and one for hot water supply. From these generators the water is circulated throughout the building both for warming and all domestic purposes, including baths and lavatories.[180]

In the 'Nightingale' infirmary wards adopted from the 1860s onwards, a fireplace or stove was often located at the centre of the room, sometimes with fresh air inlet flues routed past it so as to warm the incoming air.

(*See also*: **Gas**; **Electricity**)

HOME CHILDREN

(*See*: **Emigration**)

HOSPITAL

An establishment dating back to the Middle Ages, originally offering a wide range of care, not only medical but also non-medical provision such as shelter and food for the destitute, the education of children, and sanctuary for those incapacitated by old age or chronic infirmity. (*See also*: **Infirmary**)

HOUSE COMMITTEE

In Scotland, the House Committee was a committee of the Parochial Board with responsibilities for overseeing the operation of the parish's poorhouse, where it had such an establishment.

In England and Wales, the House Committee was introduced by the 1913 Poor Law Institutions Order as replacement for the Visiting Committee. (*See also*: **Poor Law Institutions Order; Visiting Committee**)

HOUSE OF CORRECTION

An early form of disciplinary institution dating back to the sixteenth century and a fore-runner of the prison. The 1576 Poor Act required a House of Correction to be established in each county to deal with the able-bodied poor who refused to work. Houses of Correction were often known as 'bridewells' after London's Bridewell, an institution set up for a similar purpose in 1553. (*See also*: **Bridewell**)

HOUSE OF INDUSTRY

The name commonly used for a workhouse established by a Local Act Incorporation in the eighteenth century. (*See also*: **Incorporation; Poorhouse; Workhouse**)

HOUSELESS POOR

(*See*: **Casual Poor**)

HUMOUR

The workhouse may seem an unlikely subject for humour. However, by the end of the nineteenth century when it had become an ingrained part of national life, an occasional comic take on the institution did surface.

A good example of this changing attitude can be seen in the pages of the humorous magazine *Punch*. During the 1840s, the publication usually presented the New Poor Law as a heartless, inhumane and tyrannical system. Fifty years later, however, there was more likely to be a gentle mockery of the poor law authorities or of 'Bumbledom' – pompous officialdom.

Inquisitive Guardian. "BY THE WAY, HAVE YOU ANY CHILDREN?"
Applicant for Relief. "NO."
Guardian. "BUT—ER—SURELY I KNOW A SON OF YOURS?"
Applicant. "WELL, I DON'T SUPPOSE YOU'D CALL A CHILD CHILDREN!"

Above left An 1899 Punch cartoon reveals a much-changed attitude to the once terrifying guardians' interview – the applicant is now shown trying to

Above right A 1906 postcard shows a 'casual' in the regulation workhouse bath – a regular subject for humour. 'The Beauty of Bath' was a popular musical comedy of the period.

Even the usually dolorous genre of workhouse poetry could manage a laconic take on its subject. Thomas Hardy's *The Curate's Kindness: A Workhouse Irony* describes how a long-married man is looking forward to finding peace and rest in the workhouse, where the usual arrangement is for husbands and wives to be separated:

> Life there will be better than t'other,
> For peace is assured.
> *The men in one wing and their wives in another*
> Is strictly the rule of the Board.

News that the local curate has successfully petitioned the guardians for the couple to stay together is not well received by the poem's narrator:

> I thought they'd be strangers aroun' me,
> But she's to be there!
> Let me jump out o' waggon and go back and drown me
> At Pummery or Ten-Hatches Weir.[181]

A writer with particular bent for seeing the humorous side of workhouse life was Herbert Preston-Thomas, an inspector of poor law institutions for the Local Government Board:

> When I asked an apparently strong woman why she did not earn her own living instead of staying in the workhouse, she answered solemnly that she was most anxious to do so, but 'God Almighty would not allow it.' On my subsequently applying to the Master for an explanation, he answered, 'I

think, sir, she ought to have mentioned the Gentleman at the other Extremity, for she could keep herself very well, only she can never make any money without immediately getting drunk.'[182]

Preston-Thomas also beautifully recounts an old story concerning the perils of a poorly managed workhouse kitchen:

They had two coppers so set that their tops were separated only by a space of three inches. When I was there, they were boiling clothes in one and soup in the other; and there were no lids on them. When the soup boiled over into the clothes, I raised no objection, but when the clothes boiled over into the soup, I said I would not stay to dinner.[183]

(*See also*: **Biography**; **Broadside Ballads**; **Fiction**; **Poetry**)

HUNDRED

An administrative sub-division of a county, originally representing an area containing 100 families or able to raise 100 fighting men. In the eighteenth century, many rural poor law Incorporations, particularly in Norfolk and Suffolk, were associated with county Hundreds. (*See also*: **Incorporation**)

IDIOTS AND IMBECILES

(*See*: **Mentally Ill**; **Metropolitan Asylums Board**)

ILLEGITIMACY

The 1576 Poor Act[184] pronounced that 'Bastards begotten and born out of lawful Matrimony' were 'an Offence against God's Law and Man's Law', with their mother and putative father obliged to pay for their upkeep or else face prison. It was not just for reasons of morality that such births were censured. Many illegitimate children – and their mothers – ended up being maintained by the parish for a lengthy period and so could prove an expensive liability. Fathers, if they were willing, could discharge their responsibilities towards the upkeep of such offspring by a lump sum payment in the form of a Bastardy Bond. If that did not happen, a parish could apply for a maintenance or affiliation order to recoup the costs.

Settlement

For many years, the precise location where an illegitimate child was born was highly significant. Under the early laws of settlement, such children took their place of settlement from the parish of their birth – this became the parish that then had legal responsibility for them if they were ever in need of poor relief. To avoid the financial consequences of such events, it was not unknown for parishes on occasion to forcibly transport heavily pregnant single women over the parish boundary. This could sometimes have fatal results, as in the case of Mary Simpson, an unmarried woman from Cumberland, who in 1744 died in labour the day after being bundled on horseback from the parish workhouse at Dalton in Lancashire. An alternative strategy was for the parish to pay a man from outside the area parish to marry a pregnant unmarried women, since a child born in wedlock took the husband's settlement. The situation changed slightly after the passing of the 1744 Justices Commitment Act[185] when children born out of wedlock to mothers who were vagrants now took the mother's settlement. The principle of all illegitimate children taking their mother's settlement was established in the 1834 Poor Law Amendment Act.

The Bastardy Clause

One of the most controversial parts of the 1834 Act was the so-called 'Bastardy clause' which made the obtaining of affiliation orders much more difficult and expensive than had formerly been the case. Previously, such orders were obtained through local Petty Sessions courts but after 1834 had to be heard at county Quarter Sessions and could only be initiated by overseers or guardians. Evidence of paternity claims now also had to be 'corroborated in some material particular', something that was often impossible to achieve. The Act effectively made illegitimate children the sole responsibility of their mothers until they were sixteen years old. If mothers of such children were unable to support themselves and their offspring, they would have to enter the workhouse – a measure aimed at deterring women from risking extra-marital pregnancy. Perhaps unsurprisingly, it proved a highly unpopular and contentious measure and was diluted in 1839 when affiliation claims could again be heard by local magistrates at Petty Sessions.[186] The clause was effectively overturned by a further Act[187] in 1844 which enabled an unmarried mother to apply for an affiliation order against the father for maintenance of the mother and child, regardless of whether she was in receipt of poor relief.

Unmarried Mothers

Unmarried mothers in the workhouse were unpopular with the poor law authorities. Apart from any moral disapproval, they were expensive to maintain as the woman would need medical care during and after delivery, and might not be able to support herself and her child (and possibly other children) for some time to come.

In the parish workhouse, and in the early years of the union workhouse, unmarried mothers could be stigmatised, for example by being placed in segregated accommodation, or by being made to wear uniforms of a particular style or colour, usually yellow. At the St Peter's parish workhouse in Bristol in the early 1830s, single pregnant women were given a red dress and prostitutes a yellow dress; they are kept separate from the rest and not allowed to associate with the children. In 1839, the Poor Law Commissioners issued a minute entitled 'Ignominious Dress for Unchaste Women in Workhouses' in which they deprecated such practices. However, more subtle forms of identification sometimes continued. At Gressenhall workhouse in Norfolk, unmarried mothers were made to wear a 'jacket' of the same material used for other workhouse clothing. This practice, which led to them being referred to as 'jacket women', continued until 1866.[188] Unmarried mothers (or other categories of inmate of which the guardians disapproved) might also receive an especially unappetising diet. For example, at the Strand Union workhouse, single women in the lying-in ward were kept on a diet of gruel for nine days.[189]

The 1909 Report of the Royal Commission on the Poor Laws divided unmarried mothers into three categories: 'Single Lapse Cases' who it was proposed should be dealt with in charitable institutions or, if those were not available, in homes set up by poor law authorities; 'Depraved Immoral Women' – those with several illegitimate children – who should be detained and reformed; and 'Feeble-minded Women' who should be dealt with separately under mental deficiency provisions.

As envisaged by the 1909 report, hundreds of homes and hostels were established by charities and church groups to provide accommodation for what were variously termed 'fallen and friendless women', 'girls in need of help', 'girls and women in distress', and 'morally weak and incapable women'. In many cases, these homes would only deal with those pregnant for the first time, with the birth and subsequent lying-in period still taking place in a workhouse labour ward. From the 1920s, maternity facilities and accommodation for unmarried mothers also began to be provided by some local councils, particularly in larger towns.

Moral Imbeciles

The 1913 Mental Deficiency Act[190] introduced the concept of the 'moral imbeciles', legally defined as 'persons who from an early age display some permanent mental defect coupled with strong vicious or criminal propensities on which punishment has had little or no deterrent effect.' The nebulousness of this definition allowed unmarried mothers to be brought within its scope, especially 'repeaters' – those having more than one illegitimate child. Moral imbeciles (termed moral defectives from 1927) could 'be sent to or placed in an institution for defectives or placed under guardianship', something which continued until the Mental Health Act of 1959.

The Lasting Stigma

Throughout the 1920s, unmarried mothers continued to be stigmatised by the poor law authorities compared to other comparable categories of women applying for relief with dependent children. On 1 January 1922, in England and Wales, a total of 66,755 'husbandless women with dependent children' were in receipt of poor relief. Of the 5,155 unmarried mothers included, 62 per cent were relieved through the workhouse, with 38 per cent getting out relief; for the other groups (widows, deserted and separated wives) a mere 3 per cent were in the workhouse.[191] By 1932, two years after the administration of poor relief had passed to local councils, it was a similar picture. Now, 66 per cent of unmarried mothers were being relieved in institutions while for other categories of husbandless mothers the figure was 10 per cent.[192]

Keeping unmarried mothers in the workhouse (or Public Assistance Institution, as it became after 1930) maintained its role as a deterrent against moral failings. Since the number of able-bodied women in workhouses by the 1920s was generally very low, there was also a practical use for placing unmarried women there; their labour in the daily work in running the institution had considerable practical value.

(*See also*: **Settlement**)

IMBECILES

(*See*: **Mentally Ill**; **Metropolitan Asylums Board**)

IMPOTENT POOR

(*See*: **Deserving and Undeserving Poor**)

INCORPORATION

A group of parishes jointly administering poor relief, or other local matters, under a Local Act of Parliament, usually styled themselves as an Incorporation (or sometimes Corporation). The term was also adopted by some Gilbert Unions, for example Nottinghamshire's Thurgarton Hundred Incorporation formed in 1824.

Urban Incorporations

Although a Corporation of the Poor was established in London by an ordinance of 1647, the first Local Act Incorporation was formed at Bristol in 1696. Between then and 1834, more than thirty provincial towns formed urban poor relief Incorporations as listed below:

Date	Incorporation
1696	Bristol
1697	Exeter
1698	Colchester, Crediton, Hereford, Kingston-upon-Hull, London, Shaftesbury, Tiverton
1699	King's Lynn, Sudbury
1702	Gloucester

1703	Worcester
1707	Plymouth
1711	Norwich
1727	Canterbury
1747	Bury St Edmunds
1753	Chichester
1761	Chester
1770	Salisbury
1771	Oxford
1772	Southampton
1780	Maidstone
1781	Plymouth
1783	Birmingham
1784	Shrewsbury
1785	Richmond (Surrey)
1786	Romford, Barking
1787	Highworth
1790	Manchester
1791	Sunderland
1792	Stone, Tewkesbury, Whitchurch (Shropshire)
1794	Bedford
1801	Coventry
1810	Brighthelmstone (Brighton)

The Bristol Experiment

In Bristol's pioneering experiment, the city's nineteen parishes combined to form the Bristol Corporation (or Incorporation) of the Poor which operated a joint poor relief system across the city, including the setting-up of workhouses and appointment of paid officers. The scheme's instigator was John Cary who, in 1700, published an account of the Corporation's early years.[193] The Corporation was managed by a Board of Guardians, four from each of the city's twelve 'wards' plus the Mayor and Aldermen, making a total of sixty.

In 1698, a rented property, known as the New Workhouse, was opened to house 100 pauper girls. Staff included a master, a mistress, four tutresses to teach the girls to spin, and a schoolmistress to teach them to read. Servants were initially employed to perform cooking and washing but these were soon dispensed with and the work done by the older girls. On arrival, new inmates were stripped and washed by the matron and given new clothes. Their diet included 'Beef, Pease, Potatoes, Broth, Pease-porridge, Milk-porridge, Bread and Cheese, good Beer, Cabbage, Turnips etc.' The girls worked at spinning for up to ten and a half hours a day in summer. After their initial training, they were hired out to local manufacturers. However, the coarseness of the yarn they produced soon resulted in complaints and low payment rates.

The following year, the Corporation purchased a house previously occupied by the Treasury which became known as the Mint Workhouse. In August 1699, 100 boys were moved in and were occupied in spinning cotton wool and weaving fustians. They were also taught to read and (unlike the girls) to write. Next, elderly inmates were admitted, clothed and given work suited to their age and strength. Finally, young children were taken in and put in the care of nurses.

Despite Cary's rosy picture of the Bristol scheme, it was not without its critics. In 1711, an anonymous pamphlet claimed that the workhouse was 'crowded with idle, Lazy and Lewd People.' The economics of the venture were also questioned with the cost of running the workhouse amounting to almost half of the annual poor rate (then £2,376 16s 5d) for the benefit of 170 inmates.[194]

Bristol's experience was typical of what happened in other Corporations. There was initial enthusiasm and high hopes for the scheme's financial self-sufficiency. Initial funding of the workhouse – often termed a House of Industry – could be divided among a number of parishes. The able-bodied could be required to work, reducing the numbers of relief claimants, while special provision could be made for the elderly and for children. Formation of a Corporation solved many problems relating to settlement since the whole city was treated as a single area for poor relief purposes. However, it was frequently found that the income generated by workhouse inmates was far less than hoped. An initial but relatively short-lived financial benefit was typically followed by spiralling costs and general disillusionment.

Rural (Hundred) Incorporations

In the second half of the eighteenth century, Incorporations were formed in a number of rural districts, often based on historical county Hundreds. The majority of these rural or Hundred Incorporations were in East Anglia, with a few others in Shropshire and elsewhere as shown below:

Date	Incorporation	Workhouse Location
1756	Carlford & Colneis, Suffolk	Nacton
1763	Mutford & Lothingland, Suffolk	Oulton
1764	Blything, Suffolk	Bulcamp (Blythburgh)
1764	Bosmere & Claydon, Suffolk	Barham
1764	Samford, Suffolk	Tattingstone
1764	Wangford, Suffolk	Shipmeadow
1765	Loes & Wilford, Suffolk	Melton
1770	Isle of Wight, Hampshire	Isle of Wight
1775	East & West Flegg, Norfolk	Rollesby
1775	Mitford & Launditch, Norfolk	Gressenhall
1775	Forehoe, Norfolk	Wicklewood
1778	Stow, Suffolk	One-House
1779	Cosford & Polstead, Suffolk	Semer
1779	Hartismere, Hoxne & Thredling, Suffolk	(none built)
1785	Tunstead & Happing, Norfolk	Smallburgh
1791	Oswestry, Shropshire	Morda
1792	Atcham, Shropshire	Cross Houses
1792	Ellesmere, Shropshire	Haughton
1792	Montgomery & Pool, Montgomeryshire	Forden
1792	Whitchurch, Shropshire	Whitchurch
1806	Buxton, Norfolk	Buxton

The rural Incorporations were formed for many of the same reasons as the urban ones, uppermost being a lowering of the poor rate. Relief administration based on a larger geographical area was seen as particularly attractive in thinly populated rural areas where even running a parish workhouse had presented difficulties.

Typical of these schemes was the Blything Hundred Incorporation of forty-six parishes, formed in 1764. The following year, the Incorporation began to erect its House of Industry at Bulcamp near Blythburgh. The building cost about £12,000 including £500 for rebuilding a part pulled down by a riotous mob of objectors. In 1767, the workhouse had 352 inmates in residence. Inmates were employed in spinning hemp, carding and spinning wool, weaving linen and woollen cloth for the use of the house, knitting stockings, mending shoes, and cultivating the garden and land. In 1774, income from the paupers' labour amounted to £529. In the same year, the salaries of workhouse officers (governor, chaplain, surgeons, treasurer, clerk etc.) totalled £398.[195]

Sixty years later, the workhouse was visited by Assistant Poor Law Commissioner Charles Mott. He found that the sexes were not segregated in the workhouse; men and their wives

A 1930s view of the former Shrewsbury Incorporation workhouse. Following its closure in 1871, the building was bought by Shrewsbury School.

and families were admitted, and their children grew up there until being apprenticed by the Incorporation at the age of thirteen. After serving their apprenticeship, the sons married and returned with their wives to the workhouse, had children and so repeated the cycle. A number of 'strange customs' also existed at Bulcamp. A licensed shop selling alcohol, tobacco, tea etc. had been fitted up and allowed to be run by a female pauper in the workhouse, with the local excise officer visiting periodically to 'take stock'. The small farm surrounding the workhouse was used to rear cows from which the paupers were supplied with milk and best butter, with the guardians repeatedly said to declare that they could not get such butter at their own tables as the paupers were supplied with in the Bulcamp House of Industry.[196]

INDOOR RELIEF

Poor relief provided via residence in a workhouse, poorhouse or similar institution.
(*See also*: **Out relief**)

INDUSTRIAL SCHOOLS – CERTIFIED

Certified Industrial Schools were set up from the 1850s onwards to detain vagrant, destitute and disorderly children whom the courts considered in danger of becoming criminals.

The 1854 Youthful Offenders Act allowed convicted juvenile offenders under the age of sixteen to be placed by courts in a Reformatory School for up to five years after first undergoing a fourteen-day prison sentence.[197] After an unsuccessful campaign to remove the prison requirement, reformers promoted the Industrial School, a broadly similar establishment, but catering for a slightly younger age group and without the prison element. Initially, under the Industrial Schools Act of 1857, children aged seven to fifteen who were convicted of vagrancy could be placed in an Industrial School.[198]

The majority of Industrial Schools were privately run, often by religious groups, although a few, such as the Feltham Industrial School, were operated by public authorities. Boys at Feltham were taught trades such as carpentry, bricklaying, tailoring and shoemaking and worked on the School's own farm. There was also a 'ship' rigged out to allow the boys to perform naval exercises.

The Schools had to be officially inspected and certified before they could begin operation. By 1875, there were eighty-two Certified Industrial Schools operating in England and Wales, with a further twenty-seven in Scotland. Schools generally took either just boys or girls, and some were specifically for Roman Catholic children.

The use of Industrial Schools and Reformatory Schools declined after the First World War. In 1933, The Children and Young Persons Act replaced them both with a single type of establishment known as the Approved School, catering for all classes of neglected and delinquent children.[199]
(*See also*: **Industrial Schools – Poor Law**; **Reformatory / Reformatory School**; **Training Ships**; **Truant Schools**)

INDUSTRIAL SCHOOLS – POOR LAW

The term Industrial School was used from the 1840s to refer to establishments operated by poor law authorities, separate from the workhouse, where pauper children were housed, educated and provided with industrial training. Early examples of such institutions included the Manchester Union's Industrial School at Swinton, and the Leeds Guardians' Moral and Industrial Training School. After 1856, however, the term was also adopted by a new and some-what different type of institution – the Certified Industrial School – used to detain young people placed there by magistrates' courts. The two types of institution are easily confused although the precise name of a particular establishment may help: the custodial variety was more properly known as a *Certified* Industrial School while a poor law establishment was likely to be formally titled as a *Union* Industrial School.
(*See also*: **District and Separate Schools**; **Industrial Schools – Certified**; **Industrial Training**)

INDUSTRIAL TRAINING

The training in practical skills given to inmates, usually children, in institutions such as work-house schools, Industrial Schools, Reformatories, orphanages etc.

The training of pauper children to perform useful work has a long history. The young inmates at the Bristol Corporation workhouse opened in 1698 were taught to spin and then worked at the task for more than ten hours a day. Such training could enable children to generate a useful income and so help pay for their maintenance in the workhouse. It could also equip them with employable skills and instil into them the habit of performing regular and productive work, which – it was hoped – would make them less likely to be paupers in later life.

An early photograph of the Moral and Industrial Training Schools erected in 1846–48 by the Leeds Board of Guardians to house and educate pauper children. The building now forms part of St James' Hospital.

A dressmaking class in 1896 at the St Pancras Union Industrial School at Leavesden in Hertfordshire. The children are sewing clothes both by hand and using sewing machines.

The Blacksmith's shop at the St Pancras Union Industrial School at Leavesden in 1896. The boys are engaged in various metal-working activities supervised by school staff.

In the union workhouse, industrial training for younger children – both boys and girls – could include activities such as knitting and sewing, or straw plaiting. By the age of eleven, a boy might have learned to make and mend his clothes, and by the age of thirteen to do the same for his shoes. As well as tailoring and shoemaking, training for older boys could include trades such as carpentry and joinery, plumbing, metal-working, bricklaying and agricultural work. From the 1840s, many workhouses established small farming or horticultural operations where much of the labour was provided by the inmate boys and, as a by-product, generated produce for use in the workhouse kitchens. Some workhouses also taught boys naval skills and ran a military band which could provide a path into a career in one of the services.

Industrial training for girls invariably focused on domestic skills which would equip them to work in domestic service. By the age of thirteen, a girl might have learnt to knit, sew, scrub floors, make beds and clean furniture. She could also have become accustomed to wash or iron clothes for up to six hours a day on alternate days. She would then be expected to acquire a knowledge of cooking, nursing the sick, and the management of a dairy.

The person delivering industrial training was generally known as an industrial trainer. Large establishments had trainers specialising in particular trades.

(*See also*: **Gardens and Farms**)

INFANT POORHOUSE

(*See*: **Hanway's Act**)

INFIRMARY

An establishment offering treatment for the sick and injured, usually for a defined community. Thus, the area in a workhouse where medical treatment was provided was normally described as an infirmary.

(*See also*: **Hospital**)

INS AND OUTS

The 'ins and outs' was the informal term used to refer to those who entered and left the work-house on a frequent basis, often staying for just a short period. Use of the phrase appears to date back to at least 1814 when it was used to refer to a similar situation in debtors' prisons.

Analysis of a sample of workhouse admissions in 1906–07 recorded that 83.7 per cent of inmates had entered once during the year, 13.5 per cent entered on between two and four occasions, and 2.8 per cent were admitted five or more times. It was also noted that during 1901, one eighty-one-year-old woman named Julia Blumsun had recorded 163 separate admissions to the City of London workhouse, while a forty-year-old man in the Poplar workhouse had been in and out 593 times over the period since 1884.[200]

Why did such people leave and return so frequently? Some inmates, no doubt, found that they could put up with the privations of the workhouse only for so long. Escaping for a few days provided a welcome respite, even if they ended up returning soon afterwards. When seven-year-old Charlie Chaplin, his half-brother, Sydney, and their mother, Hannah, entered the Lambeth workhouse in 1896, the two boys were soon packed off to the poor law District School at Hanwell. Two months later, the children were returned to the workhouse where they were met at the gate by Hannah, dressed in her own clothes. In desperation to see them, she had discharged herself from the workhouse, along with the children. After a day spent playing in Kennington Park and visiting a coffee-shop, they returned to the workhouse and had to go through the whole admissions procedure once more, with the children again staying there for a probationary period before returning to Hanwell.

The 'ins and outs' were a considerable irritation to workhouse staff since, upon readmission, they had to undergo all the administrative formalities required of new inmates, even though they may have only been absent for a few hours. In 1871, the Pauper Inmates Discharge and Regulation Act[201] gave officers the power to delay the discharge of such inmates: a pauper who had discharged himself in the previous month could be detained for forty-eight hours, while two or more previous discharges in the preceding two months could result in a seventy-two-hour delay. One who was considered to have discharged himself frequently and without sufficient reason, could be detained for up to a week.

(*See also*: **Admission to a Workhouse**; **Leaving a Workhouse**)

IRELAND

Prior to 1838, in contrast to the parish-based system of relief operating in England and Wales from the end of the sixteenth century, the poor in Ireland generally had to rely on support from charitable sources. Workhouses, or Houses of Industry as they were most often known, were set up in just a few towns and cities, rather along the lines of the various Local Act Incorporations established in some English towns.

Early Workhouses

In 1703 an Act of the Irish Parliament provided for the setting up of a House of Industry in Dublin for employing and maintaining the poor, to be run by a committee known as the 'Governor and Guardians of the Poor'. The main classes of inmate were 'sturdy beggars', 'disorderly women', the old and infirm, and orphan children. Up to 100 men and sixty women slept in bunk-like beds crammed into the cellars of the building on James Street. The establishment also housed abandoned and foundling children. At one of its gates, a basket was fixed to a revolving door where a child could be left anonymously. A similar scheme was instituted at Cork where a workhouse was opened in 1747, financed by a tax on coal imported into the city. Belfast opened a workhouse in 1774 after more than twenty years of fund-raising by the Belfast Charitable Society.

In 1772, the Irish Parliament passed a more general Act to allow the formation of 'Corporations' in each county which could run voluntarily funded houses of industry to relieve the poor and also to deal with beggars. As a result of this Act, a new workhouse-cum-hospital was opened at

Belfast's poorhouse and infirmary, opened in 1774 and now known as Clifton House. The building's construction was financed by subscriptions and a nationwide lottery. In 1800, children in the poorhouse were used in the first trials of vaccination in the region.

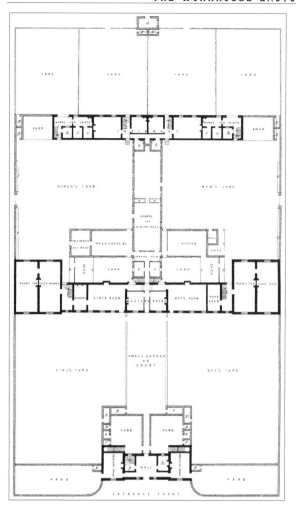

The ground plan of an Irish workhouse for between 400 and 800 inmates. The larger-capacity workhouses had essentially the same layout but could include an additional floor in the main building and attic dormitories.

A modern aerial view of the former Parsonstown Union workhouse in King's County (now County Offaly) which housed up to 800 inmates. (*Picture by kind permission of Paul Barber.*)

the north side of Dublin. Houses of Industry were also set up at Ennis (1775), Waterford (1779) and Clonmel (1811), with others being established at Kilkenny, Newtownards and Wexford.

The 1833 Royal Commission

After 1800, when Ireland was united with Great Britain under the Act of Union, the British Government made numerous but ineffectual attempts to address the widespread poverty in the country. A succession of Select Committees and Royal Commissions investigated the problems but action failed to materialise. In September 1833, in response to the growing influx of Irish immigrants to Britain, yet another Royal Commission was appointed to investigate 'the conditions of the poorer classes' in Ireland and the existing poor relief institutions. The Commission, chaired by the Protestant Archbishop of Dublin, Dr Richard Whateley, presented its final report in June 1836. During the Commission's deliberations, the British Parliament had passed the landmark 1834 Poor Law Amendment Act, introducing a new scheme for England and Wales whereby the only form of poor relief – for the able-bodied, at least – was to be via the workhouse. Whateley's report concluded that such a scheme would not be suitable for Ireland where the problem was more one of lack of available work, rather than of able-bodied men's reluctance to undertake it. The report instead proposed the setting up of a Board of Improvement and Development which would undertake such measures as a programme of public works, reclaiming wasteland and draining bog-land, the development of trade, manufacture, fisheries and mining, the provision of agricultural instruction, and the Sunday-closing of public houses.

The government's response to Whateley's proposals was lukewarm. In September 1836, George Nicholls, one of the Poor Law Commissioners (PLC), was despatched on a six-week whistle-stop tour of Ireland to give his assessment of whether the recently established English workhouse system could be made to work in the country. Rejecting (or simply ignoring) the view that the problems of poverty in Ireland were of a completely different nature to those in England, and required a different remedy (a fundamental investment in, and development of, the country's resources), Nicholls recommended that the workhouse system be introduced into Ireland.

The scheme proposed for Ireland was modelled on that operating in England and Wales, with poor relief being financed through a local poor rate, and offered only through the workhouse. Despite significant opposition, especially from Irish MPs, the Act 'for the more effectual Relief of the Destitute Poor in Ireland' passed into law on 31 July 1838.

The 1838 Act

The main provisions of the 1838 Act were: the extension of the PLC's powers to Ireland; the division of the country into Poor Law Unions based on Irish 'electoral divisions'; the creation of a Board of Guardians for each union and the setting up of a workhouse; the collection of a poor rate to finance the system; and assistance for emigration.

Initially, 130 unions were created, based upon 2,049 electoral divisions. The divisions were composed of townlands, a peculiarly Irish unit, traditionally of 120 Irish acres in area. Boards of Guardians were elected annually on 25 March by the ratepayers in each division, effectively disenfranchising most of the native Irish who were usually tenants at this time. Ratepayers were allowed between one and six votes based on a valuation of their property.

There were some significant differences between Ireland's new poor relief system and the one operating in England and Wales. In Ireland, out relief was not to be allowed in any form whatsoever. Clergymen were barred from membership of Boards of Guardians. There was no law of settlement in Ireland – England could remove destitute Irish back to Ireland, but not vice versa. The PLC had much greater control over the operation of Irish unions than those in England – they had the power to dissolve a Board of Guardians and substitute their own paid officials; they scrutinised a copy of the weekly Board minutes from each union to ensure they did not deviate from official regulations; and they were responsible for matters such as the appointment of chaplains.

An 1840 illustration of the sleeping accommodation in an Irish workhouse. On the upper floors, the able-bodied and children slept on raised platforms with a walkway in between. On the lower floor, individual wooden 'harrow' beds were provided for the elderly and infirm.

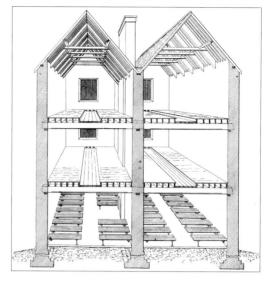

The New Workhouses

In January 1839, George Wilkinson – the architect of a number of workhouses in England and Wales – arrived in Dublin to begin work on designing the country's 130 new union workhouses. His brief from the PLC was that: 'The style of building is intended to be of the cheapest description compatible with durability; and effect is aimed at by harmony of proportion and simplicity of arrangement, all mere decoration being studiously excluded.'[202] Within two months, Wilkinson had devised model plans upon which almost all Irish workhouse buildings would be based. Only in five unions (North Dublin, South Dublin, Fermoy, Caherciveen, Clonmel) were existing buildings re-used.

Every workhouse was divided into male and female sides, with the male inmates usually placed at the right. At the front of the site was a small entrance block whose ground floor contained a porter's lodge, waiting hall and receiving rooms. Upstairs was the guardians' boardroom, with small dormitories to each side, and a store for inmates' own clothes in the attic above. The receiving rooms were used to hold new inmates prior to their moving into the main workhouse. They were also sometimes employed – to official disapproval – for housing tramps or 'night-lodgers' overnight.

Set back from the entrance was the main accommodation block, with quarters for the workhouse master and matron placed at its centre. At each side on the ground floor were separate schoolrooms for boys and girls, with the children's dormitories above. The outer parts of the block contained the accommodation for adult men and women. Unlike in England and Wales, the infirm and the able-bodied were not segregated although rooms for the aged and infirm were generally placed on the ground floor. The space in front of the main block was divided into enclosed yards for boys and girls, with a garden at the centre. To the rear of the accommodation block were the kitchen and washhouse (laundry) and a central spine containing the dining-room which also served as a chapel. At the rear, the spine connected to the infirmary and wards for 'idiots'.

Another indication of the economies applied to the new Irish workhouses was the furnishing of the dormitories, or rather lack of it. Most inmates slept on straw-filled mattresses placed on low raised platforms, running the length of the dormitory with walkways placed in between them. What were sometimes referred to as 'harrow' beds – narrow beds made from five planks of wood on raised legs – were provided for the sick and the aged and infirm. In 1896, the *British Medical Journal* reported that despite the discomfort of harrow beds, the Loughrea Board of Guardians were 'of opinion that iron and wire beds are not to be recommended on the score of expense'.[203]

Initial Problems

By April 1843, 112 of the new workhouses were finished, and eighteen others were almost complete. The new buildings did not always come into operation immediately, however, particularly if the guardians had been unable or unwilling to collect sufficient poor rates to run the workhouse.

Male inmates line up behind a feeding trough at the Bailieborough Union workhouse in County Cavan in about 1895. Food such as porridge was placed in individual compartments in the trough and eaten while standing.

A sparsely furnished dormitory at the Cootehill Union workhouse in County Cavan in about 1895. The bedding – blankets and a straw-filled mattress and pillow – was rolled back against the wall during the day and the beds used as seats.

At Westport, the new workhouse was declared fit for the admission of paupers on 15 November 1842 but stayed closed due to a lack of operating funds. For two years, the Westport guardians attempted to collect the poor rate, sometimes with the help of police and troops. Eventually, in 1844, a warship and two cruisers sailed into Clew Bay to assist – without success. The Board of Guardians resigned and a new Board was elected. The workhouse was opened only after they were served a court order and the first inmates were finally admitted on 5 November 1845. As a last resort, the PLC could forcibly dissolve a Board of Guardians and install their own vice-guardians in order to get the workhouses open – a fate which befell the Castlerea and Tuam Boards in 1846. As well as difficulties in collecting the poor rate, the people's general reluctance to sacrifice their independence meant that even by the summer of 1846, when the famine was already hitting hard, the workhouses that were open were still only half-full.[204]

Diet

The formulation of a diet for Ireland's workhouse inmates caused considerable problems. The principle of 'less eligibility', by which workhouse conditions were never to be better than those enjoyed by an independent labourer outside, was particularly difficult to apply to a population whose ordinary diet was often barely above subsistence level. An examination of the existing diets at other institutions such as Houses of Industry and prisons revealed that inmates were typically given a breakfast of oatmeal and milk, and a midday dinner of potatoes and milk, but no supper. A survey of poor labourers' diets in various parts of the country showed a frequent pattern of potatoes and milk for both breakfast and dinner, again with supper often being omitted. Herrings were sometimes substituted when milk was in short supply. The initial proposals for the workhouse dietary comprised a breakfast of stirabout (oatmeal porridge) and milk, with a dinner of potatoes and milk. However, pressure from the two Dublin unions to include meat soup dinners on two days a week resulted in unions being given the option of three different menu plans. Dietary 1 provided a two-meals-a-day menu with no meat. Dietary 2 added a twice-weekly meat soup dinner. Dietary 3 was a three-meals-a-day regime, but with no meat included.

A German visitor to the North Dublin Union workhouse in 1842 described the preparation of the inmates' potatoes:

> I was astonished by the appearance of the potato-kettle at this house. No less than 1670 pounds of potatoes are boiled at once. This enormous quantity is all divided into portions of three and a half and four pounds, and each portion is enclosed in a small net. All these nets are laid together in a large basket, and this basket, with its nets and potatoes, is deposited in the boiler. When the potatoes are supposed to have been sufficiently boiled, the basket is wound up again by a machinery, constructed for the purpose, and the poor are then marched up in military order, when each receives his net and marches away with it.[205]

The Famine

The potato was the staple food of the majority of Ireland's eight million inhabitants. In the summer of 1845, reports of potato blight began to appear, first on the Continent and then in southern England. By August it had reached Ireland, and a substantial part of that year's crop rapidly became black and inedible. Since a similar problem had occurred in 1832, it was initially assumed that only one year's crop was likely to be affected. Unhappily, the summer of 1846 saw the return of the blight and an escalation in the desperation and misery that now afflicted the country, with food in short supply and prices rocketing.

A massive surge in demand for poor relief put workhouses under enormous pressure, with conditions inside them rapidly deteriorating. Stables and washrooms were pressed into service as overflow accommodation, and additional premises were rented to try and cope with the rising numbers. However, the expense of providing extra accommodation and the increasing costs of feeding the large numbers of inmates were already pushing some unions into insolvency and they closed their doors to further admissions. On top of this, diseases such as typhus fever and dysentery were widespread leading to hundreds of deaths, including many workhouse staff.

In November 1845, the British Government set up a Relief Commission to try and generate employment through increased public works schemes. However, this proved hopelessly inadequate – there was insufficient work to satisfy demand, the wages could not keep up with escalating food prices, and food was often impossible to obtain. The Relief Commission also set up food depots around the country for the storage and distribution of 'Indian meal' (maize corn imported from America) which local relief committees could resell at cost price. Indian meal was to become a major part of many people's diet for several years.

At the start of 1847, some temporary and minimal relief for those outside the workhouse came with an Act for the Temporary Relief of Destitute Persons in Ireland Act – the so-called 'Soup Kitchen' Act.[206]

Much more significant was the legislation enacted in June which, for the first time, allowed unions to give out relief to the old, the infirm, the sick, and to poor widows with dependent children.[207] If a union's workhouse was full, or harbouring an infectious disease, out relief could also be offered to other classes of destitute persons for up to two months. In the case of able-bodied claimants, out relief was to be provided only in the form of food. The same statute also allowed land to be bought adjoining workhouses to be used for erecting a fever hospital or, reflecting the enormous numbers of deaths now taking place, as a pauper burial ground.

The following month, a further Act constituted the Irish Poor Law Commissioners (IPLC) as an independent body, no longer under the control of the Commissioners for England and Wales.[208] Although the IPLC initially took on all the rules, orders and regulations of the existing administration, the Act said nothing about the form that poor relief should take – the prohibition on out relief had effectively ended.

During 1847, to try and cope with the ravages of typhus fever and dysentery, many workhouses erected fever hospitals, although in some cases these consisted of little more than wooden sheds. Financial crises continued – Ballina Union had debts of £2,000 and Castlebar of £3,000.[209] The debts of Ennis Union were to reach £20,000 by 1849. Throughout all this, the government Exchequer continued to demand repayments on the loans taken out by most unions to finance the building of the workhouse.

The Poor Law Commissioners made considerable use of their powers to dissolve Boards of Guardians that were 'failing to provide sufficient funds, or to apply them efficiently in relieving the destitute' and to install their own officers. A total of thirty-two boards were dissolved in 1847, mostly in the west of Ireland, with six more in 1849. In the same year, some small financial relief to the twenty-two worst affected unions in the west of Ireland came via the 'Rate in Aid' Act.[210] The assisted unions received funds from the government which then had to be repaid by a 6d rate levied by all the other Irish unions.

At the end of the famine years, it was estimated that at least a million people had died, either directly from starvation, or from the diseases it brought in its wake such as typhus fever and dysentery. A further contributory factor was the nutritionally poor Indian meal which became a major part of the diet of many poor, particularly in the workhouses.

The ineffectual response of the British Government to the disaster that had struck Ireland was widely criticised, most notably by Edward Twisleton, the Chief Poor Law Commissioner in Ireland who resigned over the lack of direct funding to deal with the crisis and the imposition of Rate in Aid Act. In his evidence to a Select Committee in 1849, Twisleton asked for it to be put on record that the giving of a 'comparatively trifling sum' would allow Britain:

> to spare itself the deep disgrace of permitting any of our miserable fellow-subjects in the distressed Unions to die of starvation. From the want of sufficient food many persons in those Unions are at the present moment dying or wasting away.[211]

Between 1845 and 1850, the British Government spent £7 million on relief in Ireland – less that 0.5 per cent of the British gross national product. This made a striking contrast to the £20 million compensation given to West Indian slave-owners in the 1830s.[212]

Emigration

Emigration had been encouraged by a succession of British governments as a way of reducing the numbers claiming poor relief. Since the 1838 Irish Poor Law Act, unions had been empowered to spend up to 5 per cent of the poor rate to 'assist poor persons who would otherwise have to be accommodated in the workhouse' in emigrating. This was primarily to the British colonies of Canada, Australia and New Zealand, and from 1840 was supervised by the Colonial Land and Emigration Commission. The scheme was extended in 1848 to include other non-colonial countries such as America. In the ten years from 1845, a total of two million emigrated from Ireland.

Emigration was often encouraged by landlords who saw it as a way of clearing their land of unwanted tenants, and also reducing the poor rates to which they contributed. In some cases, estate owners chartered their own ships for the transport of emigrants.

With a surge in the demand for passages, conditions on vessels declined, becoming increasingly overcrowded and insanitary. Deaths in passage were as high as 20 per cent, and some unseaworthy vessels sank before completing their journeys. Because of this, emigrant vessels came to be known as 'coffin ships'.

New Unions

In 1848, a Boundaries Commission reviewed the existing size and composition of each of Ireland's Poor Law Unions. It proposed the creation of up to fifty new unions, of which thirty-two eventually took place between 1849 and 1850 (taking in parts of the one other new union, Dingle, which had already been established early in 1848). The new unions, predominantly in the west of Ireland, were created by subdividing some of the existing unions, together with some additional boundary adjustments where necessary. For example, in County Clare, the northern part of the Ennistymon Union was split off to create the Ballyvaughan and Corofin Unions.

Eighteen of the new unions proposed by the Boundaries Commission were not created. They were: Arvagh (to have been formed from parts of the Cavan, Granard, Longford, and Mohill unions), Ballymore (Athlone, Ballymahon, Mullingar), Blessington (Naas, Baltinglass), Cappamore (Limerick, Tipperary, Kilmallock), Castleisland (Tralee, Killarney), Cossann (Galway, Tuam, Loughrea), Drumkeeran (Manorhamiltion, Enniskillen, Carrick-on-Shannon), Ferbane (Parsonstown), Kildare (Athy, Edenderry, Naas), Killedmond (Carlow, New Ross, Enniscorthy), Killorglin (Killarney, Chairciveen, Tralee), Killybegs (Donegal, Glenties), Kilrea (Ballymoney, Coleraine, Magherafelt) Milford (Croom, Kanturk, Kilmallock, Newcastle), Mountrath (Abbeyleix, Mountrath, Roscrea), Newtown Mount Kennedy (Rathdrum), North Cork (Cork), and Riverstown (Boyle, Sligo, Tobercurry).

Medical Developments

During the 1850s and 1860s, the Irish poor relief system was involved in several significant developments in the provision of medical care in the country.

In 1851, the Medical Charities (Dispensary) Act[213] placed Ireland's charitable dispensary system under the control of the IPLC. Within each union, dispensary districts were formed, with a total of 723 initially being created. Each district had its own dispensary where the poor could obtain free medicines and medical treatment from the dispensary medical officer, with the costs being funded through the poor rate. Dispensaries were usually erected at or near workhouses.

Britain's 1840 Vaccination Act had introduced voluntary smallpox vaccination in Ireland under the management of the PLC. Its take-up had been limited, due in part to the fees paid to the doctors contracted to do the work – a shilling each for first 200, then sixpence each thereafter, compared to a flat rate of 1s 6d each received by doctors in England and Wales. In 1851, vaccination became a standard part of the duties of dispensary medical officers, with no

An 1866 *Punch* cartoon acknowledges the impact made by the Sisters of Mercy on nursing in Irish workhouses. The Dickensian beadle figure represents the 'bumbledom' which was frequently a target of the magazine.

THE UNRECOGNISED VISITOR.

Bumble. "YOU'RE THE SISTER OF MERCY, IS YOU? WELL, WE ARN'T GOT THAT NAME IN THE HOUSE; SO TODDLE!"

extra fee being paid. In 1858, efforts were made to increase the rate of vaccination by creating vaccination districts and paying a flat-rate fee for each successful vaccination.[214] Vaccination became compulsory in Ireland in 1863, ten years later than in England and Wales.

From 1856, Ireland's workhouse fever hospitals had been allowed to admit any 'poor person' i.e. those who were poor but not sufficiently destitute to require entry into the workhouse. In 1862, the Poor Relief (Ireland) Act[215] extended this provision to all other conditions – something that had been happening illegally for some years before.

The Sisters of Mercy, a Roman Catholic religious order particularly associated with caring for the needs of the poor and sick, were first allowed to act as workhouse hospital nurses in 1861 at the Limerick Union workhouse. After protracted correspondence on the matter, the appointment of three of the order's nuns was reluctantly acceded to by IPLC so long as the posts were advertised and interviewed in normal manner and that the workhouse master retained overall responsibility for the infirmary's operation. There was also official concern that such appointments should not result in demands for religious segregation within workhouse infirmaries. Within twenty years, however, the Irish Local Government Board was positively recommending the employment of Sisters of Mercy to provide workhouse medical care. A survey in 1903 revealed that eighty-five unions employed nuns as nurses, with the nursing matron in thirty-two workhouses being a nun.[216] A total of forty-eight nuns were also employed as teachers. In many cases, the nuns were given their own separate accommodation on workhouse sites.

Medical provision became an increasingly important aspect of the care provided by Irish workhouses. By the end of the 1800s, around three quarters of workhouse inmates in Ireland were officially classified either as 'sick' or as 'other' a group which probably comprised mostly the elderly and infirm.

The BMJ Commission

By the mid-1890s, workhouses in Ireland – as well as many in England and Wales – were characterised by an air of neglect, especially as regards the conditions in their infirmaries. In 1894, the *British Medical Journal* (BMJ) launched a campaign to improve workhouse medical facilities, especially in the provision of nursing care. The following year, the journal began publishing detailed reports of visits by its 'commission' to workhouses across Ireland which, almost without exception, painted a picture of lamentable squalor – a system that was denounced as 'inhuman and barbarous, unworthy of a civilised country'.[217] The BMJ report on Bailieborough was typical:

It is hard to picture a more comfortless place than these wards for the old people. They are approached through day-rooms having mud floors, a long table at one end and a bench being all the furniture in these rooms. The whole ward was dirty, and smelt so, and the patients showed – in their persons negligence and untidiness, but who could blame them when they had one basin and a towel to go round, no bath or lavatory, or decently clean clothing?

We turned into the dining hall. As the dinners were being served a few old men came in at one door, a few old women and children at another; they stood around the feeding troughs out of which they took the food, presumably porridge. No grace was said, no officer appeared to be present; it was like the feeding of animals, and not of human beings. The kitchen at the end of the hall was indescribably filthy; refuse, dirty straw, and cats were in the corners, the table was black with grease and dirt.

The epileptics and idiots are placed in the cells, which form the blocks at each end of the infirmary. These cells differ in no respect from those used for prisoners, except that they are unlocked during the day; a square flagged cell. whitewashed walls, slit in the wall for air, light and ventilation; a heavy door with ponderous bolt, crib beds filled with straw for the 'dirty cases,' and harrow beds for the less helpless two patients in each cell, no means of warming these cells in the winter, but the borrowed heat from the fire in the corridor. The pathetic look of the hapless creatures, as they stared at us out of the cribs, haunted us for a long time; the darkness, the confinement, the want of employment, the stone yard for exercise, all seemed cunningly contrived to send them out of their minds. The attendants are pauper inmates, and this department is locked at 7 p.m. Here, again, we found the pails and buckets in the cells; one most offensive case gave quite sufficient proof that this class did not receive skilled nursing.[218]

Children in the Workhouse

As in England and Wales, there were efforts by the central authorities to reduce the numbers of children residing in Irish workhouses. By 1900, however, children still comprised almost one in seven of Ireland's 41,980 workhouse inmates. The removal of pauper children to other forms of accommodation such as cottage homes or scattered homes was not adopted by any Irish union. The setting up of District Schools, which had had limited take-up in England, was even less successful in Ireland with only two such schools being established – at Trim in 1890 and at Glin in 1893. The option that proved most popular with Irish Boards of Guardians was that of boarding-out orphaned or abandoned children with foster parents. Boarding-out was introduced in 1862, initially in an attempt to reduce the mortality rates of those under five. The upper age limit for boarding-out was increased to ten in 1866, and to fifteen in 1898. In 1900, a total of 2,223 children were being boarded-out or 'out at nurse', although the majority of pauper children remained in the workhouse.[219]

Charting Poor Relief

The delays in the opening of all the country's workhouses, the onset of the famine, and the introduction of out relief in 1847, mean that useful long-term poor relief statistics for Ireland do not begin until the late 1840s. Detailed relief figures for the years 1845 to 1900 are given in Appendix B.

The chart below shows the average daily numbers of those receiving relief either in the workhouse or as out relief between 1845 and 1900. In the aftermath of the famine, accompanied by the thirty-three new unions and their workhouses, the indoor relief figure reached an all-time high of 217,388 (around 3.3 per cent of the total population) in 1851. It then dropped to around the 50,000 mark where, apart from occasional slight increases, it remained for the rest of the century.

As the famine receded, out relief numbers fell from their massive heights (830,000 in July 1848) to a low of just over 2,000 in 1856. They then rose gradually until 1880 when prolonged wet weather and a new outbreak of potato blight led to out relief numbers overtaking those in the workhouse. Another spike occurred during another period of distress in 1886, when a Poor Relief Act[220] authorised a temporary relaxation on the conditions for giving out relief.

Attempts at Reform

By the early 1900s, mounting criticism of the poor relief system led to two major reviews of its operation. In 1903, a Vice-Regal Commission was appointed to investigate whether improve-

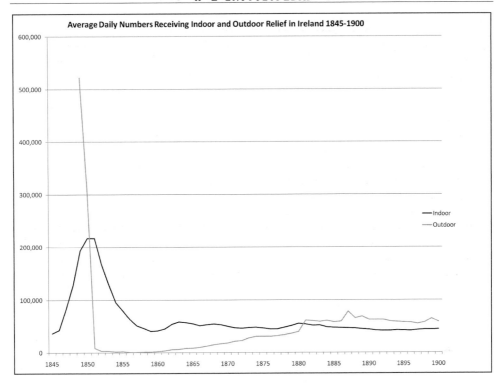

Average Daily Numbers Receiving Indoor and Outdoor Relief in Ireland 1845-1900

ments could be made in poor relief provision in Ireland and also whether financial savings were possible. Its report, published in 1906, proposed the abolition of the workhouse system with different categories of inmates – the sick, the elderly, children etc. – being placed in separate institutions such as county almshouses for aged and infirm.[221]

The 1905 Royal Commission, examining the poor relief system throughout the British Isles, broadly reached the same conclusions, emphasising the need for classification by institution as well as within institutions. No new legislation directly resulted from the Commission's work, however.

In 1911, the Local Government Board for Ireland belatedly followed the lead of its counterpart in England and Wales and overhauled the existing Irish workhouses dietaries. The new system adopted a similar scheme based on a 'rations' list from which each union could compile a weekly meal plan for its inmates. The Board also published the *Handbook of Cookery for Irish Workhouses* which, although somewhat longer than its English predecessor, followed the same basic format, and included many of same recipes. Innovations in the *Handbook* included a number of fish dishes such as fried mackerel, baked herrings and boiled ling (otherwise known as Newfoundland dried fish). New vegetable dishes included colcannon (a mixture of potatoes and cabbage), and bacon and cabbage (the cabbage to be boiled for up to an hour). Nettles were also recommended as excellent springtime vegetables. One dish that the *Handbook* did have in common with its English counterpart was the workhouse's signature dish, gruel. However, a slightly shorter second edition of the *Handbook* published in 1913 omitted this recipe – finally, a workhouse cookery book without gruel.

The First World War had relatively little impact on the Irish workhouse system. A small number of workhouses were handed over for use by the military authorities, while the Dunshaughlin workhouse served as a centre for Belgian refugees.

Independence
The Irish War of Independence, which began in January 1919 following the Irish Republic's declaration of independence, eventually led to the signing of the Anglo-Irish Treaty on 6

The 1911 *Handbook of Cookery for Irish Workhouses* included many recipes not found in its English counterpart. While nettle soup would now be widely commended for its health benefits, the same cannot be said of the preparation of cabbage – boiled for up to an hour.

> NETTLES.
>
> Nettles are excellent vegetables in the spring. They should be boiled in plenty of boiling water with a little bread soda. When cooked, drain well, and chop them up as you would spinach, then place them in the dry boiler with some gravy or dripping, salt, and pepper. Stew for about 5 minutes and serve. There are various ways of cooking them, and they are a good substitute for other vegetables in soup.
>
> The young leaf of the mangold wurzel is also excellent when cooked as above.
>
> COLCANNON.
>
> 12 ozs. potatoes. $\frac{1}{2}$ oz. dripping.
> 6 ozs. cabbage. Pepper and salt.
>
> Boil the potatoes (peeled), and cabbage.
> Mash the potatoes and mix with the finely chopped cabbage and the seasoning. Mix well with the melted dripping in pot. Put into a greased basin, make thoroughly hot in the oven, then turn out on a dish (1 lb.)
>
> To Boil CABBAGE.
>
> Take off all brown or faded leaves, remove the hard part of the stalk if the cabbage be old, and slit the stalk that it may cook more easily. Lay the cabbage in cold water with a little salt, for an hour. Must be cooked in plenty of fast boiling water with a tablespoonful of salt to every gallon, and a little bread soda. Boil quickly with the lid off, add a crust of bread to keep down smell. Time required depends upon their age—from half an hour to an hour.

December 1921. The Treaty created the independent Irish Free State containing twenty-six counties, while the remaining six (Armagh, Antrim, Derry, Down, Fermanagh and Tyrone) stayed under British rule adopting the name of Northern Ireland. In the Free State, the Boards of Guardians were soon abolished and replaced by County Boards of Health and County Boards of Public Assistance.

Between June 1922 and May 1923, a further conflict took place in the form of the Irish Civil War. During this, and the previous struggles, many workhouses underwent military occupation and were damaged or burnt down. Of those still useable, thirty-three became County Homes offering relief to the elderly and chronic invalid, with nineteen of these sites also used in part as hospitals. Nine former workhouses were converted to County Hospitals, and thirty-two more became District or Fever Hospitals.

(*See also*: **Beds**; **Royal Commission – 1905**; **Wartime**; **Appendices B, G, K**; Cassell (1997); Gray (2009); O'Connor (1995))

IRREMOVABILITY

From 1846, someone residing in a parish for at least five years became irremovable from that parish under the laws of settlement. The qualification period was reduced to one year in 1865. (*See also*: **Settlement**)

ISLE OF MAN

The Isle of Man, with its own legislature, did not follow the poor relief system established elsewhere in Britain. In the nineteenth century, a number of poorhouses and workhouses were set up in Douglas, the island's capital. These included a home on Strand Street for poor widows in 1802, and from 1817 a house on Fort Street bequeathed to the poor of Douglas by French émigré shopkeeper Francis Lasnon. A new English-style workhouse for eighty inmates was built in the town in 1837. Its management was largely in the hand of church trustees with funding based on voluntary contributions.

In 1889, following earlier criticisms of the island's poor relief provision by a Committee of Enquiry, the Tynwald (the Manx Parliament) passed an Act to establish a 'Home for the Poor' for the use of the whole island and funded by district from which each applicant came. The new home was set up at Strang in Braddan, adjacent to the Ballamona Lunatic Asylum and managed by the same committee.

ISOLATED HOMES

(*See*: **Scattered Homes**)

THE ITCH

(*See*: **Scabies**)

JEWISH BOARD OF GUARDIANS

The Jewish Board of Guardians (later known as the Jewish Welfare Board) was a charitable organisation founded in London in 1859 by the philanthropist Ephraim Alex to assist poor members of the Jewish community. The Board's funds primarily came from the United Synagogue, a confederation of synagogues in the London.

The Board's activities included the giving of handouts or loans to those in need, lending tools and machinery to workmen, giving assistance towards apprenticing poor children, and the funding of emigration. Although the Board operated industrial workrooms where employment could be provided on a limited scale, it did not operate residential institutions analogous to workhouses.

Jewish Boards of Guardians were also established in other cities with large Jewish populations such as Manchester in 1867, and Leeds in 1878.

JOINT ASYLUM / JOINT POOR LAW (ESTABLISHMENT) COMMITTEES

At the start of the twentieth century, several groups of local poor law authorities formed Joint Asylum Committees, later more usually called Joint Poor Law Establishment Committees or just Joint Committees (JCs), through which to combine their provision for what were then referred to as 'sane epileptics' and 'mental defectives'. At that time, such individuals were usually accommodated as part of the general workhouse population and received no specialised care.

The earliest of these joint management groups was the Chorlton and Manchester Joint Asylum Committee, formed in 1897. In 1902, the Committee purchased a 165-acre site at Langho, near Blackburn, where they established a 'colony' for sane epileptics. In 1905, a Joint Committee of the Birmingham, Aston and King's Norton Unions acquired the 185-acre

The former House of Industry in Douglas on the Isle of Man. The building, which dates from 1837, is now the 'Ellan Vannin' (Manx for 'Isle of Man') elderly care home.

Monyhull Hall estate near Great Barr in Stafford and three years later opened its colony for up to 250 sane epileptics and feeble-minded persons. The Walsall and West Bromwich JC purchased the Great Barr Hall and 447-acre estate in 1911, initially for use as a children's home and then from around 1914 as a colony for female mental defectives. In 1914, the Northern Counties JC (covering twenty-five unions in Cumberland, Northumberland, Durham and North Yorkshire) established a mental defectives' colony at Prudhoe Hall in Northumberland. The Surrey JC was established in 1914 and the following year acquired a property known as 'The Oaks' at Woodmansterne for use as a home for female epileptics. At around the same date, the Glamorgan JC opened a home for mental defectives at Drymma Hall, Skewen, near Neath.

By the mid-1920s, the JCs in operation comprised: Cheshire, Northern Counties, Shropshire, Staffordshire, Surrey, Walsall and West Bromwich, Warwickshire, Wiltshire and South Yorkshire. (*See also*: **Mentally Ill**)

JOINT VAGRANCY COMMITTEES

From the 1870s onwards, Poor Law Unions in several areas formed county-wide schemes to coordinate their treatment of vagrants. One aim was to ensure that regulations regarding the causal poor were consistently applied in each union. Some counties also operated a way ticket system which provided a 'passport' from one union's causal ward to a specified next one, with a portion of bread provided at a designated bread station en route.

In February 1913, the Local Government Board issued a General Order for all unions to participate in the operation of county-wide Joint Vagrancy Committees (JVCs) established for this purpose. Some Committees, such as the North Western JVC, covered several counties. In 1924, the twenty-seven JVCs then in operation were: Berks, Bucks and Oxon Joint; Cambridgeshire; Devonshire; Dorsetshire; Essex; Glamorgan, Monmouth and Brecknock Joint; Gloucestershire and Bristol; Hertfordshire; Kent; Leicestershire; Lincolnshire &c. Joint; Norfolk; North Western; Nottinghamshire and Derbyshire; Somerset and Bristol; Southampton; Staffordshire Joint; Suffolk Joint; Surrey; Sussex (East); Sussex (West); Wales (North); Wales (West); Warwick; Wiltshire; Worcestershire; Yorkshire. Some of these later merged, for example the South Midland JVC was formed in 1930 from the Warwickshire and Worcestershire JVCs. (*See also*: **Way Ticket System**)

JONES, AGNES

(*See*: **Medical Care**)

KNATCHBULL'S ACT

(*See*: **Poor Laws**; **Workhouse Test**)

LABOUR COLONY / FARM COLONY

A place, usually in a rural location, where groups such as the poor or the unemployed could live and undertake work in return for their board and lodging and, in some cases, a small wage. Among the first labour colonies in England were those set up by the Salvation Army at Hadleigh in Essex in 1891 and by the Christian Union for Social Service at Lingfield Surrey in 1897. From 1897, metropolitan Poor Law Unions and parishes could send able-bodied male paupers to Lingfield.

A view of the buildings and some of the inmates at the Poplar Union's Laindon farm colony, set up in 1904 as an alternative to the workhouse for able-bodied men. The project was never successful and was discontinued in 1912.

In 1904, the Poplar Board of Guardians established a labour colony for able-bodied male paupers on a 100-acre farm near Laindon in Essex. The scheme, financed by American philanthropist Joseph Fels, allowed the union to operate of a modified workhouse test, with the families of colony inmates receiving out relief. The colony aimed to provide productive labour instead of the usual workhouse tasks of stone breaking and oakum picking, and to encourage self-sufficiency amongst the able-bodied poor.

Initially, 100 volunteers were transferred to Laindon from the Poplar workhouse and were engaged in agricultural work and constructing earthworks. Problems soon arose, however. There was no high wall surrounding the site and men regularly slept out, begged, and frequented local public houses. Land which would normally have required only four labourers for its cultivation by plough, was repeatedly dug over by the men with spades, a practice which became as futile as the task work it was intended to replace. The scheme ended in 1912, although the site was retained by the union to accommodate able-bodied male paupers.

(*See also*: **Modified Workhouse Test**)

LABOUR RATE SYSTEM

A scheme adopted in some parishes whereby each ratepayer was required to employ, and pay at a specified rate, unemployed labourers who had settlement in the parish, regardless of whether he had any use for their labour. The number of such labourers employed was usually linked to the ratepayer's poor-rate assessment or the area of his property. The system often worked to the disadvantage of smallholders who had little need of additional labour.

(*See also*: **Allowance System**; **Roundsman System**)

LABOUR TEST

A labour (or outdoor labour) test was a provision whereby out relief could be given to able-bodied applicants, in return for their performing a task of manual labour such as stone breaking. A labour test for able-bodied relief claimants was an integral part of the 1601 Poor Relief Act which enabled parishes to provide 'a convenient Stock of Flax, Hemp, Wool, Thread, Iron, and other necessary Ware and Stuff, to set the Poor on Work'. A later variation of the same principle was the roundsman system where parishes provided out relief conditional on claimants performing work for local ratepayers.

The 1834 Poor Law Amendment Act aimed to abolish out relief for the able-bodied who should be relieved only through residence in a workhouse. However, enforcing this measure proved particularly difficult in areas such as the industrial north of England. In Nottingham, during a slump in the hosiery trade in 1836 and 1837, the large numbers of unemployed relief claimants rapidly outstripped the available workhouse accommodation and the Poor Law Commissioners (PLC) were forced to allow a labour test to be operated.

The continuation of such difficulties eventually led the PLC in April 1842 to issue the Outdoor Labour Test Order[222] which allowed out relief (at least half of which was to be in food, clothing, or in other non-monetary form) to be given to able-bodied male paupers who satisfied a labour test. The Order was initially issued to unions in northern England, such as Carlisle, Easington, Keighley, Newcastle and Sunderland, and then subsequently extended to over 100 unions.

There was a resurgence in the use of the labour test during a severe trade depression in the years 1908–10, especially in the shipbuilding and engineering districts of north-east England. Labour test yards were opened by unions including Sunderland, Middlesbrough, Stockton and South Shields and in other areas such as Nottingham, Dartford and Bromley.

In 1911, the Relief Regulation Order[223] revised and consolidated all previous Orders relating to out relief and use of the labour test. The new Order made no mention of the term 'able-bodied' but allowed, in 'exceptional circumstances', relief (at least one half to be in kind) to be given to 'a male person' in return for performing outdoor labour.

(*See also*: **Out relief**; **Workhouse Test**)

LADIES VISITING COMMITTEE

(*See*: **Visiting Committee**)

LANSBURY, GEORGE

George Lansbury (1859–1940) was a Labour politician and campaigner for improvement in the conditions of the working class, especially in the East End of London. In 1892 he had become one of the first working-class guardians in Poplar and, with his colleague Will Crooks, was one of the main proponents of more generous poor relief – what became known as Poplarism. Lansbury was a member of the 1905 Royal Commission on the Poor Law and the Unemployed and an author of its Minority Report published in 1909 which advocated a dismantling of the workhouse system. This theme was echoed in his provocatively titled 1911 pamphlet *Smash up the Workhouse* which argued that few, particularly able-bodied, people should need to be in workhouses. For those who had no alternative, there should be a softening of the workhouse regime.

Lansbury became a Labour MP in 1910 but resigned his seat two years later over the issue of women's suffrage, of which he was a forceful advocate. He spent the next ten years running the *Daily Herald* and in 1921 was one of thirty councillors imprisoned for six weeks following the Poplar rates rebellion. He returned to Parliament in 1922 and was the Labour Party's leader from 1932 to 1935.

(*See also*: **Poplarism**; **Royal Commission – 1905**)

LAUNDRY

One of the principle sources of work for women in the workhouse was the laundry where the inmates' bedding and clothing were washed and ironed each week. In the 1890s, the laundry at the large Sheffield union workhouse washed 20,000 articles every week and employed about thirty able-bodied inmates, together with a dozen women from outside who received 1s 6d a day plus three meals.

SMASH UP THE WORKHOUSE.

— BY —
GEORGE LANSBURY, L.C.C.

PUBLISHED BY THE I.L.P. PUBLICATION DEPARTMENT,
30, BLACKFRIARS STREET, MANCHESTER.

Above right A bowler-hatted George Lansbury accompanies Queen
Mary as she watches the children's march-past on her visit in 1919
to the Poplar Union's Hutton Schools near Brentwood in Essex.
The Schools, opened in 1907, were a cottage homes development
with the buildings placed around a large central green.

Above left George Lansbury's provocatively titled pamphlet *Smash up the Workhouse* was published in
1909, the same year that he put his name to the Royal Commission's Minority Report which also
advocated dismantling the poor law system.

Most workhouse laundries had distinct areas for different stages in the washing process: the
wash-house where dirty items were washed; a drying room where items were dried – often on
large wheeled racks; and the laundry proper where articles were ironed, starched, folded, and so on.

Some large institutions, particularly those with extensive infirmaries, could have several
laundries to deal with specific types of washing such as 'foul' linen or items used by staff. At the
new St Saviour's Union infirmary opened at East Dulwich in 1887, it was reported that:

> The laundry buildings consist of an officers' wash-house, 25 ft. long, 16 ft, wide, with laundry,
> 25 ft. by 21 ft. The patients' wash-house is 40 ft. long, 25 ft. wide. Adjoining it is a double
> drying-closet, containing thirty-two horses; and beyond is the laundry, 53 ft. long, 25 ft. wide;
> there is also a small wash-house for foul linen. Attached to each of the patients' wash-houses is
> a room for receiving the dirty clothes, and a delivery-room. Attached to each of the laundries
> are airing-rooms for the clothes.[224]

During the second half of the nineteenth century, the laundries in larger workhouses sometimes installed labour-saving technical innovations such as steam-powered washing machines
and driers.
(*See also:* **Work**)

LAVATORY

In the workhouse era, a lavatory was a room in which inmates washed themselves – as opposed
to its modern British usage meaning toilet.
(*See also:* **Washing and Bathing**)

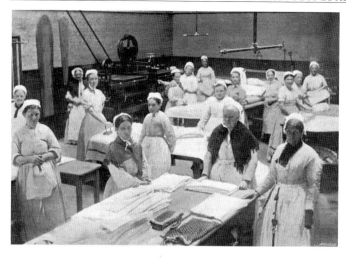

Female inmates at work in the laundry at the Mitcham workhouse in 1896.

LEAVING A WORKHOUSE

Workhouses were not prisons and an inmate could, in principle, leave at any time. However, leaving workhouse premises without permission whilst wearing the workhouse uniform would constitute an offence – the theft of workhouse property. The uniform therefore provided a useful means of control over inmates' movements.

Discharging oneself from a workhouse required notice, usually of at least three hours, to be given to the workhouse master. This allowed any necessary administrative arrangements to be carried out, and inmates' own clothes to be brought out of store. In cases where they were housed in separate establishments, all family members would need to be brought together before being discharged.

Temporary leave from a workhouse could be granted to workhouse inmates for specific purposes such as attending church, or to search for work, with disciplinary action liable to be taken against anyone staying out beyond the agreed duration.

Permission could also be given for inmates to visit friends outside, on what were known as 'liberty days'. The arrangements for such leave varied over the years and between different unions. At the Strand Union in 1838, liberty day was Monday. The inmates were divided into four groups, two male and two female, with each group allowed their day out once a month.[225] In 1844 at Southampton workhouse, each Thursday was liberty day, and was taken advantage of by the majority of inmates, leaving only twenty or thirty in the house. In the evening, those had been out frequently returned drunk.[226]

In 1909, at the Okehampton workhouse in Devon, male inmates were allowed out once a fortnight, and females once a month. At the same date, at the Smallburgh workhouse in Norfolk, men over sixty – but no other inmates – were allowed a day's leave occasionally, and also for a couple of hours on any fine afternoon. At the Kendal Unions Milnthorpe workhouse, inmates were allowed leave on application to the master. A few went out once a week and others about once a month. Young women, however, were not allowed out on leave. The most generous provision was that at the Forden and Caersws workhouses, in Montgomeryshire, where inmates were allowed visits to friends for up to seven days at a time.[227]

Prior to 1913, a married woman residing in the same workhouse as her husband could discharge herself so long as her husband had given his permission. After that date, the husband's consent was no longer required.

A Board of Guardians could order the discharge of any inmates whom they believed capable of obtaining their own means of living unless such individuals were suffering from an infectious disease which would make them a danger to themselves or others.

Some inmates, though, never left the workhouse. A parliamentary survey in 1861 found that a total of 14,216 inmates, around 21 per cent of the workhouse population, had been in continuous residence for five years or more, with 6,445 having there for ten years or more.[228] The reasons recorded for long-term residence were categorised as: old age and infirmity (42 per cent), mental disease (35 per cent), bodily defects (11 per cent), bodily disease (6 per cent), moral defects (1 per cent), and the rest 'other causes'. Some sample entries from the survey are given below for the Stoke Damerel Union in Devon:

Name	Years in Workhouse	Reason
Mary Ann Anderson	10	Infirmity
Caroline Channon	41	Imbecility
Maria Clarke	11	Illegitimate children
William Cossentine	10	Out of employ
Catherine Donovan	10	A prostitute
Peter Gunn	12	Idiocy
Agnes Jones	40	Drunkenness
William Lucas	10	Lameness
Grace Ross	30	A widow
John Stanbury	10	Insanity of wife
Thomas Soper	20	Laziness

(*See also*: **Entering a Workhouse**; **Ins and Outs**)

LESS ELIGIBILITY

The principle, usually attributed to Jeremy Bentham, that the 'eligibility' or comfort enjoyed by those living by the labour of others should not exceed that of those living by their own labour.

Under the New Poor Law, less eligibility became a yardstick for determining conditions in union workhouses which were never to be better than those of 'the independent labourer of the lowest class'.[229] In other words, life on the outside should always be more attractive than that inside the workhouse. The poverty in which some of the poor lived sometimes made this hard to achieve and matters such as the education of pauper children were sometimes questioned by Boards of Guardians as being incompatible with this doctrine.

(*See also*: **Bentham, Jeremy**)

LETTERS

Workhouse inmates were allowed to send and receive letters through the post and the institution's staff were prohibited from examining the contents of such communications.

In 1905, inmates of the Steyning workhouse in Sussex were known to be somehow secretly arranging after-dark trysts in the workhouse grounds. Extensive investigations finally revealed that the men and women were similarly communicating by letter via the general postal service which, at that date, could include six or more deliveries a day.[230]

LIBERTY DAYS

Days when workhouse inmates were allowed out, for example, to visit friends.

(*See also*: **Leaving a Workhouse**)

LINEN

A term often used in the workhouse context for underclothing.
(*See also*: **Clothing**)

LITERATURE

(*See*: **Biography**; **Broadside Ballads**; **Documentary**; **Fiction**; **Humour**; **Poetry**)

LOCAL ACT

A privately promoted Act of Parliament obtained by towns or parishes, either alone or in groups, to provide them with special powers in regulating local matters such as poor relief, street lighting, watching etc. The first such Act was that promoted by the parishes of Bristol in 1696 which enabled them to form a 'Corporation of the Poor' to jointly administer poor relief across the city. The Corporation could set up workhouses and appoint paid officers.

During the eighteenth and early nineteenth centuries, many such Local Acts were passed especially in London. Although the majority were later repealed or superseded, a few Local Acts, such as that obtained by Oxford in 1771 'for better regulating the Poor within the City', effectively remained in operation until 1930.
(*See also*: **Incorporation**; **London**)

LOCAL GOVERNMENT BOARD

In 1871, responsibility for overseeing the administration of poor relief in England and Wales passed from the Poor Law Board to the new Local Government Board (LGB). As well as poor relief, the LGB was responsible for administering the law relating to local government and public health.

A similar change took place in Ireland in 1872, when the LGB for Ireland succeeded the Irish Poor Law Commissioners. Scotland followed suit in 1894 when responsibility for poor relief passed from the Scottish Board of Supervision to the LGB for Scotland.
(*See also*: **Ministry of Health**; **Poor Laws**)

LOCK WARD

(*See*: **Venereal Disease**)

LONDON

The history of publicly funded poor relief and the operation of workhouses and related institutions is nowhere more complex and convoluted than in London. London's status as the nation's capital, its size and complexity, and its large and densely crowded population, often made it the subject of special local legislation, or with specific authorities being set up to deal with particular matters.

Even defining exactly what geographical area London covers can cause difficulties as the capital steadily grew over the centuries from the original walled city to the sprawling conurbation it had become by the twentieth century. For much of the workhouse era, the extent of

The main frontage of London's Bishopgate Street workhouse in 1819. The site was redeveloped in the 1870s with the building of Liverpool Street Station.

metropolitan London was broadly the area covered by the Bills of Mortality – weekly returns of the deaths occurring in each parish across an area encompassing the City of London, the City of Westminster, the Borough of Southwark, and a gradually increasing number of parishes in Middlesex, Surrey and, later, Kent. By the mid-nineteenth century, the metropolitan area extended north to Stoke Newington, south to Camberwell, west to Hammersmith, and east to Bromley on the northern bank of the Thames or to Woolwich on the southern bank. Following the Local Government Act of 1888, the metropolitan area was reconstituted as the City and County of London. Although this did not affect the administration of poor relief as such, metropolitan Poor Law Unions and parishes previously located in Middlesex, Surrey and Kent now fell within of the new County of London.

The Royal Hospitals
One of London's earliest provisions for the poor was introduced by Bishop Ridley's City of London Committee, set up in 1553 to tackle destitution in the capital. Ridley divided the poor into three categories: the poor by impotency (e.g. the aged, blind, lame, orphans), the poor by casualty (e.g. the sick, wounded soldiers), and the thriftless poor (e.g. the idle, vagabonds).[231] Relief was provided in four Royal Hospitals which had been closed after Henry VIII's dissolution of the monasteries but gradually restored during the reign of Edward VI. St Bartholomew's and St Thomas provided care for the sick and aged, while Christ's Hospital housed and educated homeless children. The Bethlem (or Bethlehem) Hospital, also known as 'Bedlam', operated as an asylum for the poor who were mentally ill. A new institution, Bridewell, occupied Henry VIII's former palace on the banks of the River Fleet at Blackfriars. From 1555, it provided punishment and hard labour for idlers, vagrants and prostitutes, with inmates who were classed as sturdy (i.e. able-bodied) beggars receiving a 'thin diet onely sufficing to sustaine them in health'.[232] Despite its prison-like character, Bridewell was also partly used for lodging the poor and sick. Bridewell became a model for the 'House of Correction' which each county was required to establish from 1576.

The City of London Corporation
The old City of London comprised more than 100 parishes, most lying within its ancient walls and a few just outside ('without') the walls. The city's first workhouses proper were set up by the London Corporation of the Poor, a body created by the 1647 Ordinance for the Relief and Employment of the Poor. The Ordnance's provisions included the erection of 'workhouses' – one of the earliest official uses of the word. The Corporation was given two confiscated royal properties – Heydon House in the Minories, and the Wardrobe building in Vintry – in which it established workhouses. By 1655, up to 100 children and 1,000 adults were receiving relief although residence was not a pre-requisite. Adults could perform out-work in their own homes, or carry it out each day at one of the workhouses.

As well as basic literacy, children in Corporation care were taught singing. A verse of one of their songs paints a very rosy picture of their treatment:

In filthy rags we clothed were
In good warm Raiment now appear
From Dunghill to King's Palace transferred,
Where Education, wholesome Food,
Meat, drink and Lodging, all that[s] good
For Soul and Body, are so well prepared.[233]

The Corporation's activities ended with the Restoration in 1660 when Charles II reclaimed his properties.

The 1662 Settlement Act included a provision for Corporations to be created in the City of London, Westminster, and parts of Middlesex and Surrey. As far as the City of London was concerned, shortage of funds, together with the plague (1665–66) and the Great Fire of London (1667), resulted in little activity until it was revived by a further Act in 1698. The Corporation was governed by the Lord Mayor as president, the City Aldermen, and fifty-two citizens, chosen by the Common-Council, as assistants. According to John Strype's 1720 *Survey of the Cities of London and Westminster*, the intention of the Corporation's workhouse, opened in 1700 on Bishopsgate Street, was 'to employ all the poor Children, Beggars, Vagrants, and other idle and disorderly Persons that are, or can be found within the said City of London and the Liberties thereof.' The children, up to 400 in number, were taught to read and write, and given work to do until they could be put out as apprentices, sent to sea, or 'otherwise disposed'.

The workhouse itself Strype described as 'a very strong and useful Building, and of large Dimensions, containing three long Rooms or Galleries, one over another, for Workhouses, which are all filled with Boys and Girls at Work, some Knitting, most Spinning of Wool; and a convenient Number of Women and Men teaching and overseeing them; Fires burning in the Chimneys in the Winter time, to keep the Rooms and the Children warm.' The building also included a 'large and convenient Brewhouse'.

The workhouse food was said to be 'plain but wholesome and sufficient'. Most meals consisted of bread, butter or cheese, and beer, with the weekly inclusion of 'Pease Pottage', 'Plumb Pudding Pye', 'Furmity' and, on Saturdays, a 'plain Flower Sewet Dumpling'. A large room was used as a dining room and chapel where prayers were said at 6a.m. and 6p.m. On Sundays, the inmates all went to church at St Helen's.

The reluctance of the city's parishes to fund the workhouse forced it to drastically reduce its intake of children and for much of the eighteenth century it mainly operated as a House of Correction for beggars and vagrants. In 1829, a private Act of Parliament paved the way for the disposal of the Bishopsgate site as the workhouse had fallen into disuse and needed extensive repairs.

Parish Poor Relief

As elsewhere, parishes in London had two main options when it came to dealing with those claiming poor relief. It could either provide them with out relief or, especially after 1723, it could offer them indoor relief – the workhouse. Across the country as a whole, out relief was always by far the most dominant preference. London parishes, however, had a rather different bias. The parliamentary poor relief returns of 1804 showed that in England and Wales, excluding the metropolis, expenditure on out relief was three times that spent of indoor relief. In the metropolis, however, out relief expenditure was a little over half of that on indoor relief. The capital's indoor relief expenditure accounted for almost a fifth of the £1.2 million spent nationally each year.[234] In terms of numbers relieved, the 1804 returns show that in London, 36.1 per cent of claimants received indoor relief, compared to a figure of 11.4 per cent across the rest of the country.

London's disposition towards workhouses partly reflected it buoyant labour market, with no need to subsidise wages from the poor rates as increasingly happened in rural areas. The transient nature of much of the population and the ease of moving of between parishes made the tracking of claimants difficult and so giving ample opportunity for fraudulent claims. Offering relief in a workhouse bypassed these difficulties.

Early Parish Workhouses

Two of the earliest metropolitan workhouses were set up by the Westminster parishes of St Margaret in around 1664 and St Martin in the Fields in 1665.[235] As elsewhere, however, it was the passing of Knatchbull's Act in 1723 that generated a flurry of workhouse opening.

In the City of London, just over a third of the parishes opened workhouses in the eighteenth century, amongst the earliest being St Alban's Wood Street and St Giles Cripplegate, both in 1724. The 1732 edition of *An Account of Several Workhouses* described the St Dunstan in the West workhouse as:

> A New House... built 1728 joining to the Burying Ground in Fetter-Lane for the Reception of the Poor, wherein there are now 30 Men and Women, and 26 Children, of which 21 are daily sent to the Parish Charity-School, and work only out of School Hours. These and the grown Persons, who are not employed in keeping the House clean, and nursing the old and young, card Wool, and spin Mop Yarn for a Turner in the Parish, who furnishes the Wool for this purpose, allowing 14 pound of Wool for every 12 pound they return spun up, in regard of the Waste that is made, and the Turner pays 2d. for the carding and spinning every pound so returned.
>
> They make and mend their own Cloaths for the House, and when there is Want, spin up a Quantity of finer Wool, which is wove into Serge, for the occasions of the House, of which they have seldom less than 100 or 200 Yards in the House.
>
> They have roast or boiled Beef 4 Days in the Week for Dinner, viz. Sundays, Tuesdays, Wednesdays, and Fridays, and other Days, Rice-Milk, or Dumplins. Breakfasts of Broth, or Milk-Porridge, and Suppers of Bread and Butter, or Cheese.
>
> Prayers are read in the House every Day, and they that are able, go to Church every Sunday.

In the City of Westminster, the parish of St James erected a workhouse on Poland Street in 1725. In the same year, St Martin in the Fields set up new premises at the corner of Hemmings Row and Castle Street, on what is now part of the National Gallery site.

In the wider metropolitan area, the earliest parishes to establish workhouses included Wapping Hamlet, Stepney (1723); Ratcliffe Hamlet, Stepney (1723); St Mary Matfellon, Whitechapel (1724); Limehouse Hamlet, Stepney (1725); Mile End Old Town (1725), St Giles in the Fields (1725); and Kensington (1726). Typical of these establishments was that at Christ Church, Spitalfields, described in 1731 as:

> A Large House, formerly belonging to a Throwster in Bell-Lane... hired and fitted up Midsummer 1728, where there are now 84 poor People, of which about 30 are Children, employed in winding Bengal Raw Silk for several Throwsters, who send in the silk, and allow for winding it on Bobbins 3d. per Pound for the coarser Sort, 4d. for the middling, and 5d, for the better Sort, by which at present they earn about 70l. per Annum, and are so fully employed, that they have left off picking Ockam, and spinning Wool. The Children are taught to read and say their Catechism, and the old Women knit Stockings for the House. They have 3 Flesh Dinners in each Week allow'd them.[236]

The parliamentary summary of overseers' returns published in 1777 found that London's workhouses were amongst the largest in the country. Westminster's eight establishments had an average capacity of 415 places, with those at St George Hanover Square and St Martin in the Fields each able to hold 700. In metropolitan Middlesex, the Whitechapel and St Marylebone workhouses each housed up to 600 inmates.

Farming the Poor

Knatchbull's Act allowed parishes to hand over the operation of their workhouses to private contractors or 'farmers', which many did over the next century. This was particularly so in the City of

London where, according to the 1777 survey, the number of workhouses being run by city parishes had fallen to seventeen. Factors such as the cost of running a workhouse or the lack of suitable premises had led the majority to contract out the accommodation of their poor, either to a neighbouring parish which had a workhouse, or to a commercial 'farmer' based outside the city. By the early 1800s, the parishes of All Hallows the Less, St Augustine and St Alban were paying a pauper farmer in Hoxton the sum of 4s per head per week to house their indoor poor. In 1815, the establishment run by James Robertson at Hoxton could accommodate up to 300 paupers coming from as many as forty different parishes in the city. Thomas Tipple's pauper farm at 12 Queen's Street, Hoxton, had 230 places and served seventeen city parishes, while Edward Deacon's two houses at Mile End and Bow accommodated a total of 520 paupers from more than forty city parishes.[237]

Another variety of institution, the 'baby farm', resulted from Hanway's Act of 1766 which required that pauper children under the age of six from metropolitan parishes should be sent to school in the countryside at least three miles from London or Westminster. In 1796, at St Martin in the Fields it was reported that:

> Between 70 and 80 children are generally out at nurse in the Country, at a weekly allowance of 3s. (lately advanced to 3s. 6d.). At 7 or 8 they are taken into the house, taught a little reading, etc., for 3 or 4 years, and put out as apprentices.[238]

Parishes Adopting Special Legislation

A number of London parishes obtained Local Acts to provide them with specific powers relating to the local administration of poor relief or the funding and operation of workhouses. Despite the legal expenses involved, between 1742 and 1830, around twenty parishes pursued this route, sometimes needing to obtain more than one Act when the previous one was later found to be inadequate or defective in some respect. Parishes obtaining Local Acts included: St Botolph, Aldate (1742), St Martin in the Fields (1749), St Margaret & St John Westminster (1751), St George Hanover Square (1753), St Mary Abbots, Kensington (1756), St Luke, Middlesex (1757), St James, Westminster (1762), St John, Hackney (1764), St Clement Danes (1764), St Andrew, Holborn (1766), St Matthew, Bethnal Green (1772), St Mary, Whitechapel (1772), St Leonard, Shoreditch (1774), St James & St John, Clerkenwell (1775), St Marylebone (1775), St Paul's, Covent Garden (1775), St Mary, Islington (1776), St Bride's (1792), St Botolph's, Bishopsgate (1795), St Sepulchre (1798), St Pancras (1805), Camberwell (1813), Stepney (1817), St Mary, Newington (1814), and St Giles in the Fields & St George, Bloomsbury (1830).[239]

The Special Vestries Act, introduced by Sturges Bourne in 1819, was almost totally ignored by metropolitan parishes, especially those already operating under Local Acts which provided many of the same powers. Much better received, however, was Hobhouse's Act of 1831 which allowed the participation in vestry elections of any ratepayer who had lived in the parish for at least a year. Hobhouse's Act was adopted by the parishes of St George Hanover Square, St James Westminster, St John Westminster, St Marylebone and St Pancras.

After 1834

The 1834 Poor Law Amendment Act had a hostile reception in many parts of London, with protests both against both its principles and its implementation. Some of the proposed unions were criticised as being too large. Some richer parishes complained that being joined in a union with a poorer parish would result in them having an unfair financial burden. Particularly strong resistance came from Local Act parishes and those who had adopted Hobhouse's Act, which were exempt from the 1834 Act unless a two-thirds majority of their ratepayers voted to adopt it. In 1837, after the Poor Law Commissioners (PLC) tried to bypass this requirement and force such parishes into changing their status, a legal challenge was successfully mounted by the Local Act parish of St Pancras.

By the late 1830s, some thirty-five separate poor relief authorities were in operation in the capital. Fifteen new Poor Law Unions had been formed (City of London, East London,

The Cleveland Street workhouse, erected in the 1770s for the London parish of St Paul's, Covent Garden, then taken over by the Strand Union in 1836. A young Charles Dickens lived just a few doors away from the building, which is now generally accepted as the basis for the workhouse in *Oliver Twist*.

West London, Greenwich, Hackney, Holborn, Kensington, Lewisham, Poplar, St Olave's, St Saviour's, Stepney, Strand, Wandsworth & Clapham, and Whitechapel). Eight individual parishes (Bermondsey, Bethnal Green, Camberwell, Lambeth, Rotherhithe, St George in the East, St Martin in the Fields, and Southwark St George the Martyr) were also now operating under the 1834 Act. The remaining twelve Local Act parishes or united parishes (St George Hanover Square, St Giles in the Fields & St George Bloomsbury, St James Westminster, St James & St John Clerkenwell, St Mary Islington, St Luke, St Marylebone, St Pancras, St Leonard Shoreditch, St Margaret & St John Westminster, St Sepulchre and St Mary Newington) retained their independence from the new system.

The City of London Union

The PLC initially planned to create a single City of London Union comprising 108 parishes. Many of the parishes within the old city walls were tiny and, by 1834, none was operating a workhouse. However, some of the city's parishes outside the walls had ample workhouse accommodation which could serve the new union. To keep the size of the proposed union's Board of Guardians within reason, the Commissioners sought parliamentary approval for a scheme allowing a guardian to represent more than one parish. When this was not forthcoming, the Commissioners set up three separate unions: the City of London Union (which included ninety-six parishes inside the city walls and two outside); the East London Union (with four parishes); the West London Union (seven parishes).

The City of London was a wealthy union and was initially extremely reluctant to build a union workhouse. Most of its paupers received outdoor relief, largely in cash, supplemented by generous allowances of food and drink. Its indoor paupers were farmed out, at great expense, in accommodation run by private contractors and located miles away from the union's offices at the Mansion House. Children were placed at Mr Aubin's school at Norwood, women went to a house in Stepney, and able-bodied males were sent to Marlborough House on Peckham High Street. Marlborough House was also used for casuals, numbering up to 300 a night, which was just enough in summer but wholly inadequate in winter. In January 1841, more than 1,000 casuals besieged it every night, and were crammed three to a bed in temporary wooden huts. Eventually, the union agreed to build its own workhouse on Bow Road.

In 1869, the City of London Union, the East London Union, and the West London Union were amalgamated to form an enlarged City of London Union. The new union took over the former East London Union workhouse at Homerton and the former West London Union workhouse on Cornwallis Road in Upper Holloway. The Bow Road site became the union's infirmary.

City of London Infirmary & Mile End R.E.

The City of London's workhouse opened in 1849 on Bow Road at Mile End, well out of sight of the city's residents. The palatial design cost over £55,000 and boasted central heating, a dining hall measuring 100ft by 50ft, Siberian marble pillars, and a chapel with stained-glass windows and an organ.

Workhouse Building after 1834

The antipathy of many metropolitan parishes to the 1834 Poor Law Amendment was evident not only in the refusal of parishes such as St Pancras and St Marylebone to give up their Local Act status, but also in the general reluctance to build new workhouse accommodation. Many parishes already had large existing premises which, although often quite old, they considered adequate for continued use without the expense of erecting new buildings. The increasing difficulty and cost of finding suitable sites also became a particular problem for London parishes. In the first decade of the 1834 Act's operation, only five new workhouses were erected in the metropolis: Greenwich (1840), Wandsworth & Clapham (1840), Whitechapel (1842), Bethnal Green (1842) and Chelsea (1843).

A typical example of the old parish accommodation retained for use after 1834 was the former St Paul Covent Garden workhouse on Cleveland Street taken over by the new Strand Union in 1836. Its appearance in the mid-1850s was described as:

> A square four-storied building fronting the street, with two wings of similar elevation projecting eastwards from each corner. The necessary laundry work of the establishment, which never in my time fell below five hundred inmates, was carried on beneath the entrance hall which was filled with steam and the odours from washing the paupers' linen. On the right side of the main building was a badly paved yard, which led down to the back entrance from Charlotte Street; on each side there was first, a carpenter's shop and a dead house, and secondly, opposite to it, a tinker's shop with a forge and unceiled roof. This communicated with a ward with two beds in it, used for fever and foul cases, only a lath and plaster partition separating it from the tinker's shop.[240]

Workhouse Reform

The Cleveland Street workhouse was associated with two prominent campaigns of workhouse reform. The first, in 1853, occurred when Louisa Twining visited an old woman who was an inmate of the workhouse, something which required a special letter of permission from the Strand guardians. After witnessing the feelings of neglect experienced by the inmates, she began to press for better access for visitors to workhouses, later founding the Workhouse Visiting Society.

In 1856, Dr Joseph Rogers was appointed as the workhouse medical officer and was appalled at the cramped and dirty conditions he discovered. He became a leading light in the campaign to improve workhouse medical facilities which eventually resulted in the passing of the 1867 Metropolitan Poor Act. A highly influential contribution to the cause was made by the medical journal *The Lancet*, which in 1865 published detailed articles about the abysmal conditions in London workhouses and their infirmaries. In its report on Cleveland Street, *The Lancet* observed that:

> There are no paid nurses whatsoever! There are twenty-two pauper nurses, and twenty-two pauper helpers. Of the former, very few can be considered fitted for their work as far as regards knowledge, and many are mainly incompetent from age or physical feebleness. The helpers are, of course, mere ignorant drudges. And yet this nursing staff has to minister to the wants of a sick population, which on the 28th of January last amounted to nearly 200 sick, besides 260 infirm or insane... The wards are low-pitched and gloomy... and there is a general frowsiness perceptible throughout the house. The beds on which the patient's lie are of flock, thin, lumpy, and wretched.

It was an equally dismal story at Bethnal Green: no running water was available from 5p.m. until 7a.m.; lighting and ventilation were inadequate, with many windows 6ft from the floor to prevent the inmates seeing out; overcrowding resulted in each patient having only 300 cubic feet of space, only a quarter of official recommendations; washing facilities were severely lacking – in one children's ward, seventeen children were washed daily in one pail, several in the same water, and dried with sheets; in the male wards, forty-five men were served by two latrines which were flushed only twice a day; up to 600 sick inmates were nursed by a staff of two paid but untrained nurses, assisted by forty pauper nurses and helpers 'whose tendencies to drink cannot be controlled'.

As well as Rogers and *The Lancet*, the campaign to reform workhouse medical facilities was supported by other prominent people of the day such as Charles Dickens. Its most influential advocate was Florence Nightingale, who personally lobbied the Prime Minister and the

The Whitechapel Union workhouse, opened in about 1842 on Charles Street (now Vallance Road), was one of the few new London workhouses to be erected in the years immediately following the 1834 Poor Law Amendment Act.

The new Islington workhouse on St John's Road erected in 1868–70. Although mostly demolished in the 1970s to make way for housing, the roadside guardians' boardroom block (just right of centre) still survives.

president of the Poor Law Board. Eventually, their efforts bore fruit in the shape of the 1867 Metropolitan Poor Act which aimed to take the care of the sick poor away from individual unions and parishes. An initial scheme to form six Sick Asylum Districts, each with its own large hospital, was found to be largely impractical, although two did survive – the Central London and the Poplar & Stepney Asylum Districts. Instead, some existing unions such as Holborn were enlarged, and Boards of Guardians were pressed to separate the administration of their workhouses and infirmaries which ideally would be sited at separate locations. The Local Act status of many of London's parishes, which had allowed them to escape most of the strictures of the 1834 Poor Law Amendment Act, was also abolished.

In the years that followed, some authorities acquired new sites on which to erect infirmaries, such as Holborn (at Archway in 1879) and St Marylebone (at Ladbroke Grove in 1881). Whitechapel built a new workhouse on South Grove in 1871, with the existing workhouse site on Baker Street then becoming the union infirmary. Similarly, when Wandsworth and Clapham opened a new workhouse on Garratt Lane in 1886, its old workhouse on St John's Hill became the union's infirmary. Some unions already possessing multiple workhouse sites concentrated their medical facilities at a particular location, such as St Olave's new infirmary on the old Rotherhithe workhouse site in 1876. Finally, a new infirmary could be opened adjacent to an existing workhouse but separated from it as happened for example at Mile End Old Town in 1883 and at Paddington in 1886.

London's Last Workhouses

A steady trickle of new workhouse building continued into the early years of the twentieth century. St Olave's workhouse at Ladywell, completed in 1900, was the only new workhouse in London designed specifically for elderly inmates. The new Greenwich workhouse at Grove Park was finished in 1902 but, owing to an unexpected drop in inmate numbers, stood empty for two years. Hammersmith's new workhouse, one of the last ever to be built, was completed in 1905 with construction costs amounting to the then enormous sum of £261,000. The grandeur of the workhouse dining hall and rumours of teapots costing 18s 6d each led to the establishment being condemned by some critics as a 'Pauper's Paradise'. The cost of the project virtually bankrupted the Hammersmith guardians.

Responsibility for all aspects of poor relief (or public assistance, as it then became known) was transferred to the London County Council in 1930 by which time the gradual consolidation of Poor Law Unions and parishes had reduced their number to twenty-two.

(*See also*: **Medical Care**; **Metropolitan Asylums Board**; **Metropolitan Common Poor Fund**; **Quaker Workhouses**; Green (2010); *www.londonlives.org*)

LOVE AND MARRIAGE

Males and females in the workhouse were strictly segregated – this included husbands and wives. An exception to this rule was introduced in 1847 when elderly married couples who were both aged over sixty could request a shared room. In practice, little such accommodation was provided – in 1895 only 200 couples in the whole of England and Wales were enjoying this privilege.[241] It was often suggested that many long-married couples were glad of an excuse to be away from each other and so did not take up this option.[242] The provision for married couples to live together was extended in 1876 to include those where either partner was over sixty, or was infirm, sick or disabled.[243]

In 1896, the Hampstead Board of Guardians debated the case of two of their elderly inmates, Mr and Mrs 'Pigeon' Hill, who had left the workhouse for an hour or so, gone to church, and got married. They had then returned and demanded a place in the workhouse's special married couples' quarters. The couple were both over sixty and each had been married twice before. The guardians, who clearly felt they were being manipulated, called for an alteration in the law so that the privilege of special quarters should be extended only to those who had been married for six months previously.

If Mr and Mrs Hill had received the guardians' blessing, they would have still needed to get married outside the confines of the workhouse. Even where a workhouse had its own chapel, the solemnisation of marriage was the only service specifically prohibited from being conducted there.[244]

Despite its restrictions, the normal daily work of the workhouse did provide occasional opportunities for male and female inmates to briefly come into contact and initiate a courtship. According to the anonymous author of the 1885 'insider's story' *One of Them*:

> More progress in an intrigue is made in five minutes, by a pair of indoor paupers when they happen to meet, than is made in as many weeks by persons more fortunately placed.
>
> A couple of meetings will suffice to engage a pair. And once the engagement is formed, the parties to it must have frequent communication, and all sorts of tricks and contrivances are employed to secure it. Confidants on both sides are indispensable, and found without difficulty. All other paupers, indeed, make it a point of honour to further such an affair. Messages are exchanged; so are little notes, most of which are curiosities in their way. Many are penned on the margins of old newspapers, in the queerest possible hands, and in such spelling as is scarcely to be met with elsewhere. I have seen a pauper love-letter scratched with a nail on the bowl of an old iron spoon.
>
> As a rule, however, a pauper flirtation is evanescent – a matter of six weeks or two months. Within that time it attains full intensity. Then – no better means presenting itself – the enamoured pair discharge themselves on the same morning, and go out to spend twelve to forty-eight hours together, according to the amount of money at their disposal. This is at once the consummation of the love-fit and its close. They resume their places in the house completely cured of it.

Workhouse romances could sometimes have a happy ending, though. In the Christmas of 1910, a young widower from a northern town was admitted to the casual wards of Rugby workhouse. A painter by trade, he stayed on at the workhouse for three weeks and did some painting. Taking a fancy to one of the female inmates, a young woman with two small children, he asked her to be his wife. She declined at first, but he persisted and on leaving the workhouse in mid- January he told the workhouse master he would return and marry her on 26 March. He returned to his home where he secured regular employment, and kept up a constant correspondence with the girl. On the appointed date, he presented himself at the workhouse with an outfit for his intended bride. This she put on, was married by the Registrar at the union offices, and before midday was travelling northwards with her husband and children.[245]

LUNATICS

(*See*: **Mentally Ill**)

MALTHUS, THOMAS ROBERT

Born in 1766, Robert Malthus – he rarely used his first name – was an English political economist, best known for his theories concerning population and the factors that caused its growth or decline. Malthus believed that the effect of the poor laws was actively to worsen the situation of the poor. The giving of poor relief led to an increase in population without increasing the food for its support. It also encouraged young and improvident marriages. The poor laws thus 'create the poor which they maintain', pushing up the price of food and resulting in yet more relief claimants.[246] Malthus proposed an abolition of poor relief and its replacement by charity.

MABYS

(*See*: **Aftercare**)

MARRYOTT, MATTHEW

Matthew Marryott was a workhouse entrepreneur from Buckinghamshire. He opened his first establishment at Olney in 1714 and over the next fifteen years was involved in the setting up and management of many others in the east and south Midlands and around London. He became an advisor to the Society for Promoting Christian Knowledge (SPCK) who encouraged the use of workhouses. Marryott's activities were brought to prominence in the SPCK's 1725 book *An Account of Several Workhouses for Employing and Maintaining the Poor* which described the operation of over 100 workhouses and the financial benefits to parishes of their introduction. Marryott may also have been the originator of the workhouse 'test' – offering poor relief only to those prepared to enter the confines of a strictly run workhouse.

Marryott's reputation suffered a blow with the appearance in 1731 of an illustrated pamphlet entitled *The Workhouse Cruelty; Workhouses Turn'd Gaols; and Gaolers Executioners*, published under the pseudonym of 'Christian Love Poor'. The work accused Marryott of vicious cruelty at the St Giles in the Fields workhouse. Inmates in the 'Dark Hole' were said to have been starved to death, while the corpse of a woman who had died during childbirth was mutilated with her finger cut off and her eyes gouged out.

(*See also*: **An Account of Several Workhouses**; Hitchcock (2004))

MASTER

The man (as it usually was) in charge of the day-to-day running of a workhouse was usually known as its master although in the parish workhouse era, and also in Scotland, the term governor was often used instead. Where a parish workhouse was run under contract, the manager of the workhouse might be referred to as the contractor or the farmer.

The master of a union workhouse was required to be at least twenty-one years in age, able to keep accounts, and to provide a bond with two guarantors in case of any financial impropriety.

Amongst the master's numerous duties were:

- Admitting paupers into the workhouse.
- Ensuring that new male inmates were searched, cleansed, clothed and classified.
- Holding a daily roll-call and inspection of inmates.
- Saying grace before and after meals, and reading prayers to the inmates before breakfast and after supper each day.
- Enforcing industry, order, punctuality and cleanliness.
- Providing work, training or occupation for the inmates.
- Superintending the preparation and distribution of food.
- Checking the male dormitories at 'lights-out' time.
- Checking that the male paupers were properly clothed.
- Registering all births and deaths in the workhouse.
- Summoning the medical officer for any inmate taken ill and, in the case of dangerous sickness, sending for the chaplain or any relative or friend requested.
- Informing the medical officer and next of kin of any death in the workhouse and, if needed, making burial arrangements.
- Ensuring that the workhouse building, fixtures, fittings etc. were kept clean and in good order.
- Reporting at each guardians' meeting on the number of the inmates in the workhouse
- Bringing forward to the guardians any inmate wishing to make a complaint.

The perfect master, it was suggested, should be 'a person of sufficient education, strength of will, and firmness of purpose, whilst he is considerate and gentle in his bearing, without servility or disrespect to the guardians and the higher officers, and without intolerance or laxity to the other officers and the inmates. He should be of quick intelligence and good judgement to decide upon disputes which will arise amongst the officers and inmates, and of strict integrity in the care and use of the stores entrusted to his care. He should have due control over himself, and never exhibit, or allow others to exhibit, violence of temper, or use, or allow to be used, profane or irritating language.' He should also be 'a friend and protector of the inmates'.[247]

Not all masters attained these lofty ideals, however. In the early years of the New Poor Law, masters were often former policemen or army NCOs and often rough and poorly educated men.[248] The well-known scandal at Andover workhouse in 1845 revealed the callous and cruel activities of the master, Waterloo veteran Colin McDougal. Eight years later, the appointment of former policeman George Catch as master of the Strand Union workhouse inaugurated a career of tyranny which spanned fifteen years and three different institutions.

Such abuses, though, were not necessarily representative of the great many workhouse masters who performed their duties competently and conscientiously and with concern for their charges. George Douglas, who served as master of the St Marylebone workhouse for thirty-two years from 1862, brought a 'blending of firmness and humanity' to the role. He used his position to relax some of the harsher elements of workhouse life, for example by allowing the old women to have their own teapot and make their own tea.[249] Equally long-serving was Daniel Pickett, master at Stratford-on-Avon workhouse from 1896 to 1927. After his death, Pickett's obituary declared that 'the thousands of men who came under his care, representing the flotsam and jetsam of humanity, had a very warm regard for the "Guvnor" who, with his

The master and matron of the Caistor Union workhouse, Mr and Mrs Solomon, and their staff in 1905.

great capacity for friendship, his rare sympathy and kindly nature was always ready to do his best for the travellers who came his way.'[250] If length of service can be held as a reflection of quality then Abingdon in Berkshire was exceedingly fortunate in having only three workhouse masters in the period from 1835 to 1918.

A workhouse master held office for life, unless he resigned or became incapable of discharging his duties. Where, as often happened, the master and matron were married, and the wife died, resigned or was dismissed, then the master had to vacate his post unless the guardians and Poor Law Commissioners agreed to re-appoint him. The converse situation applied if the master died or left his post.
(*See also*: **Catch, George**; **Matron**; **Scandals**)

MATRON

The running of a workhouse was often divided between a man, the master, who was invariably the senior partner in the arrangement, and a woman, the matron, sometimes known as the mistress in Old Poor Law workhouses. The matron, was often the master's wife, generally supervised the institution's female inmates and children, and also managed the domestic activities of the establishment.

The matron of a union workhouse was, like the master, required to be at least twenty-one years in age, able to keep accounts, and to provide a bond with two guarantors in case of any financial impropriety.

Amongst the matron's duties were:

- Overseeing the admission of female paupers and children under seven.
- Overseeing the occupation of female paupers.
- Assisting the schoolmistress in training children for service.
- Checking the female dormitories at 'lights-out' time.
- Upholding the moral conduct and orderly behaviour of the females and children, and ensuring they were clean and properly dressed.

- Superintending the making and mending of the inmates' linen and clothing.
- Superintending the laundering of clothes and bedding.
- Ensuring proper care diet for the children and sick.
- Searching females entering or leaving the workhouse, when requested by the porter.

The usual preference of Boards of Guardians was for the master and matron to be a married couple without dependent children or, in the words often used in advertisements for such posts, 'without encumbrance'. Where they did have children, or they arrived after the couple were in post, there was no guarantee that they could be housed on the workhouse premises or, even if that were possible, a payment for their maintenance would be expected.
(*See also*: **Master**)

MEDICAL CARE

Although the 1601 Poor Relief Act required parishes to provide for the 'Lame, Impotent, Old, Blind, and such other among them being Poor, and not able to work' it made no direct reference to the sick. However, since not being able to work was often a consequence of being ill or injured, the sick formed a significant part of those receiving relief. Treatment of the sick, as opposed to just their maintenance, was quite another matter as medical care could be expensive. However, even in purely financial terms, there were attractions for a parish in restoring someone to health as quickly as possible and coming off the weekly relief list.

Early Medical Care for the Poor
Parish medical relief could be provided in various ways. Doctor's bills for individual patients could be paid as they arose. Alternatively, a parish doctor could be appointed and paid on an annual basis to provide treatment for the parish poor, including any workhouse inmates. This was often on a fixed price contract with extra fees for certain types of case such as broken bones or attendance at a birth. In 1792, the Isle of Wight workhouse rules stipulated the employment of a 'surgeon, apothecary, and man-midwife [to] duly attend, and administer proper medicines to all such persons in the house, and such poor out of the house, [and] when called in to any poor woman in any difficult obstetrical case, in which a midwife hath been ineffectually employed, be allowed Two Guineas for every such attendance; and shall be paid Two Shillings and Sixpence for every patient he may inoculate.' In 1808, the Wallingford Gilbert Union appointed Mr James Dehay as surgeon, apothecary and man-midwife for the poor of the union (outside the workhouse as well as inside) at a salary of 30 guineas per annum, which also covered drugs, medical applications and attendances, except for those involving venereal disease.

Ancillary medical care could also be provided by parish nurses whose role could include the wet-nursing of infants, dry-nursing of children, and sick-nursing of adults. In eighteenth-century London, nursing was one of the most common female occupations, engaged in by more than 12 per cent of women in the city.[251]

The second half of the eighteenth century saw a growth in the establishment of voluntary hospitals funded by charitable donations and by annual subscriptions. Subscribers could refer a certain number of patients to the hospital based on the size of their contribution. Many parishes took advantage of this provision with Manchester Infirmary, for example, eventually having seventy-seven Lancashire parishes amongst its subscribers.[252] Some towns also set up dispensaries funded in a similar manner where the poor could obtain basic treatment or medicines.

Workhouse Medical Care After 1834
Following the 1834 Poor Law Amendment Act, each union was required to appoint one or more medical officers to provide treatment for its sick poor, both within and outside the workhouse.

The position of medical officer was not always a particularly attractive one. Until 1842, posts could be put out to competitive tender, with the appointment usually being made to whomever demanded the lowest salary. This meant that applicants were often the least experienced members of the profession, or ones with private practice where the physician's priorities would invariably lie. Apart from attending patients, medical officers often had to pay for any drugs they prescribed.

Every union workhouse had some designated area used as an infirmary for the treatment of sick or injured inmates. Workhouse infirmaries were often poorly suited to their role, however. The buildings were often small, badly laid out, lacking in light and ventilation, or with poor sanitary facilities. Lack of space often meant that bed-sharing sometimes took place in infirmary wards. Early nursing care in union workhouses was usually in the hands of female inmates who might be deaf or not be able to read – a serious problem when dealing with labels on medicine bottles. For taking on their duties, pauper nurses were often rewarded with beer, and usually had access to 'medicinal' spirits such as brandy, with the result that drunkenness was sometimes a problem. Inmates often had to resort to bribery in order to get a nurse's attention.

The appalling conditions that existed in some workhouse infirmaries came under the spotlight in 1856 when London's St Pancras workhouse was the subject of a Poor Law Board inquiry carried out by Dr Henry Bence Jones, physician to St George's Hospital. Jones' found that the workhouse was severely overcrowded, with patients in the infirmary having to be placed on the floor. Ventilation throughout the building was deficient, with fetid air from privies, sinks, drains, urinals and foul patients permeating many of the wards and producing sickness, headaches and dysentery amongst the inmates. The staff also complained of nausea, giddiness, sickness and loss of appetite. A lying-in room, also used as a sleeping room by night nurses, had a smell that was 'enough to knock you down'. In the women's receiving wards, more than eighty women and children slept in two rooms which provided a mere 164 cubic feet of space per adult. Worst of all were the underground 'pens' where between 300 and 900 applicants for out relief crowded each day, sometimes waiting until 7p.m. without food. The poor ventilation and smell in the pens was so poor as to cause women to faint and windows to be broken to obtain fresh air. The union's relieving officer reported that his predecessor had died of typhus, thought to be contracted from the foul air. Jones' heartfelt conclusion was that 'such a state of things ought not to be tolerated by the Government.'[253]

Pressure for improvements in workhouse medical care grew steadily in the late 1850s and early 1860s. Some of the most notable campaigners were Louisa Twining – founder of the Workhouse Visiting Society, Joseph Rogers – medical officer (and severe critic) of the Strand workhouse, Florence Nightingale – pioneer of nurse training, and the medical journal *The Lancet*. In 1865, *The Lancet* began a series of detailed reports about conditions in London's workhouse infirmaries. Its description of Shoreditch was typical of what it uncovered:

> The dressings were roughly and badly applied. Lotions and water-dressings were applied in rags, which were allowed to dry and stick. We saw sloughing ulcers and cancers so treated. In fact, this was the rule. Bandages seemed to be unknown. But the general character of the nursing will be appreciated by the detail of the one fact, that we found in one ward two paralytic patients with frightful sloughs of the back: they were both dirty, and lying on hard straw mattresses; the one dressed only with a rag steeped in chloride of lime solution, the other with a rag thickly covered with ointment. This latter was a fearful and very extensive sore, in a state of absolute putridity; the buttocks of the patient were covered with filth and excoriated, and the stench was masked by strewing dry chloride of lime on the floor under the bed. A spectacle more saddening or more discreditable cannot be imagined.[254]

As a result of such reports, the government was forced into action and in 1867 the Metropolitan Poor Act was passed to improve medical facilities for the capital's poor. The new Metropolitan Asylums Board (MAB) took over the provision of care for the London's sick poor in respect of infectious diseases and mental incapacity. The MAB subsequently set up its own institutions for the care of those suffering from smallpox, fever, 'imbecility', tuberculosis and venereal diseases, effectively becoming Britain's first state hospitals. The London poor law authorities were also directed to place their infirmary facilities under separate management and preferably on sites physically separated from the workhouse.

Nursing Care

Before 1863, not a single trained nurse was employed in any workhouse infirmary outside London. In 1865, only six of the capital's thirty-nine workhouse infirmaries had paid, trained nurses.[255] Changes in this state of affairs largely resulted from Florence Nightingale's campaigning for improvements in the standard of nursing care, and the founding in 1860 of the Nightingale Fund School at London's St Thomas's Hospital. A pioneering experiment took place in 1865 at Liverpool when local philanthropist William Rathbone financed the placement in the workhouse infirmary of twelve nurses trained at the Nightingale School. They were assisted by eighteen probationers and fifty-four able-bodied female inmates who received a small salary. Although the experiment had mixed results – the pauper assistants needed constant supervision and obtained intoxicants at the slightest opportunity – it was generally perceived overall to have been a success, in large part due to the efforts of the infirmary superintendent, Agnes Jones. Eventually a skilled nursing system spread to all union infirmaries in the country. The use of workhouse inmates for nursing duties was prohibited by the Local Government Board in 1897.

In another experiment, at the Chorlton Union workhouse in south Manchester, members of the All Saints Sisterhood of Margaret Street, London – a religious order engaged in nursing duties at London's University College Hospital – were appointed as superintendent nurses in 1866. According to the principles of their order, they received no salary, only board and rations. In 1868, one of the nuns, Sister Martha, died from typhus fever contracted during her work.

Despite the gradual improvement in medical care, standards in smaller provincial workhouses often lagged behind the larger establishments in London and other urban areas. In 1894, the *British Medical Journal* (BMJ) began a campaign to expose the poor conditions that still existed in many workhouses. Over the following two years, workhouses across England and Wales, and then in Ireland, were visited by a BMJ 'commission' and their often shocking inspection reports published in the journal. The BMJ's efforts undoubtedly resulted in further improvements in the standard of care, particularly for the elderly, sick and infirm, that was provided in the nation's workhouses.

One medical provision that was in frequent demand at many workhouses was the labour and lying-in ward. This was particularly so for pregnant single women who often became destitute once they became unable to work, or perhaps were dismissed by their employer or disowned by their family. Like other workhouse medical facilities, those for delivery were often basic. An official inspection at the Whitechapel workhouse in 1866 recommended that the labour ward be relocated so that the screams of those being delivered would not be heard those awaiting their own labour in the adjacent lying-in ward.[256]

One particular burden that workhouse infirmaries

A graduate of Florence Nightingale's nursing school at St Thomas' Hospital, Agnes Jones superintended the experimental nursing scheme begun in 1865 at Liverpool's huge workhouse infirmary. Though dying of typhus fever in 1868, her efforts led to the widespread use of trained nurses in workhouses.

Typical of the growing medical facilities provided at many workhouses was the pavilion-plan infirmary erected in 1897 by the King's Norton Union in Worcestershire. The site later became Selly Oak Hospital.

had to bear was that of patients with venereal diseases, sometimes known as 'lock' cases. Such cases were often refused admission to charitable and subscription hospitals, or would be offered only one course of treatment. Many workhouse infirmaries had special sections – the 'foul' wards – set aside for this type of patient.

Wider Access to Workhouse Infirmaries

Originally, union workhouse infirmaries were intended solely to provide care for workhouse inmates. From the 1880s, however, admission was increasingly permitted to those who, though poor, were not sufficiently destitute to require entry into the workhouse itself. Like all recipients of union relief, such patients first needed to have their means assessed by a union relieving officer and, where appropriate, might be required to contribute towards their maintenance while resident in the infirmary.

Prior to 1918, receipt of poor relief disqualified the recipient from voting. The 1885 Medical Relief Disqualification Removal Act[257] recognised the widening of access to workhouse infirmaries and provided that anyone who was in receipt only of poor-rate-funded medical care no longer lost their vote.

Over the years, the workhouse acquired a reputation, particularly amongst the elderly, as a place that, once inside, you would never leave – except in a coffin. In a sense, this was true, though not necessarily because they were unhealthy places. For many poor people at the end of their lives, the workhouse infirmary was the only source of medical care available to them in their final days.

The admission of non-paupers to workhouse infirmaries marked the beginnings of Britain's state-funded medical service, proving free treatment for those who would not otherwise be able to afford it. In some workhouses, the provision of medical facilities steadily expanded to the point where it outgrew the establishment's role of housing the destitute.

England's first municipal general hospital was created in 1920 when Bradford's city council, faced with a serious shortage of hospital beds in the locality, leased the Bradford workhouse site, initially for a five-year experimental period. St Luke's, as the hospital became known, received patients on the recommendation of a medical practitioner, with patients making a small payment based on their family income. The union also continued to use the hospital for pauper patients, itself making a payment for each case. An out-patients department was operated in the workhouse entrance and administration blocks.[258] In the 1930s, when control of former workhouse sites had passed to county and borough councils, more than fifty former workhouse infirmaries were 'appropriated' as municipal hospitals.[259]

When Britain's new National Health Service (NHS) was created following the Second World War, a large proportion of its real estate came from former workhouse and poor law establishments. It was significant that when Health Minister Nye Bevan officially launched the new NHS service on 5 July 1948, the location chosen for this momentous occasion was the former Barton-upon-Irwell Union infirmary at Davyhulme.

(*See also*: **Architecture**; **Death**; **District Medical Officer**; **Tuberculosis (TB)**; **Vaccination**; **Venereal Disease**; **Workhouse Infirmary Nursing Association**; **Workhouse Medical Officer**)

MEDICAL DISTRICT

A sub-division of a Poor Law Union, usually based on a grouping of parishes, for the administration of medical relief.
(*See also*: **District Medical Officer**; **Relief District**)

MEDICAL OFFICER

(*See*: **District Medical Officer**; **Workhouse Medical Officer**)

MEDICAL OFFICERS' ASSOCIATIONS

The first professional organisation for poor law physicians was the Convention of Poor Law Medical Officers, established in 1846 by the Poor Law Committee of the Provincial Medical and Surgical Association (renamed the British Medical Association in 1856). Chaired by Thomas Hodgkin, the Convention campaigned for reforms in the employment of union medical officers but became inactive in the 1850s.

In 1853, the Poor Law Medical Reform Association was set up by a medical officer of the Weymouth Union, Richard Griffin. The Association was well organised with local branches around the country and members paying subscriptions. Its demands included a parliamentary grant for providing medicines, the setting up of pauper dispensaries, and the inclusion of medical men in the Poor Law Board's team of inspectors.[260] In 1856, the Association absorbed the Convention of Poor Law Medical Officers.

In 1866, the Association of Metropolitan Workhouse Medical Officers was founded by Dr Joseph Rogers, medical officer of the Strand workhouse. Two years later, this group merged

A notice sent in 1896 by the master of the Malmesbury workhouse in Wiltshire about the serious illness of inmate Hezekiah Coster and requesting a visit from the recipient.

with the Poor Law Medical Reform Association and became known as the Poor Law Medical Officers Association, an organisation which became widely recognised and respected.

The Association of Poor Law Medical Officers of Ireland was formed in 1870.

(*See also*: **Rogers, Joseph**; Hodgkinson (1956))

MEDICAL ORDER

An order issued by a union relieving officer confirming that the bearer was entitled to attendance by a District Medical Officer.

(*See also*: **District Medical Officer**)

MEDICAL OUT RELIEF

The provision of medical care to the destitute outside the workhouse. It could include the attendance of a union medical officer, meeting the cost of nursing or special accommodation, the supply of medicines and, depending on the policy of the particular union, other medical 'extras' such as meat, milk and brandy, or appliances such as a truss. There was no precise definition of what constituted destitution – this decision was in the hands of a union relieving officer who appraised each applicant's circumstances prior to issuing a Medical Order.

(*See also*: **Medical Order**)

MEDICINES

For most of the workhouse era, the medicines used for the treatment of the sick poor – like those available to the population at large – were, by modern standards, fairly basic. The long-standing requirement of union medical officers to pay for some or all the medicines they prescribed out of their own salaries often meant that their patients might sometimes receive an inferior or even placebo medication rather than a more effective but expensive treatment.

In the early 1860s, workhouse medical officer Joseph Rogers campaigned for Boards of Guardians to supply all medicines but was only partially successful when it was agreed that expensive medicines such as quinine and cod liver oil could be funded from the poor rates.

Rogers' autobiography mentions in passing a number of medicines and treatments that he prescribed. In addition to quinine and cod liver oil, these included opium, mustard, linseed (in the form of tea for bronchitis and tubercular conditions) and charcoal and carrot poultices (for inflamed or infected skin).

Medicines typically employed by a doctor in the 1860s included: Calomel (purgative, diuretic and fungicide), Blue Pill (purgative), Rhubarb Powder (purgative), Jalap Powder (purgative), Ipecacuanha Powder (emetic and expectorant), Dover's Powder (fever reduction), Carbonate of Magnesia (antacid and laxative), Epsom Salts (anti-toxin, laxative etc.), Tartar Emetic (emetic and expectorant), Quinine (antipyretic, analgesic and anti-inflammatory), Antimonial Powder (diaphoretic and emetic), Extract of Colocynth (purgative). Carbonate of Ammonia (stimulant, expectorant, anti-flatulence), Tincture of Opium (analgesic), Senna Leaves (laxative), Sulphur Ointment (scabies), Linseed Flour (poultices), Castor Oil (purgative, skin disorders), Oil of Peppermint (digestive and stress disorders), Ringworm ointment (anti-fungal), and Jeremie's Opiate (analgesic).

The use of 'medicinal' alcohol, in the form of brandy, rum, wine, porter or beer was widespread in the treatment of workhouse patients until the end of the nineteenth century. This not only reflected the general medical belief in the stimulant properties of alcohol, but was treated as a dietary 'extra' and so paid for out of workhouse running costs.

(*See also*: **Alcohol**; **Medical Care**; **Workhouse Medical Officer**)

MENTALLY ILL

How to deal with the poor who were mentally ill or incapacitated frequently presented a problem for the poor-relief authorities. Apart from the misunderstanding or fear with which the mentally ill were often viewed, their care often caused practical problems. They were often helpless and in need of constant supervision, or could sometimes be violent. Although some cases received treatment in private 'madhouses' or at London's Bethlehem Hospital, many were consigned to the parish workhouse and were abominably treated:

> the chaining and manacling of troublesome patients, the keeping of them in a state almost of nudity, sleeping on filthy straw, the mixture of melancholics, and persons merely subject to delusions, with gibbering and indecent idiots, the noisy with the quiet, the total lack of any sanitary arrangements.[261]

Lunatics

Most workhouses included a number of 'lunatics' amongst their inmates, with the term being used to cover all manner of mental disturbance. Although a number of public asylums existed by the end of the eighteenth century, the beginnings of a national system came with the 1808 Lunatic Paupers or Criminals Act[262] which allowed the setting up of county asylums. An obligation for counties and boroughs to erect lunatic asylums came in the Lunatics Act of 1845.[263]

As regards the insane in workhouses, section 45 of the 1834 Poor Law Amendment Act stipulated that any person 'wilfully detaining in any Workhouse any such Lunatic, insane Person, or Idiot, for more than Fourteen Days, shall be deemed guilty of a Misdemeanor'. The 1845 Lunatics Act also required that dangerous lunatics be removed from workhouses to asylums. Despite these strictures, many mentally ill paupers remained in workhouses throughout the nineteenth century. A significant factor in this was the much higher cost of maintaining a pauper in an asylum compared to the workhouse. If a lunatic could be managed within the workhouse, that was often where they ended up staying.

A striking example of how the insane could be treated was provided in an 1836 report by Assistant Poor Law Commissioner W.J. Gilbert on a female lunatic he had encountered at the Tiverton parish workhouse:

> She was confined in a small room, having neither furniture, fire-place nor bed; there was not anything in the room but a bundle of straw. She was without a single piece of clothing, perfectly naked, and had been confined in that state, during winter and summer, for that last 28 years.[264]

Workhouses had two main strategies in dealing with those mentally ill whom they chose not to pass on for treatment elsewhere – either to confine them in dedicated lunatic wards or, as was more usually the case, to disperse them amongst the other workhouse inmates. The plans of a few early union workhouses indicate segregated areas for different categories such as lunatics, idiots and epileptics. Interestingly, a plan of York workhouse in around 1850 shows a female lunatics' yard, but no equivalent on the male side of the buildings.

The reports on conditions in London workhouses by *The Lancet* in 1865 described how primitive the care for the mentally ill could be. At Clerkenwell, for example:

> The women's ward, in particular, offers an instance of thoughtless cruelty which nothing can excuse the guardians for permitting. Twenty-one patients live entirely in this ward... and the mixture of heterogenous cases which ought never to be mingled is really frightful. There is no seclusion ward for acute maniacs, and accordingly we saw a poor wretch who for five days had been confined to her bed by means of a strait-waistcoat, during the whole of which time

she had been raving and talking nonsense, having only had two hours' sleep and there was the prospect of her remaining several days longer in the same condition. There were several epileptics in the ward, and one of them had a fit while we were present, and there were imbeciles and demented watching all this with curious, half-frightened looks.

Likewise, at Shoreditch, imbeciles and lunatics were found to be:

Moping about in herds, without any occupation whatever; neither classified, nor amused, nor employed; congregated in a miserable day-room, where they sit and stare at each other or at the bare walls, and where the monotony is only broken by the occasional excitement due to an epileptic or the gibbering and fitful laughter of some more excitable lunatic, they pass a life uncheered by any of the brightening influences which in well-managed asylums are employed to develop the remnants of intelligence and to preserve them from total degradation. They have here neither fresh air nor exercise, no out-door or indoor occupation of any kind. The exercise-ground is a wretched yard with bare walls, confined in space, and utterly miserable and unfit for its purposes.

The 1890 Lunacy Act[265] finally conceded that mentally ill paupers could remain in a workhouse subject to an official declaration by a union medical officer that the individual was suitable for this arrangement and that the workhouse had facilities for such persons to be kept separate from ordinary inmates. Workhouses could also be asked to house dangerous lunatics prior to their transfer to a county asylum. Some workhouses then supplemented their accommodation for lunatics with facilities such as observation rooms or padded cells.

Idiots and Imbeciles

During the nineteenth and first half of the twentieth century, those suffering from various forms of intellectual impairment were usually referred to as 'mental defectives' and categorised as being either 'idiots' or 'imbeciles'. The precise definitions of these terms were notoriously vague other than idiocy always being considered as a more severe condition than imbecility, and generally being viewed as a congenital abnormality. Another group, having a milder degree of impairment, was often labelled as the 'feeble-minded' or 'weak-minded'.

Like other forms of mental disorder, those classed as idiots or imbeciles often ended up in the care of the workhouse. In 1861, a parliamentary survey of workhouse inmates in England and Wales who had been in continuous residence for five years or more found that for 35 per cent 'mental disease' was cited as the reason for their remaining there.[266] A further analysis of this sub-group categorised their numbers as follows:

Idiot	1,565
Weak mind	1,026
Imbecile	997
Paralysis	465
Insane	325
Lunatic	210
Fits	205
Epilepsy	175
Palsy	21

The 1913 Mental Deficiency Act[267] included revised definitions, categorising idiots as those 'unable to guard themselves against common physical dangers' whereas imbeciles were 'incapable of managing themselves or their affairs, or, in the case of children, of being taught to do so'. The 1913 Act also included two other categories of mental impairment. The 'feeble-minded' were those requiring 'care, supervision, and control for their own protection or for the protection of others' or, in the case of children, were 'incapable of receiving proper benefit from the instruction in ordinary schools'. Finally, 'moral imbeciles' were those who displayed 'some permanent mental defect coupled with strong vicious or criminal propensities on which punishment has had little or no deterrent effect.'

Between 1871 and 1891, Britain's ten-yearly census recorded whether any individuals were idiots or imbeciles. In 1901 and 1911, the term idiot' was replaced by 'feeble-minded'. Most workhouse census listings include a number who were categorised as idiots and imbeciles (as well as the blind, deaf, dumb and lunatics). In workhouses with few able-bodied inmates, many of the institution's domestic tasks could be competently carried out by imbeciles.

In London, the Metropolitan Asylums Board set up two asylums for the care of pauper imbeciles, one to the north of the capital at Leavesden in Hertfordshire and one to the south at Caterham in Surrey. The institutions both opened in October 1870, each having a capacity of more than 2,000 beds. Initially, the asylums housed both adults and children but in 1878 the Board opened a new children's asylum at Darenth in Kent. Darenth subsequently expanded with the addition of a school where 'improvable' patients were given workshop training. Further accommodation for adults was later added at Darenth and a new establishment was opened at Tooting Bec in 1903.

Outside the capital, a number of institutions dealing with various types of mental impairment were opened in the early twentieth century, usually run by adjacent unions combining to form a Joint Committee. In 1908, for example, the Monyhull Colony in Staffordshire for up to 210 'sane epileptics and feebleminded persons' was opened by the Birmingham, Aston and King's Norton Joint Committee.

Epileptics

The treatment of workhouse inmates suffering from epilepsy was generally along the same lines as those placed in other categories of mental impairment, such as lunatics, idiots and imbeciles. Although some workhouses had separate accommodation for epileptics, they were more usually mixed in amongst other inmates. At the start of the twentieth century, a number of poor law 'colony' institutions for epileptics and other groups were jointly established by groups of Poor Law Unions. These included the previously mentioned colony at Monyhull, and a colony for 'sane epileptics' at Langho in Lancashire opened in 1906 by the Chorlton and Manchester Joint Committee.

(*See also*: **Joint Asylum / Joint Poor Law (Establishment) Committees**; **Medical Care**; **Metropolitan Asylums Board**)

MERTHYR TYDFIL JUDGEMENT

A ruling by the Court of Appeal in 1900 that it was illegal for Boards of Guardians to give poor relief to healthy able-bodied men who would not accept paid employment. The families of such men could be lawfully relieved, however. The ruling was to have consequences in 1926 when, despite government antagonism, unions in mining areas were able to provide out relief to the families of striking miners.

(*See also*: **Wales**)

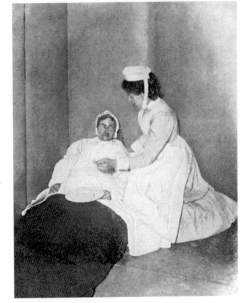

A patient and nurse in a padded room at a London workhouse, reflecting the increasing responsibilities of workhouses in the care of the mentally ill.

METROPOLITAN ASYLUMS BOARD

Between 1867 and 1930, the Metropolitan Asylums Board (MAB) played a major role in the care of London's sick poor eventually providing around forty general and specialist care establishments, many purpose-built, and staffed by well-trained personnel. The institutions set up by the MAB came to be accessible by all the capital's inhabitants, not just the poor, allowing it the claim to have provided the nation's first state hospitals and to have laid the foundations of what in 1948 became the National Health Service.

Origins of the MAB

In the late 1850s there was a growing campaign to improve conditions in workhouses, especially those for the care of the sick. In 1857, at the inaugural conference of the National Association for the Promotion of Social Science (NAPSS), Louisa Twining read a paper recounting her experiences of visiting the Strand and other London workhouses, and witnessing the poor conditions there. As a result, the Workhouse Visiting Society was formed the following year and campaigned for improvements in the treatment of the sick poor.

A Parliamentary Select Committee was appointed in 1861 to investigate the state of the poor relief system. After three years of deliberation, however, it could recommend only one change to medical provision in the workhouse – that the cost of 'cod liver oil, quinine and other expensive medicines' be met from the poor rates rather than by medical officers.[268] This was a measure that had been demanded by Dr Joseph Rogers, medical officer at the Strand Union workhouse and campaigner for reform. Even this concession was poorly publicised and many unions continued their existing practice.

In December 1864, following the much publicised death of an Irish navvy named Timothy Daly from gross neglect in Holborn workhouse, Florence Nightingale began a campaign for nursing reform in workhouse infirmaries. In January 1865, she contacted Poor Law Board president Charles Villiers, who subsequently sent out a circular to metropolitan Boards of Guardians calling on them to discontinue the use of untrained inmates for attending the sick, and instead to appoint trained nurses. However, this suggestion did not have the status of an official Order so had relatively little impact.[269]

Pressure mounted in July 1865 when the medical journal *The Lancet* began publishing a series of detailed reports on the state of London workhouses. The articles were compiled by Mr Ernest Hart, a physician attached to the staff of *The Lancet*; Dr Francis Anstie, from the staff of the Westminster Hospital; and Dr William Carr, a poor law medical officer from Blackheath. Their accounts painted a relentless picture of insanitary conditions, inadequate ventilation, poor nursing, defective equipment and overcrowding. A subsequent interview with Matilda Beeton, a former nurse at the Rotherhithe workhouse infirmary, revealed that 'many sick patients were dirty, and that their bodies crawling with vermin'; sheets were changed once in three weeks and soiled sheets had to be washed in the infirmary at night; there was 'a bad supply of towels used for every clean and dirty purpose'; beds were made of flock and 'maggots would crawl from them by [the] hundreds'; the 'sick diet was a mockery – milk was not heard of'. Similar conditions were alleged at the Strand and Paddington workhouses.[270]

In 1866, Drs Hart, Anstie and Rogers set up The Association for Improvement of the Infirmaries of London Workhouses whose aims included the setting up of 6,000-bed poor law hospitals in London staffed by trained nurses, resident medical officers, and medicines financed from the rates. Meanwhile, Florence Nightingale had approached the Prime Minister and old family friend, Lord Palmerston, who encouraged her to draft a Bill encapsulating her recommendations. Her 'ABC of Workhouse Reform' contained three main principles: 1. That the sick, insane, incurable and children should be dealt with in appropriate and separate institutions; 2. That medical relief in London should be under a single central management; 3. That the system should be financed by 'consolidation and a general rate', not from parish rates.[271]

After a change of government in 1866, Mr Gathorne Hardy, a former poor law guardian, became the new president of the Poor Law Board but initially showed little interest in Miss Nightingale's proposals. Instead, he appointed two new inspectors to the metropolitan area, Dr William Markham, former editor of the *British Medical Journal*, and Mr Uvedale Corbett, an experienced Poor Law Inspector. Their report, which reviewed the diseases common amongst the non-able-bodied poor and the existing facilities provided for their care, recommended the replacement of workhouse infirmaries by separate hospitals for the sick poor, with dispensaries to cater for paupers living outside.

Gathorne Hardy also consulted the president of the Royal College of Physicians, Sir Thomas Watson, who convened a committee to examine workhouse medical provision in the capital. Their extensive report included detailed recommendations on infirmary construction, ventilation and the space requirements for different classes of patient, together with proposals for nursing reform in an appendix contributed by Florence Nightingale. The Watson Committee again urged that the sick poor should be treated in separate accommodation, and that the insane and those suffering from infectious fevers and smallpox should be placed in specially erected hospitals.

On 6 February 1867, the government announced its intention to introduce a measure 'for improving the management of sick and other poor in the metropolis'. The Metropolitan Poor Act, sometimes known as Gathorne Hardy's Act, was passed by Parliament on 14 March 1867. The Act empowered the Poor Law Board to combine London's unions and parishes into Districts, and to raise contributions from them for a Common Poor Fund, from which they could reclaim the costs of all drugs, medical appliances, and the salaries of all poor relief officers.[272] The Fund would also be used to finance new hospitals and the maintenance of patients being treated in them. Six weeks after the Bill received its Royal Assent, Hardy announced that for the purposes of dealing with the sick poor suffering from smallpox, fever or insanity, all London's unions and parishes would be combined to form the Metropolitan Asylum District. This was to be overseen by a new body, the Metropolitan Asylums Board, whose management board was to comprise forty-five elected guardians and fifteen appointed members.

The Early Work of the MAB

The MAB immediately began to make plans for the erection of its own hospitals which would provide care for cases of smallpox, fever or insanity, and which would be easily accessible from all parts of the city. They eventually identified three sites – at Hampstead in the north-west, Homerton in the north-east, and Stockwell in the south-west – on each of which it was intended to build a 200-bed fever hospital and 100-bed smallpox hospital.

At the end of 1869, before the new hospitals were ready, there was an outbreak of relapsing fever (an infection transmitted by ticks or lice) in the east of London. To deal with this, the MAB erected temporary huts in the grounds of the London Fever Hospital at Islington and at its Hampstead site. The latter, which opened on 25 January 1870, was effectively England's first state hospital. It closed after the fever epidemic subsided in May 1870, but re-opened in December 1870 when there was a serious outbreak of smallpox in London. The two other new smallpox and fever hospitals – the South-Western Hospital at Stockwell and the Eastern Hospital at Homerton – opened shortly afterwards.

To deal with mental cases, the Board chose two locations – one north of the Thames at Leavesden in Hertfordshire, the other to the south at Caterham in Surrey – for the construction of large asylums each accommodating around 1,500 patients. The two sites opened within a few weeks of each other in the autumn of 1870. Initially, it was intended that these asylums should only deal with any pauper who had been certified to be 'a chronic and harmless lunatic, idiot or imbecile'. However, both institutions were soon filled with a wide variety of mental conditions, acute and chronic, and with patients of all ages.

To prepare for further fever epidemics, construction began in 1875 of what respectively became the Deptford Hospital and Fulham Hospital. Work also began on a new permanent school for imbecile children at Darenth near Dartford in Kent.

An aerial view of The MAB's Imbeciles' Asylum opened in 1870 at Caterham in Surrey. Ward blocks for females are at the left and those for males at the right, with the central area containing the administration block, stores, workshops, laundry, bakery etc.

The Response to Smallpox

There was a lull in smallpox outbreaks until 1876 when a major new epidemic soon outstripped all the available accommodation. Work on the new hospitals at Deptford and Fulham was speeded up and both were opened in March 1877.

During another major smallpox outbreak in 1880, a further shortage of beds led the Board to utilise two old wooden battleships, the *Atlas* and the *Endymion*, which were moored at Greenwich. A tented camp was also established on land adjacent to the Darenth asylum. In May 1881, London's first public ambulance service came into existence when hired horse-drawn ambulances were used to convey patients from Deptford Hospital to the canvas hospital at Darenth – the eighteen-mile journey took three hours.[273]

In 1882, a Royal Commission recommended that responsibility for dealing with infectious cases should be completely taken away from the poor law authorities and become part of the sanitary arrangements for the metropolis.[274] It also proposed that smallpox cases be treated in isolated hospitals on the banks of the Thames or in floating hospitals on the river itself. In addition, convalescent hospitals were to be established at some distance in the country. Finally, a central ambulance service should be established. From 1884, the existing smallpox hospitals became primarily used as fever hospitals with Deptford Hospital being renamed the South Eastern Hospital, and Fulham Hospital being renamed the Western Hospital. The hospital ships *Atlas* and *Endymion* were moved to new moorings at Long Reach near Dartford, fifteen miles below London Bridge. They were joined by a third vessel, the *Castalia*, a converted passenger ferry. In 1890, a new permanent convalescent hospital, the Southern, was built on the Gore Farm estate near Dartford, adjacent to the tented camp at Darenth.

The hospital ships continued in use until 1903 when a permanent smallpox hospital, the Joyce Green, was erected on the land next to their moorings. To provide temporary additional accommodation during a serious smallpox outbreak in 1901–02, two temporary hospitals, the Long Reach Hospital and the Orchard Hospital were erected adjacent to the Joyce Green Hospital site.

Expanding the Service

In 1891, the Public Health (London) Act[275] revised and confirmed a variety of public health legislation enacted over the previous decade. One of its most significant features was to authorise the admission of infectious non-pauper patients into MAB hospitals. However, unlike the preceding legislation, no power was given to parish authorities to charge such patients for the costs of their maintenance. Instead, these expenses were to be chargeable to the Metropolitan Common Poor Fund. The 1891 Act thus transformed the MAB fever and smallpox hospitals from pauper institutions into England's first free state hospitals for all.

As a result of the 1891 Act, the MAB was faced with the need for a major expansion of its facilities. Five new fever hospitals were planned, four located south of the Thames, each of which would accommodate 2,000 acute and 800 convalescent cases. Sites, however, were by this time becoming harder to find and more expensive to purchase. One new site at Tottenham costing £12,000 was initially vetoed by the Local Government Board. In 1892, however, a violent scarlet fever outbreak forced a reversal of the decision and approval was given for the construction of what became the North-Eastern Hospital. The following year, resurgences of scarlet fever and smallpox, together with threats of cholera and influenza, resulted in setting up of the Fountain Hospital at Tooting. Continuing high levels of scarlet fever led to the construction of three further fever hospitals beginning with the Brook Hospital opened at Shooter's Hill in 1896, the Park Hospital at Hither Green in 1897, and the Grove Hospital on an adjacent site to the Fountain at Tooting in 1899. For convalescing fever patients, the Northern Hospital at Winchmore Hill was opened in 1887.

In the field of venereal and related diseases, the MAB contracted with the City of London Union in 1916 to treat parturient women with such conditions at its Thavies Street premises. The MAB also established two specialist institutions of its own. In 1917, St Margaret's Hospital in Kentish Town was opened to treat Ophthalmia Neonatorum – a form of conjunctivitis mostly commonly contracted during delivery by an infant whose mother is infected with gonorrhoea. In 1919, the Sheffield Street Hospital was purchased from the Westminster Union and re-opened as a women's venereal disease hospital.

The MAB's hospital ships *Atlas* (left), *Endymion* (centre) and *Castalia* (right) on the Thames at Long Reach near Dartford. Between 1883 and 1903, the three linked ships formed a floating isolation hospital for smallpox patients brought by river ambulance from London.

Caring for Children

In 1875, the training ship *Goliath*, operated by the Forest Gate School District though taking boys from all across London, was destroyed by fire. The Local Government Board decided that the ship should be replaced by another vessel, the *Exmouth*, to be managed by the MAB. The *Exmouth* gave naval training to pauper boys aged from thirteen to sixteen, many of whom went on to join the Merchant or Royal Navy.

In 1897, the MAB was given additional responsibilities for: poor law children suffering from diseases of the eye, skin and scalp; educationally subnormal children; those in need of long-term nursing and convalescence; and youth offenders remanded to a workhouse under the 1866 Industrial Schools Act.

To help fulfil these new obligations, two existing seaside 'hospital-school' homes were acquired. The first, at Herne Bay, was taken over from the South Metropolitan School District and reopened as St Anne's Convalescent Home at the end of 1897. East Cliff House at Margate was purchased from the St Pancras Union to accommodate 100 children with tubercular conditions, later becoming the Princess Mary's Hospital for Children. A third establishment, the purpose-built 120-bed Millfield Sanatorium, was opened at Rustington in West Sussex in 1904. It was intended for early cases of pulmonary tuberculosis, or phthisis, and was the only poor law establishment in the country specialising in the treatment of this condition.

The MAB also acquired two sites on which to erect new hospital-schools for children suffering from ophthalmia, an inflammatory condition of the eye which was particularly common among poor law children. The White Oak School at Swanley in Kent opened in 1903, and the High Wood School at Brentwood in Essex in 1904. Each school provided for 360 children distributed among thirty cottage homes. The removal of infectious children from the ordinary schools led to a gradual reduction in the outbreaks of ophthalmia and in 1919 High Wood School was closed and converted for use as a TB sanatorium.

Another children's condition for which special establishments were set up was that of ringworm – a fungal infection affecting the scalp, the body, the feet and the nails. Accommodation for around 400 cases was provided in two further establishments acquired from the South Metropolitan School District – the Bridge School which opened in 1901 at Witham (in the former Witham Union workhouse) and the Downs School which opened in 1903 at Sutton in Surrey. The introduction of X-ray treatment for ringworm in 1905 led to much a speedier cure for the condition. In 1908, ringworm facilities were concentrated at the Downs School then transferred in 1914 to the Goldie Leigh Homes in south-east London. The Bridge School was converted to an industrial training home for 'feeble-minded' but 'improvable' boys.

A new MAB hospital erected at Carshalton in Surrey in 1907–09 was originally intended as an additional fever hospital. However, increasing demand for children's facilities led instead to its being used as a general hospital for 1,000 children under the name of the Children's Hospital. In 1910, following the accession of King George V and Queen Mary to the throne, it was renamed Queen Mary's Hospital for Children. Queen Mary's was also home to the first MAB training school for nurses.

To deal with its obligation in providing remand accommodation for juvenile offenders, the MAB adapted houses it owned in Pentonville Road, Harrow Road and Camberwell Green. These were in operation from 1902 until 1910, when responsibility for remand homes passed to the London County Council.

The Mentally Ill

In addition to the large asylums for adult imbeciles at Caterham and Leavesden, and the school for imbecile children at Darenth, the MAB operated a number of other establishments for those with various types of mental problem.

A new 'infirmary for imbeciles' was opened at Tooting Bec in 1903, with around 1,000 sick and elderly patients transferred from the Caterham and Leavesden asylums so that they could be in easier reach of their relatives. Tooting Bec was later used for housing those suffering from

Children and staff in the open air at the MAB's High Wood sanatorium at Brentford in about 1920. The institution was originally used for treating children with ophthalmia but was converted to deal with TB cases in 1919.

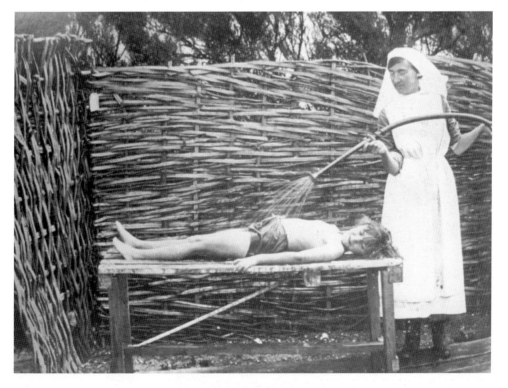

A nurse and patient at the MAB's Millfield TB sanatorium at Rustington in Sussex in about 1925. The boy is undergoing a sea-water spray treatment known as Balneotherapy.

senile dementia and eventually had 2,000 residents. In 1911, the Fountain Hospital at Tooting was converted from a fever hospital to an institution for severely subnormal children.

In the last quarter of the nineteenth century, a new category of mental deficiency came increasingly to be used – that of 'feeble-mindedness', a less severe condition than that of 'imbecility' which placed people at Caterham and Leavesden. In 1894, the MAB was given the responsibility of making provision for feeble-minded children from metropolitan poor law schools. Instead of setting up an institution for such children, the Board adopted the system of 'scattered homes' pioneered by the Sheffield Union in 1893. Houses were acquired in Fulham, Peckham, Pentonville and Wandsworth, in each of which was placed between twelve and twenty children under the care of foster parents.

To cater for the feeble-minded beyond the age of sixteen, several training colonies were set up. The largest was at Darenth, opened in 1904 on a site adjoining the existing school. Here, the less severely handicapped were taught a range of industrial skills and crafts.

In 1906, the Bridge School at Witham was converted into a working colony for feeble-minded male patients, known as the Bridge Training Home. Older feeble-minded girls were placed at the High Wood School at Brentwood. In 1915, the former Strand Union school at Edmonton was converted for use as a colony for up to 300 male 'sane epileptics'.

Tuberculosis

Although tuberculosis (TB) was particularly prevalent among the poor, the MAB was relatively slow to make special provision for its treatment, despite many of the isolation beds in its infectious hospitals being occupied by TB patients. Aided by the 1911 National Insurance Act, which included a number of TB-related provisions, the MAB eventually took on the task, initially providing 500 beds at the Downs Sanatorium at Sutton and the Northern Hospital at Winchmore Hill. This was followed by the St George's Home in Chelsea opened in 1914 for fifty female patients. In 1919, the Board took over the eighty-bed Pinewood Sanatorium at Wokingham, originally set up by voluntary effort in 1898. Another acquisition used for TB patients was the

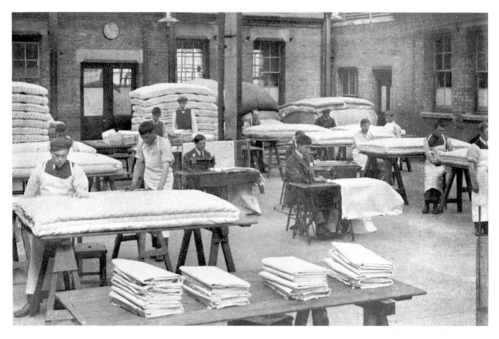

The MAB's 'training colony' at Darenth in Kent housed 'higher-grade mental defectives' who were taught industrial skills and crafts. Some of the inmates are here shown making mattresses in the 1920s.

Westminster Union's infirmary at Hendon which was reopened as the Colindale Hospital in January 1920.

The Board then purchased the Empire Hotel in Lowestoft which opened in May 1922, under the name of St Luke's Hospital. Some of the hospital's balconies were used to create open-air wards. This was followed a month later by the opening of the purpose-built 230-bed King George V Sanatorium at Godalming.

In 1926, the former Greenwich Union workhouse at Lee in south-east London was purchased and adapted for around 320 male patients, reopening as the Grove Park Hospital. As noted earlier, several of the MAB's children's establishments also provided care for TB patients.

The Houseless 'Casual' Poor

On 1 April 1912, the MAB took over the provision of relief for the capital's homeless or 'casual' poor which, according to the 1910 census, numbered over 25,000.

Prior to this, vagrants had been catered for in the casual wards operated by twenty-eight separate Boards of Guardians. Typically, a casual would stay one or two nights at each workhouse. Casuals were not allowed to return to a casual ward in the same union within thirty days without incurring an extra two days detention. With all of London counting as a single union for this purpose, this restriction was almost impossible to enforce across a large number of uncoordinated authorities.

Conditions also varied enormously between casual wards, with vagrants flocking to those where detention and work were not enforced, while beds remained unfilled in stricter establishments.

At the outset, the MAB took over control of twenty-four casual wards, with four others (Mile End, City of London, St George Hanover Square and Hampstead) being omitted from the scheme due to their being an integral part of their own workhouse premises. The Board's intention was to apply a strict and uniform policy of administration. Many of the casual wards it took over were closed or disposed of – by 1921, the number of wards had fallen to six, and by 1929 stood at nine (Chelsea, Hackney, Lambeth, Paddington, Poplar, St Pancras, Southwark, Wandsworth and Woolwich). Conditions in the remaining wards were gradually improved – the dietary was revised, newspapers were provided, and the old deterrent labour tasks such as stone breaking were largely done away with.

At the end of 1912, the Board set up a central clearing-house for casuals known as the Night Office, originally located on a disused steamboat pier near Waterloo Bridge, and from 1921 at Charing Cross Railway Bridge. The Night Office had telephone links to the remaining casual wards, and also with the Salvation Army, Church Army and other voluntary organisations. Casuals requiring accommodation were assessed at the Night Office and given a ticket to provide admission to a specific casual ward or charitable institution. Numbers applying at the Night Office fell from 3,000 a month when it first opened, to around 1,400-1,600 a month following the First World War.

As well as providing overnight accommodation, the Board also attempted to assist 'helpable' casuals to become self-supporting. In 1923, it opened The Hostel on Little Gray's Inn Lane where those genuinely seeking employment could reside in more amenable conditions than the casual wards. From 1924 to 1929, between 1,000 and 2,500 such people were admitted each year.

Ambulance Services

Growing from rudimentary beginnings in 1881, the MAB established an extensive land- and water-based ambulance service. Its land ambulances were based at six stations adjoining the Board's hospitals at Deptford, Fulham, Hampstead, Homerton, Stockwell and Woolwich. Almost the whole of London fell within a three-mile radius from one of the stations.

Until 1902, the ambulance fleet was horse-drawn. A steam vehicle carrying up to eight stretchers was then introduced to transport patients to the riverside hospitals at Dartford at a speed of up to 5mph. The first petrol-driven ambulance appeared in 1904 and could carry a

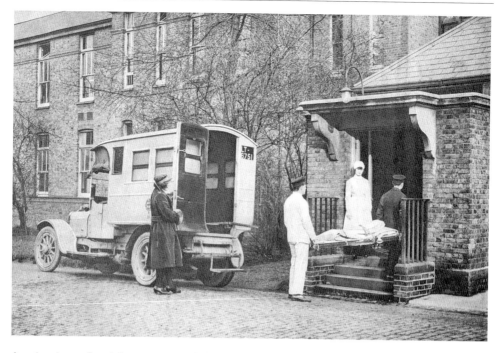

A patient is transferred from a motor ambulance to the scarlet fever receiving ward at the MAB's Park Hospital, Hither Green, in about 1908. The first petrol-driven ambulances entered service in 1904 and could carry a single stretcher at up to 15mph.

single stretcher at up to 15mph. The last horse-drawn ambulances were used on 14 September 1912, a day that marked the end of the once familiar sight of urchins pursuing the slow-moving vehicles shouting 'Fever!'[276]

From 1884, the MAB operated a river ambulance service between London and its hospital ships at Dartford. Five steamers – *Albert Victor*, *Geneva Cross*, *Maltese Cross*, *Red Cross*, and *White Cross* – ran from wharves at Blackwall, Rotherhithe and Fulham. The largest of the vessels was 143ft in length and could accommodate fifty reclining patients on its two enclosed decks on the outward journey, and 100 of those restored to health up on its bridge deck on the way back.

The First World War

At the start of hostilities in 1914, the MAB briefly undertook the provision and management of accommodation for destitute alien enemies. On 27 August, it took over Holborn's Endell Street workhouse and a total of 363 persons, mostly Germans and Austrians, were admitted. Within a few weeks, this role was taken over by the military authorities.

The Board's main wartime work, though, was the operation of institutions for housing war refugees, chiefly from Belgium. In all, around 13,000 beds were provided and about 160,000 refugees were dealt with. The first location to be adopted for this purpose was Westminster Union's disused Poland Street workhouse which, on 5 September, admitted 200 Russian Jews, mostly from Antwerp. A week later, the premises were handed over to the Jewish authorities and continued in operation as the Poland Street Institute for Jews. Refugee accommodation was provided at two other establishments taken over from the Westminster Union – the former Strand Union workhouse and Millfield School, both at Edmonton. Some of the MAB's own establishments were adopted, including the Park Hospital and the Hackney Wick and St Marylebone casual wards. By far the biggest contribution came from two vast refugee camps set up in 1914 at Alexandra Palace and the Earl's Court Exhibition Centre, each of which provided 4,000 beds.[277]

In June 1918, about 1,140 refugees from Russia arrived in England. As they had been in contact with smallpox, they were housed in isolation at the Joyce Green Hospital.

As well as dealing with refugees, the Board contributed two of its establishments, the Brook Hospital at Shooter's Hill, and the Grove Hospital at Tooting, as military hospitals for the treatment of war casualties. The Grove provided a specialist venereal disease hospital for 144 officers and 100 men. In addition, the Southern Hospital at Dartford and the North-Eastern Hospital at Tottenham were placed at the disposal of the US military authorities. The temporary buildings of the Orchard Hospital at Dartford, erected in 1902, were lent to the War Office from 1915 to 1919 for the use of overseas troops, mainly Australians.

The End of the MAB

In 1928, the government announced proposals for the reorganisation of local government in England and Wales, including the abolition of Poor Law Guardians and the transfer of their responsibilities to the county councils and county borough councils. The MAB was also included in the shake-up and on 1 April 1930 its duties and responsibilities passed to the London County Council, which also took over all the hospitals operated by the capital's Boards of Guardians.

The MAB's material legacy included a rich portfolio of infectious diseases hospitals, TB hospitals and sanatoriums, children's hospitals, and a number of specialist establishments, not to mention the ambulance services, laboratories, training and research establishments, and all the supporting administrative structures required to run them. Less tangibly, over a period of sixty years, the Board had transformed the health services of the capital and laid the foundations for the nationwide system of medical care that was to emerge in the shape of the National Health Service in 1948.

(*See also*: **London**; **Mentally Ill**; **Venereal Disease**; **Wartime**; **Appendix F**; Ayers (1971); Powell (1930))

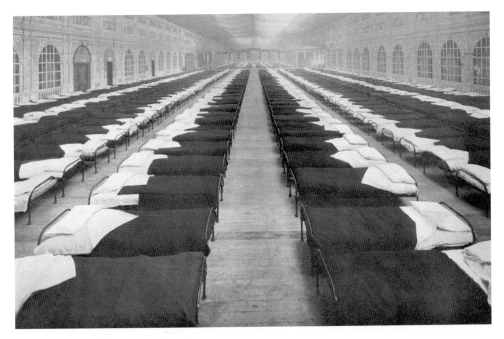

A thousand beds for refugees fill the Queen's Palace at Earl's Court in 1914 – part of the MAB's war effort.

METROPOLITAN COMMON POOR FUND

Section 69 of the 1867 Metropolitan Poor Act established the Common Poor Fund from which the capital's poor law authorities could reclaim various costs including: maintenance of the insane poor; costs of medicines and surgical appliances; salaries of officers employed in poor relief duties; costs involved in performing vaccinations; maintenance of children in separate schools; and relief of casuals. The Fund also paid the maintenance costs of patients in the asylums and fever hospitals set up by the Metropolitan Asylums Board.

The Fund was financed by a contribution from each poor law authority based on the total rateable value of all the properties in its area. This meant that London's richer unions and parishes were subsidising the poor relief expenditure of the poorer ones.

In 1870, use of the Common Poor Fund was extended to cover the maintenance of adult workhouse inmates.[278] In 1921, the costs of providing out relief could also be repaid from the Fund.[279] One expense never covered by the Fund, however, was the cost of building works.

(*See also*: **London**; **Metropolitan Asylums Board**)

METROPOLITAN POOR ACT

(*See*: **London**; **Metropolitan Asylums Board**; **Metropolitan Common Poor Fund**)

METTRAY

Mettray, a village near the French town of Tours, was the site of an influential 'agricultural colony' for reforming delinquent boys. The colony, which opened in 1839, was the result of a collaboration by penal reformer Frédéric-Auguste Demetz and architect Guillaume-Abel Blouet who believed that rural surroundings, contact with the land, and community-forming architecture, together with religious instruction, would bring about remedial changes.

The buildings were arranged around a central green with a large church at the north side. On the south side, the main entrance was flanked by the governor's house and a staff training block. The east and west sides were both lined by five three-storey houses, each home to a 'family' of forty boys supervised by a *chef de famille* and his assistant. Each house had workshops on the ground floor, a hammock dormitory on the first floor (also used as a refectory), and another dormitory for younger boys on the top floor. The colony also had extensive gardens and its own farm and quarry. A replica sailing ship was constructed in the central square, complete with masts and rigging, so that boys could be taught nautical skills.

Boys at the colony wore uniforms and had their heads shaved. Those under the age of twelve spent much of the day in basic education learning reading, writing and arithmetic. The older boys worked for most of their time either in trades they were taught or in hard manual labour in the fields or the quarry.

In its early years, the colony's success attracted much interest from other countries, with institutions such as the Philanthropic Society's boys' reformatory at Redhill being modelled on it. The cottage homes system adopted by many Poor Law Unions from the 1870s onwards was also strongly influenced by Mettray. By the 1920s, Mettray had gained a reputation for uncaring harsh discipline. Life in the colony at this period was described by Jean Genet, a Mettray inmate from 1926 to 1929, in his 1946 book *Miracle of the Rose*. The colony was finally closed in 1937.

(*See also*: **Cottage Homes**; **Rauhe Haus**)

MIDDLESEX CORPORATION WORKHOUSE

The 1662 Settlement Act included a provision for Corporations to be created in the City of London, Westminster, and parts of Middlesex and Surrey. The new bodies were empowered to erect workhouses, and in 1664, the Middlesex Corporation spent £5,000 on setting one up in Clerkenwell at the corner of what are now Corporation Row and Northampton Road. The workhouse supplied materials for the poor to work on in their own homes and was also used for 'the reception and breeding up of poor fatherless or motherless infants.'[280] The scheme was not a success and closed in 1672. A workhouse was opened on the same site by the Quakers in 1702.

(*See also*: **London; Quaker Workhouses**)

MIGRATION

At the end of 1834, the newly appointed Poor Law Commissioners (PLC) were approached by some large manufacturers in Lancashire with the suggestion that a shortage of workers in the region's rapidly expanding manufacturing industries could be filled by unemployed labourers from rural parts of southern England. The idea was not an entirely new one. Since the 1780s, large numbers of workhouse orphans from across the country had been signed over as parish apprentices and migrated to work in the textile mills in the Midlands and northern England. However, the suggestion for an officially organised and centrally administered scheme was a novel one.

The PLC took up the proposal and the first trial of the scheme took place at Bledlow in Buckinghamshire, an area of high unemployment and low wages. An Assistant Commissioner visited the area and carried out personal visits to families in distress who were living on a total income of 7s a week. Despite being offered the possibility of work at an initial wage of 24s a week (per family of four working hands), rising to 30s after a year, there was little interest. However, two families finally agreed and were followed by others, with a total of eighty-three individuals eventually migrating. Subsequent migrations took place from Princes Risborough, Chinnor, and other places in the county.[281]

The first two families from Bledlow arrived in January 1835 at Quarry Bank in Cheshire to work at the mills of Samuel Greg and Company. One of the fathers, thirty-eight-year-old John Howlett, worked twelve hours a day as a cowman and general labourer. His daughters Mary Ann (sixteen), Ann (fourteen) and Celia (twelve) did eleven and a half-hour days at the mill, while ten-year-old Timothy worked eight hours. The family received a combined wage of 24s per week during their first year, rising to 27s a week in the second. This compared with John's average weekly wage of 10s back in Bledlow.

As a result of the migration, the poor-rates of Bledlow were said to be reduced by a half. Further migration was organised from Cranfield in Bedfordshire, and from parishes in Suffolk, Kent and Sussex. Their destinations included Lancashire, Cheshire, Derbyshire and the West Riding of Yorkshire. Below is a summary of the origin and destination counties of migrations that had taken place up to July 1836.[282]

County of Origin	No. of Families	No. of Individuals
Bedford	18	144
Berkshire	13	120
Buckingham	47	414
Cambridge	5	49
Dorset	1	9
Essex	4	40
Kent	5	48

Middlesex	I	3
Norfolk	10	96
Northampton	I	8
Oxford	17	141
Southampton	4	37
Suffolk	184	1464
Sussex	14	66
Wiltshire	5	34
TOTAL	329	2673

Destination County	No. of Individuals
Cheshire	760
Derbyshire	339
Lancashire	1223
Somerset	18
Staffordshire	74
Warwickshire	57
Westmorland	39
Yorkshire	163
TOTAL	2673

By July 1837, around 10,000 persons had undergone relocation funded by parish poor-rates. The agricultural county of Suffolk was a major participant in the scheme, with 275 families, amounting to 2005 individuals (20 per cent of the total), migrating by this date. The cost of parish relief given to all the migrating families in the twelve months prior to their migration had been £1,954. However, payments for travel and outfits for those migrating cost parish funds just over £3,746, an amount which they hoped would be justified by savings in future years. One of the migrating families, from the Hoxne Union, had previously been receiving parish poor relief for thirty years.

As well as lowering the cost of relief, the PLC anticipated that the reduction in surplus labour in areas from which migration was taking place would also increase the level of wages and availability of work for those who remained. A survey of a number of unions in 1837 found mixed evidence as to the effect on the labour market in parishes from which migration was taking place. In many parishes, the numbers involved were felt to be too small to make a significant difference.

Migration was not without its critics, who viewed the Boards of Guardians of southern unions as acting with mercenary motives in its promotion, and with little care for the future condition and welfare of the migrants who would be 'out of sight, out of mind'. To counter such views, the PLC published letters of gratitude from those who were happy in their new life. One Suffolk migrant, John Brett, wrote:

> I arrived here with my family all well. I was immediately put to work in the factory, and five of my children. The employment for the first week or two was strange and rather irksome, but after that time neither myself nor children experienced any unpleasantness. My present master, who is very kind to me, employs between 400 and 500 hands in the factory in which we work, and every thing is carried on with the greatest regularity. I know it is said with you that factory children are badly used, that they are cruelly used by the over-lookers, that they are overworked for their age, and obliged to labour 14 or 15 hours each day I can assure you that this is not the case my children work twelve hours for five clays, and nine hours on Saturdays and the overlookers never beat them. With regard to the healthiness of the employment, I can say this, that during the time we have been here, about four months, my family has been very healthy, and that with having better food, and better clad, they look much better

than they did. both me and the family have now regular wages, and are well clothed and well fed, and have regular work.[283]

However, the offer of employment at a distance was often declined, with many potential candidates being stirred into finding work in their own home parishes. Despite the PLC's early optimism, home migration came to a virtual halt in the late 1830s, due to a severe downturn in the northern textile manufacturing industries. Nonetheless, they still viewed the scheme as having been successful.

(*See also*: **Apprenticeship**; **Emigration**)

MINISTRY OF HEALTH

In 1919, reflecting the increasing prominence of medical provision, central responsibility for overseeing the relief of the poor in England and Wales passed from the Local Government Board to the Ministry of Health.

In the same year, the new Scottish Board of Health took over the central administration of poor relief from Scotland's Local Government Board.

(*See also*: **Local Government Board**; **Poor Laws**)

MODIFIED WORKHOUSE TEST

(*See*: **Workhouse Test**)

MONEY

Prior to the decimalisation of UK currency in 1971, a system of pounds, shillings and pence (£ s d) was in use:

- A pound was divided into twenty shillings, and the shilling was divided into twelve pennies (or pence) – there were thus 240 (20 times 12) pennies in a pound.
- Coins in use included: the farthing (¼d), the half-penny or ha'penny (pronounced 'hayp-nee'), the penny, the threepenny (pronounced 'threp-nee') bit, the sixpence, the shilling, the florin (2s), the half-crown (2s 6d), the crown (5s), and the sovereign (£1).
- An amount such as fifteen shillings was usually written as 15s or 15/-.
- An amount such as fivepence was written as 5d (the 'd' originally stood for *denarius* – a small Roman coin); two shillings and nine-and-a-half pence was usually written as 2s 9½d or 2/9½ and said as 'two and ninepence hayp-nee'.
- For some business purposes, a unit called the guinea (21s) was used.
- In terms of its purchasing power, one pound in the year 1750 would now (2012) be worth around £150. One pound in 1850 would now be worth around £90.

(*See also*: **Weights and Measures**; **Workhouse Tokens**)

MORTUARY

A mortuary was a standard facility in union workhouses. It was used to hold the bodies of recently deceased inmates and could also include facilities for conducting post-mortems. The mortuary was usually a small separate block with high-set windows, often located next to the workhouse infirmary.

After its discovery on the morning of 31 August 1888, the body of Mary Ann Nichols, the first of Jack the Ripper's accepted victims, was brought to the mortuary of the Whitechapel workhouse infirmary. The mortuary, at that date, was a shed on Eagle Place, Old Montague Street, several hundred yards from the infirmary. The mortuary attendant, Robert Mann, was himself an inmate of the workhouse and is one of the many candidates suggested as being the true identity of the Ripper.[284]

(*See also*: **Death**)

MUSIC

(*See*: **Bands**; **Entertainment**)

NATIONAL ASSOCIATION FOR THE PROMOTION OF SOCIAL SCIENCE (NAPSS)

An organisation founded in 1857 by George W. Hastings and Lord Brougham to provide a discussion forum for those interested in promoting social reform. At its first annual conference, Louisa Twining read a paper about the poor conditions in the Strand and other workhouses, going on to form the Workhouse Visiting Society the following year under the auspices of the Association's Social Economy section. At the 1858 NAPSS conference, Florence Nightingale presented her views on the sanitary conditions in hospitals.

(*See also*: **Twining, Louisa**)

NATIONAL ASSOCIATION OF MASTERS AND MATRONS OF POOR LAW INSTITUTIONS

(*See*: **National Association of Workhouse Master**s and Matrons)

NATIONAL ASSOCIATION OF POOR LAW OFFICERS

The National Association of Poor Law Officers (also known as the National Poor Law Officers' Association) was established in 1885 to represent the interests of those employed by the poor relief system. Its foremost aim was to secure a statutory superannuation scheme for all poor law employees. Although a pension scheme had been introduced in 1864, it was discretionary and limited to those with at least twenty years service. A full superannuation scheme finally received parliamentary approval in 1896.

The Association merged with the National Association of Local Government Officers in 1930.

(*See also*: **Poor Law Workers Trade Union**; **Trade Press**)

NATIONAL ASSOCIATION OF WORKHOUSE MASTERS AND MATRONS

An organisation formed in about 1898 for the benefit of the masters and matrons of workhouses. From around 1915, following a change in official terminology, it was renamed the National Association of Masters and Matrons of Poor Law Institutions. The Association survived under a variety of titles until its demise in 1984 when it had become the Association of Health and Residential Care Officers.

NATIONAL SCHOOLS AND BRITISH SCHOOLS

British Schools and National Schools both originated in the early 1800s to provide education for poor children. Each employed a version of the 'monitorial' system where the monitored – older pupils, usually aged ten or eleven – were taught a lesson which they passed on to groups of younger children. The monitors kept order and also recommended children for promotion. Rewards and punishments were used to encourage the children in their efforts.

Credit for originating the monitorial system was disputed by two men – Andrew Bell and Joseph Lancaster. Bell, an Anglican clergyman, became superintendent at the East India Company's Male Orphanage Asylum at Madras in 1789. After seeing local schoolchildren teaching the alphabet to younger children by drawing letters in the sand, he adapted the principle for use in the Asylum using sand-trays. After his return to England, Bell opened the first school using his principles in 1798 at Aldgate. In 1811, members of the Church of England formed the National Society for the Education of the Poor in the Principles of the Established Church (or the National Society) and adopted Bell's system in all its schools, with teaching centred on the Church Liturgy and Catechism. By 1851, the Society was operating 17,000 of its National Schools.

In 1801, Joseph Lancaster, a Quaker, opened a non-denominational free school for poor children in south London. Rapidly overwhelmed by the numbers attending, he instituted a monitorial system purely to minimise on the cost of teachers. The success of the school and its methods attracted much attention and even royal patronage. Lancaster's financial problems led to the school being taken over in 1808 by the Society for Promoting the Lancasterian System for the Education of the Poor (or the Lancasterian Society), a committee of its supporters. Although he acknowledged Bell's work, Lancaster was sometimes credited as originator of the monitorial method, much to Bell's chagrin. The Lancasterian Society was renamed the British and Foreign School Society for the Education of the Labouring and Manufacturing Classes of Society of Every Religious Persuasion (or the British and Foreign School Society) and continued to establish what became known as British Schools, with around 1,500 operating by 1851.

Both National and British Schools received workhouse children into their classes.
(*See also*: **Workhouse Schools**)

NEW POOR LAW

The informal name for the legislation governing the relief of the poor based on the 1834 Poor Law Amendment Act and subsequent amendments. Many of the previous poor relief statutes, the so-called Old Poor Law, had been permissive, leading to wide variations in the poor relief arrangements adopted in different places. The New Poor Law was intended to create a compulsory, uniform national system based on the workhouse test – the principle that, for the able-bodied at least, poor relief would only be available through admission into a workhouse.
(*See also*: **Old Poor Law**; **Poor Laws**)

NICHOLLS, GEORGE

Sir George Nicholls, born in Cornwall in 1781, went to sea at the age of sixteen and by 1808 had become a financially successful captain. Following a disastrous fire on his last command in 1815, he gave up the sea. Four years later, he moved to Southwell in Nottinghamshire where he developed an interest in the operation of the poor laws and became a parish Overseer of the Poor. With the support of the local minister, the Revd J.T. Becher, he instituted a strict and deterrent poor relief regime, withdrawing out relief and instead offering only the workhouse.

In 1822, Nicholls published several letters in the *Nottingham Journal* outlining his approach and the reductions in poor relief costs that it had produced, something which received favourable attention from an 1824 House of Commons Select Committee on labourers' wages. After taking on the management of the Bank of England's Birmingham branch in 1826, he became acquainted with Home Secretary and future Prime Minister Robert Peel.

Following the passing of the 1834 Poor Law Amendment Act, Nicholls was appointed as one of the three new Poor Law Commissioners and was the most active in advancing a policy of curbing out relief and its replacement by a deterrent workhouse.

Two years later, following the government's dissatisfaction with the recommendations of the Whateley Commission's report on the poor in Ireland, the Home Secretary, Lord John Russell, despatched Nicholls on a six-week tour of the country. Unsurprisingly, Nicholls recommended the extension of the English workhouse system to Ireland, with the resulting Irish Poor Law Act being passed in July 1838. Nicholls then moved to Dublin where he remained for the next four years, overseeing the implementation of the Irish workhouse system.

On returning to London in November 1842, Nicholls found himself out of favour with the Conservative Government now in office. However, he survived the abolition of the Poor Law Commissioners in 1847, continuing as secretary to the new Poor Law Board until retiring from ill-health in 1851. For such a central and influential figure, his histories of the poor law in England, Ireland and Scotland published between 1854 and 1856 proved disappointingly dull and uncritical chronologies of events. Nicholls died in London on 24 March 1865.

(*See also*: **Ireland**; **Poor Law Commissioners**; **Royal Commission – 1832**)

NIGHT LODGERS

A term occasionally used in Ireland for the casual poor.
(*See also*: **Casual Poor**)

NIGHTINGALE, FLORENCE

Florence Nightingale (1820–1910) is perhaps best known for her nursing work during the Crimean War in the mid-1850s. However, she also made a major contribution to the welfare of the sick and poor in Britain. As well as founding her nurses' training school at London's St Thomas' Hospital in 1860, she campaigned for improvements in the care of the capital's sick poor which eventually led to the passing of the Metropolitan Poor Act in 1867.
(*See also*: **Architecture**; **Medical Care**; **Metropolitan Asylums Board**; **National Association for the Promotion of Social Science (NAPSS)**)

NURSING

(*See*: **Medical Care**; **Metropolitan Asylums Board**; **Sisters of Mercy**; **Workhouse Infirmary Nursing Association**)

OAKUM PICKING

A work task often given to workhouse and prison inmates where quantities of 'junk' – old hemp ropes from ships – were cut into short lengths and then untwisted into their raw fibres which were known as oakum (also spelled ockam, ocum etc.). Picking oakum was very hard on the fingers although a small nail or hook might

sometimes be provided to assist with the task. Oakum could be sold to ship-builders who mixed it with tar to caulk or seal the lining of wooden ships. The sale of
oakum is sometimes said to have given rise to the expression 'money for old rope'.
(*See also*: **Bone Crushing / Bone Pounding**; **Stone Breaking**; **Work**)

OLD PEOPLE

Despite the Spartan conditions that prevailed in many workhouses, inmates could live to a ripe
old age. Workhouse census records, for example, often include a sizeable number of inmates in
their seventies, eighties or nineties. Across the country, the number of workhouse inmates aged
over sixty-five rose from around 25,000 in 1851 to just over 76,000 in 1901. As a proportion of
the national total of over-sixty-fives in England and Wales, this equated to a rise from 3 per cent
to 5 per cent over the same period.[285]

In 1834, the Royal Commission, whose report formed the basis of the Poor Law Amendment
Act, had recommended that 'the old might enjoy their indulgences'. A modest concession in
this direction came in 1836 when the dietaries published by the Poor Law Commissioners
allowed the over-sixties to receive rations of tea, sugar, milk or extra meat pudding – so long as
the guardians deemed that this was 'expedient'.

From 1847, married couples who were both aged sixty or more could request to share a
separate bedroom, although little provision was made for such requests – it was often argued by
Boards of Guardians that elderly couples generally preferred the separation.

The formation of the Workhouse Visiting Society in 1858 led to many small improvements in
the treatment of inmates, particularly the elderly, many of whom received no visitors from one
year to another. By the 1860s, many workhouses had acquired some kind of library for the use
of its inmates with books and magazines being donated by the public. Concerts put on by local
groups became a regular feature at many workhouses,

Elderly married inmates' quarters at what is believed to be the Holborn Union workhouse at Merton
Lane, Mitcham. A well-dressed couple standing at the far end may be the workhouse master and matron.
A clergyman sits at the far left of the picture.

Hubert von Herkomer's illustration *Old Age – a Study at the Westminster Union* which appeared in the weekly magazine *The Graphic* in 1877.

The early 1890s saw a relaxation on the use of tobacco by elderly inmates of good character. In 1894, old women were allowed extra 'dry tea' with milk and sugar, in addition to what was already included in their dietary. This allowance was subsequently extended to include dry coffee or cocoa, and also made available to old male inmates. By 1896, the Local Government Board were recommending that well-behaved aged and infirm inmates should, within reasonable limits, be allowed to go out of the workhouse for walks, to visit friends, or attend church.[286] Other improvements for the aged and infirm during this period included a more varied diet containing items such as sago, semolina, rice pudding, stewed fruit, lettuce, onions and seed cake. By the early 1900s, entertainments provided for elderly inmates of the Stoke-upon-Trent workhouse included nine concerts during the winter months, a phonograph and gramophone, games such as dominoes and draughts, and a good supply of reading matter.[287] Workhouses could by now use the poor rates to subscribe to a lending library, buy newspapers, or install a piano or harmonium. By the 1920s, a communal radio might be installed in the dayroom.

At the end of the nineteenth century, a number of poor law authorities began to provide separate establishments for elderly paupers. In 1897, the Wandsworth and Clapham guardians converted a former college building on Church Lane Tooting to house 'deserving' elderly and infirm inmates, with amenities including a recreation room and landscaped grounds. In 1902, on the same site, the union erected a group of cottage-style homes to house twenty-two married couples, each having its own bed-sitting room and small larder, plus communal sitting rooms, sculleries and bathrooms. In 1903, Bradford Union created a development of around twenty cottages placed either side of a central green together with some communal facilities and staff accommodation. At about the same date, the Pontypridd Union opened homes for around 100 deserving elderly poor at Llwynypia. Liverpool's West Derby Union included forty-four old people's cottages on its large workhouse site at Walton-on-the-Hill. One of the largest such schemes was erected by the Salford Union in 1924–25 on a 9-acre site next to its infirmary at Pendleton. The large pavilion-plan complex of old people's homes, all at ground-floor level, was planned to accommodate up to 500 men and women.

In Victorian times, as now, women had a greater average life expectancy than men. Despite this, the elderly populations of workhouses invariably included more men than women. This is usually attributed to elderly women being better able to maintain independent lives in the community whereas elderly men, especially if widowed, were more likely to need institutional care.

The introduction of the old-age pension in 1910 led to a drop in the proportion of the nation's over-65s in the workhouse which fell from 5.0 per cent in 1901 to 2.7 per cent in 1921

Mrs Blower, an inmate of the Wandsworth Union Infirmary, who in 1896 at the age (it was said) of 107, was reckoned to be the oldest workhouse inmate in the country. She was still active and regularly ran the length of the workhouse ward. Her son, a mere youth in his eighties, was also an inmate of the workhouse.

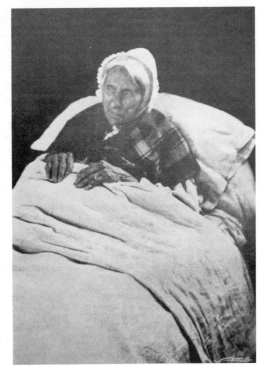

OLD POOR LAW

The Old Poor Law is the accumulating body of legislation governing the relief of the poor up to 1834. The 1601 Poor Relief Act is often taken as the point of origin for the Old Poor Law, even though it was largely a restatement of the Poor Relief Act of 1597 which had established the office of Overseer of the Poor. The 1597 Act itself incorporated many elements of legislation dating back to the 1530s.

Significant developments of the Old Poor Law came with the Settlement Act of 1662 (and its subsequent amendments), the Workhouse Test Act of 1723, Gilbert's Act of 1782, and the Sturges Bourne Acts of 1818 and 1819. Many places also promoted their own local Acts of Parliament during this period which formed another influential strand of the Old Poor Law.

The Old Poor Law can be broadly characterised as being parish-centred, haphazardly implemented, locally enforced, and with some of its most significant developments (e.g. the operation of workhouses) being completely voluntary. In contrast with what had gone before, the New Poor Law, based on the new administrative unit of the Poor Law Union, aimed to introduce a rigorously implemented, centrally enforced, universal system centred on the workhouse.

The Old Poor Law is often viewed as having been completely replaced by the 1834 Poor Law Amendment Act (the foundation of the so-called New Poor Law). However, it was the *administration* of poor relief rather than its basic principles that changed in 1834. For example, the new system was still funded by parish-based poor rates − something that continued until 1925. Applicants for relief were still subject to settlement qualifications − parts of the 1662 Settlement Act remained in force until 1948. The giving of relief was subject to a workhouse test − a principle dating from 1723. Gilbert Unions and Local Act parishes or Incorporations continued in operation − although the remaining Gilbert Unions were abolished in 1869, a few poor law authorities such as Brighton and Oxford never gave up their Local Act status. Elements of the Old Poor Law remained on the statute book until remarkably recent times, with the 1601 Poor Relief Act only being fully repealed only in 1967.

(*See also*: **New Poor Law**; **Overseers**; **Poor Laws**)

OLIVER TWIST

(*See*: **Fiction**)

OPHTHALMIA

Ophthalmia was a highly infectious inflammatory condition affecting the eyes. It was common amongst children at large poor law establishments, especially District Schools. A particularly serious outbreak in 1862 affected 686 children at the Central London District School at Hanwell, with several of the younger ones losing one or both eyes. In 1890, a specialised school known as the Ophthalmic Institute (later Park School) and accommodating 300 cases was opened in an isolated area of the Hanwell site. Any London union could, when vacancies occurred, send children to the Institute on payment of 12s 6d a week for each patient.

Two hospital-schools for children suffering from ophthalmia were also erected by the Metropolitan Asylums Board. The White Oak School at Swanley in Kent opened in March 1903, and the High Wood School at Brentwood in Essex received its first patients in July 1904. Each school provided for 360 children distributed among thirty cottage homes. The removal of infectious children from the ordinary schools led to a gradual reduction in ophthalmia cases and in 1919 High Wood School was closed and converted for use as a TB sanatorium.
(*See also*: **District and Separate Schools**; **Ringworm**)

OPPOSITION TO THE NEW POOR LAW

Southern England

In the years immediately following the passing of the 1834 Poor Law Amendment Act, the unionisation of the southern counties of England proceeded relatively smoothly, with only one or two isolated and short-lived outbreaks of resistance. At the end of April 1835, in the new Milton Union in Kent, the introduction of the new poor relief policy led to a disturbance at the village of Bapchild when a guardian and relieving officer were assaulted. Guardians leaving a board meeting at Milton were also stoned by protestors. A week later, guardians and a relieving officer were besieged in a church after confronting protestors and were only saved from the mob by the arrival of troops. A few weeks afterwards, at Ampthill in Bedfordshire, riots took place when the guardians attempted to replace out relief in cash by allowances of bread. On 23 May, the *Leicester Chronicle* reported that a mob of up to 500 people had 'commenced a most desperate attack upon the windows with stones, brick-bats, cabbage-stalks, and every missile that could be found.' The reading of the Riot Act failed to quell the protestors, and a posse of twenty-two metropolitan police arrived the next day to restore order. By and large, however, such conflict was much the exception.

Northern Resistance

In other parts of the country, especially in central Wales and the north of England, opposition to the 1834 Act was considerably more intense and sustained. Hostility was particularly strong in the textile manufacturing areas of north-eastern Lancashire and the West Riding of Yorkshire in towns such as Oldham, Rochdale and Huddersfield.

Resistance came partly from the labouring classes, led by men such as Richard Oastler, who had gained valuable experience of organising protests while campaigning to improve factory conditions. There was also hostility from the local landowners and ratepayers whose cooperation was required to operate the new system. During periods of manufacturing slump, the traditional approach to poor relief in many northern industrial towns had been to give short-term handouts to unemployed workers who were suffering hardship. A new workhouse was seen as a wasteful expense that would involve large capital expenditure, spend most of its time empty, and which would in any case be unable to cope with the large numbers of relief claimants during periodic downturns. Giving a short-term dole to a worker was viewed as much preferable to having to maintain his whole family in a workhouse.

Richard Oastler – a prominent opponent of the New Poor Law in the north of England. The scroll in his hand demands 'No Bastiles' ('bastile' was another term for the workhouse) and also refers to the 'Ten Hours Bill' – Oastler's campaign to limit the hours worked by children in textile mills.

One of the first northern protests took place in Huddersfield in December 1836. News of the imminent introduction on the New Poor Law in the town provoked a demonstration by 8,000 people in the market place at the end of which an effigy of a Poor Law Commissioner was burned. An open meeting of the Dewsbury Board of Guardians in August 1838 was halted when the audience became violent, and troops were summoned from Leeds. For the next meeting, 100 Lancers, 76 riflemen, 200 Metropolitan Police, and 600 special constables were present to keep order.

Opposition could also take a variety of more subversive forms including the boycotting of guardians' elections, the withholding of poor law rates, and the refusal of Boards of Guardians to elect a Clerk without which no union business could be conducted.

Events such as the trade slumps in the late 1830s in Nottingham and elsewhere forced the PLC to compromise on their principle of the workhouse being the only relief available to the able-bodied, and allow the use of a labour test. Even after the PLC issued its Outdoor Relief Prohibitory Order in 1844, many northern unions exploited the General Order's list of permitted exceptions and issued outdoor relief under the guise of it being medical relief or 'sudden and urgent necessity'.

One other northern obstacle which delayed the progress of unionisation in Yorkshire was the stubborn continued existence of four Gilbert Unions in West Riding – a problem that was only resolved in 1869 when all the surviving Gilbert Unions were forcibly dissolved.

Workhouse Provision

As far as workhouse provision was concerned, it was common for northern unions to retain one or more former parish or township workhouses. In Cumberland and Westmorland, for example, only three of the twelve new unions erected new workhouses, while only two of Lancashire's twenty-five new unions did so. Unfortunately for their inmates, many of the old buildings were cramped, dirty, badly ventilated and with poor sanitation. Despite often-damning inspection reports, many northern unions held out for many years against providing new workhouse accommodation that was deemed satisfactory by the central authorities. Continuing pressure from the PLC, and their successors, the Poor Law Board, eventually persuaded Boards of Guardians to erect new buildings. Among the last to do so was Todmorden, which had steadfastly refused to provided any new workhouse accommodation. It was only under the threat of dissolution that the union finally relented in 1877.

In central Wales, unions such as Rhayader, Presteigne, Crickhowell and Lampeter also stubbornly resisted the provision of the workhouse accommodation demanded by the PLC. All capitulated in the 1870s, with the exception of the Presteigne Union which was dissolved in 1877.

Opposition in Print

After the passing of the Poor Law Amendment Act, newspapers opposed to the New Poor Law campaigned vigorously for its repeal. Most prominent amongst these was *The Times* which had predicted that the proposed legislation would 'disgrace the statute-book'. The paper's news, editorial and letter columns publicised virtually any story which discredited the new system, no matter how flimsy the evidence for its veracity. According to one analysis, between 1837 and 1842 the paper reported 290 instances of individual suffering that it attributed to 'this odious law'. These included thirty-two accounts of cruel punishments, fourteen stories of overcrowding, fifteen reports of brutal separation of parents and children or husband and wife, and seven of workhouse 'murders'.[288] One notorious story first appeared in the paper on 11 July 1837, in a letter from anti-poor law campaigner Richard Oastler:

> A clergyman, a neighbour of mine, told me the other day, that two friends of his from Cambridge had told him the following anecdote:– At a union workhouse in that neighbourhood a labourer, his wife, and children, had been confined. They were, as a matter of course, separated. The poor fellow was at last tired out; he was 'tested,' as the Duke of Richmond would term it. At length, he thought he would better be half starved at liberty than half starved in prison. He gave notice to the governor 'that he, his wife, and children would leave, and that he would try to obtain work.' The governor said, 'You cannot take your wife out. You and your children may go. 'Not take my wife!' exclaimed the poor man. 'Why not?' 'We buried her three weeks ago!' replied the gaoler.

A month later, the PLC replied – also in the letter columns of *The Times* – that after 'minute and careful inquiries', they could find no evidence for such an event having taken place.

Provincial newspapers, too, sometimes published stories that were later shown to be untrue, but which generated far-reaching adverse publicity. In 1844, the *Nottingham Review* printed allegations of incompetence and corruption at the Basford workhouse. Although proved to be fallacious and probably the work of Chartist opponents of the New Poor Law, a much exaggerated version was included by Engels in his 1845 work *Conditions of the Working Class in England*:

> …the sheets had not been changed in thirteen weeks, shirts in four weeks, stockings in two to ten months, so that of forty-five boys but three had stockings, and all their shirts were in tatters. The beds swarmed with vermin, and the tableware was washed in the slop-pails.

The most comprehensive and lurid collection of anti-poor law propaganda appeared in 1841 in *The Book of the Bastiles* edited by radical Tory George Wythen Baxter. 'Bastile' (or 'Bastille') was then a popular derogatory name for the union workhouse. The book assembled extracts from virtually every newspaper and magazine article, book, letter, pamphlet and speech that had been published against the New Poor Law. Prominent amongst the press cuttings were, unsurprisingly, many from *The Times*. There were also clippings from many local papers such as *The Sheffield Iris*, *The Leeds Intelligencer* and *The Northern Star*. A typical entry is part of a letter to Baxter from the Revd Fowell Watts, former chaplain of the Bath workhouse, written in October 1840:

> The nearest relative is not allowed to carry the least thing, not even a bit of fruit, or a bun, into the House, to a dying person. I have had it said to me – 'Oh, Sir! If I had but an orange to suck to moisten my dry mouth!' and oranges I have stealthily carried to the sick and dying. A friend of mine carried a short time ago a little snuff to a man blind and dumb, whom he had long known, and who had taken it for 25 years. He was not allowed to give it. He wrote to the Board, and received for answer, that it was against the rules of the House to allow it, nor could it be allowed unless the medical officer stated it to be necessary for the man's health.

(*See also*: **Old Poor Law**, **Poor Laws**)

OUT RELIEF

Out relief, or outdoor relief, was poor relief provided outside the workhouse and given either in cash, in kind (bread, or other goods), or as a combination of the two – sometimes with an upper limit placed on the proportion of cash included.

Throughout the history of publicly funded poor relief, out relief was almost always the predominant form in which it was given, both in terms of the numbers relieved and the cost to the public purse. The escalating cost of out relief from the 1790s through to the 1820s was attributed by many to the widespread adoption of allowance schemes such as the Speenhamland system. The solution proposed by the 1832 Royal Commission on the administration of poor relief, and embodied in the 1834 Poor Law Amendment Act, was to end the giving of out relief to able-bodied men and their dependents.

Out relief was not completely abolished after 1834, however. It could still be given in cases of 'sudden and urgent necessity'; to a widow in the first six months of her widowhood or with dependent, legitimate children; to someone (or having a family member) afflicted by sickness, accident, or bodily or mental infirmity; to help pay family funeral expenses; or to the family of a man serving in the armed forces, or who had deserted them.

The 1834 Act's prohibition on out relief to the able-bodied was initially enforced in a piecemeal fashion through the issuing of a Special Order to individual unions which forbade the relief of any able-bodied male pauper, or any part of his family, except in a workhouse.[289] Such measures had proved particularly difficult to enforce, especially in the industrial areas of northern England, with the Poor Law Commissioners forced to delay and compromise. In April 1842, the Commissioners issued some unions with the Outdoor Labour Test Order which allowed relief (at least half of which was to be in food, clothing etc.) to be given to able-bodied male paupers who satisfied a daily labour test, i.e. physical work, usually stone breaking or oakum picking. This was followed in December 1844 by the Outdoor Relief Prohibitory Order which prohibited all outdoor relief to able-bodied men and women apart from in 'exceptional' circumstances. The enforcement of the two Orders was very uneven, however. In 1847, the Labour Test Order alone was in force in thirty-two unions, mostly in the industrial north, and the Prohibitory Order alone in force in 396 unions. In eighty-one unions, both Orders were in force, allowing the guardians some discretion in how to administer out relief.[290]

In August 1852, the Poor Law Board attempted to standardise the regulations and issued the Outdoor Relief Regulation Order which included new restrictions on the giving of out relief to the sick, aged and widows. Following numerous protests from Boards of Guardians who felt their discretionary powers were being interfered with, a revised version of the Order was issued in December of that year. This reverted to dealing with able-bodied males, but included additional exceptions regarding the circumstances in which out relief could be given in such cases.

Despite the Poor Law Board's efforts, a gradual growth in the numbers receiving out relief continued. In 1869, the Board's president, George Goschen, launched a new initiative to reduce out relief provision. Goschen's so-called 'minute' warned of the dangers of low wages being subsidised from public funds and suggested that the needs of those not totally destitute might often be met by charitable sources. Throughout the 1870s, the Local Government Board continued its pressure on unions to reduce out relief. The giving of out relief was increasingly made dependent on the character of the applicant, with relieving officers visiting applicants' homes and making detailed investigations to identify any 'immoral habits' or evidence of 'frequenting public houses'. Able-bodied women were particularly targeted, although the policies varied between unions. Some unions readily gave out relief to an able-bodied widow with up to two children, while others entirely refused it regardless of the size of her family. Some unions required that one or more of the children be placed in the workhouse while she found employment, or made daily labour in the workhouse a condition of receiving out relief.[291] As a result of these policies, the numbers receiving out relief fell significantly, from 3.77 per cent of the population in 1870 to 1.06 per cent in 1914.

In 1911, the Relief Regulation Order[292] revised and consolidated all previous Orders relating to out relief. It maintained the workhouse as the primary form of relief except for widows, separated married women, and those who were sick, injured, or suffering from bodily or mental infirmity, or who had a dependent family member so afflicted. The Order made no mention of the term 'able-bodied' but allowed, in 'exceptional circumstances', relief (at least one half to be in kind) to be given to 'a male person' in return for outdoor labour. Similarly, a modified workhouse test could be employed, with a man residing in a workhouse while his family received out relief.

The widespread unemployment in the 1920s was accompanied by a corresponding rise in out relief with an all-time peak of 4.44 per cent of the population being recipients in 1927. The costs of funding out relief placed many unions in severe financial difficulties, although the situation of poorer London unions was assisted by the passing in 1921 of the Local Authorities (Financial Provisions) Act which allowed out relief to be funded out of the Metropolitan Common Poor Fund.

In 1926, the government became increasingly concerned about what it viewed as excessive and improper out relief payments, including relief to those engaged in strike action. In the wake of the General Strike, the Boards of Guardians (Default) Act was passed which allowed a Board of Guardians to be replaced by civil servants. The Act was subsequently enforced at West Ham and Chester-le-Street in 1926, and at Bedwellty in 1927.

(*See also*: **Allowance Systems**; **Goschen Minute**; **Indoor Relief**; **Labour Test**; **Medical Out relief**)

OUT RELIEF UNIONS

Out relief unions originated in 1873 as a result of a proposal by Local Government Inspector Andrew Doyle. He suggested that where parts of a union fell in different counties, the creation of an out relief union within each county area could simplify the administration of out relief and also allow different counties to adopt differing out relief policies if they wished. The existing Poor Law Union would still operate the workhouse for indoor relief across the whole union. Formal provision for out relief unions came in section 58 of the 1888 Local Government Act and section 36(b) of the 1894 Local Government Act. Out relief unions were formed on 28 December 1894 at Malton and Norton (both part of the Malton Poor Law Union); Belvoir and Grantham (Grantham Union); Bishopthorpe, Escrick, Flaxton and York (York Union); and on 31 March 1895 at Keynsham and Warmley (Keynsham Union).

OUTDOOR LABOUR TEST

(*See*: **Labour Test**)

OUTDOOR RELIEF

(*See*: **Out relief**)

OVERSEERS

The function of parish overseer or Collector of Alms is first mentioned in the Vagabonds Act of 1572 along with the separate office of Supervisor of the Labour of Rogues and Vagabonds. These two roles were amalgamated in the 1597 Poor Relief Act to create the office of Overseer of the Poor – usually abbreviated just to overseer.

From the passing of the 1601 Poor Relief Act, the Overseers of the Poor, between two and four in number, were nominated by the parish vestry each Easter for approval by local Justices of the Peace. The churchwardens in a parish were also *ex officio* overseers. The duties of an overseer, an unpaid post, were to carry out the measures for relieving the poor laid down in the 1601 Act. This included the collection of the poor rate, with one of the overseers being appointed as treasurer and legally accountable for the funds raised.

The post of overseer was finally abolished by the 1925 Rating and Valuation Act, with the duties of the office passing to local rating authorities.

(*See also*: **Poor Rate**; **Vestry**)

OVERSEERS' PARLIAMENTARY RETURNS

(*See*: **Records**; **Statistics**)

PAROCHIAL BOARD

In Scotland, the Parochial Board for the Management of the Poor – normally shortened to just Parochial Board – was the body with formal responsibility for the local administration of poor relief following the 1845 Scottish poor Act. The Parochial Board was thus analgous to the Board of Guardians in England, Wales and Ireland.

In parishes where a rating assessment system had been adopted, the membership of Parochial Boards was elected by ratepayers; in non-assessed parishes, the electorate were those who would have been entitled to vote in such elections prior to the 1845 Act. A plural voting system allowed voters up to six votes based on the assessed value of their property.

(*See also*: **Scotland**)

PAUPER

A person claiming, or in receipt of, poor relief.

(*See also*: **Poor Relief**)

PEST HOUSE

A building, sometimes associated with a parish or Incorporation workhouse, for the isolation of infectious cases. The workhouse at Henley in Oxfordshire had a pest house which, in February 1794, was briefly home to the poet Samuel Taylor Coleridge. Having run away from Cambridge University where he had accumulated debts, the twenty-two-year-old Coleridge joined the Light Dragoons at Reading under the name of Silas Tomkyn Comberbache. When it was discovered he was incapable of riding a horse, Coleridge was seconded to Henley and given the job of nursing a fellow recruit who had caught smallpox. The two men were confined in a small chamber for eight days and nights in foul conditions. Coleridge's time in the claustrophobic pest house may have contributed to the imagery in the *Rime of the Ancient Mariner*.

(*See also*: **Poetry**)

PHTHISIS

(*See*: **Tuberculosis** (TB))

PIGS

(*See*: **Gardens and Farms**)

PLAYS

Few stage plays have used the workhouse as a setting. In 1847, the stage of the Shoreditch Theatre was graced by a dramatic entertainment entitled *Revolt or, The Workhouse or, A Night's Hullabaloo!* A rather more conventional production was *The Workhouse Ward*, written in 1908 by Lady Augusta Gregory and set inside an Irish workhouse. Three years later, *In the Workhouse*, by women's suffrage campaigner Margaret Wynne Nevinson, dramatised the fact that a husband could force his wife against her wishes to stay with him in a workhouse. The play caused a stir which helped lead to a change in the law in 1913. In more recent times, John Owen Smith's play *This Bloody Crew* documents riotous attacks in 1830 on the parish workhouses at Selborne and Headley in Hampshire.
(*See also*: **Fiction**)

PLURAL VOTING

The granting of multiple votes to ratepayers in elections of members to parish vestries or Boards of Guardians, or at meetings of those bodies. The practice originated in Sturges Bourne's Vestries Act of 1818 which granted ratepayers up to six votes, based on the rateable value of their property. The 1834 Poor law Amendment Act allowed property owners up to six votes and occupiers up to three votes, although from 1844 both again had up to six votes. Owner-occupiers received both allocations and so could qualify for up to twelve votes. Plural voting and property qualifications for voting were abolished by the 1894 Local Government Act.
(*See also*: **Poor Laws**)

POETRY

The workhouse was a subject which often attracted the attention of poets. An early example was the dismal picture of a parish workhouse in George Crabbe's *The Village* published in 1783. A typical section runs:

> Thus groan the old, till, by disease opprest,
> They taste a final woe, and then they rest.
> Theirs is yon House that holds the parish poor,
> Whose walls of mud scarce bear the broken door;
> There, where the putrid vapours, flagging, play,
> And the dull wheel hums doleful through the day;
> There children dwell who know no parents' care;
> Parents, who know no children's love, dwell there!
> Heart-broken matrons on their joyless bed,
> Forsaken wives, and mothers never wed;
> Dejected widows with unheeded tears,
> And crippled age with more than childhood fears;
> The lame, the blind, and, far the happiest they!
> The moping idiot, and the madman gay.

However, Crabbe's later work, *The Borough* (1810), portrayed a Suffolk Incorporation work-house in a somewhat better light:

> Be it agreed – the Poor who hither come
> Partake of plenty, seldom found at home;
> That airy rooms and decent beds are meant
> To give the poor by day, by night, content;
> That none are frighten'd, once admitted here,
> By the stern looks of lordly Overseer.

Similarly grim views were offered in 1802 by Ann Candler's *Reflections on my own Situation* and in this 1832 description of *The Village Poorhouse* by the Rev. James White:

> Within yon paper-window'd room,
> A group in sadness and in gloom
> Is sitting – and, though no-one speaks,
> Look only in their eyes and cheeks!
> It needs not language to express
> Their tale of misery and distress;
> The Village Poorhouse – paupers, they –
> Men – young, sinewy, and strong,
> Condemn'd to see, day after day,
> Their moments creep along
> In sloth – for they have nought to do,
> And – start ye not – in hunger, too!
> Yes! hunger, gnawing like a worm,
> Yet armed with more than reptile fangs,
> Wearing away the manly form,
> While scarce tobacco soothes its pangs.
> And women – young, – they might be fair,
> Save that the blackness of despair
> Is shed o'er every feature there, –
> And gives to lips that might have smil'd
> A curl of desperation wild,
> To eyes that might have beam'd, – a look
> Which virtue cannot bear nor brook!
> Such are they in that chamber dim,
> Silent, and desolate, and grim.

Written from Newmarket Union was composed by James Reynolds Withers, an unsuccessful shoe-maker from a village in Cambridgeshire. He and his family were in the Newmarket workhouse in 1846 from where his letter in verse was sent to his sister. Withers later came to the attention of literary society and was fashionable for a while but died in poverty. The poem begins:

> Since I cannot, dear sister, with you hold communion,
> I'll give you a sketch of our life in the Union.
> But how to begin I don't know, I declare:
> Let me see: well, the first is our grand bill of fare.
> We've skilly for breakfast; at night bread and cheese,
> And we eat it and then go to bed if you please.
> Two days in the week we have puddings for dinner,
> And two, we have broth, so like water but thinner;

Two, meat and potatoes, of this none to spare;
One day, bread and cheese – and this is our fare.

The walls of the workhouse casual ward often served as a repository for verse. In 1865, Poor Law Inspector Andrew Doyle collected some samples from workhouses in the north of England, including the following from a tramp known as 'Bow Street', described by Doyle as the 'laureate of cadgers':

My unfortunate friends, pray look around,
And tell me for what is this place renowned;
The room is large, but the windows are small,
But that don't much matter at all at all.
A pint of skilly for your supper to drink;
But of sleep you cannot get a wink.
You may lay on the boards or the chilly floor,
About as warm as a North American shore.
The old bed is full of fleas all alive:
I killed in number about five times five.
They are not poor, but all thorough-bred,
And before morning you will wish they were all dead;
And by this and by that it plainly is clear,
This is the worst relief in all Staffordshire.–Bow Street.

The genre of workhouse poetry was revived in 2006 when Mario Petrucci was poet-in-residence at the former Southwell workhouse, now owned by the National Trust. A book of Mario's poems was published under the title of *Fearnought* – also the name of a woollen fabric often used in workhouse uniforms.
(*See also*: **Broadside Ballads**; **Christmas**; **Humour**)

POOR FARM

In eighteenth and early nineteenth-century London, poor farms were establishments run by private contractors for housing the poor from the city. In the late nineteenth and early twentieth century, a small number of residential farm 'colonies' were set up where destitute able-bodied men were employed; a broadly similar type of institution, also known as poor farms, existed in the USA at around the same period.
(*See also*: **Farming the Poor**; **Labour Colony / Farm Colony**; **London**)

POOR LAW BOARD

In 1847, the central administration of poor relief passed from the Poor Law Commissioners to a new body known as the Poor Law Board (PLB). Unlike their predecessors, whose responsibility to Parliament had been what Home Secretary Sir George Grey described as 'indirect and imperfect', the PLB included government representation in its membership.

The new body was headed by a president, assisted by two secretaries, with the Chancellor of the Exchequer, the Secretary of State for the Home Department, the Lord Privy Seal and the Lord President of Council as *ex officio* members. The PLB's president and one of its secretaries were allowed to be Members of Parliament and were thus generally appointed by the government of the day. The other 'permanent' secretary was essentially a civil servant, with the first holder of the post being George Nicholls, one of the former Poor Law Commissioners.

During its lifetime, the Board had eleven presidents: Charles Buller (1847–48), Matthew Talbot Baines (1849–52), Sir John Trollope (1852), Matthew Talbot Baines (1852–55), Edward Pleydell Bouverie (1855–58), Thomas Sotheron-Estcourt (1858–59), Charles Pelham Villiers (1859–66), Gathorne Gathorne-Hardy (1866–67), William Reginald Courtenay (1867–68), George Joachim Goschen (1868–71), and James Stansfeld (1871).

Initially, the PLB took over the PLC's headquarters at Somerset House but in 1853 moved to a new home in Gwydyr House on Whitehall.

In 1871, the powers and responsibilities of the PLB were taken over by the new Local Government Board.

POOR LAW CERTIFIED SCHOOL

(*See*: Certified Schools (Poor Law))

POOR LAW COMMISSIONERS

The new central authority established by the 1834 Poor Law Amendment Act became known as the Poor Law Commissioners (PLC), sometimes also referred to as the Poor Law Commission. The Commissioners, of which there were three, were appointed by the government but were not themselves allowed to be MPs. It was intended that the PLC should have a large degree of political independence, being only indirectly responsible to Parliament via the Home Secretary.

The first Commissioners appointed were George Nicholls, John George Shaw-Lefevre and Thomas Frankland Lewis. They were sworn into office at noon on 23 August 1834, and shortly afterwards moved into offices in Somerset House on the Strand. Nicholls was a retired sea-captain, banker, and in the early 1820s had been a parish overseer at Southwell in Nottinghamshire where his introduction of a strict workhouse regime had dramatically reduced poor relief expenditure. Lewis, a former MP, also had a longstanding interest in poor relief having served on a Commons Select Committee on the poor laws in 1817. Shaw-Lefevre, another former MP and barrister, brought a legal background to the team. The PLC's first secretary was Edwin Chadwick, a member of the 1832 Royal Commission and one of the main authors of its report.

The 1834 Act did not go into detail about the operation of the new poor relief system. This was left up to the PLC to devise and implement. Their brief was:

> Make and Issue all such Rules, Orders, and Regulations for the Management of the Poor, for the Government of Workhouses and the Education of the Children therein... and for the apprenticing the Children of poor Persons, and for the Guidance and Control of all Guardians, Vestries, and Parish Officers, so far as relates to the Management or Relief of the Poor, and the keeping, examining, auditing, and allowing of Accounts, and making and entering into Contracts in all Matters relating to such Management or Relief, or to any Expenditure for the Relief of the Poor.[293]

One of the PLC's first tasks was to set about dividing the 15,000 or so parishes of England and Wales into the Poor Law Unions which were to form the basis of local poor relief administration under the new regime. A team of seventeen (later rising to nineteen) Assistant Commissioners was appointed, the first being Francis Head in October 1834. The Assistant Commissioners visited each district and organised meetings with local parish officials and landowners. Once the membership of the union was agreed, elections were organised to elect the union's Board of Guardians.

The implementation of the new system was specified through Orders issued by the Commissioners to Boards of Guardians which specified every aspect of the operation of a union and its workhouse. The PLC had the power to issue 'General Orders' which would apply to all unions, and 'Special Orders' which were specific to one. General Orders required parliamentary approval, while Special Orders did not. The Commission got around this restriction by repeatedly issuing identical Special Orders to multiple individual unions. In 1847, the PLC issued the Consolidated General Order, an amalgamation and revision of their exisiting General Orders, which became the 'bible' of poor law and workhouse administration.

Any plans for a workhouse that a Board of Guardians proposed to erect or modify had to be submitted to the Commissioners for their approval. The Commissioners also devised a multitude of detailed administrative procedures and sample documents, contracts, plans, diets and record forms by which the new unions would operate

The PLC was originally constituted for a period of five years. Between 1839 and 1842, its life was extended annually then in 1842 it was given a further five years.

There was a relatively small turnover of Commissioners during the PLC's lifetime. George Cornewall Lewis replaced Lewis in 1839 and Sir Edmund Walker Head replaced Shaw-Lefevre in 1841. Edward Turner Boyd Twisleton joined the PLC as the Commissioner for Ireland in 1845.

In 1847, following the Andover scandal and other bad publicity, reports of internal quarrels and divisions, together with a desire by the government to make poor law administration more directly accountable to Parliament, the Poor Law Commission was abolished and replaced by a new body, the Poor Law Board, with George Nicholls as its permanent secretary for the first three years of its life.

(*See also*: **Chadwick, Edwin**; **Nicholls, George**; **Royal Commission – 1832**; **Scandals**)

POOR LAW CONFERENCES

From around 1870, groups of Poor Law Unions in different parts of the country began to hold annual conferences and other occasional meetings, at which to discuss matters of common interest. Amongst the first of these events was the meeting held at Basingstoke in July 1870 for guardians from Hampshire and Berkshire. At the group's second conference at Reading in 1871, the topics under discussion included out relief, benefit and provident societies, the suppression of vagrancy, the training of pauper children, and the migration of labour from the south to the north of England.[294]

By 1878, conferences were being held by the Northern, North-western, South-eastern, South-western, South Midland, West Midland, Yorkshire, North Wales, South Wales and Metropolitan Districts, with an annual national conference being held in London from 1871.

(*See also*: **Association of Poor Law Unions**)

POOR LAW COUNTIES / UNION COUNTIES

For administrative purposes such as compiling statistical returns, Poor Law Unions were allocated to Poor Law or Union Counties. Although Poor Law Counties were broadly similar to geographical counties, their borders were slightly different because many unions straddled county borders. In such cases, the whole of the union area was usually allocated to the Poor Law County where the main town of the district or the largest proportion of the union's population was located.

In the 1850s, in order for Poor Law Counties to be synchronised with the corresponding areas defined for national census purposes, a few unions had their county allocation changed:

Unions Transferred	Original County	New County
Barnet	Hertfordshire	Middlesex
Dudley	Worcestershire	Staffordshire

Dulverton	Somerset	Devon
Hawarden	Flintshire	Cheshire
Kington	Herefordshire	Radnorshire
Newcastle-in-Emlyn	Carmarthenshire	Cardiganshire
St Asaph	Flintshire	Denbighshire
Shipston-on-Stour	Worcestershire	Warwickshire
Todmorden	Lancashire	West Riding of Yorkshire

(*See also*: **Poor Law Unions**)

POOR LAW EXAMINATION BOARD

(*See*: **Examinations**)

POOR LAW INSTITUTION

The official name for a workhouse or other poor law establishment in England and Wales from 1913 to 1930. Use of the term continued in Scotland until 1948.
(*See also*: **Public Assistance Institution**)

POOR LAW INSTITUTIONS ORDER

Although the 1905 Royal Commission on the poor laws did not directly result in any new parliamentary legislation, the publication of its two reports in 1909 did mark the beginning of reforms in workhouse administration. This was most clearly visible in the major update of the regulations governing the operation of workhouses and associated establishments, issued by the Local Government Board in 1913. The Order, which replaced the longstanding Consolidated General Order, included many new regulations and procedures and also incorporated changes introduced through individual orders and circulars over recent years.

The 1913 Order gave Boards of Guardians greater autonomy in matters such as setting the classification of inmates, their daily timetable and dietary, bathing regulations, and the prohibition of particular articles being brought into the workhouse. The Guardians' Visiting Committee was replaced by a House Committee which could indulge modest expenditure without consulting the full Board.

With regard to the sick, a trained nurse was now obligatory in all workhouse infirmaries. Infants below the age of eighteen months were to be medically examined at least once a fortnight. Proper medical records were to be kept, with a 'record paper' system replacing the former medical relief book. Inmates assisting in sick wards were always to be supervised by an officer. A major change for children was the instruction that from 31 March 1915, no healthy child was to reside in a workhouse for more than six weeks.

For those outside the workhouse, the 'case paper' system, developed by the Charity Organisation Society, was to be adopted for recording detailed ongoing information about each out relief claimant.

The 1913 Order was notable for a change in official terminology, with a complete absence of the terms 'workhouse' (now referred to as a 'poor law institution') and 'pauper' (now 'poor person') while infirmary inmates were now 'patients'.
(*See also*: **Consolidated General Order**; **Rules**)

POOR LAW MEDICAL OFFICERS' ASSOCIATION

(*See*: **Medical Officers' Associations**)

POOR LAW MEDICAL REFORM ASSOCIATION

(*See*: **Medical Officers' Associations**)

POOR LAW UNIONS

Poor Law Unions were groupings of parishes formed for administering poor relief following the 1834 Poor Law Amendment Act.

Unions varied widely in the number of parishes they included which could be as little as two. A few parishes, particularly in London, had a sufficiently large population to operate as single poor law parishes with equivalent status to a union. At the other end of the scale, the City of London Union's ninety-eight parishes gave it one of the largest memberships in the country, exceeded only by the 101 that comprised the Great Boughton Union in Cheshire. Generally, the largest unions both in terms of member parishes and in the physical area covered were in sparsely populated counties such as Northumberland and Lincolnshire. The Bellingham Union in Northumberland was the most sprawling, covering an area of almost 212,000 acres (330 square miles), while the West London Union encompassed a mere 122 acres (0.19 square miles).

The creation of Poor Law Unions was supervised by Assistant Poor Law Commissioners in consultation with the local parish officials and land-owners in each area. Land-owners with large estates could sometimes achieve considerable influence over the groupings of parishes forming each union, generally preferring to keep their property within a single union which would allow them the maximum of influence on its Board of Guardians. The new Potterspury Union in Northamptonshire, for example, ended up with only eleven member parishes, eight of which were owned entirely or in part by the Duke of Grafton.

Other complications could be caused by the survival after 1834 of Gilbert Unions and Local Act Incorporations. The Headington Union, for example, with its workhouse located just three miles from that of Oxford, was created as a mopping-up operation after the city had declined to relinquish its Local Act status and form a Poor Law Union in the area. The continuing existence of several large Gilbert Unions in the West Riding of Yorkshire hindered the unionisation of the area until 1869 when the surviving three were finally abolished.

Maps of the Poor Law Unions in England and Wales as they were in the 1880s are provided in Appendix J.

(*See also*: **Gilbert Union**; **Out relief Unions**; **Poor Law Counties / Union Counties**)

POOR LAW UNIONS – DISSOLVED OR DISAPPEARED

The great majority of the Poor Law Unions created following the 1834 Poor Law Amendment Act continued in operation until they were all abolished in 1930. For a variety of reasons a few were dissolved over the years, usually with their constituent parishes being absorbed into neighbouring unions. The casualties in England and Wales included:

Union	Year Dissolved
Penshurst, Kent	1836
Kensington, Middlesex	1845
Presteigne, Radnorshire	1877
Witham, Essex	1880

Radford, Nottinghamshire	1880
Chailey, Sussex	1898
West Firle, Sussex	1898
Woburn, Bedfordshire	1899
Fulham, Middlesex	1899
Guiltcross, Norfolk	1902
Hoxne, Suffolk	1908
Welwyn, Hertfordshire	1921

In Ireland, several unions were dissolved prior to the First World War, usually at their own request. Several other such requests were turned down by the Irish Local Government Board.

Union	Year Dissolved
Newport, Co. Mayo	1885
Donaghmore, Co. Leix	1886
Gortin, Co. Tyrone	1889
Glin, Co. Limerick	1891
Tulla, Co. Clare	1909

POOR LAW UNIONS - NAME CHANGES

Over the years, a number of Poor Law Unions changed their name, either to reflect changes in general usage, or to mark the increased prominence of a town within the union. A list of union name changes is given below:

Old Name	New Name	Year
Alderbury	Salisbury	1895
Altrincham	Bucklow	1895
Bedminster	Long Ashton	1899.
Bradford (Wiltshire)	Bradford-on-Avon	1895
Clifton	Barton Regis	1877
Cookham	Maidenhead	1896
Great Boughton	Tarvin	1871
Helmsley Blackmoor	Helmsley	1887
Highworth & Swindon	Swindon & Highworth	1889
Hungerford	Hungerford & Ramsbury	1896
Kensington	St Mary Abbots	1845
Melksham	Trowbridge & Melksham	1898
New Winchester	Winchester	1901
North Aylsford	Strood	1884
Penkridge	Cannock	1877
River	Dover	1837
South Stoneham	Eastleigh	1920
Stoke Damerel	Devonport	1898
Tunstead & Happing	Smallburgh	1870

POOR LAW WORKERS TRADE UNION

The Poor Law Workers' Trade Union was established in December 1918, changing its name in 1922 to the Poor Law Officers' Union. In 1930, it became the National Union of County Officers,

A member's badge for the Poor Law Workers trade union.

then was known as the Hospitals and Welfare Services Union from 1942 until 1946 when it merged with the Mental Hospital and Institutional Workers' Union to form the Confederation of Health Service Employees.
(*See also*: **National Association of Poor Law Officers**)

POOR LAWS

Early Legislation
England's earliest laws dealing with the poor were largely concerned
with suppressing beggars and itinerant vagabonds. The Black Death (1348–49) led to a severe shortage of labour and many workers took to roaming around the country in search of the highest wages. Others took to begging under the pretence of being ill or crippled. In 1349, the Ordinance of Labourers[295] included measures to keep wages at their former levels and prohibited private individuals from giving relief to able-bodied beggars.

In 1388, the Statute of Cambridge[296] introduced regulations restricting the movements of all labourers and beggars. Each county Hundred became responsible for relieving its own 'impotent poor' – those who, because of age or infirmity, were incapable of work. Servants wishing to move out of their own Hundred needed a letter of authority from a local Justice of the Peace, or risked being put in the stocks.

The 1494 Vagabonds Act[297] determined that: 'Vagabonds, idle and suspected persons shall be set in the stocks for three days and three nights and have none other sustenance but bread and water and then shall be put out of Town. Every beggar suitable to work shall resort to the Hundred where he last dwelled, is best known, or was born and there remain upon the pain aforesaid.' The Beggars and Vagabonds Act of 1531[298] required vagabonds to be whipped and returned to their birthplace for three years, and also allowed the impotent poor to beg after obtaining a licence to do so from a Justice of the Peace.

The seeds of the future direction of the poor laws were sown in the significant but short-lived Vagabonds Act of 1536,[299] which required churchwardens in each parish to collect voluntary alms in a 'common box' to provide handouts for those who could not work. At the same time, the idle and the able-bodied poor were obliged to perform labour, with punishment for those who refused. The Act also placed a prohibition on begging and on unofficial almsgiving. The 1547 Vagabonds Act[300] included further provision for the impotent poor including the erection of cottages for them to live in.

The 1552 Act for Provision and Relief of the Poor[301] required that 'collectors of alms' be appointed in each parish with every parishioner giving whatever their 'charitable devotion' suggested. In the following decades, compulsory poor-taxes were established in London, Cambridge, Colchester, Ipswich, Norwich and York. This principle was adopted nationally with the Vagabonds Act of 1572,[302] which introduced a local property tax, the poor rate, assessed by local Justices of the Peace and administered by parish overseers. The money raised was to be used to relieve 'aged, poor, impotent, and decayed persons'. This was followed in 1576 by the Act for Setting the Poor on Work,[303] which stated a principle that was to influence the administration of poor relief for centuries to come. The able-bodied were not to have 'any just excuse in saying that they cannot get service or work and be then without means of livelihood'. To achieve this, 'every city, town, and market, and market town, authorities should be enjoined to order a competent stock of wool, hemp, flax, or other stuff by taxation of all; so that every poor and needy person, old or young, able to work and standing in need of relief, shall not fear want of work, go abroad begging, or committing pilfering, or living in idleness.'

The 1597 Act for the Relief of the Poor[304] required every parish to appoint Overseers of the Poor whose responsibility it was to collect and distribute the poor rate, find work for the able-bodied, and to set up parish houses for those incapable of supporting themselves. In the same year, the Hospitals for the Poor Act[305] encouraged the founding of hospitals and 'working houses' for the poor.

The 1601 Poor Relief Act

The landmark year of 1601, the forty-third year of the reign of Elizabeth I, saw the passing of another Act for the Relief of the Poor[306] which, although essentially a refinement of the 1597 Act, is often cited as marking the foundation of the what became known as the Old Poor Law.

The main elements of the 1601 Act were: the parish being the administrative unit responsible for poor relief, with churchwardens or parish overseers collecting poor-rates and allocating relief; the provision of materials such as flax, hemp and wool to provide work for the able-bodied poor, with able-bodied paupers refusing to work liable to be placed in a House of Correction; the setting to work and apprenticeship of pauper children; and the relief of the impotent poor, including the provision of 'houses of dwelling'. The Act also made the relief and maintenance of the impotent poor the legal responsibility of their parents, grandparents, or children, if such relatives were themselves able to provide such support.

Implementation of the 1601 Act, like much legislation in this era, was often patchy or unsustained. In 1630, Charles I appointed a Select Committee of his Privy Council, known as the Commissioners of the Poor, to try and consolidate the adoption of the poor laws throughout the country – an undertaking which achieved widespread success.[307]

The Settlement Act

In 1662, another significant piece of legislation, An Act for the better Relief of the Poor of this Kingdom[308] (sometimes known as the Settlement Act), was passed. The Act allowed for the removal from a parish, back to their place of settlement, of newcomers whom local justices deemed 'likely to be chargeable' to the parish poor rates.

A further Poor Relief Act in 1691[309] specified additional ways in which settlement could be acquired – through apprenticeship or by being in continuous employment for at least a year. The 1697 Poor Act[310] gave newcomers, with settlement certificates from their own parish, protection from removal until they actually became chargeable on the poor rate. A century later, in 1795, the Poor Removal Act[311] extended this protection to all except pregnant unmarried women.

The Workhouse Test Act

The 1723 Act for Amending the Laws relating to the Settlement, Imployment and Relief of the Poor[312] often known as the Workhouse Test Act (or Knatchbull's Act after its promoter, Sir

The opening section of the 1601 *Act for Relief of the Poor* which formed the basis of what became known as the Old Poor Law. Parts of the Act remained on the statute book until 1967.

C A P. II.

An Act for the Relief of the Poor.

BE it enacted by the Authority of this present Parliament, That the Churchwardens of every Parish, and four, three or two substantial Housholders there, as shall be thought meet, having respect to the Proportion and Greatness of the same Parish and Parishes, to be nominated yearly in *Easter* Week, or within one Month after *Easter*, under the Hand and Seal of two or more Justices of the Peace in the same County, whereof one to be of the *Quorum*, dwelling in or near the same Parish or Division where the same Parish doth lie, shall be called Overseers of the Poor of the same Parish: And they, or the greater Part of them, shall take order from Time to Time, by, and with the Consent of two or more such Justices of Peace as is aforesaid, for setting to work the Children of all such whose Parents shall not by the said Churchwardens and Overseers, or the greater Part of them, be thought able to keep and maintain their Children: And also for setting to work all such Persons, married or unmarried, having no Means to maintain them, and use no ordinary and daily Trade of Life to get their Living by: And also to raise weekly or otherwise (by Taxation of every Inhabitant, Parson, Vicar and other, and of every Occupier of Lands, Houses, Tithes impropriate, Propriations of Tithes, Coal-Mines, or saleable Underwoods in the said Parish, in such competent Sum and Sums of Money as they shall think fit) a convenient Stock of Flax, Hemp, Wool, Thread, Iron, and other necessary Ware and Stuff, to set the Poor on Work: And also competent Sums of Money for and towards the necessary Relief of the Lame, Impotent, Old, Blind, and such other among them, being Poor, and not able to work, and also for the putting out of such Children to be Apprentices, to be gathered out of the same Parish, according to the Ability of the same Parish, and to do and execute all other Things as well for the disposing of the said Stock, as otherwise concerning the Premisses, as to them shall seem convenient:

Edward Knatchbull) brought workhouses to the fore. The Act, reflecting the practice already adopted by some vestries, provided a legal framework for workhouses to be set up by parishes either singly, or in combination with their neighbour. Premises could be hired or purchased for the purpose, and workhouse operation could be contracted out – a system that became known as 'farming' the poor. Knatchbull's Act also introduced the workhouse 'test' – that the prospect of the workhouse should act as a deterrent and that relief could be restricted to only those who were desperate enough to accept its regime. Although the Act was permissive, many parishes made use of its provisions. By the mid-1770s, around one in seven parishes was running a workhouse, with almost 2,000 workhouses in operation across England and Wales.

Gilbert's and Young's Acts

In 1782, MP Thomas Gilbert successfully promoted his Act for the Better Relief and Employment of the Poor.[313] Gilbert's Act aimed to organise poor relief on a larger scale with parishes forming groups or 'unions' roughly corresponding to county Hundreds. Such unions could set up a common workhouse, although this was to be for the benefit only of the old, the sick and infirm, and orphan children. Able-bodied paupers were not to be admitted but found employment near their own homes, with land-owners, farmers and other employers receiving allowances from the poor rates to bring wages up to subsistence levels. The administration of Gilbert Unions, as they became known, was through a Board of Guardians, one from each member parish, elected by ratepayers and appointed by local magistrates. This allowed a shift in power over poor relief administration from the parish vestry to the propertied classes.

In 1795, Sir William Young introduced an Act for the Relief of the Poor[314] that repealed some of the provisions of Knatchbull's Act and gave greater powers to local magistrates to order out-door relief where it had previously been refused by parish overseers. This was not a universally popular measure and may have encouraged some parishes to form Gilbert Unions which were exempt from such measures.

Sturges Bourne's and Hobhouse's Acts

In an effort to improve the administration of poor relief, and reduce costs, two Acts were promoted by the MP William Sturges Bourne in 1818 and 1819. The first of these measures, the Vestries Act,[315] introduced a plural voting system for elections to parish vestries. Resident ratepayers were allocated up to six votes depending on the value of their property.

The second statute, the Poor Relief Act[316] (also known as the Select Vestry Act) allowed parishes to appoint small committees, known as Select Vestries, to scrutinise relief-giving. In addition, a rate could be raised specifically to build or enlarge a workhouse. To help parish overseers (an unpaid post) with the growing administrative burden imposed by poor relief, a salaried assistant overseer could also be appointed. Finally, the voting rights provided in the 1818 Act were now extended to non-resident ratepayers. Overall, the 1819 Act gave parishes and their ratepayers a greater say in poor relief administration, without the expense of obtaining a local Act of Parliament for this purpose.

John Hobhouse further extended the influence of ratepayers in parish administration. His Vestries Act of 1831[317] allowed parishes to be managed by a vestry of at least twelve householders elected annually. A single vote was given to any ratepayer who had been resident in the parish for at least a year.

The 1834 Poor Law Amendment Act

In 1834, after two years of deliberation, a Royal Commission into the administration and operation of the poor laws published its report. Its main recommendations were implemented in the Poor Law Amendment Act[318] which received Royal Assent on 14 August 1834.

The 1834 Act, which formed the basis of what became known as the New Poor Law, aimed to create a national, uniform and compulsory system of poor relief administration under a new central authority, the Poor Law Commissioners (PLC). New administrative areas were to be created, known as Poor Law Unions, each managed by a Board of Guardians elected by local ratepayers – depending on the value of the property, owners had up to six votes and occupiers up to three votes. Each union was expected to provide a workhouse which was to be the only form of relief available to the able-bodied and their families. Out relief would still be available in certain situations however. Funding of the new system was from local poor rates, initially based on each parish's poor relief expenditure in the three years before it joined a Poor Law Union.

Contrary to the impression that is sometimes given, the new Act did not overturn the fundamental principles of poor relief – financial responsibility of the parish, the use of a workhouse test, the administrative grouping of parishes, local management by elected Boards of Guardians, settlement qualifications, and plural voting all featured in the Old Poor Law legislation.

The 1834 Act did not specify the details of exactly how the new system would operate – these were left for the PLC to devise. With regard to the giving of poor relief, they were empowered to:

> Declare to what Extent and for what Period the Relief to be given to able-bodied Persons or to their Families in any particular Parish or Union may be administered out of the Workhouse of such Parish or Union, by Payments in Money, or with Food or Clothing in Kind, or partly in Kind and partly in Money, and in what Proportions, to what Persons or Class of Persons, at what Times and Places, on what Conditions, and in what Manner such Out-door Relief may be afforded.[319]

The former powers of local magistrates with regard to poor relief were not entirely abolished, however. The Act allowed a Justice of the Peace to issue an order for the giving of medical relief, or for out relief to the elderly or infirm.

Amongst the other measures included in the 1834 Act was the so-called 'bastardy clause' which made it harder for a single mother to obtain an affiliation order against the child's putative father, a change intended to discourage women from risking extra-marital pregnancy.

Poor Law Commissioner George Nicholls later noted two significant deficiencies in the Act. First, it maintained the status of Gilbert Unions and Local Act Incorporations, which were allowed to continue operating in their existing form – something which seriously hindered the formation of new Poor Law Unions in some areas. Second, the PLC could not compel a union to provide a workhouse without the support of a majority of its ratepayers or its Board of Guardians, although alterating or enlarging of existing workhouse premises could be demanded.[320]

Revisions to the 1834 Act

Numerous and often small amendments to the 1834 Act were made in a succession of later legislation including further Poor Law Amendment Acts in 1842, 1844, 1848, 1849, 1850 and 1851. The 1842 Act[321] included a measure relating to the tramps and other non-settled itinerants. What were termed the 'occasional' poor could now be detained to perform up to four hours' labour in return for their night's lodging at a workhouse. The 1844 Act[322] allowed unions to combine to form School Districts for providing education to pauper children and also restored the rights of single mothers receiving poor relief to gain affiliation orders against putative fathers. The 1848 Act[323] allowed the cost of pauper burials and of relieving itinerants to be charged to a common union fund.

One of the most significant changes during this period came with the 1847 Poor Law Board Act[324] which replaced the PLC with the new Poor Law Board (PLB), a body more directly accountable to Parliament.

In 1865, the Union Chargeability Act[325] shifted the cost of poor relief from the parish to the union – each parish now contributed to a common union fund based on its rateable value not on the number of paupers it had. Prior to this change, the poorest parishes with many paupers had also been burdened with the highest rates, while in better-off parishes with few paupers rich landowners had escaped with very low rates.

The Metropolitan Poor Act

In the 1860s, increasing concern about the state of London's workhouses, and in particular their medical facilities, led to pressure for changes in their management. In 1867, the Metropolitan Poor Act[326] resulted in much of the care on London's sick poor being brought under a new body, the Metropolitan Asylums Board (MAB). Some reorganisation of London's unions was carried out, and all unions were now required to provide hospital accommodation on sites run separately from the workhouse. The MAB erected a number of its own institutions for the care the capital's fever, smallpox and tuberculosis patients, and for what were then termed 'imbeciles'. The MAB's institutions were effectively England's first state hospitals.

The Local Government Board

Under an Act of 1871,[327] the PLB was replaced by the Local Government Board (LGB) which included a much broader range of responsibilities such as sanitation and public health.

In the 1870s, the LGB mounted a campaign to reduce the levels of out relief expenditure. It also increased the pressure on the few remaining unions such as Todmorden, Rhayader and Presteigne who had held out against the building of workhouses. It was aided in this latter aim by the 1876 Divided Parishes and Poor Law Amendment Act.[328] The primary purpose of this Act was to enable the Board to tidy up the boundaries of unions, particularly those that had areas detached from the main area of the union or that crossed county borders. However, it also empowered the Board to dissolve any union 'when it is expedient to do so for the purpose of rectifying or simplifying the areas of management, or otherwise for the better administration of relief...'. Under the threat of dissolution, Todmorden and Rhayader finally agreed to build workhouses, with Rhayader taking in its first inmates in August 1879, making it the last union in the whole of England and Wales to do so. Presteigne, however, was dissolved in 1877 and its constituent parishes distributed to adjacent unions.

The Local Government Act

The Local Government Act of 1894[329] introduced a number of important changes to the election of Boards of Guardians. The term of office for guardians was increased to three years and *ex officio* guardians were abolished although Boards could co-opt up to four suitably qualified members. Plural voting and rating qualifications were also done away with. Neighbouring unions could join to form out relief unions to improve the administration of out relief.

Poor Relief Disfranchisement

Prior to 1918, acceptance of poor relief disqualified the recipient from voting. However, from the 1870s there was an increasing use of workhouse medical facilities by those for whom admission to the main institution was not appropriate. In 1885, the Medical Relief Disqualification Removal Act[330] meant that anyone who was in receipt only of poor-rate-funded medical care no longer lost their vote.

The End of the Workhouse

Despite various efforts to reform or abolish the workhouse system, most notably following the work of the 1905 Royal Commission on the Poor Law and the Unemployed, the institution continued operating with relatively little change into the 1920s. In 1919, the administration of health and poor relief was transferred from the Local Government Board to the newly created Ministry of Health.

The general depression in the years following the First World War, culminating in the miners' strike of 1926, put a tremendous strain on the system with some unions effectively becoming bankrupt. In some areas, where colliery owners also had influence with local Boards of Guardians, there were allegations that relief was deliberately reduced to break the strike. Conversely, where miners and union officials dominated a Board, there were complaints that the rates were being used to supplement strike funds.

Neville Chamberlain, Health Minister in the 1925 Conservative Government, believed that that the poor law system needed reforming and in 1926 pushed through the Boards of Guardians (Default) Act[331] which enabled the dismissal of a Board of Guardians and its replacement with government officials. The 1926 Act's provisions were subsequently made use of in the unions at West Ham, Chester-le-Street and Bedwellty Unions. Further controls were imposed by a further Poor Law Act[332] in 1927, and in 1928 Chamberlain introduced the Local Government Act[333] which would abolish the Boards of Guardians and transfer all their powers and responsibilities to local councils. These were required to submit administrative schemes to end 'poor relief' and to provide more targeted 'public assistance' on the basis of other legislation such as public health or education enactments. The Local Government Act was passed on 27 March 1929 and came into effect on 1 April 1930, a day which supposedly marked the end of the road for more than 600 Boards of Guardians in England and Wales.

Although the workhouse was officially no more, prevarication by Boards of Guardians and councils often meant that changes were very slow in taking place. Ultimately, the 1929 Act did not succeed in abolishing the poor law – it reformed how it was administered and changed a few names. Poor Law Institutions became Public Assistance Institutions and were frequently controlled by a committee of 'guardians'. Many former workhouse institutions carried on into the 1930s virtually unaltered, inheriting the same buildings, same staff and same inmates, the majority of whom continued to be the old, the chronic sick, the mentally ill, unmarried mothers and vagrants.

Under the new Labour Government elected after the Second World War, a raft of legislation heralded the creation of a comprehensive social welfare service. The 1945 Family Allowances Act[334] gave families with two or more children a weekly allowance of 5s for each child other than the first. The 1946 National Insurance Act[335] established a universal contributory scheme to fund payments such as retirement pensions and unemployment, sickness and maternity benefits, plus a new National Health Service. Contributions were made both by employees (up to 4s 9d per week for men), employers and the Exchequer. The National Health Service Act[336] of 1946 came into force on 5 July 1948 and provided a unified public health-care system, free for all at the point of delivery.

The 1948 National Assistance Act[337] was enacted 'to terminate the existing poor law' and repealed, in whole or in part, around eighty pieces of legislation dating back as far as 1718. It was intended to provide a safety net for those whose needs fell outside the National Insurance Scheme. The Act set up a new National Assistance Board which could make cash payments and also set up re-establishment centres to offer training for those not in regular employment. Reception centres were to be provided for 'those without a settled way of living'. Local authorities were also required to provide residential accommodation for the elderly and infirm and temporary accommodation for those in urgent need.

(*See also*: **Illegitimacy**; **Overseers**; **Plural Voting**; **Settlement**)

POOR RATE

A local tax, dating from 1572, based on an official assessment of the value of the property in which each contributor lived. It was collected by each parish's Overseers of the Poor and distributed under the jurisdiction of the vestry. Failure to pay the poor rate would result in a summons to appear before a Justices of the Peace, who could impose a fine or the seizure of property, or even prison. The poor rate gradually formed part of a more general rating system (colloquially known as 'the rates') which was used to pay for an growing range of local services such as maintenance of the roads, street lighting, etc.

The separate poor rate, together with the office of overseer, was abolished by the 1925 Rating and Valuation Act.[338] The rating system in England and Wales continued in operation until 1990 when it was replaced by the *per capita* Community Charge (or 'poll tax'), itself supplanted in 1993 by the Council Tax which was again based on the value of each householder's property.

POOR RELIEF

Assistance to the poor provided out of the poor rates.
(*See also*: **Indoor Relief**; **Out relief**; **Pauper**; **Poor Rate**)

POORHOUSE

In England and Wales, prior to 1834, a poorhouse was typically a place where destitute families or the elderly of a parish were given free lodging, or where the sick or disabled were housed. It might also be used as a temporary residence for paupers about to be removed to other parishes. A poorhouse typically consisted of one or more cottages or adjoining tenements although it could sometimes be a more substantial building. In some parishes, the poorhouse – often known as the Church House – was also used as a venue for village events.

Although the terms poorhouse and workhouse were often used interchangeably, differences did exist. Unlike a workhouse, a poorhouse typically had no resident governor, had few rules regarding the behaviour of inmates, placed no restrictions on what they ate, and did not require them to perform labour.

Poorhouses were also distinct from almshouses which were charitably endowed establishments providing permanent accommodation for the elderly of good character.

After 1834, the term workhouse was generally adopted in England and Wales for institutions providing indoor relief. In Scotland, the term poorhouse (or poor's house) was almost always employed, perhaps because paupers in Scotland were not generally required to labour in return for poor relief.

In the United States, a workhouse was typically an institution where petty offenders were punished with a spell of hard labour, while a poorhouse was a place where the destitute elderly and sick were housed and maintained.
(*See also*: **Workhouse**)

POPLAR EXPERIMENT

From 1871, the Local Government Board supported an experiment whereby Poplar workhouse admitted only able-bodied paupers who were subjected to a deterrent regime of hard work, strict discipline and a basic diet. Within that, some differentiation was provided in the treatment of the 'well conducted' and the 'disorderly'. Inmates were employed in stone breaking, corn grinding, oakum picking, with workshops also provided for tailors, shoemakers and for needle-working. A room for storing household goods was provided for families taking temporary refuge in the workhouse.[339]

Any spare capacity was offered to other metropolitan unions and parishes. The scheme proved to be effective with an 'Order for Poplar' proving a strong deterrent to able-bodied relief claimants. However, such Orders increasingly came to be used by unions wishing to get rid of undesirable or troublesome applicants. This could include the aged and physically defective as well as the able-bodied. As early as 1873, the workhouse medical officer was complaining of the numbers of inmates who were not able-bodied. In 1880, 235 of the 1,284 men admitted to the workhouse were aged over sixty.

During this period, Poplar had an arrangement with the adjacent Stepney Union to accommodate its other classes of inmate, with the aged and infirm going to Stepney's workhouse at Bromley and the sick to the newly opened Poplar and Stepney Sick Asylum.

The 'Poplar Experiment' continued until 1882 when the union decided that it wished to use the workhouse as additional accommodation for its own elderly and infirm inmates.
(*See also*: **Test Workhouse**)

POPLARISM

'Poplarism' was a term – often used disparagingly – describing policies of excessive expenditure, especially on poor relief, particularly associated with Labour politicians and with the East London borough of Poplar.

Poplarism had its roots in the early 1900s when the Poplar Board of Guardians, whose membership included socialist reformers Will Crooks and George Lansbury, operated an increasingly generous poor relief policy. Out relief was given to the over-sixties with no enquiry as to the earning of their other family members, and to the able-bodied without the imposition of a labour test. The level of comfort for inmates in the workhouse was said to be superior to that of a typical working labourer, with rations of beer issued to inmates amounting to over 200 pints a day on occasion. In 1906, a public inquiry by the Local Government Board into the running of the union resulted in many criticisms of the Board although Crooks and Lansbury were largely exonerated.

There was a resurgence of Poplarism following the election of Poplar's first Labour council in 1919 when George Lansbury became Mayor. The new borough council embarked on a programme of social reform, which included paying council employees' wages that were above the market rate. The Board of Guardians, too, despite an increasing level of unemployment, operated a generous out relief policy. By 1921, the cost of these measures was such that the borough refused to pay its annual rates levy to the London County Council, Metropolitan Asylums Board, Water Board and Police. The borough argued that London's rating system put it at a disadvantage – the lower values of property in Poplar meant that to raise a given amount of money, it had to charge much higher rates than would be required in a richer borough. After ignoring a court order to make the payments, thirty councillors were imprisoned. The protestors received considerable public support and were released six weeks later. Soon afterwards, the Local Authorities (Financial Provisions) Act was rushed through Parliament. Although the Act did not amend the capital's rating system in the way that Poplar had demanded, it did allow out relief to be paid for through the Metropolitan Common Poor Fund with wealthier boroughs subsidising poorer ones.

As well as in Poplar itself, Poplarist principles were adopted by other London unions, such as West Ham, and elsewhere, such as Bedwellty in South Wales and Chester-le-Street in Durham. (*See also*: **Crooks, Will**; **Lansbury, George**; **Metropolitan Common Poor Fund**; Ryan (1978))

PORTER

A resident porter was employed at virtually every workhouse, usually based in a 'lodge' at the main entrance to the site or the workhouse building itself. No special qualifications were laid down for the post whose main duties were:

- To keep the gate and prevent unauthorised persons entering or leaving the workhouse.
- To record the name and business of everyone coming or going.
- To receive all new admissions.
- To inspect all incoming parcels and goods and prevent the entry of prohibited items such as beer or spirits.
- To search any male pauper entering or leaving the workhouse suspected of carrying prohibited items.
- To inspect all parcels taken by any pauper out of the workhouse.
- To lock all the outer doors, and take the keys to the master, at 9 p.m. every night, and to receive them back from him every morning at 6 a.m.
- To assist the master and matron in preserving order in the workhouse.

Above left A uniformed porter on duty at the entrance to the Fulham workhouse in the 1890s.

Above right The decaying remains of the multi-occupancy outdoor privy at the Bawnboy workhouse in County Cavan.

As the list indicates, the overall length of the porter's day ran to fifteen hours, although at times he was probably deputised for by a trusted inmate. At some workhouses, the duties of the porter included the admission of those entering the workhouse casual ward. In such cases, a married man might be appointed to the post, with his wife supervising the female receiving or casual wards. Such a couple might subsequently be in a good position to apply for positions as a workhouse master and matron.

PRIVY

A room or small outbuilding used as a toilet or latrine where deposits fall into a pit or receptacle below which is periodically emptied.
(*See also*: **Earth Closet**; **Lavatory**; **Water Closet**)

PROBATIONARY WARD

(*See*: **Receiving Ward**)

PUBLIC ASSISTANCE INSTITUTION

After the abolition of the Boards of Guardians in 1930, many former workhouses were redesignated as Public Assistance Institutions (PAIs). PAIs were administered by local Public Assistance Committees set up by county or county borough councils and were sometimes also known as County Institutions. PAIs provided accommodation for the elderly, the chronic sick and single mothers. In many cases, PAIs also continued operating the former workhouse casual wards. The PAIs inherited their staff, inmates and buildings from the workhouse era and were often little different from their predecessors. Some cosmetic changes took place – the inmates of PAIs were no longer issued with uniforms, but with 'suitable clothing', and the governor of a PAI was usually styled the superintendent rather than the master.

The term PAI disappeared with the launch of the National Health Service in 1948. Many former PAIs became geriatric hospitals or old people's homes while others were sold off for redevelopment. (*See also*: **Poor Law Institution**)

PUNISHMENT

(*See*: **Discipline**)

QUAKER WORKHOUSES

In 1680, the Society of Friends, or Quakers, set up a scheme in London to buy stocks of flax for the Quaker poor to spin at home or in prison. The project's treasurer, John Bellers, later developed plans for a 'College of Industry' – a co-operative, self-sufficient community where up to 200 labourers and 100 of the impotent poor would live and work together. Although Bellers' utopian plans were never implemented, their influence was seen in two subsequent establishments set up by the Quakers in Bristol in 1696 and in London in 1702.

The Bristol scheme was originally intended for providing employment for seven poor Quaker weavers and the instruction of children. It was so successful that in 1700 new premises were erected in New Street, St Jude's, at a cost of £1,300 'for willing Friends to work in and the aged and feeble to live in.' The premises incorporated an orphanage, a school and an almshouse, housing a total of forty-five, including twenty-four paupers and ten apprentices. The inmates were mainly employed in manufacturing worsted cloths known as cantaloons. Old people in the workhouse received pocket money of 2s a week plus a tobacco allowance. A survey of Bristol in 1861 recorded that the site was still 'used as an asylum for poor Friends.' In 1929, the site was sold to the Bristol Churches Tenements Association for conversion to workmen's flats. The building, now known as New Street Flats, is one of the oldest surviving workhouse buildings in the country.

The London workhouse, located in the former Middlesex County workhouse at Clerkenwell, was intended to house fifty-six 'decayed Friends and Orphans'. The elderly occupied one section of the house, with the children in another where they were employed in spinning mop-yarn. The girls also made and mended the inmates' clothing, while the boys learnt to read, write and cast accounts. Cold baths were on offer to the inmates 'for their Health or Cleanliness'. The inmates brewed their own beer, and the children helped in preparing all the food.

The diary of the steward at Clerkenwell, Richard Hutton, from 1711–37 gives an insight into the operation of an early eighteenth-century workhouse. The inmates' diet included bread, butter, cheese and a pint of beer for breakfast and supper on five days a week, with broth replacing the cheese and butter on the remainder. On three days a week, the midday dinner consisted of meat, bread and beer. On the other days, it could include porridge, pudding, pottage or

The outdoor yards of the Woolwich Union workhouse before demolition of the walls that segregated different classes of inmate.

The same view of the former Woolwich workhouse following its remodelling to become a Public Assistance Institution in 1930.

'frumety' – wheat grains boiled up with milk. Sick inmates appear to have been particularly well looked after. Hutton records that the diet of one inmate, John Wilson, over a six-month period of being sick or weak, regularly included such items as: a pint of claret, half a pint of wine, fish, oysters, cheese cake, a quarter pound of chocolate, half a pound of double-refined sugar, a quarter pound of biscuits, and conserve of roses with juleps.

The workhouse ceased operating in 1786 and the buildings were demolished in around 1830. (*See also*: **Hitchcock** (1987))

RATE IN AID ACT

(*See*: **Ireland**)

RAUHE HAUS

The Rauhe Haus (or 'Rough House'), at Hamburg in Germany, was founded by Johann Wichern in 1833 as a home for parentless destitute children in Hamburg, Germany. The institution developed the 'family principle' housing children in groups of ten to twelve under the supervision of a resident 'brother'. Along with the colony at Mettray in France, the Rauhe Haus was influential in the evolution of the cottage homes system later adopted in England by some Poor Law Unions and charities.
(*See also*: **Cottage Homes**; **Mettray**)

REBECCA RIOTS

In 1842–43, the 'Rebecca Rioters' carried out a campaign of protests across South Wales which included the storming of the Carmarthen workhouse on 19 June 1843. The rioters took their name from the Bible's Book of Genesis (chapter 24, verse 60): 'And they blessed Rebekah and said unto her, Thou art our sister, be thou the mother of thousands of millions, and let thy seed possess the gate of those which hate them.' The rioters often included one or more 'Rebecca' figures dressed in women's clothes and wearing a wig of ringlets.
(*See also*: **Captain Swing Riots**; **Wales**)

RECEIVING WARD

Initial accommodation for new arrivals at a workhouse, usually located near the main entrance. Also known as a probationary ward.
(*See also*: **Entering a Workhouse**)

RECORDS

Over several centuries of operation, the poor relief system generated a vast amount of records. While many of these are concerned with the details of the numerous financial transactions that took place, others record a huge variety of information about people, buildings, procedures, scandals and political struggles, giving insights into how the poor were viewed and treated.

Some poor relief records, such as those relating to poor rates or settlement and removal, run across both the Old and the New Poor Law. Others, such as Poor Law Union records, are confined to one or other era.

Costumed Rebecca Rioters in the midst of the fray in 1843.

Poor Rates Records

From 1597, until their abolition in 1925, the Overseers of the Poor in each parish were responsible for the collection of the poor rate and its subsequent distribution. The overseers' account books typically include lists of the names of each householder and the amount of poor rate paid, together with details of all their disbursements such as weekly 'pensions' and payments for rent, food, clothing and medical treatment. The overseers themselves would often also have expenses which would be recorded, such as the costs involved in taking a pauper to visit a magistrate for a settlement examination. Other material relating to the poor rates includes rates demands or summonses issued for non-payment. Where a parish had a workhouse, expenditure on its operation could also feature in overseers' accounts.

Settlement and Removal Records

Records relating to the law of settlement and removal include a variety of documents:

- *Settlement Certificates* could, from 1697, be issued by a parish to confirm its responsibility for the bearer should they require poor relief. Carrying a certificate allowed a labourer, for example, to take up work in another parish without being threatened with removal.
- *Settlement Examinations* were conducted by magistrates to establish a person's place of settlement if this was in question. The record of the examination often included an in-depth account of the person's life including their age and place of birth, details of apprenticeship and employment, details of any marriage with names of the spouse and any children, places of abode etc.
- *Removal Orders* were issued by magistrates allowing a parish to return an incomer needing poor relief back to their place of settlement. Two copies of each order were made, one for the removing parish and one for the receiving parish.

Bastardy Records

The procedures involved in identifying the father of an illegitimate child, and the associated financial responsibility for support of the child, generated a number of records:

- *Bastardy Examinations*, conducted by magistrates, were formal interviews with the mother, usually before the child was born. As well as any information revealing the father, the record of the examination may include details of the woman's situation and family, and the circumstances by which she conceived, for example being promised marriage. If the examination took place after the child was born, its date of birth and sex may be recorded. As well as the

A 1784 removal order for the return of William Miles to his place of settlement at Rodborough in Gloucestershire from Rowde in Wiltshire. The order was signed by two Justices of the Peace and two copies were issued, one for each of the parishes involved.

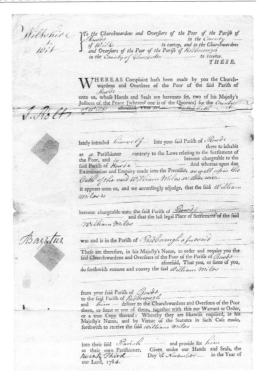

mother, such depositions could include evidence from midwives.

- *Bastardy Bonds* were agreements between fathers admitting responsibility for an illegitimate child and the parish of the mother's settlement. The father agreed to pay the costs relating to the birth of the child and its maintenance until it reached the age of seven.
- *Bastardy Warrants* were issued where the putative father of an illegitimate child refused to take responsibility for the child, typically by absconding.
- *Maintenance Orders*, issued once a child was born, include details of its birth and the payments to be made by the father.
- *Maintenance Summonses*, requiring attendance at court, could be issued to fathers who fell behind with their maintenance payments.

Apprenticeship Records

Apprenticeship agreements or 'indentures' generally include details such as the apprentice's name, age, parish, parents' names, name and occupation of the master, and the trade to be learned.

Vestry Minutes

The minute books of the vestry – the parish committee – often contain material relating to poor relief. This may include discussions of general policy, such as whether to have a workhouse and how it should be operated, or more detailed material about individual relief recipients or events inside the workhouse. Where a parish did run a workhouse, vestries occasionally kept a separate record book relating to its operation.

Parish Workhouse Records

Apart from what might appear in overseers and vestry records, parish workhouses sometimes generated various records of their own. These may include items such as workhouse rules, occasional inventories of the building's contents, and any records kept by the workhouse governor. An interesting example of the latter is the daybook kept by the master of the Knaresborough workhouse from 1788 to 1792 which records the names of the inmates, the work they performed and the income resulting from it, together with a brief daily account of life in the institution.[340]

Poor Law Union Records

The Poor Law Unions created following the Poor Law Amendment Act of 1834 were required to maintain a wide variety of records and registers.

Records kept by the union Clerk include:
- Details of guardians elected

- Minutes of board meetings
- Appointment of officers
- Union accounts (occasionally naming those relieved)

Out relief records include:
- Application and report books (including names, ages, addresses etc.)
- Out relief order books (including names, addresses, amounts etc.)
- Medical relief orders
- Loans made to paupers

Workhouse records include:
- Admission and discharge registers
- Porter's book
- Indoor pauper lists (six-monthly summaries)
- Medical examination books
- Registers of births, deaths and burials
- Register of baptisms (if workhouse had its own chapel)
- Notices to next of kin of illness or death
- Creed register (from 1869)
- Leave of absence register
- Bathing register
- Inmates' own clothing register
- Lunatics register
- Register of mechanical restraint
- Punishments book
- Casuals admission and discharge register
- Visiting Committee report book

Records relating to children included:
- Register of children under control of the guardians
- Children's home admissions and discharges
- Children's home superintendent's book
- Children's home visitor's report book
- Register of children boarded-out
- Reports on boarded-out children
- Register of persons receiving infants (from 1908)
- Register of apprentices
- Register of children placed in service
- Register of visits to under-sixteens taken as servants from workhouse
- Vaccination records (includes non-paupers)

Accessing Local Poor Law Records

Local poor law records, including those created under the Old and New Poor Law, are mostly held in county and metropolitan borough record offices. As well as online catalogues provided by record offices themselves, the 'Access to Archives' service (www.nationalar-chives.gov.uk/a2a) has details of records held by a large number of archives across England and Wales.

The survival of Poor Law Union records is especially variable. In some areas, such as Northamptonshire and Lincolnshire, extensive records exist; in other parts of the country, such as Yorkshire, relatively little remains. The directories of poor law institutions (Appendices D to G) gives the location(s) of the surviving records for each union. More detailed information is provided on the workhouse website (www.workhouses.org.uk) and in the *Poor Law Union*

A model layout for a workhouse Admissions and Discharges book in 1847.

Admission and Discharge Book

_____ UNION. _____   _____ Master of the Workhouse at _____

ADMITTED.		DISCHARGED.	

When a Pauper is admitted before breakfast, the Master is to enter in the column for "Next meal after admission" the letter B ; when before dinner, the letter D ; and when before supper the letter S. And when a Pauper is discharged after breakfast, the Master is to enter in the column for "Last meal before discharge" the letter B ; when after dinner, the letter D ; and when after supper, the letter S.

Below Samples of the different type of entry that could be made in a vaccinations register in the 1850s.

EXAMPLES shewing how Entries may be made in the Register Book of Successful Vaccinations.

I.—Extracts from the Register Book of Births, (or from the Certificates of the Vaccinator,) relating to each Child. | II.—Minute of Notices given pursuant to 16 & 17 Vict., c. 100, s. 9. | III.—Register of successful Vaccination.

		No.	When and where born: [or age according to the Vaccinator's Certificate].	Name, if any.	Sex.	Name and Surname of the Father, or, (if the child be illegitimate) of the Mother.	Rank, Occupation, or Profession of Parent.	When Registered.	When given.	To whom given.	Date of Medical Certificate of Successful Vaccination.	Name of the Medical Man by whom the Certificate is Signed.
		Col. 1	Col. 2	Col. 3	Col.4	Col. 5	Col. 6	Col. 7	Col. 8	Col. 9	Col. 10	Col. 11
First Example.	An ordinary case.	57	15 Augt. 1853. 12, King St. Birkenhead.	William.	M.	James Hudson.	Husbandman.	27 Augt. 1853.	27 Augt.	Father.	15 Septr.	I. Hutt.
Second Example.	A Child found exposed. The Notice delivered to the Master of the Workhouse in which the Child is placed.	59	26 Augt. 1853. Found exposed at Hooton.	(Named.) George Hooton.	M.			28 Augt. 1853.	29 Augt.	John Cook.	28 Septr.	H. Dale.
Third Example.	An illegitimate Child. The Notice delivered to the Person in whose custody the Child remains.	62	20 Augt. 1853. 12, King Street, Birkenhead.	—	F.	Mary Spence, (deceased.)	Lately a Milliner.	31 Augt. 1853.	31 Augt.	Paul Spence.	11 Novr.	T. Wallis.
Fourth Example.	A Child born out of the Sub-district of the Registrar. The age taken from the Vaccinator's Certificate.		185 . Aged 22 Weeks. 5, John Street, Lancaster.	Timothy.	M.	John South.	Pensioner from the 30th Regt. of Foot.	Not born in this Sub-District. 185 .			30 Septr.	M. Jones.
Fifth Example.	The Birth of the Child registered after the receipt of the Certificate of Successful Vaccination.	73	7 Septr. 1853. Rock Ferry.	Percival.	M.	Jacob Ware.	Clerk in the Inland Revenue Office.	19 Octr. 1853.			17 Octr.	G. Danby.
Sixth Example.	A Child born within the Sub-district, but the Birth not registered. The age taken from the Vaccinator's Certificate.		185 Aged 7 Weeks. Bibbingtown.	Alice.	F.	James Mills.	Clerk in Holy Orders.	Not Registered. 185			12 Decr.	S. Crane.

LIST OF OUT-DOOR POOR.
TOWNSHIP OF LEEDS.
No. 1 District.   Comprising EAST WARD.

In the latter part of the nineteenth century, some large unions began to issue annual printed versions of their proceedings such as guardians' minutes, accounts and relief lists. Here is part of the Leeds Union's outdoor relief list published in 1884.

M	F	C	Name.	Age of Head of Family.	Residence.	Cause of Relief.	Earnings of Family.	Weekly Relief.	Amount for Half-year.	Repaid H.-year
							s. d.	s. d.	£ s. d.	£ s. d
	1		Abbott Sarah Ann	61	3, Clarke Lane	...Sickness		2 6	3 2 6	
	1		Aspinall Ann ...	66	23, Wesley Terrace	...Feeble		2 6	3 2 6	
1	1		Appleyard Wm. ...	61	24, Sheffield street	..Sickness		4 0	1 0 0	
	1		Bailey Margt. ...	67	41, Bath street	. Aged		2 6	3 2 6	
	1	8	Balk Jane	46	12, Back Bow street	...Insft. Incme.	18 11	3 0	1 17 0	
	1		Ball James , Wife ..	68	Burner st.Pontfrct.In.Aged & sick			2 6	3 2 6	
	1	1	Barker Harriet ...	70	24, Old Garden walk	do ...	6 0	2 6	3 2 6	
1			Bilton Samuel ...	62	19, Weavers sq. ...	do ...		2 6	3 2 6	
1	1	1	Binks George ...	46	2, Cavalier court	...Sickness	7 6	3 0	2 13 0	
1			Birch Thomas ...	76	14, Catherine street	...Aged		2 6	3 2 6	
	1		Blackburn Elizbth.	60	St. Saviour's Alms .	. Sickness		3 0	3 3 0	
1			Blake Anthony .	75	36, Bank Farm st.	...Aged		3 0	3 15 0	
	1		Blake Miriam ...	49	36, do	...Sickness		3 0	1 1 0	
	1	3	Blamire Sarah ...	43	19, Cawood yard	.. Insft. incme.		4 0	5 0 0	
1			Bramham Christr.	61	10, Cavalier street	..Sickness		2 6	3 2 6	
	1	2	Brown Geo., Wife	32	1, Bridgefield place	...Desertion ...	4 .0	3. 0	3 15 0	
	1	3	Bunting, Julia ...	32	7, Hillhouse court	.. Insft. incme.		4 6	1 7 0	
	1		Burgess Elizabeth	75	11, Wesley terrace.	.Aged		2 6	3 2 6	

Records booklets[341] by Jeremy Gibson and Colin Rogers, with 'Access to Archives' again providing a good national catalogue.

In the case of London, the biggest collection of records is held at the London Metropolitan Archives (www.cityoflondon.gov.uk/LMA). London parish and poor law records held by the LMA are available online for subscribers to Ancestry (www.ancestry.co.uk). A substantial number of London parish records are also held at the various borough archives and local history centres, with a major collection at the City of Westminster Archives (www.westminster. gov.uk/archives). Useful guides to Middlesex and Surrey parish records have been produced by Cliff Webb.[342] Outside the capital, some records for Cheshire and Manchester workhouses are online at www.findmypast.co.uk

Free online access to some poor law records is gradually becoming available, such as the West Sussex Poor Law Records database (www.sussexrecordsociety.org.uk/plhome.asp), and the Norfolk poor law records (1796–1900) and Cheshire workhouse records (1848–1967) at the Family Search website (www.familysearch.org). Covering the period 1690–1800, the *London Lives* website (www.londonlives.org) provides a huge searchable collection of around quarter of a million manuscripts and more than three million names, many relating to the poor and workhouses. In Ireland, the Clare County Library has some transcriptions of guardians' minute books and staff and death records for the Kilrush and Ennistymon Unions (www.clarelibrary. ie/eolas/coclare/history/intro.htm).

Transcriptions of documents such as workhouse admission/discharge, birth and death registers have been undertaken by many local family history societies and are often available on CD – a good online source for such material is the Federation of Family History Society's retail operation *Genfair* (www.genfair.co.uk).

Central Poor Law Authority Records

The central authority overseeing poor law administration after 1834 was successively the Poor Law Commissioners (1834–47), the Poor Law Board (1847–71), the Local Government Board (1871–1919), and the Ministry of Health (1919–48). The main repository of records from these bodies is the UK National Archives at Kew near London. The main records held there include:

- Correspondence between unions and the central poor law authority
- Applications for workhouse officers posts including *curricula vitae*, testimonials etc.
- Letters of appointment, resignation and dismissal
- Correspondence from Assistant Commissioners and inspectors on workhouse conditions
- Architectural plans of workhouses (submitted for central approval)
- Staff appointments/departures at each workhouse (with dates, salaries, reasons for leaving)

The National Archives' poor law holdings are mostly filed in their MH (Ministry of Health) series of records as that was the government department administering the system in its latter years. The TNA website (www.nationalarchives.gov.uk/records/research-guides/poor-law-records.htm) gives an overview of these records. A useful introduction has also been produced by Kate Thompson.[343]

The extensive Poor Law Union correspondence has been the subject of a major National Archives digitisation project with the early portion of the material from over twenty unions now freely viewable and searchable online at www.nationalarchives.gov.uk/documentsonline/ workhouse.asp

The records of the Metropolitan Asylums Board, which administered certain categories of medical care for poor from 1867, and the city's casual wards from 1912, are held at the London Metropolitan Archives (www.cityoflondon.gov.uk/LMA).

Parliamentary Papers

Another valuable form of contemporary record is provided by the voluminous proceedings of the British Parliament, published each year in the form of Parliamentary Papers (also known as 'blue books' because of the colour of their original covers).

As detailed elsewhere in this book, the most significant parliamentary reports prior to 1834 are the overseers' returns published in 1777, 1804 and 1818, detailing each parish's poor relief expenditure and use of workhouses. The report of the 1832 Royal Commission on poor relief administration, running to more than 8,000 pages, also contains much valuable data, especially in the survey responses provided by 1,580 rural and town parishes.

From the arrival of the New Poor Law in 1834, until the inauguration of the National Health Service in 1948, the most useful documents are probably the annual reports of the Poor Law Commissioners and their successor authorities. They contain detailed annual relief statistics, policy discussions, details of Poor Law Unions, the texts of orders and circulars issued to unions, progress in workhouse construction, and reports by Assistant Commissioners and Poor Law Inspectors about individual institutions around the country.

In addition, there are numerous one-off reports and returns on specific topics such as children in workhouses (1841), Gilbert Unions (1852), long-term inmates of workhouses (1861), vagrancy (1866), the emigration of pauper children to Canada (1875), unions supplying expensive medicines (1877), and the consumption of spirits in workhouses (1895). The results of official inquiries into malpractice or mismanagement at particular unions generated detailed reports of their proceedings, the most notable being the Andover scandal, in 1845. Large amounts of detailed local information also feature in the reports generated by Royal Commissions (notably those on poor relief administration published in 1834 and 1909) and Departmental Committees (such as those on poor law schools in 1896, and on vagrancy in 1904 and 1929).

A surprising number of named individuals are referred to in Parliamentary Papers. Some examples include:

- Farmers, labourers etc. (Evidence to Irish Poor Inquiry, 1836)
- Atcham Union paupers and Boston Union children entering service (Poor Law Commissioners 6th Report, 1840)
- Workhouse children 'apprenticed' as miners (Children's Employment Commission, 1842)
- Selection of Irish paupers relieved (Poor Law Commissioners 10th Report, 1844)
- Complaints of inadequate relief (Scottish Board of Supervision reports, 1847–94)
- Workhouse teachers (Committee of Council on Education reports, 1849–58)
- London casual ward inmates (Reports and Communications on Vagrancy, 1848)
- Long-term workhouse inmates (Paupers in Workhouses, 1861)
- Union officers' superannuation (Irish Poor Law Commissioners and Local Government annual reports, 1867–1916)
- Workhouse boys enlisted into military bands (Poor Law Board 21st Report, 1869)

Use of Parliamentary Papers has become vastly easier since the complete collection was digitised (parlipapers.chadwyck.co.uk). Online access is available at the National Archives and via any subscribing educational institution, record office or library.

Poor Law Trade Press

The poor law system's trade press, described in a separate article, makes reference to a large number of named individuals. These are most often officials involved in the administration of the system, but others such as tradesmen or paupers may also occasionally be mentioned. The *Poor Law Unions Gazette* is unique in being entirely filled with the details of those abandoning their dependents to the care of the poor law authorities.

NAMES OF ADULT PAUPERS IN EACH WORKHOUSE IN ENGLAND AND WALES			
NAME of COUNTY AND UNION.	The Name of every Adult Pauper who has been an Inmate of the Workhouse during a continuous Period of Five Years.	The Amount of Time that each of such Paupers shall have been in the Workhouse.	The Reason assigned why the Pauper in each case is unable to maintain Himself, or Herself.
ENGLAND—*continued.* Berks—*continued.*		Yrs. ms.	
Wokingham - - -	Harriett Cheeseman -	8 0	Weak intellect - - -
	Henry Stevens -	7 0	Idiotcy from birth - - -
	Jane Paine - - -	8 0	Infirmity by asthma - - -
	John Clarke Larwill -	8 0	Infirmity by age and other causes
	Thomas White - -	14 0	Infirmity by epileptic fits from birth.
	Ann Moorcock - -	6 0	Infirmity by rheumatism and dropsy.
	Mary Batten - - -	22 0	Blindness; partial 12 years, total 10 years.
	Madelina A'Bear - -	13 0	Unable to support self and three illegitimate children; partially disabled the last four years.

Long-term inmates of the Wokingham Union workhouse from the 1861 national return listing the names of all those resident for five years or more and the reasons given.

Other Records

As well as records specifically relating to the poor law and workhouses, references to workhouse inmates can be found in a variety of other sources. These include:

- Baptism records – workhouse baptisms usually took place in the local parish church, with any surviving records now usually in county record offices.
- Burial records – pauper burial details are occasionally found in the records of parish churches or town cemeteries, now mostly held at county or borough record offices.
- Civil registration of births and deaths (1837 onwards) – indexes are widely available online e.g. www.findmypast.com and www.bmdindex.co.uk
- Census returns – each institution's resident staff and inmates each census night. Available online, e.g. www.ancestry.co.uk and 1901censusonline.com (latter has an 'institution' search)
- Local newspapers – general news, reports of guardians' meetings, elections etc. The British Library has a large digitised collection at newspapers.bl.uk/blcs
- Trade directories (e.g. Kelly's) – details of each institution and its officials at a particular date, e.g. www.historicaldirectories.org
- Passenger lists and immigration records – pauper children sent to British colonies overseas, e.g. www.collectionscanada.gc.ca
- Folk song collectors – George Gardiner gathered over 300 songs from named workhouse inmates, searchable at www.efdss.org

(*See also*: **Addresses**; **Trade Press**)

REFORMATORY / REFORMATORY SCHOOL

An establishment for housing juvenile offenders. One of the first Reformatory Schools was opened in 1849 by the Philanthropic Society at Redhill in Surrey, modelled on the reformatory colony at Mettray in France. Others followed at Kingswood in Bristol (1852), Saltley in Birmingham (1854), Stoke Farm in Worcestershire (1854) and Red Lodge Bristol – the first girls' Reformatory (1854).

The 1854 Youthful Offenders Act allowed courts to place convicted offenders under the age of sixteen in a Reformatory for up to five years, after first serving a two-week prison sentence.[344] Parents of inmates were required to contribute to the cost by a payment of up to 5s a week. Reformatories were required to be inspected and certified before opening. By 1875, there were fifty-four certified Reformatory Schools in England and Wales, with a further twelve in Scotland. A separate category of institution, the Certified Industrial School, had similarities to the Reformatory School but was aimed at a younger age group and lacked the initial prison element.

Most Reformatories were privately run, often by religious groups, though not always successfully. In 1856, the monks of St Bernard's Abbey at Whitwick in Leicestershire opened an 'agricultural colony' for up to 250 delinquent Roman Catholic boys, run with the help of lay assistants. However, the staff were unable to control their charges with several riots occurring. In 1878, sixty boys escaped after attacking the master in charge with knives stolen from the dining room. The establishment closed three years later after its certificate was withdrawn.[345]

After the passing of the Children's Act in 1908, children who broke the law were dealt with by special juvenile courts.[346] However, the Act still maintained the distinction between Reformatory and Industrial Schools. A period of probation, supervised by a probation officer, became available as an alternative to being sent to an Industrial School.

As well as land-based Reformatories, some were established as nautical training ships such as the *Clarence* on the Mersey at New Ferry, and the *Cornwall* on the Thames at Purfleet. The *Cornwall* became embroiled in a scandal in 1903 when seven boys contracted typhoid. It was discovered that cheap blankets from army hospitals, unwashed and infected, had been sold to the ship. Even more notorious was the *Akbar*, also on the Mersey at Rock Ferry, which in 1910 was accused of inflicting excessive punishments, with some boys dying as a result.

Further condemnation of Reformatories came in a series of *Daily Mail* articles, published in September 1911, which claimed that they were 'Schools for Crime' and that the boys lacked proper supervision.[347] The fact that the Reformatories and Industrial Schools were predominantly run by voluntary rather than state organisations was also criticised. In 1911, none of the existing thirty-seven Reformatories was run by a local authority, and only twenty-two of the 112 Industrial Schools.

As a result of such negative publicity, committals to Reformatory and Industrial Schools declined steeply and by 1923 forty of them had closed. In 1927, a Home Office report recommended replacing Reformatory and Industrial Schools by a single type of establishment to be known as an Approved School. This was implemented by the 1933 Children and Young Persons Act which also introduced Remand Homes for accommodating youths temporarily held in custody, for example to await a court hearing.[348] In 1969, Approved Schools were redesignated as 'Community Homes' and run by local councils rather than the prison authorities.
(*See also*: **Industrial Schools – Certified**; **Mettray**; **Training Ships**)

RELIEF COMMITTEE

A sub-committee of the Board of Guardians delegated to deal with the processing of relief applications. The use of Relief Committees, which required permission from the central poor law authorities, was mainly in large unions with many relief claimants.
(*See also*: **District Relief Committee**)

RELIEF DISTRICT

A sub-division of a Poor Law Union, usually based on a grouping of parishes, for the administration of poor relief, and usually being supervised by a single relieving officer. The areas covered by Relief Districts and Medical Districts were not necessarily the same.
(*See also*: **Medical District**; **Relieving Officer**)

RELIEF OFFICE/STATION

A place where poor-relief claimants were interviewed and also where out relief could be issued. Large urban unions often had purpose-built relief offices in town locations, sometimes as part of the union's administrative headquarters. Relief stations usually operated for just a short period each day or each week and were typically found in out-of-town locations, often in a room hired for the purpose or sometimes using a room in a relieving officer's own home.

(*See also*: **Out relief**; **Relieving Officer**)

RELIEVING OFFICER

A relieving officer was an official employed by a Poor Law Union who assessed poor relief claims and supervised the distribution of out relief. Unions were normally divided up into several Relief Districts, each covered by its own relieving officer.

A relieving officer was required to be at least twenty-one years in age, able to keep accounts, and was barred from engaging in any other employment unless he was living in the District in which he served. He also had to provide a bond with two guarantors in case any financial irregularities arose during his employment. In rural areas, it was often a condition of appointment that a relieving officer should keep a horse.

The main duties of a relieving officer were:

- To receive relief applications and assess each case, including a visit to the applicant's house.
- To periodically visit all those in his District receiving out relief.
- To arrange attendance by a District Medical Officer for those requiring it.
- To deal with any case of 'sudden or urgent necessity', either by referral to the workhouse or by giving non-monetary out relief.
- To distribute the weekly out relief allowances of all paupers in his District.

(*See also*: **Relief District**; **Relief Office/Station**)

RELIGION

In the Parish Workhouse

The 1601 Poor Relief Act placed responsibility for care of the destitute in the hands of the parish. The administration of poor relief was carried out through the parish committee, the vestry, whose members included the parish priest and churchwardens, together with annually appointed overseers. It is therefore not surprising that recipients of parish relief should be expected to follow the regular observances of the established Church while in receipt of such support.

With the gradual evolution of the workhouse during the eighteenth century, regular attendance at church usually formed part of the rules governing the behaviour of each institution's inmates. At the St Andrew's Holborn, Shoe-Lane, workhouse in the City of London, the regulations in 1730 specified that:

> All that are able, and in Health, to go every Sunday to Church, Morning and Afternoon. That they return home as soon as Divine Service is over; and if any be found loitering or begging by the way, to lose their next Meal.[349]

A visit to church could, of course, provide an opportunity to illicitly stop off at an inn, something the workhouse authorities were keen to prevent. At Croydon in February 1753, following a complaint that 'several of the Poor, let out of the House to hear Divine Service on Sabbath Days were frequently seen about Town, begging, and often drunk' it was ordered that 'no Person thus scandalously behaving, should be suffered to go out of the House, on any pretext whatsoever.'[350]

Apart from church services, the saying of prayers and of grace at mealtimes were part of the daily workhouse routine. At Romford in 1724, prayers were to be said every morning before breakfast and every evening after supper, with a recommended source being *The Whole Duty of Man*.[351] The workhouse rules in 1810 at Stone in Staffordshire required:

> That the Governor say Grace before and after meals. Read or cause to be read Prayer every morning before Breakfast, and every Evening before supper, that every person in the house, not necessarily engaged elsewhere, be required to attend.[352]

In the Union Workhouse

After 1834, requirements for religious observance were included in the national regulations for the running of union workhouses, with provision also being made for 'dissenters'. Prayers were to be read by the workhouse master before breakfast and after supper every day, with grace being said before and after each meal. 'Divine Service' was held every Sunday, Good Friday and Christmas Day, for all inmates except the sick and mentally ill, the infirm, young children and anyone 'professing religious principles differing from those of the Established Church'.

Services were usually held in the dining hall unless the workhouse had its own chapel. The Board of Guardians could also allow inmates, under supervision, to attend public worship at a local parish church or chapel.

The Chaplain

Each Board of Guardians was required to appoint a chaplain whose duties were:

- To read prayers and preach a sermon to the paupers and other inmates of the Workhouse on every Sunday, and on Good Friday and Christmas Day.
- To examine the children, and to catechise such as belong to the Church of England, at least once in every month.
- To visit the sick paupers, and to administer religious consolation to them in the workhouse.

Although the duties of a union workhouse chaplain could seem fairly modest, each appointment had to be approved by the Bishop of the local diocese in case it conflicted with the clergyman's other duties. Chaplains' salaries varied widely. Some were relatively well paid and could receive a salary on a par with that of rather more onerous full-time posts such as the workhouse master. One clergyman, writing in 1847, suggested that workhouse chaplains in Huntingdonshire received a very generous £150 per annum, while the wealthy Richmond Union in Yorkshire paid a mere £10.[353] Whatever the expense of employing a chaplain, a major incentive for doing so was that inmates did not have to be released to attend church services outside the confines of the workhouse.

Dissenters

The Poor Law Commissioners implicitly assumed that unions would appoint a chaplain from the Church of England. There was, however, considerable resistance to this in areas such as Cornwall and the north of England where 'dissenters from the Established Church' were most common. Any pressure to appoint a Church of England chaplain was seen as an attempt to proselytise non-Anglican inmates and also to provide jobs for the clergy. Since dissenters were allowed to opt out of attendance at services, appointing a Church of England chaplain also appeared to be futile in unions where dissenters were in the majority. In 1836, it was agreed that non-Anglican inmates should continue to be allowed out on Sundays, so long as a certificate of church attendance for each attendee was signed by the officiating minister. To further discourage such activities, inmates were only be allowed out under strict supervision, marching to and from church in their workhouse uniforms.[354]

Non-conformist ministers were increasingly allowed to hold services inside workhouses, invariably doing so without charge, much to the satisfaction of the guardians of such unions.

At the Ashton-under-Lyne Union in the 1870s, the holding of services was shared amongst a number of local clergy, around a third being Anglican and two-thirds of other denominations. Roman Catholic priests were generally not welcomed into the workhouse – at least in England and Wales. Even in workhouses having a high proportion of Catholic inmates, such as Liverpool, the appointment of Catholic chaplains was vetoed. In Irish workhouses, however, Catholic chaplains were in the majority, with unions in some areas employing both Protestant and Catholic chaplains.

Creed Register

From 1869, workhouses were required to maintain a register recording the admission details and religious creed of each new inmate. The register was often held at the workhouse porter's lodge where it could be inspected by any person with a legitimate interest. It thus allowed local ministers periodically to monitor for new arrivals who might be in need of their services.
(*See also*: **Baptism**; **Chapel**; **Death**)

REMOVAL

The process by which a person was returned to their parish of settlement from another parish where they had become a charge on the poor rates.
(*See also*: **Irremovability**; **Settlement**)

RINGWORM

A highly contagious fungal infection of the scalp, body, feet and nails which was often prevalent in workhouse children's establishments, particularly District Schools. In London, the

An open-air church service for workhouse inmates; location and date unknown. As usual, male and female inmates sit in separate areas.

Metropolitan Asylums Board set up two specialist treatment centres for the condition. The Bridge School (the former Witham Union workhouse) opened in February 1901, and the Downs School at Sutton opened in February 1903. The introduction of X-ray treatment for ringworm in 1905 led to much speedier treatment of the condition. In 1914, ringworm treatment was concentrated at the Goldie Leigh Homes in south-east London.
(*See also*: **District and Separate Schools; Ophthalmia**)

ROGERS, JOSEPH

From the 1850s to the 1870s, Joseph Rogers (1820–89) was one of the most prominent crusaders for the improvement of medical care for the poor, especially those in workhouses. He also campaigned for improvements in the conditions of service of poor law medical officers.

As medical officer at the Strand Union's Cleveland Street workhouse from 1856 to 1868, Rogers battled at length for improvements in the building and its management in the face of opposition from the Strand Board of Guardians and continual obstruction by the tyrannical workhouse master, George Catch. Rogers' pay at the Strand was only £50 per annum, out of which he had to pay all the costs of any medicines that he prescribed.

A growing campaign for reform of workhouse medical provision, in which Rogers played a leading part, led to the appointment in 1861 of a Parliamentary Select Committee to investigate matters. Its report, presented in 1864, recommended only one change to medical relief in the workhouse, that the cost of cod liver oil, quinine and other expensive medicines would be met by the guardians rather than by medical officers – a measure largely resulting from Rogers' testimony.

In 1865, Rogers assisted *The Lancet* in the journal's exposure of the appalling conditions that existed in many of London's workhouse infirmaries. The following year, he founded the Association for the Improvement of London Workhouse Infirmaries which aimed to create six new 1,000-bed poor law hospitals for the capital, with the cost being met from a common central fund. Many of the Association's ideas were incorporated in the 1867 Metropolitan Poor Act in whose formulation Rogers played a part.

In 1866, he founded the Association of Metropolitan Workhouse Medical Officers which subsequently became the Poor Law Medical Officers Association. The Association campaigned for better pay and conditions for doctors working in the poor law system.

From 1872 to 1883, Rogers held the post of medical officer at the Westminster Union's infirmary of Poland Street, again battling against indifferent guardians to improve the poor provision that existed for patients.
(*See also*: **Catch, George; London; Matron; Medical Care; Medical Officers' Associations**; Hodgkinson (1956); Richardson and Hurwitz (1997); Rogers and Rogers (1889))

ROUNDSMAN SYSTEM

A system adopted in some parishes prior to 1834 whereby unemployed labourers were sent around local ratepayers to be provided with work, with their wages being subsidised from the poor rate. An alternative version used a weekly auction of pauper labourers, with their wages again being raised to subsistence levels by the poor rates. The Roundsman System was also known as the billet or ticket system, because of the ticket carried by the pauper which was signed by the parish overseer as a warrant of his being employed and then countersigned by the employer after the requisite work had been performed.
(*See also*: **Allowance System; Labour Rate; Speenhamland System**)

ROYAL COMMISSION - 1832

By the late 1820s, there was growing dissatisfaction with the existing poor relief system, par-ticularly amongst ratepayers who had seen the nation's expenditure from the poor rates rise from around £1.5 million in 1776 to £7.9 million in 1818, and reaching a record high of £8.6 million in 1832.[355]

There was also growing unrest amongst the poor, particularly in rural areas afflicted by low wages and by rising unemployment for which many blamed the increasing mechanisation of farms. This turmoil culminated in the autumn of 1830 in riots and the attacking of poor-houses, notably from those who identified themselves as supporters of the shadowy figure of Captain Swing. The British Government's response, in 1832, was the appointment of a Royal Commission 'for inquiring into the administration and practical operation of the poor laws'.

The Commission was chaired by Bishop Blomfield of London, the other members being the Revd Henry Bishop (Oxford don), Walter Coulson (newspaper editor, barrister, secretary to Jeremy Bentham), Henry Gawler (lawyer), Nassau Senior (Oxford professor of political econ-omy), William Sturges Bourne (former MP, poor law legislator), John Bird Sumner (Bishop of Chester), and James Traill (lawyer). Edwin Chadwick was promoted to the Commission in 1833, following his energetic work as an Assistant Commissioner.

Several of what were to be the Commission's most influential members – Coulson, Senior and Chadwick – were advocates of the ideas of Utilitarian philosopher Jeremy Bentham. Bentham believed that people had a natural tendency to seek pleasure and avoid pain. For the good of soci-ety as whole, governments had a responsibility to make it less attractive to live off the labour of others than to work and be self-sufficient – a principle which became known as 'less eligibility'.

The Commission collected evidence from two main sources. First, a team of twenty-six Assistant Commissioners were despatched across the country with lengthy instructions speci-fying the type of information they were to gather under headings such as 'The form in which parochial relief is given' and 'The persons to whom it is given'. Second, two questionnaires were devised, one with fifty-three questions for rural parishes and one with sixty-four for town parishes, which were sent to a selection of parishes in each county. The responses were mostly provided by overseers, clergy and magistrates. A total of 1,580 replies (1,212 rural and 368 town) was received, representing just over 10 per cent of the 15,000 or so parishes in England and Wales. The wording of the queries was often unclear, or conflated different issues. Question 24 for rural parishes, for example, tried to cover both outdoor relief to the able-bodied and the giving of allowances to larger families:

> Have you any, and how many, able-bodied Labourers in the Employment of individuals receiving Allowance or regular Relief from your Parish on their own Account, or on that of their Families: and if on Account of their Families, at what Number of Children does it begin?

Rather than simply muddled thinking, it has been argued that this particular question was made deliberately confusing so that the Commissioners could turn the responses in the direc-tion they desired.[356] Whatever the reasons, it is perhaps not surprising that the replies to many of the questions were equally unclear or were just blank.

The Commission's final report, published in February 1834, was largely the work of Nassau Senior and Edwin Chadwick. Senior's contributions were primarily an 'exposition of the evils of the existing system', together with revisions of the laws of settlement and bastardy, while Chadwick compiled the bulk of the proposed 'remedial measures'. Vagrancy was dealt with by Gawler and provisions for emigration by Coulson.[357]

The report took the view that poverty was essentially caused the indigence of individu-als rather than economic and social conditions. Thus, the pauper claimed relief regardless of his merits; large families got most, which encouraged improvident marriages; women claimed relief for bastards, which encouraged immorality; labourers had no incentive to work; employers kept wages artificially low as wages were subsidised from the poor rate. The report's main legislative proposal was that: 'Except as to medical attendance... all relief whatever to able-bodied persons or to their families, otherwise than in well-regulated workhouses... shall be declared unlawful, and shall cease.'[358] In addition, the report recommended: the appointment of a central body to administer the new system; the grouping of parishes for the purposes of operating a workhouse; and that workhouse conditions should be 'less eligible' (less desirable) than those of an independent labourer of the lowest class. At the heart of the report was a revival of the workhouse test – that anyone prepared to accept relief in such a workhouse must be lacking the moral determination to survive outside it.

The conclusions presented in the Royal Commission's report have been described as 'wildly unstatistical'.[359] The report claimed that allowance systems, such as the Speenhamland system, were widespread and a major cause of the problems attributed to the Old Poor Law. However, a closer examination of the evidence they themselves collected shows that 'the Speenhamland System as such had generally disappeared by 1832'.[360] Even where the report's authors did not ignore their own findings, they twisted them to suit their preconceived opinions.

On 14 August, six months after the report's publication, the 1834 Poor Law Amendment Act received its Royal Assent.

(*See also*: **Bentham, Jeremy**; **Chadwick, Edwin**; Brundage (1978), Mandler (1990))

ROYAL COMMISSION – 1905

By the early 1900s, pressures were mounting for a major reform of the poor relief system. A number of factors contributed to this. Women were now elected to many Boards of Guardians, and there was an influx of working-class guardians following the reduction of the rate qualification to £5 in 1892. Reform was often high on the agenda of both these groups.

At a national level, it was recognised that levels of pauperism were showing no signs of decline. The cost of poor relief was also steadily rising, up from 6s 0¾d per head of the population in 1887–88 to 8s 7¾d in 1905–06.[361] Since the passing of the 1834 Poor Law Amendment Act many changes had taken place in welfare administration – the care of schoolchildren was now in the hands of local education committees, and district councils had become responsible for dealing with infectious diseases. Boards of Guardians were increasingly seen by some as inefficient and ineffective, and having an unclear relationship to other authorities.

In December 1905, a Royal Commission on the Poor Law and the Unemployed was appointed:

> To inquire: (1) Into the working of the laws relating to the relief of poor persons in the United Kingdom; (2) Into the various means which have been adopted outside of the Poor Laws for meeting distress arising from want of employment, particularly during periods of severe industrial depression; and to consider and report whether any, and if so what, modification of the Poor Laws or changes in their administration or fresh legislation for dealing with distress are advisable.

Over the next four years it carried out the most extensive investigation since the Royal Commission of 1832. Its initial membership comprised: Lord George Francis Hamilton (chairman), Frank Bentham (JP and ex-chairman of Bradford guardians), Charles Booth (social researcher), Dr Arthur Downes (Poor Law Medical Inspector), Revd Thory Gardiner (Clerk in Orders), Octavia Hill (campaigner for housing reform), George Lansbury (member of Poplar guardians and borough council), Charles Loch (secretary of the Charity Organisation Society), James Patten McDougal vice-president of LGB for Scotland), Thomas Hancock Nunn (member of Hampstead Board of Guardians and of Hampstead Distress Committee), Charles Owen O'Conor (Lord Lieutenant of Roscommon and former MP), Revd Lancelot Ridley Phelps (vice-chairman of Oxford guardians), Sir Samuel Provis (secretary to LGB for England),

Sir Henry Robinson (vice-president of LGB for Ireland), William Smart (Professor of Political Economy at Glasgow University), Revd Prebendary Henry Russell Wakefield (ex-Mayor of St Marylebone and chairman of Unemployed Body for London), Beatrice Webb (socialist reformer). Some changes in membership took place during the lifetime of the Commission. Following the death of O'Conor in 1906, he was replaced by the Revd Dr Denis Kelly (Bishop of Ross, Ireland). In the same year, Francis Chandler (trade unionist and ex-chairman of Chorlton guardians) also joined the Commission. Booth later withdrew because of ill health.

The Commission was famously divided in its views and its recommendations were published in two parts. The Majority Report was endorsed by fourteen of its members (Bentham, Bosanquet, Downes, Gardiner, Hamilton, Hill, Kelly, Loch, MacDougal, Nunn, Phelps, Provis, Robinson, and Smart). The Minority Report was signed by four members (Chandler, Lansbury, Wakefield and Webb).

Despite the split there was, however, some common ground between the two factions. Areas of broad agreement included: the abolition of Boards of Guardians, with administration moving to the county level to allow general mixed workhouses to be replaced by more specialised institutions; better administration and targeting of outdoor relief, with greater involvement of voluntary agencies; the removal of children from workhouses; and the provision of old age pensions, health insurance and unemployment support.[362]

The Majority Report recommended the replacement of Boards of Guardians by a new Public Assistance Authority in each county or county borough, together with the replacement of workhouses by more specialised institutions catering for separate categories of inmate such as children, the old, the unemployed, and the mentally ill.

The Minority Report was more radical and advocated the complete abolition of the poor laws. Those in need should be divided into two categories. The non-able-bodied would be dealt with by county and county borough council committees, such the Education Committee (school-age children), the Health Committee (aged and infirm, chronic sick, and children under school age), the Asylums Committee (the 'mentally defective'), and the Pensions Committee (those in receipt of pensions). The able-bodied in need of assistance should be dealt with by separate authority, with a new Ministry of Labour being created to coordinate the national demand for labour and to minimise unemployment. Overall, the Minority Report's emphasis was on the prevention of destitution rather than its relief.

As well as its parliamentary printing, the Minority Report was also published in a modestly priced Fabian edition and had a spectacular sale. A great propaganda campaign was organised by Sidney and Beatrice Webb in support of its recommendations for the prevention of destitution by the break-up of the poor law.

Although no new legislation directly resulted from the Commission's work, a number of significant pieces of social legislation took place in its wake. New Year's Day 1909 saw the introduction of the old age pension for those over seventy (up to 5s a week for a single person, 7s 6d for a married couple) although until 1911, anyone who had received poor relief in the previous twelve months was denied a pension. In 1911, health and unemployment insurance schemes began in a limited form.

ROYAL VISITS

Although visits by royalty to workhouses and other poor law establishments were rare, they were not completely unknown. In June 1881, St Marylebone's new workhouse infirmary at Rackham Street was opened by the Prince and Princess of Wales. On 13 July 1904, King Edward VII visited the Newmarket Union workhouse and met inmates in various wards. In 1919, Queen Mary was a guest at the Poplar Union's Hutton Schools near Brentwood in Essex.

King Edward VII talks to an inmate of the Newmarket workhouse during his visit to the establishment in 1904. The young man, TB patient John Watts, was persuaded to give a rendition of 'God Save the King' on a mandolin. His Majesty is said to have delighted the lad by saying that he had played very well.

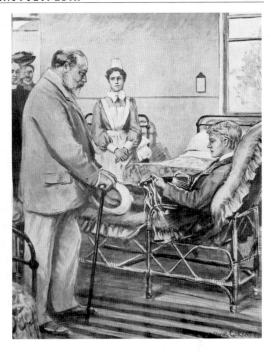

RULES

The operation of workhouses was always governed by rules – either devised locally (usually the case with a parish workhouse), or laid down by legislation (as with Gilbert Union workhouses), or imposed by some central authority (such as the Poor Law Commissioners).

Rules generally covered such matters as who was eligible for admission; the procedures for admission to and discharge from the workhouse; the inmates' diet, daily routine, work and discipline; prohibitions on the use of items such as spirits or tobacco; administrative and financial procedures; and the responsibilities and conduct of staff. If not already enshrined in legislation, more general rules might also be needed relating to such matters as the operation of an Incorporation, the election of guardians, the conduct of meetings, and so on.

In 1747, Doncaster's 'House of Maintenance for the Poor' framed set of rules or 'orders' covering each of these areas – one for the Board of Governors, one for the workhouse master and matron, and one for the inmates which included a dietary. The governors' responsibilities included ensuring that no-one was given poor relief other than through the workhouse, specifying the prayers and the dietary to be used there, and for one of their number to visit the workhouse each day – with a sixpence fine for defaulters. The master and matron's orders included setting the inmates to work (6 a.m. until 7 p.m. in summer, 7 a.m. until 4 p.m. in winter), keeping accounts of all expenditure and of the inmates' earnings, preventing inmates from smoking in the workhouse, not selling or allowing the entry of distilled liquors, and issuing clean bed-sheets every three weeks.[363]

It was usually a requirement that some or all of the workhouse rules be displayed within the building, for example on the wall of the inmates' day-rooms, and also periodically be read aloud by the master for the benefit of those who could not read.

The most comprehensive workhouse rules were the 'orders and regulations' issued by the Poor Law Commissioners from 1835 onwards which included sections on the admission of paupers to the workhouse; their classification, discipline and diet; the duties of the master, matron, porter, medical officers, and chaplain; the operation of Guardians' Visiting Committee, and so on. Specimen forms were provided for the recording of admissions and discharges, and the daily consumption of food, stores and clothing. These rules steadily evolved – for example, the rules initially demanded that 'silence, order and decorum' be maintained at mealtimes but the word 'silence' had been dropped by 1842. In 1847, all 233 rules and regulations then in force were brought together and revised in the Consolidated General Order, a document which formed the basis of union and workhouse management until 1913. A major overhaul of the regulations was then issued as the Poor Law Institutions Order.

(*See also*: **Appendix P; Consolidated General Order; Discipline; Gambling**)

The 1831 Rules and Orders from the parish workhouse at Aylesbury in Buckinghamshire.

SCABIES

Scabies, also known as 'the itch', was a common medical condition among the poor. It was caused by small parasites, similar to lice, which burrow under the skin and cause severe itching. The condition was often contracted through sharing a bed with an infected individual. Most workhouses had specially designated 'itch wards' such as the one at Preston described by Poor Law Inspector Mr R.B. Cane in 1866:

> In the midst of this ward, and in full view of the others, boys and men, an adult patient was standing upright without a fragment of clothes upon him, whilst a pauper attendant painted him over with a brush dipped in an application for his disease. The 'itch ward' is at all times the most disagreeable to enter of any. The peculiar remedy prescribed, the nature of the treatment observed, and the use in such ward of the refuse bedding and linen of the house, necessarily render it the most offensive of all.[364]

A common treatment for scabies was the application of sulphur ointment. (*See also:* **Foul Ward**)

RULES & ORDERS

TO BE OBSERVED BY
The Poor of the Parish Workhouse of Aylesbury,
IN THE COUNTY OF BUCKS.

I. That the Master and Mistress live in the House, and see that the following Rules be observed.

II. Every Person in health shall rise by six o'Clock the summer half year, and by seven the winter half year, and shall be employed in such labour as their respective age and ability will admit, and commence their work by six o'Clock in the Monday, and work till six o'Clock at Night, from Lady-day to Michaelmas; and from seven o'Clock till dark, from Michaelmas to Lady-day, allowing half an hour for breakfast, one hour for dinner, and half an hour for supper; and any one refusing to work, shall for the first offence go without their next meal, and for the second offence be reported to the Overseers, that they may otherwise be punished.

III. That all the poor in the House go to bed by eight o'Clock the summer half year, and by seven o'Clock the winter half year, and that all candles be put out by that time.

IV. That the poor shall have their provisions in a clean and wholesome manner, their breakfast by eight, their dinner at twelve, and their supper at six o'Clock; that no waste be made, nor any provisions carried away; and that Grace shall be said before and after dinner, and none may depart until Grace is said; and their dinner three times a week to be hot meat and vegetables properly cooked.

V. That the House be swept from top to bottom every morning and cleaned all over once a week, or so often as the Master and Mistress think necessary; and the windows be opened daily.

VI. That none absent themselves from the House without leave, nor stay beyond the time allowed them, on pain of losing their next meal, or of some other punishment; nor may any one be admitted into the House without leave of the Governor.

VII. Any of the poor guilty of stealing, selling their provisions or clothing, or of drunkenness, swearing, quarrelling, fighting, or in any other way disturbing the peace of the House, or of being in any way saucy or abusive to the Master or Mistress, shall be punished with the utmost severity of the law.

VIII. That all in the House who are able, and can be spared from the duties thereof, shall attend Church or some other Place of Worship twice every Sunday; and those who refuse or neglect to attend, or do not return as soon as Service is over, shall go without their next meal, or be punished in some other way, as the Overseers shall think proper.

IX. No person shall be permitted to bring spirituous liquors into the House, or smoke in any part of the premises, except the hall. Those found transgressing, shall lose their next meal, or be otherwise punished.

X. Workers shall be allowed 2d. in every shilling they earn; Cook 4d. per week; Doctor's Nurse from 1s. Washerwomen half a pint of ale each per day, and tea in the afternoon.

XI. Any of the poor acting in disobedience of the orders of the Master or Mistress, or in contempt of these Orders, shall be taken before a Magistrate, and punished as the law directs.

XII. That these Orders be placed in the hall, dinner-room, or in any other place that the Overseers may direct; and that they be read on a Sunday at dinner-time by the Master or Mistress, so that the poor may not plead ignorance of the same.

XIII. If any of the poor are found defacing or destroying these Rules, they shall be punished by being fed on bread and water only for two days.

JOHN KERSELEY FOWLER,
ROBERT READ,   } Churchwardens
JASPER JACKSON,

JOSEPH SHAW,
WILLIAM HOMEMAYER,   } Overseers.

27th JANUARY, 1831.

SCANDALS

Workhouses were involved in a number of scandals over the years, usually involving mismanagement of the institution, neglect of duty, financial impropriety, or ill-treatment of inmates.

One of the earliest workhouse scandals was that involving workhouse manager Matthew Marryott at the St Giles in the Fields workhouse. Marryott was accused of starving some inmates to death and of mutilating the body of a woman who had died in the workhouse.

In the years immediately following the 1834 Poor Law Amendment Act, numerous alleged scandals were prominently reported by newspapers opposed to the New Poor Law, most notably *The Times*. One of these concerned the Bridgwater Union in Somerset where, in 1836, the guardians adopted the Poor Law Commissioners' Dietary No. 3 which provided a breakfast of bread and 1½ pints of gruel. Oatmeal was not a normal part of the labourers' diet in the area, and it was widely held locally that gruel was unhealthy. The union medical officer reported that, after gruel replaced milk in their diet, many of children in the workhouse had become affected with 'white mouth' said to be caused by irritation of the stomach and bowels and accompanied by severe diarrhoea and dysentery. In this debilitated state, sufferers were susceptible to other conditions such as measles. It later emerged that over a six-month period during the winter of 1836–37, twenty-seven workhouse inmates had died. In March 1837, John Bowen, newly elected to the Bridgwater guardians and an opponent of much of the New Poor

Law, launched a crusade – much of it through the letters column of *The Times* – describing the union's workhouses as 'murderous pesthouses'. Bowen also provided a stomach-turning description of the effect of the gruel:

> It did not affect the poor people so much at first, but after the use of it for a few days, they became terribly bad; it ran from them while they were standing upright as they took it. It affected them upwards and downwards. All the way down the stairs, across the hall, and down the garden path, was all covered every morning, and the stench was horrible all through the house; making the people ill and sick who had not got the diarrhoea.[365]

One of the most notorious scandals occurred in 1845 when inmates at the Andover workhouse were reported as being so hungry that they were fighting over the shreds of rotting meat and marrow left on the discarded animal bones that they had been set to pound into fertiliser. At the subsequent inquiry, the workhouse master, Colin McDougal, was revealed to have been regularly drunk and having had violent and bloody fights with his wife, the matron, who had threatened suicide. McDougal had also attempted to seduce some of the young women inmates – as, too, had his seventeen-year-old son who had been taken on as workhouse schoolmaster. An inmate named Hannah Joyce, whose five-month-old baby had died in the workhouse, had been forced by McDougal to carry the baby's coffin a mile on her own to the churchyard for an unceremonious burial. Apart from criticising the McDougals, the inquiry also found: that the Andover guardians had failed to visit the workhouse and had allowed the inmates to be underfed; that the Assistant Commissioner responsible for Andover, Henry Parker, had placed too much confidence in the guardians; and, finally, that the Poor Law Commissioners had mishandled the whole affair.

At Huddersfield, there was public outcry in 1848 at conditions in the old workhouse building which appallingly cramped and unhygienic, with up to ten children sharing a bed. The inmates' diet was miserable, even by workhouse standards. Conditions in the infirmary were even worse – a living patient occupied the same bed with a corpse for a considerable period after death, and the sick were left unwashed for days on end, in some cases besmeared in their own excrement. Despite the resulting public outcry, little improved for some considerable time.[366]

In January 1849, Mr Drouet's school for pauper children at Tooting became the centre of a scandal when a cholera epidemic broke out with the eventual death toll reaching 180. Inquests on the victims founded that the effects of cholera had been aggravated by inadequate food and warm clothing, overcrowding, and poor ventilation. Drouet underwent a criminal trial for manslaughter but, to the disgust of many, including Charles Dickens, was acquitted though died soon afterwards.

Someone whose whole career might be described as a scandal was George Catch, an ex-policeman who was successively master of three London workhouses between in the 1850s and 1860s. Catch's lying, cruelty and vindictiveness finally reached public attention when, in an effort to locate a female inmate whose behaviour had affronted him, he had ordered hydrochloric acid to be added to a bowl of chloride lime beneath a chimney where he believed she was hiding. Fortunately the girl was elsewhere but the fumes created led to the collapse of sixteen pauper nurses with acute chlorine poisoning. Catch was subsequently barred from ever again holding office in a workhouse.[367]

In 1894, Ella Gillespie, a nurse at the Hackney workhouse school at Brentwood, was accused of systematic cruelty to the children in her charge including beating them with stinging nettles and forcing them to kneel on wire netting that covered the hot water pipes. Children were also deprived of water and resorted to drinking from the toilet bowls. Her most notorious practice was night-time 'basket drill' where children were woken from their sleep and made to walk around the dormitory for an hour with a basket on their heads containing their day clothes, and receiving a beating if they dropped anything. After a trial for ill-treatment of children, Gillespie was sentenced to five years penal servitude.[368]

Also in 1894, officers at the Newton Abbot workhouse became involved in a scandal after witnesses claimed that the 'jumper', a sort of sack used as a strait-jacket, was in constant use in the workhouse, and that aged inmates had been placed in it naked, and then tied to their bed-steads. A Mrs Bovey died five days after being confined in the 'jumper', and she was said to have been tied down a few hours prior to her death. Other witnesses alleged that the wards of the workhouse were in a filthy condition, and many of the inmates infested with vermin. One wit-ness, a nurse named Alice Hinton, testified that she had found an inmate named Mrs Nicholls apparently dying. The woman was very dirty and covered with vermin. Her hair had been cut off, and her toenails were like claws, being 2½in long. It was also alleged that Miss Ann Mance, workhouse matron for almost thirty years, neglected her duties, and had only been seen to visit the sick ward five times over a three-month period. Although she emphatically denied all the charges, Miss Mance was dismissed following an inquiry by the Local Government Board. She died from a heart condition a few weeks later.[369]

Not all workhouse scandals involved the ill-treatment of inmates. In March 1897, a story surfaced concerning the refreshments served at City of London guardians' board-meet-ings which were alleged to be conducted in a manner worthy of the pages of *Oliver Twist*. Proceedings began with a light luncheon of bread and cheese, beer, spirits etc. After the main business of the meeting, typically an hour to an hour and a half later, the guardians were served a repast of fish (salmon for preference), fowl, roast mutton and beef, and sundry other dishes followed by a selection of puddings and sweets. The food was accompanied by cham-pagne and other wines as well as spirits. Then came the important matter of a long series of well-lubricated toasts to the Queen and Royal Family, the chairman of the Board, the vice-chairman of the Board, the chairman for the day, the vice-chairman for the day, and so on, finally concluding with a toast for the Oldest Guardian and one for the Youngest Guardian. Finally, the members rounded off their meal with tea, coffee, biscuits, cakes and other dainties and delicacies. As well as the unseemliness of such consumption and cork-popping taking place in earshot of the workhouse inmates, concerns were raised over whether such feasts were being subsidised by the ratepayers.[370]

Guardians could also succumb to financial temptation. In 1908, seven members of the Poplar Union's Board were sent to prison for receiving gifts and bribes from a local builder named Calcutt in return for giving him work he had not tendered for and then paying his deliberately inflated bills.

In their day, such scandals attracted huge publicity as their often horrendous details were revealed in court or at some other form of public inquiry. A number of others were later revealed to have been largely hushed up by Boards of Guardians anxious to avoid bad pub-licity. It is tempting to view the whole workhouse system as being riddled with abuse. However, even just taking the period 1834–1930, such events reflect more than 60,000 institu-tion-years of workhouse activity, with many – perhaps the majority – of workhouses operating for the best part of a century without ever being tarnished in this way.

(*See also*: **Catch, George**; **Drouet's School**; **New Poor Law**; **Reformatory/Reformatory School**)

SCATTERED HOMES

The system of scattered homes (or 'isolated' homes as they were originally called) was devised in 1893 by John Wycliffe Wilson, chairman of the Sheffield Board of Guardians. Wilson criti-cised the increasingly popular cottage homes sites as isolating children from the real world in which they would eventually have to make their way. The alternative option of boarding out, though well regarded, was only suitable for orphans and deserted children, and relied on a steady supply of foster families, which were not always available. Those requiring only short-term accommodation, such as the children of the ins and outs, caused particular problems for the union. The scattered homes system was designed to deal with all these difficulties.

The scattered homes scheme placed small groups of children in ordinary houses distributed around the suburbs of Sheffield. Unlike cottage home sites which usually had their own schools, the children in scattered homes attended ordinary local Board Schools. At Sheffield, the placing of homes was arranged such that there were never more than thirty scattered homes children attending any one school. The union initially had nine homes each containing between fifteen and twenty-eight beds. Seven were allocated to Protestant children, and two to Roman Catholics. Each house was presided over by a foster mother, assisted in the household work by the elder children and an occasional charwoman.

Scattered homes schemes were implemented by many other unions beginning with Whitechapel and Bath in 1897. By 1914, over ninety unions were making use of scattered homes.

The 'scatteredness' of the homes could be rather variable. In some cases, a union took over (or even itself erected) a small row of ordinary houses in a residential area. In 1913, the West Ham Union's scattered homes included a block of four on Pelham Road, South Woodford, and blocks of two and four houses on Ferndale Road in Leytonstone.

Unions which had a large number of scattered homes often erected a 'headquarters home' which acted as a receiving or probationary home for new arrivals, short-term inmates, and those requiring special supervision. The headquarters home could also act as an administrative and supplies base for the other homes.

(*See also*: **Boarding Out**; **Children**; **Cottage Homes**; **Ins and Outs**; **Small Homes**)

SCHOOL DISTRICT

An area jointly administered by two or more Poor Law Unions or parishes for the purposes of providing residential school accommodation for pauper children.

(*See also*: **District and Separate Schools**)

An 1898 picture of children and their house-mother at 149-151 Upperthorpe in Sheffield – one of the earliest scattered homes to be set up.

SCOTLAND

Early Poor Laws

The earliest Acts of the Scottish Parliament relating to the poor date from the 1420s when a distinction was made between able-bodied 'thiggars' (beggars) and those who were unable to earn their own living. The latter could be given permission to beg by the authorities in the form of a badge or token to carry with them.[371] Over the next century and a half, a series of further Acts followed aimed at the 'staunching' of beggars, none of which proved effectual.

Public provision for the deserving poor was formalised in an Act of 1535 which made each parish liable for the support of its own aged and infirm poor and voluntary alms were to be collected for that purpose.[372]

In 1579, an Act of the Scottish Parliament 'For Punischment of Strang and Idle Beggars, and Reliefe of the Pure [Poor] and Impotent'[373] laid the basis of the system of poor relief in Scotland for the next three centuries. Amongst its provisions were for each parish to make a list of its own poor (those who had been born there or who had lived there for seven years or more), 'that the aged, impotent, and pure people, suld have ludgeing and abiding places', and to enable heritors (land-owners) to take the children of beggars into unpaid service until they were eighteen, in the case of girls, or twenty-four, for boys.

The 1579 Act was restated in 1597 with the addition that 'strong beggars and their bairns' – effectively, all the able-bodied poor – should be employed in 'common work'.[374] Implicitly acknowledging that previous legislation had been poorly implemented by the civil authorities, the Act also shifted the responsibility for carrying out poor relief directives to the Kirk Sessions – the church authorities in each parish. Money to fund poor relief was raised in a number of ways. In Aberdeen, for example, these included church door collections, donations by private individuals, fees from baptisms, marriages and burials, the income from rents and from hiring out a hearse.

Early Workhouses

An Act of 1672 ordered magistrates to erect 'correction houses' or workhouses in which beggars could be detained and made to work. One of these, 'the workhouse called Paul's work', is known to have operated in Edinburgh from at least 1720. The Edinburgh Charity Workhouse in Port Bristo opened in 1743 and was financed by voluntary subscriptions. Funds for its operation were raised by a variety of means such as a tax on the rents of the city, collections at church doors, charitable donations and other contributions including an annual benefit play at one of the city's theatres. The Charity Workhouse was a substantial building that, in 1777–78, could accommodate 484 adults and 180 children.[375]

In 1761, Edinburgh's West Kirk parish opened the Canongate Charity Workhouse at the east side of Tollbooth Wynd. It was financed by church-door collections and voluntary contributions, and managed by annually chosen members of various public societies such as the incorporated trades.

In Glasgow, a workhouse known as the Town's Hospital, was founded in 1731. The Hospital was managed by the Lord Provost and a group of forty-eight directors: twelve elected by the town council, twelve by the General Session (representing the church in each parish), twelve by the Merchants' House (the merchants' guild), and twelve by the Incorporated Trades (the producers' guild).

The 1845 Scottish Poor Law Act

The 1707 Act of Union had allowed Scotland to retain its own judicial system. Because of this, the Poor Law Amendment Act of 1834 did not extend to Scotland. However, by the 1840s, it became apparent that reform was necessary. The demand for poor relief exceeded supply and it was administered very inconsistently. A further factor, in 1843, was the Disruption where the established Church of Scotland suffered a split with 40 per cent of its clergy leaving to form the Free Church. The existing system of administration via the Church of Scotland's Kirk

A view of Edinburgh's Charity Poorhouse in 1820. Parts of the building still survive as residential accommodation and others have been incorporated into a hotel.

Sessions was no longer effective after half its members had departed. In January 1843, a Royal Commission was set up to inquire into the 'administration and practical operation' of the poor relief system in Scotland.

The Commission's report, delivered on 2 May 1844, noted that poor relief in Scotland was generally confined to the old, infirm, disabled, mentally ill and so on, and that relief to the able-bodied was rare. It therefore proposed to broadly keep relief organised at the parish level with each of the country's 880 parishes having an annually appointed Parochial Board of managers and an Inspector of the Poor to examine all applications for relief. The Parochial Board would decide whether to raise poor relief funds voluntarily, or to impose a poor rate levied on the assessed value of each householder's property. Poor relief could be given in the form of cash or in kind, or a poorhouse could be set up to shelter the sick or destitute, but not the able-bodied. Parishes, particularly in urban areas, could be united for settlement and poor-relief purposes, including the establishment of joint poorhouses, although poorhouses could be set up only by parishes, or combinations of parishes, whose population exceeded 5,000 people. The new system was regulated by a central Board of Supervision whose membership comprised the Lord Provost of Edinburgh, the Lord Provost of Glasgow, the Solicitor General of Scotland, the Sheriffs Depute of the counties of Perth, Renfrew, Ross and Cromarty, and three other persons appointed by the Crown. These proposals were put into effect on 4 August 1845 in the Poor Law (Scotland) Act.[376]

The Scottish Act was therefore significantly different from the 1834 Poor Law Amendment Act which applied in England and Wales and subsequently extended to Ireland. In Scotland, the able-bodied were exempt from receiving relief. Relief was not to be confined to the poorhouse, and the operation of poorhouses was voluntary.

After the 1845 Act, there was a steady movement away from voluntary funding towards the rate assessment system. In 1845, only 230 of Scotland's 880 parishes were using the assessment system, but by 1853 this had risen to 680.[377]

Although the 1845 Act allowed large parishes or combinations of parishes to operate poorhouses, it did not require them to do so. Approval for poorhouse schemes had to be given by the Board of Supervision which published model plans for rural and town poorhouses. In 1848, the Board reported that it had approved plans for eight new poorhouses, together with the enlargement of poorhouses in Edinburgh and Glasgow. Around seventy poorhouses were eventually in operation, about three-quarters of which were run by Combinations. However, the majority of Scotland's paupers continued to receive out relief, with many poorhouses rarely more than half full. By the 1890s, there was accommodation for over 15,000 inmates in the country's poorhouses, with the average number of inmates usually between 8,000 and 9,000.[378] Details of all the poorhouses established in Scotland are given in Appendix H, with some detailed statistics of the numbers receiving relief given in Appendix C.

Poorhouse Operation

The operation of poorhouses in Scotland was in many respects based on that adopted for workhouses in England and Wales. Inmates were classified as follows: males aged fifteen or over, boys age from two to fifteen, females aged fifteen or over, girls aged from two to fifteen, and children under two years of age. Since poorhouses were not intended to accommodate the able-bodied, they did not feature in the classification scheme. Within the poorhouse building, inmates of the different classes were segregated, although infants were allowed to stay with their mothers.

There was a prescribed daily routine and work was expected to be performed by inmates according to their capabilities. Inmates were required to wear the poorhouse uniform. An inmate's own clothing was 'purified' by steaming it for three hours and then placing it in store until the day he or she left the poorhouse. The inmates' diet was also prescribed. For working adults, the daily allowance from 1850 comprised: Breakfast – 4oz oatmeal and ¾ pint of broth; Dinner – 8oz of bread, 1½ pints of broth and 4oz of boiled meat; Supper – 4oz of oatmeal and ¾ pint of broth.[379]

Inmates were bathed once a week, under supervision, in water between 88 and 98 degrees Fahrenheit. Children under fifteen had their hair regularly cut to keep the length at 2in for boys and 3in for girls.

Although the Scottish poorhouse system was not originally intended to accommodate the able-bodied, poorhouses such as Glasgow later set up small 'test wards' for inmates who were judged to be 'bad characters' or who were suspected to be able to support themselves outside the poorhouse.[380] Test ward inmates were kept separate from other inmates and given a stricter regime. Men could be required to do stone breaking or chopping wood, while women were given knitting to do.

Edinburgh

In 1869, Edinburgh's old Charity Workhouse was replaced by a new building at Craiglockhart which had accommodation of up to 1,569 inmates. It was intended to provide both a 'comfortable home for the aged and poor' and also a reformatory for 'the dissipated, the improvident, and the vicious'.[381] The male wing had divisions for 'old men of good character', 'dissolute men', 'doubtful old men', and 'boys', with similar divisions in the women's quarters.

The city's St Cuthbert's parish established its first poorhouse on St Cuthbert's Lane in 1758. Three years later, the parish of Canongate's poorhouse was opened on Tollbooth Wynd. In 1868, St Cuthbert's erected a new poorhouse and hospital at Craigleith. The poorhouse had separate sections for 'Very Decent', 'Decent', 'Bastardy', and 'Depraved'.[382] In 1873, St Cuthbert's merged with Canongate, forming St Cuthbert's Combination, with the Tollbooth Wynd poorhouse then being closed.

Glasgow

After 1845, poor law provision in Glasgow was divided between four parishes: City, Barony, Govan and Gorbals. The City Poorhouse on Parliamentary Road was originally erected in 1809 as a lunatic asylum. With 1,500 beds, it was one of the largest institutions in Britain. Poor conditions and overcrowding in the City Poorhouse were a recurring subject of concern. It closed in 1905 following a merger with Barony parish.

The Barony Parish Poorhouse at Barnhill opened in 1853 and was described in 1882 as 'a very capacious asylum for the children of poverty and well adapted by its cleanliness, ventilation and position to mitigate the ills of their condition.' With the merger with the City parish in 1905, it was enlarged and became Scotland's largest poorhouse, housing more than 2,500 inmates.

Prior to 1872, Govan operated various establishments which were then replaced on a new site at Merryflatts by a new poorhouse, 240-bed general hospital, and lunatic asylum for 180 patients. Gorbals, which never set up a poorhouse, was absorbed by Govan in 1873.

The Highlands and Islands

Most of Scotland's poorhouses were erected in the country's more highly populated southern lowlands. The first poorhouse erected in the highlands was in 1850 at Tain, serving a combination of nine parishes in Easter Ross. Under pressure from the Board of Supervision, poorhouses were eventually erected in most parts of the highlands and islands. However, they often were larger than demand warranted and proved costly to build and to run, and never approached anywhere near their capacity. By the early twentieth century, proposals were being made for the conversion of poorhouses in the highlands and islands to other uses, such as the accommodation of the mentally ill. In 1907, the Long Island Combination poorhouse at Lochmaddy was licensed for the reception of twenty-eight 'harmless lunatics' in addition to the ordinary poor. The parishes of the Long Island Combination were thus saved the expense of sending such cases from the Hebrides to the asylum at Inverness. In 1911, a similar scheme came into operation in the Lewis Combination poorhouse at Stornoway.

The Later Years

In 1894, the Board of Supervision was replaced by a more powerful Scottish Local Government Board which was directly responsible to Parliament. At the same time, parochial boards were replaced by parish councils which held office for three years at a time. A growing emphasis was then placed on the provision of improved hospital facilities. In Glasgow, for example, following the creation of a single poor law authority in 1904, three new establishments were built: Stobhill Hospital (for the infirm and chronic sick poor, and for children), the Eastern General Hospital (an acute hospital with psychiatric assessment wards), and the Western General Hospital (for acute medical and surgical cases).

A number of poorhouse buildings were used during the First World War for military accommodation or for the treatment of military casualties. After the passing of the Local Government Act of 1929, many poorhouses became Public Assistance Institutions offering care for the elderly, infirm, chronic sick and unmarried mothers. In 1946, as part of preparations for the setting up of the National Health Service, many former poorhouse buildings were refurbished or upgraded to take on a new role within the new system. Others were condemned and sold off or demolished.

The Lewis (or Lews) Combination Poorhouse at Stornoway, Isle of Lewis, was opened in 1896 and could house up to sixty-six inmates. A number of the residents are visible at the front of the building.

Parish Homes and Almshouses

After 1845, the setting up of what were sometimes referred to as 'statutory' poorhouses – those whose operation was supervised by the Board of Supervision – was limited to larger parishes or parish combinations, However, more than 100 Scottish parishes operated smaller establishments generally referred to as parish homes or almshouses. Rather than the dormitories that characterised poorhouses, almshouse accommodation was more likely to be arranged as small apartments or cottages. The inmates ('persons of good character') could live with as much freedom as in their own homes, often with their own furniture, and buying and cooking their own food. (A list of these establishments is given in Appendix I)

(*See also*: **Wartime**; **Appendices C, H, I, L**)

SEGREGATION

In union (and some earlier) workhouses, inmates were segregated and occupied separate areas of the building. Apart from a few special instances, different classes were not allowed to communicate with each other.

Segregation was achieved in a number of ways. Within the workhouse, each class had its own dormitories, work area and day-rooms, and there were often complex arrangements of staircases, doors and passageways to maintain separation when inmates moved around the building. In the few communal areas such as the dining hall or chapel, dividing screens were sometimes used to separate different classes. Workhouse windows that might allow inmates of one class a view of another class could be fitted with frosted glass, as happened in the children's quarters at the Southwell workhouse to prevent the youngsters seeing their mothers outside. In the external areas, walls – typically 6 to 7ft high – were used to compartmentalise the inmates' exercise yards and walkways.

Keeping men and women apart sometimes proved hard to achieve. In 1905, 'unclimbable' fencing was fitted between the male and female yards at Steyning workhouse in Sussex after several men had been caught scaling the internal walls. The scheme was unsuccessful as a female inmate subsequently became pregnant during her stay in the workhouse.[383]

The exceptions to the segregation rule were fairly limited. Children up to the age of seven could, with permission, live in the women's quarters. Children were also permitted a 'daily interview' with their mother or father. From 1847, married couples over the age of sixty could request to share a separate bedroom, a privilege later extended to any couple where either partner was sick or disabled. Women sometimes entered the male sections of the workhouse to undertake nursing or cleaning duties. The workhouse kitchens, though primarily a women's domain, were an area where men might occasionally need to enter for some purpose.

(*See also*: **Architecture**)

SELECT VESTRY

The Sturges Bourne Act of 1819 allowed parish vestries to appoint a small committee of 'substantial householders' – the Select Vestry – to scrutinise the operation of its poor relief administration. The Select Vestry allowed ratepayers a greater say in matters such as how the poor rates were collected, who was to receive relief, and in what form.

(*See also*: **Poor Laws**)

SEPARATE SCHOOLS

(*See*: **District and Separate Schools**; **District and Separate Schools in Ireland**)

SETTLEMENT

The principle of settlement was that every individual had a place to which they legally 'belonged'. An early expression of this concept was the 1388 Statute of Cambridge which restricted the movements of labourers and beggars beyond their county Hundred.

The 1662 Act for the better Relief of the Poor of this Kingdom[384] – often referred to as the Settlement Act – stipulated that newcomers to a parish who were deemed 'likely to become chargeable' to the poor rates could be forcibly removed back to their home parish upon the orders of two Justices of the Peace if a complaint was made against them within forty days of arrival, provided they had not rented a house for at least £10 a year. The need for such a law was outlined in the Act's preamble:

> By reason of some Defects in the Law, poor People are not restrained from going from one Parish to another, and therefore do endeavour to settle themselves in those Parishes where there is the best Stock, the largest Commons or Wastes to build Cottages, and the most Woods for them to burn and destroy; and when they have consumed it, then to another Parish, and at last become Rogues and Vagabonds, to the great Discouragement of Parishes to provide Stocks, where it is liable to be devoured by Strangers...

The 1662 Act did not invent the idea of settlement – the concept was long established in English history. According to ancient tradition, a person's settlement was taken to be his or her place of birth. From 1503–04, three years residence in a place could also confer settlement.[385] By the seventeenth century, judicial interpretation of England's common law dictated that a legitimate child's settlement was taken to be the same as that of its father, and changed in line with any new settlement that the father acquired. At marriage, a woman took on the same settlement as her husband. Illegitimate children took their settlement from the place they were born. This often led parish overseers to try and get rid of an unmarried pregnant woman before the child was born, for example by transporting her to another parish just before the birth, or by paying a man from another parish to marry her.

In 1691, a further Act[386] specified additional ways in which settlement could be acquired. If a boy was apprenticed, which could happen from the age of seven, the place of his apprenticeship became his parish of settlement. Another means of qualifying for settlement in a new parish was by being in continuous employment for at least a year. To prevent this, hirings were often for a period of 364 days rather than a full year, or with a small amount of unpaid holiday included. Conversely, labourers might quit their jobs before a year was up in order to avoid being effectively trapped in a disagreeable parish.

Another refinement came in 1697[387] when newcomers holding settlement certificates from their own parish were protected from removal unless they actually became chargeable on the poor rate. A century later, in 1795, this protection was extended to all except pregnant unmarried women.[388] Parishes made these the least welcome because they were considered the most expensive to support. The 1697 Act also required the 'badging of the poor'. Those in receipt of poor relief were required to wear, in red or blue cloth on their right shoulder, the letter 'P' preceded by the initial letter of their parish, for example 'WP' for Woburn Parish. Badging was eventually discontinued in 1810.

The operation of the 1662 Act, and its subsequent amendments, proved complex, confusing and contentious. Expensive legal battles often took place between a parish attempting to remove a pauper, whom it claimed it had no duty to support, and the parish that it claimed did have responsibility. Where a person's place of settlement was in question, the matter was usually decided by means of a settlement examination in front of two magistrates who questioned the individual about their life history. A successful petition would result in a removal order being issued, with the pauper being escorted back to their home parish which would have to pay any relief costs incurred although not the removing parish's legal fees. It was not uncommon for a parish to spend far more

A settlement certificate for Alexander Chalk and his wife Mary issued in 1747 by the Oxfordshire parish of Newington.

on removing a pauper than it would have cost to provide relief. The legal profession, of course, benefited enormously from all the work that came its way in trying to resolve the convoluted problems which the settlement laws regularly threw up. A comic verse from the early nineteenth century illustrates such cases:

A woman having a settlement
Married a man with none:
The question was, He being dead
If that she had, was gone?
Quoth *Sir John Pratt* Her settlement
Suspended did remain,

Living the husband: But, him dead
It doth revive again.

   Chorus of Puisne Judges
Living the husband: But, him dead
It doth revive again.[389]

The settlement laws could prove particularly difficult for women who were deserted or widowed. Since they took their husband's settlement at marriage, any poor relief they might need had to be provided by that parish. In some cases, it could be a far-flung place that they might never have visited.

The 1662 Act became the target of considerable criticism, perhaps most famously by Adam Smith who suggested that:

There is scarce a poor man in England of forty years of age... who has not in some part of his life felt himself most cruelly oppressed by this ill-contrived law of settlements.[390]

What has been called the Act's 'framework of repression'[391] had the effect on labourers of:

Restricting them through life to their place of birth, destroying the incentives to independent effort, and perpetuating a low state of civilisation.[392]

In more recent times, the 1662 Act has been described as 'possibly the worst law ever passed by a British Parliament'.[393]

The 1832 Royal Commission proposed a simplification of the settlement laws so that birth in a parish would become the only means of acquiring settlement. However, this suggestion was not taken up, although the 1834 Act did remove a year's hiring and service in a parish office as options to gain settlement. A provision to allow a union, rather than its individual parishes, to become the area of settlement was only taken up by one union, Docking in Norfolk. After 1834, illegitimate children took their settlement from their mother rather than their place of birth.

In 1846, the already convoluted settlement laws were further complicated by an Act[394] which introduced the new concept of 'irremovability'. Amongst other things, this gave protection against removal to anyone who had been resident in a parish for five years. This privilege was not, however, available to those living outside their home parish and who were in receipt of non-resident poor relief from that parish. In order to prevent a flood of new relief claims from those poor who discovered that they were now irremovable, Bodkin's Act[395] was passed in 1847 to place the cost of such claims on the union's common fund rather than on individual parishes. Following the 1865 Union Chargeability Act, the union rather than the parish became the area of settlement. One year's continuous residence in a union would qualify a person as being irremovable.

Despite these changes, issues of settlement and removal continued to occupy a significant amount of unions' time and money. In 1907, more than 12,000 individuals were removed from one union to another in England and Wales, the larger number of these being from London and other large cities. The settlement laws were considerably streamlined by the 1927 Poor Law Act, and finally removed from the statute book in 1948.

(*See also*: **Illegitimacy**; **Poor Law**)

SICK ASYLUM DISTRICTS

In 1868, the year after the passing of the Metropolitan Poor Act, the Poor Law Board formed six new Sick Asylum Districts (SADs) which were to erect joint 'asylums' or hospitals for dealing with the general sick poor. The SADs created were:

Poplar and Stepney – comprising the Poplar and Stepney Unions
Central London – the Westminster and Strand Unions and the parishes of St Giles in the Fields and St George, Bloomsbury
Rotherhithe – the St Olave Union and the parishes of St Mary Magdalen, Bermondsey, and St Mary, Rotherhithe
Newington – the St Saviour Union, and the parishes of St George the Martyr, Southwark, and St Mary, Newington
Finsbury – the Holborn Union and the parishes of St James, Clerkenwell and St Luke, Middlesex
Kensington – the parishes of St Margaret and St John, Westminster, and St Mary Abbots, Kensington

Concerns about the high cost of building the proposed new hospitals led the Poor Law Board to reconsider the scheme. Under its revised plans, only the Poplar and Stepney and the Central London Districts survived. Three other SADs were reconstituted as enlarged Poor Law Unions: St Olave, St Saviour's and Holborn. The Kensington SAD was dissolved and St Margaret and St John joined with St George, Hanover Square, to form the new St George's Union.

The Poplar and Stepney SAD opened its sick asylum on Devon's Road in Bow in 1871. The Central London SAD initially took over the newly constructed St Pancras poor law infirmary at Highgate and, from 1874, the former Strand union infirmary site on Cleveland Street. In 1900, it transferred its activities to a new hospital at Colindale, Hendon.

(*See also*: **London**; **Medical Care**)

SINGING

(*See*: **Entertainment**)

An early 1900s view of the Poplar & Stepney District Asylum Devon's Road in Bow. The 572-bed hospital opened in August 1871 with just one doctor and no trained nurses. Renamed St Andrew's Hospital in 1920, it continued in operation until 2006 but has now been demolished.

SISTERS OF MERCY

An order of nuns who became widely involved in the provision of nursing care in Irish workhouses, beginning at Limerick in 1861. By 1903, a total 334 nuns were in post at eighty-five workhouses including thirty-two holding the office of matron. A further forty-eight were engaged as workhouse schoolmistresses.[396]
(*See also*: **Ireland**; **Medical Care**)

SKILLY/SKILLEY

A colloquial term, particularly associated with tramps, for workhouse gruel.
(*See also*: **Food**; **Toke**; **Tommy**)

SLOP WORK

Poorly paid sewing work done by female workhouse inmates for outside businesses.
(*See also*: **Work**)

SMALL HOMES

A rather loose term sometimes used to denote a variety of poor law children's homes which fell outside the more widely used categories of 'cottage home' and 'scattered home'. Despite their name, small homes could be quite large in a few cases, such as those run by the Cheltenham and Grimsby Unions, housing 100 or more children; most, though, accommodated no more than thirty. Unions using small homes generally operated just one or two, sometimes placing boys in one and girls in another. The person in charge of a small home, usually a woman, was variously designated as the superintendent, matron or foster mother.
(*See also*: **Children**; **Cottage Homes**; **Scattered Homes**)

SOCIAL EXPLORERS

The term often used to describe investigators such as journalists, novelists and social reformers who disguised themselves as down-and-outs to gain entry to institutions such as charity shelters, doss-houses and workhouse casual wards. Their subsequent, sometimes lurid, accounts of their experiences were avidly read by the Victorian middle classes for whom the 'underworld' held a particular fascination.

One of the earliest and best-known undercover reports was *A Night in a Workhouse*, by James Greenwood, published anonymously in 1866 in the *Pall Mall Gazette* of which his brother Frederick was editor. Greenwood's titillating prose described not only the repugnant conditions in the spike, but the characters who entered it such as an old-timer known as 'Daddy':

> The porter went his way, and I followed Daddy into another apartment where there were three great baths, each one containing a liquid so disgustingly like weak mutton broth that my worst apprehensions crowded back. 'Come on, there's a dry place to stand on up at this end,' said Daddy, kindly. 'Take off your clothes, tie 'em up in your hank'sher, and I'll lock 'em up till the morning.'
>
> Accordingly, I took off my coat and waistcoat, and was about to tie them together when Daddy cried, 'That ain't enough, I mean everything.'
>
> 'Not my shirt, Sir, I suppose?'
>
> 'Yes, shirt and all; but there, I'll lend you a shirt,' said Daddy. 'Whatever you take in of your own will be nailed, you know. You might take in your boots, though–they'd be handy if you happened to want to leave the shed for anything; but don't blame me if you lose 'em.'

The other inmates in the spike were a very rough crowd:

> Towzled, dirty, villainous, they squatted up in their beds, and smoked foul pipes, and sang snatches of horrible songs, and bandied jokes so obscene as to be absolutely appalling. Eight or ten were so enjoying themselves–the majority with the check shirt on and the frowsy

Children and staff at the Blything Union's 'small home' at Yoxford in Suffolk.

The cover of James Greenwood's *A Night in a Workhouse* articles reprinted in pamphlet form.

STARTLING PARTICULARS!

A NIGHT

IN A

WORKHOUSE.

From the PALL MALL GAZETTE.

HOW THE POOR ARE TREATED IN LAMBETH!

THE CASUAL PAUPER!

"OLD DADDY," THE NURSE!

THE BATH!

The Conversation of the Casuals!

THE STRIPED SHIRT!

THE SWEARING CLUB!!

"Skilley" and "Toke" by Act of Parliament!

The Adventures of a Young Thief!

&c. &c. &c.

F. BOWERING, 211, BLACKFRIARS ROAD,
MANSELL & SON, King Street, Borough, and all Newsagents,

PRICE ONE PENNY.

rug pulled about their legs; but two or three wore no shirts at all, squatting naked to the waist, their bodies fully exposed in the light of the single flaring jet of gas fixed high upon the wall.

Such was the interest in Greenwood's articles that they were subsequently reprinted in pamphlet form and also inspired at least two broadside ballads to be composed about the events.

Also in 1866, medical reformer J.H. Stallard published the experiences of 'Ellen Stanley', a working woman he had hired to make undercover visits to four of London's female casual wards. Her account was even more shocking than Greenwood's, as illustrated by this extract from her description of a night spent in the Whitechapel casual ward:

At this time the night was indescribably dreadful. There lay the women, naked and restless, tossing about in the dim gaslight, and getting up from time to time in order to shake off their disgusting tormentors, which speckled their naked limbs with huge black spots. When the old man came in, he motioned to me to lie down and go to sleep, but I told him I dared not, for the vermin were so bad. 'Ah,' said he, 'you are not used to it.' About twelve o'clock the closeness and heat of the room became intolerable, and every one began to feel ill and to suffer from diarrhoea. Several were drawn double with cramp, and I felt sick and ill myself. The children began to cry constantly, and seemed extremely ill. From this time the closet was constantly occupied by one or another, and the stench became dreadful. 'So help me God,' said one, 'I will never come here again. I would rather go to prison a hundred times.'

In the summer of 1902, the American writer Jack London lived incognito in London's East End, staying in doss-houses and casual wards. His experiences were detailed in *The People of the Abyss*, published the following year. Here is his account of a night at the same Whitechapel workhouse:

By seven o'clock we were called away to bathe and go to bed. We stripped our clothes, wrapping them up in our coats and buckling our belts about them, and deposited them in a heaped rack and on the floor a beautiful scheme for the spread of vermin. Then, two by two, we entered the bathroom. There were two ordinary tubs, and this I know: the two men preceding had washed in that water, we washed in the same water, and it was not changed for the two men that followed us. This I know; but I am quite certain that the twenty-two of us washed in the same water.

I did no more than make a show of splashing some of this dubious liquid at myself, while I hastily brushed it off with a towel wet from the bodies of other men. My equanimity was not restored by seeing the back of one poor wretch a mass of blood from attacks of vermin and retaliatory scratching.

A shirt was handed me which I could not help but wonder how many other men had worn; and with a couple of blankets under my arm I trudged off to the sleeping apartment. This was a long, narrow room, traversed by two low iron rails. Between these rails were stretched, not hammocks, but pieces of canvas, six feet long and less than two feet wide. These were the beds, and they were six inches apart and about eight inches above the floor. The chief difficulty was that the head was somewhat higher than the feet, which caused the body constantly to slip down. Being slung to the same rails, when one man moved, no matter how slightly, the rest were set rocking; and whenever I dozed somebody was sure to struggle back to the position from which he had slipped, and arouse me again.

Many hours passed before I won to sleep. The smell was frightful and sickening, while my imagination broke loose, and my skin crept and crawled till I was nearly frantic. Toward morning I was awakened by a rat or some similar animal on my breast.

But morning came, with a six o'clock breakfast of bread and skilly, which I gave away; and we were told off to our various tasks. Some were set to scrubbing and cleaning, others to picking oakum, and eight of us were convoyed across the street to the Whitechapel Infirmary, where we were set at scavenger work.

At eight o'clock we went down into a cellar under the Infirmary, where tea was brought to us, and the hospital scraps. These were heaped high on a huge platter in an indescribable mess pieces of bread, chunks of grease and fat pork, the burnt skin from the outside of roasted joints, bones, in short, all the leavings from the fingers and mouths of the sick ones suffering from all manner of diseases. Into this mess the men plunged their hands, digging, pawing, turning over, examining, rejecting, and scrambling for. It wasn't pretty. Pigs couldn't have done worse. But the poor devils were hungry, and they ate ravenously of the swill, and when they could eat no more they bundled what was left into their handkerchiefs and thrust it inside their shirts.[397]

Life for those frequenting the female casual ward was revisited in 1904 by Mary Higgs, a graduate of Cambridge University who became a clergyman's wife in Oldham and secretary of the Ladies Visiting Committee at the Oldham Union workhouse. She developed a particular

A line of men wait for admission to the Whitechapel Union's Thomas Street casual ward on Thomas Street in about 1902. A porter stands at the women's entrance door, with two small children just visible at the head of the women's line off to the right.

interest in vagrancy reform and determined to discover first-hand what conditions were like in casual wards and common lodging houses. Her experiences revealed the squalid conditions often to be found, and how vulnerable female vagrants could be. One of her first undercover visits, accompanied by her friend Annie Lee, was to the casual ward at Dewsbury workhouse:

We arrived a few minutes before six, at the workhouse lodge, which was occupied by a man, the workhouse buildings being a little way off. The man was a male pauper, and no one else was in sight. We had to enter his hut to answer questions, which he recorded in a book, and we were then out of sight of the house. He took my friend's name, occupation, age, where she came from, and her destination, and then sent her on, rather imperatively, to the tramp ward. She stood at the door, some way off, waiting for me. He kept me inside his lodge and began to take the details. He talked to me in what I suppose he thought a very agreeable manner, telling me he wished I had come alone earlier, and he would have given me a cup of tea. I thanked him, wondering if this was usual, and then he took my age, and finding I was a married woman, he said, 'Just the right age for a bit of funning: come down to me later in the evening.' I was too horror-struck to reply. He took my bundle, and asked if I had any money. I gave him my last penny. I received a wooden token for the bundle. I then joined my friend, and told her she had better give up her umbrella and her penny. Though I stood and waited, and she was only gone a moment, he tried to kiss her as she gave him the things.[398]

In a nod to Jack London, a collection of Mary Higgs's reports was published in 1906 under the title *A Glimpse into the Abyss*.

Perhaps inspired by Higgs, the Edwardian period saw a flurry of new explorers including Olive Malvery (*The Soul Market*, 1907), Everard Wyrall (*The Spike*, 1910), 'Denis Crane' [Walter Cranfield] (*A Vicarious Vagabond*, 1910), and the Revd George Z. Edwards (*A Vicar as Vagrant*, 1910).

In the late 1920s, former Oxford MP Frank Gray made undercover visits to a number of Oxfordshire casual wards as part of his efforts to save teenage vagrants from a life on the road. His stay at Thame was typical:

We reach the gates. It is not six o'clock yet. With some eighteen others we loaf, huddle, and cringe before the gate. There is one woman among us. Women tramps are scarce; but all tramp women look like tramps. All men tramps don't. This is curious, for in every other walk of life women are the better dissemblers.

Frank Gray disguised as a tramp in order to experience first-hand the life of such individuals, especially young men. Gray also provided temporary accommodation for a number of individuals at his own home.

The gates open; we walk up the garden. A Clerk takes particulars under a lamp at the front door, and we pass to the back, isolated from the higher grade of the workhouse, the permanent inmates. We shamble into this workhouse from the outer world, and then past the quarters of the permanent inmates to our den at the back midst the refuse heaps, well-nigh like lepers – the unclean.

I made a slip as I gave my answers, for I noticed the clerk momentarily start as he detected a pitch of voice unusual in a casual ward. I must be more careful thereafter.

In the Thame workhouse there is no strict search; there is no suggestion of a bath or a wash. We retain our clothes and sleep in some of them. To-night I have a pillow – my boots with my trousers wrapped over them. We sleep on boards on a gradient raised from the floor, and the slope helps sleep.

As we arrived at this workhouse and answered the stereotyped questions – as listlessly as they were asked – we received our hunk of bread, and with it we said good-bye to all officialdom and supervision and entered the casual ward. As the tramps have lost heart so have the officials.

Here, unclean and unhappy, I lie in a chamber already the home of body vermin and house vermin. With such hospitality as this, what do I owe to society?[399]

(*See also*: **Casual Ward**)

SOCIAL SCIENCE ASSOCIATION

(*See*: **National Association for the Promotion of Social Science (NAPSS)**)

SOCIETY FOR PROMOTING CHRISTIAN KNOWLEDGE (SPCK)

Founded in 1698, the SPCK was a small but influential London-based organisation which strongly promoted the establishment of charity schools and, later, of workhouses. The SPCK gave financial encouragement to towns setting up workhouses and also published a variety of practical resources such as its 1725 handbook *An Account of Several Workhouses*. The Society worked closely with workhouse entrepreneur Matthew Marryott and also with Sir Edward Knatchbull in the drafting of his 1723 Workhouse Test Act.
(*See also*: **Account of Several Workhouses**; **Marryott, Matthew**; **Poor Laws**; Hitchcock (1992))

SOCIETY OF INSPECTORS OF THE POOR FOR SCOTLAND

A professional body, established in Glasgow in 1858, for those employed as Inspectors of the Poor in Scotland. The Society's later names included the Society of Inspectors of Poor and Public Assistance Officials of Scotland, and the Scottish Welfare Officers' Association.
(*See also*: **Scotland**)

SPECIAL ORDER

A directive from the Poor Law Commissioners applying only to a single named Poor Law Union or parish and not requiring parliamentary approval.
(*See also*: **General Order**; **Poor Law Commissioners**)

SPEENHAMLAND SYSTEM

An allowance system named after the Berkshire parish where in May 1795 local magistrates decided to supplement labourers' wages on a scale that varied with the price of bread and the size of their family. Though never sanctioned by Parliament, the scheme was sometimes referred to as the 'Berkshire Bread Act'. It was formally expressed as follows:

> When the gallon loaf of second flour weighing 8lb. 11oz. shall cost 1s., then every poor and industrious man shall have for his own support 3s. weekly, either produced by his own or his family's labour or an allowance from the poor rates, and for the support of his wife and every other of his family 1s. 6d. When the gallon loaf shall cost 1s.4d., then every poor and industrious man shall 3s. weekly for his own, and 1s.10d. for the support of every other of his family. And so in proportion as the price of bread rises or falls (that is to say) 3d. to the man and 1d. to every other of the family on every penny which the loaf rises above a shilling.[400]

Thus, if the price of bread rose to 1s 3d, a married man with two children would be guaranteed a wage of 3s 9d for himself plus three times 1s 9d, giving a total of 9s a week.
(*See also*: **Allowance System**; **Roundsman System**)

SPIKE

A colloquial term, used especially by tramps and vagrants, for the workhouse casual ward. Theories abound as to the origin of the name including:

- A nail or similar piece of metal used in picking oakum.
- A metal spike on which admission tickets (issued in some areas at local police stations) were placed after being handed over to the workhouse porter.
- The 'spiky' nature of the beds.
- Spikes fixed to the top of the vagrants' yard wall to deter escape attempts.
- An derivation of 'spiniken', another tramps' name for a workhouse, originally based on spinning house'.
- The spike or finial that sometimes crowned a workhouse roof.

(*See also*: **Casual Ward**)

STATE OF THE POOR

The State of the Poor, published in 1797 by Sir Frederic Morton Eden, was a pioneering work of sociological investigation now regarded as one of the classic texts in the history of economics and the poor law. Eden, a disciple of the philosopher and economist Adam Smith, believed that self-help was the remedy for the problems of the poor rather than the public subsidising of workhouses or labourers' wages. Eden's writing influenced other thinkers of his day such as Malthus and Bentham.

The content of the book's massive three volumes is summarised in its appropriately lengthy subtitle: *An History of the Labouring Classes in England, from the Conquest to the Present Period; In which are particularly considered, Their Domestic Economy, with respect to Diet, Dress, Fuel and Habitation; And the various Plans which, from time to time, have been proposed, and adopted, for the Relief of the Poor; Together with Parochial Reports Relative to the Administration of Workhouses, and Houses of Industry; the State of Friendly Societies; and other Public Institutions; in several Agricultural, Commercial, and Manufacturing, Districts.*

The first part of the work contains an extensive summary of the history of the poor laws to that date. The second and third volumes include the local reports which contain considerable detail about the lives of the poor in more than 170 parishes across England and Wales.

A single-volume abridged version of Eden's work, edited by Arthur Rogers, was published in 1929.

(*See also*: **Account of Several Workhouses**; **Poor Laws**)

STATISTICS

Before 1834

Although the poor laws date back to Elizabethan times, no systematic statistics on the operation of the system were available until 1777 when an abstract of poor relief returns from (almost) every parish in England and Wales was published by Parliament.[401] An earlier national survey had, in fact, been instigated in 1750 but its results were not published at the time, perhaps because too many responses were lacking or 'defective'. The unanalysed returns were rediscovered in 1817 and a summary published the following year.[402]

The 1777 return, which covered the year running from Easter 1775 to Easter 1776 included details of numbers relieved, expenditure on out relief, and the number and capacity of workhouses in each parish. As well as parish workhouses, the return also included a number of the Local Act workhouses then in operation.

In 1775–76, the total national expenditure on poor relief in England and Wales (excluding Local Act parishes) was recorded as £1.55 million, with just over £80,000 (around 5 per cent) of that spent on workhouse accommodation. An additional £35,000 went in litigation relating to settlement and removal cases. A total of 1,978 workhouses were recorded, with a total capacity of just under 90,000 places.

Broadly similar surveys appeared in 1804 (covering 1802–03) and in 1818 (for 1812–15). The 1804 and 1818 returns included the number of paupers being maintained in workhouses and the cost of such relief but did not ask respondents to specify the number of workhouses they operated. Thus, where parishes shared a workhouse, its location is unrecorded.

Part of typical local report from Eden's *State of the Poor* which included all manner of detail about the circumstances of the nation's poor as well as details about poor relief and workhouse accommodation.

> The Poor were farmed laſt year, and ſtill continue under the care of a contractor: he received £760. for the year ending in 1794; and is to receive £860. for the preſent year; at the expiration of which, the pariſh intend to take their Poor into their own hands. The pariſh pay all expences of removals, journies, meetings, and law-charges.
>
> The work-houſe ſtands in a good ſituation; and the lodging-rooms are tolerably comfortable, but not ſufficiently ſub-divided: there are 5 or 6 beds in each room; and two or three paupers ſleep in a bed. The beds are filled with chaff; and have, each, 2 ſheets, 1 blanket, and 1 rug. The pillows are ſtuffed with chaff. Very little work is done, as the Poor in the houſe are moſtly old people and children: a few ſpin worſted and lint. No account is kept of the mortality.
>
> *The following is the uſual Bill of Fare obſerved in the Work-houſe:*

	Breakfaſt.		Dinner.	Supper.
Sunday,	Milk-pottage and bread.		Butcher's meat, potatoes, broth and bread.	Broth and bread.
Monday,	Ditto,	Ditto.	Bread and butter; 2 oz. of butter to each adult.	Milk pottage and bread.
Tueſday,	Ditto,	Ditto.	Puddings with ſauce and beer.	Ditto.
Wedneſday,	Ditto,	Ditto.	Same as Sunday.	Same as Sunday.
Thurſday,	Ditto,	Ditto.	Same as Monday.	Same as Monday.
Friday,	Ditto,	Ditto.	Same as Tueſday.	Same as Monday.
Saturday,	Ditto,	Ditto.	Puddings, &c.	Same as Monday.

In 1802–03, total expenditure on relieving the poor had risen to £4.08 million, plus a further £190,000 in legal costs. Parishes using (rather than possessing) workhouses numbered 3,765, with 83,468 paupers being maintained in them, while 957,000 received out relief. In 293 parishes poor relief was managed by a private contractor.

By 1814–15, annual expenditure on poor relief had reached £5.42 million, plus £324,000 on legal expenditure. The number of parishes using workhouses now stood at 4,094, with more than 88,115 paupers being relieved in them, and 807,858 receiving out relief. Although the poor relief bill had risen since 1802–03, the number being relieved had fallen and the cost per claimant had gone up by roughly 50 per cent.

Despite their comprehensiveness, the overseers' returns of 1777, 1804 and 1818 are not without their limitations. Exactly what was intended to be covered by the word 'workhouse' was not spelled out to respondents and their replies may have included establishments where no work was required or any other restrictions enforced. Some overseers, suspicious of the use that might be made of their return, may have given deliberately vague or misleading responses. The level of accounting and record-keeping that existed in many parishes may have resulted in some of the returns being estimates rather than accurate figures.[403]

Other detailed surveys of poor relief expenditure, though not examining the use of workhouses, were compiled at several dates including those in 1787[404] (covering the years 1782–85), in 1822[405] (covering 1815–21) and 1831–32[406] (for 1825–29).

From 1813, the national expenditure on poor relief was recorded each year and it became possible to discern trends in the ebb and flow of pauper numbers and the cost of relieving them. The year 1818 was a notable one, with 13.2 per cent of the population in receipt of poor relief – the highest level that was ever to be recorded. (Exactly a century later, in 1918, pauperism reached an all-time low at 1.23 per cent.) The regular availability of such information could now begin to influence the direction of government poor relief policy and also reflect the results of any changes that were introduced. The relentless increase in annual poor relief expenditure from £5.77 million in 1823 to a peak of £7.04 million in 1832 created a growing pressure for reform and the appointment of the 1832 Royal Commission on the operation of the poor laws. *See* Appendix A (Table 1) for a summary of poor relief expenditure in England and Wales in various years from 1688 to 1847.

After 1834

The 1832 Royal Commission initiated one of the most comprehensive exercises in the collection of poor relief data ever undertaken. Its report, published in 1834, with lengthy appendices, extended to more than 8,000 pages, including the verbatim responses from 1,580 parishes to questionnaires of either fifty-three or sixty-four items according to whether the parish was 'rural' or 'town'. Curiously, the authors of the Commission's report, published in 1834, chose not to try and tabulate this mass of raw data or produce an abstract, arguing that 'it appeared that not much could be saved in length without incurring the risk of occasional suppression or misrepresentation.'[407] More recently, it has been argued that this decision was a deliberate attempt to obscure the results and, through the use of selective extracts, allow the report's conclusions to be slanted in a particular direction.[408]

Following the 1834 Poor Law Amendment Act, the annual reports of the new Poor Law Commissioners included a mass of statistics on every aspect of the poor law system. In the early years of the new system, considerable attention was naturally given to matters such as monitoring the formation of Poor Law Unions and the provision of workhouses. However, the ongoing core of reports by the Commissioners and their successor bodies was tabulating and tracking the expenditure on different forms of poor-relief and the numbers of those who received it.

Table 2 in Appendix A presents cumulative statistics for the numbers receiving poor relief in England and Wales from 1840 to 1930. Part of that data is illustrated in the chart below which shows the numbers (per thousand of the population) receiving indoor (workhouse) relief and out relief. Both figures peak in 1848 when the Irish famine was at its height and many Irish people had sought refuge in England. Out relief declined fairly steadily apart from a brief upturn in the 1860s which then fell sharply in the wake of the 'Goschen minute' which urged unions to curtail out relief. Out relief reached an all-time low in 1918 at the end of the First World War, to be followed by a massive rise during the 1920s when a depression led to wide-spread unemployment. After its high levels during the 1840s, the number receiving workhouse relief fell to around seven per thousand, a rate which did not vary much from then until 1930.

Table 3 in Appendix A presents national poor relief expenditure between 1834 and 1930. The chart below illustrates the annual expenditure (millions of pounds) on indoor and outdoor relief, together with the total poor relief expenditure which includes additional items such as repayment of building loans. Out relief expenditure was broadly constant between 1840 and 1914, apart from small peaks in 1848 and the 1860s reflecting the upsurge in numbers at those dates. Expenditure fell sharply during the First World War, when military conscription and war work removed a number of claimants from the relief lists, followed by a massive upswing during the depression of the 1920s. Expenditure on indoor relief slowly climbed throughout the nineteenth century and only overtook that on out relief for the first time in 1904. It did not, however, mirror the drop in out relief that took place during the First World War since workhouse inmates were generally not capable of contributing to wartime activities. In the slump of the 1920s, expenditure on indoor relief increased sharply, reaching an all-time peak in 1926, the year of the General Strike.

Over the years, the poor law authorities published a mass of other statistics relating various sub-groups of inmates such as children, the elderly, the mentally ill, vagrants and so on. One of their most detailed analyses, published in 1862, was a classification 'according to character' of the 39,073 adult female inmates then resident in the country's workhouses.[409] Remarkably, a total of twenty separate categories were distinguished:

	Total	Percentage

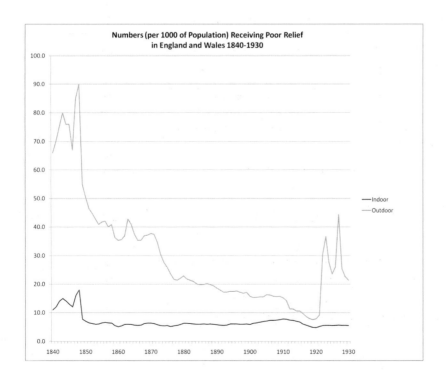

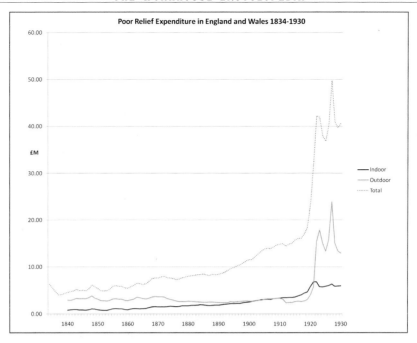

Poor Relief Expenditure in England and Wales 1834-1930

1. Single women pregnant with their first child	569	1.5
2. Single women pregnant who have one bastard child	2,847	7.3
3. Single women pregnant who have had one bastard child, and are pregnant again	292	0.7
4. Single women pregnant who have had two bastard children	1,711	4.4
5. Single women pregnant who have had three bastard children	877	2.2
6. Single women pregnant who have had four or more bastard children	782	2.0
7. Idiotic or weak-minded single-women with one or more bastard children	470	1.2
8. Women whose out relief has been taken off on account of misconduct	327	0.8
9. Women incapable, from syphilis, of getting their own living	543	1.4
10. Prostitutes	790	2.0
11. Girls who have been out at service, but did not keep their places on account of misconduct	383	1.0
12. Girls brought up in the workhouse, who have been out at service, but have returned on account of misconduct	373	1.0

13. Widows who have had one or more bastard children during their widowhood	680	1.7
14. Married women with husbands in the workhouse	1,698	4.3
15. Married women with husbands transported or in gaol	258	0.7
16. Married women deserted by their husbands	2,131	5.5
17. Imbecile, idiotic, or weak-minded women and girls	5,160	13.2
18. Respectable women and girls incapable of getting their living on account of illness or other bodily defect or infirmity	5,300	13.6
19. Respectable able-bodied women and girls	2,267	5.8
20. Respectable aged women	11,615	29.7
Total	39,073	100.0

As well as the yearly statistics, occasional longitudinal or summary tabulations were produced such as those included in the Local Government Board's *Twenty-fifth Annual Report* in 1896 and the Ministry of Health's *First Annual Report* in 1920. A massive collection of contemporary and historical statistics was published in 1911 as the *Statistical Appendix* to the report of the 1905 Royal Commission on the poor laws. Parliamentary publications such as the *Annual Abstract of Labour Statistics* also contain some yearly and occasional long-run statistics relating to poor relief.

Other good collections of poor law statistics, and informative accompanying discussions, can be found in: Aschrott (1902) Appendix II; Webb and Webb (1929), Volume 2, Appendix II; and Williams (1981) Chapter 4.

(*See also*: **Records**; **Royal Commission – 1832**; **Appendices A-C**)

STONE BREAKING

A work task sometimes performed by able-bodied male workhouse inmates, although most often used as a task for casuals or as an outdoor labour test. Large blocks of stone had to be broken up into small pieces, with the pieces sometimes required to be passed through a metal grid to check on their size. Stone breaking was popular with workhouse authorities – not only was it hard work, but the amount broken in a session (typically two or three hundredweight, depending on the hardness of the stone) was easily measured, and the resulting small stones could be sold off for other uses such as road-making.

(*See also*: **Bone Crushing / Bone Pounding**; **Oakum Picking**; **Work**)

STURGES BOURNE ACTS

Two Acts of 1818 and 1819, promoted by William Sturges Bourne MP, which gave property owners greater influence in parish poor relief administration.

(*See also*: **Poor Laws**; **Select Vestry**)

SUPERINTENDENT OF OUTDOOR LABOUR

A person employed by some Poor Law Unions whose duties were to supervise the labour of able-bodied paupers who were not resident in the workhouse, and to report to the guardians on the performance of such work.
(*See also*: **Outdoor Labour Test**)

SUPPLIES

A large workhouse, a household with a population of 2–300 inmates, had a substantial weekly shopping list. The provisions it required covered all manner of items from basic foodstuffs such as bread, milk, potatoes and oatmeal, through to coal for heating, candles for lighting, soap for washing, clothing for the inmates, linen for their beds, or even the beds themselves. For those who ended their days in the workhouse, a supply of coffins and shrouds was required.

Although some workhouses grew vegetables, raised pigs, or baked their own bread, most supplies were bought in from local suppliers, with the workhouse often forming a significant part of a town's economy. Advertisements for goods required were periodically placed in the local or trade press, inviting applications by sealed tender and accompanied by samples of the items being offered. Contracts were usually awarded to the lowest tender, with the quality of the goods generally being a secondary consideration.

Traders who supplied a workhouse sometimes saw it as an easy target for swindling. The most common deception was to provide a good-quality sample item when tendering for a contract, but to supply inferior goods afterwards. This could be done by simple measures such as watering down milk, or providing bread that was adulterated or made from an inferior grade of flour. Some frauds were more sophisticated. In 1896, Messrs Berringer & Co. had contracted to supply the South London District poor law school at Sutton with best-quality margarine from the well-known manufacturers Otto Monstead. It was later discovered that they had, in fact, been providing a much inferior foreign product packed in boxes stencilled and labelled to resemble those which Otto Monstead used.[410]

Members of the Board of Guardians and workhouse officers were forbidden by the 1834 Poor Amendment Act from being involved in the supply of goods or provisions to the workhouse in case it led to financial impropriety. Despite such regulations, workhouse officials

A stone-breaking yard set up by the Bethnal Green Employment Association during a trade depression in 1868. Although not run by the poor law authorities, the scene in a workhouse labour ward would be similar. The detail (inset top right) shows the metal gauze protective eye shields worn by some of the men.

A typical advertisement for the supply of workhouse provisions placed by the Dartford Union in 1905. All the samples of the various goods required to accompany each tender would have made a large and interesting assemblage.

frequently succumbed to temptations that were placed before them. At the Loddon and Clavering Union in 1842, the workhouse master was dismissed after being discovered replacing cheese in the inmates' diet by cheap broth, and selling off for his own gain honey and plants produced at the workhouse.

(*See also*: **Food**; **Gardens and Farms**)

SWIMMING BATHS

A number of the larger establishments set up to house pauper children – separate and district schools, and cottage homes sites – included swimming baths amongst their facilities. Among the poor law authorities making this provision were: Aston (at its Erdington children's institution), Bethnal Green (Leytonstone), Birmingham (Marston Green), Brentford (Percy House), Central London School District (Hanwell), Chorlton (Styal), Edmonton (Chase Farm), Greenwich (Sidcup), Hackney (Brentwood), Holborn (Mitcham), Kensington & Chelsea School District (Banstead), King's Norton's (Shenley Fields, Lambeth (Norwood), Leicester (Countesthorpe), North Surrey School District (Anerley), Poplar (Hutton), St Olave's (Shirley), St Marylebone (Southall), St Pancras (Leavesden), Salford (Culcheth), Shoreditch (Hornchurch), South Metropolitan School District (Sutton), Strand (Millfield House, Edmonton), West Derby (Fazakerley), Westminster (Wandsworth Common), and Wolverhampton (Wednesfield). What was possibly the only swimming pool constructed on an actual workhouse site was that in the children's block at Newcastle's Westgate Road workhouse.

Children at Islington's Hornsey Road School, which lacked its own swimming pool, learnt to swim at weekly visits to a neighbouring public baths during the summer months. The St George in the East School at Upton Park similarly made use of the Carpenters' Company baths at Stratford.

(*See also*: **Turkish Baths**; **Washing and Bathing**)

TABLEWARE

Based on inventories such as that taken in 1747 at the workhouse of St Botolph in Cambridge, a typical way of serving food to parish workhouse inmates was in a trencher – a plate or shallow dish made from a solid piece of wood, often made of sycamore which did not taint the food.[411] Food could be eaten either with the fingers, or in the case of liquids such as broth or gruel, using a wooden or metal spoon.

The trencher and spoon arrangement was still common up till the mid-nineteenth century, with tin plates or pannikins (metal pans or mugs) also being used in some workhouses. By the 1860s, the use of crockery (earthenware) plates and dishes was being encouraged as they were easier to clean and did not soak up liquids (as trenchers could) or cool food (as tin plates rapidly did). The standard provision of a knife, fork and spoon for each workhouse inmate was recommended in a report to the Poor Law Board in 1866.[412]

Dartford Union.

CONTRACT FOR PROVISIONS.

THE Guardians of the Dartford Union are prepared to receive TENDERS for the supply of the following Articles for Six Months, from the 1st day of October, 1905, to the 31st day of March, 1906, inclusive:—

1.—Meat (home fed and home killed). 2.— Fish. 3.—No. 2 Households Flour. 4. —Grocery. 5. — Provisions. 6. — Oilman's Goods. 7.—Wines and Spirits. 8.—Pale Ale and Porter. 9.—Drugs and Druggists' Sundries. 10.—Boots and Shoes. 11.—Coffins. 12.—Linen and Woollen Drapery, Hosiery, and Haberdashery. 13. — Clothing. 14. — Turnery and Brushes. 15.—Hay and Corn. 16.—Potatoes. 17.—Disinfecting Fluid and Soap. And for 12 Months, from the 1st day of October, 1905:—18. Milk.—19.—Male Officers' Uniforms.

The Tenders must include free delivery of the several articles at the Workhouse.

Tenders, addressed to the Guardians of the Poor of the Dartford Union, endorsed "Tender for Meat, &c., &c.," to be sent to the office of the Clerk, on or before Monday, the 18th day of September next, at 10 a.m.,

Tenders not containing the particulars required, or unaccompanied with the samples of articles tendered for, will be liable to be rejected.

The Guardians do not bind themselves to accept the lowest or any Tender. Samples of the different articles required may be seen at the Workhouse.

By order of the Board,
J. C. HAYWARD, Clerk.
Sessions House, Dartford, Kent,
August 30, 1905.

A rare interior view of the swimming bath at the Kensington and Chelsea District cottage homes at Banstead in Surrey in 1902.

Tableware was at its most basic in Irish workhouses where the dinner potatoes were served up to inmates in the nets in which they had been cooked. Things were no better in 1895 when representatives from the *British Medical Journal* visited the Bailieborough workhouse in County Cavan. Porridge was being served in a segmented communal feeding-trough around which the inmates gathered, with the food being eaten while standing up.
(*See also*: **Food**)

TASK WORK

Work given to able-bodied poor relief claimants, either in the workhouse or as an outdoor labour test. The tasks, intended to be deterrent in nature, included stone breaking, corn grinding and oakum picking.
(*See also*: **Labour Test; Work**)

TEA

Tea was introduced from China to Britain in the mid-1600s. A century later, it had become affordable by all and a staple item of many people's diet, including the labouring poor. Drunk without milk but with sugar, it could accompany any meal, or might substitute as a meal in itself, most often at breakfast time.

For some, however, tea was viewed as a luxury which the poor should do without. In 1729, at West Ham in Essex, it was said that 'many of those Pensioners who before spent the Alms of the Parish in Tea, and other Entertainments, now live without it, and turn themselves to Labour in their own Houses, to avoid being sent to the Workhouse.'[413]

As with tobacco and spirits, workhouses frequently placed restrictions on the consumption of tea. In the 1790s at the Ealing parish workhouse, only the sick were given tea and sugar. At the St Mary's workhouse in Reading, the elderly were allowed tea with bread and butter for breakfast. At the Bulcamp workhouse in Suffolk, tea was allowed to be drunk only on Sundays. At Chichester, in 1765, the 'pernicious and scandalous practice' of drinking tea was banned entirely from the workhouse following the scalding of two children.[414]

Women often seem to have been particularly associated with tea drinking. In 1797, Eden's *State of the Poor* revealed that breakfast for women inmates at the Empingham workhouse in Rutland comprised tea and bread and butter, while the men were given milk or broth. At Hampton in Middlesex, it was said that the female inmates 'would be riotous without tea every morning: this, however, is not allowed them by the master.' A report from Kendal noted that 'the women live much on tea but have, of late, discontinued the use of sugar.' An 1836 report to the West Riding Quarter Sessions noted that at the Hatfield parish workhouse near Doncaster 'the women find their own tea – the men their own tobacco'.[415]

Even the Local Government Board acknowledged women's particular fondness for tea – an Order in 1894 allowed guardians to 'cause dry tea, with sugar and milk, to be supplied to such of the female inmates of the Workhouse...' Not everyone was convinced of the wisdom of such relaxations. As recently as 1899, William Penney, a senior official of the Scottish Local Government Board, was convinced that 'excessive tea-drinking by women accounts largely for the number of pauper lunatics'. Another inspector pronounced that 'tea-drinking, when carried to excess, may also produce... hyper-excitability, sleeplessness, and nervousness'. Penney concluded that 'when these stages are reached by a poorly-nourished, confirmed tea-drinker, the boundary line of insanity is easily crossed.'[416]

The brewing of tea could raise problems. In 1840, Assistant Poor Law Commissioner Mr Parker complained about the practice of allowing inmates rations of dry tea, sugar and their own teapots, cups and saucers. A day ward in one workhouse he visited had three separate fires lit to heat the same number of kettles. He proposed that tea would be more efficiently prepared in a communal tea-urn which would also improve its quality.

Then, as now, the, opinions varied on how tea should be brewed. In 1866, the Poor Law Board's medical offer Dr Edward Smith – perhaps not a tea drinker himself – suggested that 'tea should not be boiled, but placed in boiling water, and the water kept quite hot for about ten or fifteen minutes. Carbonate of soda should be added to the water (and particularly if the water is hard)'.[417]

(*See also*: **Coffee**; **Food; State of the Poor**)

Typical tableware used by workhouse inmates – the bowl and mug each hold up to two pints. All such items, including cutlery, were marked with the union's name.

TEACHERS

Children in union workhouses were obliged to receive at least three hours of education each day, a figure that in 1897 rose to four hours for those aged between seven and fourteen. Exactly how that education was imparted out was up to each Board of Guardians. The low priority attached by many Boards to the education of pauper children, or resentment that it should even be provided at all, often led to teaching being carried out by someone with no qualification or experience. Adult workhouse inmates could take on the job as happened at Guisborough where, before the first (unqualified) schoolmistress was appointed in 1846, the girls were taught by a female vagrant.[418] In 1866, children at Chorley workhouse were taught by an inmate who received extra rations for his services.[419] At the same date, children at Saddleworth's remotely situated workhouse were sent to a distant school in fine weather but otherwise were taught reading and writing by one of the inmates.[420]

The teacher's role could sometimes be combined with another workhouse post. At Chorlton, early schoolmasters often doubled up as assistant overseer and workhouse porter, for which they received a total salary of £25 per year, plus board and lodging, on condition that they should be able to teach the Catechism. Several of these early teachers had themselves to be sent to school, and one or two were discharged because they could neither read nor write. At Amesbury in Wiltshire, teaching was carried out by the workhouse master.[421]

The duties of a workhouse school teacher were frequently onerous. Apart from teaching their charges for three hours or more each day, they were expected to 'regulate' the children's industrial training (practical skills to make them employable in later life); to accompany them outside the workhouse, for example on walks or attending church; and to keep them 'clean in their persons, and orderly and decorous in their conduct'; and to assist the master and matron in maintaining 'due subordination' in the workhouse. All that could add up to a working day of fourteen hours or more as indicated by the daily timetable (Monday to Saturday) included in the Chesterfield Union's regulations for workhouse teachers published in 1850.[422]

Summer	Winter	Duties
5.45am	6.45am	See the children rise, wash and dress, a few minutes allowed for private prayer, and see the windows opened and bedclothes thrown back.
6.00	7.00	Inspect the children for clean faces and hands, hair combed and shoes cleaned. Take them out for exercise.
7.45	7.45	Prayers and breakfast. See the school-room swept and fire lighted by the children. See beds are made and rooms swept.
8.45	8.45	Roll-call in school-room then lessons. 15 minutes recreation for children between 10.00 and 11.00.
12.00	12.00	Dinner. Teachers to be in attendance.
12.30pm	12.30pm	Recreation. Some degree of supervision required from teacher.
1.45	1.45	School. 15 minutes recreation at 3.00.
4.30	4.30	Recreation. Some degree of supervision required from teacher.

| 6.00 | 6.00 | Supper and prayers. Teachers to be in attendance and to read the prayers. |
| 8.30 | 7.00 | See children retire in an orderly manner to bed, and say their private prayers. |

Teachers at Chesterfield were allowed two evenings off each week from 6.30 a.m. until 10 p.m. in summer and until 9p.m. in winter.

Perhaps not surprisingly there was a large turnover in workhouse teachers. An 1852 survey of sixty-four workhouse schools in Wales and the west of England found that there had been 185 changes of teacher over the previous four years.[423] When it came to maintaining discipline, female teachers were at a particular disadvantage compared to their male colleagues in that they could not (officially, at least) themselves administer corporal punishment and girls were anyway exempt from such chastisement.

The early driving force in the improvement of workhouse teaching was James Kay (Kay-Shuttleworth from 1842). Kay had been impressed by his visits to schools in Scotland such as Wood's Session School in Edinburgh, where pupil-teachers helped assist with the teaching and where the 'simultaneous' method was used in some classes to teach several groups at once. Kay arranged for a number of Scots teachers to pass on their methods by working at the London pauper schools run by Mr Aubin at Norwood and Mr Drouet at Tooting. Kay also set up a prototype teachers' training school at his own home in Battersea with its first students all coming from Norwood.

In 1846, the government's Committee of Council on Education agreed to help fund the salaries of workhouse school teachers. As part of this arrangement, each teacher's performance was graded on a progressive scale which had four main stages: Permission, Probation, Competency and Efficiency. Each stage had three sub-sections, numbered 1 to 3, giving an overall twelve-level scale of qualification ranging from Permission Section 3 at the bottom to Efficiency Section 1 at the top. The suggested requirements for teachers in the Permission stage were: to read fluently; to write correctly a few simple sentences, read aloud from the Testament; to write from dictation sums in the first four simple rules of arithmetic, and to work them correctly; and to answer verbally a few simple questions respecting the life of our Saviour. At the top end of the scale, the requirements in the Efficiency stage were: sound attainments in biblical knowledge, English grammar, composition, etymology, decimal arithmetic, geography (especially of the British Empire and of Palestine), the outlines of English history, and in the theory and art of organising and managing a school.[424]

The government's funding of workhouse schools also required that they open to regular official inspection. The inspectors' reports were often forthright, although it was often the children rather than their teachers who bore the brunt of criticism. At Pateley Bridge workhouse in 1857, it was reported that 'the children here, as on former occasions, were deplorably ignorant. None could tell what country they lived in, or work a sum of any kind.'

The teachers' private lives also occasionally came under scrutiny. At Southwell in 1851, the inspector commented that 'the cause of the compulsory resignation of the late master and mistress is a remarkable instance of the low tone of morality so frequently exhibited by the present race of workhouse teachers. She was old enough to have been his mother.'[425] His concluding comment referred to the fact that the former schoolmistress, thirty-eight-year-old Maria Richardson, had become pregnant by the schoolmaster, William Sumner, seventeen years her junior.

In 1850, the Committee of Council opened a new training school for workhouse teachers at Kneller Hall near Twickenham. However, the scheme was not successful and failed to attract sufficient applicants. The school closed in 1855 and in 1857 the building was acquired by the army as the home for the Royal Military School of Music, which it remains to the present day. (*See also:* **Children**; **Workhouse Schools**)

KNELLER HALL TRAINING SCHOOL.

Above right An 1850 view of the training school for workhouse teachers at Kneller Hall near Twickenham. After the school's closure in 1855, the building was acquired by the army as the home for the Royal Military School of Music.

Above left An 1877 job advertisement for a workhouse resident schoolmistress. The duties of the post went beyond the classroom – the successful applicant was required to give her whole time to the care of the children.

TEST WORKHOUSE

A 'test' workhouse accommodated only able-bodied paupers and enforced a particularly strict regime of work and discipline.

The first test workhouse was operated by the London's Poplar Union from 1871 to 1882 in what became known as the 'Poplar Experiment', with spare capacity being offered to other London unions and parishes. It was established following the 'minute' published in 1869 by Poor Law Board president George Goschen which aimed to reduce out relief, especially to those not totally destitute.[426] Offering able-bodied relief claimants the test workhouse provided means of deterring those with less pressing needs that could be met from other sources, such as charitable organisations.

From 1882, Poplar's role was taken on by the St Mary Abbot's workhouse at Mary Place, Notting Hill. Some new metropolitan workhouses erected during this period also included test sections where stricter conditions could be imposed on able-bodied inmates. These included Lambeth's workhouse on Renfrew Road, opened in 1874, and the Wandsworth and Clapham workhouse on Garratt Lane opened in 1886. In 1888, Lambeth rebuilt its Princes Road premises as a test workhouse. In all these establishments, there was some differentiation between the treatment of those classed as being of good or of bad character, with the latter usually being required to work in isolation rather than with a group of other inmates.

A few authorities outside the capital also set up test workhouses. At Birmingham, in 1881, a 'test house' for 100 men was erected on the existing workhouse site. The facilities included cubicles for stone breaking and chopping wood, and a laundry where inmates were required to wash their own clothing. Other unions erecting test workhouses included West Derby (Belmont Road, 1890), Manchester (Tame Street, 1897), and Bradford (Daisy Hill, 1912) – possibly the last new workhouse ever to be opened.

(*See also*: **Labour Test; Poplar Experiment**)

TOBACCO

As with spirits, the use of tobacco by workhouse inmates was frequently banned or severely restricted. In 1725, *An Account of Several Workhouses* recorded that at the St Giles's Cripplegate workhouse in London none of the inmates was to 'smoak Tobacco in their Lodgings, or the Workhouse'. Some establishments were a little more tolerant, however. At the Portsea workhouse in 1795, those who used tobacco were each given a weekly allowance of 2oz. Some workhouses gave tobacco allowances only to those who were well behaved – at Stone in Staffordshire, in 1810, such inmates could receive up to 1oz a week.[427]

During this period, tobacco would have been smoked in a clay pipe, sniffed in the form of snuff, or chewed – cigarettes did not come into widespread use in England until the second half of the nineteenth century.

If tobacco was allowed in a workhouse, there were often restrictions on where or when smoking could take place. Smoking in bed, a great fire hazard, was often specifically prohibited – the rules for Hackney parish workhouse in the 1750s stipulated that 'no person of either sex be allowed to smoke in Bed, or in any bed-chamber of the house'. At the Kendal workhouse in 1793, anyone caught smoking in their bed or in their room could be put in the dungeon for six hours. At Lacock in Wiltshire in the 1770s, smoking was forbidden in the workhouse except in the workrooms. Anticipating present-day trends in this matter, smoking was often restricted to outdoors areas. The Leeds parish workhouse placed a ban on smoking after 7 p.m. in winter and 8 p.m. in summer.[428]

At Manchester in the 1790s, no tobacco was to be brought into the workhouse unless ordered by the workhouse surgeon or weekly Board meeting. Such prescriptions were apparently issued reasonably often – in 1792–93, the workhouse spent a total of £39 10s 6d on snuff and tobacco. Snuff was usually treated in much the same way as tobacco except presumably for the restrictions on where it could be used. At Halifax workhouse, tobacco users and snuff users were each allowed 8oz a month of their preferred pleasure.[429]

In the union workhouses established following the 1834 Poor Law Amendment Act, regulations decreed that 'No pauper shall smoke in any room of the Workhouse, except by the special direction of the Medical Officer'. As with beer, an exception could be made on special occasions such as Christmas Day, or the marriage of Queen Victoria in 1840.

Restrictions in the use of tobacco led to an undercover economy at many workhouses. At the inquiry into the Andover scandal in 1845, an inmate named Samuel Green described how workhouse bread could be used as a currency to buy tobacco:

> I did not eat my bread any one morning in the week. I did not eat it, but not because I had too much. I used to sell it to buy a bit of 'bacco. I used to sell it in the workhouse. Most all the people who take 'bacco, sell their bread. 'Bacco is a very wholesome thing, especially in such a place as the workhouse.[430]

By the 1870s, tobacco allowances for certain inmates were being provided in some workhouses. A visitor to the Chorlton Union workhouse at Withington observed screws of snuff and tobacco awaiting distribution but noted that 'the quantity of the latter given out weekly does not appear to be sufficient for the smokers, and is usually eked out with tea-leaves'.[431] A decade later, a visitor to the same establishment recorded that the old men smoked 'tobacco when they can get it, and dandelion leaves, or even old rags when they cannot come by the genuine article'.[432]

A relaxation in the general prohibition came in 1892 when the Local Government Board pronounced that tobacco and snuff could be allowed to inmates who 'are not able-bodied or are employed upon work of a specially disagreeable character'.[433] It was up to each Board of Guardians to decide whether and how to make use of this measure. In 1902 at Stoke-on-Trent, for example, elderly men were given 1oz of tobacco each week while the women instead received an extra 2oz of tea and 8oz of sugar.[434]

(*See also*: **Alcohol**; **Tea**)

Looking almost like city gents on their lunch-break, elderly male inmates at St Marylebone workhouse in 1901 enjoy a quiet smoke and perusal of the day's newspapers.

TOKE

A colloquial name for bread, particularly associated with those frequenting the workhouse casual ward.
(*See also*: **Casual Ward**; **Skilly**; **Tommy**)

TOKENS

(*See*: **Workhouse Tokens**)

TOMMY

A tramp's term for food.
(*See*: **Casual Ward**; **Skilly**; **Toke**)

TRADE PRESS

From the 1830s onwards, the poor relief system developed its own trade press providing guardians, union officers and workhouse employees with news, information, advice and a forum for discussion. The publications also provided a platform for advertisers to promote their wares, and for unions to advertise for staff and the supply of goods.

One of the earliest poor law publications was *The Guardian; or Poor Law Register* published monthly by William Potts of Banbury. Its inaugural issue, on 5 April 1838, declared that its aim was:

To record, and to present in a cheap and convenient form, the general proceedings and statistics of the Unions surrounding Banbury; to diffuse information respecting the New Poor Law; and to afford a medium for fairly canvassing and discussing its principles.

The Guardian continued in operation until May 1843 when it became a weekly general newspaper.

The Poor Law Guide, and Union Advertiser, launched in 1843, was a weekly publication produced in London and edited by Charles Mott. The paper traded on the fact that Mott was a former Assistant Poor Law Commissioner – he had lost his post at the end of 1842 when the number of Assistant Commissioners was reduced. The *Guide* contained a mixture of articles on poor law topics, news items from unions around the country, readers' letters, and a few advertisements. A running feature for the first few months was a column on workhouse management. Issue 15, for example, included advice and recipes for making soup. The paper was not successful, however, and ceased publication at the end of 1843 after forty-three issues.

The even shorter-lived *Municipal & Poor Law Gazette and Local Functionary* ran for a mere fifteen editions between January and April 1844. By comparison, *The Poor Law Chronicle*, launched in July 1866, was a runaway success. Catchily proclaiming itself as a 'journal of intercommunication for the officers administering the poor law in England and Wales,' it survived a whole seventy-four issues before folding in 1869.

The creation of county councils following the 1888 Local Government Act spawned several new titles including the *County Council Gazette* and the *County Council Times*. The weekly *Parish Councillor*, launched in 1894, briefly became the *Councillor* then in 1897, perhaps still struggling to gain a foothold, tried to cover all bases as the *Councillor and Guardian*. Optimistically, the paper subtitled itself as 'the leading organ of local government and the poor law' but finally closed in 1904.

Not all poor law papers were short-lived, however. The weekly *Poor Law Unions Gazette* ran for sixty years from 1843 to 1903. It was also unusual in another respect. It consisted entirely of 'wanted' advertisements, placed by Poor Law Unions, for persons who had deserted their spouses or families, leaving them to be supported by the poor rates. The advertisements often contained detailed pen-portraits of their subjects, specifying their physical appearance, clothing, and so on. Because of its particular purpose, unions could charge their use of the paper to the poor rates.

Another long-running title was the *Poor Law Officers' Journal* (subtitled *The Organ of the Service*), published from 1892 through to the abolition of the Boards of Guardians in 1930 when it was re-titled the *Public Assistance Journal and Health and Hospital Review*. The *Journal* was effectively the house paper of the National Association of Poor Law Officers and lobbied for changes that would improve staff conditions, especially for those employed in workhouses. It therefore welcomed Labour-dominated Boards of Guardians, as these were expected to be

A delightful pen portrait of absconding husband John Rowlands – a typical 'wanted' ad from the *Poor Law Unions Gazette* in 1860.

> ### RUTHIN UNION.
>
> Clerk—Mr. BENJAMIN DAVIS, Ruthin.
>
> JOHN ROWLANDS, of Llanarmon, miner, aged 24, about 5 feet 7 inches high, stout, curly red hair, scanty whiskers, a mark on left eye, the tip of one of his little fingers cut off, fond of drink, and rather quarrelsome, knows a little English ; he has taken with him a dark plaid waistcoat with white buttons, black Jim Crow hat ; left his family the end of May chargeable to the above parish : is supposed to be in the neighbourhood of Llanrwst, or somewhere in Canarvonshire.
>
> Ten Shillings Reward and all reasonable expenses will be paid for his apprehension.

THE

Local Government Chronicle

AND

KNIGHT'S OFFICIAL ADVERTISER,

SENT TO ALL

Boards of Guardians and Sanitary Authorities

PUBLISHED EVERY SATURDAY.

| No. 691.] { Registered at the General Post Office as a Newspaper. } | SEPTEMBER 6, 1880. | { WEEKLY, 3d., or 3½d. by Post. SUBSCRIPTION, 12s. PER ANNUM, Paid in Advance, Including Postage. |

St. Pancras, Middlesex.
CONTRACTS FOR PROVISIONS, CLOTH-ING, AND SUNDRIES.

THE Guardians of the Poor of this Parish hereby give notice that they are prepared to receive and consider proposals for the supply of the following Articles for the Workhouse and Leavesden School, viz. :—

1. Meat.
2. Australian Pre-served Meat.
3. Pickled Pork.
4. Meat to Out-door Poor.
5. Flour.
6. Tea.
7. Cheesemongery.
8. Grocery.
9. Cornchandlery.
10. Horse Provender.
11. Eggs.
12. Milk.
13. Spirits.
14. Drugs.
15. Soap.
16. Oilman's Goods.
17. Haberdashery.
18. Hosiery.
19. Linen Drapery.
20. Woollen Drapery.
21. Boys' Clothing.
22. Leather & Grind-ery.
23. Printing.
24. Stationery.
25. Brushes, Brooms, &c.
26. Ironmongery.
27. Oils, Colours, &c.
28. Timber.
29. Officers' Uniforms.
30. Sweeping Chim-neys at the Work-house.

The Guardians are also prepared to receive proposals for the purchase of Bones, Old Iron, &c. Samples of Provisions, Clothing, and Sundries may be seen on application to the Master of the Workhouse, King's-road, Pan-

Leeds Union.
FEMALE COOK.

THE Guardians of this Union require the services of an intelligent, active, practical, and trustworthy Female Cook for their Workhouse.

Applicants must have a prior knowledge of the duties of the office, and be unmarried, or widows without encumbrance, not exceeding forty years of age, and willing to render such general assistance to the Matron as may be required.

Applications to be in candidates' own hand-writing, stating age, whether single or widow, present and prior employments, and accom-panied by three recent testimonials as to cha-racter and competency, to be sent to me not later than Saturday, 18th September instant. Canvassing the Guardians will disqualify an applicant.—By order,

JNO. KING, Clerk to the Guardians.
Union Offices, East Parade, Leeds,
September 1, 1880.

Tonbridge Union.
PORTER AND LABOUR MASTER WANTED.

WANTED, a strong, able-bodied Man, be-tween the ages of 23 and 45, as a Porter and Labour Master, at the Workhouse of the

Prescot Union.

THE Guardians of this Union are desirous of receiving applications from persons competent to undertake the duties of MASTER and MATRON of the Workhouse. Candidates must be man and wife, prepared to enter upon their duties immediately on their appointment receiving the sanction of the Local Government Board, and the Master must be fully competent to keep the books and accounts, and to perform the duties required by the Guardians and the Local Government Board.

The Matron must likewise be able to perform all the duties required of her by the Orders of the Local Government Board, and to superin-tend the whole of the domestic arrangements of the Workhouse. The salary of the Master will be £100, and that of the Matron £60 per annum, with rations and furnished apartments.

Applications, in candidates' own handwrit-ing, stating age, previous occupation, and num-ber of family (if any), with copies of recent testimonials (which will not be returned), to be delivered to me not later than six o'clock p.m. on Monday, the 18th instant.

Canvassing the Guardians will be a disquali-fication.

S. H. HARTLEY, Union Clerk.
Union Offices, Whiston, Prescot,
September 1, 1880.

A selection of advertisements from the *Local Government Chronicle*, still in production today after more than 150 years. Some items would fall foul of modern legislation – the cook required at Leeds was to be female, under forty, single or widowed, and 'without encumbrance' i.e. having no dependent children.

more generous towards union employees, and criticised the 1905 Royal Commission's major-ity report proposals for county-based poor-relief authorities which the *Journal* believed might bring heavier workloads or redundancies.[435]

The most enduring publication of all, though, was *Knight's Official Advertiser of Local Management in England and Wales* which began life in 1855. *Knight's* was originally a monthly paper, becoming fortnightly from 1866 then weekly from 1872 when it was renamed the *Local Government Chronicle and Knight's Official Advertiser*. The paper is still in production today as the *Local Government Chronicle*. Originally, copies were distributed free to bodies such as Poor Law Unions, boards of health and town councils, with income largely being derived from advertis-ing. Editorially, the paper's aim was 'to furnish information of a practical character upon every essential question that belongs to our Local Management System, Metropolitan and Provincial; and to supply a Current Register of Official Appointments and Elections.'

North of the border, the *Poor Law Magazine for Scotland*, published monthly with several variations of name from 1858 to 1903, was, as its name suggests, more of a journal than a news-paper. Although news reports and correspondence did feature in its content, the magazine was largely concerned with reporting legal matters of concern to parochial boards.

For poor law medical officers, the main publication of interest was the *British Medical Journal*, both for its general medical content and also for the information it regularly carried about the activities of the Poor Law Medical Association. From 1911 until just after the First World War it carried a short monthly supplement entitled *The Poor Law Medical Officer*.

TRAINING SHIPS

Training ships were residential sailing vessels where boys were trained in seafaring skills, often as a prelude to entering service in the Royal or Merchant Navy.

The earliest training ships were run by the Marine Society, an organisation founded in 1756 by Jonas Hanway who was also a governor of the London Foundling Hospital and promoter of the 1766 Act removing young children from London workhouses. The Marine Society began life recruiting boys and young men for the Royal Navy at the beginning of the Seven Years War against France. In an effort to reduce desertions, it started to train its boys before they were sent to sea. In 1876, the Society acquired the *Warspite* for use as a training ship, and by 1911 had sent 65,667 men and boys to sea, of whom 28,538 had gone into the Royal Navy.

The Royal Navy's own first training ship was HMS *Implacable* at Plymouth in 1855, followed by HMS *Illustrious* at Portsmouth. The vessels aimed to give a training in naval life, skills and discipline to teenage boys (or 'lads' as they invariably called) and to provide a ready source of recruits for Her Majesty's ships. Over the next fifty years, around thirty other training ships were set up by a variety of other organisations, both public and private. The various ships – mostly old wooden battleships – catered for boys from a diverse range of backgrounds. These ranged from fee-paying prospective Merchant Navy officers on the *Worcester*, to boys from workhouses on ships such as the *Exmouth*, and those placed by magistrates on vessels operating as Reformatory or Industrial Schools such as the *Cornwall*. Some ships, such as the *Wellesley*, moored on the Tyne off North Shields, were both certified as Industrial Schools and also took boys placed there by poor law authorities. Training ships that took boys from poor law establishments are listed in the table below.

Training Ship	Location
Arethusa and *Chichester*	Greenhithe, Kent
Clio	Menai Straits, North Wales
Cumberland and *Empress*	River Clyde, Glasgow
Formidable / *National Nautical School*	Portishead, near Bristol
Goliath and *Exmouth*	Grays, Essex
Indefatigable	New Ferry, Birkenhead
Mercury	Hamble, Southampton
Mount Edgcumbe	Saltash, Cornwall
Southampton	Hull
Warspite	Woolwich
Wellesley	North Shields
Lancashire Sea Training Homes	Liscard, Cheshire (land-based)

A paper read by Geoffrey Drage (MP for Derby) at the Central Poor Law Conference in February 1904 extolled the virtues of training ships such as the *Exmouth*:

> In the first place the life is a healthy one for the boys, their physical development is carefully attended to, their education from an intellectual point of view is adequate, and they receive at the age at which they can most readily profit by it that technical training which at any rate as far as the sea is concerned, can only be properly acquired at an early age. More than all, the so-called stigma of pauperism is removed, and the boys are sent out into the world with a profession of national utility and under the aegis of the name of their training ship, and, when the training ship has an established position, it is an enormous advantage to a boy in after-life, to be able to claim association with it.
>
> The advantages of the Navy as a career can hardly be over-estimated. Quite apart from the great traditions of the service and the universal respect which the uniform inspires, there is the substantial fact that a boy who goes from the *Exmouth* into a naval training ship can at the age of 40 secure a pension of over £50 for life. What is more, there are few, if any, recorded instances of a blue-jacket receiving relief from the poor law.

The *Exmouth* was the only vessel whose intake was entirely from poor law establishments, largely confined to those run by metropolitan authorities. In January 1911, it had a full complement of 641 boys resident. At the same date, the national total of pauper boys placed on vessels other than the *Exmouth* was only 463, coming from just 131 unions.[436] One factor in this limited take-up may have been the cost of maintaining boys on training ships, typically 8 or 9s a week or a one-off lump sum, which was generally a little higher than keeping them in a workhouse or union children's establishment. A payment might also be required for a boy's uniform.

With the advent of steam power, naval crews became smaller and the demand for boys steadily declined, particularly in the Merchant Service. Many of the original wooden training ships also became unseaworthy or, as in the case of the *Warspite* and *Wellesley*, were destroyed by fire. Those that continued increasingly transferred their operations onto land-based premises. Some survived until the end of the twentieth century but were then forced to close by a reduction in demand for places and in their funding.

The Chichester

Typical of the ships taking boys from poor backgrounds was the *Chichester*, originally established in 1866 under the patronage of Lord Shaftesbury, a philanthropist and campaigner for children's rights. Shaftesbury persuaded the Admiralty to loan the *Chichester*, a redundant fifty-gun frigate, on which fifty boys from a London children's refuge would be housed and trained. The scheme was managed by a committee of the 'National Refuges for Homeless and Destitute Children'.

The ship's first commanding officer was the recently retired Captain A.H. Alston, a devout Christian but stern disciplinarian. Other staff included a chief officer, a schoolmaster and two instructors – all lived on board and worked a seven-day week. The chief officer's wife taught the boys how to cut out and make their own clothes from material supplied by the Naval Yard at Deptford.

An early task was teaching the boys to swim, although there were several instances of boys falling overboard and drowning. To help with this problem, a barge was moored to the head of the ship and filled with water to act as makeshift swimming pool. Training on the *Chichester* include work in compass and lead, knotting and splicing, sail-making, knowledge of all running gear and parts of ship, reefing and furling sails, and rowing and steering, not to mention time spent in swimming, cooking, carpentry and tailoring.

One bureaucratic problem that afflicted training ships was that the Royal Navy refused to accept anyone not in possession of a birth certificate. Many of the boys had no idea of their parentage let alone a birth certificate. Lord Shaftesbury managed to persuade the Admiralty to waive this rule for *Chichester* boys, provided they declared their age and agreed to serve for a specified period.

The ship had strict rules about use of the birch as a punishment – birchings could only be administered by the captain and up to a maximum of twenty-four 'cuts'. The birching scale ranged from twenty-four cuts and dismissal with disgrace for any act of gross indecency or immoral behaviour, to twelve cuts and dismissal for stealing, and six cuts for being in an

Lads aboard the training ship *Arethusa* being taught the finer points of compass drill in about 1900.

A dramatic view of the training ship *Wellesley* destroyed by fire at its North Shields mooring in 1914. Several other wooden training ships met a similar fate.

improper place. Absconding earned twelve cuts, although a second offence brought dismissal from the ship.

Food on the vessel was limited in both quantity and variety. The daily dietary scale for many years comprised 1lb soft bread, 8oz biscuit, 7oz fresh meat, 8oz potatoes, ¾oz cocoa, ⅛oz tea and ⅔oz sugar, plus occasional green vegetables and twice-weekly rations of pea soup and rice, and treacle pudding as a treat on Sundays.

The *Chichester* began taking workhouse boys from early in 1895, with forty-three being received over the following year. By the end of 1897, eleven of these had entered the Royal Navy, twelve had entered the Merchant Service, one had joined the training ship *Worcester* as a steward, six had been sent back to their unions as unfit, and thirteen were still on board.
(*See also*: **Exmouth and Goliath**; **Industrial Schools – Certified**; **Reformatory / Reformatory School**)

TRAMP MAJOR

A person, usually a tramp or former tramp himself, sometimes employed in a workhouse casual ward to undertake tasks such as supervising new admissions and the preparation of food.
(*See also*: **Casual Ward**)

TRAMPS

(*See*: **Casual Poor**; **Casual Ward**)

TREASURER

The Treasurer was an officer appointed by each Poor Law Union's Board of Guardians who was responsible for administering the union's financial transactions. The Treasurer had to be at least twenty-one years of age and to provide a bond with two guarantors in case any financial irregularities arose during his tenure. At Abingdon in 1835, the newly appointed treasurer, Henry Knapp, was required to give sureties for the then very substantial sum of £2,000.

The post of Treasurer could be paid or unpaid; in the latter case, any profits arising from the use of union funds while in the Treasurer's hands were deemed to be payment for his services.

TRUANT SCHOOLS

So-called 'Truant Schools' were a special type of Certified Industrial School which appeared in the wake of the 1876 Elementary Education Act. Children who persistently refused to attend elementary schools could be detained at a Truant School, typically for one to three months, under a very strict regime, and then released on a renewable licence to attend a normal school. The first Truant Schools to be established were in London (1878), Liverpool (1878) and Sheffield (1879), with fifteen in operation in England and Wales by 1893.
(*See also*: **Industrial Schools – Certified**)

TUBERCULOSIS (TB)

Tuberculosis (TB) or 'consumption' is a contagious bacterial disease which most often affects those living in overcrowded or insanitary conditions, or who have a poor diet or a weakened immune system. TB often attacks the lungs, a condition known as phthisis. Tuberculosis, especially in the form of phthisis, became a major concern in the latter part of the nineteenth century, and was particularly common in urban areas where the poor generally lived in cramped and unhealthy accommodation. Its nature was not properly understood until the identification of the tubercle bacillus in 1882.

Prior to the development of anti-bacterial drugs, the most usual treatment for TB was confinement to a suitably located sanatorium which provided fresh air, regarded as especially beneficial for phthisis sufferers, and isolation from the community. An early example of such an establishment was the London Open Air Sanatorium opened in 1901 in woodlands near Wokingham by the recently formed National Association for the Prevention of Tuberculosis. Wider provision for the treatment of TB came in the wake of the 1911 National Insurance Act which included a 'sanatorium benefit'. Since the poor were often especially vulnerable to TB, arrangements for its treatment also began to be made by some poor law authorities.

In London, the Metropolitan Asylums Board initially provided beds at two of its existing institutions at Sutton in Surrey and at Winchmore Hill in north London, then in 1919 took over the Open Air Sanatorium at Wokingham. This was followed by the conversion in 1920 of the Colindale Hospital at Hendon, and in 1922 of St Luke's Hospital, a former hotel at Lowestoft. Shortly afterwards, the purpose-built King George V Sanatorium was opened at Godalming. Finally, in 1926, the former Greenwich Union workhouse at Lee in south-east London was converted to become the Grove Park Hospital. For children with TB, the Board acquired and expanded the East Cliff Home at Margate (known as Princess Mary's Hospital from 1910). Surgical cases were also treated at the Queen Mary's Hospital in Carshalton.

Outside London, the Liverpool, West Derby and Toxteth Park Joint Committee established a sanatorium in 1902 at Heswall, on the Wirral, for the treatment of phthisis in children. Tuberculosis sanatoriums were also opened by the Bradford Union in 1903 at Eastby, by Rotherham (for men only) in 1911 at Badsley Moor, by Gateshead in 1912 at Shotley Bridge, and by Merthyr Tydfil in 1913 at Pontsarn. Some other unions added provision at an existing site, such as the new isolation block and tuberculosis ward completed in 1903 at the Mansfield Union workhouse or the phthisis wards opened in 1908 at Kettering workhouse, in 1911 at Sunderland, and in 1914 at Hull and Portsmouth. Poor law TB facilities generally included more beds for men than for women since curing a male breadwinner might result in a whole family no longer needing poor relief.[437] The Public Health (Tuberculosis) Act of 1921 gave county authorities responsibility for TB care, with provision for the poor being free.

Young tuberculosis patients take outdoor exercise on specially constructed trolleys at Queen Mary's Hospital for Children, opened by the Metropolitan Asylums Board in 1909 at Carshalton in Surrey.

The Merthyr Tydfil Union's tuberculosis sanatorium opened near Pontsarn, Vaynor, in 1913.

Care for TB patients in Wales was provided by the King Edward VII Welsh National Memorial Association, set up in 1910 to combat the prevalence of TB in the country. The Association operated a number of TB hospitals on behalf of Welsh county and borough councils, including two located in former workhouses – at Tregaron from 1915 and at Machynlleth from 1920.

(*See also*: **Medical Care**)

TURKISH BATHS

A Turkish bath provides a flow of hot dry air in which the bather sweats profusely, usually followed by a cold water body wash. Turkish baths became popular in Britain in the 1860s and also made their way into a few workhouses and other institutions, usually at the recommendation of an enthusiastic medical officer. The first recorded instance of such use appears to be at the Cork district lunatic asylum in 1861 with the Dundrum criminal asylum in Dublin and Limerick district lunatic asylum following shortly afterwards. A number of lunatic asylums in England and Wales also installed baths including the Sussex county asylum at Brighton in 1862 where it was thought beneficial in cases of melancholia.

The first workhouse Turkish bath was installed in 1863 at Lismore in County Waterford. All of the inmates, apart from the extremely old and infirm, used it weekly. Turkish baths were subsequently installed at other Irish workhouses including Midleton, Fermoy and Clones.[438] In 1895, the Croom workhouse in County Limerick had a Russian bath, slightly different to the Turkish bath in that it employed steam or vapour rather than dry air.

In England, the King's Lynn workhouse had a Turkish bath in operation by 1864. One was also installed in 1876 at the Metropolitan Asylums Board imbeciles' asylum at Leavesden, using hot air from the adjacent laundry. It was for the benefit of both staff and patients, but was to be used only on Sundays and Wednesdays. The medical superintendent reported that it would 'be of a great advantage to the Staff, especially the Female portion, who suffer to a large extent from biliousness consequent on their restricted and somewhat repressed life.'[439]

(*See also*: **Swimming Baths; Washing and Bathing**)

TWINING, LOUISA

Louisa Twining, born in 1820, was a granddaughter of Richard Twining, the head of the firm of tea and coffee merchants. In 1853, she was granted permission by the Strand Union's Board of Guardians to visit a Mrs Stapleton, a former nurse of her acquaintance, now resident in the union's Cleveland Street workhouse. Her discovery of the feelings of neglect experienced by the inmates led her to organise a scheme amongst her friends for visiting the Strand and other London workhouses. Although initially co-operative, the Strand guardians withdrew their permission in 1857 after the Poor Law Board expressed reservations about such activities. However, Twining continued her vigorous campaigning through lectures, pamphlets, letters to the press, and the founding in 1858 of the Workhouse Visiting Society, a body which did much to make the life of workhouse inmates more tolerable.

Becoming known as an authority on workhouses, she was consulted by the Poor Law Board on matters such as pauper schools and her proposals also led to the appointment of Mrs Nassau Senior as the first female Poor Law Inspector in 1872. In 1879, she set up the Workhouse Infirmary Nursing Association to help increase the use of trained nurses in workhouses. In 1881, she helped finance the Association for Promoting the Return of Women as Poor Law Guardians and was herself elected as one of the first female guardians at Kensington in 1884, later continuing this activity at Tunbridge Wells where she died in 1912.

(*See also*: **Workhouse Visiting Society; Workhouse Infirmary Nursing Association**; Twining (1880))

UNIFORMS

(*See*: **Clothing**)

UNION

A grouping of parishes or townships jointly administering poor law affairs, usually in order to achieve economy or efficiency of operation. The term first came into general use following the passing in 1782 of

An 1869 portrait of workhouse reformer Louisa Twining.

Gilbert's Act which encouraged the formation of such alliances. The word 'union' was also used as an informal name for the union workhouse.

(*See also*: **Poor Law Unions**)

UNION COUNTIES

(*See*: **Poor Law Counties / Union Counties**)

UNMARRIED MOTHERS

(*See*: **Illegitimacy**)

VACCINATION

In 1840, Poor Law Unions were given charge of a new national smallpox vaccination scheme. Although funded from the poor rates and largely carried out by union medical officers, the service offered free vaccination for all, not just the poor. From 1853, smallpox vaccination became compulsory for all infants under four months old. Workhouse children were a prime target for the scheme and could be vaccinated without their parents' consent.

Where they survive, vaccination registers – part of each Poor Law Union's records – may include information such as a child's parents, home address, and date of birth.

(*See also*: **Ireland**; **Medical Care**)

VAGRANTS

(*See*: **Casual Poor**; **Casual Ward**)

VENEREAL DISEASE

Institutional treatment for venereal diseases such as syphilis is usually said to have its origin at the 'Lock lazar-house' at Southwark, with 'lock' subsequently becoming a synonym for 'venereal'. In the sixteenth century, two of London's Royal Hospitals – St Thomas's and St Bartholomew's – offered treatment for the city's poor afflicted with venereal diseases.

From the early 1700s, the medical provision in parish workhouses, in London at least, increasingly included care for lock cases. They were usually treated – ineffectually – with mercury, which was believed to purge the body of the disease through increased salivation. Those being treated in workhouse were mainly women, the elderly and children under sixteen, while adult men were more likely to resort to fee-paying hospitals.[440]

An alternative source of treatment came through London's charitably funded Lock Hospital which was opened in 1747. Forty years later, when the associated Lock Asylum for the Reception of Penitent Women was founded, both institutions had as much the aim of moral reform as of medical treatment. Some voluntary hospitals would offer a one-off course treatment for venereal cases, but any recurrence – a not unlikely event – would not be dealt with.

The workhouse continued to be the primary refuge of many poor venereal patients who were generally placed in their own segregated part of the workhouse known as the lock wards or foul wards. This situation continued into the era of the New Poor Law, with conditions in foul wards sometimes being described in abysmal terms, such as in the 1866 report by Poor Law Inspector R.B. Cane on Blackburn workhouse:

> There are large wards near the entrance lodge which contain cases of 'venereal disease,' and 'bad legs.' The porter and his wife are supposed to look after these cases, but they appear for the most part to be left to themselves. In the male ward were eight or ten men walking about almost naked. I was told 'they were getting their dinners.' The condition of the inmates of this ward was most distressing and painful to witness.[441]

Provision for venereal treatment improved from 1910 onwards with the development of the anti-syphilitic drug Salvarsan. The Venereal Diseases Act of 1917 provided for local authority clinics to give free and confidential treatment to venereal patients, while London's Metropolitan Asylums Board set up two specialist women's hospitals.
(*See also*: **Medical Care**; **Metropolitan Asylums Board**)

VESTRY

The governing committee of a parish. Its name derived from the room in a church building in which it usually met, which in turn came from its function as a room where the priest put on his vestments. Its membership comprised a chairman (the minister of the parish), the church-wardens, and a number of respected householders from the parish.
(*See also*: **Select Vestry**)

VISITING COMMITTEE

The Visiting Committee was a sub-committee of a union's Board of Guardians which visited the workhouse at regular intervals. Its role was to check that the workhouse was being run in accordance with regulations, that the inmates were being treated properly, and to listen to any complaints. The results of the inspections were recorded in an official Visitors' Book. As guidance, the Committee was given fourteen specific questions to address at each visit covering various aspects of the operation of the workhouse, the condition of the workhouse premises, and the treatment of the inmates – especially children and the sick.

In 1893, Boards of Guardians were empowered to set up a Ladies Visiting Committee, whose members were not required themselves to be guardians, to inspect and report on parts of the workhouse used by children or female inmates.
(*See also*: **Board of Guardians; House Committee**)

VISITING WORKHOUSE INMATES

The regulations instituted by the Poor Law Commissioners allowed union workhouse inmates to receive visitors subject to the permission of the workhouse master. Except in the case of sick inmates, such visits had to take place in a separate room and in the presence of the master, matron or porter. This was all subject 'to such conditions and restrictions as the Guardians may prescribe', so arranging a visit was not necessarily straightforward. Louisa Twining, visiting an inmate of the Strand Union workhouse in the 1850s, first needed to obtain an order from the chairman of the Board of Guardians.[442]

Later on in the century, following the efforts of the Workhouse Visiting Society, access for visitors generally improved. Some workhouses specified fixed (though not necessarily frequent) visiting periods, at least for the sick, with an admission ticket needing to be obtained prior to the visit. Presents for inmates were allowed only by permission of the workhouse master. At Manchester's Crumpsall workhouse in 1879, sick and infirm inmates could receive visits of up to thirty minutes on the first Saturday in each month.[443] At the same date, Bradford workhouse allowed hour-long visits to the sick, aged and infirm on Monday morning each week, with children being allowed to receive a monthly visit. Except in case of sickness, Bradford prohibited visits to women in the disorderly wards, women with illegitimate children, pregnant unmarried women, and women deserted by their husbands. Similar regulations were still in force in 1920.[444]

Sadly, many workhouse inmates never had a visitor. In 1909, a report on the Kendal's union's Milnthorpe workhouse noted that visitors were permitted at any time, but that of its 101 inmates, only fifteen ever had any, and then often only once or twice a year.[445]

(*See also*: **Leaving a Workhouse**; **Workhouse Visiting Society**)

VISITOR

A person, appointed by Justices under Gilbert's Act of 1782, to oversee the operation of a Gilbert Union and its workhouse. The Visitor had the power to issue orders to the treasurer of the union and to the governor of the workhouse.

(*See also*: **Gilbert Union**)

VOLUNTARY HOMES

Voluntary homes were independently run residential establishments, often operated by charitable or religious bodies, providing accommodation and care for persons in need such as orphans or single mothers. Some homes were officially regulated and certified for taking particular categories of inmate, such as children placed by poor law authorities or magistrates' courts.

(*See also*: **Certified Schools (Poor Law)**; **Children**; **Industrial Schools – Certified**)

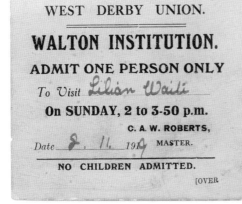

A ticket issued in 1919 by Liverpool's West Derby Union allowing the bearer to visit Lilian Waite, an inmate of the Walton-on-the-Hill workhouse. As noted on the reverse, the taking of alcohol into the workhouse was strictly forbidden.

WALES

Following the Acts of Union (1536–43) Wales was generally administered under the same laws as England. Thus, the Poor Law Acts of 1597 and 1601 and successive poor law legislation applied to Wales as well as England.

One Welsh county, the border county of Monmouthshire, has a peculiar status. After its name was omitted from the second Act of Union in 1543, the misguided notion arose that it was not truly part of Wales. Monmouthshire is thus often found listed in the English section of old directories, and administrative references to Wales often use the term 'Wales and Monmouthshire'.

Up to 1834

Prior to 1834, parishes in Wales predominantly supported their poor with out relief and relatively little use was made of indoor relief through the establishment of a workhouse. A parliamentary survey of 1777 recorded around 2,000 workhouses operating in England but only nineteen in Wales, of which more than half were in Pembrokeshire.

Wales also made little use of Gilbert's Act of 1782 which allowed parishes, either alone or in groups, to establish workhouses for the aged and infirm, and children. A rare exception was Llantrisant in Glamorgan where in December 1783, the parish vestry resolved to establish a workhouse in or near the town. Initially, and contrary to Gilbert's Act, able-bodied paupers were admitted but were subsequently barred from residence.

In 1792, Montgomery, Pool, and thirteen other nearby parishes, promoted a local Act of Parliament to establish the Montgomery and Pool Incorporation. The Incorporation, run by a twenty-four-man board of directors, spent £12,000 on erecting a workhouse or 'House of Industry'. The building was to house up to 1,000 inmates, making it amongst the largest in the whole of England and Wales at that time.

A further parliamentary survey in 1815 found that fifty-nine Welsh parishes were now 'maintaining the greater part of their poor' in workhouses. Since several parishes could share a workhouse, the number of workhouses in operation may well be somewhat less than this figure.

In the spring of 1836, Assistant Poor Law Commissioner George Clive visited the southern part of Wales and catalogued a multitude of malpractices and poor conditions:

> Many workhouses are rented in the county of Monmouth; in the parishes now forming the Monmouth Union, nearly £150 is annually paid in rent for them, exclusive of course of cottages rented for the poor. In only one or two of these houses is there any attempt at

The Montgomery and Pool Incorporation workhouse opened in 1795 near Forden in Montgomeryshire. The building was capable of holding up to 1,000 inmates.

a dietary or employment, in none classification, in the generality every kind of abuse. In Monythusloine poorhouse the contractor keeps a shop; different families have apartments in the house; the whole is filthy to the last degree. In one room was a woman who has had nine bastard children, the last confessedly born in the house and from the time she had been resident there, doubtless many more.

In Coleford poorhouse I found an idiot, who had been there 48 years during all this time, winter and summer, this poor wretch had had no other covering than a canvass shirt, no shoes even or stockings. At night he was, as the master expressed it, 'ticed' or forced into an out-house, a place unfit even for an animal a hole in the wall was the only window; there he slept in some damp straw on the bare ground, for there was not even a stone floor.[446]

After 1834

Following the 1834 Poor Law Amendment Act, forty-seven Poor Law Unions were created in Wales. The only anomaly was the Montgomery and Pool Incorporation whose Local Act status exempted it from most of the provisions of the 1834 Act. It continued in operation until 1870 when it was dissolved and replaced by a new Forden Poor Law Union.

Despite the successful unionisation of Wales, several areas, most notably the north-west, and the rural central region, resisted the provision of a union workhouse as required by the 1834 Act. Those workhouses that had been opened were amongst the targets of the 'Rebecca Rioters' who, in 1842–43, carried out a campaign of protests across South Wales which included the storming of the Carmarthen workhouse on 19 June 1843. The Rebecca Rioters took their name from the Book of Genesis (Chapter 24, Verse 60): 'And they blessed Rebekah and said unto her, Thou art our sister, be thou the mother of thousands of millions, and let thy seed possess the gate of those which hate them.' The rioters often included one or more 'Rebecca' figures dressed in women's clothes and wearing a wig of ringlets. Attacks also took place on the workhouse at Llanfyllin where the Montgomeryshire Yeomanry prevented a mob from destroying the building, and at Narberth where special constables were employed to protect the site after a mob attempted to burn down the new workhouse.

In 1845, the Poor Law Commissioners recorded seventeen out of forty-seven Welsh unions as still 'not having efficient workhouses in operation'. This compared to nineteen out of 544 English unions lacking operational workhouses at the same date. Steady pressure from the Commissioners, and their successors the Poor Law Board, gradually reduced this number but by the late 1860s five unions in the centre of Wales (Builth, Lampeter, Presteigne, Rhayader and Tregaron) were still holding out, together with Crickhowell refusing to replace its ageing and inadequate former parish workhouse. Further pressure and threats resulted in compliance from Crickhowell (1870), Lampeter (1874), Builth (1875) and Tregaron (1876). Finally, in 1876, the Local Government Board obtained new powers under The Divided Parishes and Poor Law Amendment Act which would let it dissolve any union 'when it is expedient to do so for the purpose of rectifying or simplifying the areas of management, or otherwise for the better administration of relief...'. In the face of this threat, Rhayader finally proceeded to build a workhouse. It received its first inmates in August 1879, making Rhayader the last union in the whole of England and Wales to open a workhouse complying with the requirements of the 1834 Act. Presteigne, however, stood its ground and was dissolved in 1877 with its constituent parishes being redistributed amongst adjacent unions.

New Unions

In addition to the original forty-seven unions originally created in Wales, six additional ones were eventually formed. These were mainly in the industrial south where the population in some existing unions had grown unmanageably large: the Bedwellty union was formed in 1849 from the western part of the Abergavenny union; the Gower union was created in 1857 from part of Swansea union; Pontypridd was formed in 1863 from parts of the Cardiff and Merthyr Tydfil unions; Pontardawe was formed in 1875 from part of the Neath union. In the north of Wales, a

Rhayader, in mid-Wales, was the last union in England and Wales to provide a workhouse, something which it resisted until 1879. The building is now a hotel.

new Holyhead union was created in 1852 from the western part of the Anglesey union, and the following year the Hawarden Union was formed from parishes in Flintshire and Cheshire.

Since parish workhouses were rare in Wales, almost all of the Welsh Poor Law Unions had to erect new workhouse buildings rather than the frequently cheaper option of adapting existing accommodation. The latter course was initially taken by Swansea, Monmouth and Crickhowell, although in each case a new purpose-built workhouse was eventually erected. The Bala Union was particularly unfortunate in that the new workhouse it erected in 1839–41 was no longer satisfactory by 1875 and a replacement was built at a different site.

Most of the new workhouses in Wales were designed by relatively local architects such as William Owen who designed the Narberth and Haverfordwest workhouses in Pembrokeshire. Of the major architects associated with the workhouse building boom years of 1835–40 – Sampson Kempthorne, George Gilbert Scott and William Bonython Moffatt, and George Wilkinson – only Wilkinson undertook commissions in Wales. He was responsible for the work-houses at Aberayron, Abergavenny, Bridgend and Pembroke, all of which survive, at least in part.

Cottage Homes

Although often reluctant to countenance workhouses, Wales was a pioneer when it came to another type of Poor Law establishment. The 'cottage homes' system was intended to provide an alternative form of accommodation for children who would otherwise have been in the workhouse. The homes were usually planned as self-contained 'villages' set in rural locations, and sometimes set around a green, where groups of up to twenty children lived in each home under the care of a house 'mother'. Some of the first poor law cottage homes in Britain were established at Swansea in 1877, Neath in 1878 and Bridgend in 1879, with more than 100 such schemes eventually being set up in England and Wales. As well as houses and a school, larger cottage homes sites often included workshops, an infirmary, chapel and even a swimming pool.

Hard Times

In the 1870s, a fall in the price of coal and iron led to a recession with a reduction in workers' wages in South Wales industrial towns such as Merthyr Tydfil. A number of strikes resulted, the most significant of which began on 1 January 1875 after a 10 per cent reduction in colliers' wages. The employers responded to this action with a lockout. At Merthyr Tydfil, the guardians, themselves mostly mine and iron-works owners, initially refused to offer any relief whatsoever to single men on strike. Then, at the end of January, able-bodied men were offered a labour test – out relief in return for performing manual labour such as stone breaking. From 19 February, the guardians decided that all single men should thenceforth only be relieved via admission to the workhouse. The situation escalated on 27 February when 900 single, able-bodied men arrived at the workhouse demanding relief. The master admitted as many as there was room for, then turned away the rest. Those who had been admitted tried to destroy workhouse discipline and four policemen were moved in to keep order. In mid-March, when the supply of suitable task work ran out, the Dowlais Iron Company offered colliery work as a substitute, which would have effectively broken the strike. The workers held out against this but, by May, they had been starved out and the strike collapsed.[447]

A similar situation occurred in 1898 when wage-cuts by the employers resulted in another five-month-long strike. With the support of the Local Government Board, strikers were again offered an outdoor labour test. At the end of the dispute, colliery owners challenged the legality of providing such relief to strikers. In 1900, the Court of Appeal issued what became known as the Merthyr Tydfil Judgement. It decreed that, regardless of his being on strike or not, an able-bodied man who could obtain work was not entitled to poor relief unless he was too exhausted by his situation to be capable of working. It was ruled, however, that the wives and families of strikers could claim poor relief. Unmarried strikers thus had no access to poor relief until they had become too debilitated to work.

The post-war depression in the 1920s again saw heavy unemployment in South Wales and subsequent escalations in poor relief claims. The Bedwellty Union in South Wales was particularly badly affected following the closure in May 1926 of local collieries resulting from the miners' dispute with pit-owners over reductions in wages. In one week, the union had 42 per cent of the population on its out relief lists, something which it could not afford to sustain. By the start of 1927, the union was more than £1 million in debt and its Board of Guardians was 'superseded' with its operation taken over by government officials.

Despite the financial strain, many unions continued to apply the Merthyr Tydfil Judgement although, in practical terms it was of course impossible to prevent a wife passing poor relief onto her husband. Many single men, who did not qualify for poor relief, took to the road, with vagrancy in Wales during 1926 jumping by 41 per cent compared to the previous year.

In 1928 and 1929, the plight of distressed miners in Wales and in other areas was assisted by public donations to the Lord Mayor's Fund which raised over £1 million.
(*See also*: **Labour Test**; **Merthyr Tydfil Judgement**)

A group of elderly male inmates, accompanied by a nurse, at the Cardiff Union's Cowbridge Road workhouse.

WARDSMAN

A wardsman was an individual appointed to assist in the running of a workhouse ward for the sick or mentally ill, performing such tasks as lifting or restraining patients, and usually sleeping in the ward at night, to assist in case any problems arose. The wardsman was often an inmate who was rewarded for his duties with items such as extra food or with beer, but he could also be a paid servant of the workhouse. A female performing the same role was known as a wardswoman or wardsmaid.

WARTIME

Like virtually every other sphere of national life, the workhouse was affected when Britain was at war. This was especially so during the First World War when many workhouses, workhouse infirmaries and other poor law premises were given over, entirely or in part, to war-related use.

English workhouses taken over for use as First World War military hospitals included: Atcham, Bradford-on-Avon (used as a Red Cross hospital), Brighton, Bristol – Southmead, Carlisle, Chester, Devonport (Red Cross hospital for soldiers), Eastbourne, East Preston, Elham, Greenwich – Grove Park, Guildford, Hampstead, Leeds, Lewisham, Oxford, Paddington, Reading, Richmond [Surrey], Truro (Red Cross hospital for sailors), Uppingham (Red Cross hospital) and Wellington [Shropshire]. Those taken over in Wales were: Aberayron, Bangor, Bedwellty, Bridgend, Builth, Carmarthen, Carnarvon, Holywell, Knighton (Red Cross hospital), Aberdare, Merthyr Tydfil – Trecynon, Newport, Neath, Pontardawe, Pontypool, Pontypridd – Llwynpia, Ruthin and Wrexham. Existing inmates from the affected workhouses were usually dispersed amongst other institutions in the area. Staff, however, were generally kept on to assist with the institution's new role. Workhouse medical superintendents were often given military rank for the duration of the war.

Unions housing military patients in only part of their workhouse or in other premises (as detailed below) included: Alcester (infirmary used by Red Cross), Bakewell, Barnet (new infirmary block), Barnsley, Birmingham (infirmary and part of workhouse; children's section of Monyhull Colony), Blean, Bradford, Brentford (Percy House school), Bristol (female infirmary block at Stapleton workhouse), Bury St Edmunds, Chorley, Chorlton (Nell Lane schools and homes), Crediton (isolation hospital used by Red Cross), Darlington, Dewsbury (infirmary blocks), Doncaster, Ecclesall Bierlow, Edmonton (infirmary), Epping, Exeter (children's home used by Red Cross), Faversham, Gateshead (Shotley Bridge), Glossop, Gloucester (infirmary used by Red Cross), Grimsby (Brighowgate schools), Halifax (Salterhebble infirmary), Hastings, Hollingbourne, Huddersfield, Ipswich, Keighley (Fell Lane infirmary), Kingston (infirmary used by Red Cross), Knaresborough, Leicester (North Evington infirmary), Leeds, Liverpool (Highfield infirmary and Kirkdale homes), Maidstone, Manchester (New Bridge Street site), Newark (Kilton Hill infirmary), Newcastle-upon-Tyne, Newton Abbot, North Bierley, Nottingham (infirmary and part of workhouse), Orsett, Penistone, Preston (workhouse infirmary block), Prestwich (Booth Hall hospital), Reigate (infirmary used by Red Cross), Romford, Ross, Rotherham, Rugby (infirmary used by Red Cross), St Alban's, Sheffield, Skipton, Sleaford (workhouse used for naval cases), Steyning, Stockport (Stepping Hill infirmary), Stroud, Sudbury, Tetbury, Thanet, Tonbridge, Wakefield, Wayland (Attleborough infirmary), West Derby (Alder Hey hospital), Wigan (Billinge infirmary) and York.

The treatment of battle casualties was not the only wartime medical facility to be provided in workhouses. Two or three unions in Sussex and Kent provided venereal clinics and maternity centres. Some, such as Tenterden, received 'mental defectives' who would have otherwise gone into county asylums, many of which were also being used for war purposes. Wellingborough provided some accommodation for the Royal Army Medical Corps.

A number of workhouses were used for billeting soldiers and/or housing prisoners of war (POWs). These included Axbridge, Aylsham, Banbury, Blything, Bosmere & Claydon,

The Greenwich Union's workhouse at Grove Park, Lewisham, during its First World War occupation as a barracks for the Army Service Corps. The site later became Grove Park Hospital for TB and chest conditions but is now in residential use.

Chelmsford, Chesterfield (Brampton Schools), Derby, Docking, Dore, Dunmow, East and West Flegg, East Retford, Frome, Gainsborough, Halstead, Hitchin, Honiton, Howden, Kingsbridge, Langport, Ledbury, Maldon, Martley, Mitford & Launditch (Gressenhall), Mildenhall, Newark (Kilton Hill), Newton Abbot, Northleach, Pateley Bridge, Pershore, Rochford, Saffron Walden, Selby, Shepton Mallet, Smallburgh, Stamford, Tadcaster, Taunton, Wangford, Wetherby, Wharfedale, Worksop and Yeovil. Soon after the outbreak of war, several unions in Cornwall housed passengers and crews of two German ships detained at Falmouth. At the end of the war, Boston workhouse received British POWs returning from Germany, with Germans also passing through the workhouses in the course of repatriation.

Workhouse premises served a variety of other uses during the First World War. Several housed refugees including Holborn's Endell Street workhouse, the Strand Union's workhouse and children's home at Edmonton, and the Loughborough Union workhouse. Westminster's Poland Street workhouse became a centre for Jewish refugees. Holbeach provided a guard room in connection with east coast defences. Blandford was used by the RAF. The Willesden workhouse and the Dartford Union's workhouse and children's homes were used to house munitions workers. The casual wards at Luton were used as military detention barracks, while those at Grantham were requisitioned for a Forestry Corps base. At Lincoln, the imbecile blocks and guardians' boardroom became a military administrative centre with up to 200 Clerks being accommodated. The War Office occupied Patrington and Skirlaugh workhouses. Land girls were housed in part of Selby workhouse. The Ministry of Pensions took over a block in grounds of Newcastle workhouse and the Gateshead Union's hospital at Shotley Bridge was leased to the Ministry of Health to house military casualties, later being taken over by the Ministry of Pensions for ex-servicemen who still required medical treatment.

Scotland also made a significant contribution to the war effort. Glasgow's Stobhill and Western District hospitals were entirely turned over to military use together with the following poorhouses: Aberdeen (Oldmill), Edinburgh (Craigleith), Hawick Combination, Leith (Seafield), Peebles Combination, Perth, and Renfrewshire Combination. Partial use was also made of the poorhouses at Dundee East, Dunfermline, Govan, Greenock (Smithston), Leith, Paisley and Perth. Dundee's West poorhouse was used for billeting troops, as were parts of the Falkirk and Black Isle poorhouses. Lochgilphead poorhouse was used as a temporary annexe to the Argyll District Asylum.[448]

Relatively little use was made of Irish workhouses during the First World War. At the start of the war, Belgian refugees were briefly accommodated at a number of workhouses in the Dublin area and the Dunshaughlin workhouse was given over for use as a Belgian refugee centre or 'colony'. In 1915, the workhouses at Antrim, Mallow, Mitchelstown, Oldcastle and Tipperary were handed over to the military authorities for unspecified purposes.[449] The Oldcastle workhouse in County Meath is said to have been used to hold suspected German spies or sympathisers. Some use was made of the Belfast workhouse for treating military personnel.

At the end of the war, the military were sometimes slow in returning premises to the poor law authorities. At Bangor and Neath, for example, parts of the workhouses were retained as hospitals for disabled officers and men. When they were eventually handed back, there was often haggling about the state of repair and decoration in which the buildings were left. In some cases though, wartime occupation actually resulted in positive benefits such as the installation of X-ray and other equipment in some workhouse infirmaries. Workhouse staff employed for military work had sometimes received higher salaries and war bonus payments, together with shorter hours of duty.

Some workhouses never re-opened after the war. These included Docking, Dunmow, East and West Flegg, Foleshill, Halstead, Helmsley, Mildenhall, Pateley Bridge, Patrington, Skirlaugh, Smallburgh, Southam, Swaffham, Witney and Wycombe.

(*See also*: **Metropolitan Asylums Board**)

WASH-HOUSE

A room or out-building in a workhouse where clothes and linens were washed. (*See also*: **Laundry**)

WASHING AND BATHING

The belief that 'cleanliness is next to Godliness' was clearly held by many of those in charge of running a workhouse. The lists of rules governing establishments set up under the Old Poor Law often laid down the requirements in such matters. In 1724, at the parish workhouse of St Paul's, Bedford, the master and mistress were to 'take Care that all the poor People be kept clean and neat in their Persons and Apparel.'[450] At Hackney workhouse in the 1750s, it was decreed that 'all the Children be washed, combed and cleaned by Eight in the Morning'.[451] The rules of the Isle of Wight Incorporation's workhouse in 1792 demanded that 'the children's heads and hands to be kept clean' – the expectations as to the rest of their persons, or indeed, the cleanliness of adults, were not indicated.[452]

In many cases, the cleanliness of the workhouse premises or of the clothing and bedclothes used by the occupants often received rather more attention than that which was demanded of the inmates. At Trentham, in 1810, the workhouse regulations ordered that:

> The Larder, Kitchen, back kitchen and other offices, together with the Utensils and Furniture thereof, be kept sweet, clean and decent. That the Dining Room, table and Seats be cleaned immediately after each meal, and the several Wards or dormitories every Morning before or immediately after breakfast when the Windows thereof shall be thrown open, the Door Locked and the Keys delivered to them; and that the strictest Cleanliness and Decency be observed in every part of the House.

...the Wards of Dormitories be supplied with clean sheets once a Month or oftener if necessary, and the Poor with clean linen once a week.

...The children and Grown Up Persons as far as may be possible shall be made to clean themselves and to attend Divine Service on Sunday.[453]

After 1834, every inmate of a union workhouse was required to 'duly cleanse his person', with failure to do so being a disciplinary matter.[454] Daily ablutions were usually carried out in a room referred to in Victorian times as a lavatory. In less well-endowed establishments, washing might be done under an outside pump or with water in a bucket. Facilities for more extensive bathing were very variable.

The expectations of the Poor Law Commissioners with regard to bathing were made clear in 1844 in a list of recommended improvements at Southampton workhouse:

Baths, both hot and cold, as well as shower ones, should be in a constant state of readiness in a place where 220 persons reside. The expense is very trifling, and where persons are sometimes brought in a state of deplorable filth, covered with dirt and vermin, as the lowest class of tramps sometimes are, it really is a matter of no small consideration to have baths which can be had resource to without delay, as the unfortunate creatures cannot be admitted into the wards with others until they have been freed from the pedicules which cover them. Now, in the event of sudden illness, a bath cannot be obtained till the water is heated for the purpose, whilst under other circumstances, by means of a steam boiler, hot water could always be available and ready at a moment's notice.[455]

Two areas of the workhouse where baths were most commonly found were in the receiving ward, so that new arrivals could be washed, and in the workhouse infirmary, to aid the cleanliness and hygiene of patients. Even this basic provision sometimes did not exist. In 1865, *The Lancet* medical journal reported that at the Walsall Union workhouse there were no baths except in the receiving ward, which had to be shared by all the inmates, including the sick and venereal patients. The fifty inmates of one male ward block all washed in a sink with two towels provided each day for them all to share.[456] At Farnham workhouse, the inmates 'after washing or bathing (which they did in the chamber utensils), dried themselves *on the sheets of their beds.*'[457]

Baths for new arrivals were also a requirement in the casual ward which provided overnight accommodation for passing tramps and other travellers in need. The lack of piped water and

A reconstruction of the tramps' bath at the former Guildford workhouse casual ward, now restored as a workhouse museum.

the numbers of admissions needing to be bathed in a relatively short period meant that in many cases, the same bathwater was re-used by a great many of those entering each evening. The facilities in the casual ward at the Lambeth workhouse were described by one visitor in 1866 as 'three great baths, each one containing a liquid... disgustingly like weak mutton broth.'[458]

For many workhouse inmates, taking a bath could be a completely new experience. It was sometimes said that the change in the colour of someone's skin following their first ever bath could make some inmates unrecognisable to their own mothers. The novelty, or even shock, of taking a bath was vividly recalled by the experience of a seven-year-old inmate, later writing under the name 'W.H.R.', on receiving his first ever hot bath on entering the Greenwich Union workhouse in around 1849:

> After dinner an old woman came and took all my clothes and then showed me into the bathroom, telling me to get in and not be afraid. I should think I was not afraid, indeed, I had been too much used to water. I was in the bath in a moment with a jump, but the next moment my screams and yells could be heard far and wide. The fact was, the water was hot, to me it appeared scalding hot. Mr Willis the master came and several more, but could not get me in again. They lifted me, smacked me, coaxed, and at last used sheer force. I never was so afraid. in all my life; I thought they were going to kill me: Never before had I had such a thing as a hot bath; and never shall I forget it.[459]

Despite regular complaints from official inspectors, washing and bathing facilities in many workhouses were slow to improve. In 1894, at Blofield in Norfolk, investigators from the *British Medical Journal* found that in the female infirmary:

> There are no baths except small hip baths, and no hot water is obtainable except from the main kitchen at some little distance from the wards. There is a cold water tap on the matron's landing, otherwise all water, hot and cold, must be carried by the inmates; this applies to the female wards; in the male infirmary we saw no arrangements for any bathing, nor any supply of water, hot or cold.[460]

The use of chamber-pots for washing in was also observed at the St George Hanover Square workhouse, something which evoked caustic comments from the *BMJ* reporters:

> On the female side there are fixed basins outside the dormitories with hot and cold supply; on the male side the fixed basins are out of doors, with the result, as the master said, that the old men do not wash in cold weather, or they make use of the chamber utensil in the dormitory. The old women, as we were informed by an inmate, preferred to make this use of the chamber vessel instead of that for which it is intended; we can understand that among this large number of paupers, many coming from the very lowest class, there will be some who, if left to themselves, will show every trace of the state of savagery out of which they have come, but we do not see the necessity of the workhouse lowering itself to their level.[461]

New bathing regulations introduced in 1886 required that every inmate should be bathed once a month, with the option of being bathed as frequently as once a fortnight. The cold water was to be placed in the bath before the hot and the water temperature was to be between 80 and 90 degrees Fahrenheit, checked with a thermometer. It was 'desirable' that a member of the workhouse staff should remain present in the bathroom. The hot water tap should be lockable with a key. Inmates had the right to demand water that had not been previously used and a separate clean towel was to be provided for each person.[462]

Showers, also known as shower baths or spray baths, were occasionally found in workhouses. In 1867, one was provided in the infirmary at Windsor workhouse.[463] From the 1870s onwards, showers were commonly installed in children's accommodation such as separate schools and

cottage homes where their hygienic benefits were recognised as beneficial in reducing the spread of diseases such as ophthalmia and ringworm.
(*See also*: **Casual Ward**; **Turkish Baths**; **Water Supplies**)

WATER CLOSET

A sanitary device or fitting used as a toilet, using water to flush deposits into a waste-pipe below. The term also became used for a room containing such a device.
(*See also*: **Earth Closet**; **Lavatory**; **Privy**; **Water Closet**)

WATER SUPPLIES

Until the second half of the nineteenth century, most people obtained their water from sources such as a well, spring or river, perhaps supplemented by the collection of rain water. The domestic water supplies that did exist were mostly provided by private water companies. They were thus expensive and generally only available in towns and cities. Union workhouses were often sited on the edges of towns and aimed to be run as economically as possible. Even if piped water was available in their locality, the cost would probably be more than the guardians would be prepared to pay. The principle of 'less eligibility', that a workhouse inmate should be no better off than the lowliest of independent labourer outside the workhouse, also weighed against the use of commercially supplied water.

Water for the Shrewsbury workhouse was hand-pumped from the river by the paupers using a 'small machine'. At Longtown in Cumberland, water for the workhouse was supplied by a pump in the kitchen supplemented by water from a stream adjoining the premises. At Neath in South Wales in the 1870s, water for washing and cooking was sometimes taken from the nearby canal.

A large workhouse might have four or five wells, with the water being raised by a bucket or hand-pump. Water might also be pumped to an elevated storage tank for distribution around the rest of the workhouse. The Malton workhouse in North Yorkshire had a treadmill, which was used both to pump water for the workhouse, and to provide a labour task for the inmates. When a new workhouse was opened in Tamworth in 1859, the main cold water tank was placed in the central tower, to which the water was supplied by a crank pump from the well in the able-bodied men's yard. Hand pumping was gradually replaced by the use of powered pumps. At the new Medway Union workhouse which opened in 1859, the initial plan was that water for the new building would be manually pumped from a well but a steam pump was later included in the scheme.

Large elevated water storage tanks were erected at many workhouses. The simplest method was to place the tank above a simple metal framework. In other cases, it could be placed on top of brick constructed block. Later workhouse designers usually located

A hand-pump in one of the inmates' yards at the Holywell Union workhouse in Flintshire.

The main building of the Rochdale Union's Birch Hill workhouse opened in 1877. The upper part of the central tower concealed a large water storage tank.

tanks inside the main building. In 1872, at Huddersfield's new Crosland Moor workhouse, the upper part of the central tower concealed a large tank able to contain 10,000 gallons of water. This supplied all the water closets, lavatories, baths etc. Provision was also made to attach a plug and hose on each landing in case of fire.

Building engineers often had to go to great lengths, or rather depths, in order to locate suitable sources of water. In 1881, the St Marylebone guardians opened a new infirmary at Rackham Street in Ladbroke Grove. To provide water for the establishment, a well had to be sunk to a depth of 500ft from which powerful pumps were able to raise 6,000 gallons per hour. This was said to save the St Marylebone ratepayers at least £250 a year. Even more severe difficulties were encountered at Brighton in the 1850s when it was decided to erect a new workhouse on an elevated site at Race Hill, together with a nearby workhouse school at Warren Farm. The guardians were reluctant to pay for piped water from the local pumping station to supply the new buildings so workhouse labour was used to dig a new well at the Warren Farm site. Progress was slow and the lack of water resulted in a long postponement of the building work on the new workhouse. On Sunday 16 March 1862, after four years of digging by workhouse inmates, down to a world record depth of 1,285ft, water was finally reached. Church bells were rung and there were great celebrations locally, but it was the engineers that were honoured with a parade, medals and a banquet, not the pauper labour force. One man is said to have died during the digging work and his wife was given £6 in compensation.

Some workhouse sites made use of artesian wells, where natural pressure was sufficient to bring water to the surface. New artesian wells were being drilled at the Aylsham workhouse in Norfolk as late as the 1920s.

WAYFARERS

From the mid-nineteenth century onwards, the term 'wayfarers', or 'casual' wayfarers, was sometimes used in official documents to describe those on the road and making use of workhouse casual wards. The National Assistance Act of 1948 provided for the establishment of wayfarers' reception centres, with tramps and vagrants now officially being referred to as 'persons without a settled way of living'.

(*See also*: **Casual Poor; Casual Ward**)

WAY TICKET SYSTEM

A way ticket was a certificate issued by a casual ward or police-station to casuals judged to be the 'honest unemployed'. The ticket gave the holder preferential treatment at a specified destination workhouse casual ward, such as early release or exemption from performing a task of work. In conjunction with way tickets, many casual wards also issued vagrants with meal tickets or bread tickets which could be redeemed for food at a designated 'bread station' – often a policeman's house – en route. These were intended to try and ensure that casuals kept to their supposed destination, and also aimed to reduce begging.

Although owing much to the recommendations in the 1848 Buller Memorandum, the implementation of the way ticket system is often attributed to the fourth Earl of Carnarvon who in the late 1860s promoted its use as a response to a huge rise in vagrant numbers in Hampshire. It was then adopted in other areas including Berkshire and Dorset in 1870, in Kent in 1871, in Wiltshire and Gloucestershire in 1882, and in North Wales in 1884. Despite early enthusiasm, take-up of the scheme was uneven and its use declined. However, in the early 1900s, a revival of interest took place, helped by encouragement from the Local Government Board and by the creation of County Vagrancy Committees. By 1920, way ticket schemes were operating in forty-five counties in England and Wales.

(*See also*: **Buller Memorandum; Casual Poor**; **Casual Ward**)

WEIGHTS AND MEASURES

Below is a list of some of the weights, measures and monetary units used during the workhouse era, together with their approximate metric equivalents. Common abbreviations are given in brackets.

Weight

1 ounce (oz)	–	= 28.4 grams
1 pound (lb)	= 16 ounces	= 450 grams
1 stone	= 14 pounds	= 6.3 kilograms
1 hundredweight (cwt)	= 112 pounds	= 50 kilograms

Volume

1 fluid ounce	–	= 28.4 cubic centimetres
1 pint	= 20 fluid ounces	= 570 cubic centimetres

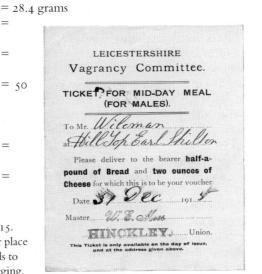

LEICESTERSHIRE
Vagrancy Committee.

TICKET FOR MID-DAY MEAL
(FOR MALES).

To Mr. *Wileman*
at *Hill Top Earl Shilton*

Please deliver to the bearer **half-a-pound of Bread** and **two ounces of Cheese** for which this is to be your voucher

Date *31 Dec* 191 *5*

Master *W. E. Moss*

HINCKLEY Union.

This Ticket is only available on the day of issue, and at the address given above.

A meal ticket issued by Hinckley workhouse in 1915. The holder could redeem it for food at a particular place en route. Such tickets were intended to keep casuals to their purported destination, and also to reduce begging.

| 1 quart | = 2 pints | = 1.1 litres |
| 1 gallon | = 8 pints | = 4.5 litres |

Length

1 inch (in)	–	= 2.5 centimetres (cm)
1 foot (ft)	= 12 inches	= 30 centimetres
1 yard (yd)	= 3 feet	= 90 centimetres
1 mile	= 1,760 yards	= 1.6 kilometres

(*See also*: **Money**)

WOMEN

(*See*: **Casual Poor**; **Classification**; **Clothing**; **Guardians / Guardians of the Poor**; **Illegitimacy**; **Out relief**; **Segregation**; **Statistics**; **Tea**; **Work**)

WORK

The workhouse, as its name implied, was an institution whose inmates were expected to labour. The work they performed varied considerably over the years, ranging from highly productive occupations to ones whose purpose was largely to act as a deterrent to those, particularly able-bodied, individuals who were contemplating claiming poor relief.

Workhouse Labour Under the Old Poor Law

The most common occupations in early workhouses were related to the production of textiles or clothing, such as spinning wool and flax, winding silk, sewing, knitting and shoe-making. In 1624, wealthy woollen draper John Kendrick left bequests to the towns of Newbury and Reading to establish workhouses for the benefit of unemployed clothiers. As was often the case at this period, the workhouses were largely non-residential with the premises acting as workshops where the destitute could labour in return for poor relief. Materials could also be provided to be worked on in people's own homes and then brought back to exchange for payment. Those managing the workhouses also took on the business of trying to sell the woollen cloth that was produced although their lack of success soon led to a failure of the enterprise.

Residential workhouses soon became the norm and inmates, especially women, were expected to provide the labour required for the day-to-day domestic operation of the establishment. This could include tasks such as baking, brewing, cleaning, washing, ironing, bed-making, tending fires, nursing, and supervising or teaching any children in the workhouse.

For those not engaged on the domestic front, textile work was again the most common occupation with spinning and knitting taking place in most parish workhouses. In an inventory of the Abingdon workhouse in 1834, the contents of its 'factory' included twenty-five sacks, a shoemaker's last, a tailor's goose (a type of iron), nine looms, thirteen spinning wheels, thirty-one foot-wheels and three winding wheels. Shrewsbury workhouse had a woollen manufactory where inmates were trained in scribbling, cording and spinning, with several weavers being kept employed. Sunderland workhouse manufactured sail cloth, Kendal inmates produced a type of coarse sacking known as 'hardens', and the workhouse at Bromsgrove produced nails.

Such enterprises were not always without problems, however. Local businesses might complain if they felt they were being subjected to unfair competition by the workhouse with its zero labour costs. In times of slump, disposing of workhouse manufactured goods might prove difficult while in better times the house might lose its skilled inmates who could find paid employment outside. Where workhouse inmates received no payment for their work, there was little incentive for them to be industrious.

Children in a workhouse often formed a significant part of its workforce. As well as any immediate benefit from their labour, there was a belief that giving a child practical skills would make it employable in later life. In the late 1690s, the newly formed Bristol Incorporation set up two workhouses where boys and girls were taught to spin cotton and wool and weave fustian (a coarse twilled cotton). Thirty children at the Whitechapel workhouse in 1731 were employed in the winding onto bobbins of Bengal raw silk, sent in by local throwsters who paid up to 5d per pound. At the St James, Middlesex, workhouse in 1776, the children worked at knitting, spinning, opening horse-hair and making lace.

In the parish workhouse era, inmates could not only work inside the workhouse but also for outside employers such as cotton or silk mills, farmers and brick-makers. At Oxford, workhouse inmates swept the city's streets, for which the guardians were paid £100 a year.[464] As specified by Knatchbull's Act of 1723, the income from such work normally went to the parish overseers, or to the contractor in the case of farmed workhouse. In practice, inmates were often allowed to keep a small proportion of their earnings to encourage their industry. At Derby's St Alkmund workhouse, those working in local textile mills earned about 16s a week of which they could keep 2d in each shilling.

Early proponents of the workhouse such as John Cary, the instigator of the Bristol Incorporation in 1696, had expected that labour of the inmates would generally make workhouses self-sufficient. By 1711, however, it was claimed that half the city's poor rate was being spent on maintaining 170 workhouse inmates.[465]

Workhouse Labour after 1834

The new union workhouses established following the 1834 Poor Law Amendment Act were intended to be deterrent in nature, and the work demanded from the inmates, especially able-bodied men, reflected this. Inmates were to be kept employed 'according to their capacity and ability; and no pauper shall receive any compensation for his labour.'[466]

As in the parish workhouse, able-bodied females were primarily occupied in domestic tasks such as cleaning, bed-making, cooking, laundry work and sewing. In some workhouses, women were employed in the making of the inmates' uniforms. Less physically capable women were often used in child care or infirmary nursing duties

For able-bodied men, the occupations favoured by the Poor Law Commissioners included stone breaking, oakum picking, pumping water and milling corn – either by cranking a hand-mill or with a number of men pushing a rotating capstan. In 1836, William Hawley, Assistant Poor Commissioner for Sussex, reported that the Westbourne Union had installed a corn mill requiring the effort of sixteen men to operate it. Becoming wise to this, local men organised themselves so that the number of able-bodied males in the workhouse in any one time never reached this number so that the task could not be imposed. The Westbourne guardians responded by installing a four-man corn mill.[467]

The task, used by some unions, of crushing or pounding old bones into dust for use as fertiliser was banned in 1845 following the Andover workhouse scandal where men engaged in the work were discovered to have been driven by hunger into fighting over the scraps of marrow and shreds of meat that were still attached to the bones. The Poor Law Commissioners suggested that unions who favoured the use of bone crushing might switch to the pounding of gypsum, a mineral used in the making of plaster.

Although the work performed by inmates was usually either part of the institution's domestic chores, or an unproductive labour task, there were occasional instances of inmates performing work paid for by outside customers. In 1843 it was reported that 'slop work' – poorly paid sewing work – was frequently carried out by female inmates, especially in

London workhouses:

> In the thirteen weeks ending 18th September, 1841, there were made by the female pau-
> pers, chiefly for the slopsellers, 2064 articles; in St. George's in the East workhouse there
> are made from 8 to 12 dozen articles per week; and in the Bermondsey workhouse occa-
> sionally, 1300 garments of various kinds per week, and upon an average 200 shirts per
> week.[468]

In the 1850s, the Strand Union's Cleveland Street workhouse ran a carpet-beating business
which generated an unhealthy amount of noise and dust.[469]

From the 1840s onwards, many workhouses turned parts of their grounds over to agricultural use, growing vegetables that could be used by the workhouse or sold off locally. Much
of the work was performed by the older boys as a form of industrial training. If the workhouse made its own bread, the bakehouse was usually operated by male inmates.

The prohibition on 'compensation' for inmates' labour was often disregarded, particularly
for those engaged in particularly onerous or exceptional household duties such as nursing, laundry work, coffin bearing and so on. Inducements to take on these tasks included
extra food, dry tea, snuff or beer. Such practices were strongly disapproved of by the central
authorities and could lead to illicit trading activities amongst inmates.

By the end of the nineteenth century, the number of able-bodied inmates entering workhouses had declined significantly, with separate test workhouses being established in some
urban areas for those that remained. The nature of the labour tasks reflected this change, with
chopping wood and gardening becoming common. Making use of inmates' own skills and
trades, something which had been discouraged by the central authorities, also became more
widely used. In the 1890s, the Holborn Union's workhouse at Mitcham replaced tasks such
as oakum picking and stone breaking with more productive work. The workhouse had its
own farm, piggery and gas works, and made all its own clothing and footwear. All repairs and
maintenance of the buildings was undertaken by the inmates.

The potential diversity of employment amongst inmates is well illustrated by the
Macclesfield workhouse where, in 1886, the jobs assigned to the able-bodied females included:
twenty-one washers, twenty-two sewers and knitters, twelve scrubbers, twelve assisting
women, four in the kitchen, four in the nursery, and four stocking darners. On the men's side
there were two joiners, one slater, one upholsterer, one blacksmith, three assisting the porter
with the tramps, six men attending the boilers, three attending the stone-shed, four white-
washers, four attending the pigs, two looking after sanitary matters, one regulating the coal
supply, eighteen potato peelers, one messenger, twenty-six ward men, and two doorkeepers.
There were twelve boys at work in the tailor's shop.[470]

The steady decline in the numbers of able-bodied inmates meant that workhouses increasingly lacked the labour to perform all the domestic chores of the institution, with outside
help having to be hired. In some cases, women applying for out relief could be pressurised
into taking on such work, often at low pay rates, since they could not use the excuse that no
work was available to them. In 1880, women on out relief in the Merthyr Tydfil Union were
ordered to work in the workhouse laundry for 6d a day plus officers' rations. Three years
later, the Merthyr Tydfil guardians demanded that relieving officers send able-bodied female
paupers with two children to work in the workhouse for three days each week, for which
they received food, outdoor relief and some wages.[471]

(*See also*: **Bone Crushing / Bone Pounding**; **Gardens and Farms**; **Industrial Training**;
Oakum Picking; **Stone Breaking**)

A woman (centre) engaged in oakum picking – solid chunks of old rope, visible on the floor, had to be picked apart into their raw fibres.

The Mitcham workhouse's shoe-making workshop in 1896. The introduction of such occupations was intended to replace deterrent and unproductive tasks such as stone-breaking.

The majority of the workhouse population were the elderly, sick and infirm. For such inmates, less strenuous tasks such as wood-chopping became popular, with the resulting firewood being saleable to local householders.

WORKHOUSE

A workhouse, in England and Wales, may be broadly defined as an institution, funded from the local poor rates, voluntarily entered into, where the destitute were housed and maintained, and usually with an obligation upon inmates to perform labour according to the capability of each individual. As well as the work requirement, a workhouse typically had a resident governor, strict rules relating to the behaviour of the inmates, and a restricted and plain diet. However, the nature and character of the institution varied considerably, both over time and between different establishments.

The workhouse never existed in isolation, but always as a part of a larger and ever evolving system of publicly funded poor relief dating back to the middle of the sixteenth century. A dilemma which preoccupied poor relief administrators from the outset was how to distinguish those deemed to be deserving of poor relief (because they were destitute through no fault of their own and were powerless to remedy their situation, the so-called 'impotent' poor) and those who were undeserving (because they were capable of supporting themselves but chose not to do so). One early solution to this was to provide separate establishments for these different groups, an approach adopted by London in the mid-sixteenth century when the old Royal Hospitals took in various categories of impotent poor, while the undeserving laboured in the less congenial confines of Bridewell.

In 1576, four years after the introduction of the poor rate, parishes were permitted to rent or purchase premises and to provide stocks of materials – wool, hemp, flax and iron – to set the poor to work in return for receiving poor relief. These were not usually residential establishments, however. The work of spinning, carding, weaving etc. was performed by the poor either in a workshop area on the premises or in their own homes. Those refusing to work could be detained in a House of Correction, a forerunner of the prison.

The 1601 Poor Relief Act continued this bipartite approach. The deserving poor – 'the lame, impotent, old, blind, and such other among them being poor' – were to be relieved through the provision of 'sums of money' and 'places of habitation'. For the undeserving – those able to work – stocks of materials could be provided, with imprisonment for those refusing to work.

In a parallel development, encouragement to the founding of charitably (rather than parish) funded hospitals and 'working houses' for the poor was given in an Act of 1597. In 1617, Dorchester set up such an establishment where fifty poor children learned a trade and the idle poor were put to work.[472]

During the seventeenth century, workshop establishments – usually related to the production of textiles – were set up in a number of towns. They were still largely non-residential, with some providing training for poor children as well as work for adults. The word 'work-house' began to appear in written records by the late 1620s when towns such as Newbury, Reading, Cambridge, Newark and Sheffield all embarked on schemes, followed by Abingdon, Taunton, Halifax, Exeter St Thomas, Salisbury and Plymouth in the following ten years. London's first workhouse was set up by the city's Corporation of the Poor in around 1649.

The second half of the seventeenth century witnessed much experimentation and debate about how best to fulfil the 1601 Act's requirement for 'setting the poor on work'. A few London parishes such as St Margaret, Westminster (1664) and St Martin in the Fields (1665) set up workhouses although both appear to have been unsuccessful.[473] The Chief Justice, Sir Matthew Hale, proposed that groups of parishes should establish joint premises where the poor could be supplied with materials for work and where children could be taught a trade. Sir Joshua Child, the chairman of the East India Company, suggested a similar scheme across the whole of London run by a body which he proposed calling 'The Fathers of the Poor'.

In 1676, philanthropist Thomas Firmin set up a workhouse at Little Britain near Smithfield. More than 1,700 carders, combers, spinners and weavers were employed to manufacture linen from flax, much of which was done in their own homes. The establishment 'was at once school and factory, wholesale warehouse and retail shop.'[474] The workforce were treated well and their wages supplemented by handouts of coal. Children were admitted from the age of three and taught to read and spin. However, the scheme, which was financed from Firmin's own pocket, lost upwards of £200 each year. A similar approach was adopted in 1680 by the Society of Friends, or Quakers. Stocks of flax were bought and given to the Quaker poor to spin up at home or in prison. The scheme's treasurer, John Bellers, also developed plans for a 'College of Industry' – a co-operative, self-sufficient, humanitarian community where up to 200 labourers and 100 of the impotent poor would live and work together. The College building was planned to consist of four wings: one for married people, one for single young men and boys, one for single women and girls, and one for sick and invalid members. The College was also to have a library, a 'physick-garden', and laboratories for the preparation of medicines.[475] Although Bellers' utopian plans were never implemented, their influence can be seen in the workhouses opened by the Quakers in Bristol (1696) and Clerkenwell (1702).

The 1690s witnessed a new era in the evolution of the workhouse when the city of Bristol obtained a parliamentary local Act of 'for the better employing and maintaining of the poor'. The Act allowed the city's eighteen parishes to jointly administer poor relief through a Corporation managed by a Board of Guardians. It also provided for the establishment of workhouses, of which the Corporation opened two. These were residential establishments providing accommodation for the elderly and also the training for children, whose labour was then hired out to local manufacturers. Over the next century, around thirty more towns followed Bristol's example and were incorporated under local Acts, with large workhouses usually forming a significant part of their schemes. A similar path was followed in the mid-eighteenth century by a number of rural areas, particularly in East Anglia.

A further development came with the appearance of parish-run workhouses in the early 1700s. The growth in popularity of the parish workhouse, given official encourage-ment through Knatchbull's Act in 1723, owes much to the activities of workhouse manager Matthew Marryott in promoting their financial benefits. Offering a workhouse as the only form of relief, it was claimed, discouraged the undeserving poor (who were required to perform labour) and offered savings over providing large numbers of individual out relief payments. The Act also allowed parishes to hand over the operation of their workhouse to a private contractor, or 'farmer', who received a payment for each inmate and also benefited from any income generated by the inmates' labour. Many parishes found this a convenient way of having a workhouse without all the effort involved in running it themselves.

The poor relief establishments operated by parishes were not uniform in character, how-ever. The 1601 Act's provision for parishes to install individuals or families in a 'cottage or house' for the impotent and poor sometimes resulted in a type of establishment known as the poorhouse or parish house. These were rather informally run institutions, usually just offering free lodging for a parish's elderly, disabled or sick, and without a requirement for the inmates to work.

After an initial surge of workhouse openings in the 1720s, interest often waned if the promised financial benefits failed to materialise. In some places, the workhouse was closed after a few years, then perhaps re-opened, often with a contractor being employed to run it. Overseers' returns published in 1777 revealed that in England and Wales, almost 2,000 parish workhouses were in operation, with about one in seven parishes adopting this option. Of course, this also meant that in six out of seven parishes out relief was still the sole form of poor relief. The exact character of the workhouses enumerated in these returns was unspecified, relying on the overseers' judgements about what to include.

Larger-scale workhouses that served a group of parishes had come into being through the various urban and rural Incorporations formed by local Acts during the eighteenth century. Adopting this approach became simpler with the scheme introduced by Gilbert's Act in 1782, which allowed 'unions' of parishes to set up workhouses for the elderly, the sick and infirm, and orphaned children. The Act included mention both of workhouses and poorhouses, with the establishments it promoted falling somewhere between the two in character. Around eighty Gilbert Unions were eventually formed, some comprising more than forty parishes. It could be more economically attractive for a parish to have a share in a Gilbert Union workhouse than to run its own. The able-bodied were excluded from Gilbert workhouses but instead were to be helped find employment near their own homes, with land-owners, farmers and other employers receiving allowances from the poor rates to bring wages up to subsistence levels.

The use of parish workhouses reached its peak in around 1800.[476] By this date, the inmates were largely the impotent poor, with parishes increasingly preferring to give out relief which was both a cheaper option and also viewed as more appropriate to those made destitute through unemployment or discharge from the military forces. Of the 368 returns from Town Queries to the 1832 Royal Commission, only two expressed an interest in relieving the able-bodied in workhouses.[477] The work being performed by inmates was also in decline, partly reflecting the changing capabilities of the inmate population and also increasing difficulties in disposing of the products of the traditional inmates' occupations of spinning, weaving etc.

Workhouses were increasingly viewed by many as 'houses of idleness and vice'.[478] They could certainly be unhealthy places – in 1797, Eden's *State of the Poor* noted fevers raging in the workhouses in Manchester, North Shields and Nottingham. However, they were not entirely repugnant places. The diet provided in many establishments was more than adequate, or even generous. In some instances, the conditions they offered proved far more attractive than what might be available outside.

An increasing use of allowance systems at the end of the eighteenth century steadily pushed up the national cost of poor relief. In 1815, this situation was made worse by the ending of the Napoleonic wars, which increased the number of poor relief claimants, and by the introduction of the Corn Laws, which increased the cost of feeding them. The growing financial strain imposed on the poor rate led to a growth of interest in the 'reformed' workhouse. The most notable examples were the Southwell parish and Thurgarton Incorporation schemes in Nottinghamshire which convinced many that a strictly run workhouse as the sole option offered to poor relief claimants was the most effective solution to the escalating poor relief bill.

The 1832 Royal Commission into the operation of the poor laws agreed with this diagnosis while highlighting the deficiencies of many parish-run workhouses. The Commission's report characterised the typical parish workhouse as containing:

A dozen or more neglected children, twenty or thirty able-bodied adults of both sexes and probably an equal number of aged and impotent persons who are proper objects of relief. Among these the mothers of bastard children and prostitutes live without shame, and associate freely with the youth, who also have the example and conversation of the inmates of the county gaol, the poacher, the vagrant, the decayed beggar, and other characters of the worst description. To these may be added a solitary blind person, one or two idiots, and not infrequently are heard, from among the rest, the incessant ravings of some neglected lunatic.[479]

The 1834 Poor Law Amendment Act, based on the Commission's recommendations, grouped parishes into new administrative areas known as Poor Law Unions, each run by a Board of Guardians who were to provide a deterrent workhouse. The Commission originally proposed separate workhouses for different categories of pauper inmate: 'At least four classes are necessary:– 1. The aged and really impotent; 2. The children; 3. The able-bodied females; 4. The able-bodied males.' As well as providing different types of accommodation to suit the particular needs of different groups, separate establishments would also have allowed many former parish workhouses to be reused under the new system. However, running four or more institutions for unpredictable numbers of inmates soon began to look expensive and difficult, especially when it came to dispersing and reuniting families entering or leaving the workhouse. Thus, most unions adopted the 'general mixed workhouse' as the single establishment for the whole union.

The union workhouse became the face of the poor relief system for almost a century. Although it evolved considerably during that period, with major improvements in areas such as diet, medical care and the treatment of children and the mentally ill, the workhouse of 1930, when the Boards of Guardians were abolished, was still an institution that was contemplated with dread. Many former workhouses, now under the control of county and borough councils, became Public Assistance Institutions though still invariably referred to by local people for a good many years afterwards as 'the workhouse'.

(*See also*: **Architecture**; **Poorhouse**; **Poor Laws**; **Statistics**)

WORKHOUSE INFIRMARY NURSING ASSOCIATION

An organisation founded in 1879 by Louisa Twining to promote the use of trained nurses in all workhouse infirmaries, with the staff in such institutions supervised by a trained lady superintendent. The organisation's rather cumbersome full title was the 'Association for Promoting Trained Nursing in Workhouse in Workhouse Infirmaries and Sick Asylums, in co-operation with the Local Government Board and Poor Law Guardians'.

(*See also*: **Twining, Louisa**)

WORKHOUSE MEDICAL OFFICER

Poor Law Unions were obliged to appoint a medical officer to attend to medical matters within the workhouse premises, with the sick poor outside the workhouse dealt with by the union's District Medical Officers. In either case, the officer was required to possess one of the various formal qualifications detailed in Article 168 of the Consolidated General Order. The original list, issued in 1842, included only those issued by London-based institutions. Following complaints from northern unions, such as Berwick-upon-Tweed, qualifications from medical bodies in Scotland and Ireland were added the following year.

Initially, the Poor Law Commissioners encouraged unions to open medical appointments to competitive tender, with the successful candidate usually being whoever required the lowest salary or fee per case.[480] This meant that applicants were often the least experienced members of the profession, or ones with private practice where the physician's priorities would invariably lie. By 1842, the Commissioners had changed their views and ordered that appointments should be offered at a particular salary.

Among the duties of a workhouse medical officer were:

- To attend the workhouse at agreed times, or when sent for by the master or matron.
- To deal with inmates requiring medical attendance, and supply any medicines needed.
- To examine paupers on their admission to the workhouse.
- To give supervise the diet and treatment of the sick, and also those of unsound mind –reporting any deemed to be dangerous or fit to be sent to a lunatic asylum.
- To supervise the diet or treatment of children, and (from 1840) vaccinate them if required.
- To report any problems in the workhouse affecting the health of inmates such as the diet, drainage, ventilation, warmth, overcrowding etc.
- To report any problems in the infirmary or in the performance of nurses.
- To records any deaths in the workhouse, and their apparent cause.

For many years, union medical officers were required to supply any drugs they prescribed, with the result that some were effectively working for almost nothing. Matters improved a little in 1864, when it was agreed that the cost of cod liver oil, quinine and other expensive medicines could be met from the poor rates rather than by medical officers themselves. In 1877, however, less than 10 per cent of unions were supplying *all* the medicines prescribed by medical officers and even then, in most cases, that only went as far as those used within the workhouse.[481]

Despite their frequently unhappy financial situation, workhouse medical officers often wielded considerable power in their institutions since few guardians would rarely presume to contradict the advice they received on medical matters. The diets of workhouse inmates, especially the sick, the elderly and malnourished new inmates could all be considerably enhanced by 'extras' prescribed by the medical officer – these typically included such items as beer, brandy, fish, eggs, beef tea and milk puddings. Advice concerning the workhouse premises, particularly if it proposed significant expenditure, was more likely to meet resistance however. Instances of such battles were described by Dr Joseph Rogers, medical officer at the Strand Union's Cleveland Street workhouse from 1856 to 1868. His plan to increase the gruel-only diet fed to single mothers for nine days after giving birth in the workhouse labour ward was, despite strong criticism from the guardians, endorsed by the Poor Law Board. However, the guardians did successfully resist his efforts to end the noisy and dirty carpet-beating business that was conducted each day in the workhouse yard.

As the provision of medical care became a more significant aspect of poor relief provision, so did the status of workhouse medical officers. This was particularly the case in London where, following the 1867 Metropolitan Poor Act, unions were obliged to place their workhouse infirmaries under separate management.

(*See also*: **District Medical Officer**; **Matron**; **Medical Care**; **Medical Officers' Associations**)

WORKHOUSE SCHOOLS

Poor Law Unions were required to provide at least three hours a day of schooling for workhouse children who were to be taught 'reading, writing, arithmetic, and the principles of the Christian Religion, and such other instruction as may fit them for service, and train them to habits of usefulness, industry and virtue.'

Despite this requirement, Boards of Guardians were sometimes reluctant to spend money on even the most basic equipment such as writing slates. Some even questioned whether pauper children actually needed to be taught basic literacy. This was partly justified by the 1834 Act's principle of 'less eligibility' which, it was argued, demanded a lower quality of education than would be enjoyed by the children of those of modest means outside the workhouse. In 1836, the guardians of the Bedford Union suggested a compromise by teaching workhouse children to read but not to write. Likewise, in 1839 the guardians of the

Pershore Union decided that it was 'quite unnecessary to teach the children in the union workhouse the accomplishment of writing'.[482] Those holding such views were eventually persuaded that teaching pauper children to read and write would, in the long run, make them less likely to need poor relief.

In the 1840s, St Marylebone operated the timetable below in its workhouse school for children between seven and sixteen years of age.[483] There were striking differences between the sexes. The girls were not required to undertake gymnastics, history, geography, grammar, telling the time, or reading 'with explanations'. Their afternoons were filled with needlework and domestic employment which continued after supper when the boys were presumably allowed some recreation.

Boys' School		Girls' School	
6.00–7.00	Rise, make beds, prayers, clean shoes and wash.	6.00–8.00	Rise, make beds, prayers, clean shoes, wash. Prayers and religious instruction.
7.00–7.45	Gymnastics exercises (Saturdays excepted)		
7.45–9.00	Prayers. Breakfast. Play.	8.00–9.00	Breakfast. Recreation.
9.00–10.00	Historical reading, with explanations.	9.00–11.30	Reading, spelling, tables, arithmetic.
10.00–11.00	General and mental arithmetic, tables, use of clock dial for learning the time of day.		
11.00–12.00	Grammar. Parsing and Dictation.	11.30–12.30	Working in copy books. Dictation.
12.00–2.00	Dinner. Recreation.	12.30–2.00	Dinner. Recreation.
2.00–3.00	Writing in copy books & arithmetic.	2.00–5.00	Needlework, knitting and domestic employment.
3.00–4.00	Reading with explanations.		
4.00–5.00	Geography, with maps.	5.00–6.00	Supper. Recreation.
6.00	Supper	6.00–8.00	Needlework, knitting & domestic employment.
8.00	Prayers. Retire to bed.	8.00	Prayers. Retire to bed.

The premises where teaching was carried out also varied widely. Most workhouses had at least a room designated for the purpose, with larger establishments having their own school block. Some even set up schools on separate sites, or joined in the operation of District Schools where children were housed, educated and also provided industrial training.

In 1868, a report by Poor Law Board Inspector Mr Bowyer described an ordinary workhouse school at that time:

It generally opens on a yard enclosed by a high wall, with a circular swing in its centre for exercise during play hours. The room is usually about 20 feet long by 10 broad, with a flat ceiling 10 or 11 feet high, imperfectly ventilated by means of openings high up in the wall, or perforated zinc tubes traversing the room from wall to wall, and opening outside. The windows are small and square, and if they should look out upon an adult ward they are darkened by whitewashing the panes. During the dark days in winter the instruction of the children is much hindered by want of light, while their spirits and probably their health must be affected by the closeness occasioned by the lowness of the ceiling... In the older schoolrooms the desk and the benches are placed against the walls; in the new ones or in the old ones that have been refurnished parallel desks have been introduced.

During the latter half of the nineteenth century, workhouses increasingly sent their children out to local schools such as one of the British or National Schools, or from 1873, to one of the new schools set up by a local School Board following the 1870 Elementary Education Act. In 1890, 200 workhouse schools were still operating in unions in England and Wales; by 1900, the number had fallen to forty-five.

(*See also*: **Board School**; **Children**; **National Schools and British Schools**; **Teachers**)

WORKHOUSE TEST

The workhouse test was the principle whereby eligibility for poor relief was determined by willingness to take up residence in a workhouse. The 'test' assumed that the prospect of the workhouse should act as a deterrent and that relief should only be available to those who were desperate enough to accept its regime. The workhouse test, which may owe its origin to Matthew Marryott, was one of the provisions of the Knatchbull's Act of 1723, also known as the Workhouse Test Act.

The workhouse test was a cornerstone of the New Poor Law established by the Poor Law Amendment Act of 1834. It was implemented on the principle that relief to a man was to be treated as relief to any of his dependants: if he entered the workhouse, the rest of his family had to accompany him.

In the 1880s, the idea of a 'modified' workhouse test emerged, which allowed an able-bodied man to be detained in the workhouse while his family received out relief. An early instance of this was in 1888 when the Local Government Board issued an order to the Whitechapel Union allowing out relief to be given to a man's family if he resided in the workhouse for seven days or more.[484] It thus provided an alternative to a labour test in unions where the Outdoor Relief Prohibition Order was in force. The advantages of the modified workhouse test were said to be that: it was a test of distress but did not break up family homes; the relief went to the family rather than the man who might not share it; the burden of sacrifice was placed on the man; and it removed superfluous labour from the market.[485] An Order allowing use of a modified workhouse test was also issued in 1905 at Poplar, allowing the union to send men to its labour colony at Laindon while their families received out relief.

(*See also*: **Labour Colony / Farm Colony**; **Outdoor Labour Test**; **Workhouse**)

WORKHOUSE TOKENS

In the early 1800s, a scarcity of copper and silver led to a national shortage of coins and corresponding difficulties in small monetary transactions. To help remedy the situation, some poor law authorities (and a variety of other organisations) had special tokens minted for local use, for example as part of out relief payments. Places that issued tokens included Birmingham, Bradford, Halesowen, Leeds, Sheffield, Tunstead and Happing in Norfolk, and Worcester.

Tokens were produced in a number of denominations, the most common being 1*d*, 3*d* and 1*s*. A trader who received such tokens could then redeem them at the workhouse. In 1817,

A penny token issued by the Birmingham Guardians of the Poor in 1812. The design includes an image of the workhouse which stood near the city centre, between Lichfield Street and Steelhouse Lane. The building, which housed more than 600 inmates, was in use until 1852.

such tokens were declared illegal although a temporary exception was made for those issued by the Birmingham and Sheffield workhouses.

(*See also*: **Withers** (1999))

WORKHOUSE VISITING SOCIETY

The Workhouse Visiting Society was a campaigning organisation founded in 1858 by Louisa Twining, under the aegis of the National Association for the Promotion of Social Science. The Society's aims were to 'promote the moral and spiritual improvement of workhouse inmates', to 'provide a centre of communication and information for all persons interested in that object', and to 'establish a system of visiting, especially by ladies, for: befriending destitute and orphan children, both while at school and after they were placed in situations; instructing and comforting the sick and afflicted; and benefiting the ignorant and depraved, for example by forming classes for instruction or encouraging useful occupation during hours of leisure.'[486]

Members of the Society, subject to the Board of Guardians' agreement, undertook activities such as: visiting inmates who otherwise never or rarely received them; reading from the Bible and other religious works, especially for the benefit of those unable to attend church services; conducting small classes of religious instruction; reading from secular works of fiction and non-fiction, and encouraging the establishment of workhouse libraries; providing pictorial religious materials for those unable to read; and teaching inmates skills such as knitting.

As well as providing religious material, the Society advised its members that readings from 'entertaining and books will help to cheer and enliven many a dull and vacant hour, especially in the workroom.'[487] Louisa Twining's own 300-page volume of *Readings for Visitors to Workhouses and Hospitals* fell rather short in this respect, mostly comprising sermons on gloomy themes such as 'Sickness – God's Chastisement' and 'The Christian's Desire to Depart'.

Workhouses did not always welcome these new visitors. Some feared that the ladies could uncover information that might discredit officials. Others were concerned about potential religious issues, such as Roman Catholic visitors ministering to Protestant inmates.

The Society published a journal from January 1859 until 1865. It also established several homes. The Industrial Home for Girls, opened in 1861 at 22 New Ormond Street WC, was funded by subscriptions and donations and housed girls aged from thirteen to eighteen who were taken from workhouses, or were about to enter them. The girls were trained for employment in domestic service and also provided with 'moral discipline'. Two other homes took in paying residents – the Home for Incurable Women was established in 1861 at 21 New Ormond Street and a Home for Epileptic and Incurable Women and for the Training of Ladies and Nurses in the Care of the Sick was opened in 1866 at 20 Queen Square, WC.

(*See also*: **National Association for the Promotion of Social Science (NAPSS)**; **Religion**; **Twining, Louisa**)

A 1930s view of the former Cerne Union workhouse at Cerne Abbas in Dorset, one of several to find later use as a youth hostel. During the Second World War, the building housed evacuees from a London school.

X-RAY TREATMENT

(*See*: **Metropolitan Asylums Board**; **Ringworm**; **Wartime**)

YOUNG'S ACT

(*See*: **Poor Laws**)

YOUTH HOSTELS

A number of former workhouses later saw use as youth hostels, including those at Cerne Abbas (1932–55), Cleobury Mortimer (1932–36), and Neath (1933–46).

ZULU

Workhouses often became the place where 'problem' individuals ended up. In 1880, London's St George's Union admitted a South African Zulu to its Fulham Road workhouse – the man appeared to be very nervous and in a state of exhaustion. Not being able to find a suitable regulation to deal with the matter, the Board of Guardians agreed to write to the Colonial Office for instructions.

APPENDIX A

POOR RELIEF STATISTICS FOR ENGLAND AND WALES

Table 1 – Poor Relief in England and Wales in Various Years from 1688 to 1847
The table below shows the total poor relief expenditure and numbers relieved at various dates between 1688 and 1847 for which the relevant data is available.[488]

Year	Estimated population	Total poor relief expenditure (£)	Expenditure per head of population (s d)	Estimated number receiving relief	Percentage of population receiving relief
1688	5,500,000	700,000	2 6	140,000	2.5
1701	5,600,000	900,000	3 2	180,000	3.2
1714	5,750,000	950,000	3 3¾	190,000	3.3
1760	7,000,000	1,250,000	3 6¾	250,000	3.5
1776	8,000,000	1,529,780	3 10	306,000	3.8
1784	8,250,000	2,004,238	5 0¼	400,000	4.8
1801	9,172,980	3,750,000	8 3	750,000	8.1
1803	9,210,000	4,077,891	8 10¼	800,000	8.6
1813	10,505,800	6,656,106	12 8	1,331,000	12.7
1818	11,876,000	7,870,801	13 3	1,574,000	13.2
1821	11,978,875	6,959,251	11 7	1,444,000	11.7
1824	12,517,000	5,736,900	9 2	1,147,000	9.2
1831	13,897,187	6,798,889	9 9	1,369,000	10.2
1832	14,105,600	7,036,969	10 0	1,400,000	9.9
1834	14,372,000	6,317,255	8 9½	1,263,000	8.8
1835	14,564,000	5,526,418	7 7	1,105,000	7.6
1836	14,758,000	4,717,630	6 4¾	943,000	6.4
1837	14,955,000	4,044,741	5 5	809,000	5.4
1841	15,906,741	4,760,929	5 5¼	952,000	5.9
1847	17,076,000	5,298,787	5 8¾	1,059,000	6.2

Table 2 – Numbers Relieved in England and Wales 1840–1930

The table below lists the numbers of individuals receiving indoor relief and out relief in England and Wales between 1840 and 1930, with each figure also being expressed as a proportion of the estimated population at that date.[489]

Over the years there were changes in the form of the returns presented and in their method of calculation. In most cases, the totals are derived by averaging snapshot censuses taken on 1 January of a particular year and on 1 July in the previous year. From 1859, separate figures for casual and insane paupers were recorded, with the latter who were in asylums being classed as outdoor lunatics. A change in the counting procedure in 1901 resulted in more accurate figures for casuals who, until that date, could have been double-counted if moving from one workhouse to another.

Year	Indoor paupers	Rate per 1,000 of pop.	Outdoor incl. casuals and insane	Rate per 1,000 of pop.	Total excl. casuals and insane	Per 1,000 pop.	Total of all relieved	Per 1,000 pop.
1840	169,232	11.0	1,030,297	66.0			1,199,529	77.0
1841	192,106	12.0	1,106,942	70.0			1,299,048	82.0
1842	222,642	14.0	1,204,545	75.0			1,427,187	89.0
1843	238,560	15.0	1,300,930	80.0			1,539,490	95.0
1844	230,818	14.0	1,246,743	76.0			1,477,561	90.0
1845	215,325	13.0	1,255,645	76.0			1,470,970	88.0
1846	200,270	12.0	1,131,819	67.0			1,332,089	79.0
1847	265,037	16.0	1,456,313	85.0			1,721,350	101.0
1848	305,938	18.0	1,570,565	90.0			1,876,503	108.0
1849	133,513	7.7	955,146	55.0			1,088,659	62.7
1850	123,004	7.0	885,696	50.4			1,008,700	57.4
1851	114,367	6.5	826,948	46.5			941,315	53.0
1852	111,323	6.2	804,352	44.7			915,675	50.9
1853	110,148	6.0	776,214	42.7			886,362	48.7
1854	111,635	6.1	752,982	40.9			864,617	47.0
1855	121,400	6.5	776,286	41.7			897,686	48.2
1856	124,879	6.6	792,205	42.1			917,084	48.7
1857	122,845	6.5	762,165	40.0			885,010	46.5
1858	122,613	6.4	786,273	40.8			908,886	47.2
1859	108,022	5.5	705,943	36.3	813,965	41.8	865,446	44.4
1860	101,160	5.1	694,559	35.3	795,719	40.4	844,633	42.9
1861	107,526	5.4	708,941	35.6	816,467	41.0	883,921	44.4
1862	118,782	5.9	742,785	36.9	861,567	42.8	917,142	45.6

Year	Indoor paupers	Rate per 1,000 of pop.	Outdoor incl. casuals and insane	Rate per 1,000 of pop.	Total excl. casuals and insane	Per 1,000 pop.	Total of all relieved	Per 1,000 pop.
1863	122,724	6.0	871,729	42.8	994,463	48.8	1,079,382	53.0
1864	120,464	5.9	844,417	40.9	964,881	46.8	1,014,978	49.2
1865	118,034	5.7	783,409	37.5	901,443	43.2	951,898	45.6
1866	118,198	5.6	746,145	35.3	864,343	40.9	916,152	43.3
1867	122,116	5.7	754,990	35.3	877,106	41.0	931,546	43.5
1868	133,570	6.2	800,882	36.9	934,452	43.1	992,640	45.8
1869	139,642	6.4	816,660	37.2	956,302	43.6	1,018,140	46.4
1870	140,778	6.4	838,295	37.7	979,073	44.1	1,032,800	46.5
1871	140,467	6.2	843,455	37.5	983,922	43.7	1,037,360	46.1
1872	132,825	5.8	791,448	34.7	923,941	40.5	977,200	42.9
1873	127,964	5.5	702,435	30.4	830,143	35.9	883,688	38.3
1874	126,657	5.4	646,456	27.6	772,819	33.0	827,446	35.3
1875	128,979	5.5	615,658	25.9	744,271	31.4	800,914	33.8
1876	124,827	5.2	566,980	23.6	691,355	28.8	749,476	31.2
1877	130,377	5.4	530,024	21.7	659,927	27.1	719,949	29.5
1878	139,364	5.6	527,390	21.4	666,537	27.0	729,089	29.5
1879	147,055	5.9	554,939	22.1	701,812	28.0	765,455	30.6
1880	158,554	6.3	582,241	22.9	740,620	29.2	808,030	31.8
1881	160,881	6.3	560,906	21.8	721,612	28.1	790,937	30.8
1882	161,114	6.2	557,127	21.4	718,104	27.6	788,289	30.3
1883	161,538	6.1	550,638	20.9	712,023	27.0	782,422	29.7
1884	159,969	6.0	534,388	20.1	694,219	26.1	765,914	28.8
1885	162,386	6.0	533,113	19.8	695,368	25.8	768,938	28.6
1886	164,289	6.1	542,325	19.9	706,447	26.0	780,712	28.7
1887	166,620	6.0	554,907	20.2	721,384	26.2	796,036	28.9
1888	169,615	6.1	554,375	19.9	723,844	26.0	800,484	28.8
1889	168,417	6.0	547,879	19.5	716,144	25.5	795,617	28.3
1890	165,603	5.8	530,233	18.7	695,653	24.5	775,217	27.3
1891	163,357	5.7	514,653	17.9	678,830	23.6	759,730	26.4
1892	163,471	5.6	496,921	17.2	662,144	22.8	744,757	25.6
1893	169,155	5.7	505,449	17.2	674,443	22.9	758,776	25.8

Year	Indoor paupers	Rate per 1,000 of pop.	Outdoor incl. casuals and insane	Rate per 1,000 of pop.	Total excl. casuals and insane	Per 1,000 pop.	Total of all relieved	Per 1,000 pop.
1894	179,881	6.1	518,810	17.4	698,603	23.5	787,933	26.5
1895	183,532	6.1	522,562	17.4	705,967	23.5	796,913	26.5
1896	186,504	6.1	534,602	17.6	720,964	23.7	816,019	26.8
1897	185,863	6.0	530,307	17.1	716,170	23.1	814,887	26.5
1898	187,663	6.0	525,389	16.8	713,052	22.8	813,986	26.2
1899	190,397	6.1	537,858	17.1	728,255	23.2	831,938	26.5
1900	188,423	5.9	500,214	15.7	688,637	21.6	792,367	25.0
1901	203,924	6.3	494,251	15.3	698,175	21.6	777,097	24.3
1902	212,936	6.5	502,125	15.4	715,061	21.9	797,243	24.4
1903	220,959	6.7	510,594	15.5	731,553	22.2	817,697	24.8
1904	229,035	6.9	516,036	15.5	745,071	22.4	832,454	25.0
1905	239,894	7.1	547,446	16.3	787,340	23.4	878,514	26.1
1906	247,758	7.3	549,796	16.2	797,554	23.5	891,637	26.2
1907	250,544	7.3	542,160	15.8	792,704	23.1	886,886	25.8
1908	255,958	7.4	540,098	15.6	796,056	23.0	892,972	25.7
1909	267,130	7.6	550,878	15.7	818,008	23.3	916,245	26.1
1910	275,075	7.8	539,642	15.2	814,717	23.0	916,377	25.9
1911	275,070	7.7	507,922	14.2	782,992	21.9	886,177	24.8
1912	267,426	7.4	408,106	11.3	675,532	18.7	780,329	21.6
1913	265,410	7.3	411,575	11.3	676,985	18.6	783,916	21.5
1914	254,624	7.0	387,208	10.6	641,832	17.6	748,019	20.4
1915	252,525	6.8	391,900	10.6	644,425	17.4	752,041	20.3
1916	225,767	6.1	364,888	9.8	590,655	15.9	695,600	18.7
1917	213,447	5.7	327,663	8.7	541,110	14.4	642,463	17.1
1918	199,422	5.3	302,431	8.0	501,853	13.3	596,163	15.8
1919	184,167	4.9	285,237	7.6	469,404	12.5	555,639	14.8
1920	180,927	4.8	297,834	7.9	478,761	12.7	563,045	14.9
1921	193,069	5.2	346,866	9.2	539,935	14.3	627,202	16.6
1922	208,881	5.5	1,146,913	30.3	1,355,794	35.8	1,448,611	38.3
1923	213,527	5.6	1,398,246	36.6	1,611,773	42.2	1,710,344	44.8
1924	215,477	5.6	1,062,402	27.7	1,277,879	33.3	1,379,038	36.0

Year	Indoor paupers	Rate per 1,000 of pop.	Outdoor incl. casuals and insane	Rate per 1,000 of pop.	Total excl. casuals and insane	Per 1,000 pop.	Total of all relieved	Per 1,000 pop.
1925	213,131	5.5	914,749	23.6	1,127,880	29.1	1,229,449	31.7
1926	216,636	5.6	1,010,582	26.0	1,227,218	31.6	1,331,002	34.2
1927	221,174	5.7	1,734,675	44.4	1,955,849	50.1	2,064,365	52.9
1928	220,770	5.6	996,992	25.4	1,217,762	31.0	1,329,882	33.9
1929	221,074	5.6	891,456	22.6	1,112,530	28.2	1,227,560	31.1
1930	216,984	5.5	849,804	21.4	1,066,788	26.9	1,182,885	29.9

Table 3 – Poor Relief Expenditure in England and Wales 1840–1930

The table below shows the expenditure on poor relief in England and Wales between 1834 and 1930.[490] For each year, the average expenditure per head of the population is included and, from 1840 onwards, separate subtotals are provided for direct expenditure on indoor and outdoor relief. The total expended in each of these years includes other costs such as staff salaries, loan interest and repayments, building repairs etc. and is therefore always greater than the sum of the direct relief sub-totals.

Year ended March	Expended on indoor relief (£)	Expended on outdoor relief (£)	Total expended on poor relief (£)	Expended per head of population (s d)
1834			6,317,255	8 9½
1835			5,526,418	7 7
1836			4,717,630	6 4¾
1837			4,044,741	5 5
1838			4,123,604	5 5¼
1839			4,406,907	5 8¾
1840	808,151	2,931,263	4,576,965	5 10½
1841	890,883	2,925,330	4,760,929	6 0½
1842	934,158	3,090,884	4,911,498	6 1¾
1843	958,057	3,321,508	5,208,027	6 5¼
1844	833,856	3,223,618	4,976,093	6 0¾
1845	844,816	3,272,629	5,039,703	6 0¾
1846	804,101	3,207,819	4,954,204	5 10½
1847	899,095	3,467,960	5,298,787	6 2½
1848	1,102,822	3,853,297	6,180,764	7 1¾
1849	1,052,515	3,359,270	5,792,963	6 6½
1850	914,264	3,155,097	5,395,022	6 1

Year ended March	Expended on indoor relief (£)	Expended on outdoor relief (£)	Total expended on poor relief (£)	Expended per head of population (s d)
1851	789,914	2,873,588	4,962,704	5 6½
1852	763,399	2,808,298	4,897,685	5 4½
1853	762,718	2,775,556	4,939,064	5 4½
1854	924,938	2,887,630	5,282,853	5 8
1855	1,093,712	3,192,909	5,890,041	6 3
1856	1,139,902	3,239,535	6,004,244	6 3¾
1857	1,088,588	3,152,278	5,898,756	6 1¾
1858	1,067,803	3,117,274	5,878,542	6 0½
1859	954,509	2,923,199	5,558,689	5 8¼
1860	912,360	2,862,753	5,454,964	5 6
1861	1,033,689	3,012,251	5,778,943	5 9
1862	1,133,286	3,155,820	6,077,922	6 0
1863	1,127,142	3,574,136	6,527,036	6 4½
1864	1,095,814	3,466,392	6,423,381	6 2½
1865	1,111,478	3,258,813	6,264,966	6 0
1866	1,188,784	3,196,685	6,439,517	6 1¼
1867	1,375,627	3,358,351	6,959,840	6 6¼
1868	1,517,495	3,620,284	7,498,059	6 11½
1869	1,546,580	3,677,379	7,673,100	7 0¾
1870	1,502,807	3,633,051	7,644,307	6 11½
1871	1,524,695	3,663,970	7,886,724	6 11¼
1872	1,515,790	3,583,571	8,007,403	6 11½
1873	1,549,403	3,279,122	7,692,169	6 7¼
1874	1,649,333	3,110,896	7,664,957	6 6
1875	1,577,596	2,958,670	7,488,481	6 3¼
1876	1,534,224	2,760,804	7,335,858	6 0¾
1877	1,613,757	2,616,465	7,400,034	6 0½
1878	1,727,340	2,621,786	7,688,650	6 2½
1879	1,720,947	2,641,558	7,829,819	6 2¾
1880	1,757,749	2,710,778	8,015,010	6 4
1881	1,838,641	2,660,022	8,102,136	6 3
1882	1,831,595	2,626,375	8,232,472	6 3¾
1883	1,869,505	2,589,937	8,353,292	6 4

Year ended March	Expended on indoor relief (£)	Expended on outdoor relief (£)	Total expended on poor relief (£)	Expended per head of population (s d)
1884	1,992,502	2,517,693	8,402,553	6 3¼
1885	1,921,857	2,469,846	8,491,600	6 3
1886	1,837,624	2,490,025	8,296,230	6 0½
1887	1,778,367	2,528,250	8,176,768	5 10½
1888	1,855,304	2,537,686	8,440,821	5 11¾
1889	1,862,799	2,503,838	8,366,477	5 10¼
1890	1,899,648	2,453,860	8,434,345	5 9¾
1891	1,951,486	2,400,089	8,643,318	6 0
1892	2,044,062	2,374,380	8,847,678	6 1
1893	2,105,760	2,370,613	9,217,514	6 3¼
1894	2,198,312	2,640,503	9,673,505	6 6
1895	2,216,231	2,530,574	9,866,605	6 6¾
1896	2,254,350	2,644,650	10,215,974	6 8¾
1897	2,256,667	2,680,296	10,432,189	6 9½
1898	2,384,135	2,732,909	10,828,276	6 11¾
1899	2,462,008	2,764,854	11,286,973	7 2¼
1900	2,548,295	2,697,684	11,567,649	7 3½
1901	2,663,075	2,721,517	11,548,885	7 2¼
1902	2,814,938	2,836,171	12,261,192	7 6¼
1903	2,920,556	2,932,745	12,848,323	7 9½
1904	3,050,806	2,901,130	13,369,494	8 0¼
1905	3,077,239	3,133,708	13,851,981	8 2½
1906	3,125,152	3,233,505	14,035,888	8 2¾
1907	3,073,752	3,211,280	13,957,224	8 1
1908	3,220,730	3,245,791	14,308,426	8 2¼
1909	3,332,454	3,344,969	14,717,098	8 4
1910	3,357,533	3,343,389	14,849,584	8 3¾
1911	3,473,706	3,130,348	15,023,180	8 4¾
1912	3,451,381	2,373,471	14,463,902	8 0
1913	3,520,444	2,458,717	14,935,605	8 2½
1914	3,489,332	2,421,689	15,055,863	8 2¾
1915	3,604,855	2,612,911	15,804,073	8 6½
1916	3,843,365	2,718,528	16,085,586	8 7½

Year ended March	Expended on indoor relief (£)	Expended on outdoor relief (£)	Total expended on poor relief (£)	Expended per head of population (s d)
1917	4,075,235	2,615,182	16,187,748	8 7½
1918	4,438,950	2,765,245	17,039,623	9 0¾
1919	4,673,709	3,053,974	18,423,883	9 10
1920	5,902,746	4,109,278	23,501,241	12 6½
1921	7,341,643	5,793,383	31,924,954	17 0¼
1922	6,808,854	15,443,084	42,272,555	22 3¾
1923	5,800,219	17,909,869	41,934,437	21 11¾
1924	5,760,968	15,066,059	37,882,282	19 8¾
1925	5,902,343	13,374,653	36,841,768	19 0¼
1926	6,027,614	15,735,527	40,083,372	20 7¼
1927	6,332,189	23,914,059	49,774,916	25 5¾
1928	5,886,898	15,146,879	40,918,528	20 10
1929	5,915,887	13,470,845	39,670,895	20 1¼
1930	5,968,091	12,972,027	40,630,903	20 6¼

APPENDIX B

POOR RELIEF STATISTICS FOR IRELAND

Table 1 – Poor Expenditure and Numbers Relieved 1845–1900
The table below shows the total poor relief expenditure and numbers relieved in Ireland between 1845 and 1900.[491] The left-hand part of the table shows the average daily number of inmates in workhouses and, from 1849, of those receiving out relief, in each case also expressed as a percentage of the estimated population of Ireland. The right-hand side of the table shows expenditure on poor relief with, from 1848, subtotals for direct expenditure on indoor and outdoor relief. The total relief expenditure (final column) includes other costs such as staff salaries, loan interest and repayments, building repairs etc. and is therefore greater than the sum of the direct relief subtotals.

Year	Average Daily no. in workhouses	Percentage of population	Average Daily no. receiving out relief	Percentage of population	Expended on Indoor Relief (£)	Expended on Outdoor Relief (£)	Total Relief Expenditure (£)
1845	36,497	0.44					316,026
1846	42,807	0.52					435,001
1847	83,283	1.04					803,684
1848	128,020	1.68			577,300	671,326	1,732,597
1849	193,650	2.67	522,068	7.19	797,294	679,604	2,177,651
1850	217,257	3.16	308,959	4.49	710,945	120,789	1,430,108
1851	217,388	3.34	8,359	0.13	692,914	11,399	1,141,647
1852	166,855	2.63	3,227	0.05	517,445	4,917	883,267
1853	129,390	2.09	3,022	0.05	416,030	4,920	785,718
1854	95,197	1.56	1,617	0.03	463,858	3,715	760,152
1855	79,598	1.32	2,150	0.04	432,842	4,702	685,259
1856	63,286	1.06	886	0.01	358,943	2,245	576,390
1857	50,688	0.86	954	0.02	292,685	2,412	498,889
1858	45,781	0.78	1,265	0.02	266,070	3,135	457,178
1859	40,369	0.69	1,296	0.02	234,202	3,239	413,712

Year	Average Daily no. in workhouses	Percentage of population	Average Daily no. receiving out relief	Percentage of population	Expended on Indoor Relief (£)	Expended on Outdoor Relief (£)	Total Relief Expenditure (£)
1860	41,341	0.71	2,001	0.03	272,682	5,514	454,531
1861	45,071	0.78	3,536	0.06	327,970	9,675	516,769
1862	53,605	0.93	5,593	0.10	373,216	14,750	578,789
1863	58,301	1.02	6,263	0.11	380,737	18,372	605,981
1864	56,957	1.01	7,859	0.14	366,732	21,473	596,465
1865	54,399	0.97	8,748	0.16	365,180	25,335	600,549
1866	50,740	0.92	10,045	0.18	371,363	29,748	611,831
1867	52,657	0.96	12,205	0.22	418,269	40,075	676,776
1868	54,197	0.99	14,940	0.27	436,842	44,785	707,556
1869	52,777	0.97	16,862	0.31	403,255	48,184	675,884
1870	49,737	0.92	18,296	0.34	381,884	59,181	668,202
1871	46,611	0.86	21,474	0.40	382,566	69,744	685,668
1872	45,903	0.85	22,552	0.42	401,840	80,477	729,331
1873	47,325	0.89	27,509	0.52	446,760	91,154	790,560
1874	47,624	0.90	30,176	1.51	457,944	93,587	817,281
1875	46,548	0.88	30,319	0.57	416,172	94,775	771,553
1876	44,346	0.84	30,246	0.57	399,097	97,403	763,155
1877	44,343	0.84	31,600	0.60	405,755	102,227	780,326
1878	47,749	0.90	33,547	0.64	449,634	110,415	845,608
1879	50,727	0.96	36,374	0.69	443,936	117,275	847,955
1880	54,976	1.06	39,629	0.76	481,710	153,586	929,967
1881	53,584	1.04	60,883	1.18	465,498	182,049	965,128
1882	51,383	1.01	60,196	1.18	466,216	180,575	967,483
1883	51,907	1.03	58,835	1.17	470,922	186,064	1,042,845
1884	48,386	0.97	60,384	1.21	443,761	181,210	945,930
1885	47,281	0.96	57,829	1.17	406,888	183,298	887,906
1886	46,961	0.96	58,965	1.20	381,194	235,500	904,018
1887	46,385	0.95	78,241	1.61	368,246	207,425	857,820
1888	46,105	0.96	65,506	1.36	369,197	201,152	850,252
1889	44,699	0.94	68,680	1.44	369,345	196,070	853,912
1890	43,427	0.92	62,286	1.32	368,375	194,750	856,008

Year	Average Daily no. in workhouses	Percentage of population	Average Daily no. receiving out relief	Percentage of population	Expended on Indoor Relief (£)	Expended on Outdoor Relief (£)	Total Relief Expenditure (£)
1891	41,893	0.90	62,231	1.33	370,042	198,838	871,424
1892	41,448	0.89	62,229	1.34	372,822	196,754	869,192
1893	41,414	0.90	59,137	1.28	352,638	188,566	857,910
1894	42,282	0.92	57,979	1.26	356,520	186,231	869,674
1895	41,648	0.91	57,435	1.26	353,262	185,936	863,944
1896	41,498	0.91	56,619	1.25	354,836	177,673	868,969
1897	42,518	0.94	54,469	1.20	374,160	178,687	824,846
1898	43,771	0.97	57,133	1.26	407,611	216,170	981,333
1899	43,570	0.97	64,604	1.43	402,353	213,864	1,007,420
1900	43,960	0.98	58,012	1.30	407,005	200,053	945,099

APPENDIX 6

POOR RELIEF STATISTICS FOR SCOTLAND

Table 1- Numbers relieved in Scotland 1864–1906

The table below shows the number of 'ordinary' poor (i.e. excluding lunatics) receiving poor relief, either in a poorhouse or as outdoor relief, in Scotland on each 15 May between 1864 and 1906.[492] Additionally, each of the totals is given in terms of the rate it represents per 1,000 of Scotland's estimated population, together with the ratio of the outdoor to indoor totals. The number of statutory poorhouses in operation in each year is also included.

Year	No. poor-houses in operation	No. receiving indoor relief	Indoor relief per 1000 pop.	No. receiving outdoor relief	Outdoor relief per 1000 pop.	Ratio of out-door to indoor recipients
1864	52	7,257	2.3	115,237	59.2	36.6
1865	56	7,348	2.3	115,637	59.7	36.3
1866	58	7,070	2.2	113,513	58.6	35.4
1867	60	7,929	2.5	114,806	64.6	35.4
1868	62	8,794	2.7	121,652	67.4	37.2
1869	63	8,346	2.5	121,657	64.2	36.9
1870	63	7,928	2.4	118,311	62.8	35.5
1871	62	7,749	2.3	115,160	61.9	34.3
1872	62	7,402	2.2	108,954	63.6	32.0
1873	62	7,899	2.3	101,736	72.0	29.6
1874	62	7,769	2.2	95,919	74.9	27.6
1875	62	7,673	2.2	91,195	77.6	26.0
1876	62	7,586	2.2	88,096	79.3	24.8
1877	62	8,046	2.3	85,334	86.2	23.8
1878	62	8,763	2.4	83,032	95.5	22.9
1879	62	9,140	2.5	85,998	96.1	23.5
1880	62	9,296	2.5	85,793	97.8	23.2
1881	63	9,040	2.4	84,918	96.2	22.8

Year	No. poor-houses in operation	No. receiving indoor relief	Indoor relief per 1000 pop.	No. receiving outdoor relief	Outdoor relief per 1000 pop.	Ratio of out-door to indoor recipients
1882	63	8,964	2.4	81,060	98.9	21.7
1883	63	8,722	2.3	79,494	98.9	21.0
1884	64	9,041	2.4	76,567	105.6	20.0
1885	65	9,007	2.3	77,355	104.3	20.1
1886	65	9,495	2.4	78,575	107.8	20.3
1887	65	9,095	2.3	77,889	104.6	20.0
1888	66	8,863	2.2	77,531	102.6	19.7
1889	66	8,471	2.2	76,295	99.9	19.2
1890	66	8,182	2.0	74,272	99.2	18.6
1891	66	8,160	2.0	72,294	101.4	18.0
1892	66	8,527	2.1	71,487	106.6	17.6
1893	66	8,824	2.2	72,178	108.9	17.5
1894	66	9,212	2.2	73,108	111.0	17.6
1895	66	9,083	2.2	75,234	108.7	17.9
1896	65	9,569	2.3	76,494	111.2	18.0
1897	64	9,908	2.3	77,313	113.6	18.0
1898	65	10,032	2.3	76,909	115.4	17.8
1899	65	9,965	2.3	75,004	117.3	17.1
1900	65	9,868	2.2	75,982	114.9	17.2
1901	65	10,306	2.3	70,126	120.6	16.8
1902	66	10,865	2.4	76,134	124.9	16.8
1903	67	11,711	2.6	77,112	131.8	16.8
1904	68	12,827	2.8	78,413	140.6	16.9
1905	70	13,255	2.8	80,772	141.0	17.3
1906	70	13,187	2.8	81,216	139.7	17.2

PRE-1834 WORKHOUSES IN ENGLAND AND WALES

1. An Account of Several Workhouses
The SPCK's publication *An Account of Several Workhouses...*, published in 1725 and with a second edition in 1732, provided the first extensive (though probably far from complete) catalogue of parish and local Act workhouses then operating. The establishments mentioned in the two editions are listed below. Spellings are as in the original text.

Bedfordshire. Ampthill, Bedford–St Cuthbert, Bedford–St Mary, Bedford–St Paul, Biggleswade, Cranfield, Kempston, Layghton, Lidlington, Luton, Shefford Cum Compton, Steventon, Turvey.

Berkshire. Faringdon, Newbury, Reading.

Buckinghamshire. Agmondesham [Amersham], Ailesbury, Asheton Clenton, Buckingham, Hanslope, Lavington, Newport Pagnell, North Crowle, Olney, Wingrave, Winslow.

Cambridgeshire. Chateris, Ely, Mershe, Wisbeche, Wittlesea.

Cheshire. Knutsford, Stockport.

Devonshire. Exeter, Tiverton.

Essex. Baddow, Billerica, Braintree, Brentwood, Barking alias Bury-king, Chelmsford, Colchester, Eppin, Fobbin, Grayes, Harlow, Hatfield Broad-Oak, Hornchurch, Maldon, Rumford, Saxfield, Southminster, Springfield, Westham, Wittham, Writtle.

Gloucestershire. Cirencester, Gloucester, Stroud

Hertfordshire. Abbots Langley, St Alban's, Aldenham, Arnum, Berkhamstead, Cheston, Gubbings, Hatfield, Hemel-hempstead, Hertford, Hitchin, St Stephen's near St Alban's, Stevenage, Tring, Ware, Watford.

Isle of Wight. Newport, Northwood.

Kent. Ashford, Canterbury, Chatham, Dartford, East Greenwich, Maidstone, Rochester (two Houses), Tunbridge.

Lancashire. Ashton under Line, Warrington.

Leicestershire. Harborough, Leicester–St Margaret, Leicester–St Martin, Leicester–St Mary, Lutterworth.

London and five miles around. Allhallows, Bread-Street; Bishopsgate-Street; St Andrews, Holborn; St Andrews, Saffron Hill; St Andrews, Woodstreet; St Botolph without, Bishopsgate; St Brides; Camberwell, Surrey; Christ-Church in London; Christ-Church, Spitalfields; Deptford, Kent; St Dunstans in the East; St Dunstans in the West; St George, Hanover Square; St George, Southwark; St Giles Cripplegate within; St Giles Cripplegate without;
St Giles in the Fields & St George, Bloomsbury (shared workhouse); Hampsted; St James, Clerkenwell; St James, Clerkenwell–Quakers Workhouse; St James Westminster; St Katherine near the Tower; Lambeth, Surrey; St Lawrence, Jewry; St Leonard, Shoreditch; St Margaret, Westminster, & St John the Evangelist (shared workhouse); St Martin in the Fields; St Martin, Ludgate; St Martin, Vintry; St Mary le Bow; St Mary Magdalen,

Bermondsey; St Mary Overee, or St Saviours; St Mary, Rotherhithe; St Mary Whitechappel; Stepney–Limehouse; Stepney–Mile End Old Town; Stepney–Ratcliff; Stepney–Wapping Hamlet (later St George in the East); St Paul, Shadwell; St Sepulchres within; St Sepulchres without.

Middlesex. Enfield, Harrow on the Hill.

Norfolk. Lynn.

Northamptonshire. Barton, Daventry, Densehanger, Grundon [Grendon], Northampton–All Saints, Northampton–St Peter, Oundle, Peterborough, Rowell [Rothwell], Stanford, Towcester, Wellingborough, Yarley [Yardley] Hastings.

Shropshire. Worfield.

Somersetshire. Bristol.

Suffolk. Mildenhall.

Surrey. Chertsey, Croydon.

Warwickshire. Coventry.

Wiltshire. Bradford, Marlborough.

Worcestershire. Worcester.

Yorkshire. Beverley, Hull.

2. The 1777 Overseers Returns

In 1777, an abstract of national poor relief returns by parish overseers in England and Wales, for the year 1776–77 (Easter to Easter), published by Parliament. The list below gives the name of each parish or township with a workhouse, and the capacity of each establishment.

ENGLAND

Bedford. Ampthill (25), Great Barford (20), Bedford–St Paul (60), Biggleswade (50), Cardington (20), Chalgrave (10), Clophill (20), Cranfield (24), Dunstable (20), Dunton (20), Eaton Bray (20), Flitton (11), Hawnes (12), Heath and Reach (14), Henlow (26), Houghton Conquest (20), Houghton Regis (20), Kempston (30), Leighton Bussard (60), Luton (80), Maulden (30), Northill (30), Old Warden (20), Polton (20), Potsgrove (8), Sandy (20), Shittlington (40), Silso (22), Southill (35), Stepengley (20), Sutton (11), Thurleigh (12), Tuddington (28), Wilden (2), Wimmington (10), Woburn (20).

Berkshire. Abingdon–St Helen's (120), Abingdon–St Nicholas (12), Aldermaston (35), Bray (?), Chievely (12), Cookham (90), Cumner (30), Great Farringdon (60), Hampstead Norris (10), Hungerford (30), Langford (12), Stratfield Mortimer and Oakfield (100), Newbury (120), New Windsor (90), Reading–St Giles (100), Reading St Lawrence (150), Reading–St Mary (90), Shalborn (16), Shinfield (42), Thatcham (40), Tilehurst (100), Wallingford–St Mary the More (50), Winkfield (40), Wokingham Town (50), Woodley and Sanford (50), Wantage (75), Wargrave (50).

Buckingham. Amersham (75), Aylesbury (50), Beaconsfield (40), Brill (?), Buckingham (40), Chalfont St Giles (80), Chalfont St Peter (80), Chesham (90), Edelsborough (30), Ellesborough (?), Eton (40), Great Missenden (30), Hambleden (60), Hanslop (40), Hitcham (60), Iver (60), Ivinghoe (50), Lavendon (15), Marlow (162), Little Marlow (40), Little Missenden (10), Moulsoe (?), Newport Pagnell (80), Olney (30), Princes Risborough (50), Stoke Goldington (18), Stony Stratford–St Giles (14), Wavendon (12), Wing (30), Wingrove (20), Winslow (20), Woburn (60), Chepping Wycomb (90), Borough of Chipping Wycomb (80), West Wycomb (44).

Cambridge. Basingbourn (?), Burwell (20), Cambridge–St Andrew (20), Cambridge–St Benedict (15), Cambridge–St Bottolph (10), Cambridge–St Edward (13), Cambridge–St Giles (20), Cambridge–St Mary the Great (20), Cambridge–St Mary the Less (10), Cambridge–St Peter's (8), Cambridge–Trinity (24), Chatteris (35), Chesterton (20), Cottenham (30)), Ely St Mary (35), Ely Trinity (80), Gamlingay (12), Guilden Mordern (12), Haddenham (40), Isleham (30), Linton (23), Littleport (30), March Hamlet (100), Rampton

(6), Soham (60), Sutton (33), Thorney (60), Waterbeach (20), Whittlesea (90), Whittlesford (40), Wicken (28), Wisbech St Peter's (150), Witchford (12), Wood Ditton (30).

Chester. Adlington (42), Altrincam (50), Audlem (10), Baddily (9), Barnshaw cum Goostrey (15), Brereton cum Smethwick (16), Bollington (18), Chester City (250), Chorley (80), Eaton (12), Faddiley (4), Gawsworth (28), Groppenhall (50), Macclesfield (160), Marple (9), Nether Knutsford (20), Newton (50), Mobberley (30), Nantwich (30), Over (30), Poole (18), Pott Shrigley (20), Rainow (30), Rode (6), Sandbach (20), Stockport (60), Sutton (20), Tarporley (40), Utkinton (12), Weaver (30), Weston (12).

Cornwall. Blisland (4), Bodmin (70), Breage (30), Budock (15), St Colan [Columb] Major (60), Gwennop (50), Mabe (13), Crowan (8), Guinear (40), Helleston (200), Kenwyn (50), Launceston (40), Lelant (14), Liskeard (60), Marazion (8), Padstow (100), Penryn (50), Penzance (30), Redruth (60), St Austell (60), St Blazey (12), Stratton (20), Truro (56).

Cumberland. Ainstable (10), Aldston (40), Arthuret (50), Bewcastle (25), Brampton (25), Caldbeck (80), Castle Carwicke (9), Cockermouth (70), Cumwhitton (7), St Cuthbert's– Botherby, Botchergate & Carleton Quarters (12), St Cuthbert's–Briscoe, Harraby & Upperby Quarters (7), Great Clifton (10), Crosthwaite (30), Nether Denton (21), Farlam (30), Hayton (7), Heskett (20), Kirkandrew–Middle Quarter (50), Kirkandrew–Mote Quarter (50), Kirkandrew–Nether Quarter (45), Kirkandrew–Nichol Forest Quarter (50), Kirklinton– Hethersgill Quarter (20), Kirklinton–Middle Quarter (20), Kirklinton–Westlinton Quarter (20), Leonard Coast–Askerton Quarter (20), Penrith (36), St Mary's–Caldewgate Quarter (20), St Mary's–Richergate Quarter (10), Rockcliffe–Castle Town Quarter (8), Rockcliffe– Church Town Quarter (8), Stapleton–Stanwix Quarter (12), Stapleton–Stapleton Quarter (20), Stapleton–Trough Quarter (3), Weatheral Parish (12), Whitehaven (135).

Derby. Ashbourne (60), Ashover (60), Barlow (10), Hamlets of Boden Edge, Bradshaw Edge & Combs Edge (60), Bolsover (20), Bonsall (40), Bradwell (30), Castleton (10), Chesterfield (50), Crich (40), Derby–St Alkmund's (34), Derby–All Saints (60), Derby–St Michael (14), Derby–St Peter (40), Derby–St Werburgh (50), Dore (60), Dronfield (12), Duffield (20), Eckington (36), Fairfield (70), Flagg (70), Hartington Quarter (70), Hartington Middle Quarter (70), Norton (16), Prescliff Tadington (70), Stanton (20), Tidswell Township (20), Walton (4), Winster (40), Wirksworth (60).

Devon. Alverdiscott (6), East Allington (20), West Alvington (30), Ashburton (100), Ashford (12), Aveton Gifford (40), Awliscombe (10), Axminster (80), Bampton (60), Barnstaple (80), Berryn Harbour (12), Berey Pumerey (40), Bicton (6), Bideford (75), Bigbury (20), Blackawton (34), Bridford (12), Brixham (60), Brixton (23), Burrington (20), Cadbury (10), Chagford (20), Chawley (24), Cheriton Fitzpaine (30), Chittlehampton (40), Christow (15), Chudleigh (20), Chulmleigh (36), Clist–Hydon (14), Clist–St Lawrence (10), Colaton Rawleigh (27), Collumpton (120), Colyton (66), Comb Martin (2), Compton Tefford (3), Cornworthy (40), Crediton (90), Cruwys Morchard (30), Culmstock (20), Feniton (8), Hartland (90), Heanton-punchardson (16), Hemyock (10), Holcombe Burnell (6), Honiton (60), Huntsham (Two families), Ilfordcombe (60), Kenton (150), Kingsbridge (20), Knowstone (28), Langtree (16), Lifton (50), Loddiswell (25), Loxbear (6), Malborough (28), Membury (18), Merton (30), North Molton (45), South Molton (100), Moreton-hampstead (60), Newton Abbot (70), Northam (80), Northcott (4), Bishops Nympton (60), Otterton (20), Parkham (20), Pilton (30), Plymouth (200), Plympton St Mary (100), Plymstock (30), Ringmore (20), St Mary Ottery (100), St Saviour within the Borough of Clifton (40), St Thomas the Apostle's (52), Sampford Courtenay (30), Sandford (60), Seaton and Beer (24), Shobrooke (40), Sidbury (40), Sidmouth (20), Silverton (60), Staverton (30), Stoke Damerell (175), Tavistock (50), Thorncombe (60), Thurlestone (20), Tiverton (400), Topsham (82), Great Torrington (20), Totness (40), Uffculme (50), Uplime (10), Wear Gifford (8), Woolfordisworthy (8), Yealmpton (26).

Dorset. Beaminster (100), Blandford Forum (50), Buckland Newton (20), Burton Bradstock (12), Charminster (20), Cranborne (60), Dorchester–Holy Trinity (80), Fordington (20),

Frampton (12), Gillingham (70), Haslebury Bryan (20), Lyme Regis (32), Lytchett Minster (15), Marnhull (60), Marshwood (12), Melcombe Regis (44), St James in the Town and County of the Town of Pool (80), Portesham (50), Puddletown (20), Sherborne (130), Stalbridge (50), Stockland (30), Sturminster Newton (50), Sturton Caundle (6), Tarrant Gunvil (5), Wimborne Minster (200), Wyke Regis (20).

Durham. Barnard Castle (50), Bedlington (60), Bishop Auckland (150), Bishop Weremouth (20), Bishopton (20), Chambois and North Blyth (40), Chester le Street (100), Coatham Mundaville (12), Cockerton (10), Cornforth (16), Crawcrook (20), Crosgate (18), Darlington (100), Durham St Giles (20), Durham St Nicholas (50), Egleston (12), Elvet (20), Framwelgate (24), Gainford (20), Gateshead (50), Hartlepool (20), Heighington (10), Nether Heworth and High Heworth (15), Houghton le Spring (16), Kyo (20), Lambton (100), Middleton (12), Monkton Tarrow and Hedworth (15), Newbiggin (12), Norton (24), Offerton (10), Pensher (30), Plausworth (100), Ryton Woodside (20), Sedgfield (30), South Shields (50), Stella (10), Stockton (80), Sunderland (90), Tanfield (30), Tweedmouth (36), Wakefield (12), Walsingham (60), Wearmouth (35), Westoe (18), Whickham (60), Winlaton (36).

Essex. Aberton (16), Aldham (20), Ardleigh (40), Ashdon (30), Aveley (40), Great Baddow (20), Bardfield Saling (12), Barking (70), Great Braxted (16), Beaumont with Mose (14), Belchampotton (9), Belchampotton St Paul (15), Little Bentley (26), Great and Little Birch (24), Bocking (140), Boxstead (30), Bradfield (12), Bradwell (13), Braintree (60), Brentwood (14), Great Bromley (30), Broomfield (20), Bumpstead Steeple (25), Bures (9), Burnham (24), Great Burstead (40), Buttsbury (10), Canewdon (30), Chelmsford (100), Chigwell (33), Great Clacton (30), Great Coggeshall (50), Little Coggeshall (15), Colchester–All Saints (28), Colchester–St Botolph (35), Colchester–St Giles (30), Colchester–St James (24), Colchester–Loxden (34), Colchester–St Martin (12), Colchester–St Mary at the Walls (30), Colchester–St Nicholas (14), Colchester–St Peter (20), Great Earls Colne (42), Engain Colne (30), Copford (30), Corringham (20), Dagenham (30), Danbury (18), Dedham (48), Fordham (22), Great Dunmow (50), High Easter (33), Epping (20), Faulkbourn (25), Felsted (20), Finchingfield (25), Foulness and North & South Shoebury (30), Fryerning (20), Goldhanger (18), Gosfield (20), Great Hallingbury (24), Halsted (80), West Ham (155), South Hanningfield (9), Harlow (20), Harwich–Dover Court (8), Harwich–St Nicholas (60), Hatfield Broad Oak (60), Hatfield Peverel (30), Hedingham Castle (65), Hedingham Sible (30), Hockley (20), Great Horkesley (26), Kelvedon (30), Kirby (24), Langham (25), Lamborne (40), Lawford (22), Layer de la Hay (15), Great Leigh (15), Leyton (30), Malden–St Mary (40), Mannington [Manningtree?](20), Great Maplestead (100), West Mersea (18), Messing (100), Navestock (25), Black Notley (16), Great Oakley (20), Pebmarsh (12), Pitsey (12), Purleigh (20), Ramsey (14), Rayleigh (20), Ridgewell (24), Rivenhall (25), Rochford (24), Roxwell (20), St Osyth (30), Shenfield (30), Southminster (30), Southweald (17), Springfield (35), Stanford (30), Stanford le Hope (20), Stansted (40), Stanway (18), Stebbing (30), Steeple (6), Stisted (20), Stock (10), Stow Maries (10), Tendring (20), Terling (20), Great Tey (28), Thaxted (50), Theydon Garnon (30), Thorock Grays (10), Thorpe (50), Tillingham (6), Tollesbury (30), Tolleshunt Darcy (10), Tolleshunt Major (10), Toppesfield (30), Great Totham (20), Little Totham (16), Upminster (20), Great Waltham (100), Little Waltham (20), Waltham Holy Cross (100), Walthamstow (50), Weathersfield (25), Weeley (16), Great Wigborough (20), Willingale Spain (12), Witham (60), Wivenhoe (30), Wix (25), Woodham Ferris (30), Writtle (100), Great Yeldham (20).

Gloucester. Admington (17), Aust (8), Avening (20), Berrington, Bisley (50), Bitton (25), Bristol City (450), Bristol–St Philip etc. (100), Broad Campden, Chipping Campden, and Wessington (70), Cheltenham (36), Chipping Sodbury (40), Cirencester (120), Dymock (30), Elberton (20), Gloucester City (200), Horsely (100), King's Stanby [Stanley] (70), Leatclade [Lechlade] (70), Littleton (20), Mangotsfield (60), Minchinhampton (100), Minty (20), Newent (150), Oldland (20), Stapleton (100), Stroud (100), Tetbury (60), Tewkesbury (36),

Thornbury (80), Winchcomb (70), Westerleigh (22), Wotton Underidge [Under Edge] (50), Yate (40).

Hereford. Dilwyn (20), Eardisland (15), Hereford–All Saints (18), Hereford–St John Baptist (20), Hereford–St Martin (7), Hereford–St Nicholas (10), Hereford–St Peter (15), Kington (40), Ledbury (100), Pembridge (30), Ross (100), Shobdon (20).

Hertford. Abbotts (44), Albury (40), Aldenham (30), Great Armwell (20), Little Armwell (4), Ashwell (12), Ayott St Peter's (4), Baldock (45), Barkway (30), Barley (25), Chipping Barnet (25), Bengeo (15), Berkhamstead–St Peter's (50), Bishop Stortford (70), Caddington (16), Cheshunt (70), Codicote (20), Digswell (9), Flampstead (30), Great Gaddesden (30), Great Hadham (50), Harpenden (20), Hatfield Bishop (60), Hemel Hempstead (60), Hertford–All Saints (30), Hertford–St Andrew (50), Hertford–St John (24), Hertinfordbury (30), Hitchin (80), Hodsdon (35), Ippollits (20), Kensworth (18), King's Langley (30), North Church (34), Northaw (20), Northmyms (30), Offley (30), Pirton (40), Redburn (40), Rickmersworth (80), Ridge (40), Royston (38), St Alban–Borough (60), St Alban–St Michael (30), St Alban–St Peter (70), St Alban–St Stephen (50), Sabridgworth (50), Sandon (25), Standon (70), Stansted Abbott (50), Tewin (20), Therfield (35), Tring (50), Paul's Walden (20), Walkern (20), Ware (90), Watford (100), Wellwyn (8), Weston (35), Wheathamsted (36).

Huntingdon. Alconbury and Weston (20), Bluntisham and Erith (28), Brampton (25), Broughton (23), Buckden (16), Connington (35), Ellington (12), Elton (10), Eynesbury (30), Hailweston (11), Huntingdon–All Saints (20), Huntingdon–St Benedict (14), Kimbolton (35), Holywell with Needingworth (30), Midlow (50), Ramsey (80), St Ives (80), Saltree [Sawtry] St Andrews & All Saints (30), Great Staughton (25), Little Stukeley (12), Yaxley (21).

Kent. Allhallows (6), Ash (50), Ashford (70), Aylesford (40), Beckenham (35), Benenden (40), Bersted (27), Bethersden (20), Bexley (40), Bidborough (6), Biddenden (52), Birling (28), Bordern (8), Boughton under the Blean (40), Boxley (36), Brabourne (30), Brasted (12), Brenchley (60), Bridge (36), Bromley (80), Buckland (10), City of Canterbury (250), Charing (20), Chatham (250), Chevening (20), Chiddingstone (30), Chislehurst (17), Chislett (33), Cobham (30), Cowden (24), Cranbrook (100), Crayford (26), Cudham (35), Darenth (36), Dartford (65), Deal (115), Deptford–St Nicholas (130), Deptford–St Paul (125), Down (24), East Church (40), Eastwell (10), Eaton Bridge (40), Elham (60), Eltham (36), Erith (40), Eynesford (15), East Farleigh, Linton and Loose (100), Faversham (70), Frindsbury (54), Frittenden (40), Gillingham (60), Goudhurst (55), Gravesend (50), Greenwich (350), Hadlow (16), Halsted (6), Hamhill (25), Harbledown–St Michael (10), Hartlip (10), Hawkherst (100), Hayes (20), Hearne (30), Hollingbourne (40), Horsmonden (20), Hougham (1), Ightham (20), Iwade (4), Kemsing (13), Kingsnorth (12), Lamberhurst (24), Leigh (30), Lenham (40), Lewisham (25), Linsted (100), Lydd (40), Maidstone (150), West Malling (20), Marden (40), Mereworth (14), Mersham (12), Milton [Gravesend] (50), Milton [Sittingbourne] (40), Minster [Isle of Sheppey] (26), Minster [Isle of Thanet] (30), Nackington (12), Nonington (15), Northfleet (40), Otford (20), East Peckham (40), West Peckham (20), Plumstead (45), Rainham (20), Ramsgate (84), Ripple (4), River (3), Rochester–St Margaret (70), Rochester–St Nicholas (90), Rolvenden (50), St Dunstan (26), St Lawrence (40), Sandwich–St Mary (36), Sandwich–St Peter the Apostle (24), Sandwich–St Clement (30), Sea Salter (16), Seven Oakes (80), Sheldwick (16), Shipborne (11), Shorne (20), Sittingborne (25), Southfleet (12, at Northfleet), Speldhurst (30), Stapleherst (45), Steeplegate (6), Stone (20), Strood (63), Sturry (50), Sundrish [Sundridge] (40), Sutton Athone [Sutton At Hone] (40), Sutton Valence (20), Swanscomb (16), Thanington (12), Throwley (12), Tonbridge (130), Wateringbury (15), Westerham (50), Holy Cross–Westgate (30), Westwell (10), Whitstable (42), Wittersham (20), Woolwich (100), Wouldham (5), Wrotham (80), Wye (40), Yaldinge (30).

Lancaster. Allerton (50), Ashton under Line (64), Aughton (114), Barrowford (14), Barton (30), Blackburn (30), Great Bolton (60), Brindle (60), Burnley with Habergham (50), Bury (50), Butterworth (45), Castleton (40), Chedderton (25), Chethem (25), Childwall (60), Churchnew (120), Colne (17), Colton (18), Cuerdley (50), Culceth (50), Dalton (20), Ditton

(50), Eccleston near Knowsley (50), Edgeworth (16), Elton (16), Failsworth (20), Hale (50), Halewood (40), Harpurhey (10), Heap (30), Great Heaton (6), Lancaster Borough (80), Liverpool Borough (600), Manchester (180), Marsden (20), Melling with Cunscough (50), Middleton (40), Oldham (60), Ormskirk (114), Pemberton (60), Pendleton (28), Pilkington (60), Prescott (80), Preston (90), Rainford (15), Great Sankey (45), Speak (50), Standish with Langtree (40), Sutton (30), Tottington Lower End (30), Warrington (100), Wavertree (50), Widnes (50), Wigan Borough and Parish (200).

Leicester. Ashby-de-la-Zouch (50), Barrow (50), Barwell (20), Bottesford (12), Bowden Magna (20), Burbage (20), Burton Obery (10), Coleorton (30), Cossington (16), Earl Shilton (30), Easton Magna (36), Enderby (-), Foxton (12), Gilmorton (18), Great Glen (20), Halloughton (16), Harborough (30), Hinkley (90), Hoton (6), Houghton on the Hill (15), Hugglescote and Donnington (30), Humberston (12), Keyham (20), Knighton (12), Leicester–All Saints (55), Leicester–St Margaret (80), Leicester–St Martin (90), Leicester–St Mary (112), Leicester–St Leonard's (7), Leicester–St Nicholas (14), Loughborough (70), Lubbenham (20), Lutterworth (30), Melton Mobray [Mowbray] (40), Mountsorrel North-End (16), Narborough (8), Oadby (30), Ratby (14), Rearsby (14), Sheepstead [Shepshed] (80), Smeeton Westerby (20), Syston (14), Thringstone (30), Wigston Magna (32).

Lincoln. Alford (15), Barrow (8), Barton upon Humber–St Mary (20), Belton [north Lincs.] (12), Bolingbroke (40), Boston (26), Bourn (44), Branston (20), Butterwick (10), Crowland (45), Deeping–St James (12), Denton (30), Digby (15), Dorrington (8), Epworth (20), Freiston (16), Gainsborough (70), Glamford Briggs (10), Gosberton (28), Grantham (60), Haxey (24), Hecking (12), Helpringham (6), Holbeach (35), Kirton (15), Leak (35), Leverton (16), Lincoln (60), Louth (40), Metheringham (15), New Sleaford (22), Newton (10), Pinchbeck (25), Great Ponton (10), Potterhanworth (10), Market Raisin (17), Ruskington (10), St Swithin (30), Sibsey (20), Skirbeck (12), Spalding (56), East Stockwith (40), Surfleet (12), Sutton–St Mary's (20), Swineshead (30), Waddington (20), Welbourn (8).

London City – Within the Walls. Allhallows–Barking (70), St Andrew Undershaft (50), St Anne and St Agnes Within–Aldersgate (28), Christ Church (80), St Dunstan's in the East (70), St Ethelburga (48), St Katherine Coleman (30), St Katherine Creechurch (45), St Olave in Hart Street (56).

London City – Without the Walls. St Andrew–Holborn (120), St Botolph Without–Aldersgate (240), St Botolph Without–Aldgate (300), St Botolph Without–Bishopsgate (250), St Bridget (220), St Dunstan in the West (72), St Sepulchre Without–Newgate (279), St Giles Without–Cripplegate (260).

Westminster. St Anne (150), St Clement Danes (350), St George–Hanover Square (700), St James (650), St Margaret and St John the Evangelist (420), St Martin in the Fields (700), St Mary le Strand (50), St Paul–Covent Garden (300).

Middlesex. Acton (16), St Anne (90), Old Artillery Ground (60), St Botolph Aldersgate (240), St Botolph Aldgate (200), New Brentford (50), Bromley–St Leonard (56), Chiswick (90), Christ Church (340), St Dunstan–Mile End New Town (50), St Dunstan–Mile End Old Town (90), St Dunstan–Stepney (150), Ealing Parish (100), Edmonton (76), Enfield (70), Finchley (18), Fulham (90), St Giles in the Fields & St George–Bloomsbury (520), St George (500), St George the Martyr's and St Andrew–Holborn (350), Hammersmith Hamlet (60), Hampton Town (30), Hampton Wick (6), Harlington (40), Harmondsworth (40), Harrow on the Hill (60), Hendon (30), Heston (30), Hillingdon (70), Hillingdon Parish (60), Hornsey (30), St James–Clerkenwell (300), St John–Hackney (22), St John–Hampstead (80), St John–Wapping (260), Isleworth (110), St Leonard's–Shoreditch (250), St Luke (400), St Luke–Chelsea (20), St Mary–Islington (60), St Mary le Bone (600), St Mary–Stratford Bow (40), St Mary Matfellon–Whitechapel (600), St Matthew–Bethnal Green (400), South Mims (55), Monkin Hadley (30), Norton Falgate (90), Paddington (12), St Pancras (120), St Paul–Shadwell (350), Pinnor (30), Poplar and Blackwall Hamlet (60), Rolls Liberty (50), Ruislip (30), Saffron Hill, Hatton

Garden and Ely Rents Liberty (140), St Sepulchre (20), Shepperton (35), Stanes (50), Sunbury (25), Tottenham High Cross (60), Twickenham (90).

Norfolk. Aylsham (80), Billingford (6), Denver (16), East Dereham (65), Dickleborough (60), Diss (50), Downham Market (20), Edgefield (50), Gissing (60), Harpley (4), City of Norwich (600), Norwich–Cathedral Precinct (16), Pulham–St Mary Magdalen (40), Paston (10), Redenhall with Harleston (45), Reedham (3), Scole alias Osmondeston (10), Stow Bardolph (20), Swaffham (50), Trowse Newton (8), Upwell (70), Walpole–St Andrew (12), North Walsham (80), Wymondham (100), Great Yarmouth (330).

Northampton. Abthorpe (30), Apethorpe (8), Earls Barton (36), Benefield (30), Bozeat (10), Chapel Brampton (8), Branston (20), Brigstock (30), Broughton (10), Long Buckby (14), Bugbrook (16), Byfield (14), Middleton Cheney (14), Clipston (20), Cosgrove (9), Crick (9), Culworth (18), Daventree (55), Denford (12), Everdon (15), Finedon or Thingdon (36), Geddington (14), Gretton (30), Great Oakley (18), East Haddon (20), West Haddon (6), Hardingstone (16), Irchester (10), Irthingborough (100), Kettering (80), Kingscliff (30), Kingsthorpe (20), Newnham (8), Moulton (32), Northampton–All Saints (60), Northampton–St Giles (15), Northampton–St Peter's (6), Northampton–St Sepulchre (45), Norton (12), Old otherwise Wold (21), Oundle (45), Great Oxendon (15), Paulerspury (20), Peterborough–City and Hamlets (110), Pisford (16), Raunds (36), Rowell [Rothwell] (26), Rushden (18), Rushton–St Peter's and All Saints (20), Scaldwell (12), Spratton (12), Stanion (20), Stoke Albany (12), Towcester (40), Thrapston (16), Titchurch (15), Walgrave (10), Great and Little Weldon (20), Weedon Beck (15), Welford (20), Wellingborough (70), Werrington (14), Welton (15), Wilbarston (30), Wollaston (10), Yardley Hastings (25), Yarwell (6).

Northumberland. Alnwick Parish (32), Ashholm (80), Bellister (80), Birling (30), Blenkinsopp (80), Byker (10), Carham Parish (30), Coanwood (40), Corbridge (100), Fetherstone (40), Heddon on the Wall (50), Hexham (55), Hollinghill Ward (22), Horsley (8), Kerton (60), Morpeth (24), Newcastle upon Tyne–All Saints (100), Newcastle upon Tyne–St John (26), Otterburn Ward (24), Plenmeller (80), Rochester (24), Rothbury (22), Elswick in St Johns (40), Westgate in St Johns (12), Thirlwall (80), Walltown (42), Warkworth (30), Whitton (22), Wooler Parish (56).

Nottingham. Basford (44), Beeston (12), Bingham (30), Bulwell and Hemshall (16), Bunney (8), Clarbrough (60), South Collingham (10), Greasley (30), Kneesal (12), Lound (30), Mansfield (56), Newark Borough (60), Nottingham–St Mary (150), Nottingham–St Nicholas (60), Nottingham–St Peter (60), East Retford (30), Snenton (10), Southwell (35), Sutton [near Newark] (30), Sutton [near East Retford] (40), Worksop (50).

Oxford. East Adderbury (12), Alverscott (8), Bampton (30), Banbury (60), Bicester–Market End (40), Blackbourton (30), Bloxham (35), Burford (30), Charlbury (40), Chipping Norton (40), Clanville (24), Coomb (20), Deddington (25), Dorchester (20), Hailey (40), Hanborough (20), Henley (70), North Leigh (35), Northmore (20), Oxford City (200), Standlake (14), Stokenchurch (20), Thame (30), Watlington (20), Witney (60).

Rutland. Barlythorpe (8), Lond's Hold (40), Uppingham (40), Whitsunding (12).

Salop [Shropshire]. Baschurch (6), Borough of Bishops Castle (25), Broseley (40), Buildwas (12), Chetwynd (-), Church Stretton (66), Claverley (20), Cleobury Mortimer (60), Drayton in Hales (75), Edgmond (16), Ellesmere (45), Hales Owen (260), Hodnett (20), Leighton (20), Ludlow Town (40), Lydham (12), Madeley (20), Newport (18), Oswestry (30), Oswestry Town (30), Pontesbury (20), Preese (60), Shiffnall (40), Shrewsbury–St Alkmond (15), Shrewsbury–St Chad (80), Shrewsbury–Holy Cross (30), Shrewsbury–St Julian (26), Shrewsbury–St Mary (40), Wellington (56), Wem (30), Much Wenlock (30), Westbury (24), Whitchurch (40), Whittington (20), Worfield (12), Worthen (-).

Somerset. Babcarry (10), Banwell (25), Bath–St James (35), Bath–Saints Peter and Paul (35), Bedminster (56), Berkley (60), Bicknoller (10), Bishop Hull (22), Bleadon (7), Brewton (50), Bridgwater (80), Brislington (12), Buckland (8), Carhampton (30), Chard (80), Chard Borough (50), Charleton Musgrave (24), Chedder (24), Chew Stoke (12), Clatworthy (8),

Old Cleeve (50), Comb St Nicholas (40), Crewkerne (80), Croscombe (20), Crowcombe (7), North Curry (20), St Decumans (60), Ditcheat (33), Dunkerton (8), Dunster (30), Fitzhead (10), Frome Selwood (54), Ham (10), Hornbloton (4), Ilminster (90), Keinton Mandfield (8), Keynsham (6), Lamyatt (12), Lincomb and Widcomb (10), Lyddiard St Lawrence (16), Lyng (10), Mells (80), Middlezoy (10), Milverton (100), Minehead (60), Nettlecombe (24), Ninehead (16), Nunny (60), Oake (4), Otterford (-), Overstowey (20), East Pennard (24), North Petherton (90), South Petherton (40), Pilton (30), Radstock (12), Road (30), Shepton Mallet (140), Stockland Bristol (8), Nether Stowey (14), Swanswick (8), Taunton–St James (40), Taunton–St Mary Magdalen (80), Walcot (100), Wedmore (40), Wellington (150), Wells–St Cuthbert (30), Weston (10), Wincanton (50), Winford (14), Winscombe (25), Winsham (40), Wiveliscombe (65), Wotton Courtenay (16), Yeovil (60).

Southampton [Hampshire]. Alton (60), Alverstoke (200), Andover (120), Basing (30), Basingstoke (56), Bedhampton (15), Bentley and Odiham (40), Bewley (35), Bishop's Waltham (40), Boldre (26), Brockenhurst (20), Catherington (30), Christchurch (150), Crondall (50), Eling (50), Fareham (60), Faringdon (8), Fawley (40), Fordingbridge (70), Greatham (12), Havant (50), Hinton Ampner (6), Isle of Wight ('A general workhouse'), Kings Somborne (35), Lymington (50), Eastmeon (60), Milford (40), Minstead (12), Petersfield (40), Portsea (210), Portsmouth (200), Ringwood (160), Romsey Extra (150), Romsey Infra (60), Seberton (24), Shamblehurst (45), Sherborn St John (40), Southampton (130), Southwick (18), Titchfield (80), Vernham Dean (30), Warblington (30), Whitchurch (120), Winchester–St Mary Callendar (12), Winchester–St Maurice (30), Winchester–St Thomas (40).

Stafford. Abbots Bromley (30), Audley (50), Biddulph (40), Bilston (60), Brewood (30), West Bromwich (100), Burslem (60), Burton upon Trent (60), Cannock (20), Cheadle (150), Chesland Hay (12), Castle Church (16), Forton (10), Ipstones (20), Kinfare (20), Leek Frith (20), Leek and Lowe (70), Leigh (30), High Offley (30), Litchfield St Mary (50), Newcastle under Lyme (40), Norton in the Moors (24), Pattingham (10), Penkridge (40), Rowley Regis (60), Sedgley (60), Stafford–St Mary and St Chad (31), Stoke upon Trent (80), Tamworth (80), Tattenhall (20), Tipton (30), Uttoxeter (80), Walsall Borough (130), Walsall Foreign Township (70), Wednesbury (60), Wigginton (15), Willenhall (25), Woodstanton (50), Woolverhampton (60).

Suffolk. Aldeburgh (15), Aldham (20), Alpheton (35), Assington (20), Barnardiston (30), Barrow (30), Belton (3), Bildestone (30), Boxford (30), Brampton (10), Brandon (22), Brettenham (20), Buers St Mary's (50), St Mary in Bungay (25), Bury St Edmunds–Thingoe Hundred 1747 (250), Cavendish (30), Clare (30), Cockfield (30), Coddenham ('House of Industry at Farnham'), Combs (36), Great Cornard (20), Little Cornard (14), Dalham (14), Debenham (40), Derediston (10), Edwardston (40), Elmsett (12), Farnham (6), Framlingham (100), Framsden (40), Fressingfield (26), Glemsford (50), Groton (30), Hadleigh (100), Hartest (30), Haverhill (40), Hitcham (30), Hoxne (40), Hundon (20), Ilkesthall St Margaret (6), Ipswich–St Clement (70), Ipswich–St Helen (10), Ipswich–St Lawrence (25), Ipswich–St Margaret (100), Ipswich–St Mary at Elms (10), Ipswich–St Mary at the Key (25), Ipswich–St Mary Stoke (30), Ipswich–St Mary Tower (30), Ipswich–St Matthew (30), Ipswich–St Nicholas (20), Ipswich–St Peter (28), Ipswich–St Stephen (24), Kelsall (40), Kersey (30), Lavenham (80), Lawshall (20), Laxfield (30), Mattlesden (26), Melford (150), Mendham (20), Mendlesham (30), Metfield (30), Mettingham (12), Mildenhall (70), Monks Eleigh (15), Mutford (10), Nacton (350), Nayland (40), Newton (24), Orford (20), Palgrave (30), Pettaugh (15), Polsted (30), Preston (16), Saxmundham (60), Snape (20), Somerleyton (3), Sotterley (14), Stoke [by Clare] (23), Stoke next Nayland (40), Stoven (6), Stowmarket (85), Stow Upland (20), Stradishall (16), Sudbourn (30), Sudbury (30), Syleham (40), Walpole (6), Walsham (20), Westhall (10), Wetheringset (25), Whitton with Thurleston (6), Wickhambrook (42), Woodbridge (100), Worlingworth (35), Wortham (30).

Surrey. Abinger (30), Albury (18), Barnes (20), Battersea (70), Beachworth (30), Beddington (10), Bermondsey (291), Blechingly (50), Burstow (15), Camberwell (100), Carshalton

(20), Chaldon (12), Cheam (14), Chertsey (70), Chiddingfold (12), Chobham (30), West Clandon (4), Cobham (40), Christ Church (150), Croydon (80), Dorking (80), Effingham (6 families), Egham (36), Epsom (60), Esher (34), Farnham (65), Frimley (12), Godalming (76), Guildford–Holy Trinity (20), Guildford–St Mary (24), Guildford–St Nicholas (20), Hambledon (8), Haselemere (30), Horne (20), Kingston (288), Lambeth (270), Limpsfield (30), Mauldon (12), Mitcham (60), Moredon (18), Mortlake (40), Newington (200), Ockley (25), Oxted (50), Petersham (6), Pirbright (30), Pirford (12), Putney (70), Reigate Borough (30), Reigate Foreign (40), Richmond (90), Rotherhith (200), Send and Ripley (4), Shiere (40), Southwark–St George (220), Southwark–St John (250), Southwark–St Olave (220), Southwark–St Saviour's (600), Southwark–St Thomas (23), Stoke Dawbernon (12), Streatham (30), Thames Ditton (30), Walton upon Thames (50), Wandsworth (120), Weybridge (20), Wisley (8), Witley (30), Wokeing (40), Wootton (25).

Sussex. Aldingborne (30), Angmering (20), Ardingly (20), Arlington (60), Arundell Borough (40), Ashington (8), Barnham (14), Battle (55), Beeding (14), Berkley (40), Bersted (25), Bexhill (40), Billingshurst (45), Birdham (23), Bolney (15), Bosham (26), Brede (30), Brighthelmston (70), Brightling (40), Burwash (70), Buxted (25), Chayley (40), City of Chichester (140), Chiddingly (25), West Chiltington (15), Chithurst (6), Cowfold (15), Crawley (8), Cuckfield (60), West Dean (18), Ditchling (20), Easebourne (26), Eastbourne (50), Ewhurst (45), Fairlight (30), Farnhurst (16), Finden (15), Fletching (38), West Grinstead (30), Hailsham (40), Hastings–All Saints (30), Hastings–St Clement (60), Hastings–St Mary of the Castle (20), Heathfield (40), Heene (6), Herfield (60), Herstmonceux (45), Heyshott (12), West Hoathly (40), Hollington (24), Hooe (30), Horsham Borough (80), Horstedkeyns (60), Hurstpierpoint (25), Iden (20), Ifield (20), Itchener (6), Itchingfield (4), Kirdford (60), Lameing (10), Lewes Borough (30), Lindfield (32), Littlehampton (20), Maresfield (20), Mayfield (50), Midhurst and Liberty of St John (30), Midlavant (12), Mountfield (30), North Mundham (16), Ninfield (15), Northam (40), Oving (12), Petworth (70), Poleing (12), Portslade (8), Poynings (20), Pulborough (46), Ringmer (24), Rogate (18), Rotherfield (50), Rottingdean (17), Rudgwick (30), Rusper (40), Rustington (10), Rye (60), Salehurst (100), Seddlescombe (30), Selsey (35), Shermanbury (15), Shipley (26), New Shoreham Borough (20), Slangham (24), Slindon (10), Slynfold (13), Sompting (15), Steyning Borough (18), Storrington (34), Stoughton (50), Terwick (5), Thakeham (20), St Thomas in the Cliff (30), Ticehurst (40), New Timber (9), Trotten (24), Uckfield (30), Wadhurst (30), Waldron (30), Warbleton (60), Warnham (20), Wartling (40), Westborne (90), Westfield (36), Wilmington (8), Winchelsea–St Thomas the Apostle (24), Wisborough Green (80), Withyham (43), Wivelsfield (16), Worth (20).

Warwick. Alcester (36), Aston (90), Atherstone (60), Bedworth (50), Birmingham–St Martin and St Philip (340), Brailes (40), Buckington (40), Chilvers Cotton (33), Coleshill (44), Coventry–Holy Trinity (140), Coventry–St Michael (180), Foleshill (30), Grandborough (20), Long Lawford (8), Napton (20), Nuneaton (70), Preston Baggott (20), Rugby (25), Solihull (60), Southam (20), Stoke (25), Stratford upon Avon (50), Old Stratford (40), Sutton Coldfield (45), Tamworth (50), Tamworth Borough (70), Warwick–St Mary (89), Warwick–St Nicholas (44), Wootton Wawen (80).

Westmorland. Brough (12), Crosby Ravensworth (11), Hartley (10), Old Hutton (10), Kirkby Lonsdale (15), Kirkby Stephen (30), Lambrigg (6), Ormside (4), Preston Richard (20).

Wiltshire. Ashton Keynes (20), Great Bedwin (30), Box (24), Bradford (140), Brinkworth (50), Burbage (18), Calne (100), Little Chalfield (16), Christian Malford (30), Corsley (50), Cricklade–St Sampson (40), Crudwell and Estcourt (26), Dauntsey (40), Downton (140), Highworth (38), Hilperton (10), Horningsham (50), Lacock (40), Market Lavington (24), Liddiard Millicent (10), Lyddiard Tregooze (20), Maiden Bradley (26), Marlborough–St Mary (52), Marlborough–St Peter and St Paul (50), Melksham (70), Mere (60), Pewsey (100), Purton (30), Ramsbury (70), Rowde (13), New Sarum–St Edmund, St Martin and St Thomas (200), New Sarum–Liberty of the Close (20), Stratton St Margaret (20), Tidcombe

(12), Tisbury (80), Warminster (120), Westbury (100), White Parish (60), Wilton (80), Wootten Bassett (40).

Worcester. Beoley (10), Bewdley (80), Blockley (40), Bromsgrove (100), St Clements (3), Dudley (100), Holy Cross (80), St John (40), Kidderminster Borough (70), Longdon (60), Mathen (10), Overbury (11), St Peter (20), Powick (20), Shipston upon Stower (30), Stourbridge (40), Old Swinford (40), Tardibigg (40), Upton upon Severn (70), Worcester–St Clement (20), Worcester–St Martin (40), Worcester–St Nicholas (30).

York, East Riding. Ampleforth (2), Beverley (100), Bridlington and Key (30), Broomfleet (2), South Dalton (2 families), Drypoole (4), Howden (20), Kilnwick (4), Kingston upon Hull (200), Lockington (4), Minster Yard with Bedern (10), North Newbald (4), South Newbald (6), Osbaldwick (100), Pocklington (12), Preston (24), Shipton (4), Sutton and Stoneferry (16).

York, North Riding. Abbotside High Quarter (24), North Allerton (28), Ampleford [Ampleforth] (2), Arkingarthdale (30), Askrigg (24), Bainbridge (24), Bedale and Ascough (80), Bowes (20), Burton cum Walden (8), Carlton and Carlton High Dale (20), Cloughton (6), Danby Wisk (8), Easingwould (25), Fylingdales (30), Grinton [near Reeth] (40), Grinton [near Leyburn] (35), Guisborough (14), Hawes (34), Helmsley (18), Hutton near Rudby (30), Ilton (20), Kirby Moor Side (20), Marsh [Marske] (6), Middleham (24), Pickering (30), Reeth (50), Scorton (18), Skelton (40), Stokesley (50), West Tanfield (8), Thirsk (56), Whitby (70), Whorlton (20), East Witton (12), Yarm (40).

York, West Riding. Aldmonbury (60), Allerton (30), Chapel Allerton (2), Alverthorp with Thorns (35), Armley (40), Aserley (6), Attercliffe with Darnall (24), Barnsley (30), Batley (40), North Bierley and Bowling (70), Bingley (40), Birstwith Hamlet (40), High and Low Bishop Side (30), Bolton Parish by Bowland (10), Bradfield (60), Bradford (70), Brightside Bierlow (24), Burton (14), Calverley with Farsley (40), Carlton Parish (12), Clapham with Newby (2), Clayton (20), Conisbrough Parish (20), Crigglestone (20), Dewsbury (30), Ealand with Greetland (80), Ecclesall Bierlow (45), Ecclesfield Parish (60), Eccleshill (36), Errinden (20), Farnley (10), Fellicliffe (40), Fishlake (26), Gildersome (20), Gomersall (70), Grassington (22), Guiseley (80), Halifax (100), Nether Hallam (20), Handsworth Parish (16), Harthill Parish (8), Hatfield Parish (8), Haworth (28), Heaton (8), Heckmondwike (26), Heptonstall (24), Hipperholm with Brighouse (40), Holbeck (45), Horbury (20), Horsforth (80), Horton (40), Huddersfield (50 or 60), Hunslet (45), Idle (60), Kettlewell (20), Keighley Parish (40), Kirkheaton (19), Knaresborough (60), Langfield (14), Leeds (200), Livesidge (40), Lockwood (15), Manningham (36), Menwith with Darley Hamlet (40), Midgley (24), Mirfield (30), Norland (12), Ossett (80 or 100), Otley (35), Ovenden (40), North Owram (70), South Owram (60), Pannal Parish (16), Potter Newton (2 families), Pudsey (60), Quick Parish (24), Ripon (30), Rotheram (40), Rothwell Parish (200), Rushworth (9), Scriven with Ten (8), Sedberg (30), Selby (20), Sheffield (160), Shircoat (30), Skipton (40), Sowerby (60), Soyland (60), Stainland (50), North Stainley with Sleiningford (10), Stanley with Wrenthorp (30), Stansfield (25), Tadcaster Bridge–West Side (8), Thorn (40), Thornton (30), Wakefield Town (120), Warley (30), Wetherby (30), Wortley (35).

WALES

Carmarthen. Laugharne (6).
Denbigh. Llansillin (40), Wrexham (70).
Glamorgan. Cardiff–St John the Baptist and St Mary (200), Swansea Town (100).
Merioneth. Llandderfel (8).
Montgomery. Llanfyllin (10), Myfod (8).
Pembroke. Begelly (3), Camrose (10), St Florence (5), Jeffreston (5), Lampeter Velfrey (6), Lanunda [Llanwnda] (3), Lawrenny (10), Lyfurvrane (4), Manerbier [Manorbier] (20), Mouncton [Mounton] (26), North Narberth (10).

APPENDIX E

NEW POOR LAW INSTITUTIONS IN ENGLAND AND WALES

The list below gives details of poor law institutions that operated in England and Wales after 1834.[493] The format of each entry is described by means of the following (fictitious) example:

Camberwick (PU 1/5/1836 10+12. SP 1920.) **W**: 23 Green Lane (now) Road, Camberwick SP123456 *c.*1823, enl. 1837 by G. Wilkinson. (PAI then St Joseph's Hospital from 1948. Dem. 1975) **CtH**: 22-24 Broad Lane, Trumpton *c.*1912. NRU). WAR

The above entry indicates that the Camberwick Poor Law Union was formed on 1 May 1836. It comprised ten parishes with twelve members on its Board of Guardians. It was reconstituted as a Single Parish in 1920. Its (only) workhouse was at 23 Green Lane, now known as Green Road, with UK National Grid Reference SJ123456. The workhouse first opened in about 1823 then enlarged in 1837 with G. Wilkinson as architect. After 1930, the building was a Public Assistance Institution then in 1948 became St Joseph's Hospital but was demolished in 1975. The union had a cottage home site in Trumpton from about 1912 – the building is now in private residential use. Surviving local records are held at Warwickshire County Archives.

Abbreviations used in the list are shown below:

<	before	**MH**	Military Hospital
Ab	Able-bodied inmates	**NRU**	Now residential use
bt	bought	**OP**	Old People
aka	also known as	**OPH**	Old People's Home
appr	appropriated	**PAI**	Public Assistance Institution
c.	circa	**PU**	Poor Law Union
cnv	converted	**POW**	Prisoner-of-War
CtH	Cottage Home	**PT**	Poor Law Township
CvH	Convalescent Home	**rb**	rebuilt
Dsp	Dispensary	**ren**	renamed
dem	demolished	**RH**	Receiving Home
diss	dissolved	**San**	Sanatorium
enl	enlarged	**ScH**	Scattered Home
GP	Gilbert Parish	**Scl**	Residential School
GU	Gilbert Union	**SD**	School District
Ify	Infirmary	**SmH**	Small Home
JC	Joint Committee	**SP**	Poor Law Parish
LI	Local Act Incorporation	**V**	Vagrant / Casual Ward
LP	Local Act Parish	**W**	Workhouse
m/w	merged with	**WW1**	First World War
MAB	Metropolitan Asylums Board	**WW2**	Second World War
Men	Mental institution		

Note that a few unions that straddled county borders changed the county to which they were allocated. In the list below, unions are placed under the county to which they were originally assigned, for example Todmorden is under in Lancashire rather than the West Riding of Yorkshire. *See* the main entry on **Poor Law Counties** for more information.

Bedfordshire

Ampthill (PU 10/5/1835 19+25) **W**: 1 Dunstable Street, Ampthill TL033375 1836 by J. Clephan. (PAI. St George's Hospital from 1942, later Cedars OPH. NRU.) BDF.

Bedford (PU 21/9/1835 44+45) **W**: 3 Kimbolton Road, Bedford TL055504 1796 by J. Wing. (St Peter's Hospital *c.* 1929–48 then Bedford General Hospital North Wing. Mostly dem. 2007.) **CtH**: Kempston Lodge, Bunyan Road, Kempston TL031474 cnv. 1910. (Closed 1993.) BDF.

Biggleswade (PU 14/5/1835 25+32) **W**: Great North Road House, London Road, Biggleswade TL200440 1836 by T.G. Elger. (The Limes PAI then OPH until 1969. Dem. 1972.) BDF.

Leighton Buzzard (PU 1/7/1835 15+20) **W**: Grovebury Road, Leighton Buzzard SP922243 1836 by W.P. Roote. (PAI. PoW camp *c.* 1946–48. Industrial use from 1960s. Part dem.) BDF.

Luton (PU 16/5/1835 15+21) **W**: 11a Dunstable Road, Luton TL086214 1836 by J. Williams. (St Mary's Hospital from *c.* 1948. Part dem.) **CtH**: Beech Hill Homes, Dunstable Road, Luton TL078220. (Dem.) BDF.

Woburn (PU 10/5/1835 16+20; diss. 23/8/1899) **W**: Off Duck Lane, Woburn SP948329 1836. (Closed 1899. Dem.) BDF.

Berkshire

Abingdon (PU 1/1/1835 14+17) **W**: 2 Oxford Road, Abingdon SU500977 1835 by S. Kempthorne. (Closed 1930. Dem. 1932.) BRK, ABG.

Bradfield (PU 2/3/1835 29+30) **W**: Central House, Union Road, Bradfield SU606716 1835 by S. Kempthorne. (PAI. Wayland Hospital *c.* 1948–1990s. Mostly dem. NRU.) BRK.

Cookham (ren. Maidenhead 1899) (PU 20/7/1835 7+15) **W**: 112 St Mark's Road, Maidenhead SU872814 1836 by Cooper & Son. (PAI. St Mark's Hospital from *c.* 1948.) **ScH**: Cookham Rise, Cookham; Leopold House, Grenfell Road, Maidenhead; The Gables, Court House Road, Maidenhead; Boyne Hill, Maidenhead; Furze House, Cannon Court Lane, Furze Platt. BRK.

Easthampstead (PU 27/7/1835 5+10) **W**: Crowthorne Road, Easthampstead SU864675 1826. (PAI then Church Hill House Institute for 'mental defectives', later Church Hill House Hospital.) **CtH**: Wokingham Road, Bracknell. (Closed *c.* 1925.) **CtH**: 76 Binfield Road, Bracknell SU864698 *c.* 1925. (Later St Anthony's home. Now child care centre.) BRK.

Faringdon (PU 2/2/1835 30+34) **W**: Ferndale Street, Faringdon SU291955 1801. (Rebuilt 1846, dem. 1960s. Site now Brackendale OPH.) BRK.

Hungerford (ren. Hungerford & Ramsbury 1896) (PU 1/5/1835 20+27) **W**: Park Street, Hungerford SU339683 1847 by S.O. Foden. (PAI. Hungerford Hospital *c.* 1948–1990s. Dem. except chapel.) BRK.

Newbury (PU 17/5/1835 18+23) **W**: 214 Newtown Road, Newbury SU473655 1836 by S. Kempthorne. (PAI, later Sandleford Hospital. Dem. 2004.) BRK.

Reading (PU 10/8/1835 3+15; SP 1905) **W1**: Thorn Street, Reading SU711734 <1834. (Closed *c.* 1867 then became Union offices and casual wards. Dem.) **W2**: Pinkney's Lane, Reading SU710729 1790s. (Closed *c.* 1867. Dem.) **W3**: 344 Oxford Road, Reading SU697738 1867 by Woodman. (MH 1914–20; Battle Infirmary from 1921; Battle Hospital from 1930. Dem. 2005.) **RH**: 109 London Road, Reading SU728731. (Dem.) **ScH**: 82-84 Crescent Road; 'Camarra' and 'Rosemont', King's Road; 109 London Road; 11-13 Millman Road; 59 Queen's Road; 23-25 and 40 Russell Street; 'Wilson' and 'Clifford', South Street; 'Ashberry' and 'Sutton', Southampton Street. **Dsp**: 72 Friar Street. BRK.

Reading & Wokingham SD (SD 28/11/1849) **Scl**:Victoria Road,Wargrave SU790786
<1834. (Closed early 1900s. Dem. by 1930.) BRK.

Wallingford (PU 2/6/1835 29+29) **W**: 1 Wantage Road,Wallingford SU600898 1807. (PAI.
St Mary's Hospital c.1948–1990s. Dem.) **CtH**:Wantage Road,Wallingford SU598900 1900.
(Now social services use.) BRK.

Wantage (PU 4/4/1835 33+36) **W**: Manor Road,Wantage SU397855 1836 by S. Kempthorne.
(PAI.The Downs Hospital c.1948. Later used as stables. Mostly dem.) **SmH**: Manor Road,
Wantage. BRK.

Windsor (PU 7/9/1835 6+18) **W**: Crimp Hill House, Crimp Hill, Old Windsor SU977737
1839 by G.G. Scott & W.B. Moffatt. (PAI. Part of King Edward VII Hospital, later Old
Windsor Hospital. Closed 1991. NRU.) **CtH**: (Boys) Albany House, Croft Corner, Old
Windsor SU984746. (Dem.) **CtH**: (Girls) Ashdene, St Jude's Road, Englefield Green
SU993707. (Dem.) BRK.

Wokingham (PU 1/8/1835 16+20) **W1**:Victoria Road,Wargrave SU790786 <1834.
(Reading & Wokingham District School from c.1850. Dem.) **W2**: 41 Barkham Road,
Wokingham SU803685 1850 by R. Billings. (PAI.Wokingham Hospital from c.1948.) **CtH**:
Oxford Road,Wokingham. BRK.

Buckinghamshire

Amersham (PU 25/3/1835 7+14) **W**:Whielden Street,Amersham SU955970 1838 by G.G.
Scott & W.B. Moffatt. (PAI later St Mary's Hospital, then Amersham General Hospital.
NRU.) BKM.

Aylesbury (PU 6/7/1835 40+48) **W1**: Oxford Road,Aylesbury SP816137 1830. (Closed 1844.
Dem.) **W2**: 100 Bierton Hill,Aylesbury SP825146 1844 by S.O. Foden. (PAI.Tindal Hospital
from c.1948, now Tindal Centre.) **ScH**:The Mount, Kimble, Princes Risborough. BKM.

Buckingham (PU 13/7/1835 30+32) **W**: 19 Stratford Road, Buckingham SP697343 1836 by
G.G. Scott. (PAI. Closed 1930s. Dem.) BKM.

Eton (PU 25/3/1835 19+22) **W**:Albert House,Albert Street, Slough SU976794 1835 by
S. Kempthorne. (PAI. Upton Hospital from c.1948.) BKM.

Newport Pagnell (PU 26/9/1835 45+48) **W**: 1 London Road, Newport Pagnell SP886432
1836 by W.P. Roote. (PAI. Renny Lodge Hospital from c.1948. Dem. 1994.) BKM.

Winslow (PU 9/6/1835 17+18) **W**: 1 Buckingham Road,Winslow SP768281 1835 by G.G.
Scott. (PAI.Winslow Hospital from c.1948. Mostly dem.) BKM.

Wycombe (PU 25/3/1835 33+41) **W**:Wycombe Road, Saunderton SU815980 1843 by G.G.
Scott & W.B. Moffatt. (Closed c.1918. Dem.) **Scl**: Bledlow Ridge Road, Bledlow SP781022
<1834. (After 1930 became Bledlow Homes for children. Burnt down 2010.) BKM.

Cambridgeshire

Cambridge (PU 2/5/1836 14+30) **W**: 81/81a Mill Road, Cambridge TL461579 1838 by
J. Smith. (County Hospital from 1932. Maternity Hospital 1948–83. Now sheltered housing.
Part dem.) **SmH**: 138 Ross Street, Cambridge TL469580 1915. (Dem.) CAM.

Caxton & Arrington (PU 18/6/1835 26+27) **W**: Ermine Street, Caxton TL301590 1837 by
W.T. Nash. (PAI. Dem. 1940s.) CAM.

Chesterton (PU 2/5/1836 37+39) **W**: 29 Union Lane, Chesterton TL460599 1838 by
J. Smith. (PAI, later Chesterton Hospital. Dem. 2003.) **SmH**: 83 Newmarket Road,
Cambridge TL460588. CAM.

Ely (PU 25/3/1836 14+26) **W**:Tower House, Cambridge Road, Ely TL533799 1837 by
W.J. Donthorn. (PAI.Tower (House) Hospital c.1948–93. NRU.) CAM.

Linton (PU 18/6/1835 22+25) **W**: Red House, Symonds Lane, Linton TL558473 1837 by
Hallett & Newman. (PAI aka Symonds House. Now OPH.) CAM.

Newmarket (PU 30/12/1835 29+36) **W**:White Lodge, Exning Road, Newmarket TL639642
1836 by W.P. Roote. (PAI then White Lodge Hospital, later Newmarket General. NRU.)

SFB, CAM.

North Witchford (PU 9/5/1836 7+25) **W**: Benwick Road, Doddington TL395912 1838. (Later Doddington Infirmary then Doddington County Hospital. Dem. 2003.) CAM.

Whittlesey (SP 29/9/1836 1+20; PU from 1894) **W1**: Broad Street, Whittlesey TL268971 1834. (Closed 1874. Dem.) **W2**: Eastrea Road, Whittlesey TL277972 1874 by F. Peck (Dem. Sir Harry Smith Community College erected 1954.) CAM.

Wisbech (PU 23/5/1836 12+31) **W**: 33 Lynn Road, Wisbech TL463101 1838 by W.J. Donthorn. (PAI. Clarkson Hospital c.1948–83. Dem.) CAM.

Cheshire

Altrincham (ren. Bucklow 1895) (PU 25/8/1836 40+45) **W**: Cranford Lodge, Bexton Road, Knutsford SJ748784 1840. (MH in WW1. Later Cranford Lodge Hospital, then Knutsford Hospital. Mostly dem.) **RH**: Clifton House, Cranford Avenue, Knutsford SJ747784. (Later known as Racefield. Dem.) **ScH**: Mobberley Road, Knutsford; 'Kilrie', Northwich Road, Knutsford. CHS.

Birkenhead (PU 2/3/1861 9+13) **W**: 56 Church Road, Tranmere SJ318875 1863 by T. Layland. (PAI. Birkenhead Municipal Hospital c.1933–48 then St Catherine's Hospital. Mostly dem.) **RH**: 591 New Chester Road, Rock Ferry SJ333862 Until c.1925. (Dem.) **RH**: Manor Grange, 2 Egerton Road, Birkenhead SJ337852 From c.1925. (NRU.)
RH: 47-49 Church Street, Birkenhead. **ScH**: Ashford House, Ashford Road; 66 & 76 Bridge Street; 100 Camden Street; 36 Carlton Road; 5 Lowwood Road; 297 & 305 Old Chester Road; 28 Pilgrim Street; and 93 Westbourne Road (all Birkenhead); 59 Albion Street, 6/10 Mill Lane, 141 Seaview Road and 66 Falkland Road (all Wallasey); 33 & 226 Bedford Road, Rock Ferry; 16 & 84-86 Highfield Road, Rock Ferry; The Tors, Thorburn Road, New Ferry. WIR.

Chester (LI from 1762; PU from 1869 9+19) **W1**: Kitchen Street, Chester SJ399662 1757. (Closed 1873. Dem. early 1900s.) **W2**: 57 Hoole Lane, Chester SJ420670 1873 by W. Perkin & Son. (St James' House PAI/Hospital from 1930, later Chester City Hospital. Dem.) **RH**: 2-4 Wrexham Road, Chester SJ401649. (NRU.) **ScH**: Dodleston Home; Saughall Home; Upton Home. CHS.

Congleton (PU 13/1/1837 31+34) **W**: Newcastle Road, Arclid SJ788624 1845 by H. Bowman. (PAI. Arclid Hospital from 1948. Dem. c.1995.) CHS.

Great Boughton (ren. Tarvin 1871) (PU 17/5/1837 101+103) **W**: Tarvin House, Heath Lane, Great Boughton SJ424659 1857 by J. Harrison. (PAI then Heath Lane Hospital. Dem. 1970s.) CHS.

Macclesfield (PU 26/9/1836 41+50) **W1**: Walker Lane, Sutton SJ924709 1785. (Closed c.1845. NRU.) **W2**: Tower Hill, Rainow SJ949757 <1834. (Closed c.1845. NRU.) **W3**: Town's Yard, Waters Green, Macclesfield SJ920737 <1834. (Closed c.1845. Dem.) **W4**: Prestbury Road, Macclesfield SJ909739 1845 by G.G. Scott & HB Moffatt. (West Park Hospital c.1929–48 then Macclesfield Hospital, West Park Branch.) **ScH**: (Girls) Ash Mount, Peter Street, Macclesfield 1912. **ScH**: (Boys) Holm Lea, Chester Road, Macclesfield. CHS.

Nantwich (PU 18/2/1837 86+88) **W**: 100 Barony Road, Nantwich SJ654533 1780. (Later Barony Hospital. Now offices etc. Part dem.) **Scl**: 100 Barony Road, Nantwich SJ653533 1880 by J. Davenport. (Now offices.) **CtH**: The Mount, Crewe Road, Nantwich SJ660523. CHS.

Northwich (PU 20/10/1836 61+59) **W**: 160 London Road, Northwich SJ658731 1839 by G. Latham. (PAI, later Weaver Hall OPH until 1964. Now Salt Museum. Part dem.) **CtH**: The Lymes, 271 London Road, Leftwich cv. 1924. CHS.

Runcorn (PU 26/8/1836 40+42) **W**: 50 Northwich Road, Dutton SJ575793 1857. (Dutton Hospital PAI. Dem.) **SmH**: Dutton Lodge, Lodge Lane, Dutton SJ581778. (NRU.) CHS.

Stockport (PU 3/2/1837 16+21) **W**: 59A Shaw Heath, Stockport SJ895895 1842 by H. Bowman. (PAI. Shaw Heath Hospital from 1949; St Thomas' Hospital from 1954. Now Stockport College.) **Ify**: 26 Poplar Grove, Stepping Hill, Stockport SJ912875 1905 by

W.H. Ward. (Stepping Hill Municipal Hospital from *c.*1938. Now Stepping Hill Hospital. Part dem.) **ScH**: 2 Hall Street; 1 Mount Vernon, Turncroft Lane; 20-26 St Thomas's Place; Brook House, 41 Bank Lane; The Cottage, Heaton Road, Heaton Norris. STC.

Wirral (PU 16/5/1836 56+57) **W**: Clatterbridge Road, Bebington SJ320821 1837 by W. Cole. (Clatterbridge County Hospital from 1930s, Clatterbridge Hospital from *c.*1950. Dem.) **RH**: Hoylake . WIR.

Cornwall

Bodmin (PU 10/5/1837 21+36) **W**: Cross Lane, Bodmin SX074673 1842 by W. Dwelly. (NRU.) **ScH**: 17 (now 22) Beacon Road, Bodmin. **ScH**: Berrycombe Hill, Bodmin. CON.

Camelford (PU 1/2/1837 14+22) **W**: Sportsman's Road, Camelford SX101834 1858. (NRU.) CON.

Falmouth (PU 13/6/1837 10+23) **W1**: Gyllyng Street, Falmouth SW808327 *c.*1820. (Children's home from 1852 then school. Dem 1970s.) **W2**: Falmouth Parish <1834. (Closed *c.*1852.) **W3**: Church Lane, Penryn <1821. (Closed *c.*1852) **W4**: Union Road, Budock SW788333 1852 by F.W. Porter. (Budock House PAI. Budock Hospital from *c.*1948. Dem. 2008.) **SmH**: 11 Clare Terrace, Falmouth SW807326. (NRU.) CON.

Helston (PU 12/6/1837 18+37) **W1**: Wendron Street, Helston SW660275 *c.*1828. (Closed *c.*1857) **W2**: Ashton, Breage <1834. (Closed *c.*1857) **W3**: 78a Meneage Street, Helston SW662272 1857 by F.W. Porter. (PAI. Meneage Hospital from *c.*1948. NRU.) CON.

Launceston (PU 2/2/1837 21+39) **W**: Hurdon Road, Launceston SX335838 1839 by C. Lang. (PAI, then Page's Cross Hospital, later St Mary's Hospital. Dem.) CON.

Liskeard (PU 16/1/1837 26+46) **W**: Station Road, Liskeard SX247640 1839 by G.G. Scott & W.B. Moffatt. (Lamellion House PAI. Lamellion Hospital from *c.*1948. Mostly dem.) **SmH**: 5 Wadeland Terrace, New Road, Liskeard SX239642 1914. (NRU.) **SmH**: 6 Westwood, Old Road, Liskeard SX246646. (NRU.) CON.

Penzance (PU 10/6/1837 19+44) **W**: Fore Street, Madron SW450321 1838 by G.G. Scott & W.B. Moffatt. (Tally Ho' from *c.*1930, industrial/residential use. Part dem.) CON.

Redruth (PU 13/5/1837 8+29) **W**: Illogan Highway, Redruth SW685416 1838 by G.G. Scott & W.B. Moffatt. (PAI, later Barncoose Hospital, now Camborne–Redruth Hospital. Part dem.) CON.

St Austell (PU 30/4/1837 15+33) **W**: Priory Road, St Austell SX011526 1839 by G.G. Scott & W.B. Moffatt. (PAI. Sedgemoor Priory Hospital from *c.*1948. Dem.) **ScH**: 'Slades', 'Tregonissey', 'St Blazey Gate', 'Godolphin', 'Trewhiddle'. CON.

St Columb Major (PU 9/5/1837 16+31) **W**: New Road, St Columb Major SW916637 1840 by G.G. Scott & W.B. Moffatt. (In 1935 became The Retreat home for 'mental defectives'. NRU.) **ScH**: (Boys) Fore Street; (Girls) Bank Street; New Road. CON.

St Germans (PU 14/1/1837 14+23) **W**: Union Road (now Marine Drive), Torpoint SX437547 1838 by C. Lang. (PAI. Dem. 1960s.) **SmH**: Anderton Villas, Lower Anderton Road, Millbrook SX430521. (NRU.) CON.

Stratton (PU 28/1/1837 11+24) **W**: Union Hill, Stratton SS226064 1856. (PAI. Later industrial use. Dem.) CON.

Truro (PU 12/5/1837 24+45) **W1**: St Mary's, Truro <1834. (Closed *c.*1850.) **W2**: St Clement's, Truro <1834. (Closed *c.*1850.) **W3**: Probus <1834. (Closed *c.*1850.) **W4**: Union Hill (now Tregolls Road), Truro SW838456 1850 by W. Harris. (1915–19 naval hospital. PAI. Later St Clement's Hospital. NRU.) CON.

Cumberland

Alston with Garrigill (SP 4/3/1837) **W**: Wide Way, Alston NY717460 <1834. (NRU.) CUC.

Bootle (PU 12/6/1837 12+16) **W1**: Bootle <1834. (Closed *c.*1856.) **W2**: Millom <1834. (Closed *c.*1856.) **W3**: Church Lane, Bootle SD100884 1856. (Now council depot. Mostly dem.) CUW.

Brampton (PU 12/6/1837 14+20) **W1**: Gelt Road, Brampton NY530605 <1834. (Closed 1875. NRU.) **W2**: Union Lane, Brampton NY530613 1875 by C.S. & A.J. Nelson. (PAI. Dem. School now stands on site.) CUC.

Carlisle (PU 2/5/1838) **W1**: Devonshire Walk, Carlisle NY396562 1784. (Used for infirm until c.1863. Dem.) **W2**: Moorhouse Road, Carlisle NY377561 1829. (Closed c.1863. Became St Mary's Home for Friendless Girls. NRU.) **Scl**: Harraby Hill, Carlisle NY411547 by 1809. (Used for children until c.1930. Dem.) **W4**: 2 Broad Street, Carlisle (entrance later on Fusehill Street) NY409556 1863 by H.F. Lockwood & W. Mawson. (Fusehill House PAI. MH in WW1/2 then City General Hospital. Now Univ. of Cumbria.) **CtH**: Home Lane, Shap (former West Ward workhouse) NY564142 cnv. 1924. (NRU.) CUC.

Cockermouth (PU 1/12/1838 47+58) **W**: Sullart Street, Cockermouth NY118304 1840. (Closed 1935. Used by RASC in WW2. Dem. 1949.) **Scl**: Flimby Lodge, Flimby NY025342 1879. (Workhouse school and vagrant wards from 1887. Dem.) **CtH**: 34 North Street, Maryport 1915-31. CUW.

Longtown (PU 19/6/1837 14+18) **W**: Longtown NY410689 1828. (PAI. Dem.) CUC.

Penrith (PU 26/12/1836 39+50) **W**: Greystoke Road, Penrith NY504300 1838. (PAI, later Station View House OPH. Dem.) **CtH**: Lark Hall, Penrith NY510308. (Now business use.) CUC.

Whitehaven (PU 5/12/1838 23+32) **W1**: Scotch Street, Whitehaven NX974180 1743. (Closed c.1856. Dem.) **W2**: Ginns, Preston Quarter NX973169 <1834. (Closed c.1856. Later orphan girl's training school. Dem.) **W3**: Low Road (now St Bees Road), Whitehaven NX975163 1856 by Porter. (PAI, later Meadow View House. Dem. 1960s.) **CtH**: Main Street, St Bees. **CtH**: (Catholic) 26 Rose Hill, Harrington NX989249. CUW.

Wigton (PU 22/6/1837 30+41) **W**: Cross Lane, Wigton NY248490 1842. (Highfield House PAI, later Wigton Hospital.) CUC.

Derbyshire

Ashbourne (PU 4/1/1845 61+63) **W1**: The Street, Brassington SK232543 1615. (Closed c.1847. NRU.) **W2**: Dark Lane (now Belle Vue Road), Ashbourne SK174464 1847 by H.J. Stevens. (PAI. St Oswald's Hospital from c.1948.) **CtH**: 58-60 Mayfield Road, Ashbourne SK173461. (NRU.) DBY.

Bakewell (PU 31/7/1838 50+57) **W**: Baslow Road, Bakewell SK220691 1840 by Johnson. (PAI. Newholme Hospital from c.1948.) DBY.

Belper (PU 5/5/1837 32+47) **W**: Derby Road, Belper SK346470 1838 by G.G. Scott & W.B. Moffatt. (Babington House PAI. Babington Hospital from c.1948.) **CtH**: Park Side, Belper SK353474. **CtH**: 50-52 Holbrook Road, Belper SK351465. (Now care home.) DBY.

Chapel-en-le-Frith (PU 4/12/1837 16+22) **W**: Manchester Road, Chapel en le Frith SK051805 1840. (PAI, later The Elms OPH. Dem.) **SmH**: Manchester Road, Chapel en le Frith SK055806. (Later Cromwell House children's home. Now offices.) DBY.

Chesterfield (PU 19/10/1837 34+40) **W**: 12a Newbold Road, Chesterfield SK382715 1840 by G.G. Scott & W.B. Moffatt. (PAI. Scarsdale Hospital from c.1948. Mostly dem.) **Scl**: Ashgate Road, Brampton SK364716 1881. (Later known as Ashgate Homes. Dem.) DBY.

Derby (PU 30/3/1837 7+27) **W1**: Osmaston Road, Derby SK357351 1838 by J Mason. (Part of Royal Crown Derby works. Mostly dem.) **W2**: Uttoxeter Road, Derby SK327353 1876 by W Giles, R & T Brookhouse. (Boundary House PAI. Manor Hospital from c.1948.) **Ify**: Uttoxeter Road, Derby SK327350 1929 by TH Thorpe. (City General Hospital from c.1930. Dem.) **RH**: 2 Mount Street and Burton Road, Derby SK350355. (Dem.) **ScH**: 2 & 3 Friary Street, 27-29 Clarence Road, 42-44 Park Grove, 89-91 Porter Road, 35 Gerard Street. DER.

Glossop (PU 5/12/1837 2+16) **W**: Bute Street, Glossop SK043952 1834. (PAI. Shire Hill Hospital from c.1948.) DBY.

Hayfield (PU 10/11/1837 4+) **W**: Low Leighton Road, Low Leighton SK008857 1839. (Ollersett View PAI then Hospital from c.1948. NRU.) DBY.

Shardlow (PU 30/3/1837 46+57) **W**: London Road, Shardlow SK429305 1795 enl. 1839 by H.J. Stevens (1839). (The Grove PAI. Grove Hospital *c.*1948–2005. Dem. 2007.) DBY.

Devon

Axminster (PU 16/4/1836 17+25) **W**: Box House, Musbury Road, Axminster SY292979 1838 by S. Kempthorne. (Box House PAI. Box House Hospital from *c.*1948. Dem.) DEV.

Barnstaple (PU 2/12/1835 39+50) **W**: 19 Alexandra Road, Barnstaple SS562331 1837 by S. Kempthorne. (PAI. Alexandra Hospital from *c.*1948. Dem.) **CtH**: Alexandra Road, Barnstaple SS562332. DVN.

Bideford (PU 1/12/1835 18+25) **W**: Meddon Street, Bideford SS449263 1837 by G.G. Scott & W.B. Moffatt. (The White House PAI. Torridge Hospital from *c.*1948. Dem. except chapel.) DVN.

Crediton (PU 19/4/1836 29+34) **W**: Western Road, Crediton SS820005 1837 by S. Kempthorne. (Western Lodge PAI. Western Hospital from *c.*1948. NRU.) DEV.

East Stonehouse (SP 3/1/1837) **W**: Clarence Place, Plymouth SX466545 1801. (Later Clarence House Reception Centre. Dem.) **SmH**: 13 Clarence Place, Plymouth SX467545. (NRU.) DVW.

Exeter, City of (LI 1697; PU from 1877; SP from 1900) **W**: 77 Heavitree Road, Exeter SX932927 1707 by R Mitchell. (PAI. City Hospital from 1939, later Heavitree Hospital. Major destruction in WW2.) **RH**: 79 Heavitree Road, Exeter SX932926 1913 by R. Challice. (Later housed medical services.) DEV.

Holsworthy (PU 31/1/1837 23+30) **W**: Rydon Road, Holsworthy SS340042 1853 by E. Ashworth. (PAI, later Dawfield Hospital, then Holsworthy Hospital. NRU.) DVN.

Honiton (PU 18/4/1836 28+35) **W**: Marlpits House, Marlpits Lane, Honiton ST164002 1836 by G. Wilkinson. (PAI, later Marlpits Hospital, then Honiton Hospital. Dem.) DEV.

Kingsbridge (PU 22/6/1836 26+41) **W**: Union Road, Kingsbridge SX732444 1837 by T. Ponsford. (Homelands PAI, now commercial use. Part dem.) DEV.

Newton Abbot (PU 20/6/1836 39+56) **W**: 50 East Street, Newton Abbot SX861710 1837 by G.G. Scott & W.B. Moffatt. (PAI. Newton Abbot Hospital *c.*1948–2002.) **RH**: Meadowside, 41 Highweek Road, Newton Abbot SX854715. (Now Mencap home.) **ScH**: (Boys) 28-30 Highweek Street; (Boys) 64 St Leonard's Terrace; (Boys) 4 Totnes Road; (Girls) 29 Highweek Rod; (Girls) 25-27 Prospect Road; (Girls) 75 Wolborough Street. DEV.

Okehampton (PU 20/4/1836 28+33) **W**: 1 Castle Walk, Okehampton SX586946 1837 by S. Kempthorne. (PAI. Castle Hospital from *c.*1948–2004. Dem. 2008.) DEV.

Plymouth (LI 1708; LP from 1898) **W1**: Catherine Street, Plymouth SX478543 *c.*1630. (Closed *c.*1853. Dem.) **W2**: Longfield Terrace, Plymouth SX487553 1853 by O.C. Arthur & W. Dwelly. (Greenbank House PAI, later City Hospital then Freedom Fields Hospital. Dem.) **RH**: 13 Hill Park Crescent, Plymouth SX484554. (NRU.) **ScH**: 6 Ashord Road, Mutley; 55 and 168 Alexandra Road; 20 Channel View Terrace; 19 Egerton Road; 2 Gifford Terrace; 80 Mount Gold Road; 13 & 36 Hill Park Crescent; 5 Saltram Villas, Laira; Southern Villa, Park Road, Compton; Priory House, Priory Lawn Terrace, Lower Compton. DVW.

Plympton St Mary (PU 10/10/1836 19+35) **W**: Market Road, Plympton St Mary SX535560 1841 by W. Dwelly. (Underwood House PAI, later Plympton Hospital. Dem.) **CtH**: 12-13 Beaumount Terrace, Crownhill, Plymouth cnv. 1912. DEV.

South Molton (PU 28/11/1835 29+36) **W**: 1 North Road, South Molton SS711261 1839 by S. Kempthorne. (Beech House PAI, later Quince Honey Farm.) **SmH**: 41 East Street, South Molton SS718259. (NRU.) DVN.

St Thomas (PU 21/4/1836 49+61) **W**: Exwick Road, Exeter SX907924 1836 by S. Kempthorne. (PAI. Redhills Hospital from *c.*1948. NRU.) **SmH**: Chase, Villa, 49-51 Church Road, Exeter SX912917 cnv. 1908. (NRU.) DEV.

Stoke Damerel (ren. Devonport 1897) (LP 1777; SP from 1900) **W1**: Duke Street,

Devonport SX452545 1777. (Closed c.1854. Dem.) **W2**: Ford House, Wolseley Road, Devonport SX460565 1854 by A. Norman. (PAI. Later Wolseley Home OPH. Dem.) **RH**: Stoke House, Ford Hill, Devonport SX461558 cnv. 1927. (Dem.) **ScH**: 15-16 Cotbele Villas, Stoke. DVW.

Tavistock (PU 8/10/1836 24+35) **W**: 42 Bannawell Street, Tavistock SX478749 1837 by G.G. Scott & W.B. Moffatt. (PAI. Later Gwynntor Welfare Institution. NRU.) **ScH**: 33 West Street, Tavistock; Gunnislake. DEV.

Tiverton (PU 30/11/1835 28+39) **W**: Water Lane, Tiverton SS958130 1837 by G.G. Scott & W.B. Moffatt. (PAI, later Belmont Hospital. Disused.) **SmH**: Shillingford 1913-249; Ayshford from 1924. DEV.

Torrington (PU 30/11/1835 23+28) **W**: New Street, Great Torrington SS485192 1837 by S. Kempthorne. (PAI, later Torridge View OPH. Dem.) DVN.

Totnes (PU 21/6/1836 28+44) **W**: 13 Plymouth Road, Totnes SX795603 1839 by T. Ponsford. (PAI, later Broomborough Hospital. NRU.) DEV.

Dorset

Beaminster (PU 28/3/1836 26+31) **W**: Stoke Water, Stoke Abbott ST467009 1837 by H.J. Whitling. (PAI. Military use WW2, then Stoke Water House OPH. NRU.) DOR.

Blandford (PU 5/12/1835 33+35) **W1**: East Street, Blandford Forum <1834. (Closed c.1857.) **W2**: Salisbury Road, Blandford Forum ST887069 1857 by C.C. Creeke. (WW1 use by RAF. PAI, later Castleman House. Mostly dem. Now care home.) DOR.

Bridport (PU 28/3/1836 19+27) **W**: 1 Bedford Place, Bridport SY469931 1837 by H.J. Whitling. (Bedford House PAI, later Port Bredy geriatric hospital. NRU.) DOR.

Cerne (PU 23/12/1835 20+21) **W**: Sherborne Road, Cerene Abbas ST661017 1837 by C. Wallis. (Youth hostel 1932-55, then Giant View flats. Part dem. Now care home.) DOR.

Cranborne (PU 30/9/1835 14+17; m/w Wimborne 1836) **W**: See Wimborne & Cranborne. DOR.

Dorchester (PU 2/1/1836 39+43) **W**: 4 Damers Road, Dorchester SY687903 1836 by G. Wilkinson. (Damers House PAI, later Damers Hospital then Dorset County Hospital. Mostly dem.) DOR.

Poole (PU 2/10/1835 8+11) **W**: 1 Shaftesbury Road, Poole SZ018914 1839 by J. Tulloch. (Longfleet Gardens PA; Poole General Hospital (St Mary's Block) from c.1948. Dem.) **ScH**: Broadstone. DOR.

Purbeck (PU 25/3/1836 9+11; m/w Cranborne 1836) **W**: See Wareham & Purbeck. DOR.

Shaftesbury (PU 25/10/1835 19+23) **W**: Breach Lane, Shaftesbury ST856227 1840 by W. Walker. (PAI. Dem. c.1947.) DOR.

Sherborne (PU 24/12/1835 30+34) **W**: Horsecastles, Sherborne ST636163 1837 by E. Percy. (PAI. Dem. c.1938.) DOR.

Sturminster (PU 4/12/1835 19+22) **W**: Bath Road, Sturminster Newton ST787148 1836 by L. Vulliamy. (PAI, later Stour View House OPH. Now arts venue and learning disability care. Part dem.) DOR.

Wareham (PU 25/3/1836 18+20; m/w Purbeck 1836) **W**: See Wareham & Purbeck. DOR.

Wareham & Purbeck (PU 29/9/1836 27+31) **W**: Streche Road, Wareham SY918874 1837 by O.B. Carter & H. Hyde. (Christmas Close House PAI later Hospital. NRU.) DOR.

Weymouth (PU 14/1/1836 18+22) **W**: 1 Wyke Road, Weymouth SY675785 1836 by T. Dobson & T.H. Harvey. (PAI. Portwey Hospital from c.1948. NRU.) DOR.

Wimborne (PU 28/9/1835 10+13; m/w Cranborne 1836) **W**: See Wimborne & Cranborne. DOR.

Wimborne & Cranborne (PU 29/9/1836 20+26) **W**: East Borough, Cranborne SU010003 1780. (Allen House PAI. Dem. c.1958.) DOR.

Durham

Auckland (PU 9/1/1837 33+40) **W1**: Newgate Street, Bishop Auckland <1834. (Closed c.1855.) **W2**: 100 Cockton Hill, Bishop Auckland NZ208289 1855. (Oakland PAI. Bishop Auckland General Hospital from 1945. Mostly dem.) **CtH**: Escomb Road, Bishop Auckland NZ205290 1903. (Now offices.) DUR.

Chester-le-Street (PU 12/12/1836 20+32) **W**: Durham Road, Chester-le-Street NZ274508 1856 by M Thompson. (PAI, later Chester-le-Street Hospital. Dem.) DUR.

Darlington (PU 20/2/1837 41+50) **W1**: Lead Yard, Darlington NZ291144 <1834. (Closed c.1868. Dem.) **W2**: 90-108 Yarm Road, Darlington NZ301142 1868 by C.J. Adams. (Feetham Infirmary from 1920s. Darlington Municipal Hospital from 1930s, later East Haven Hospital. Dem.) **CtH**: (Boys) Dodmire, Eastbourne, Darlington NZ300138. (Later Park View Boys' Home.) **CtH**: (Girls) 107 Eastbourne Road, Darlington. **CtH**: (Girls) Queen (now Commercial) Street, Darlington NZ301140. (Dem.) DUR.

Durham (PU 10/1/1837 24+33) **W**: 37 Crossgate, Durham NZ269424 1837 by G. Jackson. (PAI, later Crossgate Hospital; St Margaret's Hospital from c.1948. Now mixed use.) **ScH**: (Boys) 198 Gilesgate, Durham NZ279426. (NRU.) **ScH**: (Girls) 8 Church Street, Durham NZ276420. (Now business use.) **CtH**: Redhills Lane, Crossgate Moor, Durham NZ261426 c.1925. (NRU.) DUR.

Easington (PU 25/1/1837 19+22) **W**: Seaside Lane, Easington NZ419435 1850. (PAI, later Leeholme Hospital. Dem.) **SmH**: Small Walks, Easington NZ413435 cnv. 1921. (Later Seaton Holme OPH, now Heritage Centre.) DUR.

Gateshead (PU 12/12/1836 9+30) **W1**: Rector's Field, Union Row, Gateshead NZ249622 1841. (Dem. 1890s to construct Woodbine Street.) **W2**: Saltwell Road, Bensham, Gateshead NZ247612 1890 by J Morton, W. Newcombe & W Knowles. (High Teams PAI, ren. Fountain View 1948. Dem. 1969. Infirmary became Bensham Hospital 1941.) **San**: Shotley Bridge, Consett NZ103527 1912 by W. Newcombe. (TB Sanatorium from 1912; Mental Defectives Colony from 1926; Shotley Bridge Hospital from 1948.) **CtH**: Corbridge Road, Medomsley NZ110534 1901 by W. Newcombe. (Dem. Now Hassockfield secure training centre.) TAW.

Hartlepool (PU 25/3/1859 12+22) **W**: Howbeck House, Throston, Hartlepool NZ500345 1861 by M. Thompson. (Later Howbeck Infirmary, then Hartlepool General Hospital. Now University Hospital. Mostly dem.) **CtH**: 2 Park Road, West Hartlepool. **SmH**: 63 Blakelock Road (now Gardens), West Hartlepool NZ501315. (Now a hostel.) TEE.

Houghton-le-Spring (PU 20/1/1837 16+32) **W1**: Sunderland Street, Houghton-le-Spring NZ342501 1824. (Closed 1864. Dem.) **W2**: William Street, Houghton-le-Spring NZ343500 1864 by M. Thompson. (PAI, later Heath Lane Hostel, then Heath House. Dem.) **CtH**: 1 Cottage Homes, Houghton-le-Spring NZ342500 c.1910. (Dem.) DUR.

Lanchester (PU 4/1/1837 18+21) **W**: 1 Newbiggin Road, Lanchester NZ164475 1863. (PAI, Lee Hill Hospital from c.1948. Mostly dem. 1980.) **CtH**: Front Street, Lanchester NZ165475 1905 by chesterf. (Also known as Lee Hill Cottages.) DUR.

Sedgefield (PU 7/2/1837 23+24) **W1**: King William Street, Sedgefield NZ359290 <1834. (Closed c.1861. Dem.) **W2**: West End, Sedgefield NZ353286 1861. (PAI, later Ivy House Hostel. Dem.) DUR.

South Shields (PU 10/12/1836 6+25) **W1**: German Street (now Ocean Road), South Shields NZ369675 1837 by J. & B. Green. (Closed c.1880. Dem.) **W2**: 1 Moor Lane, West Harton; later as 169 Harton Lane, South Shields NZ366643 1880 by J.H. Morton. (Harton Institution/Hospital from 1930; South Shields General Hospital from c.1948; later South Tyneside District Hospital. Mostly dem.) **CtH**: Sunniside Lane, Cleadon NZ385629 1909. (Now a special school. Mostly dem.) TAW.

Stockton on Tees (PU 22/2/1837 41+54) **W1**: Workhouse (now Knowles) Street, Stockton NZ445191 <1834. (Closed 1851.) **W2**: 50 Portrack Lane, Stockton NZ451196 1851 by J. & W.

Atkinson. (PAI, later Portrack Hospital; ren. St Anne's Hospital 1972. Dem.) **ScH**: 52–54 and 59–61 Hartington Road; 44–50 Windsor Road. DUR.

Sunderland (PU 13/12/1836 11+34) **W1**: Gill Bridge Avenue, Bishopwearmouth NZ394571 1827. (Closed 1856. Dem.) **W2**: Hylton Road, Sunderland NZ380566 1856 by J.E. Oates. (Highfield PAI and Municipal Hospital from 1930; later Sunderland General. Dem.) **CtH**: 288 Hylton Road, Sunderland NZ380567. (Highfield Cottage Homes until 1950s then hospital use.) **RH**: Havelock Tower, 288 Hylton Road, Sunderland NZ377567. (Now community centre.) TAW.

Teesdale (PU 18/2/1837 44+52) **W**: 107 Galgate, Barnard Castle NZ054169 1838 by J. Green. (PAI. Later Cambridge House Hostel OPH. NRU. Mostly dem.) DUR.

Weardale (PU 5/1/1837 4+16) **W1**: Union Lane, Stanhope NY998390 <1834. (Closed c.1867. NRU.) **W2**: Union Lane, Stanhope NY999390 1867 by M. Thompson. (Weardale House PAI. NRU.) DUR.

Essex

Billericay (PU 10/10/1835 26+29) **W**: Norsey Road, Billericay TQ678952 1839 by G.G. Scott & W.B. Moffatt. (PAI. St Andrew's Hospital from c.1948. NRU.) **SmH**: Foxcroft, 100 High Street, Billericay TQ673944. (Later hostel. Now offices.) ESS.

Braintree (PU 16/12/1835 14+22) **W**: 142 Rayne Road, Braintree TL751231 1838 by W.T. Nash. (PAI. St Michael's Hospital from c.1948. NRU.) **CtH**: Poplar Hall, Hatfield Road, Witham TL816140 cnv. 1908. (Closed 1915. NRU.) **CtH**: Friars, 31 Bradford Street, Bocking TL760238 cnv. 1915. (Now hotel.) ESS.

Chelmsford (PU 10/8/1835 26+32) **W**: 48 Wood Street, Chelmsford TL699049 1837 rb. 1869 by W. Thorold (1837). F. Chancellor (1869). (PAI. St John's Hospital from c.1938.) **CtH**: (Girls) Baddow Road, Great Baddow cnv. 1908. **CtH**: (Boys) The Green, Writtle TL676062 cnv. 1905. (Closed 1970s. NRU.) ESS.

Colchester (PU 19/10/1836 16+21; SP from 26/3/1897) **W**: 14 Pope's Lane, Colchester TL991253 1837 by J. Brown. (PAI. St Mary's Hospital from c.1948. Dem.) ESS.

Dunmow (PU 26/3/1835 26+33) **W**: Chelmsford Road, Great Dunmow TL631212 1840 by G.G. Scott & W.B. Moffatt. (WW1 refugee/army billets and POW camp. Closed c. 1923.. NRU.) ESS.

Epping (PU 16/1/1836 18+22) **W**: 42 The Plain, Epping TL469028 1837 by L. Vulliamy. (PAI. St Margaret's Hospital from c.1938. Mostly dem.) **CtH**: Coopersale Common TL475026. (Later Forest Side children's home. Dem.) ESS.

Halstead (PU 6/11/1835 16+23) **W**: North Street (now Hedingham Lane), Halstead TL814311 1839 by W.T. Nash. (Closed 1916. German POWs housed in 1918. Dem 1922. Site now almshouses.) ESS.

Lexden & Winstree (PU 1/2/1836 35+38) **W**: 1 London Road, Stanway TL959249 1836 by S.O. Foden & Henman. (St Albright's Hospital PAI, later OPH. NRU.) **SmH**: Stanway Villa, Villa Road, Stanway TL952241. (Dem.) ESS.

Maldon (PU 14/12/1835 32+36) **W1**: Market Hill, Maldon TL845068 c.1715 enl. 1835 by J. Sadd (1835). (Closed 1873. NRU.) **W2**: 32a Spital Road, Maldon TL845068 1873 by F. Peck. (PAI. St Peter's Hospital from c.1948.) **CtH**: Tiptree. ESS.

Ongar (PU 8/4/1836 26+29) **W**: 43 London Road, Stanford Rivers TL541002 1830. (Closed 1920. Used by Piggots tent/flag-makers from 1926.) ESS.

Orsett (PU 10/10/1835 18+21) **W**: Rowley Road, Orsett TQ643817 1837 by S. Kempthorne. (Orsett Lodge PAI then Hospital from c.1948. Dem. c.1960. Now Orsett Hospital.) **CtH**: 61–63 Whitehall Road, Little Thurrcok TQ625788. (NRU.) ESS.

Rochford (PU 30/10/1835 23+26) **W**: West Stree, Rochford TQ874908 1837 by W. Thorold. (Housed Germans POWs in WW1. Rochford House PAI, later part of Rochford Hospital. Dem.) **SmH**: Acacia House, East Street, Rochford TQ876904. (Now council offices.) **SmH**: The Homestead, 12 Bulwood Road, Hockley TQ835924 *c*.1925. (NRU.) ESS.

Romford (PU 31/5/1836 10+24) **W**: 1 Oldchurch Road, Romford TQ510881 1838 by
F. Edwards. (PAI. Oldchurch Hospital *c*.1935–2006. Dem.) **CtH**: 1-2 The Croft, Heath Park
Road, Romford. **RH**: 5-8 Laurie Square, Romford TQ513891. (Dem.) **ScH**: 26-28 Manor
Road; 42-44 Brentwood Road; Dudbrook and Fernbank, King Edward Road;
3 Adelaide Villas, Mawneys; 36-38 Peham Road, Ilford. ESS.

Saffron Walden (PU 6/5/1835 24+31) **W**: Sewards End Road, later Radwinter Road, Saffron
Walden TL550386 1836 by J. Clephan. (PAI, later St James' Hospital. NRU. Part dem.) ESS.

Tendring (PU 16/11/1835 30+35) **W**: Heath Road, Tendring Heath TM135265 1838 by G.G.
Scott & W.B. Moffatt. (PAI. Heath Hospital from *c*.1948, later Tendring Meadow care home.
Part dem.) ESS.

West Ham (PU 31/5/1836 7+24) **W1**: 13 Union Road (now Langthorne Road), Leytonstone
TQ390860 1840 by A.R. Mason. (Central Home from 1930; Langthorne Hospital from
1948. NRU.) **W2**: Forest Lane, Forest Gate TQ399852 bt. 1911 from Poplar. (Forest Gate
Hospital *c*.1930–73. Newham Maternity Hospital 1973-85. NRU.) **Ify**: Whipps Cross Road,
Leytonstone TQ389886 1903 by F.J. Sturdy. (Forest House in 1894; Union Infirmary 1903;
Whipps Cross Hospital from *c*.1917.) **RH**: Aldersbrook Road, Aldersbrook E11 TQ409869
1910. (Part later Aldersbrook Hostel. NRU.) **ScH**: Ashford Road, Pulteney Road, and 21-27
Pelham Road, South Woodford; Davies Lane, 31-31A and 96-102 Ferndale Road, Leytonstone;
Capel Road, Forest Gate; Keogh Road, Stratford; Savage Gardens, East Ham. **CvH**: 25
Northdown Road, Margate TR358711 bt. 1900. NEW, WAF.

Witham (PU 15/12/1835 17+23; diss. 25/3/1880) **W**: Hatfield Road, Witham TL815140 1839
by G.G. Scott & W.B. Moffatt. (Bt. by S. Met. School District 1882. Later Bridge Home/
Hospital. NRU.) ESS.

Gloucestershire

Bristol (LI 1696; SP from 1897) **W1**: Peter Street, Bristol ST591731 1612. (The Mint work-
house, later St Peter's Hospital. Destroyed 1940.) **W2**: 100 Manor Road, Fishponds, Bristol
ST627762 *c*.1779. (Stapleton Institution for Mental Defectives from 1918; ren. Stapleton
Hospital 1948, Manor Hospital 1956, later Blackberry Hill Hospital. Closed 2008.) **CtH**:
Frenchay Road, Downend, Bristol ST644768 1905 by La Trobe & Weston. (Later became
The Crescent school. Dem.) **RH**: 11-19 Snowdon Road, Bristol ST628759 *c*.1900. (Now
mixed use.) **ScH**: 3-4 Summerhill Road, St George's; 114-115 Beaufort Road, St George's;
1-2 Park Road, Staplehill; 1-2 Teewell Hill, Staplehill; 71-73 Church Road, Horfield;
2-3 Churchways Crescent, Horfield; 6-7 & 9-10 Charlton Road, Fishponds; 255 & 256
and 260 & 262 Beechwood Road, Charlton Road. **Hostel**: Service Boys Home, Pritchard
Street, Bristol ST594736. BRI.

Cheltenham (PU 16/11/1835 13+27) **W1**: Knapp Lane, Cheltenham SO943225 1809.
(Closed *c*.1851. Then site of Parish Church Infants School. Dem.) **W2**: Swindon Road,
Cheltenham SO945231 1841 by Cope. (PAI. St Paul's Hospital from *c*.1948. Dem.) **SmH**:
The Elms, Swindon Road, Cheltenham SO945231. (Dem.) GLS.

Chipping Sodbury (PU 30/3/1836 23+29) **W**: 244 Station Road, Chipping Sodbury
ST718824 1838 by G.G. Scott & W.B. Moffatt. (County Hospital PAI, later Ridgewood
OPH. Now office/commercial use.) GLS.

Cirencester (PU 21/1/1836 29+43) **W**: 24 Querns Hill (formerly Workhouse Lane),
Cirencester SP024014 1837 by J. Plowman. (PAI. Watermoor Hospital from 1948; Council
Offices from *c*.1981.) GLS.

Clifton (ren. Barton Regis 1877) (PU 9/4/1836 12+32) **W1**: Pennywell Road, Easton,
Bristol ST599736 <1834. (Closed 1847. Vestry Hall erected on site in 1880.) **W2**: Hudds
Vale Road, St George, Bristol ST623739 <1834. (Closed 1847. Later Crown Pottery. Mostly
dem.) **W3**: Church Lane, Cliftonwood, Bristol ST575725 <1834. (Closed 1847. Dem.) **W4**:
100 Fishponds Road, Eastville, Bristol ST613748 1847 by ST Welch. (PAI, later OPH. Dem.

1972.) **W5**: 388 Southmead Road, Bristol ST591777 1902 by A. Cotterell & W. Thorpe. (Military use in WW1. Southmead Hospital from 1930.) BRI.

Dursley (PU 4/4/1836 11+20) **W**: Union Street, Dursley ST755979 1839 by T. Fulljames. (PAI, later children's reception home. Dem. 1960s.) GLS.

Gloucester (PU 30/5/1835 35+49) **W**: 95 Great Western Road, Gloucester SO838186 1840 by G.G. Scott & W.B. Moffatt. (PAI. Later Great Western House OPH. Dem. 1961.) **Ify**: 70 Great Western Road, Gloucester SO841186 1912. (WW1 Red Cross Hospital. City General c.1932, later Gloucestershire Royal. Mostly dem.) **SmH**: 73-75 Bristol Road, Gloucester SO826173. (Now Linden Tree pub.) **ScH**: Bristol Road; (Aged women) Ladybellegate Lodge, Ladybellegate Street; (Aged men) Somerset Lawn, Spa Road; (Girls) 1-2 Theresa Terrace; (Boys) Tuffley Court, Tuffley Lane, Tuffley. GLS.

Newent (PU 23/9/1835 18+25) **W**: Ross Road, Newent SO719263 c.1804. (Closed 1918. Later used as school, then youth centre.) GLS.

Northleach (PU 18/1/1836 30+33) **W**: East End, Northleach SP118144 1836 by G. Wilkinson. (Burford Road House PAI. Northleach Hospital from c.1948. Now OPH.) GLS.

Stow-on-the-Wold (PU 25/1/1836 28+30) **W**: Union Street, Stow-on-the-Wold SP195257 1836 by G. Wilkinson. (East View PAI. Dem.) GLS.

Stroud (PU 2/4/1836 15+31) **W**: 1 Bisley Road, Stroud SO863049 1840 by W. Mason. (PAI. Military use in WW2. NRU.) GLS.

Tetbury (PU 31/3/1836 13+15) **W**: Union Street (now Gumstool Hill), Tetbury ST 892931 1790 rb. 1906 by V Lawson (1906). (PAI. Now care home.) GLS.

Tewkesbury (PU 16/11/1835 23+30) **W**: Gloucester Road, Tewkesbury SO889321 1796. (PAI. Holm Hospital from c.1948. NRU.) GLS.

Thornbury (PU 5/4/1836 21+26) **W**: Gloucester Road, Thornbury ST641904 1837 by S. Kempthorne. (PAI. Thornbury Hospital from c.1948. NRU.) GLS.

Westbury-on-Severn (PU 28/9/1835 13+18) **W**: 1 High Street, Westbury on Severn SO715141 1790 rb. 1869 by A. Maberley (1869). (PAI, later Westbury Hall Welfare Home. Dem.) GLS.

Wheatenhurst (PU 21/9/1835 14+18) **W**: Chippenham (or Chipman's) Platt, Eastington SO782063 1785 enl. 1836 by T. Fulljames (1838). (PAI, later The Willows OPH. Now care home for learning diifficulties.) GLS.

Winchcomb (PU 16/1/1836 30+32) **W**: Gloucester Street, Winchcombe SP019281 1836 by S. Kempthorne. (PAI. Dem.) GLS.

Hampshire

Aldershot (GP 1812–46) **W**: Hospital Hill Road, Aldershot SU861511 c.1629. (District School 1849–55, then army hospital. Now community centre.) SRY.

Alresford (PU 31/3/1835 18+19) **W**: Tichborne Down, Alresford SU587315 1836 by E. Hunt. (PAI. Tichborne Down House Hospital c.1948–1980s. NRU.) HAM.

Alton (PU 2/4/1835 19+21) **W**: 59 Anstey Road, Alton SU725400 c.1793. (PAI, later Alton General Hospital. NRU. Part dem.) HAM.

Alverstoke (GP 1799; SP 22/10/1868) **W**: Park Road, Alverstoke SZ609992 1801 by F. Carter. (Park House PAI then industrial use. Mostly dem.) HAM.

Andover (PU 9/7/1835 32+36) **W**: 45 Junction Road, Andover SU360457 1836 by S. Kempthorne. (PAI. St John's Hospital c.1948–1980s. NRU.) HAM.

Basingstoke (PU 18/5/1835 37+41) **W**: Basing Road, Basingstoke SU654528 1836 by S. Kempthorne. (PAI. Basing Road Hospital from c.1948–69. Dem.) HAM.

Catherington (PU 6/4/1835 5+9) **W**: Portsmouth Road, Horndean SU703129 1835. (Closed c.1930, Later used as a factory. Dem.) HAM.

Christchurch (PU 28/7/1835 3+9) **W1**: Quay Road, Christchurch SZ159927 c.1764. (Closed c.1886. Now the Red House Museum) **W2**: Fairmile House, Jumpers Road, Christchurch SZ150939 1886 by C.C. Creeke & E.H. Burton. (WW1 Red Cross Hospital. PAI. Fairmile

Hospital from *c*.1948, later Christchurch Hospital. Mostly dem.) **CtH**: Fairmile Road, Christchurch SZ147943 1896. (Later known as Bournemouth Children's Homes. Dem. 1960s.) HAM.

Droxford (PU 30/3/1835 11+14) **W**: Union Lane, Droxford SU604185 1836 by S. Kempthorne. (Waltham House PAI later OPH. Dem *c*.1986.) HAM.

Fareham (PU 26/5/1835 9+15) **W**: 52 Wickham Road, Fareham SU582070 1835 by T. Owen. (PAI. St Christopher's Hospital from *c*.1948.) HAM.

Farnborough (GU 1798; diss. 1869) **W**: Workhouse Lane (later Union Street), Farnborough SU864558 *c*.1798. (Closed 1869. Dem.) HAM.

Farnham & Hartley Wintney SD (SD 19/6/1849) **Scl**: Hospital Hill Road, Aldershot SU861511 *c*.1629. (Former Aldershot GP workhouse. Used 1849-55.) **Scl**: Wimble Hill, Crondall SU802468 1856. (Later Wimble Hill Hospital. NRU. Mostly dem.) HAM.

Fordingbridge (PU 30/7/1835 9+11) **W1**: Shaftesbury Street, Fordingbridge SU145141 17C. (Closed *c*.1885. Dem.) **W2**: Bartons Road, Fordingbridge SU146143 1885 by F. Bath. (PAI. Fordingbridge Infirmary from *c*.1948, now Fordingbridge Hospital.) HAM.

Hartley Wintney (PU 8/4/1835 13+18) **W1**: Hartley Row (now Hartley Wintney) SU773573 <1834 by 18C. (Closed *c*.1871. Dem. Now golf course site.) **W2**: Pale Lane, Winchfield SU781541 1871 by E. Woodthorpe. (PAI. Winchfield Hospital from *c*.1948–84. NRU.) HAM.

Havant (PU 27/5/1835 6+10) **W**: West Street, Havant SU714063 1819. (PAI. Dem. 1950s.) HAM.

Headley GU (GU 1794; diss. 1869) **W**: Liphook Road, Headley SU825355 1795. (Closed 1869. NRU.) HAM.

Hursley (PU 11/8/1835 5+9) **W1**: Collins Lane, Hursley SU429252 1828. (Closed *c*.1900. NRU.) **W2**: Hursley Road, Chandler's Ford SU430220 1900 by Cancellor & Hill. (TB Sanatorium from *c*.1925. Leigh House Hospital *c*.1960–2002. NRU.) HAM.

Isle of Wight (LI 1770; PU from 1865 3+54) **W**: Parkhurst Road, Newport SZ495905 1771. (Forest House PAI. St Mary's Hospital from *c*.1948.) **ScH**: Arreton; East Cowes; (Infants) Wootton Bridge. IOW.

Kingsclere (PU 3/6/1835 15+18) **W**: Union Lane / Newbury Road, Kingsclere SU524592 1837 by G. Adey. (PAI. Kingsclere Hospital *c*.1948–1960s. Dem.) HAM.

Lymington (PU 18/5/1835 6+12) **W**: 20 New Street / Union Hill, Lymington SZ322959 1837 by S. Kempthorne. (PAI. Lymington infirmary *c*.1948–2002. NRU. Part dem.) HAM.

New Forest (PU 29/8/1835 9+17) **W**: Lyndhurst Road, Ashurst SU336102 1836 by S. Kempthorne. (PAI. Ashurst Hospital from *c*.1948.) HAM.

Petersfield (PU 27/4/1835 13+16) **W**: Love Lane, Petersfield SU751233 1835. (PAI. NRU. Mostly dem.) HAM.

Portsea Island (ren. Portsmouth 1900) (PU 18/7/1836 2+21; SP 1900) **W1**: Warblington Street, Portsmouth SZ634996 1723. (Closed *c*.1847. Dem.) **W2**: Elm Lane, Landport, Portsea SU646016 by 1764 rb. 1798. (Closed *c*.1847. Dem.) **W3**: St Mary's Road, Portsmouth SU660005 1845 by A. Livesay & T.E. Owen. (St Mary's PAI and Hospital from *c*.1930. Part NRU.) **CtH**: 140 St Mary's Road, Portsmouth SU659005. **Dsp**: 70 Commercial Road, Portsmouth. POR.

Ringwood (PU 29/7/1835 5+9) **W**: Verwood Road, Ringwood SU138048 1725. (Ashley House PAI. Closed 1936. NRU.) HAM.

Romsey (PU 25/3/1835 12+20) **W**: Winchester Road, Romsey SU362215 1774 enl. 1836. (PAI, later The Gardens OPH. NRU. Part dem.) HAM.

South Stoneham (ren. Eastleigh 1920) (PU 25/3/1835 9+16) **W**: Botley Road, West End, Southampton SU474145 *c*.1800 rb. 1848 by W. Henman (1848). (West End PAI. Moorgreen Hospital from *c*.1948. Part dem.) SOU.

Southampton (LI 1772; SP from 1/4/1912) **W**: 154 St Mary Street, Southampton SU426123 1776 rb. 1867 by T.A. Skelton (1867). (St Mary's PAI. Southampton Technical College from 1952, now City College. Part dem.) **Ify**: 1a/2a Chilworth Road, Shirley

Warren, Southampton SU399150 1902 by A.F. Gutteridge. (Borough Hospital from
*c.*1930, later Southampton General Hospital. Dem.) **CtH**: Hollybrook House, Shirley,
Southampton SU406150 1911. (NRU and school.) **Dsp**: Houndwell Place, Southampton.
SOU.

Stockbridge (PU 6/6/1835 15+19) **W**: Stockbridge SU360349 1837 by Hopgood. (PAI, later
Lancaster House. Dem.) HAM.

Whitchurch (PU 4/6/1835 7+10) **W1**: Dellands, Overton SU511493 early 19C. (Closed 1848.
dem.) **W2**: London Road, Whitchurch SU473481 1848 by S.O. Foden. (PAI. NRU.) HAM.

(New) Winchester (PU 10/8/1835 32+36) **W**: 1d Upper Stockbridge Road (now St Pauls
Hill), Winchester SU476298 1837 by W. Cole. (MH in WW1-2. PAI. St Paul's Hospital from
*c.*1948–98. NRU.) HAM.

Herefordshire

Bromyard (PU 20/5/1836 33+35) **W**: Bromyard Downs, Bromyard SO670541 1836 by G.
Wilkinson. (PAI, later Bromyard Hospital. NRU.) HEF.

Dore (PU 27/3/1837 29+33) **W**: Riverdale, Abbeydore SO384326 1839 by J. Plowman.
(Tractor factory in WW2. NRU.) HEF.

Hereford (PU 28/4/1836 45+53) **W**: Commercial Road, Hereford SO515402 1836 by J.
Plowman. (Longfield Buildings PAI. Hereford County Hospital from *c.*1948. Part dem.)
SmH: Ivy House, 218 Ledbury Road, Tupsley SO526402. (Dem.) HEF.

Kington (PU 25/8/1836 26+29) **W**: Kingswood Road, Kington SO298558 1837 by H.J.
Whitling. (PAI. Later Kingswood Hall OPH. Dem.) HEF.

Ledbury (PU 2/6/1836 22+27) **W**: Belle Orchard House, Union (now Orchard) Lane,
Ledbury SO707381 1836 by G. Wilkinson. (PAI, later OPH. NRU.) HEF.

Leominster (PU 15/6/1836 25+32) **W**: The Priory, Leominster SO499593 enl. 1838 by G.
Wilkinson. (PAI. Old Priory Hospital from *c.*1948. Now offices.) **SmH**: 46 Etnam Street
(Later Norfolk House Children's Home, now OPH.) HEF.

Ross (PU 12/4/1835 29+34) **W**: 3 Alton Street, Ross SO600239 1837 rb. 1872 by J. Plowman
(1837) Haddon Bros (1872). (PAI. Dean Hill Hospital from *c.*1948, now Ross Community
Hospital. Mostly dem.) HEF.

Weobley (PU 9/4/1836 21+24) **W**: Whitehill House, Kington Road, Weobley SO393521 1837
by G. Wilkinson. (PAI, later council offices, NRU.) HEF.

Hertfordshire

Barnet (PU 4/7/1835 9+14) **W**: 17 Wellhouse Lane, Barnet TQ235963 1837 by J. Griffin.
(MH in WW1. Wellhouse Home PAI. Barnet General Hospital from *c.*1948. Dem.) **ScH**:
'Moray House', Victoria Road, New Barnet; 'Guyscliffe', 27 High Street, Barnet; Rosendale,
18 King Edward Road, New Barnet. HRT.

Berkhampstead (PU 12/6/1835 10+15) **W**: High Street, Berkhampstead SP986080 1831.
(Nugent House PAI until 1935. Dem.) HRT.

Bishop Stortford (PU 26/3/1835 20+27) **W**: 2 Haymeads Lane, Bishop's Stortford
TL500209 1836 by T.L. Evans. (Haymeads PAI. Haymeads Hospital from *c.*1948, later Herts
& Essex General. NRU.) **CtH**: 'Haroldene', Recreation Ground, Stansted TL510248 1912.
HRT.

Buntingford (PU 29/6/1835 16+19) **W**: Union Terrace, Buntingford TQ324294 1837 by W.T.
Nash. (PAI. Later Bridgefoot House hostel and council offices. Now mixed use. Part dem.)
HRT.

Hatfield (PU 4/7/1835 4+8) **W**: 1 Union Lane (now Wellfield Road), Hatfield TQ225088
1788 by J Donowell. (PAI. Later Wellfield Hospital. Dem.) HRT.

Hemel Hempstead (PU 12/6/1835 6+14) **W**: Redbourn Road (now Allendale), Hemel
Hempstead TL061079 1836 by J. Griffin. (Hempstead House PAI. St Paul's Hospital from
*c.*1948. Dem.) HRT.

Hertford (PU 18/6/1835 18+21) **W**: Ware Road, Herftford TL344131 1869 by F. Peck. (Kingsmead Special School for 'mental defectives' from 1924. Dem.) HRT.

Hitchin (PU 15/6/1835 28+39) **W**: Chalkdell House, Oughton Head Way, Hitchin TL178298 1836 by T. Smith. (PAI. Lister Hospital *c.*1943–73, then Hitchin Hospital. Mostly dem.) **CtH**: 28–32 Ridge Road, Letchworth TL223328 1910. (NRU.) HRT.

Royston (PU 29/6/1835 29+32) **W**: Baldock Road, Royston TL351407 1836 by W.T. Nash. (Heath Lodge PAI. Dem. 1972.) HRT.

St Albans (PU 23/5/1835 8+17) **W**: Union Lane (now Normandy Road), St Albans TL144081 1837 by J. Griffin. (Waverley Lodge PAI. Later St Albans City Hospital. NRU. Part dem.) **CtH**: Luton Road, Harpenden *c.*1911. HRT, STA.

Ware (PU 16/5/1835 15+21) **W**: Collett Road, Ware TL359147 1840 by Brown & Henman. (Western House PAI, later Western House Hospital. NRU. Part dem.) HRT.

Watford (PU 23/5/1835 6+16) **W**: 60 Vicarage Road (formerly Hagden Lane), Watford TQ105957 1837 by T.L. Evans. (Shrodell's PAI/Hospital, then Watford General Hospital (Shrodell's Wing).) **RH**: Ashby Road, Callow Land, Watford TQ103984. (NRU.) HRT.

Welwyn (PU 4/7/1835 4+5; diss. 1921) **W**: London Road, Welwyn TQ231155 1830. (Closed 1921. Used as school by Hatfield Union until 1924. NRU.) HRT.

Huntingdonshire

Huntingdon (PU 19/1/1836 33+35) **W**: St Peter's Road, Huntingdon TL234723 1837 by S. Kempthorne. (Walnut Tree House PAI. Petersfield Hospital from *c.*1948, later offices. Dem.) HUN.

St Ives (PU 18/1/1836 24+30) **W**: London Road, Hemingford Grey, St Ives TL307703 1838 by W.T. Nash. (PAI. NRU.) HUN.

St Neots (PU 24/9/1835 30+34) **W**: St Neot's Road, Eaton Socon TL173597 1842 by W. Abbott. (White House PAI. NRU.) HUN.

Kent

Blean (PU 20/5/1835 16+19) **W**: Canterbury Road, Herne Common TR176652 1835 by F. Head & W. Edmunds. (Blean PAI. Herne Hospital *c.*1948–1990s. NRU.) **ScH**: Mill Lane, Herne. KEN.

Bridge (PU 20/5/1835 22+22) **W**: Union Road, Bridge TR179544 1836 by F. Head & G. Lancefield. (PAI. Later The Close OPH. NRU.) KEN.

Bromley (PU 19/5/1836 16+17) **W1**: London Road, Bromley TQ399695 1731. (Closed *c.*1844) **W2**: Wellbrook Road, Locksbottom, Bromley TQ433650 1844 by J. Savage & S.O. Foden. (Farnborough Hospital from *c.*1934. Dem.) **ScH**: Farnborough. BRO.

Canterbury (LI 1727; PU 1881; SP 1897) **W1**: Stour Street, Canterbury TR147577 cnv. 1727. (Closed *c.*1850. Now Museum of Canterbury.) **W2**: Nunnery Fields, Canterbury TR150567 1850 by H. Marshall. (The Home PAI. Nunnery Fields Hospital from *c.*1948. NRU.) **CtH**: 113 Wincheap Street, Canterbury TR138567 1911. (Later Woodville Homes then Key House Training Centre.) KEN.

Cranbrook (PU 3/11/1835 6+12) **W**: Hartley Road, Hartley TQ760350 1838 by J. Whichcord. (Hartley House PAI later OPH. Dem.) KEN.

Dartford (PU 19/5/1836 21+24) **W**: West Hill, Dartford TQ538743 1836 by J. Whichcord. (WW1 housing for munitions workers. PAI. West Hill Hospital from *c.*1948. Now commercial use. Part dem.) **SmH**: Manor Gate, Common Lane, Wilmington TQ523725. (Dem.) KEN.

Dover (named River 1835-7) (PU 29/5/1835 22+22) **W**: 75 Union Street (now Coombe Valley Road), Dover TR302420 1836 by F. Head & G. Lancefield. (PAI. County Hospital from 1943. Buckland Hospital from *c.*1948.) KEN.

East Ashford (PU 3/6/1835 22+22) **W**: Willesborough Lees Road (now Kennington Road), Ashford TR034423 1837 by F. Head & J. Whichcord. (Gill House PAI. Willesborough Hospital from *c.*1948. Now mixed use. Part dem.) **SmH**: The Hostel, Wye 1915. KEN.

Eastry (PU 27/5/1835 26+27) **W**: 2 Mill Lane, Eastry TR308545 1836 by F. Head & W. Spanton. (PAI. Eastry Hospital from *c*.1948. Mostly dem.) KEN.

Elham (PU 3/6/1835 18+18) **W**: Hill House, Lyminge TR167393 1835 by F. Head. (PAI. St Mary's Hospital from *c*.1948. Dem. except chapel.) **CtH**: High Street, Cheriton TR190369 1888 by J. Gardner & J. Ladds. (Now social services offices.) KEN.

Faversham (PU 25/3/1835 25+26) **W**: Gravel Pit House, Gravel Pit Road (now Lower Road), Faversham TR001614 1836 by F. Head & J. Day. (PAI. Bensted House Hospital from *c*.1948. Dem. *c*.1995.) KEN.

Gravesend & Milton (PU 9/9/1835 2+8) **W1**: Stone Street, Gravesend TQ646739 1797. (Closed *c*.1847. Now residential/commercial use.) **W2**: 10 Trafalgar Road, Gravesend TQ644736 1847 by J. Gould. (PAI. St James' Hospital from *c*.1948. Dem.) **SmH**: 28-29 (later 32-33) Clarence Place, Gravesend TQ648734. (NRU.) KEN.

Hollingbourne (PU 12/10/1835 23+23) **W**: Ashford Road, Hollingbourne TQ820548 1836. (Closed *c*.1921. Dem.) KEN.

Hoo (PU 9/9/1835 7+8) **W**: Main Road, Hoo St Werburgh TQ778721 1836 by F. Head. (Council offices from *c*.1921. Dem. 1960s.) KEN.

Isle of Thanet (PU 20/5/1835 9+13) **W**: Tothill Street, Minster in Thanet TR311655 1836 by F. Head. (Hill House MH 1915-20. PAI. Hill House Hospital *c*.1948–86. Dem.) **CtH**: Preston Road, Manston TR348663 1901. (NRU.) KEN.

Maidstone (PU 15/10/1835 15+18) **W**: Heath Road, Coxheath TQ744509 1836 by F. Head & J. Whichcord. (Coxheath Home PAI. Linton Hospital from *c*.1948. Dem. except chapel.) KEN.

Malling (PU 12/10/1835 22+22) **W**: King Hill, West Malling TQ671562 *c*.1901 by J. Whichcord. (PAI. Later King Hill Hostel for homeles families. Dem. 1980s.) **ScH**: West Malling; Snodland; East Peckham. KEN.

Medway (PU 7/9/1835 7+14) **W**: 42 Magpie Hall Road, Chatham TQ763670 1859 by F. Peck & E. Stephens. (Medway Hospital 1932-6; County Hospital 1936-48; All Saints Hospital 1948-99. Dem.) **CtH**: Pattens Lane, Chatham TQ752662 1903. (Mostly dem.) MED.

Milton (PU 25/3/1835 18+20) **W**: 1 North Street, Sittingbourne TQ903650 1835 by F. Head & W. Bland. (PAI. Milton Regis Hospital from *c*.1948. Dem. *c*.1994.) **SmH**: (Girls) Church House, North Street, Milton Regis TQ908653 cnv. 1905. (Later Green Porch children's Home. Now offices.) **SmH**: (Boys) Langley House, Brewery Road, Milton Regis TQ904648 1914. (Dem.) KEN.

North Aylesford (ren. Strood 1884) (PU 7/9/1835 15+15) **W**: 2 Gun Lane, Strood TQ735695 1837. (PAI. Clinic after 1948. Mostly dem. by 1950s.) **ScH**: 49-51 Goddington Road and 32 Bryant Road, Strood. KEN.

Penshurst (PU 25/3/1835 m/w Sevenoaks 1836 14+14) **W**: Bough Beech Green 1835. (Closed 1836) KEN.

Romney Marsh (PU 14/11/1835 14+14) **W**: Buttfield House, Church Road, New Romney TR065246 <1834. (Closed *c*.1930. Dem. *c*.1950s.) **SmH**: Glan Morfa. KEN.

Sevenoaks (PU 14/5/1835 10+19) **W1**: St John's Hill, Sevenoaks <1834. (Closed *c*.1845.) **W2**: Birchfield House, Church Lane, Sundridge TQ482537 1845 by Mason. (PAI. Sundridge Hospital from *c*.1948–99. NRU.) **SmH**: 96 Chipstead Lane, Riverhead TQ510561 cnv. 1911. (Later Rock House. NRU.) KEN.

Sheppey (PU 25/3/1835 7+14) **W**: Cliff House, Wards Hill Road, Minster TQ955733 <1834. (PAI. Minster Hospital *c*.1938–48; Sheppey Hospital until *c*.2004. Dem.) KEN.

Tenterden (PU 2/11/1835 11+11) **W**: Plummer Lane, Tenterden TQ874328 1843 by J. Savage. (West View 'Mental Institution' from *c*.1930. West View Hospital from *c*.1948. Dem. *c*.2002.) KEN.

Tonbridge (PU 5/11/1835 10+11) **W**: Tonbridge Road, Pembury TQ615413 1836 by J. Whichcord. (PAI. Pembury County Hospital from *c*.1938. Part dem.) **SmH**: (Girls) Silverleigh, 46 Hill View Road, Rusthall TQ561398. (NRU.) **SmH**: (Boys) Chalfont,

Romford Road, Pembury. KEN.

West Ashford (PU 3/6/1835 10+10) **W**: Chapel Lane, Hothfield Common TQ968464 1835 by F. Head. (Hothfield PAI. MH c.1941–45. Hothfield Hospital from c.1948–79. Now care centre. Part dem.) KEN.

Lancashire

Ashton-under-Lyne (PU 3/2/1837 13+20) **W1**: Market Street, Ashton-under-Lyne SJ940991 c.1729. (Closed c.1850.) **W2**: Fountain Street, Ashton-under-Lyne SJ954995 1850. (Darnton House PAI. Ashton General Hospital from c.1948–56 then Tameside General. Dem. 2010.) **ScH**: 'Kelvin', Millbrook, Stalybridge; 'West Villa', Dukinfield; 306-8 Mossley Road, Ashton. TMS.

Barrow-in-Furness (SP 19/4/1876) **W**: 1, Rampside Road, Barrow in Furness SD221689 1880 by J.Y. Macintosh. (MH in WWI. PAI. Roose Hospital from c.1949–93. Dem. c.1995.) **CtH**: Roose Road, Barrow in Furness SD213690 1905. (Now residential/commercial use.) CUB.

Barton-upon-Irwell (PU 30/10/1849 6+12) **W**: 21 Green Lane, Patricroft, Eccles SJ763985 1853 rb. 1894 by W. Mangnall & J. Littlewood (1894). (Green Lane PAI. Bridgewater Hospital from c.1949. Dem. c.1992.) **Ify**: Moorside Road, Davyhulme SJ755953 1926 by Elcock & Sutcliffe. (Davyhulme Park Hospital, later Trafford General. Mostly dem.) LAN.

Blackburn (PU 17/1/1837 24+29) **W1**: Merchant Street (now Hutchinson Street), Blackburn SD683273 1791. (Closed c.1864. Dem.) **W2**: 129 Haslingden Road, Blackburn SD694268 1864 by J.D. & J.E. Oates. (PAI. Queen's Park Hospital from c.1939, now Royal Blackburn Hospital. Part dem.) **CtH**: Queen's Road, Blackburn SD694271 c.1892. (Dem.) **ScH**: Cherry Street and Hickory Street, Blackburn. LAN.

Bolton (PU 1/2/1837 26+33) **W1**: Fletcher Street, Bolton SD714083 c.1810. (Closed c.1861. Dem.) **W2**: Goose Cote Farm, Turton SD719144 <1834. (Closed c.1861. Dem.) **W3**: Off Wash Lane (now Broadway), Farnsworth SD718064 1861 by Hall & Woodhouse. (Fishpool PAI. Bolton District General Hospital from c.1948, now Royal Bolton.) **CtH**: Plodder Lane, Farnsworth SD717061 c.1877. (Later known as Hollins Cottage Homes) **V**: Idle Lane (now Central Street) SD7149093 (Dem.). BOL.

Burnley (PU 20/1/1837 26+33) **W1**: Royle Road, Burnley SD838329 1821. (Closed c.1876. Dem.) **W2**: Blackburn Road, Padiham SD780333 <1834. (Closed c.1855. Later used as farm. Disused.) **W3**: 118 Briercliffe Road, Burnley SD850346 1876 by W. Waddington. (Primrose Bank PAI. Burnley General Hospital from c.1948. Dem. 2008.) **CtH**: Briercliffe Road, Burnley SD849344 c.1890. (As above for workhouse site.) **Hostel**: Working Boys' Home, 31 Hind Street, Burnley SD847347. (NRU.) **Hostel**: Working Girls' Home, Shuttleworth House, Burnley. LAN.

Bury (PU 8/2/1837 12+25) **W1**: Manchester Road, Bury SD804088 1775. (Closed c.1853. Dem.) **W2**: Blackburn Street, Radcliffe SD783073 <1834. (Closed c.1856. Dem.) **W3**: Moss Lane, Pilkington SD812061 <1834. (Closed c.1853. Dem.) **W4**: Bury Old Road, Heywood SD842106 <1834. (Closed c.1856. Dem.) **W5**: 1 Broad Oak Lane (aka 380 Rochdale Old Road), Jericho, Bury SD833116 1856. (Jericho PAI. Decontamination centre c.1940. Fairfield Hospital from c.1948. Mostly dem.) BRY..

Caton GU (GU 1822; diss. 1869) **W**: Caton Green SD546639 c.1823. (Closed 1869. NRU.) LAN.

Chorley (PU 26/1/1837 25+27) **W1**: Golden Hill Lane, Leyland SD541227 <1834. (Closed c.1846. Dem.) **W2**: Out Lane, Croston SD492189 <1834. (Closed c.1846. Dem.) **W3**: Top o'th'Lane, Brindle SD594230 <1776. (Closed c.1872. dem.) **W4**: 152 Eaves Lane, Chorley SD592178 1788 rb. 1872 by J.J. Bradshaw (1872). (PAI. Eaves Lane Hospital from c.1948. Dem.) **CtH**: Stump Lane, Chorley. LAN.

Chorlton (PU 3/2/1837 12+19) **W1**: Stretford Road, Manchester SJ836968 <1834. (Closed c.1855. Dem.) **W2**: 20 Nell Lane, Withington SJ836924 1855 by W. Hayley & L. Hall.

(Withington Hospital from *c.*1915. Closed *c.*2002. Part dem.) **CtH**: Styal Road, Styal SJ844828 1895 by J.B. Broadbent. (Closed 1956. Refugee housing 1956–59. Styal Prison from 1962. Part dem.) MAN.

Chorlton and Manchester Joint Asylum Committee (1897) **Men**: Epileptic Colony, Longsight Road, Langho SJ690339 1906 by Giles, Gough & Trollope. (Closed 1984. Part dem.) MAN.

Clitheroe (PU 14/1/1837 33+35) **W1**: Aighton SD694399 *c.*1817. (Closed *c.*1873. NRU.) **W2**: Bolton-by-Bowland SD774496 *c.*1790. (Closed *c.*1873. Dem.) **W3**: Chatburn Road, Clitheroe SD766430 1873 by J.J. Bradshaw. (Coplow View PAI. Clitheroe Hospital from *c.*1948.) LAN.

Fylde (PU 27/1/1837 24+26) **W1**: Back Lane (now Marsden Street), Kirkham SD424320 *c.*1726. (Closed *c.*1844. Dem.) **W2**: Moor Lane, Kirkham SD422321 1844. (Closed *c.*1907, used as children's home until *c.*1915. Dem.) **CtH**: Moor Lane, Kirkham SD422321 1916 by F. Harrison. (Now offices.) **W3**: 1 Derby Road, Wesham SD420329 1907 by C. Haywood & F. Harrison. (MH in WW1. PAI. Wesham Park Hospital from *c.*1948. Closed 2001. Part dem.) LAN.

Garstang (PU 31/1/1837 23+24) **W1**: Stubbins Lane, Claughton SD505427 1795. (Closed *c.*1876. Part dem. NRU.) **W2**: Bonds Lane, Bowgreave SD497444 1876. (The Beeches PAI. Dem.) LAN.

Haslingden (PU 17/1/1837 10+18) **W1**: Spring Lane, Haslingden SD786237 1749. (Closed *c.*1869. Dem.) **W2**: Mitchell Field Nook, Waggoner Tunstead SD854223 1757. (Closed *c.*1869. Dem.) **W3**: Haslingden Road, Higher Pikelaw SD797225 1869 by H. Lockwood & W. Mawson. (Moorland House PAI. Rossendale General Hospital from *c.*1948–2010.) **CtH**: Moorland Cottages, Sandown Road, Haslingden SD793226. (NRU.) MAN.

Lancaster (PU 10/12/1839 19+26) **W**: 2 Quernmore Road, Lancaster SD486614 1788 enl. 1841. (Parkside PAI than Bay View OPH. Mostly dem. Now part of Lanacaster Grammar School.) **SmH**: 2 Quernmore Road, Lancaster SD486615 1908. (Now part of Lanacaster Grammar School.) LAN.

Leigh (PU 15/2/1837 8+18) **W1**: Common Lane, Culcheth SJ655952 <1834. (Closed *c.*1851. Dem.) **W2**: Newton Road, Lowton SJ614966 <1834. (Closed *c.*1851. Dem.) **W3**: 702 Leigh Road, Atherton SD658013 1851. (Atherleigh Hospital from *c.*1948. dem.) WIG.

Liverpool (SP 25/3/1841; m/w West Derby 1922) **W**: 144a Brownlow Hill, Liverpool SJ357902 1772 enl. 1843. by J. Brooks (1772); H.F. Lockwood & T. Allom (1843). (Dem 1931. RC Cathedral now on site.) **Scl**: Bootle Lane (now Westminster Road), Kirkdale SJ350941 1843 by H.F. Lockwood & T. Allom. (Homes for aged from 1904; Westminster House Home from 1950–68. Dem.) **CtH**: Mill Lane, Wavertree SJ395898 1899. (Later Olive Mount Children's Hospital. Now offices. Mostly dem.) **Ify**: Highfield Infirmary, Old Swan SJ404909 1906 by E. Kirby & W.E. Willink. (WW1 MH; Highfield Sanatorium 1922–29 then Broadgreen Hospital. Dem.) LIV.

Liverpool, West Derby & Toxteth Park JPLC (1900) **San**: Oldfield Road, Heswall SJ257824 1902 by C.H. Lancaster. (Cleaver Sanatorium *c.*1920–50. Closed *c.*1980. Dem.) LIV.

Lunesdale (PU 15/3/1869 22+22) **W**: Hornby SD584677 1872. (Hornby Hostel PAI, later council offices. NRU.) LAN.

Manchester (PU 11/12/1841 12+24; SP from 1850) **W1**: New Bridge Street, Manchester SJ840991 1793 rb. *c.*1880. (Used by War Office in WW1. Dem 1920s for railway yards.) **W2**: Tib Street, Manchester SJ845986 cnv. 1847. (Closed 1847. Dem.) **W3**: Canal Street, Manchester SJ844979 cnv. 1847. (Closed 1858.) **W4**: 123 (later 223) Crescent Road, Crumpsall SD849023 1857 by A.W. Mills & J. Murgatroyd. (Crumpsall PAI. Park House *c.*1939–48 then Springfield Hospital. Part dem.) **Ab/V**: Tame Street, Ancoats SJ856981 <1896 rb. 1900. (Dem.) **Scl1**: Rainsough, Prestwich SD809022 1819. (Girls school/home *c.*1840–46. Prestwich workhouse from 1850. Dem.) **Scl2**: Moston Lane, Blackley SD866019 <1834. (Boys school/home *c.*1840–46. Silk mill from 1846. Dem.) **Scl3**: Chorley Road,

Swinton SD775016 1845 by R. Tattersall. (Dem. 1930s for Swinton Town Hall.) **CvH**: Rose Hill, Northenden SJ835894 1830s by A. Watkin. (Later a boys' remand home. NRU.) MAN.

Oldham (PU 3/2/1837 8+21) **W1**: Side o'th' Moor, Oldham SD937051 1731. (Closed *c*.1851. Dem.) **W2**: Hollin Lane, Middleton SD865077 <1834. (Closed *c*.1851. Dem.) **W3**: Mill Lane, Haggate, Royton SD912076 <1834. (Closed *c*.1851. Dem.) **W4**: Stockfield Road, Chadderton SD911050 <1834. (Closed *c*.1851. Dem.) **W**: 449 Rochdale Road, Oldham SD920062 1851 by Travis & Mangnall. (Westwood Park *c*.1913–29; Boundary Park Hospital *c*.1930–55. Dem.) **RH**: Fir Bank Road, Royton SD917086 1898 by Wild, Collins & Wild. (Now residential/office use.) **ScH**: 1 Low Crompton Road, Crompton; Coldhurst; Freehold; 16-18 Mayall Street, Greenacres; Hollins; Middleton. OLD.

Ormskirk (PU 31/1/1837 21+24) **W1**: Moor Street, Ormskirk SD416081 <1834. (Closed *c*.1853. Dem.) **W2**: 74 Wigan Road, Ormskirk SD421080 1853 by W. Culshaw. (PAI. Ormskirk County Hospital *c*.1949–63 then Ormskirk General. Part dem.) LAN.

Prescot (PU 31/1/1837 21+27) **W1**: Ormskirk Street, St Helen's SJ511955 <1834. (Main workhouse until closed *c*.1843. Dem.) **W2**: Marshall's Cross, St Helen's SJ523926 <1834. (Elderly inmates until closed *c*.1843. Dem.) **W3**: Poorhouse Lane (now Hillfoot Road), Hunt's Cross SJ429850 <1834. (Child inmates until closed *c*.1843. Dem.) **W4**: 1 Warrington Road, Whiston SJ479919 1843 by W. Culshaw. (PAI. Whiston Hospital from *c*.1948. Part dem.) LAN.

Preston (PU 31/1/1837 29+35) **W1**: Deepdale Road, Preston SD544303 1788. (Closed *c*.1868. Dem.) **W4**: Woodplumpton Road, Woodplumpton SD499357 1824. (Closed *c*.1868. Dem.) **W5**: Preston Road, Francis Green, Ribchester SD627366 1823 rb. 1913. (Closed *c*.1868. Mostly dem.) **W6**: 32 Watling Street Road, Fulwood, Preston SD539328 1868 by L. Hall. (PAI. Later Preston Civic Hostel then offices etc.) **Ify**: House of Recovery, Deepdale Road, Preston SD544302 1828. (Closed *c*.1868. Dem.) **Sch1**: Station Road, Bamber Bridge, Walton-le-Dale SD565260 1796. (Union boys' school *c*.1837–68. Dem.) **Sch2**: Greenbank Road, Penwortham SD532276 1796. (Union girls' school *c*.1837–68. NRU.) **SmH**: 232-234 Brockholes View, Preston SD553295. (Later Sunnybank.) LAN.

Prestwich (PU 13/2/1850 11+18) **W1**: Rainsough Brow, Prestwich SD809022 1819. (Closed *c*.1870.) **W2**: 72 Delaunays Road, Manchester 8 SD849025 1870. (Delaunay's Road Institution, later Delaunay's Hospital. Dem.) **Ify**: Charlestown Road, Blackley SD865031 1909. (Booth Hall Children's Hospital *c*.1948–2009. Mostly dem.) MAN.

Rochdale (PU 15/2/1837 6+19) **W1**: Primrose Street, Spotland Bridge SD887136 <1834. (Closed *c*.1877. Dem.) **W2**: Syke Lane, Hollingworth SD943148 *c*.1785. (Closed *c*.1877. Dem.) **W3**: Whitehall Street, Wardleworth SD896140 <1834. (Closed *c*.1877. Dem.) **W4**: Wardle Fold, Wuerdle & Wardle SD914173 <1834. (Closed *c*.1865. NRU.) **W5**: Marland Fold, Marland SD877119 <1834. (Closed *c*.1865. Dem.) **W6**: Bolton Road, Marland SD877118 1865. (Marland Infectious Diseases Hospital from 1887. Closed 1988. Dem.) **W7**: Birch Hill House, New Road, Dearnley, Rochdale SD921161 1877 by G. Woodhouse & E. Potts. (PAI and Birch Hill Hospital from 1930.) **CtH**: Birch Hill Lane, Wardle SD920169 1898 by P. Butterworth & Duncan. (Military use in WW2. Dem. 1950s.) LAN.

Salford (PU 12/7/1838 4+18) **W1**: Greengate (now Trinity Way), Salford SJ834990 1793. (Closed *c*.1853. Dem. Collier Street baths erected on site.) **Sch**: Broughton Road, Pendleton SJ812995 18C. (Closed *c*.1853. Dem.) **W2**: 92 Eccles New Road, Salford SJ808982 1852 by Pennington & Jervis. (Closed *c*.1920. Dem. 1930s.) **Ify**: 2 Stott Lane, Salford, aka 91 Eccles Old Road, Hope SJ786991 1882 by L. Booth. (Later Hope Hospital. Part dem.) **CtH**: Twiss Green Lane, Culcheth SJ650960 1903. (Newchurch Hospital *c*.1948–92. NRU.) SLF.

Todmorden (PU 15/2/1837 6+18) **W1**: Gauxholme Bridge, Gauxholme SD930232 1801. (Closed *c*.1877. NRU.) **W2**: Spinks Hill, Wadsworth SD998305 <1834. (Closed *c*.1877. NRU.) **W3**: Badger Lane, Blackshaw Head SD963275 <1834. (Closed *c*.1877. NRU.) **W4**: Lee Bottom, Mankinholes SD962238 1877. (PAI. Stansfield View Hospital *c*.1948–87. Dem. 1996.) **CtH**: Mankinholes. YWC.

Toxteth Park (SP 24/6/1857 1+18; m/w West Derby 1922) **W**: 126 Smithdown Road, Toxteth SJ378888 1859 by W. Culshaw. (Smithdown Road Institution from *c*.1923. Sefton General Hospital *c*.1950. Dem. 2001.) **SmH**: Richmond Lodge, Church Road, Wavetree SJ391885. (Dem.) LIV.

Ulverston (PU 26/8/1836 27+36) **W**: 27 Stanley Street, Ulverston SD284786 1839 by E.W. Trendall. (PAI. Stanley Hospital from *c*.1948; Ulverston Hospital from 1971. Dem.) CUB.

Warrington (PU 2/2/1837 15+18) **W1**: Church Street, Warrington SJ613883 1728. (Closed *c*.1851. Dem.) **W2**: Bridge Street, Newton-le-Willows SJ576952 <1834. (Closed *c*.1851. Dem.) **W3**: 99 Guardian Street, Warrington SJ596888 1851. (WW1 MH. Whitecross PAI then Homes, later Warrington General Hospital. Part dem.) **CtH**: Green Lane, Padgate SJ636897 1881. (Later Green Lane Schools. Now business use. Part dem.) LAN.

West Derby (PU 31/1/1837 23+31) **W1**: Low Hill, Liverpool SJ361909 *c*.1731. (Closed *c*.1841 then rented to Liverpool Select Vestry. Dem.) **W2/Ify**: 147a Mill Road, Liverpool SJ363915 1841 rb. 1893 by C.H. Lancaster (1893). (Mill Road Infirmary from *c*.1893–1947 then Mill Road Maternity Hospital. Dem. *c*.1996.) **W3/OP**: 107a Rice Lane, Walton, Liverpool SJ358954 1868 by W. Culshaw. (Later Walton Hospital. Part dem.) **Ify**: Eaton Road, West Derby SJ404919 1915 by C.H. Lancaster. (Aged/infirm home. MH in WW1 then Alder Hey Children's Hospital. Part dem.) **Ab**: 42 Belmont Road, Liverpool SJ372924 1890. (Test workhouse. PAI. Newsham Hospital from 1950. Closed 1988. Dem) **CtH**: Longmoor Lane, Fazakerley SJ387976 1889 by C.H. Lancaster. (Now social services offices etc.) **SmH**: (Boys) 101-3 Shaw Street, Everton SJ355915 adopted 1914. (Later St Francis Xavier's school.) **SmH**: (Girls) 57 Shaw Street, Everton SJ356913. (Now other use.) **CvH**: Deysbrook House, Deysbrook Lane, West Derby SJ409934 19C. (Children's convalescent home 1920s–30s. Later Deysbrook Barracks. Dem.) **Men**: Seafield House, Waterloo Road, Seaforth SJ325966 19C. (Mental defectives' home 1920-30s. Dem.) LIV.

Wigan (PU 2/2/1837 20+28) **W1**: Liverpool Road, Hindley SD613039 <1834. (Closed *c*.1857. Dem.) **W2**: 75 Frog Lane, Wigan SD574060 1857 by W. Magnall. (PAI. Frog Lane Welfare Home from *c*.1948, later Frog Lane Hospital. Closed *c*.1970. dem.) **Ify**: 154 Upholland Road, Billinge SD528028 1906. (Billinge Infirmary, later Billinge Hospital. Closed 2004. dem.) WIG.

Leicestershire

Ashby-de-la-Zouch (PU 28/6/1836 23+30) **W**: 1 Nottingham Road, Ashby-de-la-Zouch SK367171 1826 enl. 1836. (PAI. Dem. 1940s. Site became council depot.) **SmH**: Burton Road, Ashby. LEI.

Barrow-upon-Soar (PU 11/9/1837 30+30) **W**: 240 Leicester Road, Mountsorrel SK585142 1840 by W. Flint. (PAI. Laters Glenfrith Hospital then Mountsorrel Hospital. Mostly dem. NRU.) **SmH**: Rothley. LEI.

Billesdon (PU 5/4/1836 34+36) **W1**: Newton Lane, Great Glen SP651972 <1834. (Closed *c*.1846. Dem.) **W2**: Coplow Lane, Billesdon SK718029 1846. (PAI. Dem. *c*.1935.) LEI.

Blaby (PU 6/2/1836 22+32) **W**: Leicester Road, Enderby SP548985 1837 by W. Parsons. (Enderby House PAI, later OPH. Dem.) LEI.

Hinckley (PU 9/2/1836 11+25) **W**: London Road, Hinckley SP435939 1838 by J.A. Hansom. (Mostly dem. *c*.1950. Now North Warwickshire & Hinckley College.) **CtH**: Burbage. LEI.

Leicester (PU 20/6/1836 8+35; SP 1896) **W**: 2 Swain Street, Leicester SK595042 1838 rb. 1851 by W. Flint (1838); W. Parsons & M.J. Dain (1851). (PAI later Hillcrest Hospital. Dem. *c*.1977.) **Ify**: Gwendolen Road, North Evington SK622039 1905 by Giles, Gough & Trollope. (WW1 MH. North Evington Infirmary until 1920 then Leicester General Hospital.) **CtH**: Cosby Road, Countesthorpe SP569955. 1884 by I. Baradale. (Children's homes until 1970s. NRU.) **RH**: 8-10 Mill Hill Lane, Leicester SK597036. (Later The Oaks boys' home. NRU.) **ScH**: 2 Dorothy Road, 86 St Saviour's Road, 50 Halstead Street, 86 and 109 St Saviours' Road. LEI.

Loughborough (PU 9/9/1838 24+28) **W**: 59a Regent Street, Loughborough SK530199 1838 by G.G. Scott & W.B. Moffatt. (Hastings House PAI. Regent Hospital and OPH from c.1948. Dem.) **SmH**: Meadow Lane, Loughborough. LEI.

Lutterworth (PU 10/12/1835 35+36) **W**:Woodmarket Road, Lutterworth SP539841 1840 by G.G. Scott & W.B. Moffatt. (The Home PAI then Woodmarket House OPH. Dem. 1969.) LEI.

Market Bosworth (PU 11/2/1836 28+33) **W**: Station Road, Market Bosworth SK401030 1836 by Mr Knightley. (West Haven PAI. Later Westhaven OPH. Mostly dem. NRU.) LEI.

Market Harborough (PU 3/12/1835 38+42) **W**: 33 Leicester Road, Market Harborough SP726883 1837 by S. Kempthorne. (PAI. St Lukes's Hospital from c.1948. Dem.) **CtH**:The Mount, Back Lane, East Farndon SP717852 cnv. 1912. (NRU.) LEI.

Melton Mowbray (PU 26/3/1836 54+56) **W**:Thorpe Road, Melton Mowbray SK759193 1836 by C. Dyer. (PAI. St Mary's Hospital from c.1948.) **SmH**: Brookfield House, Snow Hill, Melton Mowbray SK755195. (Dem.) LEI.

Lincolnshire

Boston (PU 22/9/1836 27+38) **W**: 35 Skirbeck Road, Boston TF333433 1838 by G.G. Scott. (St John's Home PAI then OPH. Mostly dem.) **CtH**: Brothertoft Road, Boston. LIN.

Bourne (PU 25/11/1835 37+44) **W**: Union Road (now St Peter's Road), Bourne TF092199 1837 by B. Browning. (Well Head House PAI later St Peter's Hospital until 1980s. Dem. 2001.) LIN.

Caistor (PU 13/12/1836 76+80) **W**: Kelsey Road, Caistor TA102013 1802. (Certified Institution for 'mental defectives' from 1931. Caistor Hospital c.1948–90. Dem 2001.) LIN.

Gainsborough (PU 19/1/1837 45+47) **W**: 181 Lea Road, Gainsborough SK819855 1837 by G.Wilkinson. (PAI then Oakdene OPH. Dem.) **CtH**: 13-15 North Marsh Road, Gainsborough SK811908. (NRU.) LIN.

Glanford Brigg (PU 18/1/1837 50+54) **W**: 34 Wrawby Road, Brigg TA003074 1835 by W.A. Nicholson. (PAI. Glanford Hospital c.1948–91. Mostly dem.) LIN.

Grantham (PU 14/1/1836 52+62) **W1**:Workhouse Lane, Grantham SK912352 1837 by S. Kempthorne. (Closed c.1892. Site sold to Great North Railway. Dem.) **W2**: 119 Dysart Road, Grantham SK904355 1892 by V. Green. (PAI. Hill View Hospital from c.1948. Dem 1960s.) LIN.

Grimsby (PU 15/4/1890 25+44) **W**: 100 or 110a Scartho Road, Grimsby TA263073 1894 by E. Farebrother & H.C. Scaping. (Scartho Road PAI. Grimsby District General Hospital from c.1948. Part dem.) **ScI**: Brighowgate, Grimsby TA266089 1913. (WW1 billets/hospital. Later Salvation Army hostel.) LIN.

Holbeach (PU 7/12/1835 11+25) **W**:The Shrubbery, 13 Turnpike Road, Fleet TF369249 1837 by R. Ellis Jnr. (PAI. Fleet Hospital c.1948–91, later Holbeach House nursing home.) LIN.

Horncastle (PU 16/1/1837 68+71) **W**: Foundry Street, Horncastle TF265693 1838 by G.G. Scott & W.B. Moffatt. (PAI then Holmeleigh Welfare Centre. Now offices and nursery. Part dem.) LIN.

Lincoln (PU 28/11/1836 86+89) **W**: Lincoln Home, 8a Burton Road, Lincoln SK972721 1838 by W..A Nicholson. (Burton Road PAI then West View elderly care home. Dem. 1965) **ScH**: (Boys) Scothern, Lincs. **ScH**: (Girls) Long Leys Road, Lincoln. **ScH**: 27-32 Saxon Street, Lincoln; Rasen Lane, Lincoln. LIN.

Louth (PU 12/4/1837 88+90) **W**: Holmes Lane (now High Holme Road), Louth TF326878 1837 by G.G. Scott & W.B. Moffatt. (PAI then Louth County Infirmary, later County Hospital.) **SmH**: Nichol Hill, Louth. LIN.

Sleaford (PU 20/9/1836 56+59) **W**: East Gate, Sleaford TF076463 1838 by W.J. Donthorn. (PAI later Slea View elderly care home. Dem. 1960s.) LIN.

Spalding (PU 30/11/1835 8+25) **W**: Pinchbeck Road, Spalding TF248234 1837 by B. Browning. (Myntling Home PAI. Pinchbeck Road Hospital from c.1948. Dem.) LIN.

Spilsby (PU 13/4/1837 66+89) **W**: The Gables, Hundleby Road, Hundleby TF392662 1838 by G.G. Scott & W.B. Moffatt. (The Gables Hospital from *c.*1948. Dem.) LIN.

Stamford (PU 17/11/1835 37+43) **W1**: Barnack Road, Stamford TF036069 1837 by B. Browning. (Closed 1902. Part dem.) **W2**: Bourne Road, Stamford TF037078 1902 by J.H. Morton. (St George's Home PAI. St George's Hospital from *c.*1948. Dem.) **SmH**: Bourne Road, Stamford TF038079. (Now Ryhall House.) LIN.

London

Bermondsey, St Mary Magdalen (SP 21/3/1836 1+18; jd. St Olave's PU 1869) **W**: Russell (now Tanner) Street, Bermondsey TQ333797 1791. (Closed 1920s. Dem.) LMA.

Bethnal Green, St Matthew (SP 26/3/1836) **W1**: Waterloo House, Waterloo Road, Bethnal Green TQ351835 1842 by Bunning. (Dem. 1930s.) **W2**: Well Street, Hackney TQ353842 cnv. 1891. (Vacated *c.*1900; Later used by Willesden, Poplar and West Ham Unions. Dem.) **Ify**: Cambridge Heath Road, London E2 TQ350832 1900 by Giles, Gough & Trollope. (WW1 MH. Bethnal Green Hospital *c.*1930–90. Mostly dem. NRU.) **Scl**: Whipps Cross Road, Leytonstone TQ397878 bt. 1868; rb. 1889 by A&C Harston. (Closed 1937 then Leytonstone House Hospital, Closed *c.*2000. NRU. Part dem.) **V**: Hollybush Gardens, Bethnal Green Road TQ349827 *c.*1910. (Dem.) LMA.

Camberwell, St Giles (SP 28/10/1835) **W1**: Havil Street / Brunswick Square, Camberwell TQ332769 1818. (Infirmary from *c.*1875. St Giles' Hospital *c.*1930–83. Mostly dem. NRU.) **W2**: 22 Gordon Road, Camberwell TQ346764 1878 by Berriman. (PAI then Camberwell Reception Centre. NRU.) **W3**: Constance Road, Camberwell TQ333752 1892 by T.W. Aldwinckle. (St Francis Hospital from *c.*1930–48 then Dulwich Hospital North Wing. Dem *c.*1982.) **W4**: Willowbrook Road, Peckham TQ338776 cnv. *c.*1895. (Temporary workhouse in former Birkbeck schools. Dem.) **V**: Albert Road, Peckham TQ345764. **RH**: 1-6 Newlands Cottages, Stuart Road, Peckham Rye TQ355751. (Now Bredinghurst School.) **ScH**: 270-272 and 341-343 Crystal Palace Road, 14-16 Derwent Grove, 22-24 and 263 Friern Road, 2 Gowlett Road, 335-337 Lordship Lane, 1-3 and 9-11 Matham Grove, 158 and 253 Underhill Road, 32 and 328 Upland Road, and 17-19 Zenoria Street (alll East Dulwich); 2-4 and 18 Barforth Road, 7 Waveney Avenue, and 21/25/29/33 Rye Road (all Peckham Rye). LMA.

Chelsea, St Luke (In Kensington PU 1837-41 then SP) **W**: 2 Arthur (now Dovehouse) Street / 250 King's Road, Chelsea TQ271782 1843 by Coleman. (PAI then King's Mead OPH. Dem. 1960s.) **Ify**: Cale Street, Chelsea TQ271783 1872 by J. Giles & Gough. (St Luke's Hospital *c.*1925–74. Dem.) **V**: Milman's Street, Chelsea TQ268775 1894 by A&C Harston. (Dem.) LMA.

City of London (PU 30/3/1837 98+101; m/w E & W London PUs 1869) **W**: 2a Bow Road, London E3 TQ367826 1849 by R. Tress. (Union Infirmary *c.*1870–1909. City of London Institution until 1936 then St Clement's Hospital. Part dem.) **V/Ify**: Robin Hood Court, Shoe Lane TQ314814 1893 by F. Hammond. (Used by MAB from 1916. Dem.) **Dsp**: Northumberland Alley, Fenchurch Street; 61 Bartholomew Close. LMA.

Clerkenwell, St James & St John (LP 1775; jd. Holborn PU 1869) **W**: Farringdon Road, Clerkenwell TQ313822 1727. (Dem. 1883.) ISL, LMA.

East London (PU 12/12/1837 4+20; jd. City of London 1869) **W1**: 128 Aldersgate Street TQ321817 <1834. (Dem.) **W2**: Dunning's Alley, Bishopsgate Street TQ332817 <1834. (Dem. Now site of Liverpool Street Station.) **W3**: 42 Clifden Road, Clapton, Hackney TQ355853 1852. (Eastern Hospital *c.*1930–82. Dem.) **Dsp**: 22 Commercial Road East, Stepney. (Dem.) LMA.

Fulham (In Kensington PU from 1837 ; PU with Hammersmith 1845–99 then SP.) **W1**: 102-103 St Dunstan's Road, Fulham TQ236780 1849 by A. Gilbert. (WW1 MH. Fulham Hospital from *c.*1925. Dem. *c.*1957.) **W2**: Belmont Institution, Brighton Road, Sutton TQ255626 Leased *c.*1908–16. (WW1 MH. Later Belmont Hospital. Dem.) **V**: Margravine

Road, Fulham TQ237780. (Dem.) **RH**: Henniker House, 9 Parson's Green, Fulham TQ251765. (Now part of Lady Margaret School.) LMA.

Greenwich (PU 18/11/1836 4+20) **W**: Woolwich Road, Greenwich (Infirmary at 48 Vanbrugh Hill) TQ396782 1840 by R.P. Browne. (St Alfege's Hospital *c.*1931–68 then Greenwich District Hospital. Dem. 1960s.) **W**: Marvel's Lane, Grove Park, Greenwich TQ410727 1902 by T. Dinwiddy. (WWI barracks. Grove Park TB Hospital *c.*1926–77. Part dem. NRU.) **CtH**: Burnt Oak Lane, Sidcup TQ460734 1902 by T. Dinwiddy. (Later Lamorbey Schools then The Hollies. Closed 1980s. NRU.) **CtH**: 9-19 Calvert Rd, East Greenwich TQ395781 cnv. *c.*1926. (Dem.) **Dsp**: 14 Union Street (later 24 Creek Road), Deptford; Peyton Place, Royal Hill, Greenwich. (Dem.) LMA.

Hackney (PU 26/1/1837 2+18) **W**: 2 Sidney Road / 230 High Street, Homerton TQ360851 <1834. (Hackney Hospital *c.*1930–95. Now John Howard Centre. Mostly dem.) **RH**: 42 Sidney (now Kenworthy) Road, Homerton TQ361850 *c.*1897. (Closed *c.*1931. Dem.) **Scl**: Brentwood Hill (now London Road), Brentwood TQ587936 bt. 1885 from Brentwood SD. (Branch workhouse from 1908. Bt. by MAB *c.*1917. St Faith's Hospital *c.*1930–95. Dem.) **CtH**: Chipping Ongar TL553038 1905 by W. Finch. (Public Assistance School 1930–39, later Great Stony School until 1994. NRU.) **V**: Gainsborough Road (now Eastway), Hackney Wick TQ367849 1904 by W. Finch. (Closed 1960s. Dem.) **Dsp**: 68 Roseberry Place, Dalston. (Dem.) LMA, STB.

Hammersmith (In Kensington PU from 1837; PU with Fulham 1845–99 then SP) **W**: Du Cane Road, Hammersmith TQ225813 1905 by Giles, Gough & Trollope. (WWI MH. Ministry of Pensions hospital 1919-26. Hammersmith Hospital from 1930. Mostly dem.) **RH**: 206a Goldhawk Road, W12 TQ225794. (Dem.) LMA.

Hampstead, St John (In Edmonton PU 1837-48 then SP 1+11) **W**: 12 New End, Hamspstead TQ264860 *c.*1801 rb. 1851 by H.E. Kendall (1851). (WWI MH. New End Hospital *c.*1930–86. NRU.) **SmH**: Homesfield, Erskine Hill, Golder's Green NW11 TQ252890. (NRU.) CAM, LMA.

Holborn (PU 27/4/1836 2+20) **W1**: 158 Grays Inn Road, EC1 TQ310821 <1834; part rb. 1901. (Closed *c.*1890s. Later used as factory premises.) **W2**: Western Road, Mitcham TQ276693 1886 by H. Saxon Snell. (WWI MH. Closed *c.*1922 then industrial use until 1960s. Dem.) **V**: Vine Street (now Hill), EC1 TQ311821. (Closed *c.*1901. Dem.) **V**: Little Grays Inn Lane (now Mount Pleasant), EC1 TQ310821 1901 by Smith & Coggan. (Casual wards until 1930s. Still used as hostel.) **Ify**: Archway House, Archway Road, Islington TQ293870 1879 by H. Saxon Snell. (Archway Hospital from 1930. Whittington Hospital, Archway Wing *c.*1948–98. Now university use.) **Scl**: Eagle House, High Street, Mitcham TQ278694 bt. 1870 from Southwark St George the Martyr. (Closed *c.*1930. Mostly dem.) **RH**: 11 Lloyd Street, WC1 TQ310828. (NRU.) LMA.

Islington, St Mary (LP 1776; SP from 1867) **W1/Dsp**: 279a Liverpool Road (later via Upper Barnsbury Street), Islington TQ314841 <1834. (Closed *c.*1870 then used as union dispensary/offices. NRU. Part dem.) **W2**: 129 St John's Road (now Way), Islington TQ297873 1870 by R.H. Burden. (PAI then Hillside OPH. Closed 1972. Dem.) **W3**: Cornwallis Road, Upper Holloway TQ301867 bt. 1882 from West London by Searle & Yelf. (POWs housed in WWI. Later storage depot. Dem.) **Scl**: Hornsey Road, Hornsey TQ307866 1853. (Closed *c.*1930. Dem.) **RH**: 59 Hornsey Rise, N19 TQ299875. (Dem.) **Ify**: 77a Highgate Hill, London N19 TQ290869 1900 by W. Smith. (St Mary's Hospital *c.*1930–46 then Whittington Hospital, St Mary's Wing. Part dem.) LMA.

Kensington (St Mary Abbots) (PU 1837 5+26; SP from 1845) **W1**: Butts Field (now Kensington Gate), Kensington TQ262794 1778 by T. Callcott. (Closed 1849. Dem.) **W2**: 28 Marloes Road, Kensington TQ256793 1848 by T. Allom. (St Mary Abbots Hospital *c.*1922–89. Part dem. NRU.) **Ab/V/Dsp**: Mary Place, Notting Hill TQ240807 cnv. 1882. (Dem. Site is now Avondale Park Gardens.) **Dsp**: 49-51 Church Street, Kensington. (Dem.) LMA.

Lambeth, St Mary (SP 28/12/1835) **W1**: Prince's (now Black Prince) Road, Lambeth
TQ308785 <1834; rb. 1888 by T.W. Aldwinckle (1888). (Dem. *c.*1930.) **W2**: 43 Renfrew
Road, Lambeth TQ316788 1873 by T.W. Aldwinckle & R. Parris. (Lambeth Hospital
*c.*1922–76. Mostly dem. Now cinema museum.) **V**: 25a Lucretia Road (now Wincott
Street), Lambeth TQ313787 1877. (Now St Luke's Centre.) **Scl**: 62 Elder Road, Norwood
TQ322711 bt. 1809; enl. 1885. (Part OPH by 1920s later known as Norwood House, and
Norwood Children's Home. Mostly dem. NRU.) **Dsp**: 35 Lambeth Palace Road; 112
Westminster Bridge Road; 55 Stockwell Road. LAM, LMA.

Lewisham (PU 28/11/1836 7+20) **W**: 390 High Street, Lewisham TQ378745 1817. (WW1
MH. Lewisham Hospital from *c.*1930. Part dem.) **RH**: 28 Sangley Road, Catford SE
TQ377735. (Now business use.) **RH**: Cumberlow, Lancaster Road, South Norwood
TQ340687. (Dem. Now grounds of Harris Academy.) LMA.

Mile End Old Town (In Stepney PU until 1857 then SP 1+18; jd. Stepney PU 1925) **W**:
Bancroft Lodge, Bancroft Road, Mile End TQ359825 1859 by W. Dobson. (Mile End
Hospital from *c.*1930. Mostly dem.) **ScH**: 14-17 Cottage Grove, Bow; Coborn Road, Bow;
Bow Road, Bow. LMA.

Newington, St Mary (LP 1814; SP 1836 1+18; jd. St Saviour's PU 1869) **W1**: Walworth
Road, Walworth TQ324779 <1834. (Dem. 1850s) **W2**: 182 Westmoreland Road, Newington
TQ331780 1850. (St Saviour's Union Infirmary from 1870s. PAI then Newington Lodge
OPH. Dem. *c.*1970) LMA.

Paddington (In Kensington until 1845 then PU) **W**: 289 Harrow Road, Paddington TQ252819
1850. (WW1 MH. Paddington Hospital 1932-68. St Mary's (Harrow Road) 1968-86. Dem.)
RH: Trenmar House, 12 Trenmar Gardens, NW10 TQ226828. (Dem.) COW, LMA.

Poplar (PU 20/12/1836 3+15; SP from 1907) **W**: 100 High Street, Poplar TQ376807 1757, enl.
1817 and 1872 by J. Walker (1817); J. Morris (1872). (PAI. Later LCC supplies depot. Dem.
*c.*1960.) **V**: St Leonard Street, Bromley TQ380825. (Dem.) **Ab**: Dunton Road, Laindon,
Essex TQ663884 1904. (Later Dunton Farm colony. Dem.) **Scl**: Forest Lane, Forest Gate
TQ399852 bt. 1897 from Forest Gate SD. (Sold to West Ham Union 1911. NRU.) **RH**: 54
East India Dock Road, London E14 TQ371810 cnv. *c.*1903. (Langley House. Dem.) **Dsp**: 7
Fairfield Road, Poplar. **CtH**: Rayleigh Road, Hutton, Essex TQ621953 1906 by Holman &
Goodman. (Later Hutton Residential School. Closed 1982. Mostly dem.) LMA.

Rotherhithe, St Mary (SP 15/2/1836; jd. St Olave's 1869) **W**: 48a Lower Road, Rotherhithe
TQ351793 1829. (St Olave's Union Infirmary erected on site 1875.) LMA.

Shoreditch, St Leonard's (LP. SP from 17/1/1868) **W1**: 204 Hoxton Street, Shoreditch
TQ334834 <1834; rb. 1865 by Lee (1865). (St Leonard's Hospital from *c.*1920. Part dem.) **W2**:
The Mansion, Alexandra Park Road, Wood Green TQ298904 cnv. *c.*1901. (Closed *c.*1906.
Dem.) **W3**: Hazellville Road, Hornsey TQ298875 cnv. *c.*1906. (Dem. *c.*1927.) **V**: Nuttall
Street, Shoreditch TQ334834. (Dem.) **Scl**: Brentwood Hill, Brentwood TQ587936 1854. (Sold
to Brentwood SD in 1877.) **Scl**: Harold Court Road, Harold Wood TQ559911 cnv. 1885.
(Later Harold Court Hospital. Closed *c.*1960. NRU.) **RH**: 26-28 Lower Clapton Road, E5
TQ351853. (Now commercial use.) **CtH**: Hornchurch Road, Hornchurch TQ529872 1889 by
F.J. Smith. (Later Hornchurch Children's Home.) LMA, STB.

Southwark, St George the Martyr (SP 26/10/1835; jd. St Saviour's 1869) **W**: Mint Street,
Southwark TQ322799 1782. (Closed 1920s. Dem.) **Scl**: Eagle House, High Street, Mitcham
TQ278694 1856. (Sold to Holborn 1870.) LMA.

St George in the East (SP 25/3/1836 1+18; jd. Stepney PU 1925) **W**: 3 Raine Street, E1
TQ349804 1824. (St George In the East Hospital *c.*1930–56. Dem. 1963.) **Scl**: Gipsy Lane
(now Green Street), Upton Park, East Ham TQ412842 1852 by A. Wilson. (Cinema *c.*1927–
83. Dem.) **V**: 9 Raine Street, E1 TQ349804. (Dem.) **V**: Raymond Street, E1 TQ347801.
(Dem.) LMA.

St George's (ren. City of Westminster 1913) (Formed 1870 from St George's, Hanover
Square and Westminster St Margaret & St John.) **W/V**: 20 Wallis's Yard, Buckingham Palace

Road TQ290794 1886. (Dem.) **Dsp**: 31 Stockbridge Terrace, Pimlico; 128 Victoria Street, Westminster. **Scl**: Milman's Street, Chelsea TQ268776 1902. (Taken over by MAB 1914. LCC hostel from 1956. Dem. 1980s.) COW, LMA.

St George's, Hanover Square (LP 1753; jd. St George's PU 1870) **W1**: Mount Street, Westminster TQ285806 1726 by Timbrell & Phillips. **W2**: 367-9 Fulham Road, London SW10 TQ264777 1786; rb. 1850s; enl. 1878 by H. Saxon Snell (1878). (Fulham Road PAI. St Stephen's Hospital *c.*1931–89. Dem.) COW, LMA.

St Giles in the Fields & St George, Bloomsbury (LP 1774; SP from 1868; jd. Holborn PU 1914) **W**: Endell Street, St Giles TQ302813 1727; rb. 1882 by Lee & Smith (1882). (Closed 1914. WWI Endell Street Refuge. Later known as Dudley House. Dem. *c.*1980.) **RH**: 52 Broad Street (now High Holborn), Bloomsbury TQ302813 1902 by J. Izzard. **V**: 25-27 Macklin Street, Drury Lane TQ304814. (Dem.) LMA.

St Luke's, Old Street (LP 1771; jd. Holborn PU 1869) **W**: 1a Shepherdess Walk, Hoxton TQ323829 <1834; rb. 1871; enl. 1879 by H. Saxon Snell (1870–09). (St Matthew's Hospital 1936–86. Mostly dem. NRU.) **Dsp**: 97 Old Street, Finsbury. LMA.

St Martin in the Fields (SP 29/4/1836 1+24; jd. Strand PU 1868) **W**: Hemming's Row, St Martin's TQ300806 1772 by R. Palmer. (Dem. 1871. Part of National Gallery now occupies site.) COW, LMA.

St Marylebone (LP 1775; SP from 1867) **W**: 1 Northumberland Street and 2 Luxborough Street, St Marylebone TQ281819 1775; rb. 1890s by A. Saxon Snell. (PAI. Luxborough Lodge OPH 1949–65. Dem.) **Ify**: Rackham Street, Ladbroke Grove TQ237819 1881 by H. Saxon Snell. (Casual ward housed refugees and military prisoners in WWI. St Charles's Hospital from 1930.) **V**: 86 East (now Chiltern) Street, St Marylebone TQ280819 1881 by H. Saxon Snell. (Dem.) **Dsp**: Little Union (later Golford) Place, Lisson Grove; East (now Chiltern) Street, St Marylebone. (Dem:) **Scl**: South Road, Southall TQ126801 1859. (WWI Australian MH. Dem *c.*1931.) COW, LMA.

St Olave's (ren. Bermondsey 1904) (PU 1/2/1836 3+15) **W1**: Parish (now Druid) Street, Bermondsey TQ334799 <1834. (Closed 1920s. Dem. *c.*1930.) **W2**: 82 Ladywell Road, Lewisham TQ373745 1900 by H. Saxon Snell. (WWI MH. PAI then Ladywell Lodge OPH. Mostly dem. Now training centre.) **Inf/V**: 48a Lower Road, Rotherhithe TQ351793 1875 by Newman & Newman. (Later Bermondsey Infirmary then St Olave's Hospital. Closed 1985. Dem.) **CtH**: Wickham Road, Shirley TQ357658 1903 by Newman & Newman. (Shirley Residential Schools until 1983. Mostly dem. NRU.) **CtH**: Elmside, 180–182 Peckham Rye TQ344752. (NRU.) **CtH**: The Hawthorns, 43 The Gardens, Peckham Rye TQ344752. (Dem.) **Dsp**: 36-38 Abbey Street, Bermondsey; 98 Bermondsey Street, Bermondsey; 44 Lower Road, Rotherhithe. LMA.

St Pancras (LP; SP from 10/6/1867) **W1**: 4 Kings Road (now St Pancras Way), St Pancras TQ297836 1809 by T. Hardwick. (St Pancras Hospital (South) from *c.*1922. Part dem.) **W2**: St Anne's Home, Streatham Hill TQ305732 cnv. 1890. (Bt. by Bermondsey Union *c.*1915. Dem. 1930s.) **Ify**: Cook's Terrace, Pancras Road TQ297836 1885 by H. Bridgman. (Part of St Pancras Hospital (South) from *c.*1922.) **Ify**: 199 Dartmouth Park Hill, N19 TQ288869 1869 by J. Giles & Biven. (Used by Central London SAD *c.*1869–93. Later Highgate Hospital then Whittington Hospital Highgate Wing.) **V**: 41 Holmes Road, Kentish Town TQ288850. (Now St Pancras Hostel.) **Scl**: Asylum (now College) Road, Leavesden TL101014 1872 by J. Giles & Biven. (Leavesden Hospital 1930s–1995. Dem.) **RH**: St Margaret's, 25 Leighton Road, Kentish Town NW5 TQ291852. (Later St Margaret's Hospital. Dem.) **CvH**: Eastcliff House, Alexandra (now Northdown) Road, Margate TR362710 cnv. 1895. (Bt by MAB 189. Now offices.) LMA.

St Saviour's (ren. Southwark 1901) (PU 11/2/1836 2+17) **W**: 81 Gray (formerly Marlborough) Street, Southwark TQ315799 1820s by G. Allen. (PAI. Dem 1940s?) **Ify**: 72a East Dulwich Grove, Southwark TQ334751 1887 by H. Jarvis. (WWI MH. Southwark Hospital 1921-31 then Dulwich Hospital.) **V**: Great Guildford Street, Southwark. **RH**:

Boyson Road, Walworth SE17. (Dem.) **RH**: 173 South (now Dawes) Street, Walworth. (Dem.) **Dsp**: 55 Blackman (now Borough High) Street; 302 Borough High Street. LMA.

St Sepulchre (LP 1798; jd Holborn PU 1845) **W**: West Street, Smithfield TQ317817 c.1806. (Closed c.1845. Dem.) LMA.

Stepney (PU 19/12/1836 5+23) **W1**: Alderney Place, Globe Road, Mile End TQ356822 <1834. (Closed c.1857. Dem.) **W2**: Green Bank, Wapping TQ347801 <1834. (Closed c.1863. Dem.) **W3**: St Leonard's Street, Bromley-by-Bow TQ379826 1862 by H. Jarvis. (Bromley House PAI. Reception centre c.1948–66. Dem.) **W/V/RH**: Corner of Salmon's Lane and York Street West (now Barnes Street), Ratcliff TQ361813 <1834. (RH from c.1909. Included Stepney guardians' offices. Dem.) **V**: Eastfield Street, Limehouse. (Dem.) **V**: White Horse Street (now Road), Stepney TQ364816. (Dem.) **Scl**: Ropemaker's Fields, Limehouse TQ367808 <1834. (Closed c.1870. Dem.) **CtH**: Clockhouse Lane, North Stifford, Essex TQ597800 1901 by F. Baggallay. (Approved school 1935–59 then Ardale School until 1995. Mostly dem. NRU.) **RH**: 17 Cottage (now Rhondda) Grove, Bow E3 TQ364827. (NRU.) LMA.

Strand (PU 25/3/1836 5+21; jd. City of Westminster PU 1913) **W1**: Cleveland Street, London W1 TQ292818 1778. (1873–1913 used by Central London SAD. Part of Middlesex Hospital c.1924–2006.) **W2/V**: Bear Yard, Portsmouth Place, Lincoln's Inn Fields TQ307812 c.1870. (Dem. c.1900.) **W3/V**: Sheffield Street, Aldwych TQ307812 1903. (1914 bt. by MAB. Sheffield Street Hospital c.1930–48 then St Philip's Hospital. Now part of LSE.) **W3**: Tanner's End (now Silver Street), Edmonton TQ334924 1870. (Closed 1913. WW1 Edmonton Refuge. Silk factory after 1930. Dem.) **Scl**: Wye Hall Road (now Silver Street), Edmonton TQ329926 cnv. 1849. (Bt. by MAB 1914. WW1 Millfield Refuge. St David's Hospital c.1936–71. Part dem. Now arts centre.) **V**: Bear Yard, Aldwych TQ306812 1890; rb. 1903. (Closed c.1914. Site now part of London School of Economics.) **Dsp**: 29 Maiden Lane, Covent Garden. COW, LMA.

Wandsworth & Clapham (ren. Wandsworth 1904) (PU 25/3/1836 6+19) **W1**: St John's Hill, Wandsworth TQ265751 1840 by G.L. Taylor. (St John's Hospital c.1930–85. Mostly dem. NRU.) **W2**: 77 Swaffield Road, Wandsworth TQ260737 1886 by T.W. Aldwinckle. (PAI then Brocklebank OPH, and Wandsworth Hostel. Dem.) **OP**: Church Lane, Tooting TQ281711 cnv. 1897; enl. 1902. by C. Sharp (1902). (WW1 MH. St Benedict's Hospital c.1930–81. Dem.) **Ify**: St James' Road, Upper Tooring TQ277732 bt. from Westminster c.1904; enl. 1910 by J.S. Gibson. (St James Hospital c.1920–88. Dem. 1992.) **RH/Scl**: Swaffield Road, Wandsworth TQ259738 1903 by Landsell & Harrison. (Later Earlsfield House. NRU.) **Dsp**: Latchmere Road, Battersea; 127 Plough Road, Battersea; 342 Wandsworth Road. LMA, WAN.

West London (PU 12/12/1837 7+20; jd. City of London 1869) **W1**: West Street, Smithfield TQ317817 <1834. (Dem. Now site of Smithfield Market.) **W2**: Cornwallis Road, Upper Holloway TQ301867 1864 by Searle & Yelf. (Acquired by Islington in 1882.) **Scl**: Meeting House Lane, Edmonton TQ340921 <1834. (Dem.) **Dsp**: 18 Thavies Inn, Holborn. LMA.

Westminster, St James (LP 1762; Westminster PU from 1868) **W**: 49 Poland Street, Westminster TQ293812 1757; rb. 1859 by C. Lee (1859). (Closed 1913. WW1 Jewish refugee centre. Dem.) **Scl**: St James Road, Wandsworth TQ277732 1852 by C. Lee. (Bt. by Wandsworth Union c.1904.) COW, LMA.

Westminster, St Margaret & St John (LP 1752; PU from 1867; jd. St George's PU 1870) **W1**: Dean Street, Westminster TQ299794 c.1787. (Closed 1852. Dem.) **W2**: York Street (now Petty France), Westminster TQ294794 c.1850. (Closed and dem. c.1870.) **W3**: 28 Marloes Road, Kensington TQ256793 1853 by H.A. Hunt. (Closed 1878 then bt. by St Mary Abbots. Dem.) COW, LMA.

Whitechapel (PU 16/2/1837 9+25) **W1**: Charles Street (later Baker's Row, now Vallance Road) Whitechapel TQ344820 1842 enl. 1859 by T. Barry (1859). (St Peter's Hospital from 1924. Closed 1960s. Dem.) **W2**: South (now Southern) Grove, Bow TQ367825 1871. (PAI. Later Southern Grove Lodge OPH. Now day centre. Part dem.) **V**: 35 Thomas (later

Fulbourne) Street, Whitechapel TQ345819 *c.*1860. (Dem.) **Scl**: Forest Lane, London E7 TQ399852 1854. (Bt. by Forest Gate SD 1869.) **RH**: 403-409 Mile End Road, E3 TQ364825. (Also known as Jewish Homes and St Philip's House. Dem.) **RH**: Whitehall Lane, Grays, Essex TQ622783 1899 by C.M. Shiner. (NRU.) **ScH**: Whitehall Cottages, Whitehall Lane; Park Cottages, Clarence Road; Dene Cottages, Palmers Avenue; Harold Cottages, Bridge Road (all at Grays, Essex). LMA.

Woolwich (PU 10/3/1868 4+17) **W**: 79b Tewson Road, Woolwich TQ454784 1870 by Church & Rickwood. (PAI. St Nicholas Hospital *c.*1930–86. Dem.) **V**: Hull Place, Plumstead TQ454785 1872 by Church & Rickwood. (Dem.) **OP**: (Women) Furze Lodge, 138 Shrewsbury (now Plum) Lane, SE18 TQ440773. (Dem.) **CtH**: Goldie Leigh Homes, Lodge Lane, Bostall Heath TQ471776 1899. (Used by MAB from 1914. Goldie Leigh Hospital from 1933.) **RH**: 43-47 Parkdale Road, Plumstead TQ452782. (Dem.) **Dsp**: 30 Rectory Place, Woolwich; Cage Lane, Plumstead. LMA.

London School Districts

Brentwood SD (SD 1877) **Scl**: Brentwood Hill, Brentwood TQ587936 bt. 1877. (Taken over by Hackney Union 1885. St Faith's Hospital *c.*1930–95. Dem.) LMA.

Central London SD (SD 1849) **Scl**: Church Road, Upper Norwood TQ335705 <1834. (Closed *c.*1857. Dem.) **Scl**: Cuckoo Lane, Hanwell TQ156815 1858 by Tress & Chambers. (Closed 1933. Hanwell Community Centre from 1945. Part dem.) LMA.

Forest Gate SD (SD 1868 diss.1897) **Scl**: Forest Lane, London E7 TQ399852 bt. 1869. (Closed 1897. Poplar workhouse 1908–11. Forest Gate Sick Home 1913–30; Forest Gate Hospital *c.*1929–73. NRU.) LMA.

Kensington & Chelsea SD (SD 1876) **CtH**: Firtree Road, Banstead, Surrey TQ240603 1880 by A&C Harston. (Rn. Beechholme 1951. Closed 1974. Dem.) **Scl**: Marlesford Lodge, 241/253 King Street, Hammersmith TQ224786 1883 by A&C Harston. (Now Palingswick House library/musem etc.) LMA.

North Surrey SD (SD 1849) **Scl**: Anerley Road, Upper Norwood TQ342699 1850 by C. Lee. (Closed 1937. Later Anerley House OPH then Orchard Lodge. Dem 1970s.) **CvH**: Marlborough House, Granville, Broadstairs TR395674 cnv. 1886. (Convalescent home 1886–91.) **CvH**: Wainwright Convalescent Home, Park Road, Broadstairs TR398688 1891. (Wanstead House & Wainwright School by 1950s. NRU.) LMA.

South Metropolitan SD (SD 1849) **Scl**: Brighton Road, Sutton TQ255626 1855 by E. Nash. (Bt. by MAB *c.*1904. Belmont workhouse from 1908. WW1 MH then Belmont Hospital. Dem.) **Scl**: Banstead Road, Sutton TQ259622 1883 by W. Wallen. (Bt. by MAB *c.*1902. Later Downs School/Hospital then Sutton Hospital. Part dem.) **San**: St George's Terrace, Herne Bay, Kent TR173681 bt. 1875. (Bt. by MAB 1897 rn. St Anne's Home. TB sanatorium from 1919. Dem.) **Scl**: Hatfield Road, Witham TL816140 bt. 1882 by G.G. Scott & W.B. Moffatt. (Bt by MAB 1901; later Bridge Home/Hospital. NRU.) LMA.

West London SD (SD 1868) **Scl**: District (now Woodthorpe) Road, Ashford, Surrey TQ058715 1872 by H.H. Collins. (Closed 1955 then used as remand centre. Dem.) LMA.

London Sick Asylum Districts

Central London SAD (SAD 1868; diss. 1913) **Ify**: Cleveland Street, London TQ293818 appr. 1873. (Closed *c.*1913. Now annexe to Middlesex Hospital.) **Ify**: Dartmouth Park Hill, Highgate TQ288869 appr. 1869 by J. Giles & Biven. (St Pancras Infirmary *c.*1913, later Highgate Hospital then Whittington Hospital Highgate Wing.) **Ify**: Colindale Avenue, Hendon TQ211900 1900 by Giles, Gough & Trollope. (Later Colindale Hospital. Mostly dem. 2009.) LMA.

Poplar & Stepney SAD (SAD 1868; diss. 1925) **Ify**: 73a Devons Rd, Bow TQ379824 1869 by A&C Harston. (St Andrew's Hospital from 1920. Dem. 2008.) LMA, RLH.

Middlesex

Brentford (PU 30/6/1836 10+24) **W1**: Twickenham Road, Isleworth TQ164764 1838 by L. Vulliamy. (Replaced by new union infirmary 1894–96.) **W2**: Warkworth House, Twickenham Road, Isleworth TQ165762 1902 by W.H. Ward. (PAI then part of W Middlesex Hospital from 1948. Mostly dem.) **Ify**: 30 Twickenham Road, Isleworth TQ164764 1896. (West Middlesex Hospital from 1920. Dem.) **Scl**: Percy House Schools, Twickenham Road, Isleworth TQ162762 1883 enl. 1901. (MH in WW1. Admin use until 1935. OPH c.1948–75. Dem.) **RH**: Dundee House, Twickenham Road, Isleworth TQ163761. (Dem.) **ScH**: 57 and 82-84 Oaklands Road, Hanwell; 1-4 Montague Avenue, Hanwell; 24-26 Greenford Avenue, Hanwell; 23 Sunnyside Road, Ealing; 40-42 Llammas Park Road, Ealing; 21-23 Campbell Road, Twickenham; 41-47 Beaconsfield Road, St Margarets. LMA.

Edmonton (PU 3/2/1837 7+38) **W**: 77 Bridport Road, Edmonton TQ335923 1839 by G.G. Scott & W.B. Moffatt. (Canadian MH in WW1. Edmonton House PAI. Later part of North Middlesex Hospital. Mostly dem.) **Scl1**: Chase Side, Enfield TQ326976 1827 enl. 1842. (Adult use from 1886. Enfield House PAI, later St Michael's Hospital. Dem.) **Scl2**: Chase Farm, Enfield TQ312980 1886 by T.E. Knightly. (Adult use from 1930s. Chase Farm Hospital from 1948.) **SmH**: 71-73 Downhills Park Road, South Tottenham. LMA.

Hendon (PU 1/5/1835 8+18) **W**: Edgware Road, Red Hill TQ200908 1838. (Redhill PAI. Redhill House OPH from 1948. Dem.) **Scl**: Edgware Road, Burnt Oak TQ197911 1859. (Men's Home from 1930, later Redhill Lodge. Dem.) **Ify**: Edgware Road, Burnt Oak TQ198912 1927 by Paine & Hobday. (Redhill Hospital from 1927. Edgware General from 1948. Dem.) LMA.

Staines (PU 28/6/1836 13+21) **W**: The Hall, London Road, Stanwell TQ062724 1841. (PAI. Staines County Hospital from 1941. Ashford Hospital from 1948. Dem.) **ScH**: Stanwell. LMA.

Uxbridge (PU 20/6/1836 10+20) **W**: Pield Heath Road, Hillingdon TQ069821 1747 enl. 1837 by W. Thorold (1837). (Hillingdon County Hospital 1931-48 then Hillingdon Hospital. Dem.) **SmH**: Wycombe House, Yiewsley. **SmH**: Tavistock Villa, Yiewsley. **SmH**: Bartram Lodge, Harlington Road, Hillingdon TQ075820 cnv. c.1927. (Dem.) LMA.

Willesden (SP 13/8/1896) **W**: Twyford Lodge, 494 Acton Lane, London NW10 TQ202828 1908 by A. Saxon Snell. (WW1 hostel for munitions workers. Park Royal Hospital c.1921–31, then Central Middlesex County Hospital.) **SmH**: 2 Hill Side, Stone Bridge, Willesden TQ207839. (Dem.) **ScH**: Sixteen in Cricklewood and Harlesden. LMA.

Norfolk

Aylsham (PU 9/4/1836 46+47) **W1**: Aylsham Road, Oulton TG156276 <1834. (Used for aged and infirm. Closed 1849. Now farm buildings.) **W2**: Coltishall Road, Buxton TG239214 <1800. (Closed 1849. Dem.) **W3**: Cawston Road, Aylsham TG184266 1849 by W.J. Donthorn. (PAI. St Michael's Hospital from c.1948.) NFK.

Blofield (PU 5/10/1835 32+41) **W**: Norwich Road, Lingwood TG361082 1837 by J. Brown. (Homelea PAI. Closed c.1948. Dem.) NFK.

Brinton GU (GU 1783; diss. 1869) **W**: Melton Road, Melton Constable TG038307 1783. (Closed 1869. NRU.) NFK.

Depwade (PU 14/4/1836 43+53) **W**: Norwich Road, Pulham Market TM186876 1836 by W. Thorold. (PAI. Hill House Hospital from 1948. Later Beadle Hotel. NRU.) **SmH**: Briardale, Long Stratton TM195919. (NRU) NFK.

Docking (PU 1/8/1835 36+53) **W**: The Red House, Heacham Road, Docking TF749370 1836 by J. Brown. (WW1 troop/POW barracks then became housing known as Burntstalk.) **SmH**: Lyde Cottage, Fakenham Road, Docking TF773366. (NRU.) NFK.

Downham (PU 23/8/1836 34+35) **W**: London Road, Downham Market TF614030 1836 by W.J. Donthorn. (PAI. Howdale Home from 1948. Dem. c.1968. Now OPH.) NFK.

Erpingham (PU 11/4/1836 49+53) **W1**: Gimingham 1805. (Closed 1851.) **W2**: Park Road,

Upper Sheringham TG143419 1805. (Closed 1851. Later used as a school. NRU.) **W3**: Mill Road, West Beckham TG147386 1851 by W.J. Donthorn. (Beckham House PAI aka Beckham Palace. Mostly dem. Derelict.) **SmH**: Old Rectory, Holt Road, Gresham TG160383. NFK.

Flegg, East & West (LI 1775) **W**: Court Road, Rollesby TG456151 1775 by C. Elder. (Closed *c.*1920? Later known as the Old Court House. NRU.) NFK.

Forehoe (LI 1775) **W**: Wymondham Road, Wicklewood TG079019 1776. (PAI. Hill House Hospital *c.*1947, then St George's School. NRU.) NFK.

Freebridge Lynn (PU 16/11/1836 32+36) **W**: 1 Old Swaffham Road, Gayton TF736210 1836 by W.J. Donthorn. (Eastgate House PAI. OPH 1948-63. NRU.) NFK.

Great Yarmouth (SP 29/3/1837 1+16; PU 15/4/1891) **W**: 150a Caister Road, Yarmouth TG526087 1838 by J. Brown. (PAI. Northgate Hospital from 1948. Part dem.) **SmH**: The Hollies, Burnt Lane and Clarence Road (now Addison Road), Gorleston TG524052 1902 by A.S. Hewitt. (Hostel for aged and infirm' from 1950s then social services use.) NFK.

Guiltcross (PU 6/11/1835 21+24; diss. 1902) **W**: Garboldisham Road, Kenninghall TM019846 1837 by W. Thorold. (Closed 1902. Housed 'inebriates' 1904–11, 'mental defectives' 1911–16, POWs 1917-18. Dem.) NFK.

Henstead (PU 19/12/1835 37+38) **W**: Church Road, Swainsthorpe TG212012 1836 by J. Brown. (PAI. Vale Hospital *c.*1948–84. NRU.) NFK.

King's Lynn (PU 30/9/1835 2+21) **W1**: London Road, King's Lynn TF621197 13C?. (Building collapsed 1854.) **W2**: 39 Extons Road, King's Lynn TF627196 1856 by J. Medland & A.W. Maberley. (PAI. St James' Hospital *c.*1948–85. Now offices. Part dem.) NFK.

Loddon & Clavering (PU 7/5/1836 42+44) **W**: Yarmouth Road, Hales, Heckingham TM386973 1764. (PAI. Hales Hospital *c.*1948–90. Disused.) NFK.

Mitford & Launditch (PU 14/5/1836 60+64) **W**: Beech Hill House, Litcham Road, Gressenhall TF974169 1775. (Beech House PAI. Elderly care until 1974. Now Greseenhall museum.) NFK.

Norwich (LI 1712; LP 1890) **W1**: Bridge Street (now St George's Street), Norwich TG231088 15C enl. 1802. (Closed 1860. Later Technical Institute and College of Art. Dem.) **Ify**: Magpie Road, Norwich TG228096 <1834. (Closed 1860.) **W2**: The Lodge, Bowthorpe Road, Norwich TG209090 1860 by J. Medland & A.W. Maberley. (Woodlands PAI. West Norwich Hospital *c.*1948–2003. Dem.) **RH**: 110-112 Turner Road, Norwich TG212094. (Dem.) **ScH**: (Boys) 18 St Faith's Lane 1853-1932; (Girls) 55 Botolph Street 1897-1922; 83-85 Pottergate Street 1904-24; (Nursery) 96 Aylsham Road 1918-41; 6-8 & 10-12 North Walsham Road (later Constitution Hill) 1905-41; (Girls) Llandaff House, 80 Grove Road 1922-41. NFK.

St Faith's (PU 11/1/1836 30+33) **W**: Manor Road, Horsham St Faith TG218161 1805. (Closed after fire in 1922. Dem.) NFK.

Swaffham (PU 1/8/1835 28+41) **W**: Watton Road, Swaffham TF826078 1836 by W.J. Donthorn. (WW1 POW/troop barracks then closed. Dem. 1926.) NFK.

Thetford (PU 23/12/1835 34+43) **W**: Bury Road, Thetford TL869822 1837 by W. Thorold. (PAI. St Barnabas Hospital *c.*1948–70. Dem.) **CtH**: 23 Old Market Street, Thetford TL873827. (NRU.) NFK.

Tunstead & Happing (Smallburgh) (LI 1785; PU 1869) **W**: Workhouse Road, Smallburgh TG325241 1785. (Closed *c.*1920. Mostly dem.) **SmH**: 60-62 Norwich Road, North Walsham TG278295. (NRU.) NFK.

Walsingham (PU 12/4/1836 50+53) **W**: Thursford Road, Great Snoring TF967352 1836 by W. Thorold. (PAI aka Thursford Castle. Smallpox hospital in 1950s. Mostly dem.) **CtH**: Red House, Holt Road, Little Snoring TF962322. (NRU.) NFK.

Wayland (PU 19/9/1835 25+30) **W**: The Street, Rockland All Saints TL993969 1837 by W. Thorold. (Closed *c.*1920? Mostly dem. NRU.) **Ify**: Ellingham Road, Cades Hill, Attleborough TM030961 1912 by H.J. Green. (MH in WW1. Attleborough Infirmary until 1948 then Wayland Hospital. Now St Luke's. Part dem.) **SmH**: New Buckenham. NFK.

Northamptonshire

Brackley (PU 8/6/1835 30+33) **W**: The Home, Banbury Road, Brackley SP580372 1837 by G.G. Scott. (PAI. Dem 1930s.) NTH.

Brixworth (PU 9/7/1835 30+35) **W**: Spratton Road, Brixworth SP746705 1836 by Milne. (PAI. Part dem. Now business use.) NTH.

Daventry (PU 29/10/1835 28+34) **W**: London Road, Daventry SP574610 1837 by J. Plowman. (PAI. Danetre Hospital from *c.*1948.) **CtH**: 34-36 High Street, Braunston SP541662 1901. (NRU.) NTH.

Hardingstone (PU 20/7/1835 20+22) **W**: Newport Pagnell Road, Hardingstone SP764572 1839 by Milne. (Closed *c.*1927. Later used as council deport. Part dem. NRU.) NTH.

Kettering (PU 23/9/1835 28+34) **W**: 77 London Road, Kettering SP870780 1838 by G.G. Scott. (PAI. St Mary's Hospital from *c.*1948.) **CtH**: 1-2 High Street, Burton Latimer SP901745 1897. (NRU.) NTH.

Northampton (PU 27/8/1835 17+33) **W**: 137a Wellingborough Road, Northampton SP764610 1837 by G.G. Scott. (PAI. St Edmund's Hospital from *c.*1930. Now business use.) **Scl**: Portland Street (now Place), Northampton SP869780. **RH**: 2 Watkin Terrace, Bailiff Street, Northampton SP758614. (NRU.) **ScH**: 21 Marriott Street, 43 Semilong Road, 1 Adelaide Terrace, Leicester Road, 15 Colwyn Road, 95 St Michael's Road. NTH.

Oundle (PU 1/12/1835 37+40) **W**: 1 Glapthorn Road, Oundle TL036887 1837 by G.G. Scott. (PAI. Later Glapthorne Road Hospital. Mostly dem. Now various uses.) NTH.

Peterborough (PU 3/12/1835 39+45) **W**: Thorpe Road House, Thorpe Road, Peterborough TL183987 1836 by B. Browning. (PAI. Peterborough District Hospital from *c.*1948. Dem.) **CtH**: Midland Road, Peterborough. **CtH**: Alderman's Drive, Peterborough. NTH.

Potterspury (PU 20/5/1835 11+13) **W**: The White House, Yardley Gobion SP766446 <1834. (Closed 1917. WW1 POW camp. NRU.) BKM, NTH.

Thrapston (PU 30/11/1835 26+30) **W**: Cedar House, Denford (now Midland) Road, Thrapston SP995782 1836 by W.J. Donthorn. (PAI. Now council offices.) **SmH**: The Delves, Marshall's Road, Raunds SP991728. (Dem.) NTH.

Towcester (PU 20/5/1835 23+31) **W**: Brackley Road, Towcester SP690486 1836 by G.G. Scott. (PAI. Later council depot. Part dem. NRU.) NTH.

Wellingborough (PU 28/7/1835 27+36) **W**: 3a Castle Street (now Irthlingborough Road), Wellingborough SP898675 1837 by J. Clephan. (PAI. Park Hospital from *c.*1938. Later Isebrook Hospital. NRU) **CtH**: Finedon. **CtH**: Rockleigh, Wellingborough Road, Irthlingborough SP939701. (NRU 'Rock Villa'.) NTH.

Northumberland

Alnwick (PU 15/11/1836 62+68) **W**: Wagonway Road, Alnwick NU190128 1840. (PAI. Later OPH, now offices.) **CtH**: Wagonway Road, Alnwick NU191125. (NRU.) NBL.

Belford (PU 19/11/1836 34+35) **W**: West Street, Belford NU106338 1839 by B. Green. (PAI. Later Bell View OPH then day centre. Dem. *c.*2003.) BWK.

Bellingham (PU 20/10/1836 37+37) **W**: High Street, Bellingham NY839835 1839. (Council offices. Now various uses.) NBL.

Berwick-upon-Tweed (PU 21/11/1836 17+30) **W**: Featherbed Lane (Now Brucegate), Berwick NT997534 <1834. (PAI. Later elderly care known as Greenhaven and Castlegate. Part dem. NRU.) BWK.

Castle Ward (PU 30/9/1836 77+79) **W**: North Road, Ponteland NZ165733 1848 by J. & B. Green. (PAI. Ponteland Hospital from *c.*1948. Dem.) **SmH**: Ponteland. NBL.

Glendale (PU 18/11/1836 45+51) **W**: High Street, Wooler NT998281 1839. (Council offices, later field study centre, now community use.) BWK.

Haltwhistle (PU 18/11/1836 17+18) **W**: Greenholme Road, Haltwhistle NY703642 1839. (Housed 'mental defectives' from *c.*1924. Dem. *c.*1950s.) NBL.

Hexham (PU 22/10/1836 69+80) **W**: Dean Street, Hexham NY941640 1839 rb. 1883 by J.H. Morton (1883). (PAI. Hexham General Hospital from *c.*1948.) NBL.

Morpeth (PU 27/9/1836 72+79) **W**: Newgate Street, Morpeth NZ196862 <1834 rb. 1867 by F.R. Wilson. (PAI. Offices during WW2. Dem. 1951.) **CtH**: Pottery Bank, Morpeth NZ193865. (Now a nursery.) NBL.

Newcastle-upon-Tyne (PU 26/9/1836 11+34; SP 1914) **W**: 416-8 Westgate Road, Newcastle-upon-Tyne NZ228645 1840. (Wingrove Hospital 1921-30; Newcastle General Hospital from 1930. Part dem.) **CtH**: North Road, Ponteland NZ154741 1903 by T. Oliver, R. Leeson, W. Wood. (Later a teacher training college, now Northumbria Police HQ.) **SmH**: Myrtle Cottage, Bentick Road NZ227639. (Later Cedar Lodge. Dem.) TAW.

Northern Counties JPLC Men: Moor Road, Prudhoe NZ106619 1914 by J.H. Morton & J.G. Burrell. (Prudhoe Hall Colony for 'mental defectives. Leter Prudoe Hospital.) TAW.

Rothbury (PU 8/10/1836 71+72) **W1**: Town Foot, Rothbury NU061018 <1834. (Closed 1904. NRU.) **W2**: Silverton Lane, Rothbury NU063012 1904 by J. Stevenson. (PAI. Later housed epileptics and 'mental defectives'. NRU.) NBL.

Tynemouth (PU 5/9/1836 24+47) **W**: 50 Preston Road, North Shields NZ354689 1838 rb. 1848. (PAI. Preston Hospital from *c.*1948. dem. 1990s.) **RH**: Military Road, North Shields. **ScH**: Earsdon; Monkseaton; Park Crescent and Queen Alexandria Road, North Shields. TAW.

Nottinghamshire

Basford (PU 2/5/1836 43+46) **W**: 121 Highbury Road, Bulwell, Nottingham SK544443 1815. (PAI. Highbury Hospital from *c.*1948. Mostly dem.) **CtH**: 107-119 Highbury Road, Bulwell, Nottingham SK544443 *c.*1910. (Later known as The Woodlands. Dem.) NTT, NTU.

Bingham (PU 27/5/1836 40+41) **W**: Nottingham Road, Bingham SK699396 1837 by H. Sudbury. (PAI then OPH. Dem. 1967.) **SmH**: Union Street, Bingham. **SmH**: Fairfield Street, Bingham. NTT.

East Retford (PU 1/7/1836 50+51) **W**: 1 Leverton Road, East Retford SK712825 1838 by H.J. Whiting. (PAI. Hillcrest Hospital from *c.*1948. Dem. 1970s.) NTT.

Mansfield (PU 29/6/1836 17+22) **W**: 105 Stockwell Gate, Mansfield SK533608 1838 by S. Kempthorne. (Victoria Hospital from 1948, now Mansfield Community Hospital. Mostly dem.) **ScH**: Brownlow Road; (Girls) West Lodge, Chesterfield Road; (Boys) Rock House, Ratcliffe Gate. NTT.

Newark (PU 24/3/1836 44+47) **W**: Claypole Bridge SK843490 *c.*1817. (Closed *c.*1912. Dem. 1978.) **Ify/V**: Bowbridge Lane, Newark SK801529 1878. (PAI. Hawtonville Hospital from *c.*1948, later Newark General Hospital. Part dem.) **CtH**: Balderton. NTT.

Nottingham (PU 6/7/1836 3+24; SP from 1899) **W1**: York Street, Nottingham SK573405 1841. (Dem. 1896) **W2**: Beech Avenue, Forest Fields SK561419. (Temporary workhouse *c.*1896–1903. Now factory premises.) **W3**: 700 Hucknall Road, Nottingham SK567440 1903 by Marshall & Turner. (Valebrook Lodge PAI then part of Nottingham City Hospital. Mostley dem.) **Scl**: Hartley Road, Nottingham SK556406 cnv. C1860. (Dem. 1961.) **RH**: Norton Street, Nottingham SK556405. (Dem. 1961.) **ScH**: 31 Addison Street; 4 Alberta Terrace; 59 Beech Avenue; 1 Ben Street; 317 Castle Boulevard; 9 Church Drive; 20 Gorsey Road; 82 Gregory Boulevard; 174 & 176 Radford Boulevard; 449 & 451 Mansfield Road; 102 Robin Hood's Chase; 5, 9 & 10 Victoria Villas, Sneinton. NTT.

Radford (PU 4/7/1836 4+19; diss. 1880) **W**: Hartley Road, Nottingham SK556406 1837. (Closed 1880. Later used as workhouse school. Dem. 1961.) NTT.

Southwell (PU 25/4/1836 60+62) **W**: Greet House, Upton Road, Southwell SK711542 1824 by J.T. Becher & W. Nicholson. (PAI. OPH until 1990s. Now workhouse museum.) NTT.

Worksop (PU 2/7/1836 26+29) **W**: East Gate, Worksop SK587795 1837. (PAI then OPH. Dem. 1965.) **W**: Kilton Hill, Worksop SK594803 1904 by H.C. Scaping. (Kilton Hill Infirmary, later Bassetlaw Hospital.) **SmH**: Abbeyhurst, 55 Cheapside, Worksop SK592788. (Now other use.) **SmH**: (Girls) 37 Potter Street, Worksop SK585787. (Now other use.) NTT.

Oxfordshire

Banbury (PU 3/4/1835 38+45) **W**: 192 Warwick Road, Banbury SP447411 1835 by S. Kempthorne. (WW1 POW camp. PAI. Neithrop Hospital from *c.*1948. Dem. 1980s.) **SmH**: Horley House, Horley SP416441 1914. (NRU.) OXF.

Bicester (PU 1/8/1835 38+40) **W**: Market End House, Bicester SP575233 1836 by J. Plowman. (PAI then boys' home. Residential use from *c.*1950. Dem. 1968.) OXF.

Chipping Norton (PU 18/9/1835 33+37) **W**: 26 London Road, Chipping Norton SP317275 1836 by G. Wilkinson. (PAI. Cotshill Hospital from *c.*1948. NRU.) OXF.

Headington (PU 15/9/1835 22+25) **W**: London Road, Headington SP522074 1838. (London Road Hospital from *c.*1930–48 then The Laurels OPH. Dem. 1968.) OXF.

Henley (PU 15/6/1835 21+27) **W**: 78 West Hill/Street, Henley-on-Thames SU756828 1790 by W. Bradshaw. (PAI. Townlands Hospital from *c.*1948.) **CtH**: Radnor House, 35 New Street, Henley SU762828. (Dem.) **CtH**: Belmont House, 23 New Street, Henley SU761828. (NRU.) OXF.

Oxford (LI 1771) **W1**: Rats and Mice Hill (now Wellington Square), Oxford SP510068 1775 by J. Gwynn. (Closed *c.*1865. Dem.) **W2**: Cowley Road, Oxford SP532058 1865 by W. Fisher. (MH in WW1. Cowley Road Hospital from *c.*1930. Dem. 1980s.) **Scl**: Cowley Fields, Oxford SP554041 1854 by E. Bruton. (Later known as The Poplars. Dem 1988.) OXF.

Thame (PU 16/9/1835 34+38) **W**: Oxford Road, Thame SP701064 1836 by G. Wilkinson. (PAI. Rycotewood College *c.*1938–2004. WW2 troop billets. NRU. Part dem.) OXF.

Witney (PU 25/3/1835 42+47) **W**: Razor Hill (now Tower Hill), Witney SP345099 1836 by G. Wilkinson. (WW1 POW camp. Factory use from 1940. NRU. Mostly dem.) OXF.

Woodstock (PU 13/7/1835 33+37) **W**: Hensington Road, Woodstock SP447168 1837 by G. Wilkinson. (Hensington House PAI then OPH. Dem. 1969.) OXF.

Rutland

Oakham (PU 29/4/1836 30+31) **W**: The Ashes, Ashwell Road, Oakham SK862093 1837 by W.J. Donthorn. (PAI. Catmose Vale Hospital from *c.*1948. Now part of Oakham School.) LEI.

Uppingham (PU 23/4/1836 35+36) **W**: The Larches, Leicester Road, Uppingham SP861998 1837 by W.J. Donthorn. (MH in WW1 then closed. Part of Uppingham School from 1930.) LEI.

Shropshire (Salop)

Atcham (& Shrewsbury from 1871) (PU 18/11/1836 45+46) **W**: Cross Houses, Berrington SJ539076 *c.*1817 by J.H. Haycock. (Berrington MH in WW1, then Cross Houses Hospital. NRU. Part dem.) **RH**: 143 Abbey Foregate, Shrewsbury SJ502123. (Now business use.) **ScH**: Besford House and Belle Vue House, Trinity Street; Pen-y-Bont, Betton Street; Grasmere, London Road; Holywell Street (all Shrewsbury). SAL.

Bridgnorth (PU 31/5/1836 29+35) **W1**: Bernard's Hill, Low Town, Bridgnorth SO722927 <1834. (Closed *c.*1848) **W2**: 1 Innage Lane, Bridgnorth SO714934 1848. (PAI then Innage House OPH. NRU. Part dem.) SAL.

Church Stretton (PU 20/7/1836 14+15) **W**: Shrewsbury Road, Church Stretton SO455944 1838 by T.D. Duppa. (PAI. Dem. *c.*1959.) SAL.

Cleobury Mortimer (PU 15/7/1836 17+20) **W**: Charlton House, Catherton Road, Cleobury Mortimer SO660763 <1834. (Youth hostel 1932–36; WW2 Refugee camp. Dem 1960s.) SAL.

Clun (PU 18/7/1836 19+21) **W**: 13 Union Street, Bishop's Castle SO322888 1844 by H.J. Whitling & J.H. Haycock. (PAI. Stone House Hospital from *c.*1948. Dem. 1960s.) SAL.

Drayton (PU 3/10/1836 12+18) **W1**: Shropshire Street, Market Drayton SJ672339 1772. (Closed *c.*1851.) **W2**: 4 Common Edge, Buntingsdale Road, Little Drayton SJ661334 1851 by T.D. Barry. (Quarry House PAI then OPH.) SAL.

Ellesmere (PU 14/11/1836 9+14) **W**: Swan Hill, Ellesmere SJ404355 1792. (Dem. 1930s.) SAL.

Ludlow (PU 15/7/1836 32+38) **W**: Gravel Hill, Ludlow SO514753 1836 by M. Stead. (PAI. East Hamlet Hospital from *c*.1948, now Ludlow Hospital. Mostly dem.) SAL.

Madeley (PU 6/6/1836 12+30) **W1**: 13 Belmont Road, Madeley SJ677035 1797. (Closed *c*.1875. NRU.) **W2**: Spout Lane, Benthall SJ668028 <1834. (NRU The Croft.) **Scl**: Harris's Green, Broseley SJ674039 *c*.1734. (Closed 1851.) **W3**: The Beeches, Beech Road, Ironbridge SJ674039 1875 by G.C. Haddon. (PAI then Beeches Hospital. Lincoln Grange OPH from 1991.) SAL.

Newport (PU 5/10/1836 16+22) **W1**: Newport <1834. (Closed *c*.1856.) **W2**: Gnosall <1834. (Closed *c*.1856.) **W3**: Audley Avenue, Newport SJ753188 1856 by J.H. Haycock. (PAI then Audley House OPH. NRU.) **SmH**: Doley, Gnosall. SAL.

Oswestry (LI 1791) **W**: Morda Bank, Morda SJ289279 1790. (Morda House PAI then OPH. Mostly dem. 1982. NRU.) SAL.

Shifnal (PU 2/6/1836 15+20) **W**: Park Street, Shifnal SJ748072 1817. (PAI. Park Street Hospital from *c*.1948, later Shifnal Hospital.) SAL.

Shrewsbury (LI 1784; m/w Atcham 1871) **W**: Canonbury, Shrewbury SJ486120 1765 by T.F. Pritchard. (Closed 1871. Shrewsbury School from 1882.) SAL.

South East Shropshire SD (SD 7/7/1849) **Scl**: Quatt SO756883 1690s. (Closed 1901. Residential use until 1982, now Dower House School.) SAL.

Wellington (PU 4/6/1836 11+19) **W1**: Walker Street, Wellington SJ649114 1797. (Closed *c*.1875 then used as brewery. Mostly dem.) **W2**: Waters Upton, Ercall Magna SJ629197 <1834. (Closed *c*.1875. Dem.) **W3**: 181-2 Holyhead Road (formerly Street Lane), Wellington SJ648109 1875 by Bidlake & Fleming. (PAI. Wrekin Hospital from *c*.1948. Now OPH.) **SmH**: Brooklyn House, 135 Watling Street, Wellington SJ659110 cnv. 1916. (Later council depot. Dem.) **SmH**: The Mount, Haygate Road, Wellington SJ648113 cnv. 1928. (Now day hospital.) SAL.

Wem (PU 16/11/1836 12+16) **W**: Love Lane, Wem SJ514304 1837 by Graham. (PAI. Various later uses, then residential care home.) SAL.

Whitchurch (LP 1792; PU 1853 25+37) **W**: Claypit Street, Whitchurch SJ545420 1794. (Deermoss Hospital from *c*.1948, later Whitchurch Hospital. Part dem.) SAL.

Somerset

Axbridge (PU 28/1/1836 38+49) **W**: Ilex Lodge, West Street, Axbridge ST428545 1837 by S.T. Welch. (PAI. St John's Hospital from *c*.1948. NRU and OPH.) **CtH**: Cliff View House, Tweentown, Cheddar ST457538 *c*.1916. (Now offices.) SOM.

Bath (PU 28/3/1836 24+41) **W**: Frome Road House, Odd Down, Bath ST741622 1838 by S. Kempthorne. (St Martin's Hospital from *c*.1930. NRU.) **RH**: Three Ways House, Frome Road, Odd Down, Bath ST743619. (Dem.) **ScH**: Five Way House, Batheaston; Avon House, Batheaston; 15 Lambridge Place, Bath; 1 Larkhall Place, Bath; 3-4 Butty Piece Cottages, Bath; 32 Thomas Street, Bath; 1-2 Bridge Road, Twerton. BTH.

Bedminster (ren. Long Ashton 1899) (PU 11/4/1836 23+34) **W**: Old Weston Road, Flax Bourton ST518696 1837 by G.G. Scott & W.B. Moffatt. (Cambridge House 'mental deficiency' colony 1929–56, then Farleigh Hospital. Now offices.) **CtH**: West Hill, Portishead. SOM.

Bridgwater (PU 11/5/1836 40+48) **W**: Northgate, Bridgwater ST297373 1836 by S. Kempthorne. (Northgate Lodge PAI. Northgate Hospital *c*.1948–1990s. Mostly dem.) **CtH**: Rodway, Cannington ST257396 by NRU. SOM.

Chard (PU 14/5/1836 34+43) **W**: Sunnylands, Crewkerne Road, Chard ST331087 1838 by G. Wilkinson. (PAI then OPH. Dem. 1974.) SOM.

Clutton (PU 2/2/1836 29+37) **W**: Cambrook House, Temple Cloud ST629577 1837 by J. Gane. (POWs resident 1918. PAI then OPH until 1967. NRU. Part dem.) SOM.

Dulverton (PU 11/5/1836 11+12) **W**: Bridge Street, Dulverton SS912279 1856 by E. Ashworth. (Later Exmoor House council offices. Now National Park offices.) SOM.

Frome (PU 26/3/1836 28+36) **W**: 29 Weymouth Road, Frome ST770475 1838 by S. Kempthorne. (Weymouth House PAI. Selwood Hospital c.1958–88. NRU. Part dem.) **SmH**: Whitewell Home, Whitewell Road, Frome ST770475 1913. (Dem.) SOM.

Keynsham (PU 29/3/1836 19+26) **W**: St. Clements Road, Keynsham ST656678 1838 by W. Armstrong. (Clements House PAI. Keynsham Hospital from c.1948. Dem. 2007.) SOM.

Langport (PU 10/5/1836 29+34) **W**: Picts Hill, Langport ST434275 1839. (PAI. American military prison 1942–45. Dem. c.2004.) SOM.

Shepton Mallet (PU 30/12/1835 25+31) **W**: West End House, West Shepton ST612434 1836 by J. Gane. (Colony for 'mental defectives' c.1930–58; Norah Fry Hospital c.1958-90. NRU.) SOM.

Taunton (PU 12/5/1836 38+51) **W**: Trinity Road, Taunton ST236244 1838 by S. Kempthorne. (Holmoor House PAI. Trinity Hospital from c.1948. Mostly dem.) **SmH**: Cheddon Road, Taunton c.1912. SOM.

Wellington (PU 17/5/1836 24+34) **W**: North Street, Wellington ST132209 1838 by R. Carver. (The Lodge PAI then OPH. Dem. 1970s.) **SmH**: 5 Mantle Street, Wellington ST136204. (NRU.) SOM.

Wells (PU 1/1/1836 18+27) **W**: Glastonbury Road, Wells ST540455 1837 by S.T. Welch. (Rowdens House PAI. Priory Hospital from 1948. Now health centre. Part dem.) **ScH**: Magdalene Street and 42 Northload Street, Glastonbury; 14 Lawson Terrace, Wilfrid Road, Street; Wraxhall Road, Street. SOM.

Williton (PU 19/5/1836 36+41) **W**: Long Street, Williton ST083415 1840 by G.G. Scott & W.B. Moffatt. (Townsend House PAI. Williton Hospital c.1948–1990s. NRU.) SOM.

Wincanton (PU 30/12/1835 39+43) **W**: Town View, Shadwell Lane, Wincanton ST707287 1838 by G. Wilkinson. (PAI then OPH until 1973. Dem.) **SmH**: Rock Hill House, 23 North Street, Wincanton ST711287 1914. (NRU.) **SmH**: (Girls) Linden Cottages, North Street, Wincanton ST710288. (NRU.) **SmH**: (Boys) Rodber House, Shadwell Lane, Wincanton ST709286. (NRU.) SOM.

Yeovil (PU 13/5/1836 35+47) **W**: Preston Road, Yeovil ST545165 1837 by S. Kempthorne. (Preston Close PAI. Summerlands Hospital from 1948. Mostly dem.) **CtH**: Rosebery Avenue, Yeovil c.1914. SOM.

Staffordshire

Alstonefield (GU 1817; diss. 1869) **W**: Alstonefield SK130555 c.1817. (Closed 1869. NRU.) STS.

Burton-upon-Trent (PU 30/3/1837 48+55) **W1**: Horninglow Street, Burton-upon-Trent SK248238 1838 by G.G. Scott & W.B. Moffatt. (Closed c.1884. Dem. 1890s.) **W2**: 145 Belvedere Road, Burton-on-Trent SK234244 1884 by J.H. Morton. (Belvedere House PAI. Burton District Hospital c.1948–96, now Queen's Hospital.) **CtH**: (Girls) The Ferns, Station Road, Barton-under-Needwood. LCH.

Cheadle (PU 31/5/1837 15+23) **W**: Bank Street, Cheadle SK007430 1775. (PAI. Cheadle Hospital c.1948–87. NRU.) **SmH**: The Birches, Cheadle SK007429. (Now The Newlands care home.) STS.

Leek (PU 2/12/1837 19+28) **W**: 251 Ashbourne Road, Leek SJ995562 1839 by J. Bateman & G. Drury. (PAI. Moorlands Hospital from c.1948.) STS.

Lichfield (PU 21/12/1836 29+40) **W**: Burton Road (now Trent Valley Road), Lichfield SK126098 1840 by G.G. Scott & W.B. Moffatt. (PAI. St Michael's Hospital from 1948.) **SmH**: Wissage Lane (now Scotch Orchard), Lichfield SK129101. (Later The Poplars. Now children's care home.) LCH.

Newcastle-under-Lyme (PU 3/4/1838 9+18) **W**: Keele Road, Newcastle-under-Lyme SJ838457 1838 by G.G. Scott & W.B. Moffatt. (PAI. Dem. c.1938.) STS.

Penkridge (ren. Cannock 1877) (PU 29/9/1836 21+30) **W1**: Bargate Street, Brewood SJ881089 *c.*1800 enl. 1838. (Closed *c.*1872. Convent from 1920.) **W2**: 202 Wolverhampton Road, Cannock SJ975096 1872. (PAI then Ivy House OPH. Mostly dem. Now offices.) **CtH**: New Penkridge Road, Cannock SJ975104. (Later a remand home then Lynwood children's hime. NRU.) STS.

Seisdon (PU 17/10/1836 12+19) **W1**: Upper Green, Tettenhall SJ886001 <1834. (Closed *c.*1860. Dem.) **W2**: Union Lane, Trysull SO856947 1860 by G. Bidlake & Lovatt. (Closed *c.*1930. Later used as warehouse etc. Derelict.) STS.

Stafford (PU 28/9/1836 19+27) **W**: 52 Marston Road, Stafford SJ920244 1838 by T. Trubshaw. (PAI then Fernleigh OPH. Dem. *c.*1973.) STS.

Stoke-upon-Trent (SP 30/5/1836 1+24; PU 1894) **W**: 578 Newcastle Road (formerly London Road), Stoke-on-Trent SJ858452 1833 enl. 1845 by H. Ward (1845). (PAI and London Road Hospital from *c.*1930 then City General. Part dem.) **CtH**: Newcastle Lane, Penkhull SJ866449 1900. (Closed *c.*1980s. NRU.) STK.

Stone (PU 3/2/1838 10+20) **W**: Stafford Road, Stone SJ899338 1793 by W. Leigh. (PAI. Trent Hospital 1948–1990s. NRU.) STS.

Tamworth (PU 25/3/1836 22+27) **W1**: Lady Bank, Tamworth SK205039 1750. (Closed 1859. Later known as Brewery House. Now hotel annexe.) **W2**: Wigginton Road, Tamworth SK208058 1859 by G.B. Nicholls. (PAI. St Editha's Hospital *c.*1948–98. Mostly dem. NRU.) LCH.

Uttoxeter (PU 29/5/1837 16+22) **W**: Holly Road, Uttoxeter SK084340 1840 by G.G. Scott & W.B. Moffatt. (PAI. Dem. *c.*1950.) STS.

Walsall (PU 10/12/1836 8+19) **W**: 100 Pleck Road, Walsall SP003984 1838 by W. Watson. (Beacon Lodge PAI and Manor Hospital from *c.*1930. Part dem.) WAL.

Walsall & West Bromwich JPLC (1912) **Men**: Great Barr Park, Great Barr SP54953 cnv. 1912 enl. *c.*1918–30 by G. McMichael. (Mental defectives' colony from 1918; St Margaret's Hospital 1948–1990s. Dem.) WAL.

Walsall & West Bromwich SD (SD 1869) **Scl**: Pennyhill Lane, Wigmore SP017934 1870 by S.E. Bindley. (Borstal *c.*1935–1950s then offices. Mostly dem. 2002.) WAL.

West Bromwich (PU 5/11/1836 6+26) **W1**: Workhouse Lane (St Clement's Lane), West Bromwich SP008917 1735. (Closed *c.*1858.) **W2**: Meeting Street, Wednesbury SO984951 1766. (Closed *c.*1858. Dem. 1920.) **W3**: 88 Hallam Street, West Bromwich SP009921 1858 by Briggs & Everall. (Hallam Hospital from *c.*1930, later Sandwell General. Mostly dem.) SAN.

Wolstanton & Burslem (PU 2/4/1838 2+16; m/w Stoke 1922) **W**: Turnhurst Road, Chell SJ867531 1840 by Boulton & Palmer. (Westcliffe PAI then Westcliffe Hospital. Mostly dem.) **ScH**: (Boys) 55 Macclesfield Street, Burslem; (Girls) 152 High Lane, Burslem; (Girls) Victoria Road, Tunstall; 2 Stanley Street, Tunstall. STK.

Wolverhampton (PU 11/10/1836 4+25) **W1**: Bilston Road, Wolverhampton SO925980 1838 by G. Wilkinson. (Closed 1903. Dem.) **W2**: 376 Wolverhampton Road, Heath Town, Wolverhampton SJ935004 1903 by A. Marshall. (New Cross PAI and Hospital from *c.*1930. Mostly dem.) **CtH**: Amos Lane, Wednesfield SJ942009 1888 by G.H. Stanger. (Dem. 1980s.) WOL.

Suffolk

Blything (PU 25/6/1835 49+60) **W**: Red House, Bulcamp, Blythburgh TM440762 1766 by T. Fulcher. (PAI. Blythburgh & District Hospital from *c.*1948. NRU.) **CtH**: Hope House, High Street, Yoxford TM392692 cnv. *c.*1912. (NRU.) **CtH**: Halesworth from *c.*1926. SFI.

Bosmere & Claydon (PU 8/9/1835 38+40) **W**: Workhouse Lane, Barham TM122512 1766. (Closed 1920. Housed Troops/POWs in WW1 then used as training/work camp. Italian POWs in WW2. Dem. 1963.) **SmH**: Hurstlea, 131 High Street, Needham Market TM086552. (Now offices.) SFI.

Bury St Edmunds (LI 1747; PU 1907) **W**: College Street, Bury St Edmunds TL854640 cnv. 1748 ad. 1841 by W. Mason (1841). (Closed *c.*1880. Mostly dem. NRU.) **SmH**: Alexandra

Home, Hospital Road, Bury St Edmunds TL844636 c.1925. (NRU.) SFB.

Cosford (PU 1/8/1835 28+36) **W**: Semer TM008452 1780. (Closed 1923. Mostly dem. NRU.) SFB.

Hartismere (& Hoxne, from 1907) (PU 1/9/1836 32+37; m/w Hoxne 1907) **W**: Castle Hill, Eye TM147737 18C enl. 1854. (Dem 1970s.) **Scl**: Union Lane, Wortham TM093788 18C. (Closed c.1898. NRU.) **Ify**: Castleton's Way, Eye TM143739 1916 by H.J. Green. (PAI then Hartismere House Hospital, later Hartismere Hospital.) **SmH**: Wilton House (later Willow House), 50 Castle Street, Eye TM147736. (NRU.) SFI.

Hoxne (PU 24/6/1835 24+36; m/w Hartismere 1907) **W**: Barley Green, Stradbroke TM250732 1835. (Closed 1871. POW camp in WWI. Mostly dem. NRU.) SFI.

Ipswich (PU 9/9/1835 14+20) **W1**: Great Whip Street, Ipswich TM165437 1837 by W. Mason. (Closed c.1899. Dem.) **W2**: Woodbridge Road, Ipswich TM192450 1899 by S. Salter, W.L. Newcombe & H.P. Adams. (Heathfields PAI. Ipswich Hospital (Heath Road Wing) from 1948. Mostly dem.) **Scl**: St John's Children's Home, Bloomfield Street, Ipswich TM187446 1878. (Later known as Freelands. Dem c.1970s.) SFI.

Mildenhall (PU 12/11/1835 13+15) **W1**: The Churchyard, Mildenhall TL708746 1720s enl. 1836. (Closed c.1896. Part dem. NRU.) **W2**: King's Way, Mildenhall TL717749 1896 by F. Whitmore. (WWI troop/POW barracks then closed. Dem.) SFB.

Mutford & Lothingland (LI 1763; PU 1893) **W**: Lothingland House, Union Lane, Oulton TM523953 1765 enl. 1836 by J. Brown (1836). (PAI. Lothingland 'mental deficiency' Hospital from c.1948. Dem.) **SmH**: 52 Acton Road, Kirkley TM535908. (NRU.) **SmH**: Bridge Road, West Lowestoft. SFL.

Plomesgate (PU 30/12/1835 40+41) **W**: Plomesgate House, Chapel Lane, Wickham Market TM304556 1837 by J. Brown. (PAI. Converted to housing c.1948.) SFI.

Risbridge (PU 3/11/1835 26+28) **W**: Union Square, Queen Street, Haverhill TL671456 <1834. (Closed c.1856. Dem.) **W**: Hill Lane, Kedington TL702470 1856 by J.F. Clark. (Mental defectives' home c.1934. Risbridge Home c.1948 then Hospital. Dem. 1990s.) SFB.

Samford (LI 1764; PU from 1849 28+35) **W**: Tattingstone House, Tattingstone TM135373 1766. (PAI then St Mary's Hospital. Closed 1991. NRU.) SFI.

Stow (PU 24/10/1835 31+32) **W**: Onehouse Road, Stowmarket TM034591 1781 by T. Fulcher. (Stow Lodge PAI. Stow Lodge Hospital c.1948–91. NRU.) **SmH**: 18 Bury Street, Stowmarket TM048587. **SmH**: Hill House, Violet Hill Road, Stowmarket TM044591 c.1925. (Later Eastward Ho then Evelyn Fison House. Now empty.) SFI.

Sudbury (PU 24/9/1835 42+46) **W**: Walnut Tree House, Walnut Tree Lane, Sudbury TL870414 1837 by J. Brown. (PAI then Walnut Tree Hospital.) **CtH**: Crofton House, Croft Road, Sudbury TL870415. (Now hostel use.) SFB.

Thingoe (PU 21/1/1836 45+45; m/w Bury St Edmunds 1907) **W**: 36 Mill Lane (now Road), Bury St Edmunds TL847638 1836. (St Mary's Hospital PAI c.1930–77. Dem. c.1990.) SFB.

Wangford (PU 25/6/1835 28+47) **W**: Shipmeadow TM378898 1767 by M. Barn. (PAI then. Later poultry farm. NRU.) **SmH**: Uppoer Olland Street, Bungay. **SmH**: Ravensmere Road, Beccles. SFL.

Woodbridge (PU 3/10/1835 46+49) **W**: Nacton TM223406 1758. (Closed c.1898. Later Nacton House. Amberfield School from 1952.) **SmH**: Grundisburgh. SFI.

Surrey

Ash GU (GU 1806; diss. 1846) **W**: Foxhills Lane, Ash SU902512 c.1790. (Closed 1846. Dem.) SRY.

Chertsey (PU 6/11/1835 9+15) **W**: Murray Road, Ottershaw TQ026639 1836 by S. Kempthorne. (Murray House 'mental defectives' home c.1930. Later Ottershaw Hospital. Part dem. NRU.) **CtH**: Ottershaw. SRY.

Croydon (PU 21/5/1836 10+20) **W**: 66a Queens Road, Croydon TQ320673 1865 by J. Berney. (Queen's Road Homes PAI. Queen's Hospital c.1948–87. Mostly dem.) **Ify**: 76 Eridge Road, (39 Woodcroft Road from 1939), Croydon TQ316674 1882 by Berney & Monday. (Mayday Hospital from c.1932.) **CtH**: Norrington Hall, Bingham Road, Croydon Road, Croydon. **CtH**: (Girls) 218-220 London Road, Croydon TQ318665. **CtH**: (Boys) Pawson's Road, Croydon TQ321674 1905. (Dem. c.2006.) **CtH**: Mayday Road, Croydon TQ317671 1897. (Dem.) CRO.

Dorking (PU 10/6/1836 8+14) **W**: 2 Horsham Rd, Dorking TQ165487 1841 by W. Shearburn. (PAI. Dorking General Hospital c.1948. Mostly dem.) SRY.

Epsom (PU 31/5/1836 15+22) **W**: Middle House, 49 Dorking Rd, Epsom TQ204598 1836 by W. Mason. (PAI. The Oaks OPH c.1952–63. Now Epsom General Hospital. Dem.) **SmH**: 38 Wilmerhatch Lane (now Woodcote Green Road), Epsom TQ204597. (Dem.) SRY.

Farnham (PU 27/2/1846 6+19) **W**: 44 Hale Road, Farnham SU850475 1770. (PAI. St Andrew's Home OPH then Farnham Hospital. Dem.) SRY.

Godstone (PU 31/10/1835 14+18) **W**: Church Lane, Bletchingley TQ328509 enl. 1839 by J. Whichcord. (Clerk's Croft Mental Deficiency Institution (later Hospital) c.1930–80. Dem.) SRY.

Guildford (PU 11/4/1836 21+26) **W**: Guildford House, 10 Warren Road, Guildford TQ008495 1836 by G.G. Scott & W.B. Moffatt. (WW1 MH. St Luke's Home PAI. St Luke's Hospital from 1948. Dem. except casual ward, now museum.) **ScH**: Elsinore, Springfield Road; Providence, Artillery Road; 36 & 37 Recreation Road; 14 Springfield Road; 48 and 68a Woodbridge Road; 1 Cooper Road, Guildford. SRY.

Hambledon (PU 25/3/1836 16+18) **W**: Wormley Lane, Hambledon SU957381 1786. (Hambeldon Hospital c.1930–40; OPH 1950s–70s. NRU. Part dem.) SRY.

Kingston-upon-Thames (PU 4/6/1836 13+23) **W**: 50 Kingston Hill, Kingston TQ195697 1839 by W. Mason. (Central Relief Institution c.1930–48 then Kingston Hospital. Mostly dem.) **RH**: Moira House, 13 Old Bridge Street, Hampton Wick TQ176674. (Dem.) **RH**: 163 Kingston Road, New Malden TQ205684. (Now offices.) **ScH**: 174 Merton Road, Kingston; 3 Gap Road and 36 & 65 Griffiths Road, Wimbledon; 4 Adelaide Road, 94 Church Road, 81 Coburg (now Connaught) Road, 6 Hampton Road and 7 Stanley Road, and Connaught Villa, Connaught Road, Teddington; Beech Holme, Wellington Road and Fairlight, Uxbridge Road, Hampton Hill; Tudor Lodge, Vicarage Road, Hampton Wick; Franklyns, Cedars Road, Hampton Wick. SRY.

Reigate (PU 25/3/1836 16+23) **W**: Earlswood Common, Redhill TQ272491 c.1795. (PAI. Redhill County (later General) Hospital from c.1936. NRU. Mostly dem.) **CtH**: 25-27 Hardwick Road, Meadvale, Redhill TQ265491. (Dem.) SRY.

Richmond (PU 6/6/1836 5+13) **W**: Grove Road, Richmond TQ188742 1787. (PAI. Kingsmead and Grove Road Hospital c.1948–74. NRU.) **RH**: Parkshot, Richmond. **RH**: 17-19 Peldon Avenue, Richmond. (Dem.) **ScH**: 1 and 16-18 St Leonard's Road, Mortlake. **CtH**: 11-13 Cleveland Road, Barnes c.1895-1901. RIC.

Surrey JPLC (1914) **Men**: The Oaks, Croydon Lane, Woodmansterne TQ275612 cnv. 1919. (Home for female epileptics until c.1933. Part dem.) SRY.

Sussex

Arundel (GP 1780s; diss. 1869) **W**: Poorhouse Hill (now Mount Pleasant), Arundel TQ013071 1831. (Closed 1869. NRU.) SXW.

Battle (PU 10/6/1835 14+18) **W**: North Trade Road, Battle TQ732159 1840 by F. Thatcher. (PAI. Battle Hospital c.1948–1990s. NRU.) SXE.

Brighton (LP 1810) **W1**: Church Hill, Brighton TQ306046 1821 by W Mackie. (Closed 1867. Dem. 1867.) **W2**: 250 Elm Grove, Brighton TQ328052 1867 by J. & G. Lansdown & G Maynard. (Kitchener Indian Hospital 1915-20; Brighton Municpal Hospital 1930–48, then Brighton General.) **Scl**: Warren Farm, Woodingdean TQ354957 1862. (Closed 1930. St John the Baptist (later Fitzherbert) School 1955-87. Dem. 1990s.) SXE.

Chailey (PU 26/3/1835 11+13; m/w Lewes 1898) **W1**: North Common, Chailey TQ383210 <1834. (Closed 1873. Industrial School 1875–1903; Heritage Craft Schools 1903-48 then Chailey Heritage School and Hospital.) **W2**: Corner Green, Ringmer TQ445124 <1834. (Closed 1873. Dem.) **W3**: South Street, Ditchling TQ326151 <1834. (Closed 1873. Dem.) **W4**: Pouchlands House, Honeypot Lane, East Chiltington TQ383173 1873 by H. Card. (PAI. Pouchlands Hospital c.1948–90. NRU.) SXE.

Chichester (LI 1753; SP 1896) **W**: New Broyle Road, Chichester SU861056 1625. (PAI. Partly dem. NRU.) **CtH**: Lavant House, Lavant SU850083 cnv. 1913. (Closed 1929. Now a school.) SXW.

Cuckfield (PU 26/3/1835 15+18) **W**: West Hylands, Ardingley Road, Cuckfield TQ308257 1843 by S.O. Foden & H.W. Parker. (PAI. Canadian MH in WW2. Cuckfield Hospital c.1948–91. NRU.) SXW.

East Grinstead (PU 23/9/1835 7+14) **W1**: London Road, East Grinstead 1747. (Closed 1859.) **W2**: Church Street, Hartfield TQ478357 <1834. (Closed 1859. Pub from 1861, now the Anchor Inn.) **W3**: Newchapel Road, Lingfield TQ380436 <1834. (Closed 1859. NRU.) **W4**: London Road, Worth, Crawley TQ269376 1729. (Closed 1859. NRU.) **W5**: 98 Railway Approach (formerly Glen Vue Road), East Grinstead TQ390382 1859 by F. Peck. (PAI then St Leonard's House OPH. Dem. c.1980.) SXW.

East Preston (GU 1791; PU 1869 23+27) **W**: North View, The Street, East Preston TQ070023 1792 rb. 1873 by G.B. Nicholls. (PAI then OPH. Dem. 1969.) SXW.

Eastbourne (PU 25/3/1835 14+17) **W**: 123 Church Street, Eastbourne TV596994 1794. (PAI. St Mary's Hospital from c.1948. Dem. 1990.) **RH**: 2-4 Birling Street, Eastbourne TV592997. (NRU.) SXE.

Hailsham (PU 10/4/1835 11+16) **W**: Union Road (now Hawks Road), Hailsham TQ588112 1835. (PAI. Dem. c.1932.) SXE.

Hastings (PU 20/7/1835 13+18) **W1**: Frederick Road, Hastings TQ832113 1836 by S. Kempthorne & A. Voysey. (PAI. St Helen's Hospital 1948–94. Part dem. NRU.) **W2**: 40 Frederick Road, Hastings TQ831114 1903 by A. Jeffrey & W. Skiller. (Hastings Municipal Hospital from 1930. St Helen's Hospital 1948–94. Dem.) **ScH**: 100 Ashburnham Road, 59 Vicarage Road, 65 & 121 Mount Pleasant Road, 14 Edmund Road and 11 Wellington Square, Hastings. SXE.

Horsham (PU 14/9/1835 10+19) **W**: 78 Crawley Road, Horsham TQ189317 1839 by Hallett & Newman. (PAI. The Forest Hospital c.1948–90. NRU.) **SmH**: 5–7 Bedford Road, Horsham. SXW.

Lewes (PU 10/8/1835) **W1**: St Nicholas Lane, Lewes TQ416100 <1834. (Closed c.1868.) **W2**: South Street, Lewes TQ422101 <1834. (Closed c.1868.) **W3**: De Montfort Road, Lewes TQ407103 1868 by H. Currey. (Closed 1898. Inebriate reformatory 1902–10. Dem. 1960.) **ScI**: 31 High Street, Lewes TQ416101 1730. (Closed c.1868. Now office/residential use.) **CtH**: St Anne's, Lewes. SXE.

Midhurst (PU 12/5/1835 26+28) **W**: Budgenor Lodge, Dodsley Lane, Easebourne SU890232 1794. (PAI. NRU.) SXW.

Newhaven (PU 2/2/1835 16+18) **W**: Church Hill, Newhaven TQ440011 1836 by S. Kempthorne. (PAI. Later Newhaven Downs Hospital. Pert dem.) SXE.

Petworth (PU 14/9/1835 5+16) **W1**: North Street, Hampers Green, Petworth SU976226 1820. (Dem.) **W2**: School Road, Wisborough Green TQ052258 1815. (Now community/residential use.) **W3**: Kirdford TQ17265 17C. (NRU.) SXW.

Rye (PU 27/7/1835 11+18) **W1**: Station Road, Northiam TQ827254 <1834. (Closed 1845.) **W2**: Cackle Street, Brede TQ822186 <1764. (Closed 1845. Later 'Alpha Place' shop and housing. Dem. 1939.) **W3**: Watchbell Street (now Church Square), Rye TQ921202 <1834. (Closed 1845.) **W**: Rye Hill TQ919214 1845 by S.O. Foden & H.W. Parker. (The Retreat PAI. Military use in WW2. Hill House Hospital c.1948–80. Part dem. NRU.) SXE.

Steyning (PU 25/7/1835 23+31) **W1/CtH**: Ham Road, Shoreham-by-Sea TQ218052 1836 by Mr Elliott. (St Wilfrid's children's home from 1901. Dem.) **W2**: 2 Upper Shoreham Road,

Kingston-by-Sea TQ227060 1901 by Clayton & Black. (PAI. Southlands Hospital from 1948. Mostly dem.) SXE, SXW.

Sutton GU (GU 1791; diss. 1869) **W**: Sutton End SU983165 1791. (Closed 1869. NRU.) SXW.

Thakeham (PU 14/5/1835 14+16) **W**: Rock Road, Heath Common TQ101149 1791 by S. Rowland. (PAI. Dem. *c.*1936.) SXE, SXW.

Ticehurst (PU 11/9/1835 8+18) **W**: Union Street, Flimwell TQ705313 1836 by S. Kempthorne. (PAI. Furze House OPH. Dem *c.*1980.) SXE.

Uckfield (PU 25/3/1835 11+18) **W**: High View House, Ridgewood, Uckfield TQ478198 1839 by H. Kendall. (PAI. High View House OPH. Dem. 1980s.) SXE.

Westbourne (PU 25/3/1835 12+16) **W**: Commonside, Westbourne SU759083 <1834. (Children's home *c.*1925–33. Dem 1950s.) **CtH**: Stein Road, Southbourne. SXW.

West Firle (PU 25/3/1835 8+9; m/w Lewes 1898) **W**: Burgh Lane, West Firle TQ484081 1836. (Closed 1898. Ren. Stamford Buildings. Part dem. NRU.) SXE.

Westhampnett (PU 25/3/1835 37+45) **W**: St Anne Street, Westhampnett SU879059 16C. (Closed after by fire in 1899. Site later isolation hospital then council depot. Dem.) SXW.

Warwickshire

Alcester (PU 31/5/1836 22+29) **W**: Kinwarton Road, Alcester SP094577 1837. (PAI. Alcester Hospital from *c.*1948. NRU.) WAR.

Aston (PU 7/11/1836 5+25; m/w Birmingham 1912) **W**: 1 Union Road, Erdington (infirmary at 18 Union Road) SP108912 1869 by Thomason. (Erdington House PAI. Highcroft Hospital *c.*1942–96. NRU. Part dem.) **CtH**: Fentham Road, Erdington SP108913 1901 by Cross & Nicholls. (Erdington Cottage Homes until 1980s. Now offices.) BHM.

Atherstone (PU 31/3/1836 14+18) **W**: Long Street, Atherstone SP310976 1836. (PAI. Dem. by 1937.) WAR.

Bedworth GU (GU 5/12/1816; diss. 1851) **W**: Industry Yard (now George Street), Bedworth SP356871 *c.*1817. (Closed 1851. Dem.) WAR.

Birmingham (LP 1783; PU 1912) **W1**: Lichfield Street, Birmingham SP073873 1733. (Closed 1852. Dem.) **W2**: 1 Western Road (workhouse); 77-99 Dudley Road (infirmary), Birmingham SP047878 1852 by J. Bateman & G. Drury. (Western House PAI. Summerfield Hospital 1948-74 then Dudley Road Hospital later City Hospital. Mostly dem.) **Scl**: Asylum Road, Summer Lane SP071888 1797. (Closed *c.*1852. Dem.) **CtH**: Coleshill Road, Marston Green SP179858 1879. (Coleshill Mental Hospital from 1930, then Chelmsley Hospital. Most dem. NRU.) **RH**: Summer Hill, 19 Summer Hill Terrace, Ladywood SP058872 cnv. 1905. (Closed 1939. NRU.) **Hostel**: Working Boys Home, 205 Vauxhall Road, Aston SP086877 cnv. 1913. (Closed 1952. Dem.) **Hostel**: Working Girls Home, Riversdale, 258 Bristol Road, Edgbaston SP059837 cnv. 1921. (Pebble Nill House children's home from 1952. NRU.) **CvH**: Oaklands, Worcester Road, Droitwich SO894620 cnv. 1924. (Later children's nursery. Dem.) **CvH**: Wassell Grove, Hagley SO933825 cnv. 1917. (Residential nursery 1940-55.) BHM.

Birmingham, Aston & King's Norton JPLC (*c.*1905) **Men**: Monyhull Hall Road, King's Norton SP067791 1908. (Colony for 'feeble-minded'. Later Monyhull Hall Hospital. Part dem. Now school.) BHM.

Coventry (LI 1801; PU 1874) **W**: 6/11 London Road, Coventry SP340787 cnv. 1804. (Gulson Road Hospital and Salvation Army hostel from 1930. Mostly dem.) **SmH**: 1a Argyll Street; 699 Foleshill Road; 66–68 Hill Street; Abbot's Lane; Whitley. COV.

Foleshill (PU 23/7/1836 11+18) **W1**: Brick Kiln Lane (now Broad Street), Foleshill SP343810 1797. (Closed *c.*1859. Dem.) **W2**: Vicarage Lane, Exhall SP338851 <1834. (Closed *c.*1859.) **W3**: Little Heath Road (now Foleshill Road), Foleshill SP344823 1859 by E. Holmes. (Closed during WW1. Later used as housing then council depot. Dem 1960s.) **RH**: Bedlam Lane, Foleshill. COV.

Meriden (PU 29/3/1836 18+24) **W**: 1 Maxstoke Lane, Meriden SP237825 1793. (PAI. The Firs OPH and Hospital. Dem.) **ScH**: Leys Lane, Meriden. WAR.

Nuneaton (PU 6/4/1836 7+19) **W**: 52 College Street, Chilvers Coton SP358906 1800.

(PAI. George Eliot Hospital from *c*.1948. Mostly dem.) **SmH**: 23 Henry Street, Nuneaton SP360910. (Dem.) WAR.

Rugby (PU 29/3/1836 38+43) **W**: Lower Hillmorton Road, Rugby SP510749 1818 by T. Harrall & R. Over. (St Luke's Hospital *c*.1949–93. Mostly dem.) **ScH**: Mitchison Home, Cromwell Road; McClure Home and Townsend Home, Charles Street. WAR.

Solihull (PU 3/6/1835 11+20) **W**: 1 Lode Lane, Solihull SP154798 1838. (PAI. Solihull Hospital from 1948. Dem.) **SmH**: The Woodland, Friday Lane, Hampton-in-Arden SP185798. (NRU) WAR.

Southam (PU 30/4/1836 19+26) **W**: Welsh Road, Southam SP416621 1836 by J. Plowman. (Closed during WW1. Converted to housing 1923. Dem 1960s.) WAR.

Stratford-on-Avon (PU 30/5/1836 36+44) **W**: 50 Arden Street, Stratford-on-Avon SP196553 1837 by J. Bateman & G. Drury. (PAI. Stratford-on-Avon Hospital from *c*.1948. Dem.) SHA. WAR.

Warwick (PU 29/6/1836 34+45) **W**: Infirmary at 91 Union Road (now Lakin Road), Warwick SP285659 1838 by W. Watson. (PAI. Warwick Hospital from *c*.1934. Dem.) **RH**: 1–3 Wharf Street, Warwick SP290653. (Now Mencap offices.) **ScH**: 40 Grove Street, 9–13 Charlotte Street, and 16 Willes Road Leamington; Lammas, Linen Street, Warwick; Pinley House, Rowington. WAR.

Westmorland

East Ward (PU 31/10/1836 30+38) **W**: Church View, Kirkby Stephen NY776089 cnv. 1810. (Eden House PAI. Dem. 1960s.) CUK.

Kendal (PU 15/7/1836 57+67) **W1**: 1a Windemere Road, Kendal SD512932 1789. (PAI. Kendal Green Hospital *c*.1948–70. NRU. Part dem.) **W2**: Main Street, Milnthorpe SD505818 1813 by F. Webster. (Milnthorpe Mental Home *c*.1918–48 then Milnthorpe Hospital. NRU.) **V**: Mill Brow, Kirkby Lonsdale SD613788 1811. (Former GU workhouse used as casual ward from *c*.1895. NRU.) **SmH**: The Abbey Home, Main Street, Staveley SD470983 cnv. 1899. (Now care home.) CUK.

West Ward (PU 6/9/1836 22+24) **W1**: Kemplay Bank, Eamont Bridge NY523286 cnv. 1832. (Closed 1877. PartDem. Now 'The Mansion House' offices.) **W2**: Home Lane, Shap NY564142 1877. (Closed *c*.1924 then used as Carlisle Union children's home. NRU.) CUK.

Wiltshire

Alderbury (ren. Salisbury 1895) (PU 12/10/1835 22+27) **W**: Tower House, Coombe Road, East Harnham SU143283 1837 rb. 1879 by E. Hunt (1837); GB Nicholls (1879). (PAI. Later Meyrick Close County Welfare Home. Dem 1970s.) WIL.

Amesbury (PU 9/10/1835 23+24) **W**: South Hill, Amesbury SU158409 1837 by W.B. Moffatt. (PAI. Dem. 1960s.) WIL.

Bradford-on-Avon (PU 25/3/1835 15+25) **W**: The Square, Avoncliff ST802599 1792. (Closed 1917 then Red Cross Hospital. Later Old Court Hotel. NRU.) WIL.

Calne (PU 25/3/1835 11+18) **W**: 77 Curzon Street, Calne ST994714 1848 by T. Allom. (PAI. Mostly dem. 1930s. NRU.) WIL.

Chippenham (PU 1/12/1835 29+37) **W1**: Mac's Yard, The Butts, Chippenham ST924729 *c*.1753. (Closed *c*.1859. Dem.) **W2**: Church Street, Lacock ST917686 1833. (Closed *c*.1859. NRU.) **W3**: 1 Rowden Hill, Chippenham ST913727 1959 by C. Creeke. (PAI. St Andrew's Hospital from *c*.1948.) **CtH**: Velley Hill, Corsham. WIL.

Cricklade & Wootton Bassett (PU 24/11/1835 14+17) **W**: North View, High Street, Purton SU085874 1837 by G. Wilkinson. (North View Hospital *c*.1948–89. Now doctor's surgery. Mostly dem.) **SmH**: Red Gables, Restrop Road, Purton SU083873. (Closed 1997. Dem.) WIL.

Devizes (PU 3/11/1835 28+36) **W**: 7 Commercial Road, Devizes SU007616 1837 by G. Wilkinson. (PAI. St James' Hospital *c*.1948–90. Dem.) WIL.

Highworth & Swindon (ren. Swindon & Highworth 1895) (PU 23/11/1835 16+21) **W**: 8 Highworth Road, Stratton St Margaret SU175876 1846 by S.O. Foden & H.W. Parker.

(PAI. St Margaret's Hospital *c*.1948–90. Dem.) **ScH**: 2 The Villas, Stratton; The Limes, Stratton; Olive House, 11 Prospect Place, Swindon. WIL.

Malmesbury (PU 4/12/1835 25+30) **W**: 1 Bristol Road, Brokenborough ST926874 1838 by G. Wilkinson. (PAI then converted to council housing. Dem. *c*.1972.) **CtH**: Charlton Road, Charlton ST961887 *c*.1905. (NRU Homefield.) WIL.

Marlborough (PU 24/11/1835 14+16) **W**: 4 The Common, Marlborough SU184695 1837 by W. Cooper. (PAI. Children's convalescent hospital *c*.1948–81. NRU.) WIL.

Melksham (ren. Trowbridge & Melksham 1898) (PU 2/11/1835 6+20) **W**: Semington Lodge, Melksham ST893603 1838 by H. Kendall. (PAI. St George's Hospital *c*.1948–88. NRU.) **SmH**: (Boys) Fern Cottage, 98 Ashton Street, Trowbridge ST862579. (NRU.) **SmH**: (Girls) Honeywell House, 39 King Street, Melksham. WIL.

Mere (PU 14/10/1835 12+15) **W**: Castle Street, Mere ST809323 1839 by G.G. Scott & W.B. Moffatt. (Closed 1930 the retail/laundry use. Mostly dem.) WIL.

Pewsey (PU 8/12/1835 23+25) **W**: 1 Wilcot Road, Bowling (Green) Way, Pewsey SU157603 1836 by W. Cooper. (Mental defectives' colony *c*.1930–48; Pewsey Hospital 1948-95. NRU.) WIL.

Salisbury (PU 1770; m/w Alderbury 1869) **W**: Crane Street, Salisbury SU141297 1634 enl. 1728. (Closed 1869. Church offices from 1880s.) WIL.

Tisbury (PU 4/10/1835 20+21) **W1**: Church Street, Tisbury ST944291 <1834. (Closed 1868 the used as brewery. Burnt down 1885.) **W2**: Monmouth House, Union Road, West Tisbury ST941288 1868 by C. Creeke. (PAI. Non-combatant corps housed in WW2. Dem 1960s.) WIL.

Warminster (PU 2/11/1835 22+31) **W**: 33 Sambourne, Warminster ST864441 1837 by S. Kempthorne. (PAI. Sambourne Hospital *c*.1948–1990s. NRU.) WIL.

Westbury & Whorwellsdown (PU 14/11/1835 10+17) **W**: Eden Lodge, Westbury ST867508 enl. 1837 by T.L. Evans. (Closed *c*.1930. NRU. Part dem.) WIL.

Wilton (PU 13/10/1836 22+24) **W**: Kingsway House, Warminster Road, Wilton SU099318 1837 by E. Hunt. (Mental defectives' home from *c*.1930 then furniture store until 2004. NRU.) WIL.

Worcestershire

Bromsgrove (PU 7/11/1836 13+19) **W**: 12a (later 165a) Birmingham Road, Bromsgrove SO965716 1838 by J. Bateman & G. Drury. (PAI. All Saints Hospital *c*.1948, later Bromsgrove General. Part dem. Now offices.) **CtH**: Stourbridge Road, Bromsgrove SO961719. (NRU.) WOR.

Droitwich (PU 11/10/1836 26+29) **W**: Union Lane, Droitwich SO895635 1838 by S. Kempthorne. (PAI. Closed 1930s. Later used as factory premises. Dem.) WOR.

Dudley (PU 14/10/1836 4+27) **W1**: Tower Street, Dudley SO944903 <1834. (Closed *c*.1859. Dem.) **W2**: Vicar Street, Sedgley SO917935 <1834. (Closed *c*.1859. Site later used as police station.) **W3**: Workhouse Lane (now Alexandra Road), Tipton SO965925 <1834. (Closed *c*.1859. Dem.) **W4**: 10 Burton Road, Sedgley SO930912 1859 by G.B. Nicholls. (Burton House PAI. Burton Road Hospital *c*.1948–93. Dem.) **CtH**: Dibdale Road, Dudley. **CtH**: Woodcross House, Woodcross Street, Cinder Hill, Bilston SO928946. (Now a care home.) **CtH**: Ashleigh, Hurst Hill, Bilston. DUD.

Evesham (PU 7/4/1836 32+35) **W**: 5 Avonside, Hampton, Evesham SP037430 1837 by J. Plowman. (PAI. RAF hospital 1940-46. Evesham General Hospital from *c*.1948. Dem.) **CtH**: Peewit Road, Great Hampton SP025431. (Later Evesham Children's Home. Dem.) WOR.

Kidderminster (PU 14/10/1836 13+21) **W**: 1 Sutton Road, Kidderminster SO822764 1838 by W. Knight & J. Nettleship. (PAI. Kidderminster General Hospital from *c*.1948. Mostly dem.) **SmH**: Sunnyside, 8 Wolverley Road, Franche SO817781 1922. (NRU.) WOR.

King's Norton (PU 12/12/1836 5+20; m/w Birmingham 1912) **W1**: The Green, King's Norton SP049788 <1834. (Closed *c*.1870.) **W2**: 1/1a/1b/2 Raddlebarn Road, Kings Norton SP045821 1870 by E. Holmes. (Selly Oak Hospital and Institution from *c*.1930.) **CtH**: Woodcock Hill, Shenley Fields SP015817 1880s. (Dem 1980s.) BIR.

Martley (PU 8/10/1836 28+31) **W**: Red House, Martley SO753598 1838 by S. Kempthorne. (PAI then OPH. Dem.) WOR.

Pershore (PU 14/10/1835 40+43) **W**: Station Road, Pershore SO946463 1836 by S. Kempthorne. (Heathlands PAI. Now residential care home. Part dem.) WOR.

Shipston-on-Stour (PU 8/2/1836 37+44) **W**: Shipston House, Darlingscote Road, Shipston-on-Stour SP254410 1838. (PAI then commercial use. Part dem. Derelict in 2010.) WAR.

Stourbridge (PU 13/10/1836 14+24) **W**: 12 Stream Road, Wordsley, Kingswinford SO893874 <1834 rb. 1904 by A. Marshall (1904). (WWI MH. Wordsley Hospital from 1930s–2005. Part dem. NRU.) **CtH**: Norton SO893834 1904. (Dem.) STS, WOR.

Tenbury (PU 27/8/1836 19+22) **W**: Teme Street, Tenbury Wells SO596685 1837 by G. Wilkinson. (Council offices and fire-station from 1930s. Part dem.) WOR.

Upton-upon-Severn (PU 16/11/1835 22+28) **W**: Laburnum Walk, Upto-upon-Severn SO855400 1836 by S. Kempthorne. (Laburnum House PAI. OPH. Dem.) WOR.

Worcester (PU 13/12/1836 12+22) **W**: 1a Tallow Hill, Worcester SO857550 1794 by G. Byfield. (Hillborough PAI/OPH and Shrub Hill Hospital c.1930–1980s. Mostly dem.) **CtH**: Wyld's Lane, Worcester SO857545 1894. (Municipal Homes 1930–47 then Perryfields. Closed c.1961. Dem. 1992.) WOR.

Yorkshire, East Riding

Beverley (PU 15/11/1836 36+38) **W1**: Minster Moor Gate, Beverley TA036392 <1834. (Closed 1861. Dem.) **W2**: Westwood, Beverley TA027395 1861 by J. & W. Atkinson. (PAI. Westwood Hospital from c.1948.) **RH**: Norwood, Beverley. YKE.

Bridlington (PU 28/10/1836 32+34) **W1**: Church Green, Bridlington TA176679 <1834. (Closed 1846.) **W**: Marton Road, Bridlington TA174682 1846. (PAI. Later Burlington House OPH. Mostly dem.) YKE.

Driffield (PU 12/10/1836 43+44) **W1**: Middle Street, Driffield TA022581 c.1839. (Closed c.1868. Part dem. Now mixed use.) **W2**: 19 Bridlington Road, Driffield TA033585 1868 by J. Oates. (PAI. East Riding General Hospital c.1950–90. Dem. 1992.) YKE.

Howden (PU 4/2/1837 40+42) **W**: Knedlington Road, Howden SE743280 1839 by J. & W. Atkinson. (PAI then Howden Hospital. Dem. 1947.) YKE.

Kingston-upon-Hull (LI 1698; LP 1907) **W1**: Charity Hall, 51 Whitefriargate, Hull TA098287 1698. (Closed c. 1852. Dem.) **W2**: 188 Anlaby Road, Hull TA084289 1852 by H. Lockwood & W. Mawson. (PAI. Western General Hospital from 1948 rn. Hull Royal Infirmary 1967. Dem.) **RH**: 16-18 Linnaeus Street, Hull TA084284 c.1915. (Dem.) **ScH**: 131 Coltman Street, 37 Derringham Street, 20/58 Cholmley Street, 34 Fountain Street, 23 Linnaeus Street, 64 Mayfield Street. HUL.

Patrington (PU 23/9/1836 25+26) **W**: Station Road, Patrington TA310227 1837. (War Office use in WWI. PAI. Closed 1947. Later used as factory. Dem.) YKE.

Pocklington (PU 22/10/1836 47+49) **W1**: Hungate, Market Weighton SE879418 <1834. (Closed 1851. Dem.) **W2**: Burnby Lane, Pocklington SE806488 1852 by J. & W. Atkinson. (PAI. Poplars OPH. Dem. mid-1970s.) **CtH**: Pocklington. YKE.

Sculcoates (PU 6/7/1837 18+27) **W**: 160 Beverley Road, Hull TA091301 1845 by H. Lockwood. (PAI. Kingston General Hospital 1948-2002. dem.) **CtH**: Hull Road, Hessle TA043266 1898 by T. Beecroft-Atkinson. (Now residential and community use.) HUL.

Skirlaugh (PU 5/7/1837 42+42) **W**: Main Road, Skirlaugh TA138399 1839 by J. & W. Atkinson. (Closed 1915. War Office use in WWI then used as housing. Now council offices.) YKE.

York (PU 15/7/1837 79+79) **W1**: 26 Marygate, York SE598522 cnv. 1768. (Closed c.1849. then used as boys' Industrial School. Dem. 1875.) **W2**: 75 Huntington Road, York SE608530 1849 by J. & W. Atkinson. (PAI and City Hospital, later The Grange and St Mary's Hospital. Part dem. Now student hall.) **RH**: Haxby Road, York SE606531 1912. (Now student residence.) **ScH**: 120 Haxby Road; 68 Wiggington Road; 44 East Mount Road; (Infants) The Elms, Hull Road. YRK.

Yorkshire, North Riding

Bainbridge GU (ren. Aysgarth 1869) (GU 1812; PU 1869 12+16) **W**: Cam High Road, Bainbridge SD933901 1810. (PAI. High Hall OPH *c.*1948–2007. NRU.) YKN.

Bedale (PU 28/3/1839 23+25) **W**: South End, Bedale SE269879 1839 by J. & W. Atkinson. (Mowbray Grange TB Sanatorium later Mowbray Grange Hospital. NRU.) YKN.

Easingwold (PU 20/2/1837 28+29) **W**: Oulston Road, Easingwold SE534704 1837 by J. & W. Atkinson. (Claypenny 'mental deficiency' colony from *c.*1930. NRU.) YKN.

Guisborough (PU 25/2/1837 27+28) **W**: Northgate, Guisborough NZ614163 1839 by J. & W. Atkinson. (PAI. MH in WW2. Guisborough General Hospital from *c.*1948.) **SmH**: 109 Bolckow Street, Guisborough NZ610161. (NRU.) TEE.

Helmsley Blackmoor (PU 18/2/1837 45+47) **W1**: Kirkbymoorside enl. 1773. (Closed 1850.) **W2**: Helmsley 1776. (Closed 1843.) **W3**: Pottergate, Helmsley SE615838 1843. (Closed *c.*1859. Dem.) **W4**: High Street, Helmsley SE610839 1859 by J. & W. Atkinson. (Closed in WW1. NRU.) YKN.

Kirkby Moorside (PU 6/3/1848 23+24) **W**: Gillamoor Road, Kirkbymoorside SE693870 1850 by J. & W. Atkinson. (Dale End House PAI. Housed Vietnamese refugees in 1970s. NRU.) YKN.

Leyburn (PU 22/2/1837 41+43) **W1**: Moor Road, Leyburn SE109906 <1834. (Closed *c.*1877. Dem.) **W2**: Quarry Hills Lane, Leyburn SE115905 1877 by J. Jackman. (PAI. Later offices. NRU.) YKN.

Malton (PU 12/1/1837 68+70) **W**: Spring Hall, Castlegate, Malton SE791715 1735 rb. 1789. (PAI. Closed *c.*1940. Mostly dem. Now fire station and nursery.) **CtH**: St Leonard's House, 45 Old Maltongate, Malton SE788717. (cnv. *c.*1913. NRU.) YKN.

Middlesbrough (PU 25/6/1875 12+) **W**: 101 St Barnabas Road, Middlesbrough NZ485190 1878 by Perkin & Son. (Holgate PAI/Hospital from *c.*1930. Middlesbrough General Hospital *c.*1948. Dem. 1980s.) **CtH**: Broomlands, Cambridge Road, Middlesbrough NZ488180 1900. (Dem.) **ScH**: Bonanza House, Thornaby Road; 76-78 East Grange Road, 91-95 West Grange Road, 28-29 and 400-404 Imeson Terrace, Middlesbrough. TEE.

Northallerton (PU 23/2/1837 52+55) **W1**: Sunbeck, Northallerton SE368941 1730. (Closed *c.*1858. Dem.) **W2**: Ware Banks (now Bullamoor Road), Northallerton SE371942 1858 by W. Moffatt. (PAI. RAF use 1943–37. Friarage Hospital from 1948.) YKN.

Pickering (PU 10/1/1837 28+29) **W**: 5 Whitby Road, Rysea, Pickering SE801844 1837. (Children's hospital from 1930s, later OPH. Dem.) **ScH**: Hallgarth, Pickering. YKN.

Reeth (PU 27/4/1840 7+11) **W**: Market Place, Reeth SE039992 cnv. 1840. (Closed 1930. NRU.) YKN.

Richmond (PU 24/2/1837 46+48) **W**: Long Hill (now Westfields Court), Richmond NZ166010 1794 enl. 1841 by J. Foss (1794); I. Bonomi (1841). (Richmond House PAI then OPH. Dem. *c.*1968.) YKN.

Scarborough (PU 10/1/1837 33+35) **W1**: Waterhouse Lane, Scarborough TA042886 1728. (Closed *c.*1859. Dem.) **W2**: Dean Street, Scarborough TA039888 1859 by G. Styan. (PAI. St Mary's Hospital *c.*1948–2000. Mostly dem.) **SmH**: Snowdrift Cottage, Scarborough. **SmH**: Whin Bank, Scarborough. YKN.

Stokesley (PU 27/2/1837 28+29) **W1**: High Green, Stokesley *c.*1755. (Closed *c.*1848.) **W2**: Springfield, Stokesley NZ526089 1848. (PAI then OPH.) YKN.

Thirsk (PU 21/2/1837 40+41) **W**: Sutton Road, Thirsk SE434822 1838. (PAI. WW2 hospital use then factory and poultry rearing station. NRU. Part dem.) YKN.

Whitby (PU 9/1/1837 22+24) **W**: Green Lane, Whitby NZ902105 1794 enl. 1858. (PAI. St Hilda's Hospital *c.*1948–78. Now business use.) YKN.

Yorkshire, West Riding

Barnsley (PU 15/1/1850 17+22) **W**: 80 Gawber Road Barnsley SE332070 1852 by H. Lockwood & W. Mawson. (The Limes PAI/OPH. St Helen Hospital 1935–60 then Barnsley District General Hospital. Dem.) **SmH**: Ashley House, Princess Street, Barnsley. BAR.

Barwick (in Elmet) GU (GU 1825; diss. 1869) **W**: Rakehill Road, Barwick-in-Elmet SE391373 *c*.1825. (Closed 1869. NRU.) YAS.

Bradford (PU 10/2/1837 20+32; SP 1897) **W1**: Barkerend Road, Bradford SE172334 rb.1790. (Closed *c*.1852. Dem.) **W2**: Windhill Old Road, Idle SE171387 <1834. (Closed *c*.1852. NRU.) **W3**: 217 Horton Lane, Little Horton SE158320 1852 by H. Lockwood & W. Mawson. (St Luke's Hospital from 1920.) **Ab/Men**: Heights Lane, Daisy Hill, Bradford SE129349 1912 by F. Holland. (Home for 'feeble-minded' males by 1917, later Lynfield Mount Hospital. Part dem.) **San**: Barden Road, Eastby SE025550 1903 by F. Holland. (TB sanatorium closed 1940s. Mostly dem. NRU.) **Men**: 283 Rooley Lane, Bradford SE171304 *c*. 1916. (Bowling Park 'colony' for 'feeble-minded' females, later OPH. Closed 1970s. Dem.) **Men**: Odsal Institution, Rooley Avenue SE162299 *c*.1923 (Later Northern View Hospital. Closed 1980s. Dem.) **RH**: 85-93 Park Road and 9 Osborne Street, Bradford SE159321. (Dem.) **ScH**: 25 Bishop Street, 20 Cumberland Road, 22 Ellercroft Terrace, 15 Farcliffe Place, 151 Kensington Street, 131 and 385 Killinghall Road, 4-6 Lapage Street, 58 Leamington Street, 132 Lilycroft Road, 86 Lister Avenue, 80 Lower Rushton Road, 32 Marsh Street, 32 Marshfield Terrace, 57 Paley Road, 52 Rugby Place, 157 Salt Street, 13 and 168 St Leonard's Road, 15 St Margaret's Terrace, 7 West View, 196 Westwood Terrace, 40 Woodroyd Road (all Bradford); Cavendish House, the Grove, Idle. **OP**: Daisy Hill Back Lane, Bradford SE131348 *c*.1903. (Homes for aged poor. Now residential care unit.) YWB.

Bramley (PU 27/12/1862 2+7) **W**: 3 Green Hill Road, Bramley SE256338 1872 by C. & A. Nelson. (St Mary's Hospital from *c*.1934.) **ScH**: 11 Outgang, Bramley; 'Southville' and 32 & 36 Hill End Road, Armley. YWL.

Carlton GU (GU 1818; diss. 1869) **W**: East Carlton SE221431 *c*.1818. (Closed 1869. Dem.) **W**: Cross Green, Otley SE206457 <1834. (Closed 1869. Dem.) YWL.

Dewsbury (PU 10/2/1837 11+23) **W1**: Balk Hill, Dewsbury SE232214 <1834. (Closed *c*.1855. Dem.) **W2**: Flush Lane (now Muffit Lane), Gomersal SE214259 <1834. (Closed *c*.1855. NRU.) **W3**: White Lee Road, Batley SE223250 1738. (Closed *c*.1855. Dem.) **W4**: 58 Heald's Road, Staincliffe SE233228 1855 by H. Lockwood & W. Mawson. (MH in WW1. PAI. Beech Towers from 1950, dem *c*.1970. Staincliffe Hospital from 1930s.) **CtH**: Heald's Road, Staincliffe SE233227 *c*.1902. (Later The Mount children's homes. Dem.) YWK.

Doncaster (PU 4/7/1837 54+58) **W1**: Hexthorpe Lane, Doncaster SE570027 1839. (Railway works from 1901. Dem. 1960s.) **W2**: Springwell House, Springwell Lane, Balby SE556005 1900 by J. Morton. (PAI. Western Hospital from 1950. Dem. 1974.) DNC.

Ecclesall Bierlow (PU 3/7/1837 7+12) **W**: 32 Union Road, Ecclesall, Sheffield SK337849 1840 by W. Flockton. (Nether Edge Hospital *c*.1930–97. NRU.) **CtH**: Blackbrook Road, Fulwood SK294857 1905 by Holmes & Watson. (Cottage homes closed 1960, then girls' approved school. NRU.) SHF.

Goole (PU 24/10/1837 18+20) **W**: 65 Boothferry Road, Goole SE742239 1839 by J. & W. Atkinson. (PAI. St John's Hospital from *c*.1948. Dem) **SmH**: Riverside House, Riverside, Rawcliffe SE683231. (Dem.) YKE.

Great Ouseburn (GU 1828; PU 1854 41+41) **W**: Roman Road, Great Ouseburn SE435618 *c*.1828 rb. 1857. (PAI. Closed early 1930s. WW2 POW camp. Warehouse from *c*.1953.) YKN.

Great Preston GU (GU 1809; diss. 1869) **W**: Great Preston Hall, Great Preston SE402297 <1834. (Closed 1869. Dem.)

Halifax (PU 10/2/1837 19+31) **W**: Gibbet Lane (later Street), Halifax SE083253 1840. (St John's PAI later Hospital. Dem. *c*.1970.) **Ify**: Dudwell Lane, Salterhebble SE096232 1901 by R. Horsfall & W. Williams. (MH in WW1. St Luke's Hospital *c*.1901–48, Halifax General 1948-2001, now Calderdale Royal. Part dem.) **SmH**: Craigie Lea, Ovenden, Halifax SE082271. (Now nursery.) YWC.

Hemsworth (PU 12/8/1850 25+27) **W**: Southmoor House, Southmoor Road, Hemsworth SE429126 1859. (PAI. Southmoor Hospital from *c*.1948. Mostly dem.) **CtH**: Barnsley Road, Hemsworth. YWL.

Holbeck (PT 29/9/1862 1+8; PU 1869; SP 1904) **W**: 2 Lane End Place, Holbeck, Leeds SE295319 1864 by W. Hill. (South Lodge PAI. Dem. *c*.1970.) YWL.

Huddersfield (PU 16/2/1837 34+41) **W1**: Blacker Lane, Birkby SE138177 <1834. (Closed *c*.1872 then became fever hospital. Dem early 1900s.) **W2**: Kaye lane, Almondbury SE162147 <1834. (Closed 1862. Dem.) **W3**: Scapegoat Hill, Golcar SE085161 <1834. (Closed *c*.1869. Dem.) **W4**:Victoria Place, Honley SE137118 1763. (Closed 1862. Dem.) **W5**:Workhouse Lane (now Moorside Road), Kirkheaton SE181185 <1834. (Closed *c*.1872.) **W6**: 61 Deanhouse, Holmfirth SE137099 1862 by J. Kirk. (PAI. Deanhouse Hospital from *c*.1948. Dem. 1970s.) **W7**: 291a Blackmoorfoot Road, Crosland Moor, Huddersfield SE126154 1872 by J. Kirk. (St Luke's Hospital from *c*.1936. Closed 2010. Part dem.) **RH**: 24/32 Ramsden Street, Huddersfield SE145164. (Dem.) **ScH**: New Hey Road, Outlane SE087179 *c*.1905. (Club House fom *c*.1930. Now hotel.) **ScH**: 18 South Street, Huddersfield. **CtH**:The Leas, Scholes SE162074. (NRU.) YWK.

Hunslet (PT 29/9/1862 1+9; PU 1869) **W1**: Hillidge Road, Hunslet SE306317 1761. (Closed 1903. Dem.) **W2**:Wood Lane, Rothwell Haigh SE331290 1903. (St George's Hospital *c*.1934–91. Dem.) **CtH**:Wood Lane, Rothwell Haigh SE335290 1895. (Rothwell Children's Homes *c*.1930–60 then Home Lea House care home. Mostly dem.) YWL.

Keighley (PU 10/2/1837 6+10) **W1**: Myrtle Place, Bingley SE107390 <1834. (Closed 1858. Dem.) **W2**: Oakworth Road, Exley Head SE048400 <1834. (Closed 1858. Dem.) **W3**: Oakworth Road, Keighley SE055408 1858. (Hillworth Lodge PAI then OPH. Later used by Keighley College. NRU.) **Ify**: 121 Fell Lane, Keighley SE049406 1871. (WW1 MH. St John's Hospital *c*.1930–70. Dem.) **RH**: Nashville Road, Keighley SE054407 *c*.1906. (Dem.) **ScH**: 18 & 30 Clarendon St. Keighley; Cliffe Street, Keighley; 16 Haincliffe Road, Ingrow; Hillside House, Haworth. KEI.

Knaresborough (PU 25/3/1854 21+27) **W**: High Street, Starbeck SE326558 1811. (Closed 1858. Now offices.) **W**: 2-11 Stockwell Road, Knaresborough SE351573 1857 by Shutt. (PAI. Knaresborough Hospital *c*.1948–96. Dem.) **SmH**: Stockwell Lane, Knaresborough. YKN.

Leeds (SP 21/11/1844 1+18; PU 1869) **W1**: Lady Lane, Leeds SE304338 1726. (Closed *c*.1860. Dem. 1936) **W2**: 123 Beckett Street, Leeds SE317347 1860 by W. Perkin & E. Backhouse. (WW1 MH. St James Hospital from 1925. PAI. Now museum. Part dem.) **ScI**: Moral & Industrial School, Beckett Street, Leeds SE316346 1848 by W. Perkin & E. Backhouse. (Hospital use from *c*.1901.) **RH**: 123 Street Lane, Leeds SE321388 1901 by P. Robinson. (Central Children's Home until *c*.1970. Now business use.) **ScH**: 62 Belle Vue Road; 15 Banstead Terrace; 55 Brudenell Mount; 11 Claremont Grove; 19 Cross Green Crescent; 61 East Park Parade; 34 Hamilton Avenue; 20 and 24 Hartley Avenue; 43 Hartley Crescent; 25 Hessle View; Leopold House, Leopold Street; 103 Markham Avenue; 12 Osmandthorpe Lane; 22 Seaforth Avenue; 24 Stanmore Place; 28 Strathmore Drive; 310 York Road, Leeds; 'Southfield', Halton. **Hostel**: Home for working girls, Hill End Road, Armley. YWL.

North Bierley (PU 16/9/1848 16+17) **W**: 1 Highgate Road, Clayton SE124311 1858 by H. Lockwood & W. Mawson. (PAI. Thornton View geriatric hospital *c*.1948–84. Now school.) **ScH**: 5 The Grove, Idle. **ScH**: Beaconsfield Road, Clayton; 28 Gaythorne Terrace, Clayton; 9 Hope View, Windhill, Shipley. KEI.

Pateley Bridge (PU 15/2/1837 10+17) **W1**: Pateley Moor, Knott SE171655 <1834. (Closed 1868. NRU.) **W2**: King Street, Pateley Bridge SE158658 1868 by J. & W. Atkinson. (Closed 1914. WW1 POW camp. Later offices, now museum.) YKN.

Penistone (PU 27/7/1849 15+16) **W**: Huddersfield Road, Penistone SE243039 1859 by H. Lockwood & W. Mawson. (PAI then Netherfields OPH. Now part of Penistone Grammar School.) BAR.

Pontefract (PU 15/2/1862 19+23) **W**: 1 Paradise Gardens, Tanshelf, Pontefract SE456223 1864. (PAI. Northgate Lodge Hospital from 1948, later Headlands Hospital. Part dem. NRU.) **CtH**: Moor Lane, Carleton SE468201 *c*.1906. (Eastwell Lodge children's homes from 1930. Dem.) YWW.

Ripon (PU 25/10/1852 32+36) **W**: 75 Allhallowgate, Ripon SE313715 1854 by W. Perkin & E. Backhouse. (PAI then Sharow View OPH. Now museum and council offices.) YKN.

Rotherham (PU 1/7/1837 28+31) **W**: 42 Alma Road, Rotherham SK428922 1839 rb. 1894 by H. Tacon (1894). (PAI. Rotherham Municipal Hospital from c.1938. Moorgate Hospital c.1948–80. Dem.) **CtH**: Alma Road, Rotherham SK429923. (Used as nurses' homes after 1930. Dem.) **ScH**: 37 St Ann's Road; 22 Clifton Terrace. **San**: Badsley Moor Lane, Rotherham SK447928 1911. (Dem. c.1930) ROT.

Saddleworth (**'with Quick' until 1853**) (GU c.1810; PT 1853; PU 1894) **W**: Running Hill Lane, Dobcross SE007069 <1834 enl. 1855. (PAI. Farm use by 1940. NRU. Part dem.) NON.

Sedbergh (PU 11/1/1840 3+14) **W1**: Main Street, Sedbergh SD660921 <1834. (Closed c.1857. Dem.) **W2**: Hall Bank, Dent SD712873 <1834. (Closed c.1857. NRU.) **W3**: Lofthouse (now Loftus) Hill, Sedbergh SD659917 1857 by J. Oates. (PAI. POWs resident WW2. Book warehouse by 1970. NRU.) CUK.

Selby (PU 15/2/1837 27+29) **W**: Union Lane, Selby SE611320 1837. (PAI then Brook Lodge OPH. Now social services use. Mostly dem.) YKN.

Settle (PU 20/1/1837 31+33) **W**: 1 Raines Road, Giggleswick SD810638 1837. (Mental deficiency' colony c.1930–48 then Castleberg Hospital. NRU.) YKN.

Sheffield (PU 30/6/1837 3+11) **W1**: Kelham Street, Sheffield SK353880 cnv. 1829. (Closed c.1880. Dem.) **W2**: Hollow Meadows SK256879 1848. (Industrial School from 1879. Later Hollow Meadows Hospital. NRU.) **W3**: 2/12 Smilter Lane (later Herries Road), Sheffield SK362907 1880 by J. Hall. (Fir Vale House PAI. City General Hospital c.1930–67 then Northern General. Part dem.) **ScI**: Rock Street, Pitsmoor SK356885 1801. (Closed c.1879. Dem.) **RH**: Smilter Lane (later Herries Road), Sheffield SK361902 c.1895. (Part-dem.) **ScH**: 12–14 and 149-151 Upperthorpe; 14–16 Abbeyfield Road; 92 Andover Street; 279-281 Grimesthorpe Road; 71-73 Scott Road; 399-401 and 521-3 City Road; Manor Lane; 75-77 Duchess Road; 278-80 Edmund Road; 110-12 and 196-98-Heeley Bank Road. SHF.

Skipton (PU 14/1/1837 41+43) **W**: 16 Gargrave Road, Skipton SD985520 1840. (PAI. Raikeswood Hospital c.1948–90. Part dem. NRU.) **CtH**: Aireview House, Broughton Road, Skipton SD980514. (Now offices.) SKI, YKN.

Tadcaster (PU 22/2/1862 15+20) **W**: St Joseph's Street, Tadcaster SE484433 <1834. (Closed 1872. NRU.) **W**: Station Road, Tadcaster SE479431 1872. (PAI then The Beeches OPH. Dem. 1987.) **CtH**: Main Street, Bilbrough SE532465. (NRU) YKN.

Thorne (PU 24/7/1837 13+19) **W**: Union Road, Thorne SE682132 1838. (PAI, closed 1930s. Later factory and Sea Cadet HQ. Part dem.) DNC.

Wakefield (PU 10/2/1837 17+22) **W1**: George Street, Wakefield SE334206 <1834. (Dem.) **W2**: 90 Park Lodge Lane, Wakefield SE343207 1852 by J. Oates. (Stanley View PAI then OPH. Wakefield County Hospital c.1948–90. Dem.) **ScH**: 26 College Grove Road; 30 Garden Street; 57 Quebec Street; 60 Regent Street, Belle Vue; 58 Teall Street; 143 Thornes Lane; 112 Lower York Street. YWW.

Wetherby (PU 15/2/1861 19+21) **W**: Linton Road, Wetherby SE398484 1863 by J. & W. Atkinson. (PAI. Wharfe Grange Hospital c.1948–93. Part dem. NRU.) YWL.

Wharfedale (PU 15/2/1861 18+22) **W**: New Hall, Newall Carr Road, Otley SE198465 1873 by C&A Nelson. (PAI. Otley General Hospital from 1948, later Wharfedale General. Disused 2010.) YWL.

Wortley (PU 21/8/1838 12+20) **W**: Towngate, High Bradfield SK268926 <1834. (Closed c.1852. NRU.) **W**: St Mary's Lane, Ecclesfield SK354940 <1834. (Later parish offices then British Legion club. Dem. c.1968.) **W**: Salt Box Lane, Grenoside SK335935 1852 by Aicken & Capes. (PAI. Grenoside Hospital c.1948–89. Mostly dem. Now OPH.) SHF.

Anglesey

Anglesey (PU 25/9/1852 25+26) **W**: Amlwch Road, Llanerchymedd SH420848 1868. (Closed early 1920s. Later Bryn Hafod council offices. NRU and gallery.) AGY.

Holyhead (PU 1/6/1837 53+63) **W**: Holyhead Road, Valley SH290794 1868 by Thomas. (PAI. Valley Hospital *c*.1948–1990s. Dem.) AGY.

Breconshire

Brecknock (PU 5/10/1836 42+47) **W**: Bailihelig Road, Brecon SO037280 1839. (PAI. St David's Hospital *c*.1948–1990s. Now part of Christ College.) POW.

Builth (PU 2/1/1837 31+35) **W**: Brecon Road, Builth SO042507 1875. (WW1 MH. Dem. 1941.) POW.

Crickhowell (PU 6/10/1836 10+16) **W**: Dardy, Llangattock SO206183 1872. (PAI. Closed 1930s. Part dem. NRU and hotel.) POW.

Hay (PU 26/9/1836 25+27) **W**: St Mary's Road, Hay-on-Wye SO225420 1837. (Cockcroft House PAI. NRU.) POW.

Caernarvonshire (Carnarvonshire)

Bangor & Beaumaris (PU 30/5/1837 21+30) **W**: Carnarvon Road, Glan Adda SH571709 1845 by Weightman & Hadfield. (WW1 MH. Closed 1930. Later used as creamery. Dem.) **Ify**: Carnarvon Road, Glan Adda SH569710 1914. (WW1 MH. Later St David's Hospital. Closed *c*.1983. Dem.) **SmH**: Maesgarnedd Home, Llanfair PG, Anglesey. AGY.

Carnarvon (PU 1/6/1837 16+27) **W**: Bodfan, South Road, Carnarvon SH486615 1846. (WW1 MH. Bodfan Mental Home *c*.1925–48 then Eryri Hospital.) CAE.

Conway (PU 11/4/1837 15+15) **W**: Bangor Road, Conway SH774781 1859. (PAI. Conway Hospital from 1948. Closed *c*.2002. Dem.) **CtH**: Bryn Onen/Bryn Conway, Woodlands, Llanrwst Road, Conway SH779771 1909. (NRU.) **SmH**: Blodwel Home, Broad Street, Llandudno Junction SH794781 S Foulkes, 1926. (NRU.)

Pwllheli (PU 3/6/1837 32+41) **W**: Ala Road, Pwllheli SH371350. W. Thomas, 1839. (PAI. Pwllheli Hospital from 1948.)

Cardiganshire

Aberayron (PU 8/5/1837 14+16) **W**: Princes' Street, Aberayron SN461629 1838 by G. Wilkinson. (WW1 MH. Cottage hospital from 1930. Now medical centre.) CGN.

Aberystwyth (PU 5/5/1837 30+33) **W**: Penglais Road, Aberystwyth SN591818 1840 by W.R. Coulthart. (PAI. Aberystwyth General Hospital from *c*.1936–66 then Brongalis General. Dem.) CGN.

Cardigan (PU 9/5/1837 26+33) **W**: Albro Castle, St Dogmaels SN160467 1840 by W. Owen. (PAI. Closed 1930s. NRU.) CGN.

Lampeter (PU 15/5/1837 13+17) **W**: Pantfaen Road, Lampeter SN574481 1877 by Szlumper & Aldwinckle. (PAI. OPH from *c*.1948. Dem. *c*.1960s.) CGN.

Tregaron (PU 15/5/1837 22+23) **W**: Dewi Road, Tregaron SN678593 1878. (King Edward VII Hospital from 1915. Later Tregaron Hospital. Part dem.) CGN.

Carmarthenshire

Carmarthen (PU 2/7/1836 28+32) **W**: 1 Penlan Road, Carmarthen SN411206 1837. (WW1 MH. PAI. WW2 troop barracks. Later infirmary then offices. Mostly dem.) **CtH**: Waterloo Cottage, Waterloo Terrace, Carmarthen. **CtH**: Ystradwrallt, Station Road, Nantgaredig *c*.1925. (NRU.) CMN.

Llandilo Fawr (PU 14/12/1836 11+20) **W**: Ffairfach, Llandilo SN630215 1838 by G. Wilkinson. (PAI. Dem mid-1960s.) CMN.

Llandovery (PU 15/12/1836 11+21) **W**: Llanfair Road, Llandovery SN768349 1838. (PAI then hospital and children's home, later council depot. Mostly dem.) CMN.

Llanelly (PU 24/10/1836 10+17) **W**: Swansea Road, Llanelly SN514008 1838. (PAI. Bryntirion Hospital *c*.1948–2004. Part dem. NRU.) CMN.

Newcastle in Emlyn (PU 31/5/1837 20+30) **W**: Aberarad, Newcastle Emlyn SN315402 1839 by T. Rowlands. (Closed by 1922 then used as creamery. Mostly dem.) CMN.

Denbighshire

Llanrwst (PU 29/4/1837 17+20) **W**: Station Road, Llanrwst SH795622 1850. (PAI. Dem. *c*.1960s.) DEN.

Ruthin (PU 1/3/1837 21+24) **W**: Llanrhydd Street, Ruthin SJ128581 1838. (WW1 Red Cross Hospital. PAI. Dem. *c*.1960s.) DEN.

Wrexham (PU 30/3/1837 56+61) **W**: Watery Road, Wrexham SJ328504 1838. (WW1 MH. Plas Maelor PAI. Maelor Hospital from *c*.1948. Dem.) **ScH**: Coppenhall House, Wrexham; Little Acton, Wrexham. DEN.

Flintshire

Hawarden (PU 1/2/1853 15+20) **W**: Chester Road, Broughton SJ345640 1854. (Broughton Mental Hospital, later Broughton Hospital. Closed *c*.1994. Dem.) FLN.

Holywell (PU 25/2/1837 14+27) **W**: Old Chester Road, Holywell SJ189749 1840 by J. Welch. (WW1 MH. PAI. Luesty Hospital from *c*.1948.) **CtH**: Old Chester Road, Holywell SJ189750. (Dem.) FLN.

St Asaph (PU 10/4/1837 16+24) **W**: Denbigh Road, St Asaph SJ043738 1839. (PAI. HM Stanley Hospital from *c*.1948.) **CtH**: The Roe, St Asaph. FLN.

Glamorgan

Bridgend & Cowbridge (PU 10/10/1836 52+52) **W**: Quarella Road, Bridgend SS905803 1838 by G. Wilkinson. (WW1 MH. PAI. Part of Bridgend General Hospital until 1984. NRU.) **CtH**: Merthyr Mawr Road, Bridgend SS901787 1879. (Later Preswylfa Children's Home. NRU.) GLA.

Cardiff (PU 13/9/1836 41+53) **W1**: 30a Cowbridge Road, Cardiff ST173765 1839 by James, Seaward & Thomas. (City Lodge PAI. St David's Hospital *c*.1948–95. Mostly dem.) **Scl/W2**: 449-451 Cowbridge Road West, Cardiff ST142764 1862. (Union schools until 1903 then workhouse. Ely Lodge PAI. Ely Hospital *c*.1948–96. Dem.) **RH/CtH**: 449-451 Cowbridge Road West, Cardiff ST142764. (Dem.) **Dsp**: 107 Frederick Street, Cardiff. **ScH**: 433-435 and 449-451 Cowbridge Road, 145-147 Clive Road, 11-15 Romilly Crescent, 40 Llanfair Road, 34-35 Victoria Park Road and 119-121 King's Road, Canton ; 52-54 Taff Embankment, Grangetown; 13-15 Northcote Street and 3-4 Church Terrace, Roath; 22 Woodville Road and 84-86 Whitchurch Road, Cathays; 32 Windsor Terrace. Penarth; Bank, Station Road, Dinas Powis; 15-16 Park Crescent, Barry. GLA.

Gower (PU 29/9/1857 18+20) **W**: Penmaen, Swansea SS530887 1861. (PAI then OPH.) GMW.

Merthyr Tydfil (PU 3/11/1836 9+21) **W**: 44 Thomas Street, Merthyr SO051064 1853 by Aicken & Capes. (Tydfil Lodge PAI. St Tydfil's Hospital from *c*.1948.) **Scl**: Llewelyn Street, Trecynon SN990038 1871. (Union schools 1877–1912 then used a branch workhouse. Later Tegfan Hostel. Dem.) **OP**: Windsor House, Llewelyn Street, Trecynon SN991038 *c*.1914. (WW1 MH. Later Tegfan Hostel, now Tegfan OPH.) **OP**: Pantysgallog House, Pant Road, Dowlais SO063091 cnv *c*.1912. (NRU.) **CtH**: Corner House Street, Llwydcoed SN993050 *c*.1910. (Mostly dem. Now school site.) **San**: Pontsarn, Vaynor SO047094 1913. (Sanatorium until *c*.1960s. Part dem. NRU.) GLA.

Neath (PU 2/9/1836 29+33) **W**: Lletty Nedd, Llantwit Road, Neath SS758979 1838. (WW1 MH. Closed 1924. Youth hostel 1933–46. Now mixed use. Part dem.) **CtH**: Main Road, Bryncoch SN744004 1878. (Mostly dem. NRU.) **Ify**: Briton Ferry Road, Neath SS744958 1916. (Penrhiwtyn Infirmary from 1930s. Neath General Hospital *c*.1948–2003. Dem.) GMW.

Pontardawe (PU 26/3/1875 7+) **W**: 84 Brecon Road, Pontardawe SN727047 1879. (WWI MH. PAI. Danybryn Hostel *c.*1948–88. Dem.) GMW.

Pontypridd (PU 27/12/1862 6+25) **W**: Court House Street, Pontypridd ST070897 1865. (Central Homes PAI. Graig Hospital *c.*1948–65. Dem.) **OP**: Partridge Road, Llwynypia SS999942 1903. (WWI MH. Llwynypia Hospital from 1927.) **CtH**: Church Village, Llantwit Vardre ST084860 1892. (Garth Olwg from 1950. Dem.) **RH**: Maes-y-coed, Pontypridd ST066899. (Dem.) GLA.

Swansea (PU 23/10/1836 27+40) **W1**: Swansea Burrows SS651924 cnv. 1817. (Closed 1864. Dem.) **W2**: 15 Mount Pleasant, Swansea SS651936 *c.*1862. (Tawe Lodge PAI. Mount Pleasant Hospital *c.*1948–95. Part dem. NRU.) **CtH**: Station Road, Cockett SS629948 1877. (Dem.) GMW.

Merionethshire

Bala (PU 10/1/1837 5+12) **W1**: High Street, Bala SH925358 1841. (Closed 1875. Later barracks and factory use. Now shop/factory.) **W2**: Mount Lane, Bala SH928360 1875 by W.H. Spaull. (PAI then council depot. Dem.) GWY.

Corwen (PU 7/1/1837 14+23) **W**: London Road, Corwen SJ080433 1840. (Later factory use. Now retail.) GWY.

Dolgelly (PU 12/1/1837 13+19) **W**: Arran Road, Dolgelly SH733177 1857. (PAI. Llwyn View Hospital *c.*1948–93. NRU.) GWY.

Festiniog (PU 8/5/1837 15+22) **W**: Main Road, Penrhyndeudraeth SH603386 1839. (PAI. Later Bron y Garth Community Hospital, closed 2008.) GWY.

Monmouthshire

Abergavenny (PU 31/5/1836 28+36) **W**: Union Road, Abergavenny SO291143 1839 by G. Wilkinson. (PAI. Later Hatherleigh Place. NRU.) GWE.

Bedwellty (PU 26/3/1849 2+20) **W**: Whitworth Terrace, Tredegar SO151080 1852. (WWI MH. Ty Bryn PAI. St James' Hospital *c.*1948–76. Dem.) **ScH**: Nutshell, Tredegar; Defn Road, Blackwood; Mount Pleasant Road, Ebbw Vale; The Terrace, Rhymney. **CtH**: Park Row, Tredegar SO141084 1905. (Now sheltered housing.) GWE.

Chepstow (PU 16/5/1836 32+35) **W**: Regent House, Mounton Road, Chepstow ST531937 1838. (PAI then Regent House Infirmary. Mostly dem.) **CtH**: 7-10 The Terrace, Sudbrook Road, Sudbrook ST501876 cnv. 1919. (NRU.) GWE.

Monmouth (PU 11/7/1836 31+37) **W1**: Weirhead Street, Monmouth SO510127 <1834. (Closed *c.*1870. Dem. Now part of Monmouth School site.) **W2**: Old Hereford Road, Monmouth SO509136 1870 by G.C. Haddon. (PAI. Now Haberdashers' School.) GWE.

Newport (PU 1/8/1836 40+43) **W**: Woolaston House, Stow Hill, Newport ST306875 1838 rb. 1903 by T.H. Wyatt (1838). (WWI MH. St Woolos Hospital from 1949. Mostly dem.) **Scl**: Industrial School, Mill Street, Caerleon ST342908 cnv. 1859. (Closed 1902. Hospital in WWI. Later Cambria House council offices. Dem.) **V**: 67-69 Stow Hill, Newport ST310878. (Dem.) **SmH**: Ty-Gwynfa, 58 Chepstow Road, Newport ST318884. (Now business use.) **SmH**: Beeches, Chepstow Road, Newport ST327881. (Now retail use.) **SmH**: Stow Hill House, 108 Stow Hill, Newport ST309876 cnv. 1917. (Closed 1973. NRU.) **SmH**: Vale View, Caerleon. **SmH**: Brenhilda, 83 Caerleon Road, Newport ST318888. (NRU.) **SmH**: Cambria House, Newport. GWE.

Pontypool (PU 23/5/1836 22+26) **W**: Union (later Coedygric) Road, Griffithstown ST291995 1837 by G. Wilkinson. (WWI MH. PAI. Panteg County Hospital) **CtH**: Coedygric Road, Griffithstown ST291996. (As above for workhouse site.) GWE.

Montgomeryshire

Llanfyllin (PU 15/2/1837 23+27) **W**: Y Dolydd, Main Road, Llanfyllin SJ150186 1838 by T. Penson. (PAI then The Meadows OPH until 1982. Now mixed use.) POW.

Machynlleth (PU 16/1/1837 11+15) **W**: Maengwyn Street, Machynlleth SH750009 1860. (King Edward VII Memorial TB Hospital from 1920, later Machynlleth Chest Hospital. Now community hospital.) POW.

Montgomery & Pool (ren. Forden 1870) (LI 1792; PU 25/3/1870 24+34) **W**: Forden SJ216000 1795 by J. Bromfield. (PAI. Brynhyfryd Hospital *c.*1948–1990s. Now Camlad House.) POW.

Newtown & Llanidloes (PU 13/2/1837 17+21) **W**: The Lodge, Main Street, Caersws SO036924 1840 by T. Penson. (PAI. Llys Maldwyn Hospital *c.*1948–2000. NRU.) POW.

Pembrokeshire

Haverfordwest (PU 6/1/1837 63+67) **W**: Priory Mount, Haverfordwest SM955151 1839 by W. Owen. (PAI. St Thomas Hospital *c.*1948–78. NRU.) PEM.

Narberth (PU 6/1/1837 46+48) **W**: Narberth Mountain SN111133 1839 by W. Owen. (Narberth Lodge PAI then Allensbank OPH. Now holiday accommodation.) PEM.

Pembroke (PU 6/1/1837 29+35) **W**: Golden Lane (now Woodbine Terrace), Pembroke SM986016 1838 by G. Wilkinson. (Woodbine House PAI. Riverside OPH from 1948. Part dem.) **SmH**: Croft House, The Green, Pembroke SM983016. PEM.

Radnorshire

Knighton (PU 9/11/1836 20+23) **W**: Frydd Lane (now Road), Knighton SO286720 1837 rb. 1886 by Jones & Price (1837); E. Jones (1886). (WWI MH. Offa's Lodge PAI. Knighton Hospital from *c.*1948. Mostly dem.) POW.

Presteigne (PU 8/11/1836 16+17; diss. 27/2/1877) **W**: None. POW.

Rhayader (PU 10/10/1836 10+16) **W**: Builth Road, Rhayader SN978676 1878 by S.W. Williams. (PAI until 1939. Royal Deaf School 1949–1960s. Hotel from 1989.) POW.

Isle of Man

Douglas W: Kingswood Grove, Douglas SC378759 1837. (Now Ellan Vannin Home.) IOM.

Braddan W: Strang, Braddan SC361779 *c.*1900. (Dem. 1980s.) IOM.

Channel Islands

Guernsey W: Hospital Lane, St Peter Port 1741. (Later Town Hospital. Closed 1990. Now police station.) **W**: La Neuve Rue, Castel 1751. (Now Castel Hospital.) GUE.

Jersey W: Gloucester Street, Jersey 1751. (Now General Hospital.) JER, LSJ.

METROPOLITAN ASYLUMS BOARD 1869–1930

The list below gives details of the establishments operated by the Metropolitan Asylums Board (MAB).[494] The details for each institution are the date it came into use, its address location (including UK National Grid Reference indicated by an symbol) and (enclosed in brackets) its later fate.

Abbreviations used in the list are shown below:

dem	demolished	POWs	Prisoners of War
NRU	Now residential use	WWI	First World War

Isolation Hospitals – Fever and Smallpox
Eastern Hospital 1-Feb-1871 The Grove, Homerton TQ356853 (Closed 1982. Dem.)
South-Western Hospital 31-Jan-1871 Landor Road, Stockwell TQ305756 (Rebuilt 1990s. Site now Lambeth Hospital.)

Isolation Hospitals – Fever
Brook Hospital 31-Aug-1896 Shooter's Hill, Woolwich TQ423767 (Mostly dem. NRU.)
Fountain Hospital Oct-1893 Tooting Grove, Tooting Graveney TQ271714 (Hospital for mentally subnormal children from 1911. Closed 1963. Dem. Site now St George's Hospital.)
Grove Hospital 17-Aug-1899 Tooting Grove, Tooting Graveney TQ269713 (Mostly dem. 1970s. Site now St George's Hospital.)
North-Eastern Hospital 8-Oct-1892 St. Ann's Road, Tottenham TQ325885 (Now St Ann's Hospital.)
North-Western Hospital 25-Jan-1870 Lawn Road, Hampstead TQ273854 (Lawn Road branch of Royal Free Hospital after 1948. Original buildings dem. by 1973.)
Park Hospital 8-Nov-1897 Hither Green Lane, Lewisham TQ387741 (Later Hither Green Hospital. Closed 1997. Mostly dem. NRU.)
South-Eastern Hospital 17-Mar-1877 Avonley Road, New Cross TQ354774 (Later New Cross Hospital. Closed *c.*1991. Mostly dem.)
Western Hospital 10-Mar-1877 Seagrave Road, Fulham TQ257775 (Closed 1979. Dem.)

Isolation Hospitals - Smallpox
Joyce Green Hospital 28-Dec-1903 Joyce Green Lane, Dartford TQ546750 (Closed 2000. Dem.)
Long Reach Hospital 27-Feb-1902 Joyce Green Lane, Dartford TQ550773 (Rebuilt 1929. Closed 1973. Dem.)
Orchard Hospital 1902 Joyce Green Lane, Dartford TQ543768 (WWI MH. Closed *c.*1939. Dem.)
Hospital Ships *Atlas*, **Endymion** and *Castalia* 1883 Long Reach, Dartford TQ550775 (Closed 1903.)

Convalescent Hospitals – Fever

Northern Hospital 25-Sep-1887 World's End Lane, Winchmore Hill TQ306957 (Later
Highlands Hospital. Closed 1993. NRU.)

Southern (Gore Farm) Hospital - Upper 1890 Gore Farm Estate, Dartford TQ569722
(Southern Convalescent Hospital from 1908. WWI MH. Closed 1948. Dem.)

Southern (Gore Farm) Hospital - Lower 1902 Gore Farm Estate, Dartford TQ567717
(Southern Convalescent Hospital from 1908. German POWs in WWI. Closed 1948. Dem.)

Tuberculosis

Colindale Hospital 1-Jan-1920 Colindale Avenue, Hendon TQ211900 (Mostly closed by
1996. Site currently being redeveloped.)

Grove Park Hospital 9-Feb-1926 Marvel's Lane, Grove Park, Greenwich TQ410726 (TB/
chest hospital until 1977 then mentally handicapped until closure in 1994. Part dem. NRU.)

King George V Sanatorium 8-Jun-1922 Salt Lane, nr. Godalming SU971403 (Closed 1988.
Dem.)

Millfield 6-Apr-1904 Sea Lane, Rustington TQ049015 (Closed 1948. Dem.)

Pinewood 7-Jul-1919 Nine Mile Ride, Wokingham SU835660 (Closed c.1965. Dem.)

St George's Home 14-May-1914 Milman's Street, Chelsea TQ268775 (Dem. 1980s.)

St Luke's Hospital 9-May-1922 Kirkley Cliff Road, Lowestoft TM542914 (Closed c.1947.
Dem.)

Venereal Diseases

St Margaret's Hospital 16-Sep-1918 Leighton Road, Kentish Town TQ291853 (Closed
c.1947. Dem.)

Sheffield Street Hospital 21-Jun-1920 Sheffield Street, Kingsway TQ307812 (St Philip's
Hospital from 1952. Closed 1992. Dem. 2011)

Mental Hospitals

Caterham Asylum Oct-1870 Coulsdon Road, Caterham TQ326559 (Caterham Mental
Hospital 1920-41 then St Lawrence's. Closed 1994. Mostly dem. NRU.)

Darenth Schools / Training Colony Nov-1878 Darenth, Kent TQ570729 (Closed 1988.
Dem.)

Edmonton Colony for Sane Epileptics Dec-1916 Silver Street, Edmonton TQ329926 (St
David's Hospital from c.1936. Closed 1971. Part dem. Now arts centre.)

Leavesden Asylum Oct-1870 Asylum (now College) Road, Abbot's Langley TL102017
(Leavesden Mental Hospital 1920–59 then Leavesden Hospital. Closed 1995. Part dem.
NRU.)

Tooting Bec Hospital 19-Jan-1903 Tooting Bec Road, Tooting Bec TQ286718 (Tooting Bec
Mental Hospital 1924-37 then Tooting Bec Hospital. Closed 1995. Dem.)

Children's Institutions

Bridge Hospital (ringworm) 1901 Hatfield Road, Witham TL815140 (Industrial Home
for Feeble-Minded Boys' (Bridge Training Home) from 1908, later Bridge Hospital. Closed
2002. NRU.)

Downs School (ringworm) 26-Feb-1903 Brighton Road, Sutton TQ259622 (TB sanatorium from 1913. Now Sutton and Royal Marsden Hospitals.)

High Wood School/Hospital (ophthalmia) 26-Jul-1904 Ongar Road, Brentwood
TQ591944 (Children's TB cases 1922–59. Geriatric care 1960–2010. Site now being redeveloped.)

Goldie Leigh Homes (ringworm etc.) 1-Nov-1914 Abbey Wood, Woolwich TQ471776
(Now Goldie Leigh Hospital.)

Millfield (convalescent) 6-Apr-1904 Sea Lane, Rustington TQ049015 (Closed 1948. Dem.)

Princess Mary's Hospital (formerly East Cliff House) 26-Jun-1898 Wilderness Hill, Margate TR361709 (Princess Mary's Hospital for Children from 1919. Closed *c.*1981. Now nursing home and offices.)

Queen Mary's Hospital for Children (general) 29-Jan-1909 Fountain Drive, Carshalton TQ278625 (Closed 1993. Part dem.)

St Anne's Convalescent Home 26-Dec-1897 St George's Terrace, Herne Bay TR173682 (TB sanatorium from 1919. Dem.)

Training Ships Exmouth/Goliath Mar-1876 Off Grays, Essex (Replaced 1905. Scrapped 1970s.)

Training Ships' Infirmary Aug-1905 Grays, Essex TQ613776 (Dem.)

White Oak School/Hospital (ophthalmia) 20-Mar-1903 Swanley Junction, Kent TQ511689 (Closed *c.*1950. Mostly dem.)

Casual Poor

The Hostel 2-Jul-1923 Little Gray's Inn Lane, Holborn TQ310821 (Now used as hostel.)

The Night Office Nov-1912 Waterloo Pier, London TQ306806 (Under Charing Cross rail bridge from 1921.)

River Ambulance Stations

North Wharf Jan-1884 Manager's Street, Blackwall TQ384800 (Closed *c.*1932.)

South Wharf Dec-1883 Trinity Street, Rotherhithe TQ366796 (Closed *c.*1932.)

West Wharf Feb-1885 Carnwath Road, Fulham TQ257756 (Closed *c.*1932.)

POST-1838 POOR LAW INSTITUTIONS IN IRELAND

The list below gives details of poor law institutions that operated in Ireland after 1838.[486] The format of each entry is described by means of the following (fictitious) example:

Patrickstown (3-Aug-1840 13+21) **W**: 600, 1-Jul-1842, 25-Sep-1844. Dublin Street, Patrickstown R123456. (Closed 1921. DH. Part dem. NRU.) CLA.

The above entry indicates that the Patrickstown Union was officially declared on 3 August 1840, with its Board of Guardians comprising twenty-one members from thirteen electoral divisions. The union's workhouse, for up to 600 inmates, was declared fit for the admission of paupers on 1 July 1842, with the first admissions taking place on 25 September 1844. (Note that admission dates are only available for unions formed before 1845.) The workhouse building was located on Dublin Street, Patrickstown with an Irish National Grid Reference of R123456. After its use as a workhouse ended in 1921, some or all of the building was used as a District Hospital but has been partly demolished with the surviving parts now in residential use. Surviving local records are held at Clare County Library (see Appendix I).

Abbreviations used in the list are shown below:

AH	Auxiliary Home	FH	Fever Hospital
c.	circa	NRU	Now residential use
CH	County Home	OPH	Old People's Home
CHH	County Home and County Hospital	Scl	Residential School
dem	demolished	W	Workhouse
DH	District Hospital	WWI	First World War
diss	dissolved		

Co. Antrim

Antrim (13-May-1840 19+24) **W**: 700, 1-Sep-1843, 19-Sep-1843. Railway Street (now Station Road), Antrim J151869. (WWI military use. Massereene Hospital. Mostly dem. 2003.) PNI.

Ballycastle (11-Apr-1840 15+18) **W**: 300, 1-Oct-1842, 1-Jan-1843. Coleraine Road, Ballycastle D109406. (Dalriada DH. Mostly dem.) PNI.

Ballymena (13-May-1840 23+28) **W**: 900, 1-Nov-1843, 17-Nov-1843. Cushendall Road, Ballymena D109043. (Braid Valley Hospital. Part dem.) PNI.

Ballymoney (18-Jan-1840 22+37) **W**: 700, 15-Nov-1842, 1-Mar-1843. Coleraine Road, Ballymoney C944262. (Route DH. Closed c.2001. Dem.) PNI.

Belfast (21-Dec-1838 12+22) **W**: 1000, 1-Jan-1841, 11-May-1841. 55 Lisburn Road, Belfast J329728. (Now Belfast City Hospital. Mostly dem.) PNI.

Larne (13-May-1840 13+23) **W**: 400, 31-Oct-1842, 1-Jan-1843. Old Glenarm Road, Larne D402028. (Larne DH, now Moyle Hospital.) PNI.

Lisburn (8-Jan-1839 27+29) **W**: 800, 1-Jan-1841, 11-Feb-1841. Hillsborough Road, Lisburn J265636. (Now Lagan Valley Hospital.) PNI.

Co. Armagh

Armagh (25-Apr-1839 25+49) **W**: 1000, 14-Dec-1841, 14-Jan-1842. Tower Hill, Armagh H882455. (Now Tower Hill Hospital.) PNI.

Lurgan (16-Jan-1839 19+25) **W**: 800, 1-Jan-1841, 22-Feb-1841. Union Street, Lurgan J077577. (Lurgan & Portadown DH from 1929, now Lurgan Hospital.) PNI.

Co. Carlow

Carlow (14-Sep-1840 14+30) **W**: 800, 16-Sep-1844, 18-Nov-1844. Kilkenny Road, Carlow S717758. (Military use in 1920s. Dem. Site now FE Institute.) CAR.

Co. Cavan

Bailieborough (20-Nov-1839 11+18) **W**: 600, 26-Mar-1842, 20-Jun-1842. Cavan Road, Bailieborough N672969. (Closed 1921. Dem. 1970s. Site now Fairlawns OPH.) CAV.

Bawnboy (28-Apr-1850 25+25) **W**: 500. Main Street, Bawnboy H214191. (Closed 1921. Part used as school 1931-67. Derelict.) CAV, NAI.

Cavan (27-Nov-1839 23+30) **W**: 1200, 26-Mar-1842, 17-Jun-1842. Cathedral Road, Cavan H421063. (CHH & FH, now St Felim's Hospital.) CAV.

Cootehill (10-Aug-1839 12+18) **W**: 800, 15-Sep-1842, 1-Dec-1842. Station Road, Cootehill H612137. (Closed 1917. Dem.) CAV.

Co. Clare

Ballyvaughan (24-Feb-1850 11+11) **W**: 500. School Road, Ballyvaughan M227076. (Closed *c.*1923. Dem.) CLA.

Corofin (24-Feb-1850 9+9) **W**: 500. Newtown, Corofin R288887. (Mostly dem. Now storage depot.) CLA.

Ennis (27-Jun-1839 18+28) **W**: 800, 1-Dec-1841, 15-Dec-1842. Lifford Road, Ennis R341782. (CH, now St Joseph's Hospital. Mostly dem. by 1970.) CLA.

Ennistymon (3-Aug-1839 13+21) **W**: 600, 1-Jul-1842, 1-Sep-1845. 1m W of Ennistymon R115880. (DH. Mostly dem. Site now disused.) CLA.

Killadysert (24-Feb-1850 11+12) **W**: 500. Ennis Road, Kildysart R260599. (Dem.) CLA.

Kilrush (1-Aug-1838 13+29) **W**: 800, 15-Dec-1841, 1-Jul-1842. St Joseph's Terrace, Kilrush Q994556. (DH & AH. Site now school/housing.) CLA.

Scariff (25-Jul-1839 10+26) **W**: 600, 1-Oct-1841, 11-May-1842. R352, Scariff R638840. (Mostly burnt 1921.) CLA.

Tulla (diss. 1909) (24-Feb-1850 18+13) **W**: 500. Courthouse Road, Tulla R503801. (Closed 1909. Dem.) CLA.

Co. Cork

Bandon (12-Feb-1839 23+31) **W**: 900, 29-Sep-1841, 17-Nov-1841. Connolly Street, Bandon W499549. (Burnt 1921. Site now Bandon Community Hospital.) COR.

Bantry (28-Sep-1840 9+18) **W**: 800, 19-Aug-1844, 24-Apr-1845. James Gilhooly Terrace, Bantry V997481. (Burnt *c.*1921. Site now Bantry General Hospital.) COR.

Castletownbere (30-Sep-1849 7+10) **W**: 600. St Jospeh's Villas, Castletownbere V685461. (Dem. Stone used to build cottages.) COR.

Clonakilty (4-Oct-1849 20+22) **W**: 700. Convent Road, Clonakilty W393424. (CH. Sacred Heart Hospital from 1931. Now Mount Carmel. Part dem.) COR.

Cork (3-Apr-1839 14+40) **W**: 2000, 15-Feb-1840, 1-Mar-1840. Douglas Road, Cork W682706. (CH, DH & FH from 1924. Now St Finbarr's Hospital. Part dem.) COR.

Dunmanway (18-Dec-1839 7+15) **W**: 400, 16-Sep-1841, 1-Oct-1841. 1m NE of Dunmanway W247535. (Burnt *c*.1921. DH. Now St Anthony's Hospital. Mostly dem.) COR.

Fermoy (23-Feb-1839 22+28) **W**: 900, 10-Jun-1841, 1-Jul-1841. New Barracks Lane (now The Showgrounds) W807991. (Closed *c*.1857. Site now showground.) **W**: 700, 1857. Courthouse Road, Fermoy W825986. (County Hospital. Now St Patrick's Community Hospital. Part dem.) COR.

Kanturk (21-Dec-1839 14+29) **W**: 800, 23-May-1842, 18-Jul-1844. Millview Road, Kanturk R373030. (Burnt 1921.) COR.

Kinsale (30-Jan-1839 16+21) **W**: 500, 29-Sep-1841, 1-Dec-1841. New Road, Kinsale W635512. (Now Kinsale Community Hospital and council depot. Part dem.) COR.

Macroom (20-Dec-1839 16+25) **W**: 600, 1-Oct-1842, 13-May-1843. New Street, Macroom W334731. (Burnt 1921. Site now Macroom Community Hospital.) COR.

Mallow (5-Mar-1839 16+25) **W**: 700, 29-Nov-1841, 1-Aug-1842. Limerick Road, Mallow R545001. (WWI military use. CH & DH from 1922. Now Mallow General Hospital. Part dem.) COR.

Midleton (16-Feb-1839 21+32) **W**: 800, 15-Jun-1841, 21-Aug-1841. Mill Road, Midleton W881739. (DH, FH & AH from 1924. Now Our Lady of Lourdes Community Hospital. Part dem.) COR.

Millstreet (31-Mar-1850 12+14) **W**: 600. Killarney Road, Millstreet W261900. (DH 1920s. Dem. Site now Millstreet Community Hospital.) COR.

Mitchelstown (31-Mar-1850 18+18) **W**: 600. Clonmel Road, Mitchelstown R828129. (WWI military use. Dem. Now farm use.) COR.

Schull (or Skull) (4-Oct-1849 11+13) **W**: 600. 1m NE of Schull V937326. (Dem. 1920.) COR.

Skibbereen (31-Jan-1839 20+27) **W**: 800, 21-Dec-1841, 19-Mar-1842. Mill Road, Skibbereen W124352. (Dem. Site now Skibbereen County Hospital.) COR.

Youghal (9-Jun-1850 14+18) **W**: 700. Barrack Road, Youghal X097779. (Cottage Hospital from 1922. Dem. Site NRU.) COR.

Co. Derry (Co. Londonderry)

Coleraine (28-Nov-1839 20+27) **W**: 700, 11-Apr-1842, 19-Apr-1842. Mountsandel Road, Coleraine C850316. (Later Colreaine Hospital. Closed c. 2001. Mostly dem.) PNI.

Londonderry (17-Jan-1839 22+27) **W**: 800, 10-Nov-1840, 10-Nov-1840. Glendermott Road, Londonderry C443166. (Later Waterside Hospital until 1990. Part dem. Now library and musuem.) PNI.

Magherafelt (25-Nov-1839 25+30) **W**: 900, 10-Mar-1842, 11-Mar-1842. Hospital Road, Magherafelt H891912. (Margherafelt DH from 1941, now the Mid-Ulster Hospital) PNI.

Newtown Limavady (21-Sep-1839 19+24) **W**: 500, 15-Mar-1842, 15-Mar-1842. Irish Green Street, Limavady C675227. (Limavady DH from 1930, later Roe Valley Hospital. Now community use.) PNI.

Co. Donegal

Ballyshannon (15-Jun-1840 10+18) **W**: 600, 1-Oct-1842, 1-May-1843. Carrickboy Road, Ballyshannon G874610. (DH. Now council depot and day centre.) DON.

Donegal (7-Nov-1840 11+18) **W**: 500, 15-Sep-1842, 21-May-1843. Upper Main Street, Donegal G935785. (DH. Mostly dem. Still Donegal DH.) DON.

Dunfanaghy (2-Jul-1841 10+18) **W**: 300, 15-Mar-1844, 24-Jun-1845. N56, 0.3m SE of Dunfanaghy C014369. (Closed 1922 then shop, later council depot. Part dem. Now museum.) DON.

Glenties (15-Jul-1841 14+23) **W**: 500, 22-Sep-1845, 24-Jul-1846. Main Road, Glenties G816946. (DH from 1922. Dem. 1960. Site now school.) DON.

Inishowen (18-Sep-1840 21+23) **W**: 600, 18-Sep-1843, 1-Oct-1843. Convent Road, Carndonagh C465444. (DH from *c.*1922. Dem. 1958. Now Community Hospital.) DON.

Letterkenny (7-Jun-1841 14+21) **W**: 500, 16-Dec-1844, 14-Mar-1845. Kilmacrenan (now High) Road, Letterkenny C169119. (Mostly dem. Now Donegal County Museum.) DON.

Milford (28-Jun-1841 12+21) **W**: 400, 24-Dec-1845, 1-Apr-1846. R245, Glenkeen, Milford C203257. (Dem. Site now agricultural market.) DON.

Stranorlar (10-Dec-1840 10+18) **W**: 400, 16-Mar-1844, 1-May-1844. The Glebe, Stranorlar H161952. (CH. Dem. Site now St Joseph's Community Hospital.) DON.

Co. Down

Banbridge (22-Feb-1839 23+29) **W**: 800, 14-Jun-1841, 22-Jun-1841. Ballygowan Road, Banbridge J121457. (Dem. 1930. Site then Banbridge DH until *c.*2003.) PNI.

Downpatrick (3-Jan-1840 24+27) **W**: 1000, 22-Aug-1842, 17-Sep-1842. Strangford Road, Downpatrick J489459. (Later factory/offices and Quoile Hospital. Mostly dem.) PNI.

Kilkeel (29-Jul-1839 10+16) **W**: 300, 16-Aug-1841, 1-Sep-1841. Newry Street, Kilkeel J303148. (Mourne DH from 1927. Mostly dem.) PNI.

Newry (3-May-1839 23+31) **W**: 1000, 14-Dec-1841, 16-Dec-1841. Hospital Road, Newry J077268. (Now Daisy Hill Hospital. Mostly dem.) PNI.

Newtownards (3-Sep-1839 16+24) **W**: 600, 21-Dec-1841, 1-Jan-1842. Circular Street (now Road), Newtownards J481742. (Ards Hospital from 1932.) PNI.

Co. Dublin

Balrothery (1-Apr-1839 12+23) **W**: 400, 1-Feb-1841, 15-Mar-1841. R132, 2m NW of Lusk O194557. (Housed Belgian refugees in WWI. Mostly dem. Now farm use.) NAI.

North Dublin (6-Jun-1839 9+33) **W**: 2000, 25-Mar-1840, 1-May-1840. North Brunswick Street, Dublin O147349. (Closed 1918 then military use. Dem.). **Scl**: St Vincent's Home, Navan Road, Cabra O114367. (Later St Vincent's special school. Part dem.) NAI.

South Dublin (6-Jun-1839 8+33) **W**: 2000, 25-Mar-1840, 24-Apr-1840. James Street, Dublin O136337. (CHH. St Kevin's (later St James') Hospital from 1920s. Trinity College uses part of site. Mostly dem.). **Scl**: Pelletstown School, Navan Road, Cabra O112370. (AH from 1920s. Dem.) NAI.

Rathdown (8-Aug-1839 10+24) **W**: 600, 1-Sep-1841, 12-Oct-1841. Dublin Road, Loughlinstown O246230. (St. Columcille's Hospital from 1922. Part dem.) NAI.

Co. Fermanagh

Enniskillen (10-Aug-1840 20+30) **W**: 1000, 19-Mar-1844, 1-Dec-1845. Cornagrade Road, Enniskillen H235445. (Erne Hospital from 1964. Mostly dem.) PNI.

Lisnaskea (27-Jun-1840 14+18) **W**: 500, 1-Oct-1842, 25-Feb-1843. Main Street, Lisnaskea H362334. (Varied uses e.g. army billets, fire brigade HQ, residential.) PNI.

Lowtherstown (14-Sep-1840 9+18) **W**: 400, 28-Oct-1844, 1-Oct-1845. Church Street, Lowtherstown H234583. (Dem. Now Reihill Park housing estate.) PNI.

Co. Galway

Ballinasloe (6-Jun-1839 22+36) **W**: 1000, 20-Dec-1841, 1-Jan-1842. Society Street (now Sarsfield Road), Ballinasloe M847313. (Varied uses, e.g. slaughterhouse, shoe factory. Now supermarket. Mostly dem.) GAL.

Clifden (17-Aug-1840 4+12) **W**: 300, 22-Dec-1845, 1-Mar-1847. Galway Road, Clifden L665505. (Burnt *c.*1921. Dem. Now factory site.) GAL.

Galway (22-May-1839 12+37) **W**: 1000, 27-Dec-1841, 1-Mar-1842. Newcastle Road, Galway M289256. (Central Hospital 1920s-1956. Dem. Site now University College Hospital.) GAL.

Glenamaddy (24-Feb-1850 18+18) **W**: 500. Creggs Road, Glenamaddy M637617. (Mostly burnt 1921. Later orphanage and dispensary. Now farm use.) GAL.

Gort (20-Aug-1839 10+18) **W**: 500, 1-Dec-1841, 11-Dec-1841. George Street, Gort M455017. (Burnt *c.*1921. Now council depot.) GAL.

Loughrea (5-Sep-1839 15+24) **W**: 800, 17-Feb-1842, 26-Feb-1842. Lake Road, Loughrea M623156. (CH from 1923, now St Brendan's Hospital.) GAL.

Mountbellew (24-Feb-1850 14+14) **W**: 500. College Road, Mountbellew Bridge M678457. (Became vocational/technical school.) GAL.

Oughterard (9-Oct-1849 14+14) **W**: 600. Station Road, Oughterard M117422. (Burnt *c.*1921. Site now housing estate.) GAL.

Portumna (24-Feb-1850 15+16) **W**: 600. St Brigid's Road, Portumna M850054. (Later council depot, now heritage centre.) GAL.

Tuam (19-Sep-1839 13+31) **W**: 800, 15-Aug-1842, 1-May-1846. Dublin Road, Tuam M441512. (AH from *c.*1922. Dem. Now housing estate.) GAL.

Co. Kerry

Cahirciveen (19-Sep-1840 9+19) **W**: 800, 19-Aug-1844, 17-Oct-1846. Bahaghs, 3m E of Cahirciveen V512801. (DH in 1920s. Part dem. Derelict.) KER.

Dingle (22-Feb-1848 19+22) **W**: 700, opened *c.*1849. Ashmount Terrace, Dingle Q442016. (DH later Dingle Hospital. Closed 2010.) KER.

Kenmare (21-Sep-1840 7+15) **W**: 500, 19-Aug-1844, 23-Oct-1845. Now Sunnyhill Grove, Kenmare V911718. (Mostly dem. 1936. Site now Kenmare Community Hospital.) KER.

Killarney (18-Sep-1840 11+27) **W**: 800, 1-Nov-1844, 1-Apr-1845. Workhouse (now Rock) Road, Killarney V960915. (CH & DH. Now St Columbanus care home.) KER.

Listowel (27-Mar-1840 21+27) **W**: 700, 17-Aug-1844, 13-Feb-1845. Convent Road, Listowel Q981339. (DH. Dem. Site now Listowel Community Hospital.) KER.

Tralee (30-Mar-1840 18+34) **W**: 1000, 1-Sep-1842, 1-Feb-1844. Quill Street, Tralee Q854140. (County Hospital, later St Catherine's until 1980s. Now council offices.) KER.

Co. Kildare

Athy (16-Jan-1841 14+24) **W**: 600, 20-Nov-1843, 1-Jan-1844. Woodstock Street, Athy S674946. (CH. Now St Vincent's hospital. Part dem.) KID.

Celbridge (31-Jan-1839 15+19) **W**: 400, 26-May-1841, 1-Jun-1841. Big Lane (now Maynooth Road), Celbridge N972336. (Now paint factory.) KID.

Naas (12-Feb-1839 23+29) **W**: 550, 15-Jun-1841, 1-Aug-1841. Craddockstown Road, Naas N893187. (County Hospital & FH. Part dem. Now Naas General Hospital.) KID.

Co. Kilkenny

Callan (27-Mar-1839 12+25) **W**: 600, 21-Dec-1841, 25-Mar-1842. The Green (now Clonmel Road), Callan S410433. (Later knitwear factory. Now offices and council depot. Part dem.) KIK.

Castlecomer (9-Jun-1850 7+12) **W**: 500. S of St Mary's Chapel, Castlecomer S530723. (DH. Part dem. Now Castlecomer District Hospital.) KIK, NAI.

Kilkenny (1-Jul-1839 22+47) **W**: 1300, 24-Mar-1842, 21-Apr-1842. Hebron Road, Kilkenny S511563. (CH in 1920s. Later used as council depot. Dem. Site now shopping centre.) KIK, NAI.

Thomastown (9-Jun-1850 27+27) **W**: 600. Chapel Lane, Thomastown S589424. (St Columbkille's CH from 1923, now St Columba's Hospital.) KIK.

Urlingford (9-Jun-1850 16+17) **W**: 500 1-. Main Street, Urlingford S284637. (Dem. Now housing estate.) KIK, NAI.

Co. Laois (Queen's County)

Abbeyleix (3-Dec-1839 11+24) **W**: 500, 24-Mar-1842, 1-Jun-1842. Ballinakill Road, Abbeyleix S442847. (DH. Dem. Now Abbeyleix District Hospital.) LEX.

Donaghmore (diss. 1886) (9-Jun-1850 13+15) **W**: 400 1-. R435, 0.3m NW of Donaghmore S259807. (Closed 1886. Dairy use from 1927. Workhouse museum since 1989.) LEX.

Mountmellick (7-Dec-1839 16+30) **W**: 800, 31-Aug-1844, 1-Jan-1845. St Joseph's Terrace, Mountmellick N452069. (CH. Mostly dem. Now St Vincent's Hospital.) LEX.

Co. Leitrim

Carrick-on-Shannon (24-Aug-1839 15+23) **W**: 800, 1-Jul-1842, 21-Jul-1842. Summer Hill, Carrick-on-Shannon G943001. (DH & FH. Part dem. Now St Patrick's community Hospital.) LET.

Manorhamilton (30-Aug-1839 10+18) **W**: 500, 1-Sep-1842, 1-Dec-1842. Station Road, Manorhamilton G891394. (CHH. Our Lady's Hospital from 1936. Dem. c.1954.) LET.

Mohill (5-Sep-1839 13+22) **W**: 700, 25-Apr-1842, 1-Jun-1842. Hyde Street, Mohill N088966. (Dem. Now Hyde Terrace.) LET.

Co. Limerick

Croom (31-Mar-1850 20+20) **W**: 600. St Senan's Terrace, Croom R514418. (County Hospital. St Nessan's Hospital from 1956, now Mid-Western General Orthopaedic. Part dem.) LIM.

Glin (diss. 1891) (31-Mar-1850 13+13) **W**: 600. East Mall, Glin R134469. (Closed 1891). **Scl**: in former workhouse building from 1893. (Closed 1960s. Mostly dem.) LIM.

Kilmallock (9-Jan-1839 21+28) **W**: 800, 18-Feb-1841, 29-Mar-1841. Railway Road, Kilmallock R611275. (Mostly dem. Parts used as fire station and council depot.) LIM.

Limerick (20-Dec-1838 17+40) **W**: 1600, 18-May-1841, 20-May-1841. Shelbourne Road, Limerick R566576. (BHH. Part dem. Now St Camillus Hospital.) LIM.

Newcastle (28-Dec-1838 13+22) **W**: 550, 18-Feb-1841, 15-Mar-1841. Gortboy, Newcastle West R284342. (CH. Now St Ita's Hospital.) LIM.

Rathkeale (27-Dec-1838 19+30) **W**: 660, 18-Feb-1841, 26-Jul-1841. Holy Cross, Rathkeale R359422. (Later used as meat processing factory. Mostly dem.) LIM.

Co. Longford

Ballymahon (28-Apr-1850 18+20) **W**: 600. Off Main Street, Ballymahon N150565. (Closed c.1921. Site derelict for many years.) LOG.

Granard (6-Jun-1840 15+21) **W**: 600, 15-Aug-1842, 30-Sep-1842. Barrack Street, Granard N336813. (Closed c.1921. Dem. Site now school.) LOG.

Longford (13-May-1839 19+30) **W**: 1000, 24-Mar-1842, 24-Mar-1842. Dublin Road, Longford N141749. (CHH. St Joseph's Hospital from 1952. Mostly dem. c.1970.) LOG.

Co. Louth

Ardee (21-Aug-1839 13+24) **W**: 600, 25-Apr-1842, 13-May-1842. John Street, Ardee N958901. (Used as vocational school then factory from 1970s. Part dem.) LOU.

Drogheda (18-Jun-1839 12+25) **W**: 800, 18-Nov-1841, 16-Dec-1841. Dublin Road, Drogheda O095749. (DH. Mostly dem. Now St Mary's Hospital.) LOU.

Dundalk (18-Jun-1839 19+36) **W**: 800, 1-Mar-1842, 14-Mar-1842. Ardee Road, Dundalk J032056. (DH. Mostly dem. 1987. Site now care charity premises.) LOU.

Co. Mayo

Ballina (3-Jul-1840 17+33) **W**: 1200, 14-Nov-1842, 1-Nov-1843. Lord Edward Street, Ballina G237190. (DH. Dem. 1930s. Site now Ballina District Hospital.) MAY.

Ballinrobe (7-Nov-1839 14+26) **W**: 800, 24-Mar-1842, 26-May-1842. Kilmaine Road, Ballinrobe M193637. (Mostly burnt 1922. Now council depot.) MAY.

Belmullet (30-Sep-1849 13+15) **W**: 500. Bridge Road, Belmullet F704328. (FH in 1920s.

Dem. Site now Belmullet Community Hospital.) MAY.

Castlebar (9-Nov-1839 10+21) **W**: 700, 1-Aug-1842, 22-Oct-1842. Davitt's Terrace, Castlebar M146911. (CH. Dem. Site now Sacred Heart Hospital.) MAY, LSE.

Claremorris (24-Feb-1850 19+19) **W**: 800. Ballindine Road, Claremorris M343742. (Closed 1918. Barracks 1918-22. Bacon factory 1933-89. Mostly dem.) MAY.

Killala (30-Sep-1849 8+13) **W**: 500. Church Street, Killala G204298. (Closed 1917. Dem.) MAY.

Newport (diss. 1885) (9-Oct-1849 11+13) **W**: 500. Mulranny Road, Newport L985946. (Closed 1885. Part dem. NRU.) MAY.

Swineford (or Swinford) (2-Apr-1840 12+21) **W**: 700, 30-Nov-1842, 14-Apr-1846. Barrack (now Bridge) Street, Swinford M378998. (FH from c.1923. Mostly dem. Now Swineford District Hospital.) MAY.

Westport (13-Jul-1840 10+26) **W**: 1000, 1-Nov-1842, 1-Nov-1845. Quay Road, Westport L991841. (Closed c.1918. Dem. Now housing estate.) MAY, LSE.

Co. Meath

Dunshaughlin (1-Apr-1839 12+26) **W**: 400, 12-May-1841, 17-May-1841. Derrockstown, Dunshaughlin N978504. (WWI Belgian refugee depot. Part derelict. NRU.) MEA.

Kells (8-Jul-1839 14+25) **W**: 600, 25-Apr-1842, 23-May-1842. Oliver Plunkett Road, Kells N736765. (Dem. 1960s.) MEA.

Navan (25-Jun-1839 12+21) **W**: 500, 28-Mar-1842, 1-Aug-1842. Commons Road, Navan N861675. (County Hospital now Our Lady's Hospital.) MEA.

Oldcastle (6-Jan-1840 13+21) **W**: 600, 1-Jul-1842, 12-Aug-1842. Milbrook Road, Oldcastle N550798. (WWI military use. Dem. 1950s.) MEA.

Trim (22-May-1839 11+21) **W**: 500, 29-Sep-1841, 11-Oct-1841. Patrick Street, Trim N801563. (CH. St Joseph's Hospital. Part dem.) MEA. **Scl**: Dublin Road, Trim N802565. (Former prison converted 1890 into District School. Dem.) MEA.

Co. Monaghan

Carrickmacross (5-Nov-1839 14+16) **W**: 500, 25-Oct-1842, 11-Feb-1843. Shercock Road, Carrickmacross H836040. (Hosiery factory 1920s. Technical school from 1930s. Now community use. Part dem.) MOG.

Castleblayney (or Castleblaney) (8-Nov-1839 18+22) **W**: 800, 25-Oct-1842, 15-Dec-1842. New Street (now Laurel Hill), Castleblayney H821197. (CH from 1923. Now St Mary's Hospital. Mostly dem.) MOG.

Clones (3-Feb-1840 8+18) **W**: 600, 15/11/1942, 23-Feb-1843. Mccurtain Street, Clones H502252. (Dem. except fever hospital used until 1966. Later meat factory.) MOG.

Monaghan (4-Nov-1839 21+27) **W**: 900, 25-Apr-1842, 25-May-1842. Glaslough Street, Monaghan H672344. (County Hospital & FH from 1923. Dem.) MOG.

Co. Offaly (King's County)

Edenderry (7-May-1839 17+22) **W**: 600, 21-Dec-1841, 19-Mar-1842. Chapel Road (now St Mary's Street), Edenderry N623321. (Later use as school, barracks, factory, council depot. Dem. 1970s. Site now nusring home.) OFF.

Parsonstown (8-May-1839 21+29) **W**: 800, 14-Mar-1842, 1-Apr-1842. Elm Grove, Birr (formerly Parsonstown) N068047. (NRU.) OFF.

Tullamore (16-Sep-1839 15+24) **W**: 700, 25-Apr-1842, 1-Jun-1842. Emmett Road, Tullamore N338255. (CHH. Dem. 1970s.) OFF.

Co. Roscommon

Boyle (20-Aug-1839 16+19) **W**: 700, 1-Dec-1841, 31-Dec-1841. Elphin Street, Boyle G800023. (DH. Dem. Site now day centre.,) ROS.

Castlerea (14-Sep-1839 18+27) **W**: 1000, 1-Oct-1842, 30-May-1846. Knockroe, Castlerea M684794. (Dem. 1920s. Site NRU.) ROS.

Roscommon (13-Sep-1839 18+23) **W**: 900, 1-Oct-1842, 1-Nov-1843. Golf Links Road, Roscommon M878637. (CHH. Now Sacred Heart Hospital.) ROS.

Strokestown (24-Feb-1850 20+20) **W**: 600. Lisnaree, Strokestown M922802. (Closed *c.*1922. Dem. Now housing.) ROS.

Co. Sligo

Dromore West (30-Sep-1849 17+17) **W**: 400. N59, 2m W of Dromore West G401332. (Part burnt 1923. Later courthouse and store. NRU since 1983.) NAI, SLI.

Sligo (17-Jul-1839 23+39) **W**: 1200, 16-Nov-1841, 17-Dec-1841. Ballytivnan Road, Sligo G694368. (CHH from *c.*1923. Now St John's Hospital. Mostly dem.) SLI.

Tubbercurry (24-Feb-1850 21+19) **W**: 500. Humbert Street, Tubbercurry G522122. (Closed *c.*1921. Dem. Site NRU.) SLI.

Co. Tipperary

Borrisokane (9-Jun-1850 13+16) **W**: 600 1-. 1m NE of Borrisokane R920944. (Now community college.) TIP.

Carrick-on-Suir (25-May-1839 13+21) **W**: 500, 10-May-1842, 1-Jul-1842. Well Road (now Sean Treacy Park), Carrick-on-Suir S394220. (Burnt 1920s.) TIP.

Cashel (30-Jan-1839 17+24) **W**: 700, 15-Dec-1841, 28-Jan-1842. Deer Park Road, Cashel S073400. (CH. Now St Patrick's Hospital.) TIP.

Clogheen (2-Feb-1839 12+18) **W**: 500, 24/03/1942, 29-Jun-1842. Convent Road, Clogheen S004134. (Mostly burnt 1923. DH.) TIP.

Clonmel (18-Mar-1839 10+21) **W**: 600, 1-Jan-1841, 1-Jan-1841. Convent Road, Clonmel S192221. (Closed 1853.) **W**: 1200. Western Road, Clonmel S194226. (DH. Closed 1924. Now St Joseph's Hospital.) TIP.

Nenagh (9-Feb-1839 25+34) **W**: 1000, 1-Dec-1841, 28-Apr-1842. Tyone, Nenagh R870785. (Part burnt *c.*1923. DH. Dem. Site now St Joseph's Hospital.) TIP.

Roscrea (8-May-1839 19+28) **W**: 700, 24-Mar-1842, 1-May-1842. Templemore Road, Roscrea S141876. (DH & FH. Dem. Site now commercial premises.) TIP.

Thurles (28-Mar-1839 21+31) **W**: 700, 25-Apr-1842, 1-Nov-1842. Castlemeadows, Thurles S119593. (CH & DH. Dem. 2003. Now Hospital of the Assumption.) TIP.

Tipperary (30-Jan-1839 20+32) **W**: 700, 1-Jun-1841, 1-Jul-1841. Station Road, Tipperary R891351. (WW1 military use. DH. Now residential/commercial use.) TIP.

Co. Tyrone

Castlederg (7-May-1839 14+14) **W**: 200, 20-Feb-1841, 1-Mar-1841. Lurganboy Road, Castlederg H264849. (Closed 1929. Mostly dem. 1930s then school and Derg Valley Hospital.) PNI.

Clogher (17-Apr-1841 17+24) **W**: 500, 1-Mar-1844, 1-Mar-1844. Tullybroom Road, Clogher H537523. (Closed 1916. Various later uses e.g. factory, stores, OPH, offices. Part derelict.) PNI.

Cookstown (22-Aug-1839 16+21) **W**: 600, 31-May-1842, 31-May-1842. Burn Road, Cookstown H804784. (Dem. Site now council depot.) PNI.

Dungannon (20-Jul-1839 19+26) **W**: 800, 16-May-1842, 23-Jun-1842. Thomas Street, Dungannon H797631. (Dem. Site now South Tyrone Hospital.) PNI.

Gortin (diss. 1889) (7-May-1839 13+14) **W**: 200, 17-Feb-1842, 19-Feb-1842. Chapel Lane, Gortin H498859. (Closed 1889. Mostly dem. Site now St Patrick's church.) PNI.

Omagh (9-May-1839 29+30) **W**: 800, 24-Aug-1841, 24-Aug-1841. Mountjoy Road, Omagh H454733. (Dem. Site now Omagh General Hospital.) PNI.

Strabane (8-Apr-1839 24+25) **W**: 800, 18-Nov-1841, 18-Nov-1841. Londonderry (now

Derry) Road, Strabane H349986. (DH (later Strabane Hospital) from *c.*1922 and council offices. Mostly dem.) PNI.

Co. Waterford

Dungarvan (28-Mar-1839 15+30) **W**: 600, 27-Dec-1841, 1-Jul-1844. Springmount, Dungarvan X248928. (CH & DH. Now St Joseph's Hospital.) WAT.

Kilmacthomas (9-Jun-1850 16+17) **W**: 500 Union Road, Kilmacthomas S406056. (Closed 1919. Now residential/business use.) WAT.

Lismore (30-Mar-1839 9+24) **W**: 500, 1-Dec-1841, 18-May-1842. Chapel Street, Lismore X046975. (Later St Carthages Hospital. Part dem. NRU.) WAT, NAI.

Waterford (20-Apr-1839 25+34) **W**: 900, 15-Mar-1841, 20-Apr-1841. Johnstown Road (now John's Hill), Waterford S612112. (St Patrick's County Hospital from 1921. Part dem.) WAT.

Co. Westmeath

Athlone (3-Apr-1839 19+27) **W**: 900, 20-Oct-1841, 22-Nov-1841. Abbey Road, Athlone N038418. (DH. Part dem. Varied later uses. Part of site now Athlone Hospital.) WEM.

Castletowndelvin (Delvin) (11-Aug-1850 19+17) **W**: 400 1-. Ballyhealy Road, Delvin N602624. (Closed 1920s. Dem.) WEM.

Mullingar (22-Oct-1839 26+30) **W**: 800, 1-Oct-1842, 1-Dec-1842. Castlepollard Road, Mullingar N429541. (CHH. Now St Mary's Hospital.) WEM.

Co. Wexford

Enniscorthy (22-Jan-1840 14+30) **W**: 600, 1-Sep-1842, 11-Nov-1842. Munster Hill, Enniscorthy S969392. (CH from 1922. St John's Hospital since 1940s.) WEX.

Gorey (14-Dec-1839 10+24) **W**: 500, 21-Dec-1841, 22-Jan-1842. 1m SW of Gorey T145587. (DH. Later used as leather factory. Mostly dem. NRU.) WEX.

New Ross (23-Mar-1840 19+30) **W**: 900, 21-Dec-1841, 1-Jul-1842. Charleton Hill, New Ross S721269. (DH. Dem. Site now New Ross Community Hospital.) WEX.

Wexford (10-Jun-1840 14+24) **W**: 600, 1-Jul-1842, 25-Jul-1842. Old Hospital Road, Wexford T036224. (County Hospital & FH. Derelict. Site now part of Wexford General Hospital.) WEX.

Co. Wicklow

Baltinglass (21-Nov-1839 11+21) **W**: 500, 1-Sep-1841, 28-Oct-1841. R747, 1m SE of Baltinglass S887875. (Dem. Site now Baltinglass District Hospital.) WIC.

Rathdrum (25-Sep-1839 12+30) **W**: 600, 21-Dec-1841, 1-Mar-1842. Union Lane, Rathdrum T183885. (CH. Dem. Site now St Colman's Hospital.) WIC.

Shillelagh (12-Jul-1839 19+24) **W**: 400, 21-Dec-1841, 18-Feb-1842. Chapel Lane, Shillelagh S982676. (FH in 1920s. Dem. Site now Church of the Immaculate Conception.) WIC.

POST-1845 STATUTORY POORHOUSES IN SCOTLAND

The list below gives details of the 'statutory' poor law institutions that operated in Scotland after 1845, overseen by the Scottish Board of Supervision and its successor bodies.[486] The list is ordered by county based on the location of each authority's poorhouse(s). The format of each entry is described by means of the following (fictitious) example:

Lochladdy Cmb. P: Macintyre Road, Lochladdy NS691838. (Closed 1883. Dem.) **P**: 33 Johnston Street, Lochladdy NS689841 1883 by J. McGregor. (Lochside House PLI. Now OPH) STG.

The above entry indicates that the Lochladdy Combination's first poorhouse was on Macintyre Road, Lochladdy with UK National Grid Reference NS691838; the institution closed in 1838 and the building is now demolished. The Combination opened a second poorhouse in 1883 at 33 Johnston Street, Lochladdy with Grid Reference NS689846 and designed by J. McGregor.; the establishment later became Lochside House Poor Law Institution, and the premises are now an old people's home. Surviving local records for the Lochladdy Combination are held at Stirling Council Archives (see Appendix M).

Abbreviations used in the list are shown below:

c.	circa	m/w	merged with
Ch	Children's residential home/school	NRU	Now residential use
Cmb	Combination	OPH	Old People's Home
cv	converted	P	Poorhouse
dem	demolished	PLI	Poor Law Institution
H	Hospital/Infirmary	ren	renamed
Men	Mental institution	WWI	First World War
MH	Military Hospital		

Aberdeenshire

Aberdeen P: Nelson Street, Aberdeen NJ942071 1847 by T. Mackenzie & J. Matthews (Closed 1907. Later St Peter's School. Dem.) **P**: Skene (now Queen's Road), Aberdeen NJ897062 1907 by A. Brown & G. Watt (Oldmill MH in WWI/2. Woodend Hospital from 1927.) ABD, ABH.

Buchan Cmb. P: Bank Road, (New) Maud NJ925476 1868 by A. Ellis (Maud Home PLI. Maud Hospital from *c.*1948.) ABH.

Old Machar (m/w Aberdeen 1905) P: St Machar's Place (now Fonthill Road), Aberdeen NJ933051 1853 by W. Henderson (Closed 1907 then Fonthill barracks. Dem. Now housing.) ABD, ABH.

Angus (Forfarshire)

Arbroath Cmb. P: Brechin Road, Arbroath NO641417 1864 by W. Aitkenhead (Rosebank Home PLI. Closed *c.*1935. Site now housing.) ANS.

Brechin P: Infirmary Street, Brechin NO603604 1878 (SP from 1918. St Drostan's House PLI. Now OPH.) ANS.

Dundee (Cmb. From 1879) P: Duncarse House, Perth Road, Dundee NO368300 cv. 1925 by C. Wilson (Children's home until 1980s.) **P**: Molison Street, Dundee NO410317 1855 by W.L. Moffat (WWI MH. PLI. Rowans OPH from *c.*1948. Dem. 1977. Now sports ground.) DND, DNU.

Forfar P: Arbroath Road, Forfar NO463506 1861 by D. Smart (Lordburn House PLI. Now The Gables care home. Mostly dem.) ANS.

Kirriemuir P: Beechwood Place, Kirriemuir NO386532 *c.*1850 by L Falconer (SP from 1913. Beechie House PLI from 1930. Now guesthouse.) ANS.

Liff & Benvie (jnd. Dundee Cmb. 1879) P: Blackness Road, Dundee NO387303 1864 (WWI troop billets then used by Logie School. Dem. *c.*1930.) DND, DNU.

Argyll

Campbeltown P: Witchburn Road, Campbeltown NR715203 1861 by J. Honeyman (Witchburn House PLI. Witchburn Hospital from 1948. Now offices.) ARL.

Islay Cmb. P: Church (now High) Street, Bowmore NR316597 1865 by J.C. Walker (Gortanvogie House PLI. Dem. Site now Islay Hospital.) ARL.

Lochgilphead Cmb. P: Hospital Road, Lochgilphead NR869884 1861 by D. Crow. (Used for mental patients from 1919. Now offices.) ARL.

Lorn Cmb. P: Miller Road, Oban NM862293 1863 by J. McKillop (West Highland Rest PLI. Dalintart Hospital from 1948. Dem) ARL.

Mull Cmb. P: B8073 1m SW of Tobermory NM492544 1862 by D. Cousin (Closed 1923. Mostly dem. 1974.) ARL, MUL.

Ayrshire

Ayr P: Mill Street, Ayr NS341216 1756 (Closed *c.*1858. Dem. Site now flats.) AYR.

Cunninghame Cmb. P: Sandy Lane, Irvine NS310406 1858 by W.A. Railton (Cunninghame Home PLI. Ravenspark Hospital from 1948. Dem.) AYR.

Kyle Cmb. P: Holmston Road, Ayr NS342214 1860 by W.L. Moffat (Kyle Home PLI then council offices.) AYR.

Maybole Cmb. P: Ladyland Road, Maybole NS297098 1863 by J. Bowman (Closed *c.*1920. Later offices and Carrick House welfare centre. Mostly dem. *c.*2000.) AYR.

Banffshire

Rathven H: Barhill Road, Buckie NJ415646 1911 by W. Hendry & R.M. Fulton (Rathven Parish Hospital, later Seafield Hospital.) ABD.

Bute

Rothesay P: High Street, Rothesay NS087636 1926 (Thomson Home PLI, now Thomson House OPH.) GLG.

Caithness

Latheron Cmb. P: Causeway Mire Road, Braehungie ND184373 1858 by W.L. Moffat (Latheron Town & County Home PLI. Dem.) CAI.

Thurso Cmb. P: Thurso Road, Halkirk ND128599 1856 by W.L. Moffat (Closed 1917. Later residential use.) CAI.

Dumfriesshire

Dumfries P: Rosevale Street, Dumfries NX982757 1854 Henderson (Rosevale House PLI. Cresswell Maternity Hospital from *c.*1948. Dem.) DFS.

Kirkpatrick Fleming Cmb. (ren. Notwen c.1922) P: Off B7076, Kirkpatrick Fleming NY274707 1853 by J. Hodgson (Notwen House PLI then OPH.) DFS.

Upper Nithsdale Cmb. P: Gatelawbridge NX902962 1855 by W.L. Moffat (Rowantree House PLI. Closed 1970s. NRU.) DFS.

Dunbartonshire

Dumbarton Cmb. P: Townend Road, Dumbarton NS403762 1865 by J.C. Walker (Townend PLI then Hospital from 1948. Dem 1980s. Site now OPH.) DNB.

East Lothian (Haddingtonshire)

East Lothian Cmb. P: Preston Road, East Linton NT590775 1864 by Peddie & Kinnear (Prestonkirk Home PLI then OPH. Now library and day centre.) ELN.

Fife

Dunfermline P: Cemetery (now Leys Park) Road, Dunfermline NT100879 1843 by T. Brown II (WWI Red Cross Hospital. PLI. Northern Hospital from 1948. Now nursing home.) FIF.

Dysart Cmb. P: 100 Station Road, Thornton NT297978 1860 by J.C. Walker (Thornton Home PLI, closed 1943. Dem. 1960s.) FIF.

Kirkcaldy Cmb. P: Off A921 0.5m NE of Kinghorn NT275878 1849 by W.L. Moffatt (Abden Home PLI. Now Linton Court residential.) FIF, KKC.

Inverness-shire

Inverness P: Old Edinburgh Road, Inverness NH672441 1861 by J. Matthews & W. Lawrie (Muirfield PLI, later Hilton Hospital. NRU.) HHS.

Long Island Cmb. P: Lochmaddy, North Uist NF915692 1884 by Kinnear & Peddie (Asylum from 1907 then Long Island PLI. Lochmaddy Hospital *c.*1948–2001.) HEB.

Skye Cmb. P: 12 Shulishader (now Viewfield Road), Portree NG476435 1860 by A. Ross & W.C. Joass (School hostel from 1933. Now used by Portree High School.) HCA.

Kincardineshire

Kincardineshire Cmb. P: Woodcot Brae, Stonehaven NO866856 1867 by W. Henderson (Woodcot Hospital 1930–1990s. NRU.) ABH.

Kirkcudbrightshire

Kirkcudbrightshire Cmb. P: Burnside Loaning, Kirkcudbright **P**: NX691518 1850 by J.A. Bell (Burnside House PLI. Closed 1949. Dem. Now housing estate.) DFS.

Lanarkshire

Barony (m/w Glsgow 1904) P: Atlas Street (now Edgefauld Road), Glasgow NS612673 1852 by Clarke & Bell (Barnhill PLI. Foresthall Institution *c.*1945–83. Dem. Now housing estate.) GLG.

Cambusnethan (ren. Omoa 1903) Cmb. P: Park Street, Motherwell NS756567 1867 (Closed *c.*1905. Dem.) **P**: Bellside Road, Cleland NS804582 1904 by A. Cullen (County Hospital from 1930s. Cleland Hospital from *c.*1948.) NLA.

Dalziel P: Airbles Farm Road, Mothwerwell NS742560 1905 by A. Cullen (PAI then Airbles Hospital and Avon Lodge OPH. Dem. 1980s.) NLA.

Glasgow (m/w Barony 1904) P: Parliamentary Road, Glasgow NS594658 1809 (Closed *c.*1904 then dem.) GLG. **H**: 133 Balornock Road, Glasgow NS612689 1904 by J. Thomson

& R.D. Sandilands (WWI MH. Now Stobhill General Hospital. Part dem.) **H**: 247-9 Duke Street, Glasgow NS607651 1904 by AH Tiltman (Eastern District Hospital closed 1996. Dem.) **H**: 63 Possil Road, Glasgow NS586670 1904 by A. Cullen & J. Lochhead (WWI MH. Western District Hospital then Oakbank Hospital from 1965. Dem.) **Ch**: Dunclutha (home for young invalids), Shore Road (now Marine Parade), Dunoon NS183784 cv. *c*.1912 **Ch**: Girls' Training School, Dunoon cv. 1911 from former cottage hospital. **Men**: Stoneyetts, Chryston NS695717 1910 (Later Stoneyetts Hospital. Closed 1992. Dem.) GLG.

Govan P: Dale (now Tradeston) Street, Govan cv. 1845 (Closed *c*.1850. Dem.) **P**: Eglinton Street, Govan NS584637 cv. 1852 by R. Black & J. Salmon (Closed 1872. Dem.) **P/H/ Men**: 1345 Govan Road, Merryflatts NS535659 1872 by J. Thomson (WWI MH. Southern General Hospital from 1923.) GLG.

Hamilton Cmb. P: Bothwell Road, Hamilton NS717562 1867 by J.G. Peat (Hamilton Home PLI. Dem. *c*.1980.) GLG.

Lanark P: Broomgate, Lanark NS879435 <1845 (Closed *c*.1883. Dem.) **P/H**: Hyndford Road, Lanark NS892431 *c*.1883 (Crosslaw Home PLI. Now OPH and Lockhart Hospital.) GLG.

New Monkland P: Commonhead Street, Airdie NS757664 1850 by J. Thomson (Thrashbush House PLI. Dem. 1980s. Now sports ground.) NLA.

Old Monkland P: Hospital Street, Coatbridge NS731636 1861 by R. Baird (Old Monkland Home PLI. Coathill Hospital from *c*.1948.) NLA.

Midlothian

Dalkeith Cmb. P: Bonnyrigg Road, Dalkeith NT324665 1849 by W.L. Moffatt (Westfield Park PLI then OPH. Now offices etc. Part dem.) NAS.

Edinburgh (absorbed St Cutherbert's 1894) P: Port Bristo, Edinburgh NT257731 1743 (Closed *c*.1869. Mostly dem.) **P**: Glenlockhart Road, Craiglockhart NT234700 1869 by G Beattie & Son (Later Greenlea OPH. NRU.) **Ch**: Crewe Road, Craigleith NT231751 *c*.1912 by R.M. Cameron (Later used as nurses' home.) **Ch**: Balgreen Road, Craiglockhart NT221723 cv. *c*.1921 (Closed *c*.1929. Dem.) EDI.

Edinburgh Canongate (m/w St Cutherbert's 1873) P: Tolbooth Wynd, Edinburgh NT264739 1761 (Closed *c*.1873. Later used as 'epidemic hospital'. Dem.) EDI.

Edinburgh St Cuthbert's (Cmb. from 1873) P: St Cuthbert's Lane, Edinburgh NT247733 1758 (Closed *c*.1868. Dem. Site now N end of West Approach Road.) **P**: Crewe Road, Craigleith NT230750 1868 by Peddie & Kinnear (WWI MH then Craigleith Hospital. Western General from 1930. Part dem.) EDI.

Inveresk Cmb. P: Haugh Road (now Wedderburn Terrace), Inveresk NT348714 1861 by Peddie & Kinnear (Inveresk PLI later Wedderburn House. NRU.) MLN.

Leith, North (m/w South Leith 1906) P: North Junction Street, Leith NT264765 1862 by P. Hamilton (Part dem *c*.1920. Site later David Kilpatrick school. Now OPH.) MLN.

Leith, South (m/w North Leith 1906) P: Great Junction Street, Leith NT266763 1850 by J.D. Peddie (Dem. 1911 to create garden area in front of Leith Hospital.) MLN.

Leith P: Seafield Street, Leith NT285754 1908 by J.M. Johnston (WWI MH. US Navy use from 1918. Eastern General Hospital *c*.1930–2007. Dem.) MLN.

Morayshire (Elgin)

Morayshire Cmb. P: Lossiemouth Road, Bishopmill NJ214639 1864 by A. & W. Reid (Craigmory PLI. Dem. 1970s. Site now care home.) MOR.

Nairn

Nairn Cmb. P: Balblair Road, Nairn NH878557 1861 by J. Matthews & W. Lawrie (Balblair Home PLI. Dem. 2000.) HCA.

Orkney

Orkney Cmb. P: Old Scapa Road, Orkney HY443103 1883 by T.S. Peace (Orkney County Home PLI. Now sheltered housing.) ORK.

Peeblesshire

Peebles Cmb. P: Rosetta Road, Peebles NT248410 c.1858 by by Peddie & McKay (WW1 MH. Cmb. dissolved 1919. Dem. 1930s. Now council offices.) SBA.

Perthshire

Perth P: Glasgow Road, Perth NO108235 1861 by A. Heiton (Bertha Home PLI. Later council offices. NRU. Part dem.) PER.

Upper Strathearn Cmb. P: Western Road, Auchterarder NN932116 1863 by J.C. Walker (Strathearn Home PLI. Now offices.) PER.

Weem (Athole & Breadalbane from 1862) Cmb. P: A827, 0.3m NW of Logierait NN966523 1863 by J.C. Walker (Cuil-an-Daraich Home PLI. NRU.) PER.

Renfrewshire

Abbey (Paisley from 1895) P: 15-17 Craw Road, Paisley NS479629 1850 (WW1 MH. PLI then Royal Alexandra Infirmary annexe. Dem.) PAI.

Greenock P: Captain Street, Greenock NS274759 c.1850 (Closed c.1878. Dem. Site now housing.) **P/H/Men**: Inverkip Road, Greenock NS252753 1878 by J. Starforth (WW1 MH. Smithston PLI. WW2 Canadian Navy use. Ravenscraig Hospital from 1948. Part dem.) GLG.

Paisley P: Sneddon Street, Paisley NS483644 1752 (Closed c.1895. Dem.) **Ch**: Barrholm, Largs cv. 1916 (Children's home.) **Ch**: Auchentorlie House, Paisley NS494636 cv. c.1911 (Closed c.1933. Dem.) **Ch**: Woodside House, Paisley NS472640 cv. c.1933 (Burnt down 1952.) PAI.

Renfrewshire Cmb. P: 837 Crookston Road, Glasgow NS521619 1906 by Macwhannell & Rogerson (WW1 military use. Crookston Home PLI then OPH. Dem. Now housing estate.) GLG.

Ross and Cromarty

Black Isle Cmb. P: Ness Road, Fortrose NH738566 1859 by Matthews & Lawrie (WW1 troop billets. Ness House PLI. NRU.) HCA.

Easter Ross Cmb. P: Scotsburn Road, Tain NH773811 1850 by A. Maitland (Arthurville PLI. NRU.) HCA.

Lewis Cmb. P: Coulregrein Road (now Westview Terrace), Stornoway NB424340 1895 J.M. Thomson (Coulregrein PLI. Dem. Site now OPH and day centre.) HEB.

Roxburghshire

Hawick Cmb. P: Drumlanrig Square, Hawick NT500142 1857 (WW1 military use. Drumnlanrig PLI then Hospital. NRU.) SBA.

Jedburgh Cmb. P: Lanton Road, Jedburgh NT647206 1852 (Closed c.1921. NRU.) SBA.

Kelso Cmb. P: Inch Road, Kelso NT726344 1854 (Inch Home PLI then Kelso Hospital.) SBA.

Selkirkshire

Galashiels Cmb. P: Kirk Brae, Galashiels NT486364 1860 by J.C. Walker (Windyknowe PLI the Eidon View OPH.) SBA.

Shetland (Zetland)

Shetland (or Zetland) Cmb. P: Scalloway (now Clickimin) Road, Lerwick HU469409 1887 by T.S. Peace (Zetland County Homes PLI then Brevik Hospital. Now offices.) SHE.

Stirlingshire

Falkirk P: Cow Wynd, Falkirk NS887795 1849 (Closed 1904. Dem. Site now primary school.) **P**: Windsor Road, Falkirk NS877794 1904 by A. Black (WW1 troop billets. Blinkbonny Home PLI. Windsor Hospital *c.*1948-89. Dem.) FLK.

Stirling Cmb. P: Union Street, Stirling NS795944 1857 by Peddie & Kinnear (Orchard House PLI. Part dem. Now day hospital. Part dem.) STG.

Sutherland

Sutherland Cmb. P: Matheson Road, Bonar Bridge NH616915 1865 by A. Maitland (Swordale PLI. Migdale Hospital from *c.*1948-2011.) HCA.

Wigtownshire

Rhins of Galloway Cmb. P: Dalrymple Street, Stranraer NX063602 1853 (Wigtownshire PLI later Waverley Home. Dem 1977.) DFS.

West Lothian (Linlithgowshire)

Linlithgow Cmb. P: Edinburgh Road, Linlithgow NT012769 1856 (St Michael's Home PLI. St Michael's Hospital. Dem. 1977. Site now day hospital.) WLN.

POST-1845 PARISH HOUSES IN SCOTLAND

The list below gives details of small 'parish houses', also known as almshouses, in Scotland after 1845. 486 Unlike the poorhouses listed in Appendix H, these were administered by local Parochial Boards and not overseen by the Scottish Board of Supervision. The list is ordered by county and then parish. The format of each entry is described by means of the following (fictitious) example:

Craigallan On A84 SW of Bowdale NS671638 1861 (NRU. Heather Cottage); (Location unidentified) by 1905.

The above entry indicates that from 1861 the parish of Craigallen had a parish house located on the A84 road to the south-west of Bowdale with UK National Grid Reference NS671638; the building is now in residential use and known as Heather Cottage. A second parish house was in operation by 1905 but its exact location is unknown.

Abbreviations used in the list are shown below:

c.	circa	NRU	Now residential use
cv	converted	OPH	Old People's Home
dem	demolished		

Aberdeenshire

Aboyne & Glentanar A93, Aboyne NJ547001 1840s (NRU. Kirkton Cottages.)
Alford Old Military Road, Alford NJ566153 1856 (NRU. Red Gates.)
Auchterless NE of Thomastown NJ729436 by 1901 (Dem.)
Birse Marywell NO581962 by 1869 (NRU. Market Stance Cottage.); Powlair Cottage, Powlair NO617912 by 1869 (NRU.); Waterside NO544977 by 1869 (Dem.)
Chapel of Garioch Hillhead of Pitbee, Chapel of Garioch NJ72245 1845 (Dem.)
Clatt Ford, near Kirktown of Clatt 1856.
Crimond SW of Crimond NK038552 by 1872 (Dem.)
Cruden NE of Hatton NK061378 by 1901 (NRU. Braco Cottage.)
Culsalmond E of Kirkton of Culsalmond NJ664325 by 1870 (Dem.)
Ellon Station Road, Ellon NJ953304 1849 (Dem.)
Forgue (Location unidentified) by 1864.
Foveran Newburgh NK000248 1854 (Dem.)
Fyvie Lethenty NJ807408 1860 (Mostly dem.)
Gartly Gartly Station 1874.
Huntly 26 George Street, Huntly NJ527398 1850s (Dem.)
Insch Market Green, Insch 1853.
Inverurie North Street, Inverurie NJ770218 by 1869 (Dem.)

Keig NE of Castle Forbes NJ624199 by 1868 (NRU.)

Kincardine O'Neil Monboddo Road, Torphins NJ626019 by 1881 (NRU. Treetops and Westwinds.)

Kinellar W of Blackburn 1864.

King Edward SW of Netherbrae NJ791587 by 1869 (Dem.)

Kinnethmont Kinnethmont NJ539287 1854 (Dem.)

Kintore W of Kintore NJ783163 1890s (Dem.)

Leochel Cushnie NE of Leochel Cushnie NJ538121 by 1869 (Derelict.)

Leslie Duncanston 1867.

Lonmay NE of New Leeds NK010550 1854 (NRU. The Poorhouse.)

New Deer W of New Deer NJ870469 by 1873 (NRU. Turfhill Cottage.)

New Machar Disblair Road, Summerhiil (now Newmachar) 1854 (Dem. 1960s.)

Old Deer Abbey Street, Old Deer NJ974477 1851 (Dem.)

Old Meldrum Upper Cowgate, Old Meldrum NJ807272 1865 (NRU. Webster Court.)

Oyne W of Oyne NJ662258 1844 (Dem.)

Peterhead 12 Ugie Street. Peterhead NK132466 1849 reb. 1898 (Eventide Home for the Elderly from 1950s. Dem. 2008.)

Premnay Auchleven NJ622238 by 1867 (Dem.)

Rathen Spillarsford Bridge NK013590 by 1870 (Dem. by 1900.)

Rhynie Rhynie NJ494274 1864 (Dem.)

St Fergus (Location unidentified) by 1864.

Strichen (Location unidentified) by 1867.

Tarves Red Moss NJ829317 1858 (Dem.); Craigdam NJ846302 1847 (NRU. Craigdam Cottages.)

Tough NE of Kirkton of Tough NJ628132 by 1900 (Dem.)

Turriff (Location unidentified)

Tyrie Low Street, New Pitsligo NJ882561 1850 (Dem. 1960s.)

Udny Udny 1860.

Angus (Forfarshire)

Brechin City Road, Brechin NO598602 1853 (Closed c.1878); Infirmary Street NO604605 1878 (Statutory poorhouse from 1918. Now OPH.)

Kirriemuir Muirhead Road, Kirriemuir NO386532 1860 (Statutory poorhouse from 1913. Now Beechie House.)

Montrose Alfred Street, Montrose NO717574 1865 (NRU.)

Argyll

Ardnamurchan Langal NM718701 by 1881 (NRU. Old Poor's House.); Scotstown by 1881.

Kilarrow Kilarrow 1874.

Lochgoilhead Lochgoilhead NN199015 1869 (Dem.)

Morven Lochaline NM677445 1864 (Now restaurant.)

Ayrshire

Auchinleck Main Street by 1881.

Kilmaurs (Location unidentified) by 1889.

Ochiltree 5 Mill Street, Ochiltree NS508212 by 1881.

Banffshire

Cabrach N of Cabrach NJ385277 by 1872 (Dem.)

Cullen (Location unidentified) by 1904.

Deskford W of Kirktown of Deskford NJ497612 by 1867 (Derelict.)

Gamrie and Macduff (Location unidentified) by 1890.

Grange NE of Grange NJ468554 by 1881 (Dem.)
Kirkmichael (Location unidentified) by 1901.
Marnoch (Location unidentified) by 1884.

Berwickshire
Ayton High Street, Ayton by 1881.
Bunkle & Preston Near Slighhouses by 1881.
Chirnside (Location unidentified) by 1881.
Coldingham Bow Street by 1881.
Duns (Location unidentified) by 1846.
Earlston Haughhead Road, Earlston by 1881.
Stichill Near Stichill police station by 1881.

Caithness
Dunnet N of West Dunnet ND211728 by 1873 (Dem.)
Halkirk (Location unidentified) by 1900.

Clackmannanshire
Clackmannan (Location unidentified) by 1874.

Dumfriesshire
Hoddom Ecclefechan by 1881.

Dunbartonshire
Cardross Brooks Road, Cardross by 1881.
Kirkintilloch Southbank Road, Kirkintilloch ND211728 by 1855 (NRU.)

East Lothian (Haddingtonshire)
Haddington Lydgait, Haddington NT512741 1855 (Disused by 1907.)

Fife
Ceres Ceres 1854.
St Andrews 36 North Street, St Andrews NO511167 1854 (Later 'Home of Rest'. Now offices.)

Inverness-shire
Abernethy Mackenzie Crescent, Nethy Bridge NJ012203 by 1871 (NRU. Lynstock Cottages.)
Alvie (Location unidentified) by 1874.
Boleskine and Abertarff Bunoich, Fort Augustus NH377096 1879 (NRU. The Old Almshouse.)
Dores (Location unidentified) by 1884.
Duthil SE of Carrbridge NH918216 1864 (Dem.)
Glenmoriston Dalchreichart NH291127 by 1903 (NRU.); Mill of Tore by 1881.
Kilmallie N of Fort William NN121769 by 1871; Muirshearlich NN132794 1887.
Kilmonivaig (Location unidentified) by 1886.
Kilmorack Beauly NH527463 by 1905 (Dem. 1960s.)
Kiltarlity Camault Muir, Kiltarlity by 1881; Glaichbea, Kiltarlity by 1881; Knockchoille, Eskdale by 1881; Kinneras by 1881.
Kingussie Laggan Cottages, E of Kingussie NH770012 1880 (NRU. The Auld Poorhouse.)
Kirkhill (Location unidentified) by 1864.
Laggan (Location unidentified) by 1890.

Portree (Location unidentified) by 1904.

Kincardineshire
Banchory-Ternan NE of Banchory NO702966 by 1868 (NRU. Tillybrake Cottages.)
Marykirk Main Street, Luthermuir by 1881.
St Cyrus St Cyrus by 1860s.
Strachan SE of Strachan NO684517 by 1868.

Kinross-shire
Kinross (Location unidentified) by 1879.

Lanarkshire
Lesmahagow N of Lesmahagow NS813405 by 1881. (Dem. 1960s.)

Morayshire (Elgin)
Cromdale Former parochial school NJ067284 1864 (Dem.); NE of Grantown-on-Spey
    NJ046283 1854 (Dem.); (Location unidentified) by 1902.
Knockando Bridge of Capnach, Upper Knockando NJ181429 by 1871 (Dem.)
St Andrews Lhanbryde Lhanbryde NJ270611 by 1881.

Orkney
Birsay and Harray E of Dounby, Mainland HY311205 by 1861 (Now outhouse.)
Cross and Burness Sanday 1884 (Now outhouse.)
Deerness Grindigar HY578059 by 1881 (NRU.)
Eday (Location unidentified) by 1881.
Lady Sanday HY681414 1884 (NRU. Riverside.)
Orphir S of Kirbister HY253130 1864 (Now used as outhouse.)
Stenness (Location unidentified) by 1904.
Westray Kirkbrae HY456459 1883 (NRU.)

Perthshire
Alyth Springbank, Alyth NO249484 1850 (NRU.)
Blairgowrie (Location unidentified) 1900.
Coupar Angus Campbell Street, Coupar Angus 1864.
Kenmore W of Acharn NN752435 1884 (NRU.)

Ross and Cromarty
Alness (Location unidentified) 1884.
Applecross (Location unidentified) by 1881.
Dingwall High Street, Dingwall NH550586 by 1867 (Closed 1888. Later site of Royal Hotel.);
    Burn Court, Dingwall NH545587 1888 (NRU.)
Glenshiel (Location unidentified) by 1894.
Kintail (Location unidentified) by 1884.
Lochalsh Auchtertyre NG840274 1855 (NRU. Tigh Bochd and Cluarn.)
Lochcarron Lochcarron NG899395 by 1875 (NRU. Poorhouse.)
Lochs Crosbost, Lewis by 1881.
Urquhart Balvaird by 1881; 44 Conon Bridge 1881.

Roxburghshire
Canonbie N of Canonbie by 1881.

Shetland (Zetland)
Dunrossness Vatchley HU401165 1868 (NRU.); Stove, near Hoswick.
Unst Vallafield, W of Baltasound HP596082 by 1882 (Derelict.)

Stirlingshire
Logie (Location unidentified) by 1874.

Sutherland
Assynt N of Lochinver NC090239 1847 (NRU. The Old Poorhouse.); Rienachait NC045302
   by 1908 (Dem.)
Clyne W of Brora NC894043 by 1873; rb. by 1906. (Now outhouse.)
Durness (Location unidentified) by 1854.
Eddrachillis (Location unidentified) by 1870s.
Kildonan The Barracks, N of Helmsdale ND025161 1820s (Dem.)
Rogart N of Rogart station NC736044 by 1880s (Dem.)
Tongue Strathtongue 1897.

Wigtownshire
Kirkcolm (Location unidentified) by 1850s.
Penninghame Newton Stewart NX408649 1896 (NRU. Fir Tree Cottage.)

APPENDIX J

MAPS OF POOR LAW UNIONS IN ENGLAND AND WALES

Map 1. Poor Law Union Boundaries – North of England, 1880s.
(*Reproduced by kind permission of GB Historical GIS Project.*)

Map 2. Poor Law Union Boundaries – North-west England and North Wales, 1880s.
(Reproduced by kind permission of GB Historical GIS Project.)

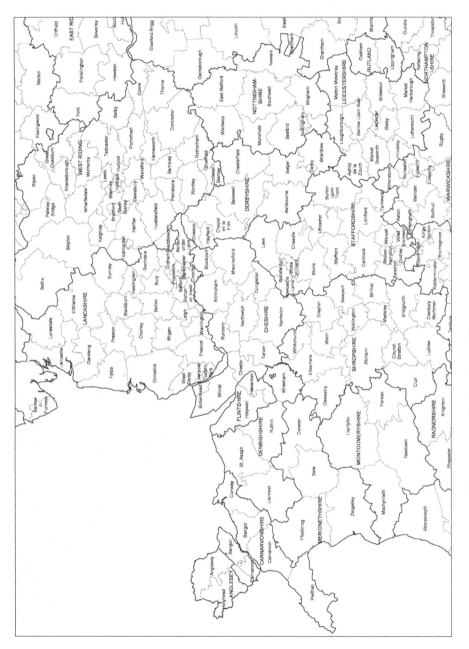

Map 3. Poor Law Union Boundaries – East Midlands and Norfolk, 1880s.
(*Reproduced by kind permission of GB Historical GIS Project.*)

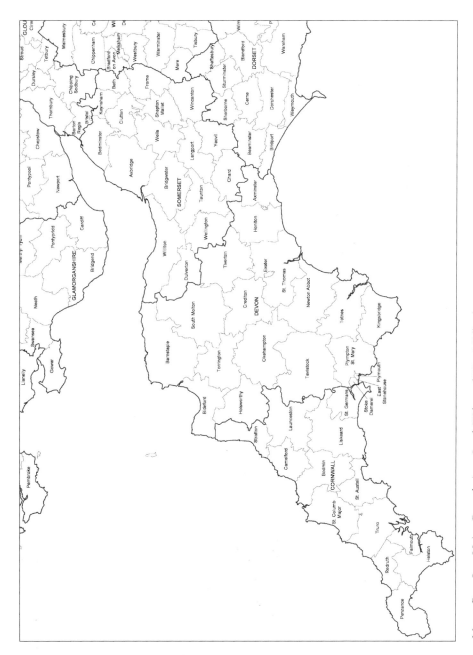

Map 4. Poor Law Union Boundaries – South Wales and West Midlands, 1880s.
(*Reproduced by kind permission of GB Historical GIS Project.*)

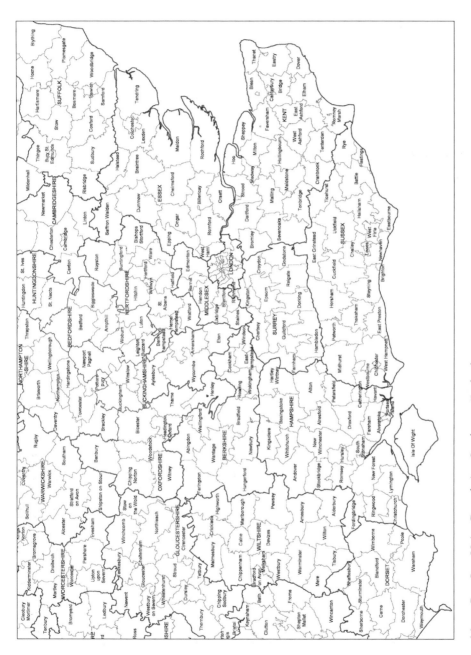

Map 5. Poor Law Union Boundaries – South–west England, 1880s.
(Reproduced by kind permission of GB Historial GIS Project.)

Map 6. Poor Law Union Boundaries – South-east England, 1880s.
(Reproduced by kind permission of GB Historical GIS Project.)

Map 7. Poor Law Union Boundaries – Metropolitan London, 1880s.
(*Reproduced by kind permission of GB Historical GIS Project.*)

APPENDIX K

MAPS OF POOR LAW UNIONS IN IRELAND

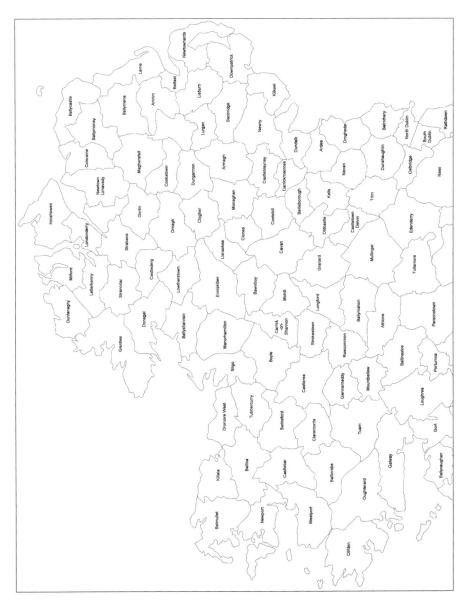

Map 1. Poor Law Union Boundaries – north of Ireland, 1871.
(Reproduced by kind permission of GB Historical GIS Project / Ian Gregory.)

Map 1. Poor Law Union Boundaries – south of Ireland, 1871.
(*Reproduced by kind permission of GB Historical GIS Project / Ian Gregory.*)

APPENDIX L

MAPS OF STATUTORY POORHOUSE LOCATIONS IN SCOTLAND

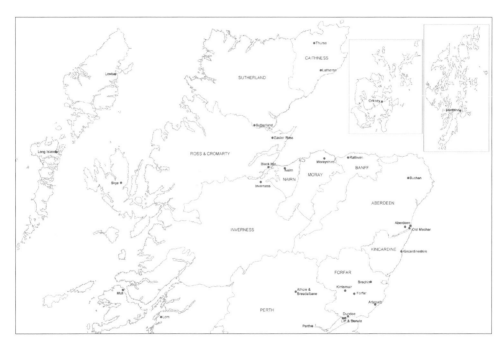

Map 1. Statutory Poorhouse Locations – north Scotland, 1845–1930.
(*Borders map by kind permission of GB Historical GIS Project.*)

Map 2. Statutory Poorhouse Locations – south Scotland, 1845-1930.
(*Borders map by kind permission of GB Historical GIS Project.*)

APPENDIX M

POOR LAW ARCHIVE REPOSITORIES IN THE UK AND IRELAND

Below is a list of the main archive repositories that hold poor law records in the United Kingdom and Republic of Ireland. The three-letter code at the start of each line is that used in the list of poor law authorities and institutions in Appendices E to G.

Before travelling to visit a repository, always check to confirm its location, opening times, and availability of the records you wish to consult. Records relating to individuals are often closed to public viewing for 100 years from the date of the latest entry in a particular volume.

ENGLAND

ABG	St Helen's Parish Office, St Helen's Court, Abingdon OX14 5BS.
BAA	Birmingham Archdiocesan Archives, Cathedral House, St Chad's Queensway, Birmingham, B4 6EU.
BAR	Barnsley Archives and Local Studies, Barnsley Central Library, Shambles Street, Barnsley, South Yorkshire S70 2JF.
BDF	Bedfordshire and Luton Archives and Records Service, Borough Hall, Cauldwell Street, Bedford. MK42 9AP.
BHM	Birmingham Archives and Heritage Service, Central Library, Chamberlain Square, Birmingham B3 3HQ.
BKM	Centre for Buckinghamshire Studies, County Hall, Walton Street, Aylesbury, Bucks HP20 1UU.
BOL	Bolton Archives and Local Studies Service, Bolton History Centre, Le Mans Crescent, Bolton BL1 1SE.
BRI	Bristol Record Office, 'B' Bond Warehouse, Smeaton Road, Bristol BS1 6XN.
BRK	Berkshire Record Office, Berkshire Record Office, 9 Coley Avenue, Reading, Berks RG1 6AF.
BRO	Bromley Archives, Central Library, High St, Bromley BR1 1EX.
BRY	Bury Archives Service, Bury Museum & Archives, Moss Street, Bury BL9 0DR.
BTH	Bath and North East Somerset Record Office, Guildhall, High Street, Bath BA1 5AW.
BWK	Berwick-upon-Tweed Record Office, Council Offices, Wallace Green, Berwick-upon-Tweed TD15 1ED.
CAM	Cambridge Archives and Local Studies, Box RES 1009, Shire Hall, Castle Hill, Cambridge CB3 0AP.
CCA	Canterbury Cathedral Archives, The Precincts, Canterbury, Kent CT1 2EH.
CHS	Cheshire and Chester Archives and Local Studies Service, Cheshire Record Office, Duke Street, Cheshire CH1 1RL.
CIR	Cirencester Bingham Library, The Waterloo, Cirencester, Gloucestershire GL7 2PZ.
CMD	Camden Local Studies and Archives Centre, Holborn Library, 32-38 Theobalds Road, London WC1X 8PA.

CON	Cornwall Record Office, Old County Hall, Truro, Cornwall, TR1 3AY.
COV	Coventry History Centre, The Herbert, Jordan Well, Coventry CV1 5QP.
COW	City of Westminster Archives Centre, 10 St Ann's Street, London SW1P 2DE.
CRO	Croydon Local Studies and Archives, Central Library, Katharine Street, Croydon CR9 1ET.
CUB	Cumbria Archive Centre, 140 Duke Street, Barrow-in-Furness, Cumbria LA14 1XW.
CUC	Cumbria Archive Centre, Petteril Bank House, Petteril Bank Road, Carlisle CA1 3AJ.
CUK	Cumbria Archive Centre, Kendal County Offices, Kendal LA9 4RQ.
CUW	Cumbria Archive Centre, Scotch Street, Whitehaven, Cumbria CA28 7NL.
DBY	Derbyshire Record Office, New Street, Matlock, Derbyshire DE4 3AG
DER	Derby Local Studies Library, 25b Irongate, Derby DE1 3GL.
DEV	Devon Record Office, Great Moor House, Bittern Road, Sowton Exeter EX2 7NL.
DNC	Doncaster Archives, King Edward Road, Balby, Doncaster DN4 0NA.
DOR	Dorset Record Office, Bridport Road, Dorchester DT1 1RP.
DUD	Dudley Archives and Local History Service, Mount Pleasant Street, Coseley, West Midlands WV14 9JR.
DUR	Durham County Record Office, County Hall, Durham DH1 5UL.
DVN	North Devon Record Office, Tuly Street, Barnstaple, EX31 1EL.
DVW	Plymouth and West Devon Record Office, Unit 3, Clare Place, Plymouth PL4 0JW.
ESS	Essex Record Office, Wharf Road Chelmsford CM2 6YT.
GLS	Gloucestershire Archives, Clarence Row, Alvin Street, Gloucester GL1 3DW.
HAM	Hampshire Record Office, Sussex Street, Winchester SO23 8TH.
HEF	Herefordshire Record Office, Harold Street, Hereford HR1 2QX.
HRT	Hertfordshire Archives and Local Studies, County Hall, Pegs Lane, Hertford SG13 8DE.
HUD	Huddersfield Local History Library, Princess Alexandra Walk, Huddersfield, West Yorkshire HD1 2SU.
HUL	Hull City Archives, Hull History Centre, Worship Street, Hull HU2 8BG.
HUN	Huntingdon Library and Archives, Princes Street, Huntingdon, PE29 3PA.
IOW	Isle of Wight Record Office, 26 Hillside, Newport, Isle of Wight PO30 2EB.
ISL	Islington Local History Centre, Finsbury Library, 245 St John Street London EC1V 4NB.
KEI	Keighley Local Studies Library, North Street, Keighley, BD2 1 3SX.
KEN	Centre for Kentish Studies, Sessions House, County Hall, Maidstone, Kent, ME14 1XQ.
KNE	East Kent Archives Centre, Enterprise Zone, Honeywood Road, Whitfield, Dover CT16 3EH.
LAM	Lambeth Archives, Minet Library, 52 Knatchbull Road, London SE5 9QY.
LAN	Lancashire Record Office, Bow Lane, Preston, Lancashire, PR1 2RE.
LCH	Lichfield Record Office, The Friary, Lichfield, WS13 6QG.
LEI	Record Office for Leicestershire, Leicester and Rutland, Long Street, Wigston Magna, Leicester, LE18 2AH.

LIN	Lincolnshire Archives, St Rumbold Street, Lincoln LN2 5AB.
LIV	Liverpool Record Office and Local History Service, Central Library, William Brown Street, Liverpool L3 8EW.
LMA	London Metropolitan Archives, 40 Northampton Road, London EC1R OHB.
LNE	North East Lincolnshire Archives, Municipal Offices, Town Hall Square, Grimsby, DN31 1HU.
LSE	London School of Economics Library, Archives Division, Lionel Robbins Building, 10 Portugal Street, London WC2A 2HD.
MAN	Greater Manchester County Record Office (with Manchester Archives), 56 Marshall Street, New Cross, Manchester, M4 5FU.
MED	Medway Archives and Local Studies, Gun Wharf, Dock Road, Chatham, Kent ME4 4TR.
MMM	Merseyside Maritime Museum, Albert Dock, Liverpool L3 4AQ.
MRN	The Marine Society, 202 Lambeth Road, London SE1 7JW.
NBL	Northumberland Archives, Woodhorn, Queen Elizabeth II Country Park, Ashington, Northumberland NE63 9YF.
NEW	Newham Archives and Local Studies Library, Stratford Library, 3 The Grove, London E15 1EL.
NFK	Norfolk Record Office, The Archive Centre, Martineau Lane, Norwich NR1 2DQ.
NTH	Northamptonshire Record Office, Wootton Hall Park, Northampton NN4 8BQ.
NTT	Nottinghamshire Archives and Southwell Diocesan Record Office, County House, Castle Meadow Road, Nottingham NG2 1AG.
NTU	Manuscripts and Special Collections, The University of Nottingham, King's Meadow Campus, Lenton Lane, Nottingham NG7 2NR.
OLD	Oldham Local Studies and Archives, 84 Union Street, Oldham, OL1 1DN.
OXF	Oxfordshire Record Office, St Luke's Church, Temple Road, Cowley, Oxford OX4 2EX.
OXS	Centre for Oxfordshire Studies, Central Library, Westgate, Oxford OX1 1DJ.
POR	Portsmouth City Museum and Records Office, Portsmouth Museum Road, Portsmouth, Hampshire PO1 2LJ.
RIC	Richmond Local Studies Library, Old Town Hall, Whittaker Avenue, Richmond TW9 1TP.
RLH	Royal London Hospital Archives and Museum, St Augustine with St Philip Church, Newark Street, Whitechapel, London E1 2AA.
ROC	Local Studies Library, Touchstones Rochdale, The Esplanade, Rochdale OL16 1AQ.
ROT	Rotherham Archives and Local Studies Service, Rotherham Central Library, Walker Place, Rotherham, S65 1JH.
SAL	Shropshire Archives, Castle Gates, Shrewsbury, Shropshire SY1 2AQ.
SAN	Sandwell Community History and Archives Service, Smethwick Library, High Street, Smethwick B66 1AA.
SFB	Suffolk Record Office, 77 Raingate Street, Bury St Edmunds IP33 2AR.
SFI	Suffolk Record Office, Gatacre Road, Ipswich IP1 2LQ.
SFL	Suffolk Record Office, Central Library, Clapham Road, Lowestoft NR32 1DR.
SHA	Shakespeare Birthplace Trust Records Office, Henley Street, Stratford-upon-Avon, Warwickshire CV37 6QW.
SHF	Sheffield Archives, 52 Shoreham Street, Sheffield S1 4SP.
SKI	Skipton Library, High Street, Skipton BD23 1JX.

SLF	Salford City Archives, Salford Museum and Art Gallery, Peel Park, The Crescent, Salford M5 4WU.
SOM	Somerset Heritage Centre, Brunel Way, Langford Mead, Norton Fitzwarren, Taunton TA2 6SF.
SOU	Southampton Archives Service, Civic Centre, Southampton SO14 7LP.
SRY	Surrey History Centre, 130 Goldsworth Road, Woking, Surrey GU21 6ND.
STA	St Albans Central Library, The Maltings, St Albans, Herts AL1 3JQ.
STB	St Bartholomew's Archives & Museum, West Smithfield, London EC1A 7BE.
STC	Stockport Central Library, Wellington Road South, Stockport SK1 3RS.
STK	Stoke on Trent City Archives, Hanley Library, Bethesda Street, Hanley, Stoke on Trent ST1 3RS.
STS	Staffordshire Record Office, Eastgate Street, Stafford, ST16 2LZ.
SXE	East Sussex Record Office, The Maltings, Castle Precincts, Lewes, East Sussex, BN7 1YT.
SXW	West Sussex Record Office, County Hall, Chichester, West Sussex PO19 1RN.
TAW	Tyne and Wear Archives, Discovery Museum, Blandford Square, Newcastle upon Tyne NE1 4JA.
TEE	Teesside Archives, Exchange House, 6 Marton Road, Middlesbrough TS1 1DB.
TMS	Tameside Local Studies and Archives Centre, Central Library, Old Street, Ashton-under-Lyne OL6 7SG.
TNA	The National Archives, Kew, Richmond, Surrey, TW9 4DU.
WAF	Waltham Forest Archives, Vestry House Museum, Vestry Road, Walthamstow, London E17 9NH.
WAL	Walsall Local History Centre, Essex Street, Walsall WS2 7AS.
WAN	Wandsworth Heritage Service, Battersea Library, 265 Lavender Hill, London SW11 1JB.
WAR	Warwickshire County Record Office, Priory Park, Cape Road, Warwick CV34 4JS.
WIG	Wigan Archive Service, Town Hall, Leigh WN7 2DY.
WIL	Wiltshire and Swindon Archives, Wiltshire and Swindon History Centre, Cocklebury Road, Chippenham SN15 3QN.
WIR	Wirral Archives, Cheshire Lines Building, Canning Street, Birkenhead CH41 1ND.
WOL	Wolverhampton Archives and Local Studies, Wolverhampton City Council, Molineux Hotel Building, Whitmore Hill, Wolverhampton WV1 1SF.
WOR	(From mid-2012) The Hive, Worcester WR1 3NZ
YAS	Yorkshire Archaeological Society, Claremont, 23 Clarendon Road, Leeds LS2 9NZ.
YKE	East Riding of Yorkshire Archives and Local Studies, The Treasure House, Champney Road, Beverley HU17 9BA.
YKN	North Yorkshire County Record Office, Malpas Road, Northallerton DL7 8TB.
YRK	York City Archives, York Explore Centre, Museum Street, York YO1 7DS.
YWB	West Yorkshire Archive Service Bradford, Bradford Central Library, Prince's Way, Bradford BD1 1NN.
YWC	West Yorkshire Archive Service Calderdale, Central Library, Northgate House, Northgate, Halifax HX1 1UN.
YWK	West Yorkshire Archive Service Kirklees, Central Library, Princess Alexandra Walk, Huddersfield, HD1 2SU.
YWL	West Yorkshire Archive Service Leeds, Chapeltown Road, Sheepscar, Leeds, LS7 3AP.

| YWW | West Yorkshire Archive Service Wakefield, Registry of Deeds, Newstead Road, Wakefield, WF1 2DE. |

WALES

AGY	Anglesey Archives, Industrial Estate Road, Bryn Cefni Industrial Estate, Llangefni, Anglesey LL77 7JA.
CAE	Caernarfon Record Office, Council Offices, Caernarfon LL55 1SH.
CGN	Ceredigion Archives, County Offices, Marine Terrace, Aberystwyth, Ceredigion, SY23 2DE.
CMN	Carmarthenshire Archives Service, Parc Myrddin, Richmond Terrace, Carmarthen, SA31 1HQ.
CNW	Conwy Archive Service, Old Board Street School, Lloyd Street, Llandudno LL30 2YG.
DEN	Denbighshire Record Office, Ruthin Gaol, 46 Clwyd Street, Ruthin, Denbighshire LL15 1HP.
FLN	Flintshire Record Office, The Old Rectory, Hawarden, Flintshire, CH5 3NR.
GLA	Glamorgan Archives, Clos Parc Morgannwg, Leckwith, Cardiff CF11 8AW.
GMW	West Glamorgan Archive Service, County Hall, Oystermouth Road, Swansea SA1 3SN.
GWE	Gwent Archives, Steelworks Road, Ebbw Vale NP23 6DN.
GWY	Gwynedd Council: Meirionnydd Archives, Ffordd y Bala, Dolgellau LL40 2YF.
NLW	National Library of Wales, Aberystwyth, Wales SY23 3BU.
PEM	Pembrokeshire Record Office, The Castle Haverfordwest, Pembrokeshire SA61 2EF.
POW	Powys County Archives Office, County Hall, Llandrindod Wells, Powys, LD1 5LG.

SCOTLAND

ABD	Aberdeen City Archives, Town House, Broad Street, Aberdeen AB10 1AQ, and Old Aberdeen House, Dunbar Street, Aberdeen AB24 3UJ.
ABH	Northern Health Services Archives, Victoria Pavilion, Woolmanhill Hospital, Aberdeen AB25 1LD.
ANS	Angus Archives, Hunter Library, Restenneth Priory, By Forfar DD8 2SZ.
ARL	Argyll and Bute Council Archives, Manse Brae, Lochgilphead PA31 8QU.
AYR	Ayrshire Archives, Watson Peat Building, SAC Auchincruive, Ayr KA6 5HW.
CAI	Caithness Archive Centre, Wick Library, Sinclair Terrace, Wick KW1 5AB.
CLK	Clackmannanshire Archives, 26-28 Drysdale Street, Alloa, FK10 1JL.
DFS	Dumfries and Galloway Archives, 33 Burns Street, Dumfries DG1 2PS.
DNB	West Dunbartonshire Archives, Strathleven Place, Dumbarton G82 1BD.
DND	Dundee City Archive & Record Centre, 21 City Square Dundee, DD1 3BY.
DNU	Archive Services, University of Dundee, Dundee DD1 4HN.
EDI	Edinburgh City Archives, Level 1, City Chambers, 253 High Street, Edinburgh EH1 1YJ.
ELN	East Lothian Local History Centre, Newton Port, Haddington, East Lothian, EH41 3NAJ.
FIF	Fife Council Archive Centre, Carleton House The Haig Business Park, Balgonie Road, Markinch, Glenrothes KY7 6AQ.
FLK	Falkirk Council Archives, Callendar House, Callendar Park, Falkirk, FK1 1YR.

GLG	Glasgow City Archives, The Mitchell Library, 210 North Street, Glasgow G3 7DN.
HCA	Highland Council Archives, Highland Archive and Registration Centre, Bught Road, Inverness IV3 5SS.
HEB	Hebridean Archives, 6 Kenneth Street, Stornoway, Isle of Lewis HS1 2DP.
HHS	Highland Health Sciences Library, University of Stirling, Highland Campus, Centre for Health Science, Old Perth Road, Inverness IV2 3JH.
KKC	Kirkcaldy Museum & Art Gallery, Abbotshall Road, Kirkcaldy KY1 1YG.
MLN	Midlothian Archive Service, 2 Clerk Street, Loanhead EH20 9DR.
MOR	Moray Council Heritage Centre, Old East End School, Institution Road, Elgin IV30 1RP.
MUL	Mull Museum, Columba Buildings, Tobermory, Isle of Mull, Argyll PA75 6NU.
NAS	National Archives of Scotland, HM General Register House, 2 Princes Street, Edinburgh EH1 3YY.
NLA	North Lanarkshire Archives & Record Centre, 10 Kelvin Road, Cumbernauld G67 2BA.
ORK	Orkney Library & Archive, 44 Junction Road, Kirkwall, Orkney KW15 1AG.
PAI	Reference and Local Studies, Central Library, 68 High Street, Paisley PA1 2BB.
PER	Perth & Kinross Council Archive, AK Bell Library, 2-8 York Place, Perth PH2 8EP.
SBA	Scottish Borders Archive and Local History Centre, Heritage Hub, Kirkstile, Hawick TD9 0AE.
SHE	Shetland Museum and Archives, Hay's Dock, Lerwick, Shetland ZE1 0WP.
STG	Stirling Archives, 5 Borrowmeadow Road, Stirling FK7 7UW.
WLN	West Lothian Archives, 9 Dunlop Square, Deans Industrial Estate, Livingston EH54 8SB.

NORTHERN IRELAND

PNI	Public Record Office of Northern Ireland, 2 Titanic Boulevard, Titanic Quarter, Belfast BT3 9HQ.

ISLE OF MAN

IOM	Manx National Heritage Library, Douglas, Isle of Man, IM1 3LY.

CHANNEL ISLANDS

GUE	States of Guernsey Island Archives, St Barnabas, Cornet Street, St Peter Port, Guernsey GY1 1LF.
JER	The Jersey Archive, Clarence Road, St Helier, JE2 4JY.
LSJ	Library of the Société Jersiaise, 7 Pier Road St Helier, Jersey JE2 4XW.

REPUBLIC OF IRELAND

CAR	Carlow County Library, Tullow Street, Carlow.
CAV	Cavan County Library, Farnham Street, Cavan, Co. Cavan.
CLA	Clare County Library, The Manse, Harmony Row, Ennis, Co.Clare.
COR	Cork City and County Archives, 33a Great William O'Brien Street, Blackpool, Cork, Co.Cork.
DON	Donegal County Record Office, Three Rivers Centre, Lifford, Co. Donegal.
GAL	Galway local archives, Island House, Cathedral Square, Co.Galway.

KER	Kerry County Library, Moyderwell, Tralee, Co. Kerry.
KID	Kildare County Library, Riverbank Campus, Main Street, Newbridge, Co. Kildare.
KIK	Kilkenny County Library, 6 John's Quay, Kilkenny, Co. Kilkenny.
LET	Leitrim County Library, Main Street, Ballinamore, Co. Leitrim.
LEX	Laois County Library, County Hall, James Fintan Lalor Avenue, Portlaoise, Co. Laois.
LIM	Limerick Studies – Archives, Lissanalta House, Dooradoyle Road, Limerick, Co. Limerick.
LOG	Longford County Library, Town Centre, Longford, Co.Longford.
LOU	Louth County Archives Service, Old Gaol, Ardee Road, Dundalk, Co. Louth.
MAY	Local History Department, Castlebar Central Library, Castlebar, Co. Mayo.
MEA	Meath County Library, Railway Street, Navan, Co. Meath.
MOG	Monaghan County Library, The Diamond, Clones, Co. Monaghan.
NAI	National Archives of Ireland, Bishop Street, Dublin 8.
OFF	Offaly County Library, O'Connor Square, Tullamore, Co. Offaly.
ROS	Roscommon County Library, Abbey Street, Roscommon, Co.Roscommon.
SLI	Sligo County Library, Stephen Street, Sligo, Co.Sligo.
TIP	Tipperary Studies, County Library, Castle Avenue, Thurles, Co. Tipperary.
WAT	Waterford County Archive Service, Dungarvan Central Library, Davitt's Quay, Dungarvan, Co. Waterford.
WEM	Westmeath County Library HQ, Dublin Road, Mullingar, Co. Westmeath.
WEX	Wexford County Archive Service, 6A Ardcavan Business Park, Ardcavan, Co. Wexford. (Visitors by prior appointment only.)
WIC	Wicklow County Archives, County Council Buildings, Station Road, Wicklow Town, Co. Wicklow.

APPENDIX N

PLACES TO VISIT

Below is a list of museums housed in former workhouse buildings. Most include displays about their workhouse past. Further information and details of opening times etc. are available on each museum's website whose current web address is also included.

United Kingdom
Derry Workhouse Museum, 23 Glendermott Road, Waterside, Derry BT47 6BG.
    www.derrycity.gov.uk/Museums/Workhouse-Museum
Gressenhall Farm and Workhouse, Gressenhall, Dereham, Norfolk NR20 4DR.
    www.museums.norfolk.gov.uk/Visit_Us/Gressenhall_Farm_and_Workhouse
Guildford Spike, Warren Road, Guildford, Surrey GU1 3JH.
    www.guildfordspike.co.uk
Nidderdale Museum, 5 King St, Pateley Bridge, North Yorkshire HG3 5LE.
    www.nidderdalemuseum.com
Red House Museum, Christchurch, Quay Road, Christchurch, Dorset BH23 1BU.
    www.hants.gov.uk/redhouse
Ripon Workhouse Museum, Allhallowgate, Ripon, North Yorkshire HG4 1LE.
    www.riponmuseums.co.uk/museums/workhouse_museum_gardens
Southwell Workhouse, Upton Road, Southwell, Nottinghamshire NG25 0PT.
    www.nationaltrust.org.uk/workhouse
Thackray Medical Museum, Leeds, 141 Beckett Street, Leeds LS9 7LN.
    www.thackraymuseum.org
Vestry House Museum, Vestry Road, Walthamstow, London E17 9NH.
    www.walthamforest.gov.uk/vestry-house
Weaver Hall Museum & Workhouse, 162 London Road, Northwich, Cheshire CW9 8AB.
    www.cheshirewestandchester.gov.uk/visiting/museums/weaver-hall.aspx

Republic of Ireland
Donaghmore Famine Workhouse Museum, Donaghmore, Portlaoise, Co. Laois, Ireland.
    www.donaghmoremuseum.com
Dunfanaghy Workhouse Heritage Centre, Figart, Dunfanaghy, Co. Donegal, Ireland.
    www.dunfanaghyworkhouse.ie
Irish Workhouse Centre, Ceadars Avenue, Portumna, Co. Galway, Ireland.
    www.irishworkhousecentre.ie

Denmark
Svendborg Forsorgsmuseet (Svendborg Social Welfare Museum)
    www.svendborgmuseum.dk/index.php?option=com_content&task=view&id=159&Ite
    mid=188

SOME USEFUL WEBSITES

Access to the websites listed below is free except for those marked (£) where a payment or subscription may be required. Some non-free sites may be accessible without payment via local libraries or record offices, or by members of educational or other institutions that hold subscriptions.

General Resources

www.workhouses.org.uk – a comprehensive resource about every aspect of workhouse history and operation, with information on hundreds of individual workhouse sites.

www.connectedhistories.org – searches across multiple online sources for Brtish history, 1500–1900.

www.pastscape.org.uk – English Heritage's 'national historic environment database'. Just search for 'workhouse'.

parlipapers.chadwyck.co.uk – (£) House of Commons Parliamentary Papers searchable online.

www.british-history.ac.uk – digital library of core printed sources for the history of the British Isles, e.g. volumes of *Victoria County History*, Ordnance Survey maps etc.

www.visionofbritain.org.uk – 'A vision of Britain between 1801 and 2001. Including maps, statistical trends and historical descriptions.'

www.historicaldirectories.org – hundreds of local and trade directories 1750–1919.

newspapers.bl.uk – (£) British Library archive of nineteenth-century newspapers.

www.archive.org – thousands of digitised books including local history, periodicals, official papers.

www.historyhome.co.uk/peel/pltopic.htm – the Peel Web section on the poor law.

www.victorianweb.org/history/sochistov.html – the Victorian Web social history section.

ezitis.myzen.co.uk – 'Lost Hospitals of London' – includes many former workhouses and MAB hospitals.

www.old-maps.co.uk – historical Ordnance Survey maps of England, Wales and Scotland.

www.motco.com – detailed historic maps of London 1746–1862.

maps.nls.uk/os – historical Ordnance Survey maps of Scotland.

maps.osi.ie/publicviewer – historical Ordnance Survey maps of the Republic of Ireland.

maps.osni.gov.uk/MapConsoleHistoricalMaps.aspx – historical maps of Northern Ireland.

www.poorhousestory.com – 'The Poorhouse Story'. Poorhouses in the USA.

www.cyndislist.com/poor/poor-law – huge collection of website links for family historians.

Locating Records

www.nationalarchives.gov.uk/records/research-guides/poor-law-records.htm – UK National Archives guide to poor law records 1834–71.

www.nationalarchives.gov.uk/a2a – A2A (Access to Archives) catalogue of archives and their holdings across England and Wales.

www.cityoflondon.gov.uk/LMA – London Metropolitan Archives guide to holdings and catalogue search.

www.westminster.gov.uk/archives – Westminster City Archives.
www.aim25.ac.uk – catalogue of over 100 archives in London and inside M25.
www.archivesnetworkwales.info – Archives Wales catalogue of over twenty Welsh archives.
www.scan.org.uk/catalogue – SCAN catalogue of archives in Scotland.
www.nationalarchives.gov.uk/hospitalrecords – Hospital Records Database. Includes many former
  workhouses and MAB hospitals.

Online Workhouse Records

Please note – the UK national census and civil registration records, available online from a
number of sources, also include inmates of workhouses and other institutions. However, the list
below focuses on resources specifically relating to the workhouse and poor relief administration.

www.nationalarchives.gov.uk/about/living-poor-life.htm – UK National Archives project to digitise
  the official correspondence of Poor Law Unions in England and Wales. *search.ancestry.co.uk/
  search/db.aspx?dbid=1557* – (£) London Poor Law Records, 1834–1940.
www.findmypast.co.uk – (£) Cheshire and some Manchester union workhouse records.
www.londonlives.org – 'Crime, poverty and social policy in the Metropolis, 1690–1800.' Includes
  a searchable database of more than 3 million names.
www.origins.net/help/aboutbo-poorlaw.aspx – (£) records of St Botolph Aldgate (settlement
  examinations 1742–1868) and St Sepulchre (settlement examinations, bastardy and apprenticeship records 1765–1844).
www.bucksfhs.org.uk/index.php?option=com_winslow – extracts of Winslow workhouse records
  (1835–49).
www.cfhs.org.uk/PoorLawPapers – Cambridgeshire poor law papers index.
www.familysearch.org – a growing collection currently includes Norfolk poor law records
  (1796–1900) and Cheshire workhouse records (1848–1967).
www.welbank.net/norwich/1570 – Norwich census of the poor (1570).
www.sussexrecordsociety.org.uk/plhome.asp – Sussex poor law records (1662–1835).
www.genuki.org.uk/big/eng/Paupers – 10 per cent sample of 1861 parliamentary survey of long-
  term workhouse inmates.
www.fdca.org.uk/FDCAPoorIndexes.html – indexes of Liff & Benvie Register of Poor (1854–65)
  and Dundee East Poorhouse Registers (1856–78).
www.workhouses.org.uk/Abingdon/AbingdonMinutes1835-6.shtml – transcription of guardian's
  minute book for the Abingdon Union, 1835–36.
www.clarelibrary.ie/eolas/coclare/history/intro.htm – transcriptions of guardians' minute books and
  staff and death records for the Kilrush and Ennistymon Unions in Ireland.

APPENDIX P

THE CONSOLIDATED GENERAL ORDER, 1847

Reproduced below is the text of the Consolidated General Order (CGO) published in 1847 by the Poor Law Commissioners who were about to be replaced by a new body, the Poor Law Board. The CGO was an amalgamation and revision of all the General Orders issued by the Poor Law Commissioners since coming to office in 1834. With periodic amendments, the CGO remained the 'bible' of poor law and workhouse administration until 1913 when a major revamp resulted in its replacement by the Poor Law Institutions Order.

To the GUARDIANS OF THE POOR of the several Unions named in the Schedule hereunto annexed;–

To the CHURCHWARDENS and OVERSEERS of the several Parishes and Places comprised within the said Unions;–

To the CLERK or CLERKS to the Justices of the Justices of the Petty Sessions held for the Division or Divisions in which the Parishes and Places comprised within the said Unions are situate;–

And to all others whom it may concern.

WE, THE POOR LAW COMMISSIONERS, in pursuance of the authorities vested in us by an Act passed in the fifth year of the reign of His late Majesty King William the Fourth, intituled 'An Act for the Amendment and better Administration of the Laws relating to the Poor in England and Wales,' and by all other Acts amending the same, Do hereby Rescind every Order, whether General or Special, heretofore issued by the Poor Law Commissioners to the Unions named in the Schedule hereunto annexed, which relates to the several subjects herein provided for, except so far as the same may have related to the apprenticeship of any poor person not yet completed, or may have required or authorised the appointment of any officer, or the giving of any security, or the making of any contract not yet executed, or the making of any orders by the Guardians for contributions and payments not yet obeyed, or may have defined the salaries of any officers, or have prescribed the districts within which the duties of any officer shall be performed, or may have provided for the class of paupers or their number to be received into any particular Workhouse, or may have provided for the election of Guardians in any case where such election shall not have been completed when this Order shall come into force, and except the Order regulating the mode of election of Guardians, bearing date the Sixth day of March One thousand eight hundred and forty-six, and addressed to the Guardians of the Poor of the Nottingham Union.

And We do hereby Order, Direct, and Declare, with respect to each of the said Unions, as follows:–

ELECTION OF GUARDIANS

ARTICLE 1.–The Overseers of every Parish in the Union shall, before the Twenty-sixth day of March in every year, distinguish in the rate-book the name of every ratepayer in their parish who has been rated to the relief of the poor for the whole year immediately preceding the said day, and has paid the poor-rates made and assessed upon him for the period of one whole year, except those which have been made or become due within the six months immediately preceding the said day.

ART. 2.–The Clerk shall at every future annual election of Guardians perform the duties hereby imposed upon him, and all other duties suitable to his office which it may be requisite for him to perform: in conducting and completing such election; and in case the office of Clerk shall be vacant at the time when any duty relative to such election is imposed on the Clerk by this Order, or in case the Clerk, from illness or other sufficient cause, shall be unable to: discharge such duties, the Guardians shall appoint some person to perform such of the said duties as then remain to be performed, and the person so appointed shall perform such duties.

ART. 3.–The Guardians shall, before or during every such election, appoint a competent number of persons to assist the Clerk in conducting and completing the election in conformity with this Order; but if the Guardians do not make such appointment within the requisite time, the Clerk shall take such measures for securing the necessary assistance as he may deem advisable.

ART. 4.–The persons appointed under Article 3 shall obey all the directions relative to the conduct of the election which may be given by the Clerk for the execution of this Order.

ART. 5.–The Overseers of every Parish in the Union, and every Officer having the custody of the poor-rate books of any such Parish, shall attend the Clerk at such times as he shall require their attendance, until the completion of the election of Guardians; and shall, if required by him, produce to him such rate books, and the registers of owners and proxies, together with the statements of owners, and appointments and statements of proxies, and all books and papers relating to such rates in their possession or power.

Provided that, where any register of owners shall have, been prepared in any Parish containing a population exceeding two thousand persons, it shall not be necessary to produce the statements of owners.

ART. 6.–The Clerk shall prepare and sign a notice, which may be in the Form marked (A.) hereunto annexed, and which shall contain the following particulars:–

    1st. The number of Guardians to be elected for each Parish in the Union.

    2d. The qualification of Guardians.

    3d. The persons by whom, and the places where, the Nomination Papers in respect of each Parish are to be received, and the last day on which they are to be sent.

    4th. The mode of voting in case of a contest, and the days on which the Voting Papers will be delivered and collected.

    5th. The time and place for the examination and casting up of the votes.

And the Clerk shall cause such notice to be published on or before the Fifteenth day of March, in the following manner:–

    1st. A printed copy of such notice shall be affixed on the principal external gate or door of every Workhouse in the Union, and shall from time to time be renewed, if necessary, until the Ninth day of April.

    2d. Printed copies of such notice shall likewise be affixed on such places in each of the Parishes of the Union as are ordinarily made use of for affixing thereon notices of parochial business.

Provided that whenever the day appointed in this Order for the performance of any act relating to or connected with the Election of Guardians shall be a Sunday or Good Friday, such act shall be performed on the day next following, and each subsequent proceeding shall be postponed one day.

ART. 7.–Any person entitled to vote in any Parish, may nominate for the office of Guardian thereof himself, or any other person or number of persons (not exceeding the number of Guardians to be elected for such Parish), provided that the person or persons so nominated be legally qualified to be elected for that office.

ART. 8.–Every nomination shall be in writing in the Form marked (B.) hereunto annexed, and be signed by one person only, as the party nominating, and shall be sent after the Fourteenth and on or before the Twenty-sixth day of March, to the Clerk or to such person or persons as may have been appointed to receive the same, and the Clerk, or such person or persons, shall on the receipt thereof, mark thereon the date of its receipt, and also a number according to the order of its receipt; provided that no nomination sent before the Fifteenth or after the said twenty sixth day of March shall be valid.

ART. 9.–If the number of the persons nominated for the office of Guardian for any Parish shall be the same as or less than the number of Guardians to be elected for such Parish, such persons, if duly-qualified, shall be deemed to be the elected Guardians for such Parish for the ensuing year, and shall be certified as such by the Clerk under his hand as hereinafter provided in Article 22.

ART. 10.–But if the number of the duly qualified persons nominated for the office of Guardian for any Parish shall exceed the number of Guardians to be elected therein, the Clerk shall cause Voting Papers, in the Form marked (C.) hereunto annexed, to be prepared and filled up, and shall insert therein the names of all the persons nominated, in the order in which the Nomination Papers were received, but it shall not be necessary to insert more than once the name of any person nominated.

ART. 11.–The, Clerk shall on the Fifth day of April cause one of such Voting Papers to be delivered by the persons appointed for that purpose, to the address in such Parish of each rate-payer, owner, and proxy qualified to vote therein.

ART. 12.–If the Clerk consider that any person nominated is not duly qualified to be a Guardian, he shall state in the Voting Paper the fact that such person has been nominated, but that he considers such person not to be duly qualified.

ART. 13.–If any person put in nomination for the office of Guardian in any Parish shall tender to the officer conducting the election his refusal, in writing, to serve such office, and if in consequence of such refusal the number of persons nominated for the office of Guardian for such Parish shall be the same as or less than the number of Guardians to be elected for such Parish, all or so many of the remaining Candidates as shall be duly qualified shall be deemed to be the elected Guardians for such Parish for the ensuing year, and shall be certified as such by the Clerk under his hand, as hereinafter provided in Article 22.

ART. 14.–Each Voter shall write his initials in the Voting Paper delivered to him against the name or names of the person or persons (not exceeding the number of Guardians to be elected in the Parish) for whom he intends to vote, and shall sign such Voting Paper; and when any person votes as a proxy, he shall in like manner, write his own initials and sign his own name, and state also, in writing, the name of the person for whom he is proxy.

ART. 15.–Provided that, if any Voter cannot write, he shall affix his mark at the foot of the Voting Paper in the presence of a witness, who shall attest the affixing thereof, and shall write the name of the voter against such mark, as well as the initials of such Voter against the name of every Candidate for whom the voter intends to vote.

ART. 16.–If the initials of the Voter be written against the names of more persons than are to be elected Guardians for the parish, or if the Voter do not sign or affix his mark to the Voting Paper, or if his mark be not duly attested, or his name be not duly written by the witness, or if a proxy do not sign his own name, and state in writing the name of the person for whom he is proxy, such Voter shall be omitted in the calculation of votes.

ART. 17.–The Clerk shall cause the Voting Papers to be collected on the Seventh day of April, by the persons appointed or employed for that purpose; in such manner as he shall direct.

ART. 18.–No Voting Paper shall be received or admitted, unless the same have been delivered at the address in each Parish of the Voter, and collected by the persons appointed or employed for that purpose, except as is provided in Article 19.

ART. 19.–Provided that every person qualified to vote, who shall not on the Fifth day of April have received a Voting Paper, shall, on application before the Eighth day of April to the

Clerk at his office, be entitled to receive a Voting Paper, and to fill up the same in the presence of the Clerk, and then and there to deliver the same to him.

ART. 20.–Provided also, that in case any Voting Paper duly delivered shall not have been collected through the default of the Clerk, or the persons appointed or employed for that purpose, the Voter in person, may deliver the same to the Clerk before twelve o'clock at noon, on the Eighth day of April.

ART. 21.–The Clerk shall, on the Ninth day of April, and on as many days immediately succeeding as may be necessary, attend at the Boardroom of the Guardians of the Union, and ascertain the validity of the votes, by an examination of the rate-books, and the registers of owners and proxies, and such other documents as he may think necessary, and by examining such persons as he may see fit; and he shall cast up such of the Votes as he shall find to be valid, and to have been duly given, collected, or received, and ascertain the number of such votes for each Candidate.

ART. 22.–The Candidates, to the number of Guardians to be elected for the Parish, who being duly qualified, shall have obtained the greatest number of votes, shall be deemed to be the elected Guardians for the Parish, and shall be certified as such by the Clerk under his hand.

ART. 23.–The Clerk, when he shall have ascertained that any Candidate is duly elected as Guardian, shall notify the fact of his having been so elected, by delivering or sending, or causing to be delivered or sent, to him a notice in the Form (D.) hereunto annexed.

ART. 24.–The Clerk shall make a list containing the names of the Candidates, together with (in case of a contest) the number of votes given for each, and the names of the elected Guardians, in the Form marked (E.) hereunto annexed, and shall sign and certify the same, and shall deliver such list, together with all the Nomination and Voting Papers which he shall have received, to the Guardians of the Union, at their next meeting, who shall preserve the same for a period of not less than two years.

ART. 25.–The Clerk shall cause copies of such list to be printed, and shall deliver or send, or cause to be delivered or sent, one or more of such copies to the Overseers of each Parish.

ART. 26.–The Overseers shall affix, or cause to be affixed, copies of such list, at the usual places for affixing in each Parish notices of parochial business.

ART. 27.–In case of the decease, necessary absence, refusal,, or disqualification to act, during the proceedings of the election, of the Clerk or any other person appointed or employed to act in respect of such election, the delivery of the nominations, voting papers, or other documents to the successor of the Clerk or person so dying, absenting himself, refusing or disqualified to act, shall, notwithstanding the terms of any notice issued, be as valid and effectual as if they had been delivered to such Clerk or person.

MEETINGS OF THE GUARDIANS

ART. 28.–The Guardians shall upon the day of the week, and at the time of day, and at the place already appointed for holding the ordinary meetings, hold an ordinary meeting once at the least in every week or fortnight for the execution of their duties; and may, when they think fit, change the period, time, and place of such ordinary meeting, with the consent of the Commissioners previously obtained.

ART. 29.–The Guardians shall at the first meeting after the Fifteenth day of April, elect out of the whole number of Guardians a Chairman and a Vice-chairman who, provided they be Guardians at the time, shall continue respectively to act as such Chairman and Vice-Chairman for the year next ensuing.

ART. 30.–The Guardians at any time may elect two Vice-Chairmen, and if such Vice-Chairmen be appointed at the same time, the Guardians shall determine their precedence; according to which precedence one of the said Vice-Chairmen shall thenceforth preside and act as in the case when only one Vice-Chairman is elected.

ART. 31.–If a Chairman or a Vice-Chairman cease to be a Guardian, or refuse or become incapable to act as Chairman, or Vice -Chairman, before the expiration of the term of office, the Guardians shall, within one month after the occurrence of the vacancy, refusal, or incapacity, elect some other Guardian to be Chairman or Vice-Chairman, as the case may be.

ART. 32.–Whereas no act of any meeting of the Guardians will be valid unless three Guardians be present and concur therein; if three Guardians be not present at any meeting, the Clerk shall make an entry of that fact in the Minute-book, and the time for holding such meeting shall be deemed to have expired as soon as the said entry shall have been made. But one hour at least shall be allowed to elapse from the time fixed for the commencement of the meeting before such entry shall be made.

ART. 33.–If three or four or more Guardians be present at any ordinary meeting, such three, or the majority of such four or more Guardians, may adjourn the same to the day of the next ordinary meeting, or to some other day previous to the next ordinary meeting.

ART; 34.–An extraordinary meeting of the Guardians may be summoned to be held at any time, upon the requisition of any two Guardians addressed to the Clerk. Every such requisition shall be made in Writing, in the Form (F.) hereunto annexed, and no business, other than the business specified in the said requisition, shall be transacted at such extraordinary meeting.

ART. 35.–Notice of every change in the period, time, or place of holding any meeting, and notice of the adjournment of any meeting, and notice of every extraordinary meeting, shall be given in writing to every Guardian. Every such notice shall be respectively in the Forms (G.), (H.), and (I.) hereunto annexed, and shall be given or sent by the Clerk to every Guardian, or left at his place of abode two days, if practicable, before the day appointed for the meeting to which it relates.

ART. 36.–If any case of emergency arise requiring that a meeting of the Guardians should immediately take place, they, or any three of them, may meet at the ordinary place of meeting, and take such case into consideration, and may make an order thereon.

PROCEEDINGS OF THE GUARDIANS

ART. 37.–At every meeting the Chairman, or, in his absence, a Vice-Chairman, shall preside; but if at the commencement of any meeting the Chairman, and Vice-Chairman or Vice-Chairmen be absent, the Guardians present shall elect one of themselves to preside at such meeting as Chairman thereof, until the Chairman or a Vice-Chairman take the chair.

ART. 38.–Every question at any meeting consisting of more than three Guardians shall be determined by a majority of the votes of the Guardians present thereat and voting on the question, and when there shall be an equal number of votes on any question, such question shall be deemed to have been lost.

ART. 39.–No resolution agreed to or adopted by the Guardians shall be rescinded or altered by them, unless some Guardian shall have given to the Board seven days notice of a motion to rescind or alter such resolution, which notice shall be forthwith entered on the Minutes by the Clerk. Provided always, that this regulation shall not extend to any resolution which immediately concerns the allowance of relief to any person, or the punishment of any pauper, or to any resolution which the Commissioners may request the Guardians to reconsider or amend, or to any question of emergency.

ART. 40.–The Guardians may, from time to time, (as occasion may require), appoint a Committee to consider and report on any special subject, and such Committee may meet at such times and places as to them may seem convenient; but no act or decision of any such Committee shall of itself be deemed to be the act of the Guardians.

ART: 41.–At every ordinary meeting of the Guardians, the business shall, as far as may be convenient, be conducted in the following order:

Firstly. The minutes of the last ordinary meeting, and of any other meeting which may have been held since such ordinary meeting, shall be read to the Guardians; and in order that such minutes may be recognised as a record, of the acts of the Guardians at their last meeting, they shall be signed by the Chairman presiding at the meeting at which such minutes are read, and an entry of the same having been so read shall be made in the minutes of the day when read.

Secondly. The Guardians shall dispose of such business as may arise out of the minutes so read, and shall give the necessary directions thereon.

Thirdly. They shall proceed to give the necessary directions respecting all applications for relief made since the last ordinary meeting, and also respecting the amount and nature of relief to be given and continued to the paupers then in the receipt of relief, until the next ordinary meeting, or for such other time as such relief may be deemed to be necessary.

Fourthly. They shall hear and consider any application for relief which may be then made, and determine thereon.

Fifthly. They shall read the report of the state of the Workhouse or Workhouses, examine all books and accounts relative to the relief of the paupers of the Union, and give all needful directions concerning the management and discipline of the said Workhouse or Workhouses, and the providing of furniture and stores and other articles.

Sixthly. They shall examine the Treasurer's account, and shall, when necessary, make orders on the Overseers or other proper authorities of the several Parishes in the Union, for providing such sums as may be lawfully required by the Guardians on account of the respective Parishes.

Seventhly. They shall transact any such business as may not fall within any of the above classes.

ART. 42.–When the Guardians have allowed relief in the Workhouse to any applicant, a written or printed order for his admission therein, signed by the Clerk, shall be forthwith delivered to the applicant, or to any person on his behalf.

ART. 43.–When the Guardians have allowed outdoor relief, in money or kind, to any applicant, the particulars of such relief shall be entered, by the proper Relieving Officer, in a ticket according to Form (K.) hereunto annexed, and such ticket shall be delivered, by him to the applicant, or to some person on his behalf.

CONTRACTS OF THE GUARDIANS

ART. 44.–All contracts to be entered into on behalf of the Union relating to the maintenance, clothing, lodging, employment, or relief of the poor, or for any other purpose relating to or connected with the general management of the poor, shall be made and entered into by the Guardians.

ART. 45.–The Guardians shall require tenders to be made in some sealed paper for the supply of all provisions, fuel, clothing, furniture, or other goods or materials, the consumption of which maybe estimated, one month with another, to exceed Ten pounds per month, and of all provisions, fuel, clothing, furniture, or other goods or materials, the cost of which may be reasonably estimated to exceed Fifty pounds in a single sum, and shall purchase the same upon contracts to be entered into after the receipt of such tenders.

ART. 46.–Any work or repairs to be executed in the Workhouse, or the premises connected with the Workhouse, or any fixtures to be put up therein, which may respectively be reasonably estimated to exceed the cost of Fifty pounds in one sum, shall be contracted for by the Guardians, on sealed tenders, in the manner prescribed in Articles 45 and 47.

ART. 47.–Notice of the nature and conditions of the contract to be entered into, of the estimated amount of the articles required, of the last day on which tenders will be received, and the day on which the tenders will be opened, shall be given in some newspaper circulated in the Union, not less than ten days previous to the last day on which such tenders are, to be received; and no tender shall be opened by the Clerk, or any Guardian, or other person, prior to the day specified in such notice, or otherwise than at a, meeting of the said Guardians.

ART. 48.–When any tender is accepted, the party making the tender shall, in pursuance of these regulations, enter into a contract, in writing, with the Guardians, containing the terms, conditions, and stipulations mutually agreed upon, and whenever the Guardians deem it advisable, the party contracting shall find one or more surety or sureties, who shall enter into a bond conditioned for the due performance of the contract, or shall otherwise secure the same.

ART. 49.–Provided always, that if from the peculiar nature of any provisions, fuel, clothing, furniture, goods, materials, or fixtures to be supplied, or of any work or repairs to be executed, it shall appear to the Guardians desirable that a specific person or persons be employed to supply or execute the same, without requiring sealed tenders as hereinbefore directed, it shall be lawful for such Guardians, with the consent of the Commissioners first obtained, to enter into a contract with the said person or persons and to require such sureties and securities as are specified in Article 48.

ART. 50.–Every contract to be hereafter made by any Guardians shall contain a stipulation requiring the contractor to send in his bill or account of the sum due to him for goods or work on or before some day to be named in the contract.

ART. 51.–The Guardians shall fix some day of days, not being more than twenty-one days after the end of each quarter, for the attendance of contractors and tradesmen, or their author-ised agents, and the Clerk shall notify such day to every contractor or tradesman to whom money may be due, or to his agent, or he shall, under the direction of the Guardians, cause the same to be advertised in some newspaper.

APPRENTICESHIP OF PAUPER CHILDREN

PARTIES

ART. 52.–No child under the age of nine years, and no child (other than a deaf and dumb child) who cannot read and write his own name, shall be bound apprentice by the Guardians.

ART. 53.–No child shall be so bound to a person who is not a housekeeper, or assessed to the poor-rate in his own name.

Or who is a journeyman, or a person not carrying on trade or business on his own account;

Or who is under the age of twenty-one;

Or who is a married woman.

THE PREMIUM

ART. 54.–No premium, other than clothing for the apprentice, shall he given upon the binding of any person above the age of sixteen years, unless such person be maimed, deformed, or suffering from some permanent bodily infirmity, such as may render him unfit for certain trades or sorts of work.

ART. 55.–Where any premium is given it shall in part consist of clothes supplied to the appren-tice at the commencement of the binding, and in part of money, one moiety whereof shall be paid to the master at the binding, and the residue at the termination of the first year of the binding.

TERM

ART. 56.–No apprentice shall be bound by the Guardians for more than eight years.

CONSENT

ART. 57.–No person above fourteen years of age shall be so bound without his consent. And no child under the age of sixteen years shall be so bound without the consent of the father of such child, or if the father be dead, or be disqualified to give such consent, as hereinafter pro-vided, or if such, child be a bastard, without the consent of the mother, if living, of such child.

Provided, that where such parent is transported beyond the seas, or is in custody of the law, having been convicted of some felony, or for the space of six calendar months before the time of executing the indenture has deserted such child, or for such space of time has been in the service of Her Majesty, or of the East India Company, in any place out of the United Kingdom, such parent, if the father, shall be deemed to be disqualified as hereinbefore stated, and if it be the mother, no such consent shall be required.

PLACE OF SERVICE

ART. 58.–No child shall be bound to a master whose place of business, whereat the child is to work and live, is distant more than thirty miles from the place in which the child is residing at the time of the proposed binding, or at the time of his being sent on trial to such master; Unless in any particular case the Commissioners shall, on application to them, otherwise permit.

PRELIMINARIES TO THE BINDING

ART. 59.–If the child whom it is proposed to bind apprentice, be in the Workhouse, and under, the age of fourteen years, the Guardians shall require a certificate in writing from the Medical Officer of the Workhouse as to the fitness in regard to bodily health and strength of such child to be bound apprentice to the proposed trade, and shall also ascertain from the Master of the Workhouse the capacity of the child for such binding in other respects.

ART. 60.–If the child be not in the Workhouse, but in the Union by the Guardians of which it is proposed that he shall be bound, the Relieving Officer of the district in which the child is residing shall examine into the circumstances of the case, the condition of the child, and of his parents, if any, and the residence of the proposed master, the nature of his trade, the number of other apprentices, if any, then bound to him, and generally as to the fitness of the particular binding, and shall report the result of his inquiry to the Guardians.

ART. 61.–If in any case within Article 60, the Guardians think proper to proceed with the binding they shall, when the child is under the age of fourteen years, direct the Relieving Officer to take the child to the Medical Officer of the district, to b examined as to his fitness in respect of bodily health and strength for the proposed trade or business; an such Medical Officer 35 shall certify in writing according to his judgment in the matter, which certificate shall be produced by the said Relieving Officer to the next meeting of the Guardians.

ART. 62.–If the child be not residing within the Union, the Guardians who propose to bind him shall not proceed to do so unless they receive such a report as is required in Article 60 from the Relieving Officer of the district in which such child is residing, and certificate from some Medical man practising in the neighbourhood of the child's residence to the effect required in Article 61.

ART. 63.–When it is proposed to give a premium other than clothing upon the binding of any person above the age of sixteen years, the Guardians shall require a certificate in writing from some Media practitioner, certifying that the person is maimed deformed, or disabled, to the extent specified in such Article, and shall cause a copy of such certificate to be entered on their minutes before they proceed to execute the indenture.

ART. 64.–When such certificate, as is required by, Articles 59, 61, 62 and 63, is received, or in case from the age of the child no such certificate is required, the Guardians shall direct that the child and the proposed master, or some person on his behalf, and in case the child be under the age of sixteen, that the parent or person in whose custody ouch child shall be then living, attend some meeting of the Board to be then appointed.

ART. 65.–At such meeting, if such parties appear, the; Guardians shall examine into the circumstances of the case; and if, after making all due inquiries, and hearing the objections (if any be made) on the part of the relatives or friends of such child, they deem it proper that the binding be effected, they may forthwith cause the indenture to be prepared, and, if the master be present, to be executed but if he be not present they shall cause the same to be transmitted to him for execution; and when executed by him, and returned to the Guardians,, the same shall be executed by the latter, and shall be signed by the child, as provided in Article 67.

ART. 66.–If the proposed master reside out of the Union, but in some other Union or Parish under a Board of Guardians, whether formed under the provisions of the first-recited Act, or of the Act of the twenty-second year of the reign of King George the Third, intituled 'An Act for the better Relief and Employment of the Poor,' or of any local Act, the Guardians shall, before proceeding to effect the binding, communicate in writing the proposal to the Guardians of such other Union or Parish, and request to be informed whether such binding is open to any objection, and if no objection be reported by such Guardians within the space of one calendar month, or if the objection does not appear to the Guardians proposing to bind the child to be sufficient to prevent the binding, the same may be proceeded with; and when the indenture shall have been executed, the Clerk to the Guardians who executed the same shall send notice thereof in writing to the Guardians of the Union or Parish wherein the said apprentice is to reside.

INDENTURE

ART. 67.–The indenture shall be executed in duplicate, by the master and the Guardians, and shall not be valid unless signed by the proposed apprentice with his name, or if deaf and dumb with his mark, in the presence of the said Guardians; and the consent of the parent, where requisite, shall be testified by such parent signing with his name or mark, to be properly attested, at the foot of the said indenture; and where such consent is dispensed with under Article 57, the cause of such dispensation shall be stated at the foot of the indenture by the Clerk.

ART. 68.–The name of the place or places at which the apprentice is to work and live shall be inserted in the indenture.

ART. 69.–One part, of such indenture, when executed, shall be kept by the Guardians; the other shall be delivered to the master.

DUTIES OF THE MASTER OF A PAUPER APPRENTICE

ART. 70.–And We do hereby prescribe the duties of the master to whom such poor child maybe apprenticed, and the terms and conditions to be inserted In the said indenture to be as follows:

No. 1. The master shall teach the child the trade, business, or employment set forth in the indenture, unless the Guardians authorise the substitution of another trade, business, or employment.

No. 2. He shall maintain the said child with proper food and nourishment.

No. 3. He shall provide a proper lodging for the said child.

No. 4. He shall supply the said child with proper clothing during the term of the binding, together with the necessary provision of linen.

No. 5. He shall, in case the said child be affected with any disease or sickness, or meet with any accident, procure at his own cost, adequate medical or surgical assistance, from some duly qualified medical man, for such child.

No. 6. He shall, once at least on every Sunday, cause the child to attend some place of Divine worship, if there be any such within a reasonable distance, according to the religious persuasion in which the child has been brought up, so, however, that no child shall be required by the master to attend any place of worship to which his parents or surviving parent may object, nor when he shall be above the age of sixteen, any place to which he may himself object.

No. 7. Where such parents or parent or next of kin desire it, he shall allow the said child to attend any Sunday or other school which shall be situated within the same parish, or within two miles distance from his residence, on every Sunday, and, if there be no such school which such child can attend, he shall, at some reasonable hour on every Sunday, allow any minister of the religious persuasion of the child to have access to such child for the purpose of imparting religious instruction.

No. 8. Where the apprentice continues bound after the age of seventeen years the master shall, in every case where the Guardians require him so to do, pay to such apprentice, for and in respect of every week that he duly and properly serves the said master, as a remuneration, a sum to be inserted in the indenture, or to be agreed upon by the Guardians and the said master when that time arrives, or, if they cannot agree, to be settled by some person to be then chosen by the said master and such Guardians, and, until such sum be agreed upon or settled, not less than one fourth of the amount then commonly paid as wages to journeymen in the said trade, business, or employment.

No. 9. The master shall, himself or by his agent, produce the apprentice to the Guardians by whom such apprentice was bound at their ordinary meeting next preceding the end of the first year of the binding, and before the receipt of the remainder of the premium, if any be due, and, shall in like manner produce the said apprentice at some one of their ordinary meetings, to be held at or about the middle of the term, and whenever afterwards, required to do so by the, said Guardians: provided, that if the apprentice reside out of the Union by the Guardians whereof he was bound, the apprentice shall be produced, as hereinbefore directed, to the Guardians of the Union or Parish, as described in Article 66, in which the apprentice may be residing.

No. 10. The master shall not cause the said apprentice to work or live more than ten miles from the place or places mentioned in the indenture according to Article 68, without the leave of the Guardians so binding him, to be given under their common seal: provided, that such Guardians may in such licence so to be given under their common seal, by express words to that effect, if they think fit, authorise the master, any time during the residue of the term of the apprenticeship, to change the place of the abode or service of the, apprentice, without any further application to them or their successors.

ART. 71.–These duties of the master set forth in Article 70 shall be enforced by covenants and conditions to be inserted in the indenture to be execute by him.

ART. 72.–The master shall also covenant, under penalty to be specified in the covenant, not to assign or cancel the indenture, without the consent of the Guardians, under their common seal, previously obtained, and to pay to the said Guardians all costs and expences that they may incur in consequence of the said apprentice not being supplied with medical or surgical assistance by the master, in case the same shall be at any time requisite.

ART. 73.–The indenture shall be made subject to the following provisoes:

No. 1. That if the master take the benefit of any Act for the relief of insolvent debtors or be discharged under any such Act, such indenture shall forthwith become of no further force or effect.

No. 2. That if, on a conviction for a breach of any one of the aforesaid covenants and conditions before a Justice of the Peace, the Guardians who may be parties to the said indenture declare by a resolution that, the indenture is determined, and transmit a copy of such resolution, under the hand of their Clerk, by the post or otherwise, to the said master, such indenture shall, except in respect of all rights and liabilities then accrued, forthwith become of no further force or effect.

ART. 74.–Nothing contained in this Order shall apply to the apprenticing of poor children to the sea service.

MODE OF OBTAINING MEDICAL RELIEF BY PERMANENT PAUPERS

ART. 75.–The Guardians shall, once at least in every year, cause to be prepared by the Clerk or Relieving Officers a list of all such aged and infirm persons, and persons permanently sick or disabled, as may be actually receiving relief from such Guardians, and residing within the district of each Medical Officer of the Union, and shall from time to time furnish to each District Medical Officer a copy of the list aforesaid.

ART. 76.–Every person whose name is inserted in such list, shall receive a ticket in the Form (L.) hereunto annexed, and shall be entitled on the exhibition of such ticket to the Medical Officer of his district to obtain such advice, attendance, and medicines, as his case may require, in the same manner as if he had received an order from the Guardians and such ticket shall remain in force for the time specified therein, unless such person shall cease to be in the receipt of relief before the expiration of such time.

RELIEF OF NON-SETTLED AND NON-RESIDENT POOR

ART. 77.–If any Board of Guardians undertake to administer relief allowed to a non-settled pauper living within the Union for which they act, on behalf of the Officers, or of the Board of Guardians, of the Parish or Union in which such pauper is deemed to be settled, every such undertaking shall be made in conformity with the rules and regulations of the Commissioners in force at the time.

ART. 78.–No money shall be transmitted to any Guardians or to any Officer of a Parish or Union, to be applied to the relief of any non-resident pauper, except in conformity with the provisions of this Order.

ART. 79.–No money shall be paid on account of any non-resident pauper to the Guardians or to the Officer, of any Union or Parish in which the relief is administered by a Board of Guardians, except in one of the three following ways:

> No. 1. By Post-office order payable to the Treasurer of the Union or Parish to the account of which the money is to be paid, or to the banker of such Treasurer.
>
> No. 2. By cheque or order payable to the Treasurer of such Parish or Union, or to his order.
>
> No. 3. By cheque payable to bearer (where the same may lawfully be drawn), and crossed as payable through the Treasurer of such Parish or Union, or his banker, or through the agent of such Treasurer or banker; and every such cheque shall be so crossed by the Clerk before it is signed by the presiding Chairman.

ART. 80.–Every account for relief duly administered to non-resident poor shall be discharged by the Guardians, within two calendar months from the receipt of such account, by the transmission of the amount due; in one of the modes prescribed in Article 79.

ORDERS FOR CONTRIBUTIONS AND PAYMENTS

ART. 81.–The Clerk shall, four weeks at least before the Twenty-fifth day of March and the Twenty-ninth day of September respectively in each year, refer to and ascertain the cost to each Parish in the Union for the maintenance of the poor, and other separate, charges, as well as for the common charges incurred in the half of the last year, corresponding to the half-year next coming, and shall estimate and, as near as may be, divide amongst the Parishes any extraordinary charges to which the Union may be liable in the coming half-year, and he shall also estimate the probable balance due to or from the Parish at the end of the current half-year, and shall then prepare the orders on the several Parishes for the sums which, upon such computation, it shall appear necessary for them to contribute to the expenses of the Union for the coming half-year; and the orders so prepared shall be laid before the Guardians for their consideration three weeks at least before the expiration of the current half-year.

ART. 82.–The Guardians shall make orders on the Overseers or other proper authorities of every Parish of the Union, from time to time, for the payment to the Guardians of all such sums as may be required by them for the relief of the Poor of the Parish, and for the contribution of the Parish to the common fund of the Union, and for any other expenses chargeable by the Guardians on the Parish; and in such orders the contributions shall be directed to be paid in one sum or by instalments, on days specified, as to the Guardians may seem fit.

ART. 83.–Every such order shall be made according to the Form (M.) hereunto annexed. It shall be signed by the presiding Chairman of the meeting and two other Guardians present thereat, and shall be countersigned by the Clerk.

ART. 84.–The Guardians shall pay every sum greater than Five pounds by an order, which shall be drawn upon the Treasurer of the Union, and shall be signed by the presiding Chairman and two other Guardians at a meeting, and shall be countersigned by the Clerk.

ART. 85.–The Guardians shall examine at their Board, or shall cause to be examined by some Committee or Guardian authorised by them for the purpose, every bill exceeding in amount One pound (except the salaries of officers) brought against the Union; and when any such bill has been allowed by the Board, or, by such Committee or Guardian, a note of the allowance thereof shall be made on the face of the bill before the amount is paid.

CUSTODY OF BONDS

ART. 86.–The Guardians shall provide for the safe custody of all bonds given in pursuance of the Regulations of the Commissioners, so always that no bond given by any person shall remain in the custody of such person himself.

ART. 87.–The Guardians shall, at the audit next after the Twenty-firth day of March in every year cause every person having the, custody of bonds given by any officer of the Union to produce such bonds to the Auditor for his inspection.

GOVERNMENT OF THE WORKHOUSE

ADMISSION OF PAUPERS

ART. 88.–Every pauper who shall be admitted into the Workhouse, either upon his first or any subsequent admission, shall be admitted in some one of the following modes only; that is to say–

> By a written or printed order of the Board of Guardians, signed by their Clerk according to Art. 42.
> By a provisional written or printed order, signed by a Relieving Officer or an Overseer.
> By the Master of the Workhouse (or during his absence, or inability to act, by the Matron), without any order, in any case of sudden or urgent necessity.

Provided that the Master may admit any pauper delivered at the Workhouse under an order of removal to a Parish in the Union.

ART. 89.–No pauper shall be admitted under any written or printed order as mentioned in Article 48, if the same bear date more than six days before the pauper presents it at the Workhouse.

ART. 90.–If a pauper be admitted otherwise than by an Order of the Board of Guardians, the admission of such pauper shall be brought before the, Board of Guardians at their next ordinary meeting, who shall decide on the propriety of the pauper's continuing in the Workhouse or otherwise, and make an order accordingly.

ART. 91.–As soon as the pauper is admitted, he shall be placed in some room to be appropriated to the reception of paupers on admission, and shall then be examined by the Medical Officer.

ART. 92.–If the Medical Officer upon such examination pronounce the pauper to be labouring under any disease of body or mind, the pauper shall be placed in the sick ward, or in such other ward as the Medical Officer shall direct.

ART. 93.–If the Medical Officer pronounce the pauper to be free from any such disease, the pauper shall be placed in the part of the Workhouse, assigned to the class to which he may belong.

ART. 94.–No pauper shall be detained in a receiving ward for a longer time than is necessary for carrying into effect the regulations in Arts. 91, 92, and 93, if there be room in the proper ward for his reception.

ART. 95.–Before being removed from the receiving ward, the pauper shall be thoroughly cleansed, and shall be clothed in a workhouse dress, and the clothes which he wore at the time of his admission shall be purified, and deposited in a place appropriated for that purpose, with the pauper's name affixed thereto. Such clothes shall be restored to the pauper when he leaves the Workhouse.

ART. 96.–Every pauper shall, upon his admission into the Workhouse, be searched by or under the inspection of the proper officer, and all articles prohibited by any Act of Parliament, or by this Order, which may be found upon his person, shall be, taken from him, and, so far as may be proper, restored to him at his departure from the Workhouse.

ART. 97.–Provided always, that the regulations respecting the admission, clothing, and searching of paupers shall not apply to any casual poor wayfarer, unless the Guardians shall so direct, or unless he is compelled to remain in the Workhouse from illness or other sufficient cause, in which case he shall be admitted regularly as an inmate.

CLASSIFICATION OF THE PAUPERS

ART. 98.–The paupers, so far as the Workhouse admits thereof, shall be classed as follows:

Class 1. Men infirm through age or any other cause.

Class 2. Able-bodied men, and youths above the age of fifteen years.

Class 3. Boys above the age of seven years and under that of fifteen.

Class 4. Women infirm through age or any other cause.

Class 5. Able-bodied women, and girls above the age of fifteen years.

Class 6. Girls above the age of seven years and under that of fifteen.

Class 7. Children under seven years of age.

To each class shall be assigned that ward or separate building and yard which may be best fitted for the reception of such class, and each class of paupers shall remain therein, without communication with those of any other class.

ART. 99.–Provided,–

Firstly. That the Guardians shall from time to time, after consulting the Medical Officer, make such arrangements as they may deem necessary with regard to persons labouring under any disease of body or mind.

Secondly. The Guardians shall, so far as circumstances will permit, further subdivide any of the classes enumerated in Art. 98 with reference to the moral character, or behaviour, or the previous habits of the inmates, or to such other grounds as may seem expedient.

Thirdly. That nothing in this Order shall compel the Guardians to separate any married couple, being both paupers of the first and fourth classes respectively, provided the Guardians shall set apart for the exclusive use of every such couple a sleeping apartment separate from that of the other paupers.

Fourthly. That any paupers of the fifth and sixth classes may be employed constantly or occasionally in any of the female sick-wards, or in the care of infants, or as assistants in the household work; and the Master and Matron shall make such arrangements as may enable the paupers of the fifth and sixth classes to be employed in the household work, without communication with the paupers of the second and third classes.

Fifthly. That any pauper of the fourth class, whom the Master may deem fit to perform any of the duties of a nurse or assistant to the Matron, may be so employed in the sick-wards, or those of the fourth, fifth, sixth, or seventh classes, and any pauper of the first class, who may by the Master be deemed fit, may be placed in the ward of the third class, to aid in the management and superintend the behaviour of the paupers of such, or may be employed in the male sick-ward.

Sixthly. That the Guardians, for a special reason to be entered on their minutes, may place any boy or girl between the ages of ten and sixteen years in a male or female ward respectively, different from that to which he or she properly belongs, unless the Commissioners shall otherwise direct.

Seventhly. That the paupers of the seventh class may be placed in such of the wards appropriated to the female paupers as shall be deemed expedient, and the mothers of such paupers shall be permitted to have access to them at all reasonable times.

Eighthly. That the Master (subject to any directions given or regulations made by the Guardians) shall allow the father or mother of any child in the same workhouse, who may be desirous of seeing such child, to have an interview with such child at some one time in each day, in a room in the said Workhouse to be appointed for that purpose. And the Guardians shall make arrangements for permitting the members of the same family who may be in different Workhouses of the Union to have occasional interviews with each other, at such times, and in such manner, as may best suit the discipline of the several Workhouses.

Ninthly. That casual poor wayfarers admitted by the Master or Matron, shall be kept in a separate ward of the Workhouse, and shall be dieted and set to work in such manner and under such regulations as the Guardians by any resolution now in force, or to be made hereafter, may direct.

ART. 100.–The Guardians shall not admit into the Workhouse or any ward of the same, or retain therein, a larger number or a different class of paupers than that heretofore or hereafter from time to time to be fixed by the Commissioners; and in case such number shall at any time be exceeded, the fact of such excess shall be forthwith reported to the Commissioners by the Clerk.

ART. 101.–No pauper of unsound mind, who may be dangerous, or who may have been reported as such by the Medical Officer, or who may require habitual or frequent restraint, shall be detained in the Workhouse for any period exceeding Fourteen days, and the Guardians shall cause the proper steps to be taken for the removal of every such pauper to some asylum or licensed house as soon as may be practicable.

DISCIPLINE AND DIET OF THE PAUPERS

ART. 102.–All the paupers in the Workhouse, except the sick and insane, and the paupers of the first, fourth, and seventh classes, shall rise, be set to work, leave off work, and go to bed, at the times mentioned in the Form (N.) hereunto annexed, and shall be allowed such intervals for their meals as are therein stated, and these several times shall be notified by the ringing of a bell provided always, that the Guardians may, with the consent of the Commissioners, make such alterations in any of the said times or intervals, as the Guardians may think fit.

ART. 103.–Half an hour after the bell shall have been rung for rising, the names of the paupers shall be called over by the Master and Matron respectively, in the several wards provided for the second, third, fifth, and sixth classes, when every pauper belonging to the respective wards shall be present, and shall answer to his name, and be inspected by the Master and Matron respectively, provided that the paupers of the third and sixth class may be called over and inspected by the Schoolmaster and Schoolmistress.

ART. 104.–The meals shall be taken by all the paupers, except the sick, the children, persons of unsound mind, casual poor wayfarers, women suckling their children, and the paupers of the first and fourth classes, in the dining-hall or day-room, and in no other place whatever, and during the time of meals order and decorum shall be maintained.

ART. 105.–No pauper of the second, third, fifth, or sixth classes, shall go to or remain in his sleeping-room, either in the time hereby appointed for work, or in the intervals allowed for meals, except by permission of the Master or Matron.

ART. 106.–The Master and Matron shall (subject to the directions of the Guardians) fix the hours of rising or going to bed, for the paupers of the first, fourth, and seventh classes, and determine the occupation and employment of which they may be capable and the meals for such paupers shall be provided at such times and in such manner as the Guardians may from time to time direct.

ART. 107.–The paupers shall be dieted with the food and in the manner set forth in the Dietary Table, which may be prescribed for the use of the Workhouse, and no pauper shall have or consume any liquor, or any food or provision other than is allowed in the said Dietary Table, except on Christmas-day, or by the direction in writing of the Medical Officer, as provided in Article 108.

ART. 108.– Provided –

Firstly. That the Medical Officer may direct in writing such diet for any individual pauper as he may deem necessary, and the Master shall obey such direction, until the next ordinary meeting of the Guardians, when he shall report the same in writing to the Guardians.

Secondly. That if the Medical Officer at any time certify that he deems a temporary change in the diet essential to the health of the paupers in the Workhouse, or of any class or classes thereof, the Guardians shall cause a copy of such certificate to be entered on the minutes of their proceedings, and may forthwith order, by a resolution, the said diet to be temporarily changed, according to the recommendation of the Medical Officer, and shall forthwith transmit a copy of such certificate and resolution to the Commissioners.

Thirdly. That the Medical Officer shall be consulted by the Matron as to the nature of the food of the infants, and of their mothers when suckling, and the time at which, such infants should be weaned.

Fourthly. That the Guardians may, without any direction of the Medical Officer, make such allowance of food as may be necessary to paupers employed as nurses or in the household work; but they shall not allow to such paupers any fermented or spirituous liquors on account of the performance of such work, unless in pursuance of a written recommendation of the Medical Officer.

ART. 109.–If any pauper require the Master or Matron to weigh the allowance of provisions served out at any meal, the Master or Matron shall forthwith weigh such allowance in the presence of the pauper complaining and of two other persons.

ART. 110.–The clothing to be worn by the paupers in the Workhouse shall be made of such materials as the Board of Guardians may determine.

ART. 111.–More than two paupers, any one of whom is above the age of seven years, shall not be allowed to occupy the same bed, unless in the case of a mother and infant children.

ART. 112.–The paupers of the several classes shall be kept employed according to their capacity and ability and no pauper shall receive any compensation for his labour.

ART. 113.–No pauper in the Workhouse shall be employed or set to work in pounding, grinding, or otherwise breaking bones, or in preparing bone dust.

ART. 114.–The boys and girls who are inmates of the Workhouse shall, for three of the working hours, at least, every day, be instructed in reading, writing, arithmetic, and the principles of the Christian religion, and such other instruction shall be imparted to them as may fit them for service, and train them to habits of usefulness, industry, and virtue.

ART. 115.–Any pauper may quit the Workhouse upon giving to the Master, or (during his absence or inability to act) to the Matron, a reasonable notice of his wish to do so; and in the event of any able-bodied pauper, having a family, so quitting the house, the whole of such family shall be sent with him, unless the Guardians shall, for any special reason, otherwise direct; and such directions shall be, in conformity with the Regulations of the Commissioners with respect to relief in force at the time.

ART. 116.–Provided nevertheless, that the Guardians may, by any general or special direction, authorise the Master to allow a pauper, without giving any such notice as is required in Art. 115, to quit the Workhouse, and to return after a temporary absence only and every such allowance shall be reported by the Master to the Guardians at their next ordinary meeting.

ART. 117.–Provided also, that nothing herein contained shall prevent the Master from allowing the Paupers of each sex under the age of fifteen, subject to such restrictions as the Guardians may impose, to quit the Workhouse, under the care and guidance of himself, or the Matron, a Schoolmaster, Schoolmistress, Porter, or some one of the assistants and servants of the Workhouse, for the purpose of exercise.

ART. 118.–Any person may visit any pauper in the Workhouse by permission of the Master, or (in his absence) of the Matron, subject to such conditions and restrictions as the Guardians may prescribe; such interview shall take place in a room separate from the other inmates of the Workhouse, and in the presence of the Master, Matron, or Porter, except where a sick pauper is visited.

ART. 119.–No written or printed paper of an improper tendency, or which may be likely to produce insubordination, shall be allowed to circulate, or be read aloud, among the inmates of the Workhouse.

ART. 120.–No pauper shall play at cards, or at any game of chance, in the Workhouse and the Master may take from any pauper, and keep until his departure from the Workhouse, any cards, dice, or other articles applicable to games of chance, which may be in his possession.

ART. 121.–No pauper shall smoke in any room of the Workhouse, except by the special direction of the Medical Officer, or shall have any matches or other articles of a highly combustible nature in his possession, and the Master may take from any person any articles of such a nature.

ART. 122.–Any licensed minister of the religious persuasion of an inmate of the Workhouse, who may at any time in the day, on the request of any inmate, enter the Workhouse for the purpose of affording religious assistance to him, or for the purpose of instructing his child or children in the principles of his religion, shall give such assistance or instruction, so as not to interfere with the good order and discipline of the other inmates of the Workhouse.

And, such religious assistance or instruction shall be strictly confined to inmates who are of the religious persuasion of such minister, and to the children of such inmates.

Except in the cases in which the Guardians may lawfully permit religious assistance and instruction to be given to any paupers who are Protestant dissenters, by licensed ministers who are Protestant dissenters.

ART. 123.–No work, except the necessary household work and cooking, shall be performed by the paupers on Sunday, Good Friday, and Christmas-day.

ART. 124.–Prayers shall be read before breakfast and after supper every day, and Divine service shall be performed every Sunday, Good Friday, and Christmas-day in the Workhouse (unless the Guardians, with the consent of the Commissioners, otherwise direct), and at such Prayers and Divine service all the paupers shall attend, except the sick, persons of unsound mind, the young children, and such as are too infirm to do so provided that those paupers who may object so to attend, on account of their professing religious principles differing from those of the Established Church, shall also be exempt from such attendance.

ART. 125.–The Guardians may authorise any inmates of the Workhouse, being members of the Established Church, to attend public worship at a parish church or chapel, on every Sunday, Good Friday, and Christmas-day, under the control and inspection of the Master or Porter, or other officer.

ART. 126.–The Guardians may also authorise any inmates of the Workhouse, being dissenters from the Established Church, to attend public worship at any dissenting-chapel in the neighbourhood of the Workhouse, on every Sunday, Good Friday and Christmas-day.

PUNISHMENTS FOR MISBEHAVIOUR OF THE PAUPERS

ART. 127.–Any pauper, being an inmate of the Workhouse,

Who shall neglect to observe such of the regulations in this Order as are applicable to him as such inmate;

Or who shall make any noise when silence is ordered to be kept;

Or who shall use obscene or profane language;

Or shall by word or deed insult or revile any person;

Or shall threaten to strike or to assault any person;

Or shall not duly cleanse his person;

Or shall refuse or neglect to work, after having been required to do so;

Or shall pretend sickness;

Or shall play at cards or other game of chance;

Or shall refuse to go into his proper ward or yard, or shall enter or attempt to enter, without permission, the ward or yard appropriated to any class of paupers other than that to which he belongs;

Or shall climb over any fence or boundary wall surrounding any portion of the Workhouse premises, or shall attempt to leave the Workhouse otherwise than through the ordinary entrance;

Or shall misbehave in going to, at, or returning from public worship out of the Workhouse,, or at Divine service or Prayers in the Workhouse;

Or having received temporary leave of absence, and wearing the Workhouse clothes, shall return to the Workhouse after the appointed time of absence, without reasonable cause for the delay;

Or shall wilfully disobey any lawful order of any officer of the Workhouse;

Shall be deemed DISORDERLY.

ART. 128.–Any pauper being an inmate of the Workhouse, who shall, within seven days, repeat any one, or commit more than one, of the offences specified in Art. 127;

Or who shall by word or deed insult or revile the Master or Matron, or any other officer of the Workhouse, or any of the Guardians;

Or shall wilfully disobey any lawful order of the Master or Matron after such order shall have been repeated;

Or shall unlawfully strike or otherwise unlawfully assault any person;

Or shall wilfully or mischievously damage or soil any property whatsoever belonging to the Guardians;

Or shall wilfully waste or spoil any provisions,, stock, tools, or materials for work, belonging to the Guardians;

Or shall be drunk;

Or shall act or write indecently or obscenely;

Or shall wilfully disturb other persons at public worship out of the Workhouse, or at Divine service or Prayers in the Workhouse;

Shall be deemed REFRACTORY.

ART. 129.–The Master may, with or without the direction of the Guardians, punish any disorderly pauper by substituting, during a time not greater than forty-eight hours, for his dinner, as prescribed by the Dietary, a meal consisting of eight ounces of bread, or one pound of cooked potatoes or, boiled rice, and also by withholding from him, during the same period, all butter, cheese, tea, sugar, or broth, which such pauper would otherwise receive, at any meal during the time aforesaid.

ART. 130.–The Guardians may, by a special direction to be entered on their minutes, order any refractory pauper to be punished by confinement in a separate room, with or without an alteration of diet, similar in kind and duration to that prescribed in Article 129 for disorderly paupers; but no pauper shall be so confined for a longer period than twenty-four hours, or, if it be deemed right that such pauper should be carried before a Justice of the Peace, and if such period of twenty-four hours should be insufficient for that purpose, then for such further time as may be necessary for such purpose.

ART. 131.–If any offence, whereby a pauper becomes refractory under Art. 128, be accompanied by any of the following circumstances of aggravation; (that is to say), if such pauper

Persist in using violence against any person;

Or persist in creating a noise or disturbance, so as to annoy other inmates;

Or endeavour to excite other paupers to acts of insubordination;

Or persist in acting indecently or obscenely in the presence of any other inmate;

Or persist in mischievously breaking or damaging any goods or property of the Guardians; the Master may, without any direction of the Guardians, immediately place such refractory pauper in confinement for any time not exceeding twelve hours; which confinement shall, however, be reckoned as part of any punishment afterwards imposed by the Guardians for the same offence.

ART. 132.–Every refractory pauper shall be deemed to be also disorderly, and may be punished as such; but no pauper who may have been punished for any offence as disorderly shall afterwards be punished for the same offence as refractory, and no pauper who may have been punished for any offence as refractory shall afterwards be punished for the same offence as disorderly.

ART. 133.–No pauper shall be punished by confinement or alteration in diet for any offence not committed in the Workhouse since his last admission, except in such cases as are expressly specified in Articles 127 and 128.

ART. 134.–No pauper who may have been under medical care, or who may have been entered in the medical weekly return as sick or infirm, at any time in, the course of the seven days next preceding the punishment, or who may be reasonably supposed to be under twelve or above sixty years of age, or who may be pronounced by the Medical Officer to be pregnant, or who may be suckling a child, shall be punished by alteration of diet, or by confinement, unless the Medical Officer shall have previously certified, in writing that no injury to the health of such pauper is reasonably to be apprehended from the proposed punishment; and any modification diminishing such punishment, which the Medical Officer may suggest, shall be adopted by the Master.

ART. 135.–No pauper shall be confined between eight o'clock in the evening and six o'clock in the morning, without being furnished with a bed and bedding suitable to the season, and with the other proper conveniences.

ART. 136.–No child under twelve years of age shall be punished by confinement in a dark room or during the night.

ART. 137.–No corporal punishment shall be inflicted on any male child, except by the Schoolmaster or Master.

ART. 138.–No corporal punishment shall be inflicted on any female child.

ART. 139.–No corporal punishment shall be inflicted on any male child, except with a rod or other instrument, such as may have been approved of by the Guardians or the Visiting Committee.

ART. 140.–No corporal punishment shall be inflicted on any male child until two hours shall have elapsed from the commission of the offence for which such punishment is inflicted.

ART 141.–Whenever any male child is punished by corporal correction, the Master and Schoolmaster shall (if possible) be both present.

ART. 142.–No male child shall be punished by flogging whose age may be reasonably supposed to exceed fourteen years.

ART. 143.–The Master shall keep a book to be furnished him by the Guardians, in the Form (o.) hereunto annexed, in which he shall duly enter.

Firstly. All cases of refractory or disorderly paupers, whether children or adults, reported to the Guardians for their decision thereon.

Secondly. All cases of paupers, whether children or adults, who may have been punished without the direction of the Guardians, with the particulars of their respective offences and punishments.

ART. 144.–The person who punishes any child with corporal correction shall forthwith report to the Master the particulars of the offence and punishment; and the Master shall enter the same in the book specified in Article 143.

ART. 145.–Such book shall be laid on the table at every ordinary meeting of the Guardians; and every entry made in such book since the last ordinary meeting shall be read to the Board by the Clerk.

The Guardians shall thereupon, in the first place, give direction as to the confinement or other punishment of any refractory or disorderly pauper reported for their decision, and such direction shall he entered on the minutes of the proceedings of the day, and a copy thereof shall be inserted by the Clerk in the book specified in Article 143.

The Guardians, in the second place, shall take into their consideration the cases in which punishments are reported to have been already inflicted by the Master or other officer, and shall require the Master to bring before them any pauper so punished, who may have signified a wish to see the Guardians. If the Guardians in, any case are of opinion that the officer has acted illegally or improperly, such opinion shall be entered on the minutes, and shall be communicated to the Master, and a copy of the minute of such opinion shall be forwarded to the Commissioners by the Clerk.

ART. 146.–If any pauper above the age of fourteen years unlawfully introduce or attempt to introduce any spirituous or fermented liquor into the Workhouse, or abscond from the

Workhouse with clothes belonging to, the Guardians, the Master may cause such pauper to be forthwith taken before a Justice of the Peace, to be dealt with according to law. And whether he do so or not, he shall report every such case to the Guardians at their next ordinary meeting.

ART. 147.–The Master shall cause a legible copy of Arts. 127, 128, 129, 130 and 131, to be kept suspended in the dining-hall of the Workhouse, or in the room in which the inmates usually eat their meals, and also in the Board-room of the Guardians.

VISITING COMMITTEE

ART. 148.–The Guardians shall appoint one or more Visiting Committees from their own body; and each of such committees shall carefully examine the Workhouse or, Workhouses of the Union, once in every week at the least, inspect the last reports of the Chaplain and Medical Officer, examine the stores, afford, so far as is practicable, to the inmates an opportunity of making any complaints, and investigate any complaints that may be made to them.

ART. 149.–The Visiting Committee shall from time to time write such answers as the facts may warrant to the following queries, which are to be printed in a book, entitled the VISITORS BOOK, to be provided by the Guardians, and kept in every Workhouse for that purpose, and to be submitted regularly to the Guardians at their ordinary meetings: –

Q. 1. Is the Workhouse, with its wards, offices, yards, and appurtenances, clean and well, ventilated in every part?–and is the bedding in proper order?–if not, state the defect or omission.

Q. 2. Do the inmates of the Workhouse, of all classes, appear clean in their persons, and decent and orderly in their behaviour; and is their clothing regularly changed?

Q. 3. Are the inmates of each sex employed and kept at work as directed by the Guardians, and is such work unobjectionable in its nature?–if any improvement can be suggested in their employment, state the same.

Q. 4.–Are the infirm of each sex properly attended to, according to their several conditions?

Q. 5.–Are the boys and girls in the school properly instructed as required by the regulations of the Commissioners, and is their industrial training properly attended to?

Q. 6.–Are the young children properly nursed and taken care of, and do they appear in a clean and healthy state?–Is there any child not vaccinated?

Q. 7. Is regular attendance given by the Medical Officer?–are the inmates of the Sick wards properly tended?–Are the nurses efficient?–Is there any infectious disease in the Workhouse?

Q. 8. Is there any dangerous lunatic or idiot in the Workhouse?

Q. 9. Is Divine service regularly performed?–are Prayers regularly read?

Q. 10. Is the established dietary duly observed?= and are the prescribed hours of meals regularly adhered to?

Q. 11. Are the provisions and other supplies of the qualities contracted for ?

Q. 12. Is the classification properly observed according to Articles 98 and 99 ?

Q. 13. Is any complaint made by any pauper against any officer, or in respect of the provisions or accommodations?–if so, state the name of the complainant, and the subject of the complaint.

Q. 14. Does the present number of inmates in the Workhouse exceed that fixed by the Poor Law Commissioners?

REPAIRS AND ALTERATIONS OF THE WORKHOUSE

ART. 150.–The Guardians shall once at least in every year, and as often as may be necessary for cleanliness, cause all the rooms, wards, offices, and privies belonging to the Workhouse to be limewashed.

ART. 151.–The Guardians shall cause the Workhouse and all its furniture and appurtenances to be kept in good and substantial repair; and shall, from time to time, remedy without delay any such defect in the repair of the house, its drainage, warmth, or ventilation, or in the furniture or fixtures thereof, as may tend to injure the health of the inmates.

GOVERNMENT OF THE WORKHOUSE BY THE GUARDIANS

ART. 152.—We do declare, that, subject to the rules and regulations herein contained, the guidance, government, and control of every Workhouse, and of the officers, servants, assistants, and paupers, within such Workhouse, shall be exercised by the Guardians of the Union.

APPOINTMENT OF OFFICERS

ART. 153.—The Guardians shall, whenever it may be requisite, or whenever a vacancy may occur, appoint fit persons to hold the undermentioned offices, and to perform the duties respectively assigned to them; namely,

1. Clerk to the Guardians.
2. Treasurer of the Union.
3. Chaplain.
4. Medical Officer for the Workhouse.
5. District Medical Officer.
6. Master of the Workhouse.
7. Matron of the Workhouse.
8. Schoolmaster.
9. Schoolmistress.
10. Porter.
11. Nurse.
12. Relieving Officer.
13. Superintendent of Out-door Labour.

And also such assistants as, the Guardians, with the consent of the Commissioners, may deem necessary for the efficient performance of the duties of any of the said offices.

ART. 154.—The officers so appointed to or holding any of the said offices, as well as all persons temporarily discharging the duties of such offices, shall respectively perform such duties as may be required of them by the Rules and Regulations of the Commissioners in force at, the time, together with all such other duties, conformable with the nature of their respective offices, as the Guardians may lawfully require them to perform. Provided always, that every regulation applying to any officer holding his office under this Order shall apply to any officer of the like denomination appointed by the Guardians, although such officer may have been appointed before this Order shall have come into force.

MODE OF APPOINTMENT

ART. 155.—Every officer and assistant, to be appointed under this Order, shall be appointed by a majority of the Guardians present at a meeting of the Board, consisting of more than three Guardians, or by three Guardians if no more be present. Every such appointment shall, as soon as the same has been made, be reported to the Commissioners by the Clerk.

ART. 156.—No appointment to any of the offices specified in Article 153, shall be made under this Order, unless a notice that the question of making such appointment will be brought before the Board has been given and entered on the minutes at one of the two ordinary meetings of the Board next preceding the meeting at which the appointment is made, or unless an advertisement giving notice of the consideration of such appointment shall have appeared in some public paper by the direction of the Guardians at least seven days before the day on which such appointment is made: provided that no such notice or advertisement shall be necessary for the appointment of an assistant or temporary substitute.

ART. 157.—The Guardians shall not, by advertisement, or other public notice, printed or written, invite tenders for the supply of medicines, or for the medical attendance on the paupers of the Union, unless such advertisement or notice shall specify the district or place for which such supply of medicines and such attendance is required, together with the amount of salary or other remuneration.

ART. 158.–The Guardians may from time to time divide the union into districts for general and medical relief, with the consent of the Commissioners; and on any change in the division of the Union into districts for general and medical relief, or in the assignment of Relieving Officers and Medical Officers to such districts, the Clerk shall report every such change to the Commissioners for their approbation.

ART. 159.–The Guardians shall not assign to any Medical-officer a district which exceeds in extent the area of fifteen thousand statute acres, or which contains a population exceeding the number of fifteen thousand persons, according to the then last enumeration of the population published by authority of Parliament.

ART. 160.–Provided that if it be impracticable, consistently with the proper attendance on the sick poor, for the Guardians to divide the Union into districts containing respectively an area and population less than is specified in Article 159, then and in such case the Guardians shall cause a special minute to be made and entered on the usual record of their, proceedings, stating the reasons which in their opinion make it necessary to form a district exceeding the said limits, and shall transmit a copy of such minute to the Commissioners for their consideration, and if the Commissioners signify their approval thereof to such Guardians, then and in such case, but not otherwise, such Guardians may proceed to assign the said district to a Medical Officer.

ART. 161.–Provided also, that the limit of fifteen thousand statute acres, prescribed in Article 159, shall not apply to any medical district situate wholly or in part within the Principality of Wales; but no medical district situate wholly or in part within that Principality shall be assigned to any Medical Officer residing more than seven miles from any part of any parish included within such district, unless such district shall have been specially sanctioned by the Commissioners in the same manner as is directed in Article 160.

QUALIFICATIONS OF OFFICERS

ART. 162.–No person shall hold the office of Clerk, Treasurer, Master, or Relieving Officer, under this Order, who has not reached the age of twenty-one years.

ART. 163.–No person shall hold the office of Master of a Workhouse, or Matron of a Workhouse having no Master, unless he or she be able to keep accounts.

ART. 164.–No person shall hold the office of Relieving Officer unless he be able to keep accounts, and unless he reside in the district for which he may be appointed to act, devote his whole time to the performance of the duties of his office, and abstain from following any trade or profession, and from entering into any other service.

ART. 165.–No person shall hold the office of Nurse who is not able to read written directions upon medicines.

ART. 166.–Provided always, that the Guardians may with the consent of the Commissioners previously obtained, but not otherwise, dispense with any of the conditions specified in Articles 162, 163, 164, and 165.

ART. 167.–No person shall be appointed to the office of Master, Matron, Schoolmaster, Schoolmistress, Porter, or Relieving Officer, under this Order, who does not agree to give one month's notice previous to resigning the office, or to forfeit one month's amount of salary, to be deducted as liquidated damages from the amount of salary due at the time of such resignation.

ART. 168.–No person shall hold the office of Medical Officer under this Order unless he possess one of the four following qualifications; that is to say–

　　1. A diploma or degree as surgeon from a Royal College or University in England, Scotland, or Ireland, together with a degree in medicine from an University in England, legally authorised to grant such degree, or together with a diploma or licence of the Royal College of Physicians of London.

2. A diploma or degree as surgeon from a Royal College or University in England, Scotland, or Ireland, together with a certificate to practise as an apothecary from the Society of Apothecaries of London.

3. A diploma or degree as surgeon from a Royal College or University in England, Scotland, or Ireland, such person having been in actual practice as an apothecary on the first day of August One thousand eight hundred and fifteen.

4. A warrant or commission as surgeon or assistant-surgeon in Her Majesty's Navy, or as surgeon or assistant-surgeon or apothecary in Her Majesty's Army, or, as surgeon or assistant-surgeon in the service of the Honourable East India Company, dated previous to the first day of August One thousand eight hundred and twenty-six.

ART. 169.–Provided always, that if it be impracticable, consistently with the proper attendance on the sick poor, for the Guardians to procure a person residing within the district in which he is to act, and duly qualified in one of the four modes recited in Article 168, to attend on the poor in such district, or that the only person resident within such district, and so qualified, shall have been dismissed from office by the Commissioners, or shall be unfit or incompetent to hold the office of Medical Officer, then and in such case the Guardians shall cause a special minute to be made and entered on the usual record of their proceedings, stating the reasons which, in their opinion, make it necessary to employ a person not qualified as required by Article 168, and shall forthwith transmit a copy of such minute to the Commissioners for their consideration; and the Commissioners may permit the employment by such Guardians of any person duly licensed to practise as a medical man, although such person be not qualified in one of the four modes required by Article 168.

ART. 170.–Provided also, that the Guardians may, with the consent of the Commissioners, continue in office any Medical Officer duly licensed to practise as a medical man already employed by any such Guardians, although such Medical Officer may not be qualified in one of the four modes required by Article 168.

ART. 171.–No person shall hold the office of Chaplain under this Order without the consent of the Bishop of the Diocese to his appointment, signified in writing.

REMUNERATION OF THE OFFICERS

ART. 172.–The Guardians shall pay to the several officers and assistants appointed to or holding any office or employment under this Order, such salaries or remuneration as the Commissioners may from time to time direct or approve.

Provided that the Guardians, with the approval of the Commissioners, may pay to any officer or person employed by such Guardians a reasonable compensation on account of extraordinary services, or other unforeseen circumstances connected with the duties of such officer or person or the necessities of the Union.

ART. 173.–The salary of every officer, or assistant, appointed to or holding any office or employment under this Order, shall be payable up to the day on which he ceases to hold such, office or employment, and no longer.

ART. 174.–If no remuneration or salary be expressly assigned to the Treasurer, the profit arising from the use of money from time to time left in his hands shall be deemed to be the payment of his services.

ART. 175.–An officer who may be suspended, and who may without the previous removal of such suspension be dismissed by the Commissioners, shall not be entitled to any salary from the date of such suspension.

ART. 176.–The Guardians shall not pay to any officer bound to account, to be hereafter appointed, who may have been removed, or who may be under suspension from his office, any salary claimed by such officer until his accounts shall have been audited by the Auditor.

ART. 177.–No salary of any District Medical Officer shall include the remuneration for operations and services of the following classes performed by such Medical Officer in that capacity for any out-door pauper, but such operations and services shall be paid for by the Guardians, according to the rates specified in this Article.

	£	s	d
1. Treatment of compound fractures of the thigh	5	0	0
2. Treatment of compound fractures or compound dislocations of the leg	"		
3. Amputation of leg, arm, foot, or hand	"		
4. The operation of a strangulated hernia	"		
5. Treatment of simple fractures or simple dislocations of the thigh or leg	3	0	0
6. Amputation of a finger or toe	2	0	0
7. Treatment of dislocations or fractures of the arm	1	0	0

The above rates shall include the payment for the supply of all kinds of apparatus and splints.

ART. 178.–Provided that, except in cases of sudden accident immediately threatening life, no Medical Officer shall be entitled to receive such remuneration for any amputation, unless he shall have obtained at his own cost the advice of some member of the Royal College of Surgeons of London, or some fellow or licentiate of the Royal College of Physicians of London, before performing such amputation, and unless he shall also produce to the Guardians a certificate from such member of the Royal College of Surgeons, or such fellow or licentiate, stating that in his opinion it was right and proper that such amputation should be then performed.

ART. 179.–Provided also, that if in any case the patient has not survived the operation more than thirty-six hours, and has not required and received several attendances after the operation by the Medical Officer who has performed the same, such Medical Officer shall be entitled only to one-half of the payments respectively prescribed above.

ART. 180.–Provided also, that if several of the fees specified in Art. 177 become payable with respect to the same, person at the same time, and in consequence of the same cause or injury, the Medical Officer shall be entitled only to one of such fees, and if they be unequal, to the highest.

ART. 181.–In any surgical case, not provided for in Art. 177, which has presented peculiar difficulty, or required and received long attendance from the District Medical Officer, the Guardians may make to the said Medical Officer such reasonable extra allowance as they may think fit, and the Commissioners may approve.

ART. 182.–In cases in which any Medical Officer, either for the Workhouse or a District, shall be called on by order of a person legally qualified to make such order, to attend any woman in or immediately after childbirth, or shall, under circumstances of difficulty or danger, without any order, visit any such woman actually receiving relief, or whom the Guardians may subsequently decide to have been in a destitute condition, such Medical Officer shall be paid for his attendance and medicines by a sum of not less than Ten shillings, nor more than Twenty shillings, according as the Guardians may agree with such Officer.

ART. 183.–Provided that in any special case in which great difficulty may have occurred in the delivery, or long subsequent attendance in respect of some puerperal malady or affection may have been requisite, any District Medical Officer shall receive the sum of Two pounds.

SECURITY OF THE OFFICERS

ART. 184.–Every Treasurer, Master, Matron of a Workhouse in which there is no Master, Collector, or Relieving Officer, every person hereafter appointed as Clerk, and every other officer whom the Guardians shall require so to do, shall respectively give a Bond conditioned for the due and faithful performance of the duties of the office, with two sufficient sureties, not, in the case of any security to be hereafter entered into, being officers of the same Union; and every officer who shall have entered into any such security shall give, immediate notice to the Guardians of the death, insolvency, or bankruptcy of either of such sureties, and shall, when required by the Guardians, produce a certificate, signed by two householders, that his sureties are alive, and believed by them to be solvent, and such officer shall supply a fresh surety, in the place of any such surety who may die, or become bankrupt or insolvent.

ART. 185.—Provided that the Guardians may, if they think, fit, take the security of any society or company expressly authorised by statute to guarantee or secure the faithful discharge of the duties of such officers.

ART. 186.—Provided also, that the Guardians may, with the consent of the Commissioners, dispense with such security in the case of any banking, firm acting as Treasurer, or in the case of a Treasurer, being a banker or partner of such firm.

CONTINUANCE IN OFFICE AND SUSPENSION OF OFFICERS – SUPPLY OF VACANCIES

ART. 187.—Every officer appointed to or holding any office under this Order, other than a Medical, Officer, shall continue to hold the same until he die, or resign, or be removed by the Commissioners, or be proved to be insane, to the satisfaction of the Commissioners.

ART. 188.—Provided always, that every Porter, Nurse, Assistant, or servant, may be dismissed by the Guardians without the consent of the Commissioners; but, every such dismissal, and the grounds thereof, shall be reported to the Commissioners.

ART. 189.—If any Master and Matron hereafter appointed be husband and wife, and one of them should be dismissed by Order of the Commissioners, or should otherwise vacate his or her office, or should die, the other or survivor shall, at the expiration of the then current quarter, cease to hold his or her office of Master or Matron, as the case may be.

ART. 190.—No officer of a Workhouse who may have been dismissed by any Order of the Commissioners, shall, after such dismissal, remain upon the Workhouse premises, or enter therein for the purpose of interfering in the management of such Workhouse, unless the Commissioners have consented to his subsequent appointment to an office in such Workhouse, under the provisions of the said first-recited Act, or to his temporary employment therein.

ART. 191.—Every Medical Officer duly appointed shall, unless the period for which he is appointed be entered on the Minutes of the Guardians at the time of making such appointment, or be acknowledged in writing by such Medical Officer, continue in office until he may die or resign, or become legally disqualified to hold such office, or be removed therefrom by the Commissioners.

ART. 192.—The Guardians may at their discretion suspend from the discharge of his or her duties any Master, Matron, Schoolmaster, Schoolmistress, Medical Officer, Relieving Officer, or Superintendent of Out-door Labour, and the Guardians shall, in case of every such suspension, forthwith report the same, together with the cause thereof, to the Commissioners; and if the Commissioners remove the suspension of such officer by the Guardians, he or she shall forthwith resume the performance of his or her duties.

ART. 193.—If any officer, or assistant, appointed to or holding any office or employment under this Order, be at any time prevented by sickness or accident, or other sufficient reason, from the performance of his duties, the Guardians may appoint a fit person to act as his temporary substitute, and may pay him a reasonable compensation for his services and every such appointment shall be reported to the Commissioners as soon as the same shall have been made.

ART. 194.—The Vice-Chairman, or some Guardian to be appointed by the Guardians, may perform any of the duties assigned to the Clerk until any vacancy in the office shall have been filled, or until a substitute be appointed in the case of the sickness, accident, or absence of the Clerk.

ART. 195.—When any officer may die, resign, or become legally disqualified to perform the duties of his office, the Guardians shall, as soon as conveniently may be after such death, resignation, or disqualification, give notice thereof to, the Commissioners, and proceed to make a new appointment to the office so vacant in the manner prescribed by the above regulations.

ART. 196.—If any officer give notice of an intended resignation to take effect on a future day, the Guardians may elect a successor to such officer, in conformity with the above regulations, at any time subsequent to such notice.

ART. 197.–In the case of any Medical Officer who holds his office for a specified term, the Guardians may provide for the continuance of such officer, or appoint his successor, within three calendar months next before the expiration of such term.

PERSONAL DISCHARGE OF DUTIES

ART. 198.–In every case not otherwise provided for by this Order, every officer shall perform his duties in person, and shall not intrust the same to a deputy, except with the special permission of the Commissioners on the application of the Guardians.

ART. 199.–Every Medical Officer shall be bound to visit and attend personally, as far as may be practicable, the poor persons intrusted to his care, and shall be responsible for the attendance on them.

ART. 200.–Every Medical Officer shall, as soon as may be after his appointment, name to the Guardians some legally qualified medical practitioner to whom application for medicines or attendance may be made, in the case of his absence from home, or other hindrance to his personal attendance, and who will supply the same at the cost of such Medical Officer, and the name and residence of every Medical Practitioner so named shall be forwarded by the Clerk to each Relieving Officer, and to the Overseers of every Parish in the District of such Medical Officer.

DUTIES OF THE OFFICERS

ART. 201.–And We do hereby define and specify the duties of the several Officers appointed to or holding their offices under this Order, and direct the execution thereof, to be as follows:

DUTIES OF THE CLERK

ART. 202.–The following shall be the duties of the Clerk:

No. 1. To attend all meetings of the Board of Guardians, and to keep punctually minutes of the proceedings, at every meeting, to enter the said minutes in a book, and to submit the same so entered to the presiding Chairman at the succeeding meeting for his signature.

No. 2. To keep, check, and examine all accounts, books of accounts, minutes, books, and other documents as required of him by the Regulations of the Commissioners, or relating to the business of the Guardians, and from time to time to produce all such books and documents, together with the necessary vouchers, and the bonds of any Officers, with any certificates relating thereto, which may be in his custody, to the Auditor of the Union, at the place of audit and at the time and in such manner as may be required by the Regulations of the Commissioners.

No. 3. To peruse and conduct the correspondence of the Guardians according to their directions, and to preserve the same, as well as all Orders of the Commissioners, and letters received, together with copies of all letters sent, and all letters, books, papers, and documents, belonging to the Union, or intrusted to him by the Guardians, and to make all necessary copies thereof.

No. 4. To prepare all written contracts and agreements to be entered into by any parties with the Guardians, and to see that the same are duly executed, and to prepare all bonds or other securities to be given by any of the Officers of the Union, and to see that the same are duly executed by such Officers and their sureties.

No. 5. To receive all requisitions of Guardians for extraordinary meetings, and to summon such meetings accordingly and to make, sign, and send all notices required to be given to the Guardians, by this or any other Order of the Commissioners.

No. 6. To countersign all orders legally made by the Guardians on Overseers, for the payment of money, and all orders legally drawn, by the Guardians upon the Treasurer.

No. 7. To ascertain, before every ordinary meeting of the Board, the balance due to or from the Union, in account with the Treasurer, and to enter the same in the Minute-book.

No. 8. At the first meeting of the Guardians in each quarter, to lay before the Guardians, or some Committee appointed by them, the non-settled poor account, and the non-resident poor account, posted in his ledger to the end of the preceding quarter, and to take the directions of the Guardians respecting the remittance of cheques or post-office orders to the Guardians of any other Union or Parish, or the transmission of accounts due from other Unions or Parishes, and requests for payment.

No. 9. Within fourteen days from the close of each quarter, to transmit by post all accounts of relief administered in the course of the preceding quarter to non-settled poor to the Guardians of the Unions and Parishes on account of which such relief was given and to state in every account so transmitted the names and classes of the several paupers to whom the relief in question has been administered.

No. 10. To communicate to the several Officers and persons engaged in the administration of relief within the Union, all orders and directions of the Commissioners, or of the Guardians; and so far as may be, to give the instructions requisite for the prompt and correct execution of all such orders and directions, and to report to the Guardians any neglect or failure therein which may come to his knowledge.

No. 11. To conduct all applications by or on behalf of the Guardians to any Justice or Justices at their Special, Petty, or General Sessions, and if he be an attorney or solicitor, to perform and execute all legal business connected with the Union, or in which the Guardians shall be engaged, except prosecutions at the assizes, actions at law, suits in equity, or parliamentary business, without charge for anything beyond disbursements.

No. 12. To prepare and transmit all reports, answers, or returns, as to any question or matter connected with or relating to the administration of the laws for the relief of the Poor in the Union, or to any other business of the Union, which are required by the regulations of the Commissioners, or which the Commissioners, or any Assistant-Commissioner, may lawfully require from him.

No. 13. To conduct duly and impartially, and in strict conformity with the regulations in force at the time, the annual or any other election of Guardians.

No. 14. To observe and execute all lawful orders and directions of the Guardians applicable to his office.

DUTIES OF THE TREASURER OF THE UNION

ART. 203.—The following shall be the duties of the Treasurer of the Union:

No. 1. To receive all monies tendered to be paid to the Guardians, and to place the same to their credit.

No. 2. To pay out of any monies for the time being in his hands belonging to the Guardians, all orders for money which shall be drawn upon him, in conformity with Art. 84, when the same shall be presented at the house or usual place of business of the Treasurer, and within the usual hours of business.

No. 3. To keep an account, under the proper dates, of all monies received and paid by him as such Treasurer, to balance the same at Lady-day and Michaelmas in every year, and to render an account of such monies to the Guardians, when required by them to do so.

No. 4. Whenever there are not funds belonging to the Guardians in his hands as Treasurer of the Union, to report in writing the fact of such deficiency to the Commissioners.

No. 5. To submit a proper account, together with the bonds of any officers which may be in his custody, to the Auditor at the place of audit, and at the time and in such manner as may be required, by the regulations of the Commissioners.

No. 6. To receive the monies payable to him as Treasurer of the Union, under any Act of Parliament or other authority of law.

ART. 204.–Provided that the regulations in Art. 203 shall not be applicable to cases in which the Governor and Company of the Bank of England may act as Treasurer of the Union or Bankers to the Guardians.

DUTIES OF A MEDICAL OFFICER

ART. 205.–The following shall be the duties of every Medical Officer appointed by the Guardians, whether he be the Medical Officer for a Workhouse or for a District:

No. 1. To give to the Guardians, when required, any reasonable information respecting the case of any pauper who is or has been under his care to make any such written report relative to any sickness prevalent among the paupers under his care, as the Guardians or the Commissioners may require of him and to attend any meeting of the Board of Guardians when requested by them to do so.

No. 2. To give a certificate respecting children whom it is proposed to apprentice, in conformity with Articles 59 and 61.

No. 3. To give a certificate under his hand in every case to the Guardians, or the Relieving Officer, or the pauper on whom he is attending, of the sickness of such pauper or other cause of his attendance, when required to do so.

No. 4. In keeping the books prescribed by this Order, to employ, so far as is practicable, the terms used or recommended in the regulations and statistical nosology issued by the Registrar General and also to show when the visit or attendance made or given to any pauper was made or given by any person employed by himself.

DUTIES OF A DISTRICT MEDICAL OFFICER

ART. 206.–The following shall be the duties of a District Medical Officer:

No. 1. To attend duly and punctually upon all poor persons requiring medical attendance within the District of the Union assigned to him, and according to his agreement to supply the requisite medicines to such persons, whenever he may be lawfully required to furnish such attendance or medicines by a written or printed order of the Guardians, or of a Relieving Officer of the Union, or of an Overseer.

No. 2. On the exhibition to him of a ticket, according to Art. 76, and on application made on behalf of the party to whom such ticket vas given, to afford such medical attendance and medicines as he would be bound to supply if he had received in each case an order from the Guardians to afford such attendance and medicines.

No. 3. To inform the Relieving Officer of any poor person whom he may attend 'without an order.

No, 4. To make a return to the Guardians at each ordinary meeting, in a book prepared according to the Form marked (P.) hereunto annexed, and to insert therein the date of every attendance, and the other particulars required by such Form, in conformity with Art. 205, No. 4.

Provided, however, that the Medical Officer may, with the consent of the Guardians, but not other wise, make the entries which he is directed to make in such book on detached sheets of paper, according to the same Form, and cause the same to be laid before the Guardians at every ordinary meeting, instead of such book; and the Guardians shall, in that case, cause such sheets to be bound up at the end of the year.

DUTIES OF THE MEDICAL OFFICER FOR THE WORKHOUSE

ART. 207. The following shall be the duties of the Medical Officer for the Workhouse:

No. 1. To attend at the Workhouse at the periods fixed by the Guardians, and also when sent for by the Master or Matron.

No. 2. To attend duly and punctually upon all poor persons in the Workhouse requiring medical attendance, and according to his agreement to supply the requisite medicines to such per sons.

No. 3. To examine the state of the paupers on their admission into the Workhouse, and to give the requisite directions to the Master according to Articles 91 and 92.

No. 4. To give directions and make suggestions as to the diet, classification, and treatment of the sick paupers, and paupers of unsound mind, and to report to the Guardians any pauper of unsound mind in the Workhouse whom he may deem to be dangerous, or fit to be sent to a Lunatic Asylum.

No. 5. To give all necessary instructions as to the diet or treatment of children and women suckling children, and to vaccinate such of the children as may require vaccination.

No. 6. To report in writing to the Guardians any defect in the diet, drainage, ventilation, warmth, or other arrangements of the Workhouse, or any excess in the number of any class of inmates, which he may deem to be detrimental to the health of the inmates.

No. 7. To report in writing to the Guardians any defect which he may observe in the arrangements of the Infirmary, and in the performance of their duties by the Nurses of the sick.

No. 8. To make a return to the Guardians, at each ordinary meeting, in a book prepared according to the Form (Q.) hereunto annexed, and to insert therein the date of every attendance, in conformity with Art. 205, and the other particulars required by such Form to be inserted by the Medical Officer, and to enter in such return the death of every pauper who shall die in the Workhouse, together with the apparent cease thereof.

No. 9. To enter in the commencement of such Book, according to the Form marked (R.) hereunto annexed, the proper dietary for the sick paupers in the house in so many different scales as he shall deem expedient.

DUTIES OF THE MASTER

ART. 208.–The following shall be the duties of the Master: –

No. 1. To admit paupers into the Workhouse, in obedience to the orders specified in Art. 88, end also every person applying for admission who may appear to him to require relief through any sudden or urgent necessity, and to cease every pauper upon admission, to be examined by the Medical, Officer, as is directed in Article 91.

No. 2. To cause every male pauper above the age of seven years, upon admission, to be searched, cleansed, and clothed, and to be placed in the proper ward.

No. 3. To enforce industry, order, punctuality, and cleanliness and the observance of all regulations for the government of the Workhouse by the paupers, and by the several officers, assistants, and servants therein.

No. 4. To read Prayers to the paupers before breakfast and after supper every day, or cause Prayers to be read, according to Article 124.

No. 5. To cause the paupers to be inspected, and their names called over, in conformity with Art. 103, in order that it may be seen that each individual is clean and in a proper state.

No. 6. To provide for and enforce the employment of the able-bodied adult paupers, during the hours of labour to assist in training the youths in such employment as will best fit them for gaining their own living to keep the partially disabled paupers occupied to the extent of their ability; and to allow none who are capable of employment to be idle at any time.

No: 7. To visit the sleeping wards of the male paupers at eleven o'clock in the forenoon of every day, and see that such wards have been all duly cleansed and are properly ventilated.

No. 8. To see that the meals of the paupers are duly provided, dressed and served, according to the directions in Articles 104 and 107, and to superintend the distribution of the food.

No. 9. To say, or cause to be said, grace before and after meals.

No. 10. To visit all the wards of the male paupers before nine o'clock every night in winter, and ten o'clock in summer, and see that all the male paupers are in bed, and that all fires and lights therein are extinguished, except so far as may be necessary for the sick.

No. 11. To receive from the Porter the keys of the Workhouse at nine o'clock every night, and to deliver them to him again at six o'clock every morning, or at such hours as shall from time to time be fixed by the Guardians.

No. 12. To see that the male paupers are properly clothed, and that their clothes are kept in proper repair.

No. 13. To cause the birth of every child born in the Workhouse to be registered by the Registrar of Births and Deaths within the space of one week after such child shall have been born; and also to enter such birth in a register kept according to Form (S.) hereunto annexed.

No. 14. To send for the Medical Officer in case any pauper is taken ill or becomes insane, and to take care that all sick and insane paupers are duly visited by the Medical Officer, and are provided with such medicines and attendance, diet and other necessaries, as the Medical Officer or the Guardians direct, and to apprise the nearest relation in the Workhouse of the sickness of any pauper, and, in the case of dangerous sickness, to send for the Chaplain, and any relative or friend of the pauper, resident within a reasonable distance, whom the pauper may desire to see.

No. 15. To take care that no pauper at the approach of death shall be left unattended either during the day or the night.

No. 16. To give immediate information of the death of any pauper in the Workhouse to the Medical Officer, and to the nearest relations of the deceased who may be known to him, and who may reside within a reasonable distance; and if the body be not removed within a reasonable time, to provide for the interment thereof.

No. 17. When requisite, to cause the death of every pauper dying in the Workhouse to be duly registered by the Registrar of Births and Deaths within five days after, the day of such death and also to enter such death in a register kept according to Form (T.) hereunto annexed.

No. 18. To deliver an inventory of the clothes and other property of any pauper who may have died in the Workhouse, to the Guardians at their next ordinary meeting.

No. 19. To keep such portion of the Workhouse Medical Relief Book prescribed in this Order as is assigned to him in the Form marked (Q.), and to keep all books or accounts which he is, or hereafter may be, by any Order of the Commissioners, directed and required to keep, to allow the same to be constantly open to the inspection of any of the Guardians of the Union, and to submit the same to the Guardians at their ordinary meetings.

No. 20. To submit to the Guardians, at every ordinary meeting, an estimate of such provisions and other articles as are required for the use of the Workhouse, and to receive and execute the directions of the Guardians thereupon.

No. 21. To receive all provisions and other articles purchased or procured for the use of the Workhouse, and before placing them in store to examine and compare them with the bills of parcels or invoices severally relating thereto; and after having proved the accuracy of such bills or invoices, to authenticate the same with his signature, and submit them to the Guardians at their next ordinary meeting.

No. 22. To receive and take charge of all provisions, clothing, linen, and other articles belonging to the Workhouse, or confided to his care by the Guardians, and issue the same to the Matron or other persons as may be required.

No. 23. To report to the Guardians from time to time the names of such children as the Schoolmaster may recommend as fit to be put out to service or other employment, and to take the necessary steps for carrying into effect the directions of the Guardians thereon.

No. 24. To take care that the wards, rooms, larder, kitchen, and all other offices of the Workhouse, and all the utensils and furniture thereof, be kept clean and in good order and as often as any defect, in the same, or in the state of the Workhouse, shall occur, to report the same in writing, to the, Guardians at their next ordinary meeting.

No. 25. To submit to the Guardians, at every ordinary meeting, a report of the number of the inmates in the Workhouse according to the Form (U.) hereto annexed.

No. 26. To bring before the Visiting Committee or the Guardians any pauper inmate desirous of making a complaint or application to the Guardians.

No. 27. To report forthwith to the Medical Officer and to the Guardians, in writing, all cases in which any restraint or compulsion may have been used towards any pauper inmate of unsound mind in the Workhouse.

No. 28. To keep a book, in which he shall enter all his written report to the Guardians or to the Medical Officer, and to lay the same before the Guardians at every ordinary meeting.

No. 29. To inform the Visiting Committee and the Guardians of the state of the Workhouse in every department, and to report in writing to the Guardians any negligence or other misconduct on the part of any of the subordinate officers or servants of the establishment;

And generally to observe and fulfil all lawful orders and directions of the Guardians suitable to his office.

ART. 209.–The Master shall not, except in case of necessity, purchase or procure any articles for the use of the Workhouse, nor order any alterations or repairs of any part of the premises, or of the furniture or other article belonging thereto, nor pay any monies on account of the Workhouse, or of the Union, without the authority of the Guardians, nor apply any articles belonging to the Guardians to purposes other than those authorised or approved of by such Guardians.

DUTIES OF THE MATRON

ART. 210.–The following shall be the duties of the Matron: –

No. 1. In the absence of the Master, or during his inability to act, to act as his substitute in the admission of paupers into the Workhouse, according to Articles 88 and 208, No. 1 and 2, and to cause every pauper upon such admission to be examined by the Medical Officer, as is directed in Art. 91.

No. 2. To cause the pauper children under the age of seven years, and the female paupers, to be searched, cleansed, and clothed, upon their admission, and to be placed in their proper ward.

No. 3. To provide, for and enforce the employment of the able-bodied female paupers during the hours of labour, and to keep the partially disabled female paupers occupied to the extent of their ability, and to assist the Schoolmistress in training up the children so as best to fit them for service.

No. 4. To call over the names of the paupers as is directed in Art. 103, to inspect their persons, and see that each individual is clean.

No. 5. To visit the sleeping wards of the female paupers at eleven o'clock of the forenoon of every day, and to see that such wards have been all duly cleansed and are properly ventilated.

No. 6. To visit all the wards of the females and children every night before nine o'clock, and to ascertain that all the paupers in such wards are in bed, and all the fires and lights, not necessary for the sick or for women suckling their children therein, extinguished.

No. 7. To pay particular attention to the moral conduct and orderly behaviour of the females and children, and to see that they are clean and decent in their dress and persons.

No. 8. To superintend and give the necessary directions for making and mending the linen and clothing supplied to the male paupers, and all the clothing supplied to the female paupers and children, and to take care that all such clothing be properly numbered and marked on the inside with the name of the Union.

No. 9. To see that every pauper in the Workhouse has clean linen and stockings once a week, and that all the beds and bedding be kept in a clean and wholesome state.

No. 10. To take charge of the linen and stockings for the use of the paupers, and the other linen in use in the Workhouse, and to apply the same to such purposes as shall be authorised or approved of by the Guardians, and to no other.

No. 11. To superintend and give the necessary directions concerning the washing, drying, and getting up of the linen, stockings, and blankets, and to see that the same be not dried in the sleeping wards or in the sick wards.

No. 12. To take proper care of the children and sick paupers, and to provide the proper diet for the same, and for women suckling infants, and to furnish them with such changes of clothes and linen as may be necessary.

No. 13. To assist the Master in the general management and superintendence of the Workhouse, and especially in

Enforcing the observance of good order, cleanliness, punctuality, industry, and decency of demeanour among the paupers;—

Cleansing and ventilating the sleeping wards and the dining-hall, and all other parts of the premises;—

Placing in store and taking charge of the pro visions, clothing, linen, and other articles belonging to the Union.

No. 14. When requested by the Porter, in pursuance of Article 214, No. 5, to search any female entering or leaving the Workhouse under the circumstances described in that Article.

No. 15. To report to the Master any negligence or other misconduct on the part of any of the female officers or servants of the establishment, or any case in which restraint or compulsion may have been used towards any female inmate of unsound mind.

No. 16. And generally to observe and fulfil all lawful orders and directions of the Guardians suitable to her office.

DUTIES OF THE CHAPLAIN

ART. 211.–The following shall be the duties of the Chaplain:

No. 1. To read prayers and preach a sermon to the paupers and other inmates of the Workhouse on every Sunday, and on Good Friday and Christmas-day, unless the Guardians, with the consent of the Commissioners, may otherwise direct.

No. 2. To examine the children, and to catechise such as belong to the Church of England, at least once in every month, and to make a record of the same, and state the dates of his attendance, the general progress and condition of the children, and the moral and religious state of the inmates generally, in a book to be kept for that purpose, to be laid before the Guardians at their next ordinary meeting, and to be termed 'THE CHAPLAIN'S REPORT.'

No. 3. To visit the sick paupers, and to administer religious consolation to them in the Workhouse, at such periods as the Guardians may appoint, and when applied to for that purpose by the Master or Matron.

DUTIES OF THE SCHOOLMASTER AND SCHOOLMISTRESS

ART. 212.–The following shall be the duties of the Schoolmaster and Schoolmistress for the Workhouse, or either of them:

No. 1. To instruct the boys and girls according to the directions in Article 114.

No. 2. To regulate the discipline and arrangements of the school, and the industrial and moral training of the children, subject to the direction of the Guardians.

No. 3. To accompany the children when they quit the Workhouse for exercise, or for attendance at public worship, unless the Guardians shall otherwise direct.

No. 4. To keep the children clean in their persons, and orderly and decorous in their conduct.

No. 5. To assist the Master and Matron respectively in maintaining due subordination in the Workhouse.

DUTIES OF A NURSE

ART. 213.—The following shall be the duties of a Nurse for the Workhouse:

No. 1. To attend upon the sick in the sick and lying-in wards, and to administer to them all medicines and medical applications, according to the directions of the Medical Officer.

No. 2. To inform the Medical Officer of any defects which may be observed in the arrangements of the sick or lying-in ward.

No. 3. To take care that a light is kept at night in the sick ward.

DUTIES OF THE PORTER

ART. 214.—The following shall be the duties of the Porter of the Workhouse:

No. 1. To keep the gate, and to prevent any person not being an officer of the Workhouse, or of the Union, an Assistant Poor Law Commissioner, or any person authorised by law, or by the Commissioners or Guardians, from entering into or going out of the house without the leave of the Master or Matron.

No. 2. To keep a book in which he shall enter the name and business of every officer or other person who shall go into the Workhouse, and the name of every officer or other person who shall go out thereof, together with the time of such officer's or person's going in or out.

No. 3. To receive all paupers who apply or present themselves for admission in conformity with Art. 88, and if the Master and Matron be both absent, to place such paupers in the receiving ward until the Master or Matron return.

No. 4. To examine all parcels and goods before they are received into the Workhouse, and prevent the admission of any spirituous or fermented liquors, or other articles contrary to any of the regulations contained in this Order, or otherwise contrary to law.

No. 5. To search any male pauper entering or leaving the Workhouse whom he may suspect of having possession of any spirits or other prohibited articles, and to require any other person entering the Workhouse whom he may suspect of having possession of any such spirits or prohibited articles, to satisfy him to the contrary before he permit such person to be admitted; and in the case of any female, to cause the Matron to be called for the purpose of searching her, if necessary.

No. 6. To examine all parcels taken by any pauper out of the Workhouse, and to prevent the undue removal of any article from the premises.

No. 7. To lock all the outer doors, and take the keys to the Master, at nine o'clock every night, and to receive them back from him every morning at six o'clock, or at such hours as shall from time to time be fixed by the Guardians and if any application for admission to the Workhouse be made after the keys shall have been so taken to the Master, to apprise the Master forthwith of such application.

No. 8. To assist the Master and Matrons in preserving order, and in enforcing obedience and due subordination in the Workhouse.

No. 9. To inform the Master of all things affecting the security and order of the Workhouse, and to obey all lawful directions of the Master or Matron, and of the Guardians, suitable to his office.

DUTIES OF A RELIEVING OFFICER

ART. 215.–The following shall be the duties of a Relieving Officer:

No. 1. To attend all ordinary meetings of the Guardians, and to attend all other meetings when summoned by the Clerk.

No. 2. To receive all applications for relief made to him within his district, or relating to any parish situated within his district, and forthwith to examine into the circumstances of every case by visiting the house of the applicant (if situated within his district), and by making all necessary inquiries into the state of health, the ability to work, the condition and family, and the means of such applicant, and to report the result of such inquiries in the prescribed form to the Guardians at their next ordinary meeting, and also to visit from time to time as requisite all paupers receiving relief, and to report concerning the same as the Guardians may direct.

No. 3. In any case of sickness or accident requiring relief by medical attendance to procure such attendance by giving an order on the District Medical Officer, in the Form (V.) hereunto annexed, or by such other means as the urgency of the case may require.

No. 4. To ascertain from time to time from the District Medical Officer the names of any poor persons whom such Medical Officer may have attended or supplied with medicines, without having received an order from himself to that effect.

No. 5. In every case of a poor person receiving medical relief, as soon as may be, and from time to time afterwards, to visit the house of such person, and until the next ordinary meeting of the Guardians, to supply such relief (not being in money) as the case on his own view, or on the certificate of the District Medical Officer, may seem to require.

No. 6. In every case of sudden or urgent necessity, to afford such relief to the destitute person as may be requisite, either by giving such person an order of admission into the Workhouse, and conveying him thereto if necessary, or by affording him relief out of the Workhouse, provided that the same be not given in money, whether such destitute person be settled in any Parish comprised in the Union or not.

No. 7. To report to the Guardians at their next ordinary meeting all cases reported to him by an Overseer in conformity with Art. 218, and to obey the directions of the Guardians with reference to the relief administered in such cases.

No. 8. To perform the duties with respect to pauper apprentices prescribed by Arts. 60, 61, and 62.

No. 9. To give all reasonable aid and assistance at the request of any other Relieving Officer of the Union, by examining into the case of any applicant for relief, or administering relief to any pauper whose name has been entered on the books of such other Relieving Officer, and who may be within his own district.

No. 10. Duly and punctually to supply the weekly allowances of all paupers belonging to his district, or being within the same, and to pay or administer the relief of all paupers within his district to the amount and in the manner in which he may have been lawfully ordered by the Guardians to pay or administer the same.

No. 11. To visit, relieve, and otherwise attend to non-settled poor, being within his district, according to the directions of the Guardians, whose officer he is, and in no other way, subject always to the obligation imposed on him in cases of sudden or urgent necessity.

No. 12. To set apart one or more pages in his Outdoor Relief List, in which he shall duly and punctually enter up the payments made by authority of his own Board of Guardians, to non-settled poor, and to take credit for such payments in his Receipt and Expenditure Book.

No. 13. To present his weekly accounts to the Clerk for his inspection and authentication before every ordinary meeting of the Guardians, and to the Guardians, at such meeting, for their approval.

No. 14. To submit to the Auditor of the Union all his books, accounts, and vouchers, at the place of audit, and at such time, and in such manner, as may be required by the Regulations of the Commissioners.

No. 15. To assist the Clerk in conducting and completing the annual or other election of Guardians, according to the Regulations of the Commissioners.

No. 16. To observe and execute all lawful orders and directions of the Guardians applicable to his office.

ART. 216.—The Relieving Officer shall in no case tales credit in his accounts, or enter as paid or given by way of relief, any money or other articles which have not been paid or given previously to the taking of such credit, or the making of such entry; and he shall not take credit in such accounts for any money paid to any tradesman or other person without producing, at the next ordinary meeting of the Guardians, a bill from such tradesman or person with voucher of payment.

DUTIES OF A SUPERINTENDENT OF OUT-DOOR LABOUR

ART. 217.—The duties of a Superintendent of Outdoor Labour shall be to superintend any able-bodied paupers not inmates of the Workhouse who may be set to work by the Guardians, to take care that they perform the work respectively assigned to them, and to report truly to the Guardians respecting the performance of such work.

RECEIPT AND PAYMENT OF MONEY BY OFFICERS

ART. 218.—No Clerk, Relieving Officer, Master, or other Officer appointed to or holding any office under this Order, shall, directly or indirectly, receive or bargain to receive any gratuity, percentage, or allowance of any kind with reference to any contract with the Guardians, or in respect of any payment made or to be made for goods supplied or work executed according to the order of such Guardians or on their behalf.

ART. 219.—No Clerk shall directly or indirectly cause to be paid to himself, or shall pay away on his own account or for his own benefit, any cheque drawn by the Guardians, and made payable to any person other than himself.

ART. 220.—Every Clerk receiving any cheque or money from the Guardians on account of any other party, shall transmit the same within fourteen days to the proper persons, and shall produce the receipt or acknowledgment for the same at the next ordinary meeting after the same has come to his hands.

ART. 221.—Every Officer of the Union who may receive money on behalf of the Guardians thereof, shall forthwith pay the same into the hands of the Treasurer of the Union, to the credit of the Guardians, notwithstanding that any salary or balance may be due from the Union to such officer.

ART. 222.—No Relieving Officer, or other officer of any Guardians, nor any Assistant Overseer or Collector, shall receive money for the relief of any non-settled pauper on behalf of any officer, or of the Guardians, of any other Parish or Union, or shall constitute himself in any way the agent of any officer or Guardians of such other Parish or Union, except as is provided in this Order.

ART. 223.—If any money be transmitted to any officer contrary to the provisions of this Order, such officer shall forthwith pay such money into the hands of, the Treasurer of the Union whose officer he is, and shall report to the Guardians at their next meeting the fact that such money has been so received and paid, and shall make a true entry accordingly in his accounts.

EXPLANATION OF TERMS

ART. 224.—Whenever the word 'Parish' is used in this Order, it shall be taken to include any place maintaining its own poor, whether parochial or extra-parochial.

ART. 225.—Whenever the word 'Overseer' is used in this Order, it shall be taken to include any person acting or legally bound to act in the discharge of any of the duties usually performed by Overseers of the Poor, so far as such duties are referred to in this Order.

ART. 226.–Whenever the word 'Commissioners' is used in this Order, it shall be taken to mean the Poor Law Commissioners.

ART. 227.–Whenever the word 'medicines' is used in this Order, it shall be taken to include all medical and surgical appliances; whenever the words 'medical attendance' are used in this Order, they shall be taken to include surgical attendance; and whenever the words 'medical relief' are used in this Order, they shall be taken to include relief by surgical as well as medical attendance.

ART. 228.–Whenever the words 'Medical Officer' are used in this Order, they shall be taken to include any person duly licensed as a medical man, who may have contracted or agreed with any Guardians for the supply of medicines, or for medical attendance.

ART. 229.–Whenever the words 'Clerk', 'Master' or 'Matron' are used in this Order, they shall be taken to mean the Clerk to the Guardians, and the Master or Matron of the Workhouse respectively.

ART. 230.–The term 'non-resident poor' in this Order shall be taken to mean all paupers in receipt of relief allowed on account of any Union in relation to which the term is used, but not residing therein.

ART. 231.–The term 'non-settled poor' in this Order shall be taken to mean all paupers residing in the Union in relation to which the term is used, but to whom relief is allowed on account of some Parish or Union other than that in which they reside.

ART. 232.–Whenever in describing any person or party, matter or thing, the word importing the singular number or the masculine gender only is used in this Order, the same shall be taken to include, and shall be applied to, several persons or parties as well as one person or party, and females as well as males, and several matters or things as well as one matter or thing respectively, unless there be something in the subject or context repugnant to such construction.

ART. 233.–Whenever in this Order any Article is referred to by its number, the Article of this Order bearing that number shall be taken to be signified thereby.

BIBLIOGRAPHY

Adams, J. (2000) 'The Last Years of the Workhouse, 1930-1965' (in J. Bornat, R. Perks, P. Thompson and J. Walsmley (eds.), *Oral History, Health and Welfare*, pp. 97-118)

Anonymous (1686) *An Account of the General Nursery or College of Infants Set up by the Justices of the Peace for the County of Middlesex*

Anonymous (1711) *Some Considerations Offer'd to the Citizens of Bristol, Relating to the Corporation for the Poor in the Said City*

Anonymous (1725) *An Account of Several Workhouses for Employing and Maintaining the Poor, Setting Forth the Rules by Which They Are Governed*

Anonymous (1732) *An Account of Several Workhouses for Employing and Maintaining the Poor, Setting Forth the Rules by Which They Are Governed*

Anonymous (1885) *Indoor Paupers, by One of Them*

Anstruther, I. (1973) *The Scandal of the Andover Workhouse*

Ayers, G. (1971) *England's First State Hospitals 1867-1930*

Baker, D. (1984) *Workhouses in the Potteries*

Baxter, G.R.W. (1841) *The Book of the Bastiles, or, the History of the Working of the New Poor Law*

Bedford, P. and Howard, D.N. (1985) *St. James's University Hospital, Leeds – a Pictorial History*

Bellers, J. (1695) *Proposals for Raising a Colledge of Industry of All Useful Trades and Husbandry*

Bennet, A. (1910) *Clayhanger*

Blaug, M. (1963) 'The Myth of the Old Poor Law and the Making of the New' (in *Journal of Economic History*, vol. 23(2), pp. 151-184)

Blaug, M. (1964) 'The Poor Law Report Re-Examined' (in *Journal of Economic History*, vol. 24(2), pp. 229-245)

Booth, W. (1890) *In Darkest England, and the Way Out*

Brodie, A., Croom, J. and Davies, J.O. (2002) *English Prisons: An Architectural History*

Brundage, A. (1975) 'Reform of the Poor Law Electoral System, 1834-94' (in *Albion*, vol. 7(3), pp. 201-215)

Brundage, A. (1978) *The Making of the New Poor Law: The Politics of Inquiry, Enactment and Implementation, 1832-39*

Brundage, A. (2001) *The English Poor Laws, 1700-1930*

Carlebach, J. (1970) *Caring for Children in Trouble*

Cary, J. (1700) *An Account of the Proceedings of the Corporation of Bristol in Execution of the Act of Parliament for the Better Employing and Maintaining the Poor of That City*

Cassell, R.D. (1997) *Medical Charities, Medical Politics: The Irish Dispensary System and the Poor Law, 1836-1872*

Chance, W. (1897) *Children under the Poor Law*

Chaplin, C. (1964) *My Autobiography*

Clark, D. (1969) *The Early Days of Retford Workhouse*

Clarke, J.J. (1955) *A History of Local Government of the United Kingdom*

Cole, A. (2000) *An Introduction to Poor Law Documents before 1834*

Cousins, D.L. (1847) *Extracts from the Diary of a Workhouse Chaplain*

Crawfurd, G.P. (1932) *Recollections of Bicester, Oxfordshire, 1894 to 1907*

Crompton, F. (1997) *Workhouse Children: Infant and Child Paupers under the Worcestershire Poor Law, 1780-1871*

Crowther, M.A. (1981) *The Workhouse System, 1834-1929: The History of an English Social Institution*

Dangerfield, M.E., Marshall, O., Stringer, E.R., *et al.* (1938) 'Chichester Workhouse' (in *Sussex Archaeological Collections*, vol. 79, pp. 131-67)

Dickens, A. (1976) 'The Architect and the Workhouse' (in *Architectural Review*, vol. CLX(958), pp. 345-52)

Digby, A. (1978) *Pauper Palaces*

Diplock, M. (1990) *The History of Leavesden Hospital*

Dumsday, W.H. (1907) *The Workhouse Officers' Handbook.*

Eden, F.M.S. (1797) *The State of the Poor: Or, an History of the Labouring Classes in England*

Edsall, N. C. (1971) *The Anti-Poor Law Movement, 1834-44*

Edwards, G. (1975) *The Road to Barlow Moor: The Story of Withington Hospital, Manchester*

Emmison, F.G. (1933) *The Relief of the Poor at Eaton Socon, 1706-1834*

Fideler, P.A. (2003) *Social Welfare in Early Modern England: The Old Poor Law Tradition*

Finer, S.E. (1952) *The Life and Times of Sir Edwin Chadwick*

Fraser, D. (1976) *The New Poor Law in the Nineteenth Century*

Garcia-Bermejo Giner, M. and Montgomery, M., Eds. (2003) *The Knaresborough Workhouse Daybook: Language and Life in 18th-Century North Yorkshire*

Gibson, J. and Rogers, C. (2004) *Poor Law Union Records: 3. West England, the Marches and Wales*

Gibson, J. and Rogers, C. (2008) *Poor Law Union Records: 2. The Midlands and Northern England*

Gibson, J., Rogers, C. and Webb, C. (2005) *Poor Law Union Records: 1. South-East England and East Anglia*

Gibson, O. (2006) *Indoor Relief: A Diary of the Life and Times of a London Workhouse*

Goodwyn, E.A. (1987) *'a Prison with a Milder Name': The Shipmeadow House of Industry 1766-1800*

Gray, F. (1931) *The Tramp*

Gray, P. (1995) *The Irish Famine*

Gray, P. (2009) *The Making of the Irish Poor Law*

Green, D.R. (2010) *Pauper Capital*

Greenwood, J. (1866) *A Night in a Workhouse*

Grey, P. (1972) 'Parish Workhouses and Poorhouses' (in *The Local Historian*, vol. 10(2), pp. 70-75)

Hall, S. (2004) *Workhouses and Hospitals of North Manchester*

Hammond, J.L. and Hammond, B.B. (1948) *The Village Labourer Vol. 1*

Hardy, T. (1909) *Time's Laughingstocks*

Hastings, F. (1889) 'Workhouse Worries' (in *The Quiver*, pp. 643-645)

Haw, G. (1907) *From Workhouse to Westminster, the Life Story of Will Crooks, M.P.*

Hepburn, J. (2000) *A Book of Scattered Leaves (Volume 1)*

Higginbotham, P. (2006) *Workhouses of the North*

Higginbotham, P. (2007) *Workhouses of the Midlands*

Higginbotham, P. (2008) *The Workhouse Cookbook*

Higginbotham, P. (2010) *The Prison Cookbook*

Higgs, M. (1906) *Glimpses into the Abyss*

Hindle, S. (2004) 'Dependency, Shame and Belonging: Badging the Deserving Poor, C.1550–1750.' (in *Cultural and Social History*, vol. 1, pp. 6-35)

Hinton, F.H. (1940) 'Notes on the Administration of the Relief of the Poor of Lacock, 1583 to 1834' (in *Wiltshire Archaeological and Natural History Magazine*, vol. XLIX, pp. 166-218)

Hitchcock, T. (1985) 'The English Workhouse: A Study in Institutional Poor Relief in Selected Counties, 1696-1750', University of Oxford).

Hitchcock, T. (1992) 'Paupers and Preachers: The Spck and the Parochial Workhouse Movement', (in L. Davison, T. Hitchcock, T. Keirn and R.B. Shoemaker (eds.), *Stilling the Grumbling Hive: The Response to Social and Economic Problems in England, 1689-1750*, pp. 145-166)

Hitchcock, T. (2004) 'Marryott, Matthew (Bap. 1670, D. 1731/2)', (in H. C. G. Matthew and B. Harrison (eds.), *Oxford Dictionary of National Biography*)

Hodgkinson, R.G. (1956) 'Poor Law Medical Officers of England: 1834-1871' (in *Journal of the History of Medicine and Allied Sciences*, vol. XI(3), pp. 299-228)

Hodgkinson, R.G. (1967) *The Origins of the National Health Service: The Medical Services of the New Poor Law, 1834-1871*

Honeyman, K. (2007) *Child Workers in England, 1780-1820: Parish Apprentices and the Making of the Early Industrial Labour Force*

Howard, J. (1777) *State of the Prisons in England and Wales*

Humphreys, R. (1995) *Sin, Organized Charity and the Poor Law in Victorian England*

Johnston, J., Ed. (1996) *Workhouses of the North West*

Knott, J.W. (1986) *Popular Opposition to the 1834 Poor Law*

Kohl, J.G. (1844) *Travels in Ireland*

Lees, L.H. (1998) *The Solidarities of Strangers: The English Poor Laws and the People, 1700-1948*

Leonard, E.M. (1900) *The Early History of English Poor Relief*

Levene, A. and King, P. (2006) *Narratives of the Poor in Eighteenth-Century Britain*

Levene, A., Powell, M. and Stewart, J. (2006) 'The Development of Municipal General Hospitals in English County Boroughs in the 1930s' (in *Medical History*, vol. 50, pp. 3-28)

London, J. (1903) *The People of the Abyss*

Longmate, N. (1974) *The Workhouse*

Mackay, T. and Nicholls, G. (1904) *A History of the English Poor Law: Being a Supplementary Volume to 'a History of the English Poor Law', by Sir George Nicholls*

Mandler, P. (1990) 'Tories and Paupers: Christian Political Economy and the Making of the New Poor Law.' (in *The Historical Journal*, vol. 33(1), pp. 81-103)

Marshall, D. (1926) *The English Poor in the Eighteenth Century: A Study in Social and Administrative History*

Marshall, J.D. and Economic History Society. (1985) *The Old Poor Law, 1795-1834*

Martin, E.W. (1972) 'From Parish to Union: Poor Law Administration, 1601-1865', (in E.W. Martin, Ed. *Comparative Development in Social Welfare*, pp. 25-56)

Martin, E.W., Ed. (1972) *Comparative Development in Social Welfare*

Maude, W. C. (1903) *The Poor Law Handbook*

McInnes, P. and Sparkes, B. (1990) *The Croydon Workhouse*

Means, R. and Smith, R. (1998) *From Poor Law to Community Care*

Monnington, W. and Lampard, F.J. (1898) *Our London Poor Law Schools*

Montair, P. (1995) *Swelling Grounds: A History of Hackney Workhouse (1729-1929)*

Morrison, K. (1998) 'Cottage Homes Villages' (in *Transactions of the Ancient Monuments Society*, vol. 42, pp. 83-102)

Morrison, K. (1999) *The Workhouse: A Study of Poor Law Buildings in England*

Morrison, K. (2004) 'The English and Welsh Workhouses of George Wilkinson' (in *The Georgian Group Journal*, vol. XIV, pp. 104-130)

Murdoch, L. (2006) *Imagined Orphans: Poor Families, Child Welfare, and Contested Citizenship in London*

Murphy, J. (1992) *British Social Services: The Scottish Dimension*

Neate, A.R. (2003) *St Marylebone Workhouse and Institution, 1730-1965*

Nicholls, G. (1854) *A History of the English Poor Law: In Connexion with the Legislation and Other Circumstances Affecting the Condition of the People*

O'Connor, J. (1995) *The Workhouses of Ireland: The Fate of Ireland's Poor*

Orwell, G. (1931) 'The Spike' (in *Adelphi*, vol. 2(1))

Oxley, G.W. (1974) *Poor Relief in England and Wales: 1601-1834*

Pearl, V. (1978) 'Puritans and Poor Relief: The London Workhouse, 1649-60', (in D. Pennington and K. Thomas (eds.), *Puritans and Revolutionaries*, pp. 206-232)

Powell, A. (1930) *The Metropolitan Asylums Board and Its Work, 1867-1930*

Poynter, J.R. (1969) *Society and Pauperism: English Ideas on Poor Relief, 1795-1834*

Preston-Thomas, H. (1909) *The Work and Play of a Government Inspector*

Railton, M. (1994) *Early Medical Services – Berkshire and South Oxfordshire from 1740*

Raynes, H.E. (1957) *Social Security in Britain: A History*

Reid, A. (1994) *The Union Workhouse: A Study Guide for Teachers and Local Historians*

Ribton-Turner, C. J. and Sterling, L.S. (1887) *A History of Vagrants and Vagrancy, and Beggars and Begging*

Richardson, R. (1987) *Death, Dissection and the Destitute*

Richardson, R. and Hurwitz, B. (1997) *Joseph Rogers and the Reform of Workhouse Medicine*

Roberts, D. (1963) 'How Cruel Was the Victorian Poor Law?' (in *The Historical Journal*, vol. 6(1), pp. 97-107)

Rogers, J. and Rogers, J.E.T. (1889) *Joseph Rogers, M. D: Reminiscences of a Workhouse Medical Officer*

Rose, M.E. (1971) *The English Poor Law, 1780-1930*

Ross, A.M. (1967) 'Kay-Shuttleworth and the Training of Teachers for Pauper Schools' (in *British Journal of Educational Studies*, vol. 15(3), pp. 275-283)

Ryan, P.A. (1978) "Poplarism' 1893-1930', (in P. Thane, Ed., *The Origins of British Social Policy*, pp. 56-83)

Scottish Record Office (1995) *Poor Relief in Scotland: Historical Background, Document Extracts and Copies*

Shaw, C. (1903) *When I Was a Child*

Sieh, E.W. (1989) 'Less Eligibility: The Upper Limits of Penal Policy.' (in *Criinal Justice Policy Review*, vol. 3, pp. 159-183)

Siena, K.P. (2004) *Venereal Disease, Hospitals and the Urban Poor: London's 'Foul Wards', 1600-1800*

Slack, P. and Economic History Society. (1995) *The English Poor Law, 1531-1782*

Smith, A. (1776) *The Wealth of Nations*

Smith, E. (1870) *A Guide to the Construction and Management of Workhouses; Together with the Consolidated Order ... Of the Poor Law Board*

Stallard, J.S. (1866) *The Female Casual and Her Lodging*

Stanley, D., Ed. (1909) *The Autobiography of Sir Henry Morton Stanley.*

Symonds, D.A., Ed. (2006) *Narratives of the Poor in Eighteenth-Century Britain - Volume 2: Voices from the Street*

Taylor, J.S. (1972) 'The Unreformed Workhouse 1776-1834', (in E.W. Martin, Ed., *Comparative Development in Social Welfare*, pp. 57-84)

Taylor, J.S. (1976) 'The Impact of Pauper Settlement 1691-1834' (in *Past & Present*, (73), pp. 42-74)

Thane, P. (1978) 'Women and the Poor Law in Victorian and Edwardian England' (in *History Workshop Journal*, vol. 7, pp. 29-51)

Thomas, E.G. (1971) 'The Treatment of Poverty in Berkshire, Essex and Oxfordshire, 1723-1834' (PhD thesis, London University)

Thomas, T. (1992) *Poor Relief in Merthyr Tydfil Union in Victorian Times*

Thompson, K. (1987) 'Sources for the New Poor Law in the Public Records' (in *Journal of Regional and Local Studies*, vol. 7, pp. 1-13)

Trollope, F. (1843) *Jessie Phillips*

Trow, M. J. (2010) *Jack the Ripper: Quest for a Killer*

Turner, I. J. (1984) 'The Guisborough, Middlesbrough and Stockton-on-Tees Poor Law Union Workhouses 1837-C.1930.', Leeds)

Twining, L. (1880) *Recollections of Workhouse Visiting and Management During Twenty-Five Years*

Vorspan, R. (1977) 'Vagrancy and the New Poor Law in Late Victorian and Edwardian England' (in *English Historical Review*, vol. XCII, pp. 59-81)

Wakefield, H. R. and Webb, B. M. (1909) *The Minority Report of the Poor Law Commission*

Webb, C. R. (1999) *A Guide to Surrey Parish Documents*

Webb, C. R. (2006) *A Guide to Middlesex Parish Documents (Including Poor Law Records)*

Webb, S. and Webb, B.P. (1913) *English Poor Law Policy*

Webb, S. and Webb, B.P. (1927) *English Poor Law History. Part I: The Old Poor Law*

Webb, S. and Webb, B.P. (1929) *English Poor Law History. Part Ii: The Last Hundred Years*

White, J. (1990) *Southlands Workhouse and Infirmary*

Williams, K. (1981) *From Pauperism to Poverty*

Withers, P.J. (1999) *British Copper Tokens: 1811-1820*

Wood, P. (1991) *Poverty and the Workhouse in Victorian Britain*

LOCAL AND REGIONAL POOR LAW AND WORKHOUSE STUDIES

The works in this section are roughly organised by region and then, for England, alphabetically grouped by county within each region. In a few cases where the location may be unclear from the title, it is indicated at the end of the item in square brackets. Copies of locally produced and commemorative publications can often be difficult to locate — local studies libraries in the area may sometimes be able to help.

England – North

Burne, R.V.H. (1965) 'The Treatment of the Poor in the Eighteenth Century in Chester' (in *Journal of the Chester and North Wales Architectural and Historic Society*, vol. LII, pp. 44-48)

Handley, M. (2007) 'Poor Law Administration in the Chester Local Act Incorporation, 1834-71' (in *Transactions of the Historic Society of Lancashire and Cheshire*, vol. 156)

Jones, J., Brigg, P.M.H. and Macclesfield Ferrets (1999) *Macclesfield Workhouse*

Langley, M. and Langley, G. (1993) *At the Crossroads: A History of Arclid Workhouse and Hospital*

Langstaff, R. (2010) *Cruel Shelter: Macclesfield's Workhouses 1836-45*

Lewis, C. (1998-9) 'Building Cheshire's First Workhouse' (in *Cheshire History*, vol. 38)

Northwich District Heritage Society (1999) *Cold Comfort at the Northwich Union Workhouse*

Rochester, M. (1988) *The Northwich Poor Law Union and Workhouse*

Utting, E.J. (1969) *The Working of the Poor Law in Chester in Tudor Times*. (B.Phil. thesis, Liverpool)

Thompson, R.N. (1978) 'The Working of the Poor Law Amendment Act in Cumbria, 1836-71' (in *Northern History*, vol. XIV, pp. 119-137)

Barker, R. (1974) *Houghton-Le-Spring Poor Law Union, 1837-1930*. (M.Litt. thesis, Newcastle-upon-Tyne)

Kitts, J.J. (1909) 'The Poor Laws, with Special Reference to the Old Sunderland Workhouses' (in *Antiquities of Sunderland*, vol. 10, pp. 133-159)

Pallister, R. (1968) 'Workhouse Education in County Durham: 1834-70' (in *British Journal of Educational Studies*, vol. 16, pp. 279-92)

Reid, D.S. (1981) *Durham under the Old Poor Law: Illustrative Documents*

Rose, D. (1970) 'Bishop Auckland Poor Law Union, 1863-6' (in *Durham County Local History Society Bulletin*, vol. 13, pp. 2-7)

Blease, W.L. (1909) 'The Poor Law in Liverpool 1681-1834' (in *Transactions of the Historic Society of Lancashire and Cheshire*, vol. LXI, pp. 97-181)

Boyson, R. (1949) *The Haslingden Poor Law Union. 1848-1930* (B.A. thesis, Manchester)

Boyson, R. (1960) 'The New Poor Law in North-East Lancashire, 1834-71' (in *Transactions of the Lancashire and Cheshire Antiquarian Society*, vol. LXX, pp. 35-57)

Cole, J. (1994) *Down Poorhouse Lane: The Diary of a Rochdale Workhouse*

Connor, B. (1989) *A Paupers' Palace: A History of Fishpool Institution 1860-1948* [Bolton]

Edwards, G. (1975) *The Road to Barlow Moor: The Story of Withington Hospital, Manchester*

Forrest, D. (2001) *Warrington's Poor and the Workhouse 1725 - 1851*

Greenwood, M. (1996) *Springfield Hospital - the Human History*

Hall, S. (2004) *Workhouses and Hospitals of North Manchester*

Hurst, P. (2009) *A History of Prescot Union Workhouse, Whiston, Lancashire*

Lofthouse, F.H. (2001) *Keepers of the House: A Workhouse Saga* [Clitheroe]

MacWilliam, H.H. (1965) *Memories of Walton Hospital, Liverpool*

Midwinter, E. C. (1969) *Social Administration in Lancashire, 1830-1860: Poor Law, Public Health and Police*

Mullineux, C. E. (1966) *Pauper and Poorhouse: Study of the Administration of the Poor Laws in a Lancashire Parish* [Worsley/Swinton]

Proctor, W. (1965) 'Poor Law Administration in the Preston Union, 1838-1948' (in *Transactions of the Historic Society of Lancashire and Cheshire*, vol. 117, pp. 145-166)

Underwood, B. (2008) *Ormskirk: Workhouse, Two World Wars, NHS Hospital*

Whitehead, J. (2006) *Lost Children; Ulverston Workhouse in the 19th Century*

Wilson, M.D. (1976) *The Paupers of Leigh: Their Persecution and Poor Relief, 1660-1860*

Bowen, J.M. (2005) *'A Poor Little House...': The Story of Belford Union Workhouse and Its People from 1836 to 1930*

Hurrell, G. and Harlan, G.P. (1996) *History of Newcastle General Hospital*

Manders, F.W.D. (1980) *The Administration of the Poor Law in the Gateshead Union, 1836-1930* (M.Litt. thesis, Newcastle upon Tyne)

Bedford, P. and Howard, D.N. (1985) *St. James's University Hospital, Leeds - a Pictorial History*

Tyson, B. (2006) 'Windermere Paupers 1749-1862 and the Undermillbeck Workhouse (1829)' (in *Transactions of the Cumberland & Westmorland Antiquarian & Archaeological Society*, vol. VI, pp. 113-137)

Anderson, P. (1981) 'The Leeds Workhouse under the Old Poor Law: 1726-1834' (in *Thoresby Society*, vol. LVI(2), pp. 75-113)

Anonymous (1903) *Hunslet Union New Workhouse and Infirmary (Opening Souvenir Brochure)*

Ashforth, D. (1979) *The Poor Law in Bradford, C.1834-1871* (Ph.D. thesis, Bradford)

Carter, P., (2004) *Bradford Poor Law Union: Papers and Correspondence with the Poor Law Commission: October 1834-January 1839*

Daniels, L. (2001) *The Workhouse, Bridlington Road, Driffield*

Diver, D. and Howsam, L. (2010) *Life in the Grenoside Workhouse*

Drinkall, M. (2009) *Rotherham Workhouse*

Drinkall, M. (2011) *Sheffield Workhouse*

Dunn, M.P. (1988) *For the Love of Children: A Story of the Poor Children of Sheffield and of Fulwood Cottage Homes*

Fallowfield, M. and Watson, I. (1986) *The New Poor Law in Humberside*

Flett, J. (1984) *The Story of the Workhouse and the Hospital at Nether Edge*

Garcia-Bermejo Giner, M. and Montgomery, M. (eds.) (2003) *The Knaresborough Workhouse Daybook: Language and Life in 18th-Century North Yorkshire*

Hastings, P. (1982) *Poverty and the Poor Law in the North Riding of Yorkshire, C1780-1837*

Howsam, L. (2004) *A Child's Life in Gawber Road Workhouse* [Barnsley]

Howsam, L. (2006) *Life in the Workhouse & Old Hospital at Fir Vale - the Story of the Northern General Hospital, Sheffield*

King, S. (1997) 'Reconstructing Lives: The Poor, the Poor Law and Welfare in Calverley, 1650-1820' (in *Social History*, vol. 22(3), pp. 318-338)

Mitchelson, N. (1953) *The Old Poor Law in East Yorkshire*

Pennock, P.M. (1986) 'The Evolution of St. James's 1845-94: Leeds Moral and Industrial Training School, Leeds Union Workhouse and Leeds Union Infirmary' (in *Thoresby Society*, vol. LIX(130), pp. 129-176)

Place, A. (2004) *Pray Remember the Poor - the Poor Laws and Huddersfield*

Rose, M.E. (1965) *The Administration of the Poor Law in the West Riding of Yorkshire (1820-1855)* (D.Phil. thesis, University of Oxford)

Scobie, J. (1996) 'Sedbergh and District Workhouse' (in *Yorkshire History Magazine*, vol. 1(6), pp. 5-7)

Speck, P. (1978) *The Institution and Hospital at Fir Vale: A Centenary History of the Northern General Hospital* [Sheffield]

Thrall, R. (2003) *Paradise Gardens* [Pontefract]

Turner, I.J. (1984) *The Guisborough, Middlesbrough and Stockton-on-Tees Poor Law Union Workhouses 1837-C.1930* (Leeds, Department of Adult and Continuing Education)

Watkinson, W.R. (1950) *The Relieving Officer Looks Back: The Last Years of Poor Law in Holderness*

Williams, G. (1997) 'The Administration of the New Poor Law in the Union of Thorne 1834-1852' (in *Journal of Regional and Local Studies*, vol. 17(2), pp. 1-15)

England – Midlands

Cashman, B. (1988) *Private Charity and the Public Purse: Development of Bedford General Hospital, 1794-1988*

Emmison, F.G. (1933) *The Relief of the Poor at Eaton Socon, 1706-1834*

Page, K. (2003) 'Biggleswade Workhouse' (in *Bedfordshire Country Life*, Summer 2003)

Tuddenham, A. (1995) *Dear Mother: The Story of a Letter, Written in 1840, at the Eton Union Workhouse, Slough*

Middleton, L.R. (2002) *Born into Poverty: Derby Workhouse*

Powell, J. (1999) *The Hayfield Union Workhouse: A History*

Watson, A.F. (1981) 'The Chesterfield Union Workhouse, 1839–47' (in *Journal of the Bakewell and District Historical Society*, vol. VIII, pp. 10–20)

Elliott, N. (1985) *Dore Workhouse in Victorian Times*

Morgan, C. and Briffett (1998) *The Ross Union Workhouse, 1836 - 1914*

Morrill, S.A. (1974) 'Poor Law in Hereford 1836-1851' (in *The Woolhope Club*, vol. 41, pp. 239–252)

Powell, J.C. (2000) *The Implementation of the New Poor Law in Herefordshire 1834-1855*

Bailey, R., Hill, L. and Wilkinson, B. (eds.) (1998) *The Lutterworth Workhouse*

Henry, M. (1978) *The Introduction and Implementation of the New Poor Law in the Barrow-Upon-Soar Union, Leicestershire, 1837-1860.*, vol. M.A.

Thompson, K. (1988) 'The Building of the Leicester Union Workhouse 1836–1839', in D.D. Williams (ed), *The Adaptation of Change*

Thompson, K.M. (1988) *The Leicester Poor Law Union, 1836-1871* (Ph.D. thesis, Leicester)

Becher, J.T. (1834) *The Anti-Pauper System*

Caplan, M. (1970) 'The Poor Law in Nottinghamshire, 1836–71' (in *Transactions of the Thoroton Society*, vol. 74, pp. 82 –98)

Caplan, M. (1984) *In the Shadow of the Workhouse: The Implementation of the New Poor Law Throughout Nottinghamshire, 1836-46*

Clark, D. (1969) *The Early Days of Retford Workhouse*

MacFine, J. (1984) *Bagthorpe to the City – the Story of Nottingham Hospital*

Smith, S. (2002) *The Workhouse, Southwell: Nottinghamshire*

Alasia, V. (2000) *The Henley Union Workhouse 1834 - 61: National Authority V Local Autonomy?*

Brown, H. (2008) *Gallon Loaves and Fustian Frocks: The Wantage Union and Workhouse 1835-1900*

Cooper, T.J. (1981) 'Aspects of the Old Poor Law in Witney 1536–1834' (in *Record of Witney*, (12), pp. 7–12)

Gray, F. (1931) *The Tramp*

Higginbotham, P. (2002) *The Oxford Workhouse*

Higginbotham, P. (2006) *West Oxfordshire Workhouses*

Mason, E. (1997) *Headington Union and the New Poor Law, 1834 - 1933*

Song, B.K. (1999) 'Continuity and Change in English Rural Society: The Formation of Poor Law Unions in Oxfordshire' (in *The English Historical Review*, vol. 114(456), pp. 314–338)

Walsh, V.J. (1974) 'Old and New Poor Laws in Shropshire' (in *Midland History*, vol. II(4))

Buchanan, C.A. (1987) 'John Bowen and the Bridgwater Scandal' (in *Somerset Archaeology and Natural History*, vol. 131, pp. 181–201)

(1968) *Poor Relief in Staffordshire 1662-1840*

Bailey, S. (1987) *My Childhood in the Workhouse*

Baker, D. (1984) *Workhouses in the Potteries*

Broadbridge, S.R. (1973) 'The Old Poor Law in the Parish of Stone' (in *North Staffordshire Journal of Field Studies*, vol. 13, pp. 12–25)

Carpenter, P.B. (1998) *A History of Walsall Hospitals (1838-1998)*

Leighfield, E.J. (1978) *The History of St Michael's Hospital, Lichfield*

Shaw, C. (1903) *When I Was a Child*

Walton, P. (1989) *A Peep into the Past - Being a History of the Premises Forming the Leek Moorlands Hospital*

Hicks, C., Ed. (2001) *St. Luke's Hospital & Rugby Union Workhouse 1819-1993.*

Hinson, M., Ed. (2001) *Highcroft from Workhouse to Modern Mental Health Service.*

Holden, J.N. (1988) *A History of Warwick Hospital 1836-1903*

Wishart, B. (1995) *Foleshill Union Workhouse Punishment Book, 1864-1900*

Wishart, B. (2000) *The Coventry Workhouse Birth Registers 1854-1930: And Births from Other Workhouse Sources*

Woodall, J. (1994) *Gin, Ale and Poultices - Lasers and Scanners: Solihull Workhouse and Hospital 1742-1993*

Tyson, B. (1987) 'The Mansion House, Eamont Bridge, Cumbria: A Tercentenary History of Its Owners, Occupiers and Associations' (in *Transactions of the Ancient Monuments Society*, vol. 31, pp. 146–174)

Crompton, F. (1997) *Workhouse Children: Infant and Child Paupers under the Worcestershire Poor Law, 1780-1871*

Land, N. (1990) *Victorian Workhouse: A Study of the Bromsgrove Union Workhouse 1836-1901*

Payne, E. (1994) The Perryfields and Cottage Homes Story

England - East

Barclay-Munro, B. and Cook, H.E. (1991) *Workhouse to Housework* [Cambridge]

Bevis, T. (2009) *From Workhouse to Hospital: Illustrated Reminiscences of Doddington Hospital*

Denton, A. (1986) *Ely Union Workhouse*

Hampson, E.M. (1934) *The Treatment of Poverty in Cambridgeshire, 1597-1834*

Heasman, D. and Melleney, J.R. (1996) *160 Years of Service to the Community: A History of Newmarket General Hospital*

Murphy, M.J. (1978) *Poverty in Cambridgeshire*

Stokes, H.P. (1911) 'Cambridge Parish Workhouses' (in *Proceedings of the Cambridge Antiquarian Society*, vol. XV)

Workers' Educational Association. (1978) *In and out of the Workhouse: The Coming of the New Poor Law to Cambridgeshire and Huntingdonshire*

Andrews, D.D. (2002) 'Historic Buildings Notes and Surveys – St. Andrew's Hospital, Formerly the Billericay Union Workhouse' (in *Essex Archaeology*, vol. 33, pp. 414-442)

Attwood, M. (ed) (2004) *Looking Back over the Bridge* [Witham]

Costello, R. (1999) "We Could Manage Our Parochial Concerns Much Better by Ourselves': Some Responses to Proposed Poor Law Unions in Essex.' (in *Essex Journal*, vol. 44, pp. 45-51)

Cuttle, G. (1934) *The Legacy of the Rural Guardians: A Study of Conditions in Mid-Essex*

Drury, J.O. (2006) *Essex Workhouses*

Edmond, P. (1999) *Maldon Workhouse, 1719-1875: An Architectural History, 1719-1997*

Edwards, C. (2010) *Lexden and Winstree Union Workhouse*

Grounds, W.M. (1968) 'The Old Billericay Workhouse' (in *Essex Journal*, vol. 3(4), pp. 218-22)

Hopkirk, M. (1949) 'The Administration of Poor Relief 1604-1834 – Illustrated from the Parochial Records of Danbury' (in *The Essex Review*, vol. LVII(231), pp. 113-121)

Moore, I.S. (1999) *Oldchurch: The Workhouse Story: How It All Began*

Noordin, R.M. (1929) *Through a Workhouse Window, Being a Brief Summary of Three Years Spent by the Youngest Member of a Board of Guardians in the Course of His Duties*

Anderson, C. L. (1986) 'How the Poor in Horncastle Were Treated [C1835-1879].' (in *SLHA Newsletter*, (50), pp. 8-11)

Brocklebank, J. (1962) 'The New Poor Law in Lincolnshire' (in *Lincolnshire Historian*, vol. 2(9), pp. 21-33)

Painter, B. (2000) *Upon the Parish Rate: The Story of Louth Workhouse and the Paupers of East Lindsey*

Russell, R., Frankish, A. and Frankish, P. (1993) *The House of Industry, Caistor*

Udell, J. (2005) *The Legacy of the Workhouse - Harsh Prison or Popular Myth [Louth and Caistor Workhouses 1834-1925]*

Bilyard, J. (1987) *Hales Hospital - a History - Workhouse to Hospital*

Crowley, J. and Reid, A. (1983) *The Poor Law in Norfolk, 1700-1850: A Collection of Source Material*

Digby, A. (1978) *Pauper Palaces*

Humphreys, D. (no date) *Born Poor, A Brief History of the Norwich Workhouse*

Pope, S. (2006) *Gressenhall Farm and Workhouse*

Reid, A. (1994) *The Union Workhouse: A Study Guide for Teachers and Local Historians*

Serreau, A. (2000) *Times and Years - a History of the Blofield Union Workhouse at Lingwood in the County of Norfolk*

Goodwyn, E.A. (1987) *'A Prison with a Milder Name': The Shipmeadow House of Industry 1766-1800*

Hardy, S.M. (2001) *The House on the Hill: The Samford House of Industry, 1764-1930*

Plumridge, P. (1998) *Riches and Rags: The History of a Site in College Street, Bury St. Edmunds 1480-1997*

Pritchard, M. (1965) 'Early Days of the Wangford Hundred Workhouse' (in *Suffolk Institute of Archaeology*, vol. 30, pp. 175-182)

Whitehand, R. (2007) *At the Overseer's Door: The Story of Suffolk's Parish Workhouses*

England – London

Adams, J. and Coll, G. (1999) *The History of Shirley Oaks Children's Home*

Barnes, W. (1996) *Down in the Battle of Life: Bermondsey Union Workhouse*

Brown, K. (1994) *Workhouse to Hospital: The Experience of Paddington General from Infirmary to St Mary's Hospital, Harrow Road*

City of Westminster Archives Centre (2003) *Information Sheet 12: Location of Westminster's Workhouses and Infirmaries*

Cleminson, F. (1983) *Beyond Recall: The Making of Mile End Hospital*

Connelly, A. (1979) *The Pauper's Paradise: Poor Relief in Hammersmith 1899-1907*

Diplock, M. (1990) *The History of Leavesden Hospital*

Drage, A. *et al.* (1985) *The Hospital on the Hill: The Story of Whittington Hospital*

Earl, E. (1996) *Queen Mary's Hospital for Children*

Gibson, O. (2006) *Indoor Relief: A Diary of the Life and Times of a London Workhouse* [Wandsworth & Clapham]

Goodman, J. and John Innes, S. (1989) *"The Unfortunate Infants": An Account of the Bermondsey Poor Law Institution for Children at the Old Church House, Merton, 1820-1845*

Green, D.R. (2010) *Pauper Capital*

Hughes, B. (1991) *From Workhouse to Hospital: The Story of St. Mary Abbots Hospital, Kensington*

Hunter, D. (2002) 'Life at Hackney Workhouse, 1920-23' (in *Hackney History*, vol. 8(37-43))

Lees, L.H. (1988) *Poverty and Pauperism in Nineteenth-Century London*

MacKay, L. (1995) 'A Culture of Poverty? The St. Martin in the Fields Workhouse, 1817' (in *Journal of Interdisciplinary History*, vol. 26(2), pp. 209-231)

Marshall, G. (1998) *Beechholme: The School on Banstead's Breezy Downs*

Monnington, W. and Lampard, F.J. (1898) *Our London Poor Law Schools*

Montair, P. (1995) *Swelling Grounds: A History of Hackney Workhouse (1729-1929)*

Murphy, E. (2002) 'The Metropolitan Pauper Farms 1722-1834' (in *London Journal*, vol. 27(1), pp. 1-18)

Neate, A.R. (2003) *St Marylebone Workhouse and Institution, 1730-1965*

Pearl, V. (1978) 'Puritans and Poor Relief: The London Workhouse, 1649-60', in D. Pennington and K. Thomas (eds.), *Puritans and Revolutionaries*, 206-232

Powell, A. (1930) *The Metropolitan Asylums Board and Its Work, 1867-1930*

Rogers, J. and Rogers, J.E.T. (1889) *Joseph Rogers, M. D: Reminiscences of a Workhouse Medical Officer*

Stewart, S. (c. 1980) *The Central London District Schools 1856-1933: A Short History*

Tanner, A. (1995) *The City of London Poor Law Union, 1837-1868* (Ph.D. thesis, University of London)

Tanner, A. (1999) 'The Casual Poor and the City of London Poor Law Union, 1837-1869' (in *Historical Journal*, vol. 42(1), pp. 183-206)

England – South-east

Bond, M. (1945) 'Windsor's Experiment in Poor-Relief, 1621-1829' (in *Berkshire Archaeological Journal*, vol. 48, pp. 31-42)

Higginbotham, P. (2001) 'The Workhouse in Berkshire' (in *Berkshire Family Historian*, vol. 24(3), pp. 122 - 134)

Higginbotham, P. (2003) 'The Abingdon Workhouse' (in *Oxfordshire Family Historian*, vol. 17(1), pp. 12-13)

Jackson, C. (2004) 'Functionality, Commemoration and Civic Competition: A Study of Early Seventeenth-Century Workhouse Design and Building in Reading and Newbury' (in *Architectural History*, vol. 47, pp. 77-112)

Jackson, C. (2004) *Newbury Kendrick Workhouse Records, 1627-1641*

Railton, M. (1994) *Early Medical Services – Berkshire and South Oxfordshire from 1740*

Railton, M. and Barr, M. (2005) *Battle Workhouse and Hospital 1867-2005* [Reading]

Coppock, J. (2003) 'Life in a Georgian Workhouse' (in *Records of Buckinghamshire*, vol. 32, pp. 179-195)

Tuddenham, A. (1995) *Dear Mother: The story of a letter, written in 1840, at the Eton Union Workhouse, Slough*

Conway, B.J. (1972) *The Berkhampstead Union Workhouse 1835-1935*

Corfield, J. *et al.* (1990) 'Buntingford Workhouse' (in *Hertfordshire's Past*, (28), pp. 10-33)

Gear, G., Ed. (2010) *Diary of Benjamin Woodock, Master of Barnet Union Workhouse, 1836-1838*

Gelder, W.H. (1984) 'Leaves from a Workhouse Register', in W.H. Gelder (ed), *Historic Barnet*, 80-91

Gutchen, R. *et al.* (1984) *Down and out in Hertfordshire: A Symposium on the Old and New Poor Law*

Allinson, H. (2005) *Life in the Workhouse - the Story of Milton Union, Kent*

Arthur, A. *et al.* (1984) *Crime and Poverty in the Dartford Area 1480-1900*

Gilham, J. C. (1991) *The Isle of Thanet Union Workhouse*

Judge, S. (1987) 'Sheppey General Hospital – a Brief History' (in *Bygone Kent*, vol. 8, June 1987)

Langridge, B. (1997) 'Bromley Workhouse and Bromley Union' (in *North-west Kent Family History Society*, vol. 7 (11), pp. 397-400)

Lansberry, H. C. F. (1984) 'The Blean Bastille: Blean Poor Law Union 1835-1846' (in K. McKintosh and G. HE (eds.), *Hoath and Herne - the Last of the Forest*, 108-112)

Nicholson, D. C. (1986) 'Tonbridge Union: 1836-1986' (in *Pembury Contact*, no. 802)

Stevens, J. and Faversham, S. (2002) *Faversham Union Workhouse: The Early Years, 1836-1850*

Avery, D. (1967) *Charity Begins at Home: Edmonton Workhouse Committee 1732-37*

Black, M. (1993) *West Middlesex University Hospital - a History* [Brentford]

Boudier, G. (2003) *History of the North Middlesex University Hospital* [Edmonton]

Gray, J.D.A. (1963) *The Central Middlesex Hospital* [Willesden]

Hitchcock, T., Ed. (1987) *Richard Hutton's Complaints Book: The Notebook of the Steward of the Quaker Workhouse at Clerkenwell 1711-1737*

Richardson, S.I. (1971) *A History of the Edmonton Poor Law Union 1837-1854*

Wingfield, H. (2003) *The Workhouse and Hospital at Hillingdon 1744-1967* [Uxbridge]

Butler, M. (1969) *The Barnes Poorhouse 1758-1836*

Davies, H. C. (2004) *The Spike: The Guildford Union Workhouse and the Vagrants' Casual Ward*

Fowler, S. (1991) *Philanthropy and the Poor Law in Richmond, 1836-1871*

McInnes, P. and Sparkes, B. (1990) *The Croydon Workhouse*

Merton Historical Society (1972) *Mitcham Workhouse*

Noyes, A. (1996) *Shere Poverty: From Parish Workhouse to Union Workhouse*

Dangerfield, M.E. *et al.* (1938) 'Chichester Workhouse' (in *Sussex Archaeological Collections*, vol. 79, pp. 131-67)

Gaston, H. (2009) *A Lingering Fear: East Sussex Hospitals and the Workhouse Legacy*

Gooch, J. (1980) *A History of Brighton General Hospital*

Hickman, M. (1944) 'Rules for the Paupers in Shipley Poorhouse' (in *Sussex Notes and Queries*, vol. X, pp. 35-36)

Jacobs, J. (1990) 'Drastic Measures for Sturdy Loafers: Brighton Guardians and the Able-Bodied Men in the Workhouse, 1900-1914' (in *Archaeological Collections*, vol. 128, pp. 225-242)

Standing, R.W. (2000) *East Preston Gilbert Union Workhouse 1791-1869*

Surtees, J. (1992) *Barracks, Workhouse and Hospital: The Story of St Mary's, Eastbourne 1794-1990*

Thomas, E.G. (1971) 'The Treatment of Poverty in Berkshire, Essex and Oxfordshire, 1723-1834' (PhD thesis, London University)

Valentine, D. (2000) *St. Helen's Hospital, Hastings (1837-1994) 'Paupers to Pacemakers'.*

Watson, I. (1991) *The Westbourne Union Life in and out of the New Workhouse*

White, J. (1990) *Southlands Workhouse and Infirmary* [Steyning]

England – South-west

Hutton, P. (2000) *The Launceston Union Workhouse*

Philp, T. (2005) *A Social History of Bodmin Union Workhouse*

Forsythe, W. J. (1985) 'Paupers and Policy Makers in Exeter, 1830-1860' (in *Devonshire Association Report and Transactions*, vol. 117, pp. 117-160)

German, A. (1986) *The Land of Goschen: Life in the Totnes Union Workhouse 1869-1870*

Morris, R.K. (2010) 'The Rise and Fall of Okehampton Workhouse' (in *Devon Buildings Group Newsletter*, (28), pp. 10-21)

Norman, V. (2003) *Scattered Homes, Broken Hearts* [Devonport]

Wheeleker, S. and Eyles, S. (1991) *Poor Relief in Devon: Two Studies*

Cockburn, E. (1972) 'The Cerne Abbas Union Workhouse 1835-8' (in *Proceedings of the Dorset Natural History and Archaeological Society*, vol. 94, pp. 89-94)

Dorset Countryside Treasures (1980) *Dorset Workhouses*

Flame, M.J. (1986) 'The Politics of Poor Law Administration in the Borough of Poole 1835-C.1845' (in *Proceedings of the Dorset Natural History and Archaeological Society*, vol. 108, pp. 19-25)

Newman, S. (2000) *The Christchurch and Bournemouth Union Workhouse*

Alcock, P. (1992) *Whispers from the Workhouse: The Story of 'the Spike'* [Chipping Sodbury]

Large, D. (1995) *Bristol and the New Poor Law*

Moss, M.S. (1968) 'The Building of, and Subsequent Running of, the Westbury-on-Trym Workhouse near Bristol' (in *Transactions of the Bristol and Gloucestershire Archaeological Society*, vol. 86, pp. 151-172)

Summers, M. and Bowman, S. (1995) *Of Poor Law, Patients and Professionals: A History of Bristol's Southmead Hospital*

Townley, C. (2009) *Stroud Workhouse - a Danger to Sick People*

Anstey, C. M. (1978) *A History of the Southampton Technical College Buildings, formerly the Workhouse, with Special Attention to Their Architecture* (unpublished)

Bennett, A. C. (1976) *Whitchurch Workhouse*

Cannon, J. (1992) *Lymington Infirmary: From the Poor Law to the NHS*

Cook, J. and Eastleigh and District Local History, S. (1997) *Eastleigh, the Guardians and Poor Relief*

Jones, M.J. (1982) *Administration of the Poor in the Isle of Wight, 1771-1836* (M.Phil. thesis, Southampton)

Moxley, C. (1987) *An Introduction to the History of St. Paul's Hospital Winchester: The New Winchester Union 1835-1846*

Norman, B. (1988) *Portsea Workhouse Project*

Pitcher, A. (1985) *Illustrated History of Winchfield and the Hospital* [Hartley Wintney]

Raffo, E.H. (2000) *'Half a Loaf' - the Care of the Sick and Poor at South Stoneham 1664-1948*

Society, E. a. D.L.H. (2003) *Leigh House - Chandlers Ford Workhouse*

Griffiths, K. (2005) *Workhouse - Brief Glimpses of the Poor Law and Life inside the Clutton Union House*

Hurley, J. (1974) *Rattle His Bones* [Williton and Dulverton Workhouses]

Jenkins, P. (1988) *Priory Hospital Wells - an Illustrated History to Commemorate Its First 150 Years*

Munckton, T. (1994) *Somerset Paupers: Unremembered Lives*

Randell, P.W. (1983) *Poor Law Relief in Somerset, with Particular Reference to the Wincanton Union, 1834-1900* (M.Litt. thesis, Lancaster)

Randell, P.W. (2010) *Life in a Rural Workhouse: Wincanton Workhouse Somerset, 1834-1900*

Blake, P. (1992) 'In and out of the Workhouse' (in *Wiltshire Family History Society*, no. 44, pp. 10-14) [Melksham and Westbury & Whorewellsdown]

E, S. and M, S. (1995) *Mere Union Workhouse*

Fuller, B.A. (1986) *Changed Times: A Short History of Devizes Union Workhouse and St. James's Hospital, 1836-1986*

Hinton, F.H. (1940) 'Notes on the Administration of the Relief of the Poor of Lacock, 1583 to 1834' (in *Wiltshire Archaeological and Natural History Magazine*, vol. XLIX, pp. 166-218)

Robbins, A. (1992) *The Workhouses of Purton and the Cricklade and Wootton Bassett Union*

Watkin, B. (1986) 'The Warminster Workhouses' (in *Hatcher Review*, vol. 3(22), pp. 67-77)

Wales

Anonymous (1989) *The 150th Anniversary of Riverside, Pembroke - Commemorative Brochure*

Brown, R.L. (1999) *Parish and Pauper: A History of the Administration of the Poor Law in the Parish of Castle Caereinion, Montgomeryshire*

Davies, A.E. (1998) 'Poor Law Administration in Cardiganshire', in G.H. Jenkins and I.G. Jones (eds.), *Cardiganshire County History*. vol. 3, pp. 323-241.

Dodd, A.H. (1926) 'The Old Poor Law in North Wales' (in *Archaeologica Cambrensis*, vol. VI, pp. 111-132)

Draper, C. (2005) *Paupers, Bastards and Lunatics: The Story of Conwy Workhouse*

Flynn-Hughes, C. (1944) 'The Bangor Workhouse' (in *Caernarvonshire Historical Transactions*, vol. 5, pp.

88-100)

Flynn-Hughes, C. (1946) 'The Workhouses of Caernarvonshire 1760-1914' (in *Caernarvonshire Historical Transactions*, vol. 7, pp. 88-100)

Foster, B. (1990) *A History of Pontypool Union Workhouse 1838-1930*

Grant, R. (1988) *On the Parish: An Illustrated Source Book on the Care of the Poor under the Old Poor Law: Based on Documents from the County of Glamorgan*

Hainsworth, J. (2004) *The Llanfyllin Union Workhouse*

Jones, D.L. (2005) 'The Fate of the Paupers: Life in the Bangor and Beaumaris Union Workhouse 1845-71' (in *Caernarvonshire Historical Transactions*, vol. 66, pp. 94-125)

Jones, G. (1992) *Carchar, Nid Cartref: Hanes Cynnar Wyrcws Pwllheli, 1840-1890*

Jones, T. (1995) *The Holywell Workhouses*

Jones, T.D. (1964) 'Poor Law Administration in Merthyr Tydfil Union 1834-1894' (in *Morgannwg*, vol. 8, pp. 35-62)

King, S.A. and Stewart, J. (2001) 'The History of the Poor Law in Wales: Under-Researched, Full of Potential.' (in *Archives*, vol. 36, pp. 134-48)

Lewis, B. and Thomas, H.M. (2003) *Swansea and the Workhouse: The Poor Law in 19th Century Swansea*

Lindsay, J. (1991-2) 'The Problems of the Caernarfon Union Workhouse from 1846 -1930' (in *Caernarvonshire Historical Transactions*, vol. 52-3, pp. 71-85)

Lindsay, J. (2000) 'Poor Relief in North Wales and East Lothian: A Comparison of the East Lothian Combination Poorhouse and the Bangor and Beaumaris Union Workhouse, 1865-1885.' (in *Transactions of the East Lothian Antiquarian and Field Naturalists Society*, vol. XXIV(41-66))

Owen, B. (1990) 'The Newtown and Llanidloes Poor Law Union Workhouse, Caersws, 1837-1847' (in *Montgomeryshire Collections*, vol. 78, pp. 115-60)

Owen, G.D. (1941) 'The Poor Law System in Carmarthenshire During the Eighteenth and Early Nineteenth Centuries' (in *Transactions of the Honourable Society of Cymmrodorion*, pp. 71-86)

Parry-Jones, E. (1981) *From Workhouse to Hospital: The Story of H.M. Stanley Hospital, St Asaph 1840-1980*

Peeling, B. and Knight, C. (2004) *The Royal Gwent and St. Woolos Hospitals: A Century of Service in Newport*

Thomas, J.H. and Wilkins, W.E. (1995) *The Bridgend-Cowbridge Union Workhouse and Guardians*

Thomas, T. (1992) *Poor Relief in Merthyr Tydfil Union in Victorian Times*

Williams, M. (2000) *Crickhowell Union Workhouse: The Spike*

Ireland

Barrett, R. (2008) *Life in the Workhouses of Co. Meath, 1838-1850*. vol. M.Litt.

Begley, A. (1989) 'Poverty, Famine, and the Workhouse at Ballyshannon' (in *Donegal Annual*, vol. 41, pp. 57-72)

Bell, M. (1997) *A Hospital at Magherafelt: The History of the Mid-Ulster Hospital from Its Origins, as Magherafelt Union Workhouse, in 1842*

Burns, C. (1988) *Pauper to Patient: A History of the Route Hospital Ballymoney 1840-1987*

Byrne, K (2008) *Time Did Not Stand Still* [Rathdrum, Co. Wicklow]

Cassell, R.D. (1997) *Medical Charities, Medical Politics: The Irish Dispensary System and the Poor Law, 1836-1872*

Clare, L. (1986) *Loughlinstown Workhouse in the 1840s*

Collins, S. (2005) *Balrothery Poor Law Union, County Dublin, 1839-1851*

Corrigan, F. (1976) 'Dublin Workhouses During the Great Famine' (in *Dublin Historical Record*, vol. XXIX(2), pp. 59-65)

Coy, N. and McCarthy, G. (eds.) (1998) *A History of Naas Hospital (1838-1998): From Workhouse to Hospital*

Crawford, E.M. (1993) 'The Irish Workhouse Diet, 1840-1900', in C. Geissler and D. Oddy (eds.), *Food, Diet and Economic Change Past and Present*, 83-100

Crossman, V. (2006) *Politics, Pauperism and Power in Late Nineteenth-Century Ireland*

Crossman, V. (2006) *The Poor Law in Ireland 1838-1948*

Crossman, V. (2009) 'Cribbed, Contained, and Confined?: The Care of Children under the Irish Poor Law, 1850–1920' (in *Eire-Ireland*, vol. 44 (1 and 2), pp. 37-61)

Dickson, D. (1988) 'In Search of the Old Irish Poor Law', in R. Mitchison and P. Roebuck (eds.),
    Economy and Society in Scotland and Ireland 1500-1939

Durnin, P. (1991) *Derry and the Irish Poor Law: A History of the Derry Workhouse*

Farrell, M. (1978) *The Poor Law and the Workhouse in Belfast, 1838-1948*

Fraher, W. and Dungarvan Museum, S. (1996) *Desperate Haven: The Poor Law, Famine, & Aftermath in
    Dungarvan Union*

Getty, D.I. (1991) *The Poor Law in Ireland 1838-1852: The Ballymoney and Magherafelt Unions*. vol. D.Phil.

Gould, M.H. (1983) *The Workhouses of Ulster*

Gray, P. (1995) *The Irish Famine*

Gray, P. (2009) *The Making of the Irish Poor Law*

Guerin, M. (1996) *Listowel Workhouse Union*

Guinnane, T. and Ó Gráda, C. (2002) 'The Workhouses and Irish Famine Mortality' (in T. Dyson and C.
    Ó Gráda (eds.), *Famine Demography: Perspectives from Past and Present*, 44-64)

Johnston, J., Ed. (1996) *Workhouses of the North West*

Kelly, S. (1985) 'The Newcastle West Workhouse' (in *Old Limerick Journal*, vol. 32, pp. 151-152)

Kiely, K. 'Naas Workhouse During the Famine', 22-46

Kinealy, C. (1989) 'The Poor Law During the Great Famine: An Administration in Crisis', in E.M.
    Crawford (ed), *Famine: The Irish Experience 900-1900*, 157-75

Kinealy, C. (1992) 'The Workhouse System in County Waterford, 1838-1923' (in W. Nolan and T.P. Power
    (eds.), *Waterford: History and Society*, 579-596)

Lanigan, A. (1995) 'Tipperary Workhouse Children and the Famine' (in *Tipperary Historical Journal*, pp.
    54-80)

Livingstone, P. (1964) 'Castleblayney Poor Law Union: The Early Years 1839-49' (in *Clogher Record*, vol.
    5(2), pp. 227-50)

Lonergan, E. (1992) *A Workhouse Story: A History of St. Patrick's Hospital Cashel, 1842-1992*

Lonergan, E. (2000) *St. Joseph's Hospital, Clonmel: An Historical and Social Portrait*

Luddy, M. (1999) '"Angels of Mercy": Nuns as Workhouse Nurses', in E. Malcolm and G. Jones (eds.),
    Medicine, Disease and the State in Ireland, 1650-1940

McCabe, D. and Ó Gráda, C. (2009) *'Better Off Thrown Behind a Ditch': Enniskillen Workhouse During the
    Great Famine*

McCusker, B. (1997) *Lowtherstown Workhouse*

McLoughlin, D. (1989) 'Workhouses and Irish Female Paupers, 1840-70' (in M. Luddy and C. Murphy
    (eds.), *Women Surviving: Studies in Irish Women's History in the Nineteenth and Twentieth Centuries*, pp. 117-
    147

Murphy, M. (2007) *Tullamore Workhouse: The First Decade, 1842-852*

Nicholls, G. S. (1856) *A History of the Irish Poor Law*

Nolan, P. (1987) 'The Irish Workhouse System' (in *History of Nursing Bulletin*, vol. 2 (2), pp. 18-21)

Nolan, T. (1995) 'The Lismore Poor Law Union and the Famine', in D. Cowman and D. Brady (eds.),
    Teacht Na Bprátaí Dubha: The Famine in Waterford 1845-50, 101-118.

Ó Cathaoir, E. (1991) 'Rathdrum Workhouse (1838-1880)' (in *Wicklow Historical Society Journal*, vol. 1(4),
    pp. 5-13)

Ó Cathaoir, E. (1994) 'The Poor Law in County Wicklow', in K. Hannigan and W. Nolan (eds.), *Wicklow:
    History and Society*, 503-80

Ó Cathaoir, E. (1995) 'The Rathdown Union Workhouse at Loughlinstown, 1838-1923' (in *Dublin
    Historical Record,*, vol. 48(2), pp. 111-124)

Ó Murchadha, C. (1995) 'Limerick Union Workhouse During the Great Famine' (in *The Old Limerick
    Journal*, vol. 32, pp. 39-43)

Ó Murchadha, C. (1998) *Sable Wings over the Land: Ennis, County Clare and Its Wider Community During
    the Great Famine*

O'Brien, G. (1982) 'The Establishment of Poor Law Unions in Ireland' (in *Irish Historical Studies*, vol. 23,
    pp. 97-120)

O'Brien, G. (1986) 'Workhouse Management in Pre-Famine Ireland' (in *Proceedings of the Royal Irish*

Academy, vol. c.,86, pp. 113-34)

O'Brien, G. and O'Brien, B. (1995) *Athlone Workhouse and the Famine*

O'Brien, G. (1985) 'The New Poor Law in Pre-Famine Ireland: A Case Study' (in *Irish Economic and Social History*, vol. XII, pp. 35-39)

O'Brien, S. (1999) *Famine and Community in Mullingar Poor Law Union, 1845-1849: Mud Cabins and Fat Bullocks*

O'Connor, J. (1995) *The Workhouses of Ireland: The Fate of Ireland's Poor*

O'Dwyer, M. (2008) *The Famine in the Kilkenny/Tipperary Region: A History of the Callan Workhouse and Poor Law Union, 1845-1852*

O'Gorman, M. (1994) *A Pride of Paper Tigers: A History of the Great Hunger in the Scariff Workhouse Union from 1839 to 1853*

O'Mahony, C. (2005) *Cork's Poor Law Palace: Workhouse Life 1838-1890*

O'Mahony, M. (2005) *The Famine in Cork City: Famine Life at Cork Union Workhouse*

O'Sullivan, J.F. (2003) *Belfast City Hospital: A Photographic History*

Scannell, J. (2006) 'St. Columcille's Hospital, Loughlinstown, Co. Dublin: From Workhouse Infirmary to General Hospital' (in *Dublin Historical Record*,, vol. 59 (2), pp. 153-165)

Scotland

Adamson, D. (1986) 'Kirkpatrick Fleming Poorhouse' (in *Transactions of the Dumfries and Galloway Natural History and Antiquarian Society*, vol. 61, p. 103)

Anonymous (2006) *Linlithgow Combination Poorhouse*

Bangor-Jones, M. (2002) 'The Building of the Sutherland Combination Poorhouse', *Northern Times*, 20 September 2002

Birnie (1938) 'The Edinburgh Charity Workhouse' (in *Book of the Old Edinburgh Club*, vol. 22, pp. 38-55)

Blackden, S. (1986) 'The Board of Supervision and the Scottish Parochial Medical Service, 1845-95' (in *Medical History*, vol. 30, pp. 145-72)

Cage, R.A. (1981) *The Scottish Poor Law, 1745-1845*

Cormack, A.A. (1923) *Poor Relief in Scotland; an Outline of the Growth and Administration of the Poor Laws in Scotland, from the Middle Ages to the Present Day*

Day, J.P. (1918) *Public Administration in the Highlands and Islands of Scotland*

Eastwood, M.A. and Jenkinson, A. (1995) *A History of the Western General Hospital: Craigleith Poorhouse, Military Hospital, Modern Teaching Hospital*

Ferguson, T. (1958) *Scottish Social Welfare 1864-1914*

Hamilton, T. (1942) *Poor Relief in South Ayrshire, 1700-1845*

Levitt, I. (1988) *Government and Social Conditions in Scotland 1845-1919*

Levitt, I. (1988) *Poverty & Welfare in Scotland 1890-1948*

Lindsay, J. (1975) *The Scottish Poor Law: Its Operation in the North-East from 1745 to 1845*

Lindsay, J. (2000) 'Poor Relief in North Wales and East Lothian' [see entry in Wales section]

Lothian Council Department of Social Work (undated) *Greenlea Old People's Home: A Brief History* [Edinburgh]

Mackay, G.A. and Macwhannell, N. (1908) *Management and Construction of Poorhouses and Almshouses*

MacNab, P.A. (1972) 'The Last Refuge' (in *The Scots Magazine*, vol. 97(3), pp. 258-263) [Mull]

Mitchison, R. (2000) *The Old Poor Law in Scotland: The Experience of Poverty, 1574-1845*

Mitchison, R. (2002) 'Poor Relief and Health Care in 19th Century Scotland', in O.P. Grell and A. Cunningham (eds.), *Health Care and Poor Relief in 18th and 19th Century Northern Europe,* 246-255

Moody, D. (1983) *The Poorhouse and Poor Relief in East Lothian*

Murray, M. (2001) *Paisley Burgh - Sneddon Poorhouse or Town Hospital 1752-64*

Nicholls, G.S. (1856) *A History of the Scotch Poor Law: In Connexion with the Condition of the People*

Scottish Record Office (1995) *Poor Relief in Scotland: Historical Background, Document Extracts and Copies*

NOTES

Abbreviations:

CCE   Committee of Council on Education
LGB   Local Government Board
MH   Ministry of Health
PLB   Poor Law Board
PLC   Poor Law Commissioners
PP   Parliamentary Papers
RCPL   Royal Commission on the Poor Laws
SBS   Scottish Board of Supervision

1. Pat Roberts, personal communication.
2. PP, 1894, *Twenty-third Annual Report of the LGB*, p. lxxxviii.
3. McInnes and Sparkes, 1990, p. 14.
4. Anonymous, 1725, p. 71.
5. *Ibid.*, p. 10.
6. PP, 1834, RCPL, p. 27.
7. http://www.workhouses.org.uk/Abingdon consulted 1 March 2011.
8. Anonymous, 1725, p. 11.
9. *Ibid.*, p. 21.
10. PP, 1836, *Second Annual Report of the PLC*, p. 314.
11. Higginbotham, 2008, p. 91.
12. *Ibid.*
13. *Ibid.*
14. *Ibid.*, p. 92.
15. *Ibid.*
16. *Ibid.*
17. Martin, 1972, p. 36.
18. PP, 1824, *Report from the Select Committee on Labourers Wages.* p. 4.
19. PP, 1834, RCPL, Appendix B1, p. 293b.
20. Blaug, 1964, p. 231.
21. Honeyman, 2007, p. 97.
22. PP, 1836, *Second Annual Report of the PLC*, p. 174.
23. PP, 1842, *Children's Employment Commission. First Report: Mines*, p. 19.
24. PP, 1842, *Coal mines. Copy of Letter from PLC to Guardians of Dewsbury and Halifax Unions*, p. 1.
25. PP, 1842, *Children's Employment Commission. First Report: Mines*, p. 579.
26. *Ibid.*, p. 142.
27. *Ibid.*, p. 26.
28. PP, 1845, *Eleventh Annual Report of the PLC*, pp. 45-47.
29. *Ibid.* p. 11.
30. 14 &15 Vict. c. 11.
31. Digby, 1978, p. 191.
32. Morrison, 1999, pp. 28-29.
33. Goodwyn, 1987, p. 13.
34. Emmison, 1933, p. 30.
35. Howard, 1777, p. 279.
36. Anonymous, 1732, p. 127.
37. PP, 1776, *Abstract of the Returns on thh Relief and Employment of the Poor*, pp. 260-61.
38. Brodie, Croom and Davies, 2002, p. 52.
39. PP, 1839, *Fifth Annual Report of the PLC*, p. 118.
40. Morrison, 2004, p. 105.
41. Edwards, 1975, p. 45.
42. PP, 1836, *Second Annual Report of the PLC*, pp. 446-450.
43. PP, 1839, *Fifth Annual Report of the PLC*, p. 97.
44. Monnington and Lampard, 1898, p. 28.
45. http://www.workhouses.org.uk/ Beaminster consulted 1 March 2011.
46. Dumsday, 1907, p. 76.
47. Anonymous, 1725, p. 65.
48. *Ibid.*, p. 71.
49. *The Lancet*, 15 July 1865.
50. *Br Med J*, 1895, vol. 2, p. 795.
51. *Illustrated Times*, 1857, vol. iv, p. 137.
52. *London*, 1896, vol. 5, p. 1128.
53. Anonymous, 1725, p. 89.

54. PP, 1842, *Eighth Annual Report of the PLC*, p. 115.

55. PP, 1845, *Tenth Annual Report of the PLC*, p 100.

56. Higginbotham, 2006, p. 108.

57. PP, 1867-68, *Poor Law (Workhouse Inspection)*, p. 358.

58. Quoted in Sieh, 1989, p. 162.

59. Chaplin, 1964.

60. Stanley, 1909.

61. Haw, 1907, pp. 107-8.

62. PP, 1874, *Third Annual Report of the LGB*, p. 255.

63. http://www.workhouses.org.uk/Golding consulted 1 March 2011.

64. Preston-Thomas, 1909, pp. 226-227.

65. Crawfurd, 1932.

66. *Boards of Guardians (Default) Act* (16 & 17 Geo.V, c20) 1926.

67. PP, 1875, *Fourth Annual Report of the LGB*, pp. 195-196.

68. Baxter, 1841, pp. 155-156.

69. http://www.christchurchscouts.org.uk/archive/xchistory05.htm consulted 1 March 2011.

70. http://www.burtonlatimer.info/history/Cottagehomes.html consulted 1 March 2011.

71. PP, 1848, *First Annual Report of the PLB*, pp. 22-23.

72. PP, 1849, *Second Annual Report of the PLB*, p. 9.

73. PP, 1837-8, *Fourth Annual Report of the PLC*, p. 44.

74. *Poor Law Amendment Act (7&8 Vict. c101) 1844, s. 41.*

75. PP, 1911, *Fortieth Annual Report of the LGB*, p. 122.

76. PP, 1856, *Eighth Annual Report of the PLB*, p. 6.

77. PP, 1911, *Fortieth Annual Report of the LGB*, p. 122.

78. Webb and Webb, 1929, pp. 416-417.

79. PP, 1906, *Report of the Departmental Committee on Vagrancy*.Volume I, p. 21.

80. *Ibid.*, p. 26.

81. *Ibid.*, pp. 24-25.

82. Gray, 1931, pp. 74-81.

83. PP, 1929-30, *Report of the Departmental Committee on the Relief of the Casual Poor*, p. 16.

84. Ribton-Turner and Sterling, 1887, p. 277.

85. Orwell, 1931.

86. 45 & 46 Vict. c.36.

87. PP, 1864-65, *Seventeenth Annual Report of the PLB*, pp. 77-79.

88. Booth, 1890, p. 70.

89. PP, 1942, *Summary Report by the Ministry of Health*, p. 9.

90. Raynes, 1957, p. 241.

91. 25 & 26 Vict. c. 43.

92. PP, 1892, *Twenty-first Annual Report of the LGB 1891-92*, p. lxxxii.

93. Finer, 1952, p. 109.

94. Maude, 1903, p. 112.

95. Hinton, 1940.

96. PP, 1839, *Report on the Continuance of the PLC*, p. 34.

97. Monnington and Lampard, 1898, p. 85.

98. PP, 1911, *Fortieth Annual Report of the LGB, 1910-11*, p. xx.

99. PP, 1922, *Persons in Receipt of Poor-Law Relief*, pp. 21-26.

100. Hansard, 26 July 1922 vol. 157 col. 446.

101. Eden, 1797, vol. 2, p. 210.

102. Longmate, 1974, p. 221.

103. PP, 1835, *First Annual Report of the PLC*, p. 60.

104. Longmate, 1974, p. 221.

105. Anstruther, 1973, p. 151.

106. PLC, *Official Circulars*, vol. 1, p.74, 1840.

107. Smith, 1870, pp. 35-36.

108. PP, 1914, *Forty-third Annual Report of the LGB 1913-14*, p. 4.

109. PP, 1835, *First Annual Report of the PLC*, p. 59.

110. PP, 1842, *Eighth Annual Report of the PLC*, p. 66.

111. PP, 1867, *Poor Law (Workhouse Inspections)*, p. 445.

112. PP, 1835, *First Annual Report of the PLC*, p. 59.

113. PP, 1842, *Eighth Annual Report of the PLC*, p. 50.

114. PP, 1834, RCPL, Appendix A, p. 512.

115. PP, 1840, *Sixth Annual report of the PLC*, p. 56.

116. http://www.workhouses.org.uk/Ongar consulted 1 March 2011.

117. PP, 1840, *Sixth Annual report of the PLC*, p. 56.

118. PP, 1895-6, *Twenty-fifth Annual Report of the LGB*, p. 111.

119. PP, 1834, RCPL – *Town Queries*, p. 189.

120. PP, 1866, *Dieteries for the Inmates of Workhouses*, p. 6.

121. PP, *Twenty-first Annual Report of the Poor Law Board* 1868–69, p. 43.

122. Haw, 1907, p. 11.

123. PP, 1867, *Poor Law (Workhouse Inspections)*, p. 274.

124. Anonymous, 1732, p. 41.

125. Crowther, 1981, p. 241.

126. Richardson, 1987, p. 274.

127. Anonymous, 'A Workhouse Probe' in *Household Words*, 7th December, 1867.

128. PP, 1867-8, *Poor Law (Workhouse Inspection) Returns*, pp. 588-9.

129. LGB, 1900, *Workhouse Regulation (Dietaries and Accounts) Order*

130. http://www.workhouses.org.uk/Doncaster consulted 1 March 2011.

131. Montair, 1995, pp. 40-41.

132. Dangerfield, Marshall, Stringer and Elch, 1938, p. 150.

133. Clark, 1969.

134. Johnston, 1996, p. 77.

135. Higgs, 1906, p. 274.

136. PP, 1871, *First Report of the LGB*, p. xxvi.

137. PP, 1839, *Fifth Annual report of the PLC*, p. 99.

138. PP, 1914, *Forty-second Annual Report of the LGB for Ireland*, p. xix.

139. PP, 1854, *Report from the Select Committee on Medical Relief*, p.177.

140. Anonymous, 'A Day in the Withington Workhouse', *The Sphinx*, 15 April 1871, p. 115.

141. Hastings, 1889, pp. 644-645.

142. Kohl, 1844, pp. 278-279.

143. *The Lancet*, 4 November 1865.

144. *Br Med J*, 1895, vol. 1, p. 344.

145. Ross, 1967, pp. 276-277.

146. *The Examiner*, 20 January 1849, p. 34.

147. Ibid.

148. PP, 1889, *Eighteenth Annual Report of the LGB*, p. xciv.

149. *Illustrated London News*, 2 December 1871.

150. http://www.workhouses.org.uk/Hunslet consulted 1 March 2011.

151. Hansard, 1843, lxviii, col. 522.

152. PP, 1844, *Tenth Annual report of the PLC*, p. 138.

153. PP, 1852, *Fifth Annual Report of the Irish PLC*, pp. 204-206.

154. PP, 1875, *Pauper Children (Canada)*.

155. PP, 1884, *Thirteenth Annual Report of the LGB 1883-84*, p. xlix.

156. PP, 1888, *Seventeenth Annual Report of the LGB 1887-88*, pp. 50-51.

157. PP, 1890-91, *Twentieth Annual Report of the LGB 1890-91*, p. xc.

158. Now in the archives of English Folk Dance and Song Society – www.efdss.org

159. Anonymous, 1885, pp. 63-67.

160. PP, 1867, *Workhouses (Metropolis)*, p. 31.

161. Higginbotham, 2008, pp. 102-103.

162. Gibson, 2006, p. 78.

163. Bedford and Howard, 1985, pp. 18-19.

164. Personal recollection to author from Mr Laurie Liddiard.

165. Green, 2010, pp. 65-67.

166. Trollope, 1843, pp. 208-209.

167. Bennet, 1910. book 1, chapter 5.

168. Anon (1742) p. 1143.

169. PP, 1834, RCPL, Appendix A, p. 532.

170. Shaw, 1903, p. 101.

171. Haw, 1907, p. 109.

172. PLB, *Official Circulars*, June 1849, p. 94.

173. PP, 1854, *Minutes of the CCE; Schools of Parochial Unions 1853-4*, p. 134.

174. PP, 1870, *Twenty-second Annual Report of the PLB*, p. xv.

175. Berkshire Record Office, GA1-1, Abingdon Union Guardians' Minutes, 1835–36.

176. PP, 1870, *Twenty-second Annual Report of the PLB*, pp. 9-12.

177. Webb and Webb, 1929, p. 234.

178. Triennial elections had already been adopted in some individual unions, e.g. in Nottingham from 1878, a change requiring a poll of a union's electorate.

179. Berkshire Record Office, GA1-1, Abingdon Union Guardians' Minutes, 1835–36.

180. Hunslet Union New Workhouse Souvenir Programme, 1903.

181. Hardy, 1909, pp. 131-133.

182. Preston-Thomas, 1909, pp. 285-286.

183. Ibid., p. 293.

184. *An Act for Setting the Poor on Work* (18 Eliz. I, c. 3) 1576.

185. *An Act to amend and make more effectual the Laws relating to Rogues, Vagabonds and other idle and disorderly Persons, and to Houses of Correction* (17 Geo. II c5) 1743.

186. *An Act to enable Justices of the Peace in Petty Sessions to make Orders for the Support of Bastard Children* (2&3 Vict. c. 85) 1839.

187. *Poor Law Amendment Act* (7 & 8 Vict. c. 101) 1844.

188. Reid, 1994, pp. 66–67.
189. Rogers and Rogers, 1889, p. 15.
190. 3 & 4 Geo.V c. 28.
191. PP, 1922, *Return of Persons in Receipt of Poor Relief (England and Wales)*, p. 28.
192. PP, 1931-2, *Return of Persons in Receipt of Poor Relief (England and Wales)*, p. 21.
193. Cary, 1700.
194. Anonymous, 1711.
195. PP, 1776, *Abstract of the Returns on thh Relief and Employment of the Poor*, pp. 252–55.
196. PP, 1835, *First Annual Report of the PLC*, p. 108.
197. 17 & 18 Vict. c. 86.
198. 20 & 21 Vict. c. 48.
199. 23 & 24 Geo.V, c. 12.
200. PP, 1909, RCPL. Appendix Vol. I, p. 222.
201. 34 & 35 Vict. c. 108.
202. PP, 1839, *Fifth Annual Report of the PLC*, p. 35.
203. *Br Med J*, 1896, vol. 1, p. 159.
204. O'Connor, 1995, p. 126.
205. Kohl, 1844, p. 280.
206. 10 & 11 Vict. c. 7.
207. 10 & 11 Vict. c. 31.
208. 10 & 11 Vict. c. 90.
209. O'Connor, 1995, p. 141.
210. 12 & 13 Vict. c. 24.
211. PP, 1849, *Fourth Report from the Select Committee of the House of Lords on the Operation of the Irish Poor Law*, p. 717.
212. Gray, 1995, pp. 94-95.
213. 14 & 15 Vict. c. 68.
214. Cassell, 1997, pp. 119-123.
215. 25 & 26 Vict. c. 83.
216. PP, 1903, *Workhouse Infirmaries (Ireland). Nuns employed*. p. 5.
217. *Br Med J*, 1895, vol. 2, p. 1055.
218. *Ibid*. pp. 1055-56 (abridged).
219. PP, *Twenty-eighth Annual Report of the LGB for Ireland*, p. xxvi.
220. 49 & 50 Vict. c. 17.
221. PP, 1906, *Report of Vice-Regal Commission on Poor Law Reform in Ireland. Volume I*, p. 35.
222. PP, 1842, *Eighth Annual Report of the PLC*, p. 103.
223. PP, 1912-13, *Forty-first Annual Report of the LGB, 1911–1912*, p. 37-43.
224. *The Builder*, 26th February, 1887.
225. PP, 1838, *Thirty-fifth Report from Select Committee on the Poor Law Amendment Act*, para. 11,888.
226. PP, 1844, *Tenth Annual Report of the PLC*, p. 102.
227. PP, 1909, RCPL. Appendix Vol. XIV, pp. 33–34.
228. PP, 1861, *Paupers in Workhouses*.
229. PP, 1834, RCPL, p. 127.
230. White, 1990, p. 9.
231. Martin, 1972, p. 27.
232. Leonard, 1900, p. 99.
233. Pearl, 1978, p. 226.
234. PP, 1804, *Abstract of Returns Relative to the Expence and Maintenance of the Poor in England*.
235. Morrison, 1999, p. 8.
236. Anonymous, 1732, p. 24.
237. http://www.londonlives.org/statis/workhouses.jsp consulted 1 March 2011.
238. Eden, 1797, vol. 2, p. 440.
239. PP, 1843, *Ninth Annual Report of the PLC*, pp. 62–66.
240. Rogers and Rogers, 1889, p. 3.
241. Longmate, 1974, p. 144.
242. PP, *Twenty-fifth Annual Report of the LGB*, p. 181.
243. *Divided Parishes and Poor Law Amendment Act* (39 & 40 Vict. c 61) 1876.
244. Dumsday, 1907, p. 77.
245. Higginbotham, 2008, pp. 100–101.
246. Malthus, T.R. (1826) *An Essay on the Principle of Population*, Book III, Chapter VI.
247. Smith, 1870, p. 99.
248. Longmate, 1974, p. 101.
249. Neate, 2003, pp. 37–38.
250. *Stratford Herald*, Friday 1 January 1937.
251. http://www.londonlives.org/static/ParishNurses.jsp consulted 1 March 2011.
252. Oxley, 1974, p. 68.
253. PP, 1856, *Report on the Accommodation in St. Pancras Workhouse*.
254. *The Lancet*, 29 July 1865.
255. Hodgkinson, 1967, pp. 562–63.
256. PP, 1866, *Report by Dr Edward Smith on Metropolitan Workhouse Infirmaries*, p. 122.
257. 48 & 49 Vict. c. 46.
258. PP, 1920, *First Annual Report of Ministry of Health 1919–20*, p. 119.
259. Levene, Powell and Stewart, 2006, pp. 25–28.
260. Ayers, 1971, p. 5.
261. Webb and Webb, 1927, pp. 300–301.
262. 48 Geo. III c. 96.
263. 8 & 9 Vict. c. 100.
264. PP, 1836, *Second Annual Report of the PLC*, p. 326.

265.   53 & 54 Vict. c. 5.

266.   PP, 1861, *Paupers in Workhouses*, p. ii.

267.   3 & 4 Geo. V c. 28.

268.   PP, 1864, *Report from the Select Committee on Poor Relief*, p. 16.

269.   Ayers, 1971, pp. 6-7.

270.   *Ibid.*, p. 7.

271.   *Ibid.*, p. 9.

272.   30 & 31 Vict. c. 6.

273.   Ayers, 1971, p. 74.

274.   PP, 1882, *Report of the Commissioners appointed to Inquire Respecting Small-pox and Fever Hospitals.*

275.   54 & 55 Vict. c. 76.

276.   Powell, 1930, p. 78.

277.   *Ibid.*, p. 89.

278.   *Metropolitan Poor Amendment Act*, 1870 (33 & 34 Vict. c. 18.)

279.   *Local Authorities (Financial Provisions) Act*, 1921 (11 & 12 Geo. 5. c. 67.)

280.   Anonymous, 1686, p. 1.

281.   PP, 1835, *First Annual Report of the PLC*, p. 22.

282.   PP, 1836, *Second Annual Report of the PLC*, p. 412.

283.   *Ibid.*, p. 421.

284.   Trow, 2010.

285.   Williams, 1981, p. 205.

286.   PP, 1895–6, *Twenty-fifth Annual Report of the LGB*, p. 111.

287.   Higginbotham, 2007, p. 94.

288.   Roberts, 1963, p. 99.

289.   PP, 1838, *A copy of the order under the new Poor Act for withholding out-of-door relief to the able-bodied.*

290.   Webb and Webb, 1913, pp. 30-31.

291.   Thane, 1978, p. 41.

292.   PP, 1912–13, *Forty-first Annual Report of the LGB, 1911-1912*, p. 37-43.

293.   4 & 5 Will. IV, c. 76, s. 15.

294.   *Hampshire Advertiser*, 1 July 1871, p. 6.

295.   23 Edw. III cc.1-8.

296.   12 Rich. II, c. 3 and 12 Rich. II, c. 7.

297.   11 Henry VII c. 2.

298.   22 Henry VII c. 12.

299.   27 Henry VIII c. 25

300.   1 Edw. VI c. 3

301.   5 & 6 Edw. VI c. 2

302.   14 Eliz. I, c. 5.

303.   18 Eliz. I, c. 3.

304.   39 Eliz. I c. 3.

305.   39 Eliz. 1, c. 5.

306.   43 Eliz. I c. 2.

307.   Webb and Webb, 1927, p. 92.

308.   13 & 14 Car. II c. 12.

309.   3 Will. & Mary, c. 11.

310.   8 & 9 Will. III, c. 30.

311.   35 Geo. III, c. 101.

312.   9 Geo. I, c. 7.

313.   22 Geo. III, c. 83.

314.   36 Geo. III, c. 23.

315.   58 Geo. III, c. 69.

316.   59 Geo. III, c. 12.

317.   1 & 2 Will. IV, c. 60.

318.   4 & 5 Will. IV, c. 76.

319.   *Ibid.* s. 52.

320.   Nicholls, 1854, p. 271.

321.   5 & 6 Vict. c. 57.

322.   7 & 8 Vict. c. 101.

323.   11 & 12 Vict. c. 110.

324.   10 & 11 Vict. c. 109.

325.   28 & 29 Vict. c. 79.

326.   30 & 31 Vict. c. 6.

327.   34 & 35 Vict. c. 70.

328.   39 & 40 Vict. c. 61.

329.   56 & 57 Vict. c. 73.

330.   48 & 49 Vict. c. 46.

331.   16 & 17 Geo. V, c. 20.

332.   17 & 18 Geo. V, c. 14.

333.   19 & 20 Geo. V c. 17.

334.   8 & 9 Geo. VI, c. 41.

335.   9 & 10 Geo. VI, c. 67.

336.   9 & 10 Geo. VI, c. 81.

337.   11 & 12 Geo. VI, c. 29.

338.   15 & 16 Geo. V, c. 90.

339.   PP, 1873, *Second Annual Report of the LGB*, p. 9.

340.   Garcia-Bermejo Giner and Montgomery, 2003.

341.   Gibson and Rogers, 2004. Gibson, Rogers and Webb, 2005. Gibson and Rogers, 2008.

342.   Webb, 1999. Webb, 2006.

343.   Thompson, 1987.

344.   17 & 18 Vict. c. 86.

345.   Higginbotham, 2010, p. 74.

346.   8 Edw. VII, c. 67.

347.   Carlebach, 1970, p. 86.

348.   23 & 24 Geo. V, c. 12.

349.   Anonymous, 1732, p. 17.

350.   McInnes and Sparkes, 1990, p. 16.

351.   Anonymous, 1725, p. 56.

352.   http://www.workhouses.org.uk/Stone consulted 1 March 2011.

353.   Cousins, 1847, p. 8.

354. Crowther, 1981, p. 129.

355. Mackay and Nicholls, 1904, p. 603.

356. Blaug, 1964, pp. 231-232.

357. Mandler, 1990, p. 81.

358. PP, 1834, RCPL, p. 146.

359. Blaug, 1964, p. 243.

360. *Ibid.*, p. 231.

361. PP, 1909, RCPL, p. 26.

362. Clarke, 1955, p. 79.

363. http://www.workhouses.org.uk/Doncaster consulted 1 March 2011.

364. PP, 1867–8, *Poor Law (Workhouse Inspection) Returns*, p. 390.

365. Baxter, 1841, p. 432.

366. Higginbotham, 2006, p. 108.

367. Rogers and Rogers, 1889, pp. 85-88.

368. http://www.workhouses.org.uk/Hackney consulted 1 March 2011.

369. *British Medical Journal*, 18 August 1894, p. 371.

370. Higginbotham, 2008, p. 84.

371. 1424, James I, c. 7, May 26, no. 7.

372. 1535, James V, c. 22, June 12, no. 29.

373. 1579, James VI, c. 74, October 26, no. 12.

374. 1597, James VI, c. 272, November 3, no. 39.

375. Scottish Record Office, 1995, p. 20.

376. *An Act for the Amendment and Better Administration of the Laws Relating to the Relief of the Poor in Scotland* (8 & 9 Vict. c. 83) 1845.

377. PP, 1853, *Eighth Annual Report of the SBS*, p. iii.

378. PP, 1892, *Forty-seventh Annual Report of the SBS 1891-92*, p. xiv.

379. Higginbotham, 2008, p. 122.

380. PP, 1895, *Departmental Committee on Habitual Offenders, Inebriates, &c. (Scotland)*, p. 26.

381. Murphy, 1992, p. 57.

382. Scottish Record Office, 1995, p. 23.

383. White, 1990, p. 9.

384. 13 & 14 Car. II c.12.

385. Taylor, 1976, pp. 47-48.

386. 3 Will. & Mar. c. 11.

387. *An Act for supplying some Defects in the Laws for the Relief of the Poor* (9 Will. III, c. 11) 1697.

388. *An Act to Prevent the Removal of Poor Persons until they shall Actually become Chargeable* (35 Geo. III c. 101) 1795.

389. Quoted in Taylor, 1976, p. 42.

390. Smith, 1776, vol. 1, p. 61.

391. Webb and Webb, 1927, p. 407.

392. Nicholls, 1854, p. 282.

393. Longmate, 1974, p. 17.

394. *An Act to Amend the Laws Relating to the Removal of the Poor* (9 & 10 Vict. c. 66) 1846.

395. 10 & 11 Vict. c. 110.

396. PP, 1903, *Workhouse infirmaries (Ireland) – (Nuns employed)*, p. 5.

397. London, 1903, pp. 107-112. (abridged)

398. Higgs, 1906, pp. 108-110.

399. Gray, 1931, p. 82. (abridged)

400. Hammond and Hammond, 1948, vol. 1, p. 160.

401. PP, 1777, *Report on the Returns made by the Overseers of the Poor.*

402. PP, 1818, *Report from Select Committee on the Poor Laws, with an Appendix*, p.8.

403. Taylor, 1972, p. 58.

404. PP, 1787, *Report from the Committee on Certain Returns Relative to the State of the Poor.*

405. PP, 1822, *Report from the Select Committee on Poor Rate Returns.*

406. PP, 1830-31, *Poor Rate Returns.*

407. PP, 1834, RCPL, p. 2.

408. Blaug, 1964.

409. PP, 1862, *Female Adult Paupers.*

410. Higginbotham, 2008, p. 82.

411. http://www.workhouses.org.uk/ Cambridge consulted 1 March 2011.

412. PP, 1866, *Metropolitan Workhouse Infirmaries*, p. 52.

413. Anonymous, 1732, p. 109.

414. Higginbotham, 2008, pp. 38-39.

415. *Ibid.*

416. PP, 1900, *Fifth Annual Report of the LGB for Scotland*, p.7.

417. PP, 1867–8, *Twentieth Annual Report of the Poor Law Board*, p.46.

418. Turner, 1984, p. 3.

419. PP, 1867–8, *Poor Law (Workhouse Inspection) Returns*, p. 357.

420. *Ibid.* p. 446.

421. *Ibid.* p. 70.

422. PP, 1855, *Minutes of the CCE; Schools of Parochial Unions 1854–-5*, p. 112.

423. PP, 1853, *Minutes of the CCE; Schools of Parochial Unions 1852–3*, p. 171.

424. PP, 1847, *Minutes of the CCE*, p. 28.

425. PP, 1852, *Minutes of the CCE; Schools of Parochial Unions 1850–2*, p. 207.

426. PP, 1870, *Twenty-second Annual Report of the PLB*, pp. 9-12.

427. Higginbotham, 2008, p. 38.

428. *Ibid.*

429. *Ibid.*

430. PP, 1846, *Report from the Select Committee on Andover Union*, p. 1336.

431. Anonymous, 'A Day in the Withington Workhouse', *The Sphinx*, 15 April 1871, p. 115.

432. Edwards, 1975, p. 16.

433. LGB, *Tobacco and Snuff Order*, 3 November 1892.

434. http://www.workhouses.org.uk/ StokeUponTrent consulted 1 March 2011.

435. Crowther, 1981, p. 144.

436. PP, 1911, *Pauperism (England and Wales)*, p. vi.

437. Morrison, 1999, p. 176.

438. PP, 1870, *Return of the Lunatic Asylums and Workhouses in the Counties of Cork and Limerick, in which Turkish baths have been erected.*

439. Diplock, 1990, p. 12.

440. Siena, 2004, p. 161.

441. PP, 1866, *Poor Law (Workhouse Inspection)*, p. 347.

442. Twining, 1880, p. 91.

443. Hall, 2004, p. 71.

444. Bradford Union Guardians' year-books.

445. PP, 1909, RCPL. Appendix Vol. XIV, pp. 231-232.

446. PP, 1836, *Second Annual Report of the PLC*, p. 364.

447. Thomas, 1992, pp. 120-124.

448. PP, 1919, *Twenty-fifth Annual Report of the LGB for Scotland*, p. liv.

449. PP, 1915, *Forty-third Annual Report of the LGB for Ireland*, pp. 5-9.

450. Anonymous, 1725, p. 84.

451. http://www.workhouses.org.uk/Hackney consulted 1 March 2011.

452. http://www.workhouses.org.uk/ IsleOfWight consulted 1 March 2011.

453. Baker, 1984, pp. 43-45.

454. PP, 1842, *Eighth Annual Report of the PLC*, p51.

455. PP, 1844, *Tenth Annual report of the PLC*, p. 101.

456. *The Lancet*, 9 November 1867, p. 585.

457. *Ibid.*, 19 October 1867, p.497.

458. Greenwood, 1866.

459. PP, 1874, *Third Annual Report of the LGB*, p. 250.

460. *Br Med J*, 1894, vol. 2, p. 1186.

461. *Br Med J*, 1895, vol. 1, p.152.

462. PP, 1887, *Sixteenth Annual Report of the LGB*, Appendix A. pp. 1-2.

463. 'Windsor Workhouse' in *The Lancet*, 28 September 1867.

464. Eden, 1797, vol. 1, p. 592.

465. Anonymous, 1711.

466. PP, 1847, *Fourteenth Report of the PLC*, p. 17.

467. PP, 1836, *Second Annual Report of the PLC*, p. 208.

468. PP, 1843, *Second Report of the Children's Employment Commission*, pp. 123-124.

469. Rogers and Rogers, 1889, p. 5.

470. *Macclesfield Courier and Herald*, 1888, *A Walk through the Public Institutions of Macclesfield*, p. 13.

471. Thomas, 1992, p. 113.

472. Victoria County History, 1908, *Dorset*, vol. II, p. 294.

473. Morrison, 1999, p. 8.

474. Webb & Webb (1927) pp.106-7.

475. Bellers, 1695.

476. Taylor, 1972, p. 60.

477. *Ibid.*, p. 85.

478. PP, 1817, *Report from the Select Committee on the Poor Laws*, p. 20.

479. PP, 1834, RCPL, p. 170.

480. PP, 1835, *First Annual Report of the PLC*, p. 30.

481. PP, 1877, *Poor Relief (Expensive Medicines) Return.*

482. Crompton, 1997, p. 154.

483. Neate, 2003, p. 29.

484. PP, 1888, *Report from the Select Committee of the House of Lords on Poor Law Relief*, p. 205.

485. PP, 1888, *Report from House of Lords Select Committee on Poor Law Relief*, p. 207.

486. *Journal of the Workhouse Visiting Society*, January 1859.

487. *Ibid.*, p. 7.

488. Table based on Webb and Webb, 1929, pp. 1038-40.

489. After Williams (1981) pp158-163. Sources include annual reports of PLC, LGB and MH.

490. After Williams (1981) pp. 169-172. Sources include annual reports of PLC, LGB and MH.

491. Sources include annual reports of Irish PLC and LGB, and the *Report of the Royal Commission on Poor Laws* (1910).

492. Data from PP, 1910, *Report of the* RCPL, *Appendix VI*, pp. 881–882.

493. Sources include Parliamentary Papers, published local studies, official and trade directories, newspapers, local record offices, the National Monuments Record, Pevsner guides, OS maps, and personal communications. Major sources for architect attributions in England and Wales were Morrison (1999) and Morrison (2004).

494. Sources include Ayers (1971) plus OS maps, Parliamentary Papers, and official and trade directories.